Baptist Faith And Martyrs' Fires

Baptist Faith and Martyrs' Fires

by

W. J. BURGESS

Published by
THE BAPTIST PUBLICATIONS COMMITTEE

Publishing Agency of
THE NORTH AMERICAN BAPTIST ASSOCIATION

716 Main Street
Little Rock, Arkansas

BAPTIST FAITH AND MARTYRS' FIRES

Copyright 1964

Baptist Publications Committee
Little Rock, Arkansas

Library of Congress Catalog Card Number 64-18767

Printed in the United States of America

Dedication

Dedicated to my wife, Dova, and the children with whom the Lord has blessed us.

CONTENTS

BOOK I — The Church, Her Doctrines and Practices

I. THE ORIGIN OF THE CHURCH	3
II. THE NATURE OF THE CHURCH	16
III. THE GOVERNMENT OF THE CHURCH	24
IV. THE IDENTITY AND PERPETUITY OF THE CHURCH	38
V. THE FUNCTIONS OF THE CHURCH	50
VI. BAPTISM	61
VII. THE LORD'S SUPPER—BAPTISTS CALLED "CLOSE COMMUNIONISTS"	75
VIII. A PERPETUAL ORDINANCE	86
IX. RESTRICTED TO THE BAPTIZED	95
X. RESTRICTED AS TO ELEMENTS	105
XI. RESTRICTED TO LOCAL CHURCH	115
XII. BAPTISTS AND EDUCATION	130
XIII. BAPTISTS AND MISSIONS	137
XIV. BAPTIST DISTINCTIVES	147

BOOK II — Baptists and Their Influence Upon Early American History

I. SOURCE OF AMERICAN BAPTISTS AND EARLY COLONIAL ACTIVITIES 155
American Baptists From Several Sources — Baptists in the South and Liberty — Baptists in the North and Independence.

II. THE AMERICAN REVOLUTION AND THE BAPTISTS 172
The Revolution and the Baptists — The Relations of the Baptists to the American Revolution.

III. VIRGINIA AND THE GENERAL ASSEMBLY 179

IV. SOME EXPERIENCES OF THE VIRGINIA BAPTISTS 187
Roanoke Association and Christian Education — Roanoke Association on Authority of Ministers — Colored Ministers in Bluestone Association — Many Baptized by Colored Persons — Lawsuit in an Association — Church Rejected by Ketocton Association — Baptist Women Present a Present to Thomas Jefferson — Minister Runs Away From Officers — Had Their Unworthies, Too — Goshen Association About Assessments — Dover Association Received Colored Churches — Charles City — Feet Washing in Dover Association — On Baptism by Unordained Person, Dover Association — Dover Association on Matter of Ordination — Sends Paper to President Thomas Jefferson, 1808 — Virginia Baptists and Slavery — Virginia Baptists and Strict Communion.

V. BAPTISTS AND THE RELIGIOUS AMENDMENT TO
   THE CONSTITUTION OF THE UNITED STATES 199
VI. SOME OF THE OLDEST BAPTIST CHURCHES
   IN AMERICA 205
   Summary of American Baptists in 1790 — First Sermon West of
   the Mississippi.
VII. THE NEW HAMPSHIRE AND THE PHILADELPHIA
   CONFESSIONS OF FAITH 209
   The New Hampshire Confession of Faith — The Philadelphia
   Confession of Faith — Influence of the Philadelphia Confession
   of Faith.

BOOK III — Origin of Other Groups Who Held Baptist
           Principles 261-375

ALBIGENSES — ANABAPTISTS — DONATISTS — DUTCH BAPTISTS — ENGLISH BAPTISTS — English Baptists (Hiscox) — John Bunyan a Baptist — English Baptist Descended From the German Baptists — GERMAN BAPTISTS — THE HENRICIANS — MENNONITES — MONTANISTS — NOVATIANS — The Churches Called "Novatian Churches" Did Not Originate With Novatian — Origin of the Novatians — PAULICIANS — PETROBRUSIANS — SEPARATE BAPTISTS (AMERICA) — Another Account of the Origin of Separate Baptists — WELSH BAPTISTS — WALDENSES — Were the Waldenses Pedobaptists? — Three Confessions of Faith — Another Testimony to the Virtue of the Waldenses — Persecutions of the Waldenses — Cathcart's Account of the Waldenses — Remarks of Mr. Jones — Later Waldenses were Heretical — ORCHARD'S LINE OF SUCCESSION — HISTORIAN BENEDICT SUMMARIZES — ST. PATRICK HELD THE LEADING DOCTRINES OF THE BAPTISTS — IN THE VALLEYS OF THE PIEDMONT.

BOOK IV — Associations of Churches

I. THE NATURE OF AN ASSOCIATION OF CHURCHES...... 379
II. ENGLISH ASSOCIATIONS 382
   Particular Baptist Associations, England — Other Associations
   in England — London Associations.
III. EARLY AMERICAN ASSOCIATIONS 386
   Hiscox's Account of Early American Churches — Oldest Baptist
   Associations in America — Virginia Associations.
IV. THE NUMBER OF ASSOCIATIONS INCREASES................ 389
   English and American Associations — A Period of Unrest.
V. NORTH AMERICAN BAPTIST ASSOCIATION 392
   State Associations Affiliated With the North American Baptist
   Association.

BOOK V — Persecutions in All Centuries............409-490

CENTURY ONE — CENTURY TWO — More Pagan Persecutions — Christianity Widespread in Second Century — CENTURY THREE — Suffering Baptists in the Third Century — CENTURY FOUR — Those Who Were in the Palace — Constantine the Great — Constantine Orders Donatists Killed — CENTURY FIVE — Catholic Relic Worship in Fifth Century — Ridiculous Superstition — CENTURY SIX — CENTURY SEVEN — CENTURY EIGHT — CENTURY NINE — CENTURY TEN — CENTURY ELEVEN — CENTURY TWELVE — The Decree of Pope Lucius II Against Heretics, A. D. 1181 — The Decree of Idlefonsus, A. D. 1194 — CENTURY THIRTEEN — Slaughter of the Albigenses — CENTURY FOURTEEN — CENTURY FIFTEEN — Driven From Bohemia — The Inquisition (Spain) — CENTURY SIXTEEN — Wife and Children See Husband and Father Burn — Sentence Against Quirius Pieters, 1545 — Sentence of Anna Heyndriks, Surnamed Ulaster — Denied a Few Moments to Pray — Another Burned at Stake — Robert Smith, the Martyr — A Peak at Popery in Luther's Day — CENTURY SEVENTEEN — Massacre of Waldenses, 1655 — Whipped and Branded — Persecution in American Colonies — Edict of the Duke of Savoy, 1686 — CENTURY EIGHTEEN — Patrick Henry, a Friend — CENTURY NINETEEN — CENTURY TWENTY — Morris in Portugal — Persecutions in New Guinea — SUMMATION OF THE CENTURIES (William Jones).

BOOK VI — Persecutions in All Countries

I. ITALY—THE MORALS OF THE PERSECUTORS.............. 493

II. NETHERLANDS, GERMANY, SWITZERLAND—
ANABAPTIST MARTYRS 498

III. ENGLAND—THE REFORMATION 506

IV. GERMANY AND FRANCE—LUTHER AND
OTHER REFORMERS 519

V. BOHEMIA — PERSECUTIONS 527

VI. FRANCE—THE GREAT SLAUGHTER OF THE
PROTESTANTS 530

VII. AMERICA—PERSECUTIONS IN THE COLONIES
AND EARLY STATES 536
Colonies were Religio-Political States — Seeds of Persecutions — Virginia (Persecutions of Baptists in America) — The Virginia Baptists — Georgia (First Colored Church) — Maryland (Early Law of Maryland Concerning Religion) — Massachusetts — First Law Against the Baptists in This Colony.

BOOK VII — Appendix — or Miscellaneous Quotes

Item 1. SEARCHING FOR BAPTISTS TO PUNISH 573
Item 2. FROM THE FIRST CENTURY TO ABOUT THE
        TIME OF CONSTANTINE 575
Item 3. FURNISHING OF JERUSALEM TEMPLE LOST AT SEA.. 588
Item 4. STRONG CONCESSIONS FROM HARNACK'S
        HISTORY OF DOGMA 589
Item 5. A POPE AND A KING 593
Item 6. ROGER WILLIAMS NEVER A BAPTIST 594

INTRODUCTION

There are several reasons why I have prepared this book, during a very busy and responsible service to my brethren.

I am fully conscious of a lack of both knowledge and ability of expression. However, it appears to me that our people are wanting in a knowledge of the simple, primary, and fundamental lessons of Baptist doctrines. Too, the age in which we live does not lend promise for improvement. The atmosphere of human society in this complex age is such that one's mind is often so preoccupied as to stifle Christian knowledge and growth.

How many Baptists of today know why they are Baptists? How many could even state the cardinal beliefs of Baptists? There was never a time when so much heresy was preached. Of those called Baptists today, very few can rightly claim the name. Some who claim it actually deny the Inspiration of the Scriptures; they do not believe in the virgin-birth of Christ, in the blood atonement which He made; they do not believe in the bodily resurrection of Christ from the grave and they deny His Deity. Their "gospel" has become a mere social gospel, nothing more. Millions of dollars are given in the name of Christianity, and these dollars do not support Bible truths.

As to the church and its ordinances, they know but little. We need to hearken anew to the Bible and its simple truths. The churches have, in a large measure, become too formal; the worship is entertaining to the carnal nature, of which, unfortunately, we still have too much about us.

Baptists have a noble heritage. But to read the dusty pages of their history is painful. Were it not that we deeply feel the necessity of doing otherwise, we would let this record of suffering rest in the history books. Those who suffered for their faith, in unspeakable tortures, are now with Jesus. He has already healed their wounds, cooled the fires and eased the pains with the balm of His blessed presence.

One would hardly believe, were it not for the written records, that humans, God's once most glorious creation, could be so cruel, so mean, so devil-possessed, as to persecute, by every means imaginable, God's meekest children as thousands of their persecutors have done in all ages since Christ. But it is true. And the half is not on record. Along with Baptists, their records also were burned.

As I have said I would be glad to let these few glimpses of the past be forgotten were it not that I believe we are facing the possibility of this all over again. Two things convince me. First, the Bible warns us. Second, we can see the very spirit that sent our fathers to the stake rising up again today. We have selected a few of the records and reprint them here to awaken us to reality, and to stir us to action, to move us toward God and toward the mission fields, which are today so white unto harvest.

This is not a history, but we have included some history in it. It is not a theological treatise, but we have tried to set forth some truths that I believe we need to re-emphasize. We especially appeal to our people to love one another. Let us not wait until we have to appreciate each other's fellowship because of a common suffering. It is my opinion that, if the Lord does not come very soon, many of us who let little petty things as envy and jealousy, selfishness and the love for the preeminence absorb us, will learn to crucify these on the altar of common interest. The world is our enemy, let us make no mistake about it.

This book comprises **Baptists Then and Now,** which is out of print, and **The Lord's Table,** both written some years ago. **The Lord's Table** is still available in original small book form. The writer had intended to write also a small booklet on baptism. When it was thought well to republish **Baptists Then and Now** it was decided to somewhat revise it, include the **Lord's Table,** and the yet unwritten treatise on baptism. So, all three are incorporated in this work.

This is not all. Although most of the history of Baptists went up in flames, along with Baptists themselves, there yet remain some accounts of their suffering. So, much of this book is a compilation of material selected from many sources—religious periodicals and histories, both religious and secular.

Most of these I select are not available to our people. Many of the accounts we here publish are about to be lost. We therefore republish them to preserve anew what our fathers went through to be Baptists the past twenty centuries. We are giving an account of some persecutions as late as the date of the book. Another reason is that we might learn anew the price of faithfulness to truth. If a full account of the history of Baptists, their sufferings, their triumphs, and their influence had been preserved libraries would be filled. It is hoped that this book will be widely read and that it will be a means of blessing lives.

A fellow servant,

W. J. Burgess

Note of Explanation

In this book the author has selected many accounts by prominent historians of various Christian sects never consonant to Catholicism. It must be remembered that Catholic writers always termed those not in her wicked Hierarchy as **heretics**. In general, these "heretics" held Baptist sentiments, bore witness to the truth in very dark times, and often paid for their fidelity with their sufferings and lives. The author of this book is aware of the many alleged doctrinal faults charged to these people. However, it will be remembered that most of the history we have of them was written by their enemies.

It may be that some individuals at some time and in some countries were, from an orthodox Baptist viewpoint, unsound in finer points of doctrine, but the main stream flowed pure as to distinctive essentials.

As of this date there are thousands who claim the name Baptists, but their personal beliefs run counter to New Testament truths.

Are sound Baptists the less sound because of them?

BOOK ONE

THE CHURCH, HER DOCTRINES AND PRACTICES

CHAPTER I

THE ORIGIN OF THE CHURCH

1. DEFINITION. A New Testament church is a congregation of believers in Christ, scripturally baptized and voluntarily associated together under a covenant for the purpose of worship, the promulgation of the gospel, the observance of the ordinances, obedience to Christ's other commandments and the edification of one another in Christian virtues.

2. NOT A COMPLEX ORGANIZATION. The church is not an elaborate or complicated organization. It is very simple. It is a local congregation, and under Christ, its head, a sovereign body. It is not a part of a more general organization with headquarters elsewhere. It owes allegiance to no one and to no authority, except Christ. Its ordained officers are of two offices only—the pastor and the deacons. It is at the same time the lowest and the highest court in matters that concern it.

3. BAPTIST CHURCHES. We associated Baptists believe that the Lord's true churches on earth today are found among us. We do not claim that every congregation that calls itself Baptist is a scriptural church, but we do say that every true, New Testament church holds the orthodox and age-long Baptist doctrines for which Baptists for nearly two thousand years have suffered. Later we shall give reasons why we believe real Baptist churches are the churches of Christ.

When we speak of the church in this study we will usually use the term in its institutional sense; as we speak of the tree, the wife or the husband, the horse or the bird, meaning no particular one of these species. We are told that God made man; mankind is represented by Adam, Genesis 2:7. Paul writes of the wife and of the husband; meaning any or all wives or husbands and no particular one, I Corinthians 7:10. What would be true with one would be true with all. He used the term institutionally. So will we speak of the church.

It is improper to speak of the church of America. There is no such thing. Many other denominations have an over-all organization with various local units scattered throughout the country and subject unto it. Not so with Baptists. Each church is a church of Jesus Christ in its own right. But we will discuss this more fully later.

4. HAD ITS ORIGIN DURING CHRIST'S PERSONAL MINISTRY. There are many theories about when the church was organized. In the worldly sense of the term it was not organized. It had a beginning when Jesus called John's prepared disciples. Some preach that the church was established in Abraham's day, or before; some, that it started with Moses. Others say it did not begin until the first Pentecost after the resurrection of Christ. We shall notice these false ideas later.

The church had its beginning while Christ was on earth. The English word church comes from an original Greek word, ecclesia. It means a called out congregation of free citizens. Keep this in mind—we shall need it later. See Ephesians 2:10.

While there evidently is a future golden kingdom prophesied in the Scriptures, there certainly is a sense in which the kingdom was here during Christ's days on earth.

"Now after that John was put in prison, Jesus came into Galilee, preaching the gospel of the kingdom of God, and saying, The time is fulfilled, and the kingdom of God is at hand: repent ye and believe the gospel. Now as he walked by the sea of Galilee, he saw Simon and Andrew his brother casting a net into the sea: for they were fishers. And Jesus said unto them, Come ye after me, and I will make you to become fishers of men," Mark 1:14-17. See also Matthew 4:17.

John the Baptist preached the same thing.

"In those days came John the Baptist, preaching in the

wilderness of Judaea, and saying, Repent ye: for the kingdom of heaven is at hand," Matthew 3:1-2.

"And from the days of John the Baptist until now the kingdom of heaven suffereth violence, and the violent take it by force," Matthew 11:12.

5. JOHN PREPARED THE MATERIAL. Though the church was not established by John the Baptist he did prepare the material that Jesus later used to build it.

"Behold, I will send my messenger, and he shall prepare the way before me: and the Lord, whom ye seek, shall suddenly come to his temple, even the messnger of the covenant, whom ye delight in: behold, he shall come, saith the Lord of hosts," Malachi 3:1.

"In those days came John the Baptist, preaching in the wilderness of Judaea, and saying, Repent ye: for the kingdom of heaven is at hand. For this is he that was spoken of by the prophet Esaias, saying, the voice of one crying in the wilderness, Prepare ye the way of the Lord, make his paths straight," Matthew 3:1-3. See also Mark 1:2-4; Luke 1:17, 76-80; John 1:6-28.

6. JESUS CALLED JOHN'S DISCIPLES. We have said that the word church means a called out congregation of free people. John had prepared material by his preaching. People had believed and were saved. Being saved they were free from sin. All saved people are free.

"If the Son therefore shall make you free, ye shall be free indeed," John 8:36.

"Being made free from sin, ye became the servants of righteousness," Romans 6:17.

"There is therefore now no condemnation to them which are in Christ Jesus," Romans 8:1.

"For he that is dead is freed from sin," Romans 5:7.

"Verily, verily, I say unto you, He that heareth my word, and believeth on him that sent me, hath everlasting life, and shall not come into condemnation: but is passed from death unto life," John 5:24.

Jesus took the men who had believed John's message and who had been baptized by him and constituted His church—His called out.

"Again the next day after John stood, and two of his disciples; and looking upon Jesus as he walked, he saith, Behold the Lamb of God! and the two disciples heard him speak, and they followed Jesus . . . One of the disciples which heard John speak, and followed him, was Andrew, Simon Peter's brother. He first findeth his own brother Simon, and saith unto him, We have found the Messiah, which is, being interpreted, the Christ. And he brought him to Jesus. And when Jesus beheld him, he said, Thou art Simon the son of Jona: thou shalt be called Cephas, which is by interpretation, a stone. The day following Jesus would go forth into Galilee, and findeth Philip, and saith unto him, Follow me. Now Philip was of Bethsaida, the city of Andrew and Peter. Philip findeth Nathanael . . .," John 1:35-45.

Later, up in Galilee, Jesus called Peter and Andrew again, then James and John.

> "And Jesus, walking by the sea of Galilee, saw two brethren, Simon called Peter, and Andrew his brother, casting a net into the sea: for they were fishers. And he saith unto them, Follow me and I will make you fishers of men. And they straightway left their nets and followed him. And going on from thence, he saw other two brethren, James the son of Zebedee, and John his brother, in a ship with Zebedee their father, mending their nets; and he called them," Matthew 4:18-21.

7. THE CHURCH WAS TO START QUIETLY. The Jews mistook the nature of the kingdom and the manner of its coming. They fully looked for a showy demonstration and for the old kingdom of Israel to be restored to them. But Christ's kingdom was not to be of this world, John 18:36. It is in the world, but not of it, John 17:14.

> "He shall not strive, nor cry; neither shall any man hear his voice in the streets," Matthew 12:19.

The church was to be started much as the temple of Solomon was built. Solomon's temple was, in many points, typical of the church. The materials for the temple were prepared previously, and in their native places were found. Each piece, timber or stone, that went into the magnificent temple, was hewn to size and shape and made exactly ready out in the mountains before being brought to Jerusalem to be erected on Mt. Moriah. Just in this way John prepared the material for the church. Read all of chapter 5 of I Kings.

> "And the house, when it was in building, was built of stone made ready before it was brought thither: so that there was neither hammer nor axe nor any tool of iron heard in the house, while it was in building," I Kings 6:7.

We have said that the church was composed of saved people, those who had been freed from their sins because they believed the preaching of the gospel message by John the Baptist. Such were stones, lively stones, that Jesus put into His church. Christ's temple is built of living stones.

You will recall, according to the Scriptures quoted from the first chapter of John, that when Peter was brought to the Lord for the first time He renamed him Cephas. This word means a stone. Peter was one of John's disciples and was one of the first members of the Lord's church. He is typical of all others, being a living stone. The church is therefore an organism, with Christ the life.

> "Ye also, as lively stones, are built up a spiritual house, an holy priesthood, to offer up spiritual sacrifices, acceptable to God by Jesus Christ," I Peter 2:5.

We have said that the church started quietly. It did not consist of a lot of earthly pomp and show, detailed organization and intricate elements. Just simply a few of John's disciples called by Jesus to follow Him and to become fishers of men. Incidentally, this is what the kingdom is like, fishers of men.

> "Again the kingdom of heaven is like unto a net, that was cast into the sea, and gathered of every kind . . ." Matthew 13:47.

Jesus went about the business of establishing His church in such manner that the Jews did not recognize His work. They were not looking for such a small thing. And the church was small at first. It is still small in the eyes of the world, and insignificant, too. But we are not to fear because of this, Luke 12:32.

> "And when he was demanded of the Pharisees, when the kingdom of God should come, he answered them and said, The kingdom of God cometh not with observation: neither shall they say, Lo here! or, Lo there! for, behold, the kingdom of God is within you," Luke 17:20-21.

Jesus certainly did not mean that the kingdom of God was in the hearts of these wicked Pharisees. He simply meant that it was there in their very midst. They had not observed it. He said that the kingdom came not with observation; that is, not with a lot of noise and worldly celebrations that would attract notice. It was to be known by its spiritual qualities instead. Such it should be today.

8. THE CHURCH WAS SMALL AT FIRST. It does not take many people to have a New Testament church. But they must be the right kind. Jesus started with a very

few. Later, there were hundreds. On the day of Pentecost there were "about an hundred and twenty" present. Jesus has promised to be with a very few when they are gathered in his name:

> "For where two or three are gathered together in my name, there am I in the midst of them," Matthew 18:20.

While in Jerusalem a few years ago this writer plucked some seed pods of the "mustard tree" and crushed them in his hand. He found the tiny seeds to be so small they could hardly be handled. The Jerusalem mustard tree that is meant in the parable is about the size of an apple tree. We are told that the mustard seed is the smallest of all but it grows into a tree in which the birds may rest in its branches. And the kingdom is like this. Birds are symbols of uncleanliness. They mar the trees, break the tender twigs and defile it with refuse from their bodies while they feast on its fruits and rest on its boughs. Exactly in this way does the worldly and unsaved affect the church. It is bad when a church becomes so popular that sinners seek its cover.

> "Another parable put he forth unto them, saying, The kingdom of heaven is like unto a grain of mustard seed, which a man took, and sowed in his field: which indeed is the least of all seeds: but when it is grown, it is the greatest among herbs, and becometh a tree, so that the birds of the air come and lodge in the branches thereof," Matthew 13:31-32.

9. FURTHER PROOF THE CHURCH WAS HERE DURING CHRIST'S MINISTRY. David foretold in Psalm 22:22 that Jesus would sing in the church. The writer to the Hebrews referred to this. It is recorded in Matthew that the prophecy was fulfilled. Jesus could not have done this if the church did not exist in His day. Matthew tells us that after the institution of His Supper THEY sang an hymn, Jesus and the disciples present, fulfilling what David had said.

> "I will declare thy name unto my brethren: in the midst of the congregation will I praise thee," Psalm 22:22.
>
> "Saying, I will declare thy name unto my brethren, in the midst of the church will I sing praise unto thee," Hebrews 2:12.
>
> "And when they had sung an hymn, they went out into the mount of Olives," Matthew 26:30.

Another proof is that Jesus gave rules of discipline while He was here. He said that when one had offended you to go to him alone. If he failed to hear, take others and go. If he still failed, "Tell it to the church." This could not have been done if the church did not exist until Pentecost.

> "And if he shall neglect to hear them, tell it unto the church: but if he will not hear the church, let him be unto thee as an heathen man and a publican," Matthew 18:17.

We are without the Commission if the church was not here while Christ was here. He gave it personally, and before He left. If given only to individuals then we have no commission, for the individuals to whom He gave it are all dead. But if in church capacity they received it, there has been a succession of churches all down the centuries. But Jesus said in the Commission, "I am with you alway." Hence, it was given to a church.

> "Go ye therefore, and teach all nations, baptizing them in the name of the Father, and of the Son, and of the Holy Ghost: teaching them to observe all things whatsoever I have commanded you: and, lo, I am with you alway, even unto the end of the world," Matthew 28:19-20.

Moreover, if the church was not here when Jesus was here we do not have the Ordinance of the Lord's Supper, for it was also given personally by Jesus while He was here. We see, therefore, that when we try to set up the church on Pentecost we get into all sorts of difficulties. Let us just take the plain Scriptures.

10. THE THEORY THAT IT WAS DURING THE OLD DISPENSATION. Some aver that it began with Abraham, with Moses, or even before either of these. The covenants the Lord made with Abraham had nothing to do with the church of Christ, as the church of the Scriptures was a New Testament body. Neither did Moses establish the church.

> "This is that Moses, which said unto the children of Israel, A prophet shall the Lord your God raise up unto you of your brethren, like unto me; him shall ye hear. This is he, that was in the church in the wilderness with the angel which spake to him in the mount Sina, and with our fathers . . ." Acts 7:37-38.

Moses was a type of Christ, both in person and ministry, in many ways. But he was not the builder of the New Testament church. In the above Scripture, Stephen was quoting from Deuteronomy 18:15. Moses was a prophet, a law-giver, a deliverer, a leader of the Israelites. He led the children of Israel out of bondage, from Egypt and into the wilderness. They were a congregation of free people. In this sense they constituted a church, for the English word comes from the Greek word ecclesia which means a called out congregation. They were even baptized **"unto Moses, in the cloud and in the sea."**

> **"Moreover, brethren, I would not that ye should be ignorant, How that all our fathers were under the cloud, and all passed through the sea; and were all baptized unto Moses in the cloud and in the sea . . .," I Corinthians 10:1-2.**

It is plain that the "church in the wilderness" was not the church of Jesus Christ. But there is much analogy between it and Christ's church. The Israelites were a called out people, a freed people, had a deliverer, a law-giver, a mediator, were baptized unto their deliverer—Moses—in the cloud and in the sea. This was all a type. As they were freed from bondage by the blood they had faith to sprinkle on their houses in Egypt, so are we saved from sin by the blood of Christ. They were led to the baptism in the sea by the pillar of cloud and fire, a type of the Holy Spirit leading us. They were completely covered or buried in the baptism as they crossed the sea. The water was on either side, the cloud covered above, a type of our baptism unto our Saviour, Jesus Christ.

However, the church of the Lord Jesus Christ is a New Testament body. It was started by Jesus Himself while He was on the earth.

11. THE PENTECOST THEORY. There is not even one word said in the Scriptures about a church being organized on the day of Pentecost. There is no hint of it, even. The assumption is based purely on the necessity to fit a false theory. Pentecost was an annual feast of the Jews and was one of three such annual feasts which all male Jews were expected to attend. The other two were Tabernacles and Passover.

The first Pentecost after the resurrection and ascension of Jesus was the scene of a great demonstration of the Holy Spirit, but no church organization. The church which was already in existence was baptized by the Holy Spirit that day, and was baptized once for all.

> "And when the day of Pentecost was fully come, they were all of one accord in one place. And suddenly there came a sound from heaven as of a rushing mighty wind, and it filled all the house where they were sitting. And there appeared unto them cloven tongues like as of fire, and it sat upon each of them. And they were all filled with the Holy Ghost, and began to speak with other tongues, as the Spirit gave them utterance," Acts 2:1-4.

But absolutely nothing is said about a church being organized or started in any form. In fact, everything that is necessary for the existence of a church was here before the day of Pentecost. There were believers, and plenty of them. There were baptized believers. John had baptized many, and John's baptism was Christian baptism, it was from heaven.

> ". . . But he that sent me to baptize with water, the same said unto me . . .," John 1:33.

> "The baptism of John, Whence was it? from heaven, or of men? And they reasoned with themselves, saying, If we shall say from heaven; then he will say unto us, why did ye not believe him?" Matthew 21:25.

John's baptism was the kind that Jesus had and the only kind the apostles had. After the death of Judas, when the church was gathered together, Peter said that one must be ordained to take his place, one that had continued all the way from "the baptism of John."

> "Wherefore of these men which have companied with us all the time that the Lord Jesus went in and out among us, beginning from the baptism of John, unto that same day that he was taken up, must one be ordained to be a witness with us of his resurrection," Acts 1:21-22.

There were many whom the disciples of Jesus had baptized. Jesus Himself did not baptize, but what His disciples did at His command is reckoned as though He did it.

> "When therefore the Lord knew how the Pharisees had heard that Jesus made and baptized more disciples than John, (though Jesus baptized not, but his disciples,) he left Judaea and departed again unto Galilee," John 4:1-3.

They had the gospel before Pentecost. The gospel age did not begin on the day of Pentecost for it had begun more than three years before. It began with the ministry of John the Baptist. This is very plainly shown by the following reference.

> "The beginning of the gospel of Jesus Christ, the Son of God; as it is written in the prophets, Behold, I send my messenger before thy face, which shall prepare thy way before thee," Mark 1:12.

The church even had a treasurer before Pentecost, though a dishonest one. Judas Iscariot had this position, John 12:6; 13:29.

They had the Lord's Supper, Luke 22:19-20.

They had a Commission, Matthew 28:19-20.

They had a Head, Christ Himself, as we have today. He was personally then present. See Ephesians 4:15; Colossians 1:18.

They had a church roll, Acts 1:15. This number were present at the business meeting when Matthias was chosen by vote to take the place of Judas Iscariot. They voted between two nominees, and one was chosen. This is exactly the way Baptists do today. Their church government is congregational, or democratic.

They had rules concerning church discipline before Pentecost, Matthew 18:15-18. The church had authority, also.

The fact that Jesus completed His work before He left the earth also proves that the church was here before Pentecost. There can be no doubt that Jesus was to establish His church, and this He did before He left the earth. He told His Father, in His dedicatory prayer in the seventeenth chapter of John, that He did so.

> "I have glorified thee on the earth: I have finished the work which thou gavest me to do," John 17:4.
> "Jesus saith unto them, My meat is to do the will of him that sent me, and to finish his work," John 4:34.

12. NOT ON THE MOUNTAIN. Some believe that the church was established on a mountain while Christ was here on the earth. This writer would not want to be dogmatic, but he believes otherwise. I shall give some reasons. Let us examine the mountain theory.

Those who believe the church was started by Jesus on the mountain cite the following Scriptures:

> "And it came to pass in those days, that he went out into a mountain to pray, and continued all night in prayer to God. And when it was day, he called unto him his disciples: and of them he chose twelve, whom also he named apostles," Luke 6:12-13.

The prophecy of Isaiah is then cited as predicting this event. We give the prophecy here as we shall note the content.

> "The word that Isaiah the son of Amoz saw concerning Judah and Jerusalem. And it shall come to pass in the last days, that the mountain of the Lord's house shall be established in the top of the mountains, and shall be exalted above the hills; and all nations shall flow unto it. And many people shall go and say, Come ye, and let us go up to the mountain of the Lord, to the house of the God of Jacob; and he will teach us of his ways, and we will walk in his paths: for out of Zion shall go forth the law, and the word of the Lord from Jerusalem. And he shall judge among the nations, and shall rebuke many people: and they shall beat their swords into plowshares, and their spears into pruning hooks: nation shall not lift up sword against nation, neither shall they learn war anymore," Isaiah 2:1-4.

First of all, no such things have happened as are prophesied in this Scripture. It has reference to a yet future time when the earth shall be subdued. Nations are still lifting up swords against other nations, and we are still learning war. The law is not now going forth from Jerusalem, nor is the Word of the Lord. This prophecy concerns "Judah and Jerusalem," and has reference, in my opinion, to a golden time that is yet to come. The "mountain of the Lord's house" means the kingdom yet to be manifest. It will be the rest of the promise made to Mary in Luke 1:32-33. See also Revelation 5:10; 11:15; I Corinthians 6:1-3; Micah 4; Daniel 2:44; Psalm 72; Luke 19:12-27; Matthew 19:28-30.

Isaiah says in the Scripture above cited that the mountain of the Lord's house would be established in the top of the mountains, plural. Jesus was on only one mountain that morning. The word mountain is used to represent a power, kingdom, etc. And while this can be said of the church in a sense, Isaiah said that what he was talking about would be on more than one mountain, and Jesus was only on one the morning He called His disciples to Him. This writer believes that Isaiah was writing of the same thing that John saw.

> "And the seventh angel sounded; and there were great voices in heaven, saying, The kingdoms of this world are become the kingdoms of our Lord, and of his Christ; and he shall reign for ever and ever," Revelation 11:15.

The proponents of the mountain theory also use another Scripture:

> "And God hath set some in the church, first apostles, secondarily prophets, thirdly teachers, after that miracles, then gifts of healing, helps, governments, diversities of tongues," I Corinthians 12:28.

If one will study the context here he will find that the subject Paul is writing about is Spiritual gifts. It was gifts that were placed in the church on the mountain, rather the first of a number of spiritual gifts. The first to be set into the church was apostles, or the aspostolic office, not the first members. After the apostolic gift was given the church, there were other spiritual gifts given. The very order is given: "secondarily, prophets, thirdly teachers," etc.

These spiritual gifts were temporary endowments to serve in a very needed way. The Bible was not yet written as we have it today. These were needed as credentials of the faith of the early church. But they ceased at the end of the Apostolic age. **"Whether there be prophecies they shall fail; whether there be tongues, they shall cease; whether there be knowledge, it shall vanish away,"** I Corinthians 13:8.

The church must have been in existence on the day the apostles were placed in it. One cannot place something in that which does not exist. It is very plain that this had reference only to the apostolic office being placed in the church, and does not mean the first members. As a matter of fact, some of these apostles named that morning were the first members, having been converts of John the Baptist, but they were in the church long before this day. But these twelve were chosen as apostles as the first spiritual gift and were sent forth to preach and were given special powers.

We have already referred to the election of Matthias in Jerusalem by the church to take the place of Judas, and how that Peter said one must be chosen who had companied with them all the time from John's baptism. A church is a company of baptized believers, and this company was with Jesus long before the mountain event.

We now come to a Scripture that is widely used but which we have not heretofore noticed. The reason is, it has nothing whatever to do with the origin of the church. It follows:

> "He saith unto them, But whom say ye that I am? And Simon Peter answered and said, Thou art the Christ, the Son of the living God. And Jesus answered and said unto him, Blessed art thou, Simon Barjona: for flesh and blood hath not revealed it unto thee, but my Father which is in heaven. And I say also unto thee, that thou art Peter, and upon this rock I will build my church; and the gates of hell shall not prevail against it," Matthew 16:15-18.

This was spoken after the church was already in existence. He does not mean that He will start the church. He simply means that He will enlarge, edify, add to, cause to grow, etc., and that nothing would be able to stop it. He did not mean, either, that He would do this on Peter, but upon Himself. The church was not built on Seth, Abraham, Noah, Moses, Paul, Peter or John the Baptist, but upon Jesus Christ. He is the foundation stone and head of the corner. See I Corinthians 3:10-33; Isaiah 28:16; I Peter 2:6; Ephesians 2:20.

It is very plain that the church was started by Jesus while He was on earth, and out of material prepared by John the Baptist. By taking your stand on this fundamental fact, you will not be embarrassed by inability to harmonize any Scriptures that might touch the origin of it.

CHAPTER II

THE NATURE OF THE CHURCH

1. IT IS AN ORGANISM. It is more than an organization. It is composed of spiritually living members, with Christ as the living entity within us.

> "Ye also as lively stones, are built up a spiritual house, an holy priesthood, to offer up spiritual sacrifices, acceptable to God by Jesus Christ," I Peter 2:5.
>
> "I am crucified with Christ; nevertheless I live; yet, not I, but Christ liveth in me: and the life which I now live in the flesh I live by the faith of the Son of God, who loved me, and gave himself for me," Galatians 2:20.
>
> "Know ye not that ye are the temple of God, and that the Spirit of God dwelleth in you? If any man defile the temple of God, him shall God destroy; for the temple of God is holy, which temple ye are," I Corinthians 3:16-17. See also Romans 8:9; Ephesians 3:17; I John 4:12.

The nature of a New Testament church can best be seen when we understand that it comes from the original Greek word EKKLESIA. All Greek lexicons of any note tell us that it means a called out group of free citizens.

Liddell and Scott, in their Greek lexicon, define the word ekklesia, "an assembly of citizens summoned by the crier, the legislative assembly."

The word ekklesia is composed of two Greek words, say scholars. Kalein, to call; and ek, out of. Therefore, the word ekklesia literally means the called out.

Dean Trench in his lexicon says: "Ekklesia, as all know, was the lawful assembly in a free Greek city of all those possessed of the rights of citizenship, for the transaction of public affairs."

Many others could be cited but these will suffice. Greek scholars tell us that the word **ekklesia** is found in the New Testament 115 times. It is used in a singular sense to designate a local congregation, or the church institution seventy six times. It is used in the plural to designate local churches thirty six times, and is used three times to designate a worldly assembly or mob.

2. IT IS CHRIST'S BODY. It is His body in the sense that it belongs to Him and in the sense that we are members and He is the head.

> "And he is the head of the body, the church . . ." Colossians 1:18.
> "But speaking the truth in love may grow up into him in all things, which is the head, even Christ; from whom the whole body fitly joined together and compacted by that which every joint supplieth, according to the effectual working in the measure of every part, maketh increase of the body unto the edifying of itself in love," Ephesians 4:15-16.

3. IT IS HIS HOUSE. A house is a place in which to dwell. God lives in His house, which is the church. There are some wonderful lessons here. Paul tells us (II Corinthians 5:1) that our fleshly bodies are only tabernacles, or tenthouses. They are temporary places in which to live. Some day our spirits will move out into a house which is from heaven, same verse.

Do you think God is always "comfortable" in His house? A house that is open, one with no windows or maybe doors, or where the walls are full of cracks which will let in the cold, is not comfortable. A roof that isn't good will let the rain in. Our churches should be tight against the world. It is God's will we be so.

> "Now therefore ye are no more strangers and foreigners, but fellow citizens with the saints, and of the household of God: and are built upon the foundation of the apostles and prophets, Jesus Christ himself being the chief corner stone; in whom all the building fitly framed together groweth unto an holy temple in the Lord: in whom ye also are builded together for an habitation of God through the spirit," Ephesians 2:19-22.

Notice that Paul says that we are a temple for the habitation of God through the Spirit. God lives in His church. It is His plan to get glory in the church, Ephesians 3:21. Jesus said that He would be with the church always even unto the end of the world, Matthew 28:20.

> "But if I tarry long, that thou mayest know how thou oughtest to behave thyself in the house of God, which is the church of the living God, the pillar and the ground of the truth," I Timothy 3:15.
> "Christ as a Son over his own house, whose house are we,"

Hebrews 3:6. See also II Corinthians 6:16; I Corinthians 3:16.

"For as the body is one, and hath many members, and all the members of that one body, being many, are one body; so also is Christ. For by one Spirit are we all baptized into one body, whether we be Jews or Gentiles, whether we be bond or free; and have been all made to drink into one Spirit. For the body is not one member, but many. If the foot shall say, Because I am not the eye, I am not of the body: is it therefore not of the body? If the whole body were an eye, where were the hearing? If the whole were hearing, where were the smelling? But now hath God set the members every one of them in the body, as it hath pleased him. And if they were all one member, where were the body? But now are they many members, yet one body. And the eye cannot say unto the hand, I have no need of thee: nor again the head to the feet, I have no need of you. Nay, much more those members of the body, which seem to be more feeble, are necessary; and those members of the body which we think to be less honorable, upon these we bestow more abundant honor: and our uncomely parts have more abundant comeliness. For our comely parts have no need; but God hath tempered the body together, having given more abundant honor to that part which lacked: that there should be no schism in the body; but that the members should have the same care one for another. And whether one member suffer, all the members suffer with it; or one member be honored, all the members rejoice with it. Now ye are the body of Christ, and members in particular," I Corinthians 12:12-27.

4. IT IS A VISIBLE BODY. There is no such thing as an invisible church, or a universal church. The first church at Jerusalem was a local body of people. These were just men and women in their flesh, but who had been saved and born again. If the church were an invisible something the rules of discipline could not be enforced. How could one "tell it to the church"? Matthew 18:17.

The Scriptures do not speak of an invisible, universal church. They speak of a local church, or churches.

"And fear came upon all the church" (the church at Jerusalem), Acts 5:11. See also Acts 8:1.

"Then had the churches rest throughout all Judaea and Galilee and Samaria, and were edified; and walking in the fear of the Lord, and in the comfort of the Holy Ghost, were multiplied," Acts 9:31.

"And he went through Syria and Cilicia, confirming the churches," Acts 15:41.

"And so were the churches established in number daily," Acts 16:5.

"Unto whom not only I give thanks, but also all the churches of the Gentiles," Romans 16:4.

"The churches of Christ salute you," Romans 16:16.

"And so ordain I in the churches," I Corinthians 7:17.

"Neither the churches of God," I Corinthians 11:16.

"As in all churches of the saints," I Corinthians 14:33.
"Let your women keep silence in the churches," I Corinthians 14:34.
"As I have given order to the churches," I Corinthians 16:1.
"The churches of Asia salute you," I Corinthians 16:19. See also II Corinthians 8:1, 19, 23; 11:8, 28; 12:13; Galatians 7:22; I Thessalonians 1:4; 1:11, 20; Revelation 2:7.

Paul said (Colossians 4:15), "Salute the brethren which are in Laodicea, and Nymphas, and the church which is in his house." See also Romans 16:5; Philemon 2.

5. THE CHURCH IS THE REPOSITORY AND SUPPORT OF THE TRUTH. The Lord has committed to us His truth. We should hold it inviolate, guard against admixture of heresy, and declare it to the world. The word faith is sometimes used in the sense of the true doctrines.

"Beloved, when I gave all diligence to write unto you of the common salvation, it was needful for me to write unto you, and exhort you that ye should earnestly contend for the faith which was once delivered to the saints," Jude 3.
"And all things are of God, who hath reconciled us to himself by Jesus Christ, and hath given to us the ministry of reconciliation . . . Now then we are ambassadors for Christ, as though God did beseech you by us; we pray you in Christ's stead, be ye reconciled to God," II Corinthians 5:19-20.
"But if I tarry long, that thou mayest know how thou oughtest to behave thyself in the house of God, which is the church of the living God, the pillar and ground of the truth," I Timothy 3:15.

In the above Scriptures we are told that the church is the "pillar and ground of the truth." God has chosen to trust His church with this grave responsibility.

Authority and privilege have been placed in the church. The churches are the executive units of His kingdom.

"All power is given unto me in heaven and in earth. Go ye therefore, and teach all nations, baptizing them in the name of the Father, and of the Son, and of the Holy Ghost: teaching them to observe all things whatsoever I have commanded you: and, lo, I am with you alway, even unto the end of the world. Amen," Matthew 28:18-20.
"And I will give unto thee the keys of the kingdom of heaven: and whatsoever thou shalt bind on earth shall be bound in heaven: and whatsoever thou shalt loose on earth shall be loosed in heaven," Matthew 16:19.

6. THE CHURCH IS NOT OF THIS WORLD. Every other organization—fraternal, economic, civic or political—had its origin in the minds of men. Not so with the church

of the Lord Jesus Christ. God is the designer. It was God that designed the tabernacle in the wilderness, and the temple that crowned Mt. Moriah, Hebrews 8:5; Exodus 25:40. He also designed His church and had it in mind from of old. Until the gospel age it was a mystery (Ephesians 3:3-6), that both Gentiles and Jews would constitute one body. Jesus said:

> "Jesus answered, My kingdom is not of the world. If my kingdom were of this world, then would my servants fight, that I should not be delivered to the Jews: but now my kingdom is not from thence," John 18:36.

The head of the church, Jesus, is not of this world, John 17:8; we are not of this world, John 17:16; and many other references.

The authority of the church is from heaven. The ordinances are from heaven. The laws and commandments given it are from heaven. It owes its allegiance to God, rather than the world. Its hopes and promises are from heaven. Its business concerns spiritual things.

7. THE CHURCH OF CHRIST AND FAMILY OF GOD ARE DIFFERENT. The family of God includes all the saved everywhere, in heaven and in earth. Everyone that is saved is "born again." They are, at the moment of salvation, born from above, born of the Spirit, and hence, children of God. Indeed, one must be born again to go to heaven. Baptists maintain that we cannot train a person into salvation. We can train a saved person and help his Christian growth after he is saved, however.

Perhaps there are many thousands of church members today that are not saved. Church membership does not save. Baptists believe that one must be saved before one is qualified to join a church. But everyone that is saved belongs to God's family.

> "Jesus answered and said unto him, Verily, verily, I say unto thee, Except a man be born again, he cannot see the kingdom of God," John 3:3.
>
> "Jesus answered, Verily, verily, I say unto thee, except a man be born of water and of the spirit, he cannot enter into the kingdom of God . . . Marvel not that I say unto thee, Ye must be born again," John 3:5-7.
>
> "Which were born, not of blood, nor of the will of the flesh, nor of the will of man, but of God," John 1:13.

> "Beloved, let us love one another: for love is of God; and every one that loveth is born of God and knoweth God," I John 4:7.
> "Whosoever believeth that Jesus is the Christ is born of of God . . .," I John 5:1. See verses 4, 18.
> "Being born again, not of corruptible seed, but of incorruptible, by the Word of God which liveth and abideth for ever," I Peter 1:23.
> "As newborn babes, desire the sincere milk of the word, that ye may grow thereby," I Peter 2:2.

There can be no such thing as a child without parents. Saved people are said to be children. Children are members of a family. God had a family, and it consists of those who have been begotten by Him. Satan has a family also. Note:

> "Ye are of your father the devil, and the lusts of your father ye will do . . ." John 8:44.

The unsaved are said to be children of this world. God's people are not of this world, as we have heretofore shown. They are "children of light." See also John 12:36; Ephesians 5:8; I Thessalonians 5:5.

> "For the children of this world are wiser than the children of light," Luke 16:8.
> "The Spirit itself beareth witness with our spirit, that we are the children of God. And if children, then heirs: heirs of God, and joint-heirs with Christ," Romans 8:16-17.
> "For ye are the children of God by faith in Christ Jesus," Galatians 3:26.

Thus we have shown that God has children, a family. However, one thing we should understand. Every person is not a child of God. The theory of the universal brotherhood of man and Fatherhood of God is not true. One is in the world, kingdom of darkness, a child of wrath, a child of this world and of Satan until born again. See Ephesians 2:1-3; Colossians 1:13.

The church of Christ is composed of those who are saved, who are born again, confess Christ and are baptized by it. It is not synonymous with the family of God. There are a lot of people outside the church who are children of God. Without doubt, too, there are many in the church who are not saved.

8. THE CHURCH IS A LIGHTHOUSE. Nothing can take the place of light. It is an indispensable thing. By it ships are saved from disaster. By it we see our way to

travel. Indeed, it lets us into a world of knowledge that would otherwise be hidden from us. The Scriptures liken the church to a light.

> "Ye are the light of the world. A city that is set on a hill cannot be hid," Matthew 5:14.

We are commanded to put our lights on the candlestick, and the candlestick is said to be the church.

> "Neither do men light a candle, and put it under a bushel, but on a candlestick: and it giveth light unto all that are in the house," Matthew 5:15.

> "The mystery of the seven stars which thou sawest in my right hand, and the seven golden candlesticks. The seven stars are the angels of the seven churches: and the seven candlesticks which thou sawest are the seven churches," Revelation 1:20. See also Matthew 5:16; Luke 12:35; Ephesians 5:8; I Thessalonians 5:5.

> The church is to radiate the light of the glorious gospel of Jesus Christ, II Corinthians 4:4.

9. THE CHURCH IS THE SALT OF THE EARTH. Salt is a preservative. It is one of the most necessary things for human health. Also with many in oriental lands salt was used as a seal of covenant. To eat salt with another was to show that there was perfect accord and fellowship; particularly with the Arabs was this true. The church is likened by Jesus Himself to salt. Like salt it fills a place nothing else can fill. We should be sure that our salt will not lose its savour.

> "Ye are the salt of the earth: but if the salt have lost its savour, wherewith shall it be salted? It is thenceforth good for nothing, but to be cast out, and to be trodden under the foot of man," Matthew 5:13.

10. A WORSHIPPING AND WORKING BODY. The church is a place for glorifying God. "**Unto him be glory in the church by Christ Jesus throughout all ages, world without end,**" Ephesians 3:21. We can glorify the Lord in worship. The church is the place where devout worship should be made. We should join with our fellow members in this first of all duties.

> "And let us consider one another to provoke unto love and to good works: not forsaking the assembling of ourselves together, as the manner of some is; but exhorting one another; and so much the more as ye see the day approaching," Hebrews 10:24-25.

So the church is a place where we should meet together and exhort one another and provoke one another or urge one another to good works. Here we sing together, pray together, praise together, and also plan together to better serve the Lord.

The church is a benevolent institution. It is especially directed to serve one another or help one another when in need. Paul had the churches to remember the poor saints at Jerusalem. See the second chapter of II Corinthians.

The church is a preaching institution and is commanded to preach the gospel in all the world. It is a training institution and should so teach that babes in Christ will become strong in the faith.

It and it only has the authority to hold and observe the ordinances Christ delivered to the church—baptism and the Lord's Supper.

Its business is purely concerning spiritual things, or things designed to terminate in the spiritual. It is not of this world but is God's representative on earth of things that are spiritual, eternal and Divine. It asks nothing from the world and is not subject unto it.

11. THE CHURCH A STOREHOUSE. Should the church be a collecting agent? Well, why not? It is the Lord's house, it is the Lord's body, His temple. It is this writer's opinion that all our work should be done through the church so that the church would get the glory. **"To Him be glory in the church."** The church is a cooperative body composed of individuals. Each should contribute his part to the whole. Giving of our time, talent or money should be for, and through, the church. Personal glory should forever be banished from our minds.

Oftentimes we hear people criticize the pastor, or someone else they think responsible, for wanting money. Most of the time these very same people spend multiple times more money on themselves, even on the world; and what is still worse, on sinful things. But they complain when they are expected to give a reasonable part of the means God gives them for the work of the church. God has a right to ALL our time, talent and means.

CHAPTER III

THE GOVERNMENT OF THE CHURCH

1. IT IS CONGREGATIONAL, OR DEMOCRATIC. There are three principal forms of church government in the religious world: Episcopal, Presbyterian and the Baptist way—congregational or democratic. The latter is the New Testament way, and has been a distinguishing mark for Missionary Baptists, by whatever name then known, in every century since Christ. Their way of government occasioned much persecution in former centuries. They would not recognize the state-churches or Rome's so-called authority.

In a New Testament church each member has the same privileges as others. There are no orders in the laity, and none among the elders. Any member of a Baptist church has the right to make motions and to vote on motions of others. They have a right to be heard when they have a matter to propose.

All questions should be decided by a majority vote of the church. The minority, if there be one, should acquiesce in the majority decision. Often times this is not done and confusion and strife result. In the case of the incestuous man in the church at Corinth, he was excluded by the "many." This literally means, by majority. See I Corinthians 5:1-5 and II Corinthians 2:1-8.

The decision of a church is final. It is at the same time the primary and the supreme court in matters touching its sphere. However, a practice of long standing has been to call councils on occasions where there is some dispute that cannot be otherwise settled. But the council can only recommend; it cannot enforce its opinion. It is up to the local church after all.

Because of the fact that the local church does have the final say, it is all the more important that it weigh well any matters that come before it. It is very important that it stay with the rules of the Scriptures.

The church calls its own pastors. It exercises its own discipline and regulates its order of worship. It being independent and a separate unit is not dependent upon any other such body, and certainly not to a super-governing power. It is not a member of a general or territorial or regional governing body and not subject to any overall impositions of any kind.

2. THE CHURCH IS AN EXECUTIVE BODY. There are three principal divisions of government: Executive, Judicial and Legislative. A Baptist church has nothing whatever to do with the legislative. The New Testament churches didn't, and we are their successors. The church cannot make laws; Jesus never authorized this function. Through the centuries Baptists, by whatever name they were known in those ages, suffered intolerably by those who took to themselves the authority to enact laws and rules in church affairs. Missionary Baptists never recognized any right by false churches to pass rules for behavior.

Jesus had laid down His laws in the New Testament and we are to follow these to the letter. We are told:

> "All scripture is given by inspiration of God, and is profitable for doctrine, for reproof, for correction, for instruction in righteousness: that the man of God may be perfect, throughly furnished unto all good works," II Timothy 3:16-17.

It must be remembered that the church is subject to Christ's laws. It does not have absolute authority except as it conforms to the will of its Head.

The Catholics, and many Protestants, superimpose what they call the voice of the church over the expressed command of Christ. With the Catholics, tradition is equal, if not a little above, the Written Word; hence, the reason for all the human innovations, pageantry, carnival spirit and "sacraments."

Not even a church of the Lord Jesus Christ has a right to do wrong, and whether a thing is wrong or not is to be determined by the New Testament.

Note that we are throughly, and thoroughly, furnished unto ALL good works. Everything then that God would have us do is given us in the Scriptures. He also said, **"Teaching them to observe ALL THINGS whatsoever I have commanded you,"** Matthew 28:20.

As an executive it is to carry out the expressed will of its Head and lawgiver. The great Commission was given to the church as His executive on the earth, to execute His commands for preaching and teaching; rules of discipline, also. It is His body, His house, and in it He lives and works. It is the business of His church to **"make known the manifold wisdom of God,"** not to follow and enforce its own wisdom, Ephesians 3:10.

3. THE CHURCH CHOOSES ITS OWN OFFICERS. There are but two ordained officers in the church, pastor and deacons. The idea of a modern bishop over a regional territory with several congregations is heretical and foreign to the Scriptures. Such was not known in New Testament times. Instead of there being some ruling bishop over several churches, the reverse was true: there were sometimes several elders in the same congregation. The term bishop is interchangeable with the term elder—they mean the same thing. There is no distinction made in the Scriptures, other denominational teaching notwithstanding. When Paul called the elders of the church to him at Ephesus, you will note there were several of them.

"And from Miletus he sent to Ephesus, and called the elders of the church," Acts 20:17.

The church being a local body, independent and separate, and being sovereign under Christ its head, calls its own pastor just as it conducts its other affairs. A church should always be prayerful in doing so, and should be willing for the Lord to have His own way. So many times possibly a preacher's personality, dress, culture, education, affability or some other trait influences people. In the matter of electing or ordaining one to take the place of Judas, the church at Jerusalem voted on two. Only one, of course, was elected, Matthias. The church prayed that the Lord might show them who was His choice, Acts 1:15-17.

There are certain qualifications that the Bible gives for ministers. Too many times these are not even considered by churches in setting someone aside for ordination. This has resulted in unprincipled men being in the ministry and is the cause of a lot of factions and confusion, a lot of strife and division. If churches would ordain only those God wants there would be much less of this among the churches. Preachers who are selfish, easily offended, lovers of preeminence, those that love the "spotlight," who are vain, are a curse to the Cause. Notice the following:

> "This is a true saying, If a man desire the office of a bishop, he desireth a good work. A bishop then must be blameless, the husband of one wife, vigilant, sober, of good behaviour, given to hospitality, apt to teach; not given to wine, no striker, not greedy of filthy lucre; but patient, not a brawler, not covetous; one that ruleth well his own house, having his children in subjection with all gravity; (for if a man know not how to rule his own house, how shall he take care of the church of God?) Not a novice, lest being lifted up with pride he fall into the condemnation of the devil. Moreover he must have a good report of them that are without; lest he fall into reproach and the snare of the devil," I Timothy 3:1-7. See also the first chapter of Titus, II Corinthians 6:3.

"Congregations elected their own deacons in New Testament times. Acts 6:3-6, 'Wherefore, brethren, look YE out among you seven men,' etc. The **church** had been called together and the apostles instructed the **church** to select seven men. These men were to look after the needy. Those elected, the apostles laid their hands on.

"When it came to choosing elders Paul and Barnabas ordained those that were elected by the churches. We read, Acts 14:23, 'And when they had ordained them elders in every church, and had prayed with fasting,' etc. The Greek word used is 'cheirotonein,' meaning to stretch forth the hands."—Ben M. Bogard, Baptist Waybook.

Phillip Schaff, the Lutheran Historian in "Apostolic

Church" page 501, says: "As to presbyters-bishops (pastors) Luke informs us (Acts 14:23) that Paul and Barnabas appointed them to office in the newly founded congregations by taking a vote of the people, thus merely presiding over the choice. Such, at least, is the usual sense of 'cheirotonein.'" This view is also held by that noted Baptist, J. M, Pendleton, author of Pendleton's Church Manual.

Early congregations elected their missionaries. Acts 11:22-24, "Then tidings of these things came unto the ears of the church which was in Jerusalem; and they sent forth Barnabas, that he should go as far as to Antioch," etc. Pendleton says in his church manual, page 118: "The churches in apostolic times sent forth ministers on missionary tours."

Jesus laid down a rule that there should be no one person in authority over His people. His church is congregational in government. Matthew 20:25-26, **"Ye know that the princes of the Gentiles exercise authority upon them, and they that are great exercise authority over them. BUT IT SHALL NOT BE SO AMONG YOU."**

Peter said, I Peter 5:3, **"Neither as being lords over God's heritage, but being ensamples to the flock."**

The fact that a church can Scripturally exist without any officers at all is proof that the government of the same is in the hand of the church itself.

We have the testimony of a Lutheran historian that the early churches were independent and democratic in government. Mosheim in his history, volume 1, page 92, says: "The churches in those ancient times were entirely independent; none of them subject to any foreign jurisdiction, but each governed by its own rules and its own laws. For though the churches founded by the apostles had this deference shown them, that they were consulted in difficult and doubtful cases; yet they had no judicial authority, no sort of supremacy over the others, nor the least right to enact laws for them. Nothing, on the contrary, is more evident than the perfect equality that reigned among the primitive churches."

Mosheim was a Lutheran historian, yet this is what he says. This testimony of the government of the early churches goes against his own church. But a historian must speak the truth, if he be sincere. This testimony is also a fatal blow to the claims of the Catholics.

Here is another testimony from an enemy of Baptists. "Such was the mild and equal constitution by which the Christians were governed for more than a hundred years after the death of the apostles. Every society formed within itself an independent republic; and although the most distant of these little states maintained a mutual, as well as a friendly intercourse of letters and deputations, the Christian world was not yet conducted by any supreme authority or legislative assembly."—Gibbons Roman Empire, Volume 1, page 555.

Gibbons therefore sounds a death knell to episcopacy or kindred governments for churches. We learn from him, and he was not a Christian, that only a government such as Baptists have today existed in the early churches.

Elders, presbyters and bishops are the same. The New Testament knows nothing of the Catholic or Protestant orders of the ministry. There is not even a hint in the Apostolic churches. A. B. Chapin, an Episcopalian, admits this in these words:

"It is evident from a comparison of certain passages of Scripture, that the terms Presbyter and Bishop are often used in the Bible to designate the same class of officers. Thus in Acts (20:27) it is said that when Paul was at Miletus, 'He sent to Ephesus and called the Presbyters of the church;' and in his address to them (verse 28), he tells them, 'to take heed to themselves and to all the flock, over which the Holy Ghost hath made them bishops.' So the Apostle ordained Presbyters in every church (Acts 14:23), but the direction of the Epistle to the Philippians is, 'to the Bishops and Deacons.'" — Chapin's Primitive Church, page 147.

Deacons are also officers of the church and the local church selects and ordains them. They should be men of sterling character. As to qualifications, much the same is required of them as of ministers. Deacons are the servants of the church, and not the bosses. Theirs is to take the lead in the material matters of the church while the pastor has charge of the spiritual work. They should be men with the following traits:

> "Likewise must the deacons be grave, not double-tongued, not given to much wine, not greedy of filthy lucre; holding the mystery of the faith in a pure conscience. And let these also first be proved; then let them use the office of a deacon, being found blameless. Even so their wives must be grave, not slanderers, sober, faithful in all things. Let the deacons be the husband of one wife, ruling their children and their own houses well," I Timothy 3:8-13.

4. A CHURCH HAS AUTHORITY OVER ITS MEMBERSHIP. The power of receiving and dismissing members is inherent in its very nature, being a self governing body. But even here it must function in harmony with the laws given it by its Head.

It is commanded, as a church, to receive members. In some modern and so-called churches the pastor or someone else receives the members. But Paul said to the church at Rome:

"Him that is weak in the faith, receive ye," Romans 14:1.

A church has the powers of discipline. Nothing is clearer than this. We have already cited the case of the adulterous man in the church at Corinth. Paul directed that the church take action. Note that he did not do it himself, but urged the church to do it. The church did; they put him out of their fellowship, and by a majority vote. Later, as you will find from his second Corinthian letter, this same man was restored, after he had suffered awhile.

The church is the court of last resort for personal offenses. Jesus gave commandment that when one was offended he should go to the offender; if he failed to effect reconciliation he should go and take others with him. If even that failed, **"Tell it to the church."** It becomes a church matter.

> "Moreover if thy brother shall trespass against thee, go and tell him his fault between him and thee alone: if he shall hear thee, thou hast gained thy brother. But if he will not hear thee, then take with thee one or two more, that in

the mouth of two or three witnesses every word may be established. And if he shall neglect to hear them, tell it unto the church: but if he neglect to hear the church, let him be unto thee as an heathen and a publican," Matthew 18:15-17.

Concerning discipline, Paul gave an explicit command when he said, II Thessalonians 3:6, **"Now we command you, brethren, in the name of the Lord Jesus Christ, that ye withdraw yourselves from every brother that walketh disorderly, and not after the tradition which ye received from us."** See also Romans 16:17.

Discipline should always be in the spirit of love and humility. It should begin with gentle and repeated admonition. Close, personal friends can often bring the erring to realize, if they are truly the Lord's children, their errors. This is one of the pastor's responsibilities. Wisdom and prudence should always be used. The Lord's admonition is, **". . . considering thyself lest thou also be tempted."**

If an offender must be brought before the church let it not be until all other measures have failed. Oftentimes persons are charged in churches out of revenge or personal animosity, or out of hurt pride. There **is** such a thing as contempt of the church. But we should be sure that it is not contempt of **us** that moves us to discipline.

Our behaviour with and in the church is a very serious matter for it is God's institution. Its peace and harmony is something that we should guard, even at great cost to ourselves. We should always remember that the church was purchased with Christ's blood, Acts 20:28.

5. RESPECTIVE DUTIES OF PASTORS AND DEACONS. As we have shown, both of these are ordained officers of the church. However, a New Testament church does not have to have either to be a church. They are necessary to the proper ministry of the church.

The Pastor. He is first of all a servant of Christ. See Romans 1:1. He is the secondary shepherd of the flock. Christ Himself is the chief shepherd.

"**And when the Chief Shepherd shall appear, ye shall receive a crown of glory that fadeth not away,**" I Peter 5:4.
"**But are now returned unto the Shepherd and Bishop of your souls,**" I Peter 2:25.
"**I am the good Shepherd,**" John 10:14.

> "Take heed therefore unto yourselves, and to all the flock, over the which the Holy Ghost hath made you overseers, to feed the church of God, which he hath purchased with his own blood," Acts 20:28. See also I Peter 5:2.

The pastor is God's messenger, and should be attentively heard. The right kind of a pastor is concerned about his people. He is, in a measure, a watchman, a guard, as well as a teacher. The pastor's primary duty is to preach the Word, but there are attendant duties. It is the writer's conviction that often the pastor is not given the important place in the life of the church that divine commission gives him, at least not every time. He occupies a unique place in the government of the church.

> "Remember them that have the rule over you, who have spoken unto you the word of God," Hebrews 12:7.
>
> "Obey them that have the rule over you, and submit yourselves: for they watch for your souls as they that must give account, that they may do it with joy, and not with grief: for that is unprofitable for you," Hebrews 13:17.

Thus we see, that in some sense, the pastor is a ruler. Certainly he is not an episcopal dictator, still he should rule. We are told why we should submit ourselves to his rule. It is that he must give account. As a shepherd is careful to bring back to the fold at night the whole number counted out to him in the morning, watching over the sheep alertly during the day in the pasture, so the pastor should consider his charges. And the church should co-operate with him in it.

The pastor is the first officer of the church. It is his duty to faithfully preach the Word, declaring the whole counsel of God, Acts 20:27. He should indoctrinate the church against grievous wolves that might seek to enter in, Acts 20:29. Paul said that he counted not his life dear unto himself to instruct and warn the Ephesian brethren, Acts 20:24.

The pastor is the presiding officer for the business meetings of the church. It is his business to see that everyone is fairly heard and that all are treated equally in the conduct of the business.

He is the ex-officio chairman of all committees. By virtue of his position and attendant responsibility he should first be consulted about all matters that affect the church.

He should rule by example, exhortation and even by rebuke. See I Timothy 5:20; II Timothy 2:15. He should rule in the sense of leadership, leading the church to do its proper business and shoulder its responsibilities in worship, discipline, missions, benevolences, teachings and otherwise. See also I Timothy 5:12.

There was still only one order or rank in the ministry in the second century. Presbyters and bishops were the same men; they were chosen by the people, not appointed by cardinals or the pope. They lived on the voluntary offerings by the people, exactly as Baptists practice today. See Ruter's Gregory, page 40.

The Deacons. Happy is the church that has only godly, consecrated deacons. Pity the church that has any other kind. Deacons primarily are to look after the material affairs of the church, and have no more to do with the pulpit than any other member unless commissioned by the church. They are the servants of the church, not the masters.

We have already given some qualifications as laid down in the Bible, and it is seen that the same standard concerning character is required for the deacon as for the minister. There is one thing, however, that needs to be emphasized. They should be men of good, sober, sound, judgment.

The primary purpose for them is to relieve the ministry of duties not directly related to the ministry of the word. This was the reason given for the first church at Jerusalem:

> "Wherefore, brethren, look ye out from among you seven men of honest report, full of the Holy Ghost and wisdom, whom we may appoint over this business. But we will give ourselves continually to prayer, and to the ministry of the word," Acts 6:3-4.

The Scriptures know nothing of the modern term, "Board of Deacons." The very word "deacon" comes from the word "diakonos," meaning servant. The modern way of imposing the rulership of the church into their hands is unscriptural. In some large and modern, worldly-minded churches today, even in Baptist ranks, this is done. But a real deacon would not want such responsibility.

6. OTHER OFFICERS OF THE CHURCH. A church can have as many special officers as is necessary to its proper functioning. Of necessity, there must be a clerk or secretary to keep the records. There must be a treasurer. Even the first church had one, though he was an unworthy one. Paul said, I Corinthians 14:40, **"Let everything be done decently and in order."** A well organized church is a better church. It is wise to get just as many of the members in places of responsibility as possible. In this way more people can help "run" the church. It is always better to pin point responsibility, if you want to get things done. "Everybody's business is nobody's business."

7. INTER-CHURCH RELATIONS. Though churches are complete as local bodies, have their own government and not dependent upon any other church and not answerable to any other church for its actions, churches can have fellowship.

Once baptized by an orthodox Missionary Baptist church, all other Baptist churches recognize the baptism and will accept members from that church by a mere recommendation. Usually, this is in the form of a "church letter." However, the letter itself is not a transfer of membership; it is only a recommendation. A person is received into a Baptist church by the sovereign vote of that church.

The ordained ministers and deacons of one Baptist church are usually welcome to help ordain candidates for the ministry or the deaconship by other Baptist churches. They meet and form a council or presbytery, examine the candidates as to their scriptural qualifications and make their recommendation to the local church. The church must authorize the presbytery to proceed if hands are laid on the candidates.

Churches may associate together in what we call Associations. This they can do by means of messengers from each church. Association Baptists believe in absolute equality of churches and pastors. We believe that a church must send only her members, not some other church's members, to represent her in the association. Equality can only be assured in this way. But we will discuss this feature under the head, The Functions of a Church.

Churches must respect each other's discipline. Much confusion and strife come from a failure to do so. Though each church has only authority over its own members yet it should respect the action of another. If a member is excluded from one church, the other churches should refuse to accept that person until he has gone back to the church and made proper amends and obtained a letter in fellowship. Sometimes, however, churches get wrong. There is always the privilege to have a council of unbiased men to come together from sister churches to consider and make recommendations. Thus, any wrong can be corrected.

8. BAPTIST INFLUENCE ON AMERICAN GOVERNMENT. It is worthy of note that the government of a Virginia Baptist Church attracted the attention of Thomas Jefferson. Its pure democracy, coming under his observation while attending its meetings, he thought to be the best form of government for the American colonies.

For documentary proof we refer to the following:

"We appeal to the opinion of Jefferson, the most eminent of American statesmen, touching Baptist church government. The following facts were communicated to the Christian Watchman, several years ago, by the Rev. Fishback, of Lexington, Kentucky.

'Mr. Editor: The following circumstance, which occurred in the state of Virginia, relative to Mr. Jefferson, was detailed to me by Elder Andrew Tribble, about six years ago, who since died when ninety-two or three years old. The fact may interest some of your readers.

'Andrew Tribble was the pastor of a small Baptist church which held monthly meetings at a short distance from Mr. Jefferson's house, eight or ten years before the American Revolution. Mr. Jefferson attended the meetings of the church several months in succession, and after one of them he asked Elder Tribble to go home and dine with him, with which he complied.

'Mr. Tribble asked Mr. Jefferson how he was pleased with their church government. Mr. Jefferson replied that it had struck him with force, and had interested him much, that he considered it the only form of pure democracy that then existed in the world, and had concluded that it would be the best plan of government for the American Colonies. This was several years before the Declaration of Independence.'" See Orchard's History of Baptists, vol. 1, page 19.

9. THE VIRGINIA CHURCH PATTERNED ITS GOVERNMENT AFTER THE PRIMITIVE CHURCH. William Jones, speaking of episcopacy, says: "This constitution of things was an entire departure from the order of worship, established under divine direction by the apostles of Christ in the primitive church. In fact, scarcely any two things could be more dissimilar than was the simplicity of the gospel dispensation from the hierarchy established under Constantine the Great.

'Let none,' says Dr. Mosheim, alluding to the first and second centuries, 'confound the bishops of this primitive and golden period of the church, with those of whom we read in the following ages. For though they were both designated by the same name, yet they differed extremely in many respects. A bishop, during the first and second centuries, was a person who had the care of one Christian assembly, which at that time was, generally speaking, small enough to be contained in a private house.

'In this assembly, he acted not so much with the authority of a master, as with the zeal and diligence of a faithful servant. The churches also, in those early times, were entirely independent; none of them subject to any foreign jurisdiction, but each one governed by its own rulers and its own laws. Nothing is more evident than the perfect equality that reigned among the primitive churches; nor does there ever appear, in the first century, the smallest trace of that association of provincial churches, from which councils and metropolitans derive their origin.'

"To which we may add, that the first churches acknowledged no earthly potentate as their head. This had been expressly prohibited by their divine Master. 'The kings of the Gentiles,' said he, 'exercise lordship over them; and they that exercise authority upon them are termed benefactors. But with you it shall not be so; let him that is greatest among you be as the younger, and he that is chief, as he that doth serve.' Again, 'Be not ye called Rabbi; for one is your master, even Christ, and all ye are brethren. And call no man your father upon the earth; for one is your father who is in heaven. Neither be ye called masters; for one is your master, even Christ. But he that is greatest among you shall be your servant; and, whosoever exalteth himself, shall be abased, while he that humbleth himself shall be exalted.'

"These divine maxims, which are in perfect unison with the whole tenor of the New Testament, were entirely disregarded by the ecclesiastics who undertook to new-model the constitution of the Christian church, under the auspices of Constantine, and whom, as a matter of courtesy, they condescended to make its earthly head."—Jones' History of the Christian Church, page 166.

CHAPTER IV

THE IDENTITY AND PERPETUITY OF THE CHURCH

1. THE CHURCH MAY BE IDENTIFIED BY ITS DOCTRINE. Association Missionary Baptists claim to believe and teach the very same doctrines that the Apostolic churches had. We believe that there have always been, since the days of Christ, a people who believed and taught exactly what we believe today. They have not always been known as Baptists. They have been known in different centuries as Anabaptists, Waldenses, Albigenses, Petrobrussians, Novatians, Montantists and many others. We would not affirm that everyone known by these names were orthodox, no more than we would affirm that all who go by the name Baptist today are sound in the faith. But the true churches were found among them, and in all ages; in Europe, Africa, Asia and the Islands. Many times they were called after the name of the leading proponent among them, but generally named by their enemies. The name does not matter. The doctrines only count.

2. JESUS PROMISED THE CHURCH WOULD CONTINUE. Nothing is more certain than that Jesus Himself promised to be with the church all the time. The idea that the church died out and had to be rebuilt by Martin Luther, or some other "reformer," is absurd. Martin Luther never got rid of all his Catholicism. He was heretical himself. If he had been the right kind of person he would have found a Baptist church and joined it. There were some at that time. Many of the "reformers" themselves were persecutors in their own right. If all the churches of the Lord died out previous to the reformation, then the promise of Jesus was of none effect. If they didn't and were still on

the earth, then there was no excuse for the "reformers" to start something new. Protestantism has persecuted Baptists much as Rome has; not only in Europe, but in the American colonies as well. But here is the promise of Jesus:

> "And, lo, I am with you alway, even unto the end of the world," Matthew 28:20.

> "And I say also unto thee, That thou art Peter, and upon this rock I will build my church; and the gates of hell shall not prevail against it," Matthew 16:18.

> "Husbands, love your wives, even as Christ also loved the church, and gave himself for it; that he might sanctify and cleanse it with the washing of water by the word, that he might present it to himself a glorious church, not having spot, or wrinkle, or any such thing: but that it should be holy and without blemish," Ephesians 5:25.

Jesus said that He would finally present it to Himself as a finished product of His grace—no chance for apostasy.

> "Unto him be glory in the church by Christ Jesus throughout all ages, world without end," Ephesians 3:21.

Jesus placed the Lord's Supper in His church while He was here on the earth. He then commanded that this Memorial Supper be observed until He comes again, I Corinthians 11:24. Manifestly, then, there must ever be churches to do this until He comes. Yes, Jesus has promised to be with the church all the way. See also Hebrews 12:28; John 14:16-17.

3. BAPTISTS ARE NOT PROTESTANTS. They are not, in the accepted sense of that term. It usually refers to those who protested against Romanism or Catholicism during the time of the reformation, and those sects that have arisen out of it. Missionary Baptists were in the world before Catholicism began. Baptists were never in the Catholic church and did not, therefore, come out of it.

4. THE RISE OF CATHOLICISM. The Catholic church was a gradual formation. A people holding our very Baptist doctrines remained entirely separate while the leaven of heresy was being planted in the measures of meal. In Revelation we have the term Nicolaitanes. This one English word is from two Greek words, "nico," meaning to rule, or subdue,

conquer, etc.; and "laos," meaning people. Hence, the idea, ruling the people. Here is how the Catholic heresy started, and it began early. Jesus Himself said He "hated" this doctrine of the Nicolaitanes. To the church at Ephesus Jesus says:

"But this thou hast, that thou hatest the deeds of the Nicolaitanes, Which I also hate," Revelation 2:6. See also verse 15.

In the beginning of the seventh century the emperor Phocas conferred upon Boniface III, bishop of Rome, the title of ecumenical, or universal bishop. In the year 755 the pope became a temporal prince.—Epitome of Ecclesiastical History, Marsh, pages 224, 231.

Paul could see the rise of this heretical monster in his day, and warned against it. Let it be understood that Baptists did not come out of Roman Catholicism; rather, Catholicism grew out of some heretical Baptists. To this very church at Ephesus that hated the deeds of the Nicolaitanes, he said, **"For I know this, that after my departing shall grievous wolves enter in among you, not sparing the flock,"** Acts 20:29. This doctrine of the Nicolaitanes probably first started in the church at Rome. At first, it was a missionary Baptist Church as established by Paul, and he was well acquainted with it. This same Apostle warned the church at Thessalonica about it: we read:

"For the mystery of iniquity doth already work," II Thessalonians 2:7.

Concerning the rise of the Catholic church, Dr. J. B. Moody says: "It did not originate in a day or year, but gradually subverted the Apostles' teaching, and in centuries inaugurated full-grown popery. But there is not a trace of a pope or universal father . . . in the first three centuries." See "My Church," by J. B. Moody.

The renowned historian Ridpath says: "This epoch in history should not be passed over without reference to the rapid growth of the papal church, in the close of the sixth century and the beginning of the seventh. Most of all by Gregory the Great, whose pontificate extended from 590 to 604, was the supremacy of the apostolic see attested and maintained. Under the triple title of Bishop of Rome, Prelate of Italy, and Apostle of the West, he gradually, by gentle insinuations or bold assertions as best suited the circumstances, elevated the episcopacy of Rome into a genuine papacy of the church. He succeeded in bringing the Arians of Italy and Spain into the Catholic fold, and thus secured the solidarity of the Western Ecclesia."—Vol. 4, page 41.

But the movement had begun a long time before this. Some historians place the ripened fruits of the tree of heresy fully a century before Gregory. But the point is that during all this time persecution was practiced, even before Constantine himself who has been glorified by some as the first Christian emperor, became the persecutor of Baptists, and had them put to death, even after he professed the Christian religion. He put Donatists to death. See Reuter's Gregory, page 80.

5. BAPTISTS IN HISTORY. First, no one has ever been able to find the origin of Baptists this side of Jesus and the apostles. Mosheim, a German historian of world renown, and himself not a friend to Baptists, said: "The true origin of that sect which acquired the denomination of Anabaptists, by their administering anew the rite of baptism to those who came over to their communion, and derived that of Menonites, from that famous man to whom they owe much of their present felicity, is **hidden in the depths of antiquity. This uncertainty will not appear surprising when it is considered that this sect started up suddenly in several countries at the same point of time.**"

Mosheim was Pedobaptist, but he continues. "Anabaptists not only considered themselves descendants of the Waldenses, who were so grievously oppressed and persecuted by the despotic heads of the Romish church, but it may be observed that they are not entirely in error when they boast of their descent from the Waldenses, Petrobrussians, and other ancient sects, who are usually considered as witnesses of the truth in times of general darkness and superstition. **BEFORE THE RISE OF LUTHER AND**

CALVIN, there lay concealed in almost all the countries of Europe, particularly in Bohemia, Moravia, Switzerland, and Germany, many persons who adhered tenaciously to the doctrine, etc., which is the true source of all the peculiarities that are to be found in the religious doctrine and discipline of the Anabaptists."

Alexander Campbell, founder of the so-called "Church of Christ," certainly would not admit any favorable consideration of Baptists if it were not necessary. He says: "From the Apostolic age until the present time, the sentiments of Baptists, and their practice of baptism, have had a continued chain of advocates, and public monuments of their existence in every century can be produced." His debate with McCalla.

Sir Isaac Newton said: "The Baptists are the only body of Christians that have not symbolized with the church of Rome."

Drs. Yepij and Dermont, two noted scholars, were appointed by the king of the Netherlands to write a history of the denominations, and this is what they said about Baptists: "We have now seen that the Baptists, who were formerly called Anabaptists, and in later times, Menonites, were the original Waldenses, and who have long in the history of the church received the honor of that origin. On this account, the Baptists may be considered as the only Christian community which has stood since the days of the apostles, and as a Christian society, which has preserved pure the doctrines of the gospel in all ages. The perfectly correct external and internal economy of the Baptist denomination tends to confirm the truth, disputed by the Romish church, that the reformation brought about in the sixteenth century, was in the highest degree necessary; and, at the same time, goes to refute the erroneous notion of the Catholics, that their communion is the most ancient."

6. BAPTISTS BY OTHER NAMES. Wales was full of Baptists even in the first century. See Davis' History of the Welch Baptists. As we have heretofore said, they were known by other names. North Africa was full of people

who were the same as Missionary Baptists today in their doctrine. In fact, in North Africa, where now Mohammedanism is so rooted, there were found some of the world's most noted preachers.

It must be remembered that about all the history we have of our people has come from our enemies. During the times when Baptists were martyred all their books and papers were also destroyed. See Fox's "Book of the Martyrs." Much of the information we do have has been taken from ancient court records, records of "trials" for the "crime" of dissenting from the apostate church or churches and for nonconformity to the rules and rites adopted by those who presumed to substitute the will of man for the commands of God.

In this short work we do not have space to give much history. We will only be able to give some names and places. If we only had the records that are forever lost it could be readily seen how numerous and how pious the people called Baptists have been through the ages. Though persecuted by Catholics and Protestants, they have adhered to the New Testament faith and practice from the days of Christ until now. Missionary Baptists suffered persecution even in America from those who should have been their helpers in the fight for religious freedom.

Historian John T. Christian, (whose works, in two volumes, should be read by all,) says concerning Baptists: "Baptist churches have the most slender ties or organization and a strong government is not according to their policy. They are like the River Rhone, which sometimes flows as a river broad and deep, but at other times is hidden in the sands. It, however, never loses its continuity or existence. It is simply hidden for a period. Baptist churches may disappear and reappear in the most unaccountable manner. Persecuted by sword and fire, their principles would appear to be almost extinct, when in a most wondrous way God would raise up a man, or some company of martyrs, to proclaim the truth. The footsteps of Baptists of the ages can more easily be traced by blood than by baptism. It is a lineage of suffering rather than a succession of bishops; a martyrdom of principle, rather than an iron chain of succession, which, while attempting to rattle its links back to the apostles, has been of more service in chaining some protesting Baptists to the stake than in proclaiming the truth of the New Testament. It is, nevertheless, a royal succession, that in every age the Baptists have been advocates of liberty for all, and have held that the gospel of the Son of God makes every man a free man in Christ Jesus."

Long before the Reformation in the Sixteenth century Baptists, by other names but in principles the same, were protesting against the corruptions of the apostate church. We are mentioning some but lack of space forbids more notice. Doubtless there were some who went under these names that were not sound in their views. But in the main they were what Missionary Baptists are today.

For information concerning many other groups who held Baptist principles, see a later section, Book III—Origin of Others Who Held Baptist Principles.

For reference books see: "The Origin of Baptists," by Ford; "A History of the Baptists," by Mason; Benedict's "Church History"; "A History of Welch Baptists," by Davis; Orchard's "History of Baptists"; March's Eccl. History and many, many others.

7. BAPTIST PERSECUTION IN AMERICA. Missionary Baptists suffered at the hands of Protestants in early America. We give but one or two instances. Joseph Craig and Aaron Bledsoe were indicted in Virginia "For preaching the gospel of the Son of God in the Colony of Virginia." Patrick Henry, a young lawyer, rushed into the courtroom as the trial began, took the paper of indictment and defended them. Hundreds of instances could be cited where Baptists suffered, even in Colonial times.

Hawkes, an Episcopalian, said: "No dissenters in Virginia experienced, for a time, harsher treatment than the Baptists."

Many laws were passed in Massachusetts, Virginia and other colonies against the Baptists. Many were hailed into court, sent to jail or fined; and not by Catholics, but by Protestants. Among those so persecuted was Dr. John Clarke, the founder of the first Baptist church in Newport, R. I., and as far as we can tell the first Baptist church on American shores. Though Roger Williams was a good and great man, he was not, however, the founder of the first Baptist church in America. True, he held many Baptist sentiments and one time gathered a group together, but it soon came to nought.

Page after page of history tells of the persecutions of Baptists here in our own country. Lack of space forbids more details.

8. BAPTIST SUCCESSION BACK TO CHRIST. We take the liberty to copy the following from "The Church That Jesus Built" by Roy Mason. It is a fine book and our readers are encouraged to read it. He gives a line of Baptist succession as follows:

"Link One. The Baptist church at Dyer, Tennessee, was organized by J. W. Jetter, who came from the Philadelphia Association.

Link Two. Hillcliff church, Wales, England. H. Roller came to the Philadelphia Association from the Hillcliff church. See Minutes of the Philadelphia Association.

Link Three. Hillcliff church was organized by Aaron Arlington, A. D. 987. See Alex Munston's Israel of the Alps, p. 39.

Link Four. Lima Piedmont church ordained Aaron Arlington in 940. See Jones' Church History, p. 324.

Link Five. Lima Piedmont church was organized by Balcaloa, A. D. 812. See Neander's Church History, Vol. 2, p. 320.

Link Six. Balcaloa came from the church at Timto, Asia Minor. See Neander's Church History, Vol. 2, p. 320.

Link Seven. Timto church was organized by Archer Flavin, A. D. 738. See Mosheim's History, Vol. 1, p. 394.

Link Eight. Archer Flavin came from the Daretha church, organized by Adromicus, A. D. 671, in Asia Minor. See Lambert's Church History, p. 47.

Link Nine. Adromicus came from Ponifossi, at the foot of the Alps in France. See Lambert's Church History, p. 47.

Link Ten. Pontifossi church was organized by Tellestman from Turan, Italy, A. D. 309. See Nowlin's Church History, Vol. 2, p. 318.

Link Eleven. Turan church was organized by Tertullan from Bing Joy, Africa, A. D. 237. See Armitage's Church History, p. 182.

Link Twelve. Tertullan was a member of the Partus church at the foot of the Tiber that was organized by Polycarp, A. D. 150. See Cyrus' Commentary of Antiquity, p. 924.

Link Thirteen. Polycarp was baptized by John the Beloved or Revelator, on the 25th day of December, A. D. 95. See Neander's Church History, p. 285.

Link Fourten. John was with Jesus on the Mount. See Mark 3:13-14; Luke 6:12-13.

9. DOCTRINAL COMPARISON. That Missionary Baptists hold the same doctrines as the Apostolic church and preach the pure gospel can be ascertained by comparing the New Testament doctrines and practices with the Baptist churches of today.

A Regenerated Church Membership. Baptists have ever demanded that a person be born again, or regenerated, before acceptance into a church. One must repent and show some signs of being saved. So did John the Baptist, and the early churches, Matthew 3:8; John 3:3; Acts 2:41, 47.

They Baptize Only Believers, and Only by Immersion. So did the Apostles and early churches.

> "And as they went on their way, they came unto a certain water: and the eunuch said, See, here is water; what doth hinder me to be baptized? And Philip said, If thou believest with all thine heart, thou mayest. And he answered and said, I believe that Jesus is the Son of God," Acts 8:36-37. See also Acts 2:41; Matthew 3; 28:19; Mark 16:15-16; Acts 10:47.

They Believe in Salvation by Grace. Many other religious sects profess to believe in this, but inconsistently so. They hold contradictory doctrines. Baptists believe that it is purely by grace that we are saved, and not of works, nor partly by works, of any kind. The Baptist view is in line with Scriptures.

> "For by grace are ye saved through faith; and that not of yourselves: it is the gift of God: not of works, lest any man should boast," Ephesians 2:8-9.
>
> "And if by grace, then it is no more of works: otherwise grace is no more grace . . .," Romans 11:6.
>
> "Being justified by his grace," Titus 2:5.

They Believe in Justification by Faith. So did Jesus and the apostles.

> "Knowing that a man is not justified by the works of the law, but by the faith of Jesus Christ, even we have believed in Jesus Christ, that we might be justified by the faith of Christ, and not by the works of the law: for by the works of the law shall no flesh be justified," Galatians 2:16. See also Galatians 3:6; 3:11; I Corinthians 6:11; Romans 5:1.

They Believe in Total Depravity of Man. The New Testament teaches this. In this we differ from almost all other people.

> "And you hath he quickened, who were dead in trespasses and sins; wherein in time past ye walked according to the course of this world, according to the prince of the power of the air, the spirit that now worketh in the children of disobedience; among whom also we all had our conversation in times past in the lusts of our flesh, fulfilling the desires of the flesh and of the mind; and were by nature the children of wrath, even as others," Ephesians 2:1-2.
>
> "Behold, I was shapen in iniquity, and in sin did my mother conceive me," Psalm 51:5.
>
> "How then can a man be justified with God, or how can he be clean that is born of a woman?" Job 25:4.
>
> "The wicked are estranged from the womb; they go astray as soon as they be born, speaking lies," Psalm 58:3.
>
> "There is not a just man upon earth that doeth good and sinneth not," Ecclesiastes 7:20. Be sure to turn and read Romans 3:9-20. See also Isaiah 64:6; Jeremiah 17:9; Ecclesiastes 8:11; John 8:44; II Corinthians 4:3-4; II Timothy 2:26; Romans 8:7-8; 7:18-30; Jeremiah 12:23; Romans 5:12.

Baptist Churches Are Local and Independent. So were the Apostolic churches. They were separate from even other churches yet held the same beliefs and had fellowship together. See Acts 9:31; 15:41; 16:5; and many others showing there were churches, plural. The church was a local body. Paul said, "Unto the church of God at Corinth," I Corinthains 1:2, etc. One of the doctrines that called down upon them the wrath of state and apostate churches through the centuries of persecution was their peculiar belief that churches were autonomous and sovereign, subject only to Christ the Head.

Baptists Preach That Every Believer Is Perfectly Secure in Christ. Christ preached this doctrine, so did Paul and others. We quote but one Scripture. Please refer to others mentioned.

> "Verily, verily, I say unto you, He that heareth my word, and believeth on him that sent me, hath everlasting life, and shall not come into condemnation; but is passed from death unto life," John 5:24. See also John 3:16; 10:5, 28-29; Romans 5:20; 6:7, 18; 8:1; John 6:35, 50-51; Psalm 97:10; 145:20; II Timothy 4:18; Psalm 103:13, see also verses 8, 10, 11, 12, 17; 27:10; Isaiah 49:15; Romans 8:35-39; Hebrews 7:25; I John 3:9; Ephesians 4:30; II Corinthians 1:21-22; Ecclesiastes 3:14; Psalm 37:24; Hebrews 5:13.

The Separation of Church and State. Baptists through all the ages have consistently maintained that there should be a difference between church and state and have therefore refused to even accept assistance from the state. Most all Protestants have, at one time or another, courted state favor. This was true in the early colonies of America. And in many European countries today Protestant as well as Catholic churches are supported by state taxes.

The Baptist way has been to keep separate and to support its own cause. They believe in obeying the laws of the country. This is taught in the Word of God. See Romans 13:1-7; Titus 3:1; I Peter 2:13-16.

However, Baptists believe in being law-abiding citizens, and they have been known for this during the centuries. In case it should come to the point that we cannot obey both the laws of a jurisdiction and the laws of Christ we have then no choice but to follow our Master. Peter said, **"We ought to obey God rather than men,"** Acts 5:29. See Romans 13:1-7; Titus 3:1; I Peter 2:13-16.

We are taught that civil rulers are ministers of God and are ordained for their place. This does not mean that they are necessarily Christians, but the civil office is ordained or chosen of God for our good. **"Rulers are not a terror to good work."**

There are many other doctrines held by Baptists that they can prove as warranted by the Scriptures. While some of the doctrines of Baptists are believed by others, no other denomination teaches all of them. We believe that the Scriptures teach everything we teach today.

A Restricted Lord's Supper. This ordinance is just that —The Lord's Supper. It is not a sacrament in the Romish sense of the term. It has no saving efficacy whatsoever. Its purpose is to remember the Lord's death until He comes again. We believe as the Apostolic churches believed.

> "**And when he had given thanks, he brake it, and said, Take, eat: this is my body, which is broken for you: this do in remembrance of me. After the same manner also he took the cup, when he had supped, saying, This cup is the New Testament in my blood: this do ye, as oft as ye drink it, in remembrance of me. For as often as ye eat this bread, and drink this cup, ye do show the Lord's death till he come,**" I Corinthians 11:24-26. See rest of chapter; Matthew 26; Mark 14; Luke 22.

We believe that one must be saved, must be scripturally baptized, must be sound in the doctrines of God's word, must be in fellowship with the other members of the church before he is a fit subject to partake of the supper. Moreover we believe that only the proper elements should be used in observing the supper; that is, the fruit of the vine and unleavened bread. We also believe that the proper motive must be had, that of showing the Lord's death until He comes again. All this, the true churches of Christ have ever practiced.

This subject is further discussed elsewhere in this volume.

CHAPTER V

THE FUNCTIONS OF THE CHURCH

1. THE SCRIPTURES A PERFECT GUIDE. Since Baptists believe that God has revealed to us all that He would have us do, and the manner in which it should be done, they resort to the Bible as the all-sufficient rule of faith and practice.

> "All Scripture is given by inspiration of God, and is profitable for doctrine, for reproof, for correction, for instruction in righteousness: that the man of God may be perfect, throughly furnished unto all good works," II Timothy 3:16-17.

We have studied the nature of the church. The very nature of the church indicates its functions. These we shall more particularly study.

2. PREACHING THE GOSPEL. The primary and paramount business of the church of the Lord Jesus Christ is to preach the gospel. Jesus Himself preached it while He was on the earth, using the very same message that John the Baptist used, **"Repent ye for the kingdom of heaven is at hand,"** Matthew 4:17.

Just before He left the world He told His disciples, in church capacity, to go into all the world, make disciples of all nations and baptize those that believed.

> "And Jesus came and spake unto them, saying, All Power is given unto me in heaven and in earth. Go ye therefore and teach all nations," Matthew 28:18-19. See also Mark 16:15.

> "And when he had so said, he showed unto them his hands and his side. Then were the disciples glad when they saw the Lord. Then said Jesus unto them again, Peace be unto you: as my Father hath sent me even so send I you," John 20:20-21.

> "And he ordained twelve, that they should be with him and that he might send them forth to preach," Mark 3:14.

> "And they went forth, and preached everywhere, the Lord working with them," Mark 16:20.

> "And how shall they preach except they be sent," Romans 10:15.

> "And Jesus said, Let the dead bury their dead: but go thou and preach the kingdom of God," Luke 9:60.

In the verse immediately above, we see the importance Jesus placed on preaching. As Paul said, **"How shall they hear without a preacher, how shall they preach except they be sent."** See also Acts 28:30; Acts 8:4; II Timothy 4:2.

3. THE KIND OF MESSAGE WE SHOULD PREACH.

We should preach the gospel of Jesus Christ. That means we should preach the good news, that Jesus Christ has died for our sins according to the Scriptures, and that He was buried and rose again according to the Scriptures. Baptists only can consistently preach the pure gospel, for their definition of the gospel, the Bible meaning of the term, is in harmony with their general beliefs.

The gospel is not an ordinance, nor works, nor law, nor rules, nor commandment, nor a religious ritual. The word itself means good news. It is, therefore, the good news that Jesus died for our sins just like the prophets said He would. It is a declaration to this effect.

> "Moreover, brethren, I declare unto you the gospel which I preached unto you, which also ye have received, and wherein ye stand; By which also ye are saved, if ye keep in memory what I preached unto you, unless ye have believed in vain. For I delivered unto you first of all that which I also received, how that Christ died for our sins according to the Scriptures; and that he was buried, and that he rose again the third day according to the Scriptures," I Corinthians 15:1-4.

Paul said he "received" it. Galatians 1:2 tells us how. It was by the revelation of Jesus Christ, not from man.

The gospel cannot be laws and commandments, for that would not be good news and would be contrary to the definition of the term. God demands perfection, and this we cannot in our own selves have. See Galatians 3:10, 13. We have it because Christ became the curse for us.

The church, therefore, has a cheerful message. It is to tell to sinners the news of something good, the news of something that Christ has done for them—that they could never do for themselves.

> "For what the law could not do, in that it was weak through the flesh, God sending his own Son in the likeness of

sinful flesh, and for sin, condemned sin in the flesh: that the righteousness of the law might be fulfilled in us, who walk not after the flesh, but after the spirit," Romans 8:4-5. See also II Corinthians 11:4; Galatians 1:4-9; Ephesians 1:13; I Timothy 1:11.

4. THE COMMISSION GIVEN TO THE CHURCH. No organization on earth has the right to preach the gospel or administer its ordinances except a New Testament church. The commission to preach and to teach was given to the church as such by Jesus Himself before He left the world. No fraternal organizations, and no so-called churches started by some man since the days of Christ, have any authority to do so. Only that church that was existing before Jesus ascended could have the Commission, for He delivered it in person. It is very plain that if Jesus gave the commission to individuals as such then we are without it today for all of them are dead. But if He gave it to the disciples as a composite body, the church, we still have it for there has been a succession of churches since His day. Jesus promised always to be with it.

"Then the eleven disciples went into Galilee, into a mountain where Jesus had appointed them. And when they saw him, they worshipped him: but some doubted, And Jesus came and spake unto them, saying, All power is given unto me in heaven and in earth. Go ye therefore, and teach all nations, baptizing them in the name of the Father, and of the Son, and of the Holy Ghost; teaching them to observe all things whatsoever I have commanded you: and, lo, I am with you alway, even unto the end of the world," Matthew 28:16-20. See also Mark 16:14-16.

"Then the same day at even, being the first day of the week, when the doors were shut where the disciples were assembled for fear of the Jews, came Jesus and stood in the midst, and saith unto them, Peace be unto you. And when he had so said, he showed unto them his hands and his sides. Then were the disciples glad, when they saw the Lord. Then said Jesus unto them again, Peace be unto you: as my Father hath sent me, even so send I you," John 20:10-21.

There is no such thing as "the church of the air" that you sometimes hear "aired" on the radio. There are a lot of radio preachers who solicit money and who ignore the local church where the authority rests only to preach the gospel. Most of them preach heresy. Yet, a lot of Missionary Baptist churches help support them, when such support should go to their own local ministry or to their own missions program sponsored by the Association of which their church is a member. Beware of deception!

5. HOW WE MAY PREACH. **By the pastor** the local church preaches through its ordained ministry. This is his primary business. Everything else takes second place. The gospel **"is the power of God unto salvation to everyone that believeth, to the Jew first and also to the Greek,"** Romans 1:16. Without it no one can be saved. The pastor should have his message at all times well seasoned with the plan of salvation as he preaches from the pulpit. But his preaching is not confined to that place. From house to house he should preach the good news in his locality. Paul said he preached from house to house, Acts 20:20. See Ephesians 4:11; Acts 8:4-5. The word of God should be preached in such a manner that it can be easily understood, I Corinthians 1:18. Not deceitfully, II Corinthians 4:2.

By the Membership. Every member should preach the word. They are witnesses. Jesus said, **". . . And ye shall be witnesses unto me both in Jerusalem, and in all Judaea, and in Samaria, and unto the uttermost part of the earth,"** Acts 1:8. When the church at Jerusalem was scattered by persecution they went **"everywhere preaching the word."** Only the Apostles remained in Jerusalem, Acts 8:1. The idea that only the minister is expected of the Lord to preach Christ is a mistaken one. True, one may preach by supporting those who do. In this sense we can all preach in foreign lands. Yet, each saved person should also present Jesus personally to those around him.

> **"And the Spirit and the Bride say, Come, And let him that heareth say, Come. And let him that is athirst come. And whosoever will, let him take the water of life freely," Revelation 22:17.**
>
> **"The woman then left her waterpot, and went her way into the city, and saith to the men, Come see a man, which told me all things that ever I did: is not this the Christ? . . . And many of the Samaritans of that city believed on him for the saying of the woman . . ." John 4:28-29, 39.**

By the Printed Page. "The pen is mightier than the sword." The printed page is one of the avenues of preaching the gospel. Good papers, pamphlets, books and other writings have been a blessing to the Cause of Christ. On the other hand, heretical ones have been a curse. Our message from God comes to us from writings. None of us alive today saw Jesus or heard His blessed words of truth. However, men wrote, inspired of God, the truths and they have come down to us through the Providence and design of God, John 20:31; I John 2:12; Hosea 8:12.

Our religious newspapers go into many thousands of homes, and many people read about the Saviour and are schooled in the doctrines of the Word.

Distribution of tracts that present the truth is another way the Word can be preached. Tracts are inexpensive, and everyone can distribute them. Only tracts that are sound should be given out, however. Many are printed that are not true to the Bible. Tracts can be used both at home and abroad. Everyone can preach the gospel by them.

World-Wide Missions. The church is exclusively responsible for missions everywhere. Jesus said:

"Go ye into ALL the world . . . make disciples of ALL nations . . ." Matthew 28:19.

"Go ye into all the world and preach the gospel to every creature," Mark 16:15.

"And ye shall be witnesses unto me both in Jerusalem, and in all Judaea, and unto the uttermost part of the earth," Acts 1:8.

"And this gospel of the kingdom shall be preached in all the world for a witness unto all nations; and then shall the end come," Matthew 24:14.

The churches of the North American Baptist Association have their Jerusalem, their Judea, their Samaria and their "uttermost part of the earth." Their local territory may well be their Jerusalem, but they owe the Lord due notice of fields beyond. Paul said he wanted to preach in regions beyond, II Corinthians 10:16.

Paul said to hold forth the word of life. To hold something forth is to make it accessible to others. This is what we do when we practice missions, whether at home or abroad, Philippians 2:16. Solomon tells us: **"As cold waters to a thirsty soul, so is good news from a far country,"** Proverbs 25:25. The gospel is the good news that Jesus has suffered for our sins so we may have eternal life. We should take the good news to earth's remotest bounds. The world's greatest Missionary, Paul, said again: **"For from you sounded out the Word of the Lord not only in Macedonia and Achaia . . ."** I Thessalonians 1:8. We should be sounding boards to take up the glad refrain and let it reverberate throughout the world. "The church that gives is the church that lives." We will grow only if we go. If we put missions first in our program God will continue to bless our churches.

6. TEACHING. Another function of the church is to teach. Probably this one part of the commission has been as sorely neglected as any other part. The result is apparent. Christians should be well grounded in the faith. This can only be done through study and teaching.

"Study to show thyself approved unto God, a workman that needeth not to be ashamed, rightly dividing the word of truth," II Timothy 2:15.

The church is a teaching institution as well as a preaching institution. In fact, there can be but little distinction between the two duties. In the Commission given by Jesus to His church which we have already quoted, He says, **"teaching them to observe all things whatsoever I have commanded you."** That means a lot. Acquila and Priscilla taught Apollos the way of the Lord more perfectly, Acts 18:26. He was a good man, but needed more teaching. Can this not be said about all of us? The Lord placed "teachers" in the early church as one of the spiritual gifts then needed, Ephesians 4:11. We should never lose sight, while in our study, that the Holy Spirit is the greatest teacher of all, and should look to Him for guidance, John 14:26.

A pastor has much opportunity, and it is his responsibility, to teach, so he must be apt to do so. That is, he must have talent along that line, I Timothy 3:2. One who has not this talent should not be ordained. He should be able to teach the young converts after they are baptized. He can do this in his sermons and he can do it in their homes.

The Teacher Should Know Something. It is tragic how many try to teach who need to be taught themselves. The Sunday school teacher should be one that is able to impart information to the class; otherwise it is mockery and is in vain. This requires some study, some training. Paul one time said:

> "For when for the time ye ought to be teachers, ye have need that one teach you again which be the first principles of the oracles of God; and are become such as have need of milk, and not of strong meat," Hebrews 5:12.

Study Courses and Teaching Clinics. The church should periodically sponsor study courses. The lessons should be so designed as to impart much needed knowledge concerning all the counsel of God, including one's personal responsibility. The government and workings of the church should be included. Missions, benevolence, consecration, the Providence of God, membership responsibility, cooperation and every other needed thing. These courses should be under the direct supervision of someone who is qualified to conduct them. If no one is available locally, then some one should be obtained from some other church.

There are many books available that are good. The Bible, of course, should be the chief text. Every teaching and every idea should "square" with it or else be rejected. In these classes, both young and old should be enlisted. None are too old to learn.

The young men and women of the church, even teen-age boys and girls, should be taught the Word and, not only that, should be taught church responsibility. Too often this is neglected. The church is responsible for the training of its young.

Christian teaching should, of course, begin in the homes of the church members. Parents should not leave it to a Sunday school teacher to do what they should do under their own roof.

Sunday Schools. The Sunday school is a part of the teaching work of the church. It should be under the direct sponsorship of the church, with church elected officers and teachers. The kind of officers and teachers selected will govern the kind of Sunday school the church will have. The most faithful, the most consecrated and the most talented should be chosen for this very important work.

Teachers in the Sunday school should make their Bible a daily companion. Their lessons should be well prepared from the quarterlies they use. Outside helps can be obtained and should be used. They should be, of course, the right kind.

A Sunday school teacher who is too lazy to prepare for his or her class should have the fortitude to resign; likewise, so should the one who is worldly-minded and loves the pleasures of this world more than the house of God.

> "But in a great house there are not only vessels of gold and of silver, but also of wood and of earth; and some to honor and some to dishonor. If a man therefore purge himself from these, he shall be a vessel unto honor, sanctified, and meet for the master's use, and prepared unto every good work," II Timothy 2:20-21.

The Auxiliary. Many Women's Auxiliaries have a lesson at their meetings. This is a good work. Just as with the Sunday school, the preaching and Worship service, the study courses and the Training Service meetings, individuals should always carry their Bibles with them.

The Weekly Training Service. This is another teaching and training service of the church. What we said about the Sunday school applies equally here.

7. WORSHIP. This is decidedly a different function of the church. It transcends everything else. Nothing can take its place. We must worship God because He is our Creator and also our Saviour. Not even angels are worthy of worship—only God. The church is His body, His very own. It is His abode in His ministrations with His own.

True worship must be in spirit and in truth. Hear Him say:

> "But the hour cometh, and now is, when the true worshippers shall worship the Father in Spirit and in truth: for the Father seeketh such to worship him," John 2:23.

There should be an atmosphere of reverence in the church building when the church comes together to worship. I have been in places where the church congregation acted more like they were at a ball game or an outing than a worship service. It should be a time of heart searching and meditation. The Jews had three annual feasts that were joyful occasions—Pentecost, the Passover and the feast of Tabernacles. But there was one day when there was none of this. It was a time of confession and remembrance of sins. It was the annual day of atonement, occurring on the tenth day of the seventh month.

Our worship service should always have a remembrance of Christ's atonement and His sufferings and death for us. We should rejoice yes, but only in the Lord, not with worldly promptings.

It should be a place of prayer. Jesus quoted from David concerning the temple, that it should be called a place of prayer, Matthew 21:12. He drove the thieves from it. The church house should be considered a sacred place. Of course the brick, the stone or the wood does not constitute the church; rather the men and women of the membership. But it is the place where they meet to worship God. It should not be a place for worldly affairs, dances, or revelries of any kind. That which is designed to glorify God, to train His people or to promote their Christian growth and fellowship is desirable.

Worship is a thing of the heart and right attitude. Just coming to a church house isn't necessarily worship. Singing, or even saying a prayer, is not. For God to accept our worship or hear our prayer we must meet His conditions. If there is not fellowship it is in vain. We are admonished to get that fixed first.

"Therefore if thou bring thy gift to the altar, and there rememberest that thy brother hath ought against thee; leave there thy gift before the altar, and go thy way; first be reconciled to thy brother, and then come and offer thy gift," Matthew 5:23-24.

"But if ye forgive not men their trespasses, neither will your Father forgive your trespasses," Matthew 6:15.

8. CHURCH SHOULD PRAISE THE LORD. Praise is one of the highest forms of worship when from a sincere heart. He is worthy of all possible praise. Members should praise the Lord when they are assembled together, and in personal contact with others by telling of His goodness out of a grateful heart.

> "By him therefore let us offer the sacrifice of praise to God continually, that is, the fruit of our lips giving thanks to his name," Hebrews 13:15.

Here we are told that we should offer our praise to Him; that is, Christ, for He is our High Priest. Every blessing is ours by Christ. It is the only way God can look mercifully upon us. Those therefore who would rule out Christ, or deny Him, have no chance to approach God. Jesus said, John 14:6, **"I am the way, the truth and the life. No man cometh unto the Father but by me."** See also Psalm 107:32. Many could be cited.

We may praise by testimony. Some of the sweetest services are those probably on the midweek worship night when only the faithful are there and they engage in a testimonial service. Members encourage one another and give God glory by relating their experiences and His merciful dealings with them. See Psalm 87:5; 67:3; Luke 2:13.

We may praise the Lord in the song service. This can either be a means of worship or of mockery. Many times it is the latter. Singing should glorify God, not man. Only songs should be sung that prompt a spirit of worship. Sometimes they move the heel more than the heart. Only songs should be sung that tell the truth. Many do not. Music has always had a place in divine worship. David had a wonderful choir in his day. The temple worship had a place for it. Song directors should be consecrated people; this should be true as well of all those who sing in the choir.

There should be some order in the song part of the worship service.

> "Speaking to yourselves in psalms and hymns and spiritual songs, singing and making melody in your heart to the Lord . . ." Ephesians 5:19.

9. CHURCH SHOULD SET EXAMPLES FOR COMMUNITY. Our space is running out, but a few words here. It is very important that church people should be examples of uprightness. A doctrine, a movement, or an organization is measured by the world by those who represent it. How careful then we should be! A church should be found standing "four-square" for the right on every issue of the community. It is the only Bible some people read.

"... Be thou an example of the believers, in word, in conversation (manner of living) in charity, in spirit, in faith, in purity," I Timothy 4:12.

"Christ suffered, leaving us an example," I Peter 2:21. See also I Corinthians 1:6.

10. ONLY THE CHURCH CAN BAPTIZE. We shall discuss this elsewhere, but a word here. The Commission being given to the church, only the church can baptize. The administrator is but an agent of the church in performing this ordinance. One can baptize only on the authority of a New Testament church. Individuals as such have no authority.

11. THE CHURCH OBSERVES THE LORD'S SUPPER. Note this is a memorial supper, and not a sacrament. It can be celebrated only by a New Testament church and in church capacity. It is an ordinance that Jesus gave to His church, and He placed restrictions upon it. Inasmuch as this, too, is treated elsewhere, we desist here.

CHAPTER VI

BAPTISM

True Baptists of today hold to the same kind of baptism that Jesus and the apostles had.

All Greek scholars of note will agree that the first baptisms were by immersions. Since the mode of baptism at the first was immersion, it follows that it is the only authorized way, for nowhere has anyone been given the right to change it. Churches cannot enact laws, or change those already given by the Head of the Church, Jesus Himself.

THE ORIGIN AND MEANING OF THE WORD

We have only to find out what the word **baptize** means to know the way the act is performed.

The English word **baptize** is an Anglicized word, not a translation. It comes from the original Greek **baptizo** and every Greek lexicon gives its primary meaning as **dip, immerse, plunge** or some similar term. If the original **bapto** had been translated we would have immersion in the place of baptize in the New Testament.

When the King James version of the Scriptures was made, the church of England was well established and it practiced sprinkling. In order not to disturb the practice in the State Church of England, the word was NOT translated, but rather ANGLICIZED. That is, it was given an English spelling, thus **Baptize**. So, it is an Anglicized word, not a translated word. But what does it mean? We have said that all Greek scholars, of note, regardless of their faith, have long since admitted that the word means immersion.

We quote from several Greek Lexicons.

Liddel and Scott, **Greek Lexicon**—Baptizo, to dip.

Sapulo: Baptizo, to dip, to immerse.

Thayer: Greek-English Lexicon of the New Testament—Properly, to dip repeatedly, to immerse, to submerge.

Bagster: **The Analytical Greek Lexicon of the New Testament**—Baptizo, primarily to dip, immerse; to cleanse or purify by washing; to administer the rite of baptism, to baptize.

Maltby: **Greek Gradus**—Baptizo, immerge, to plunge; to immerse.

Sophocles: **Greek and English Lexicon**—Baptizo, to dip, to immerse, to sink.

Hinds and Noble: **New Greek-English Lexicon of the New Testament,** by George Ricker Berry, Ph. D. (1897)—Baptizo, of the Christian ordinance, to immerse, submerge, to baptize.

Cremer: **Biblico-Theological Lexicon of New Testament Greek**—Baptizo, immerse, submerge. The peculiar New Testament use of the word to denote immersion, submersion for a religious purpose—baptize.

Parkhurst: **Greek and English Lexicon of the New Testament**— Baptizo, from bapto to dip. To dip, immerse, or plunge in water.

Bass: **Greek and English Lexicon of the New Testament**—Baptizo, 1. to dip, immerse, or plunge in water, **middle and passive,** to wash, to bathe oneself (Mark 7:4; Luke 11:38). 2. To baptize, administer baptism, **figuratively,** to be immersed in sufferings or afflictions.

Jones: **Greek and English Lexicon**—Baptizo, I plunge—plunge into water, dip, baptize, John 4:2—plunge in sleep, bury, overwhelm.

Dunbar: **Greek and English Lexicon**—Baptizo, to dip, immerse, submerge, plunge, sink, overwhelm; to soak.

Robinson: **Greek and English Lexicon of the New Testament**—Baptizo (bapto;—to submerge, sink). 1. To wash, to perform ablution, cleanse, Mark 7:4. 2. To baptize, immerse, administer the rite of baptism; spoken of the religious institution of that name. 3. Metaphorical, to overwhelm one with anything. To bestow liberally, to imbue largely, largiter profundo. 4. Metaphorical passive, to be overwhelmed with miseries, oppressed with calamities, Matthew 20:22-23; Mark 10:38-39; Luke 12:50. Baptisma (pp. what is immersed) 1. Baptism, immersion, spoken of as a religious rite.

Laing: **Greek and English Lexicon of the New Testament**—Baptizo, to dip, to baptize, to plunge in water.

Groves: **Greek and English Dictionary**—Baptizo, to dip, immerse, immerge, plunge; to wash, cleanse, purify; to baptize; to depress, humble, overwhelm.

Green: **Greek-English Lexicon to the New Testament**—Baptizo, to dip, immerse; to cleanse or purify by washing; to administer the rite of baptism; to baptize. **Baptisma**, immersion; baptism; ordinance of baptism.

Ewing: **Greek and English Lexicon**—Baptizo... 1. to plunge or sink completely under water.

We could quote scores of others such as: Valpy, Kontopoulos, Loveland, Greenfield, Leith, Dunbar, Bloomfield, Wright, Schwarz, Simson, Schrevelius, Schoettgen, Estienne, Mintert, Cyril, Stephens, Sessa and De Ravanis, Alstedius, Pasor, Bretschneider, Dalmer, Scapula, Suidas, Robertson, Dugard, Hederic, Stock, Wilke, Schleusner, Morel, Constantin, Wahl, Suicer, and Pollux. Every one of them give the meaning of **baptize** as DIP or a similar word. Julius Pollux wrote about the year A.D. 180.

The above are as quoted by Lawson in, Did Jesus Command Immersion?

SOME PASSAGES EXAMINED

Matthew 3:6, **"And were baptized of him in Jordan, confessing their sins."**

It will be noted that John baptized IN the river Jordan. It would be quite unnecessary to go **into** the river to sprinkle water upon a person. Those who came to him from Jerusalem, the region of Judea and the Jordan, he baptized in Jordan.

Matthew 3:1, **"In those days came John the Baptist, preaching in the wilderness of Judea."** Plainly, this simply means that John the **Immerser** came preaching in the wilderness of Judea.

On this passage Dean Stanley says: **"It is quite correct to translate John the Baptist by John the Immerser."** Nineteenth Century, article Baptism, page 39, October, 1879.

Matthew 3:11, **"I indeed baptize you with water unto repentance: but he that cometh after me is mightier than I, whose shoes I am not worthy to bear: He shall baptize you with the Holy Ghost, and with fire,"** etc.

Matthew 3:16, **"And Jesus, when he was baptized, went up straightway out of the water: and, lo, the heavens were opened unto Him, and He saw the Spirit of God descending like a dove, and lighting upon Him: and lo a voice from heaven, saying, This is My Beloved Son, in whom I am well pleased."**

According to all scholars of note as to the meaning of baptism, Jesus was immersed. It is well to note that Jesus went straightway OUT OF THE WATER. So, He was IN the water when He was baptized; that is, immersed.

On the above passage, with Acts 8:38 and Romans 6:4, Gurtlerus, a Presbyterian, says in Institutes Theology, chapter 38—"The action in this element of water is immersion; which rite continued for a long time in the Christian church, until, in a very late age, it was changed to sprinkling; of which an example is hardly to be found in ancient history, except what relates to the clinics, or sick persons, who, when confined to their beds, were to be initiated by the sign of the covenant of grace. Hence, baptized persons are said to have descended into the water, and to be buried with Christ into death (Matthew 3:16; Acts 8:38; Romans 6:4); for they who are immersed in water are covered with it, and, as it were, buried in it, until they arise out of it."

Jesus said that His baptism was necessary to fulfill all righteousness. By this act He set forth His own future death, burial, and resurrection. This is a picture of the very Gospel that saves. Paul says, Romans 1:16, the gospel is the power of God unto salvation. The same apostle says, I

Corinthians 15:1-3, that the gospel saves and that the gospel is the declaration of Christ's death, His burial and His resurrection on the third day. His baptism, therefore, was prophetic.

John 3:23, **"And John was baptizing in Aenon near Salim, because there was much water there."**

A reason is given for John baptizing here. That reason? Because there was much water. The conclusion is simple, John baptized by immersion, else there would not have been need for MUCH water.

Romans 6:4, **"Therefore we are buried with Him by baptism into His death; that like as Christ was raised up from the dead by the glory of the Father, even so we also should walk in newness of life. For if we have been planted together in the likeness of His death, we shall be also in the likeness of His resurrection."**

Note the word **buried.** One qualified for Christian baptism is one who is **dead to sin.** In our unsaved state we are dead in sins, Ephesians 3:1. Repenting and believing we become dead TO sin; that is, sin no longer has power over us, its fury having been fully spent upon the Divine Sacrifice, and by faith we have become heirs of this vicarious death and atoning blood.

Only immersion can be likened unto a burial. Then, there is the word **plant.** Planting is done by putting under and in the soil. So, Christian baptism, in water.

Of the above passage Conybeare and Howson say in **Life and Epistles of Paul**—"This passage cannot be understood unless it be borne in mind that the primitive baptism was by immersion."

Dr. Schaff says on this same passage: "All commentators of note (except Stuart and Hodge) expressly admit or take for granted in this verse the ancient mode of baptism by immersion and emersion is implied, as giving additional force to the idea of going down of the old, and the rising up of the new, man."—In Lange on Romans.

Professor Moses Stuart, in speaking of the Greek word from which "baptism" comes, says, **"Baptize means to dip,** to plunge, to immerse, in any liquid. All lexicographers and critics of any note agree in this."

There is an interesting story told of this Professor Stuart in The Story of Baptists in All Ages and Countries, by Cook. It goes like this:

The Professor had before him a class, reading and translating from the Greek New Testament. When they came to the 16th verse of the 16th chapter of Mark, one of the students translated, "He that believeth and is sprinkled shall be saved."

"Sprinkled," the Professor replied, "is not correct."

"Is it not in accordance with the practice of the denomination?" asked the student.

"That is not the question," replied the Professor, "you are now translating the Greek New Testament, and the word means, immerse."

Bingham says—"Represents the death, burial, and resurrection of Christ, as well as our own death to sin and rising again unto righteousness."

C. G. Barth, D. D. (He was a Lutheran), **Bible Manual and Practical Commentary,** on Romans 6:3-4 states, "The expression appears particularly appropriate when we recollect the custom prevalent at the time of immersing the whole body in baptism."

Benson (A Methodist), **The Bible With Notes,** on Romans 6:3-4 writes, "Therefore we are buried with Him—alluding to the ancient manner of baptizing by immersion."

Bloomfield (Episcopal), Greek Testament With Notes, on Romans 6:3-4, ". . . we were thus buried (in the water of baptism)—for the term has allusion to Baptism, according to that mode in which it was originally administered, viz., by immersion practiced in the case of adults," etc.

Diodati (Presbyterian), Annotations, on Romans 6:4, "In baptism being dipped in water according to ancient ceremony, is a sacred figure unto us, that sin ought to be drowned in us."

Estius (Catholic), Commentary on the Epistles, on Romans 6:3, "For immersion represents to us Christ's burial; and also His death . . . Moreover the emersion, which follows the immersion, has a resemblance to a resurrection. We are therefore, in baptism, conformed not only to the death of Christ, as he has just said, but also to His burial and resurrection."

Le Cleric (Arminian), Commentary on Romans 6:4, "The manner of baptizing at that time, by plunging into water those whom they baptized, was an image of the burial of Jesus Christ."

Machnight (Presbyterian), Literal Translation, Note on Romans 6:4, "Buried together with him in baptism. Christ's baptism was not the baptsm of repentance; for He never committed any sin: but, as was observed at the beginning, He submitted to be baptized, that is, to be buried under water by John, and to be raised up out of it again, as an emblem of His future death and resurrection. In like manner the baptism of believers is emblematical of our death and resurrection."

We could continue the parade of witnesses, unfriendly to immersion, but who, because of their honesty and integrity and reputation as scholars must write the truth. We deem it entirely unnecessary to list more.

Acts 8:38-39, "**. . . and they went down both into the water, both Philip and the eunuch; and he baptized him. And when they were come up out of the water, the Spirit of the Lord caught away Philip, that the eunuch saw him no more.**"

This passage needs no comment from us. It simply means that Philip and the eunuch went down into a river, or a pool, or a lake, or some such body of water, and while there Philip immersed him. Then they both came out of the water. But we will let the following of our adversaries give their version of this verse.

Calvin (Reformed), Commentary, on Acts 8:38, "Here we see how baptism was administered among the ancients; for they immersed the whole body in water."

Dobb (Episcopal), Commentary, on Acts 8:38, "Considering how bathing was used in those hot countries, it is not to be wondered that baptism was generally administered by immersion; though there does not appear any proof that it was essential to that institution. It would be very unnatural to suppose, that when they went down into the water merely that Philip might take a little water in his hand to pour on the eunuch."

Bishop Elliott (Episcopal), Commentary on Acts 8:38, "They went down into the water. The Greek preposition might mean simply 'unto the water,' but the universality of immersion in the practice of the early church supports the English version."

Colossians 2:12, "Buried with Him in baptism, wherein also ye are risen with Him."

This passage is very plain. We can only wonder why any one cannot see that baptism must be immersion. We give some views of others, even those who practice sprinkling.

Dean Alford (Episcopal), Annotated Greek Testament, on Colossians 2:12, "Buried together with Him in your baptism . . . an image familiar alike to Jews and Christians . . . the process itself of baptism is regarded as the burial of the former life: originally, perhaps owing to the practice of immersion, which would most naturally give rise to the idea."

Dr. Adam Clarke (Methodist), Commentary, on Colossians 2:12, "Buried with Him in baptism . . . alluding to the immerson practiced in the case of adults," etc.

Roell (Lutheran), Exegesis of the Epistle to the Colossians, on Colossians 2:12, "It is certain that immersion into water, and emersion out of it, were practiced in Christian baptism in the beginning."

Wolfius (Lutheran), Notes, on Colossians 2:12, "Here the apostle alludes to immersion in baptism, practiced of old."

Many more noted authorities could be cited on Colossians 2:12, but these will suffice.

WHAT SOME OTHERS HAVE SAID

Dean Stanley says: "For the first thirteen centuries the almost universal practice of baptism was that of which we read in the New Testament, and which is the very meaning of the word 'baptize'—that those who were baptized were plunged, submerged, immersed into the water."—Article on Baptism, Nineteenth Century, 1879, page 39.

Dr. Schaff says: "There can be no doubt that immersion, and not sprinkling, was the original form."—Church History, page 488.

Neander, a converted Jew and a Lutheran, who stands as a front rank scholar and church historian says: "It is certain, that Christ did not ordain infant baptism."—Christian Religion, page 360, 1879. Remember, these men were Pedobaptists.

Dean Stanley says: "It is quite correct to translate John the Baptist by John the Immerser."—Nineteenth Century, Article Baptism, page 39, October, 1879.

Mosheim, **Ecclesiastical History:** "In this (the first) century **Baptism** was administered, in convenient places, without the public assemblies; and by immersing the candidates wholly in water."

Gregory and Ruter, **Church History,** page 53: "The initiatory rite of baptism was usually performed by immersing the whole body in the baptismal font."

Schaff, **History of the Apostolic Church,** Volume 2, book 4: "Finally, as to the outward mode of administering this ordinance; immersion, and not sprinkling, was unquestionably the original, normal form. This shown by the very meaning of the original Greek words **baptizo, baptisma, baptismos,** used to designate the rite. Then, again, by the analogy of the baptism of John, which was performed in the Jordan. (Matthew 3:6, compare with verse 16 and Mark 1:9.) Furthermore, by the New Testament comparisons of baptism with the passage through the Red Sea —with the flood—with a bath—with a burial and a resurrection. Finally, by general usage of ecclesiastical antiquity, which was always immersion (as it is to this day in the Oriental and also the Graeco-Russian churches); pouring and sprinkling being substituted only in cases of urgent necessity, such as sickness or approaching death."

Tertullian (he wrote in second century): "**As for**

baptism itself there is a bodily act, that we are immersed in water," etc.

Grotius (Lutheran), Annotation, on Matthew 3:6, "That the rite was accustomed to be performed by immersion, and not by pouring, appears both from the propriety of the word, from the places chosen for its administration (John 3:23; Acts 8:38), and from many allusions of the apostles, which cannot be referred to sprinkling (Romans 6:3-4; Colossians 2:12)."

Cornelius A. Lapide (Catholic), Commentary, on John 3:23, " 'Because there was much water there.' So much, as Grotius has remarked on this place, as would easily suffice for the immersion of a man's body in which mode baptism was then administered."

Maldonatus (Roman Catholic), Commentary on the Gospels, on Matthew 20:22, "For in Greek, to be baptized is the same as to be submerged."

We feel it unnecessary to multiply quotations.

This writer had a peculiar experience several years ago relating to the Greek manner of baptism. While in Cairo, Egypt, we were taken by a guide to an old church built, it is said, over the place where Mary and Joseph and the young child Jesus lived in that country. The church is Greek Orthodox. Coming across a baptistry, I asked the priest showing us through, about it. He said, "We Greeks know what our own language means. The New Testament was written in Greek." They immerse to this day.

In view of abundance of evidence on every hand we must conclude that Jesus gave His great marching orders to the church in Matthew 28:19-20, He said Go make disciples and IMMERSE the ones made.

SCRIPTURAL SUBJECTS

Nowhere in all the Scriptures do we have an example or precept for baptizing any who are not believers. This forever does away with infant baptism.

When the Ethiopian eunuch asked what hindered his being baptized, Philip said he could **if he believed,** Acts **8:37.**

On the day of Pentecost those that **gladly received the word** were baptized. Since babies cannot gladly receive the Word, they were not included in this great baptizing, Acts 2. Baptism is for those who are old enough to repent and receive the Word, none others.

In the great commission to His church, Jesus said make disciples, then baptize, Matthew 28:19-20. So, only those who become disciples were to receive baptism. This is plain.

The case of the Philippian jailor proves the point. Paul and Silas had told him to believe. He did, he was baptized, Acts 16.

It is objected by the pedobaptists that their household was also baptized, for this reason there must have been babies in it. Pure assumption. We can find tens of thousands of homes where there are no babies. We emphasize again, there is not even one instance—precept or example—in the New Testament for baptizing a person who is not old enough to believe. The writer, himself, has baptized whole households, but each member had repented, believed and was saved.

One of the most able pedobaptist historians was **Dr. Wall.** He defended, as best he could, the practice of sprinkling. But he says:

"Among all the persons that are recorded as baptized by the apostles, there is no express mention of any infant." —First page of his preface to History of Infant Baptism, quoted by Pendleton.

Says Neander: "It is in the highest degree probable . . . that the practice of infant baptism was unknown, in the apostolic churches."—The Gospel in Water, Jarrell, page 3.

The Romish church relies, **not** on Scripture for infant baptism, but on its assumed right to originate and change the ordinances. Says Dollinger, the Romish historian: "There is no proof or hint in the New Testament that the Apostles baptized infants or ordered them to be baptized." —First Age of the Church, pp. 318, 319. Quoted by W. A. Jarrell in The Gospel in Water.

Since every scholar of note, of every religious group,

those who hold to sprinkling and those who do not, are on record saying that those old enough to believe and have done so, are fit subjects and that the very word baptize means to plunge, immerse, or dip, and since this discussion has already gone far beyond what was first in mind, there is no good reason for piling quotations upon one another; though this could easily be done.

We have shown conclusively that immersion, and immersion alone, was the form of baptism at the first. John immersed. The disciples of Jesus immersed, for such is the very meaning of the word used concerning them.

Immersion was practiced even in the case of infants after this great heresy of the baptism of infants started subsequent to the apostolic age.

The first "Church Council" to authorize sprinkling was the Council of Ravenna in 1311. They voted to leave it to the choice of the officiating minister. We quote from the Encyclopedia Britannica: "The usual mode of performing the ceremony was by immersion. In the case of sick persons (clinics), the minister was allowed to baptize by pouring water upon the head, or by sprinkling. In the early church, clinical baptism, as it was called, was only permitted in cases of necessity; but the practice of baptism by sprinkling gradually came in spite of the opposition of Councils and hostile decrees. The Council of Ravenna, in 1311, was the first council of the church which legalized baptism by sprinkling—by leaving it to the choice of the officiating minister."—Volume 3, page 351.

Though the Council of Ravenna was the first council to legalize sprinkling there were some instances of it before that time. The idea of baptismal regeneration began soon after the apostles and the first fathers fell asleep. Some sort of rite was thought necessary in cases of illness; hence, the innovation of pouring and sprinkling. If all had continued to believe in justification by faith, salvation by grace through faith, all this would have been thought useless, as indeed it was. Let us emphasize that there were many who stood true to the faith of the New Testament while these terrorists plunged the world into chaos and kindled martyr fires in many countries. Baptists died by the millions as a result.

The learned Dr. Wall, who wrote a history and defense of infant baptism, could not find an earlier example, even of clinic baptism, than that of Novatian.

From the year 62 to 600 the Welsh Baptists knew nothing but immersion for baptism. We quote from Davis' History of the Welsh Baptists:

"Infant baptism was in vogue long before this time in many parts of the world, but not in Britain. The ordinances of the Gospel were administered exclusively there according to the primitive mode. Baptism by immersion, administered to those who professed repentance toward God and faith in our Lord Jesus Christ, the Welsh people considered the only baptism of the New Testament. That was their unanimous sentiment as a nation, from the time the Christian religion was embraced by them in 62, until a considerable time after the year 600."—Page 14, Davis History.

A long time after the baptizing of infants became common, the mode was still immersion. Not until the Council of Ravenna in 1311, was sprinkling substituted for that of immersion. In Wales, after Austin, the Roman monk, succeeded in sowing the heresy of infant baptizings and other Romish innovations, in the year 597, immersion continued for a thousand years after. See Davis History of the Welsh Baptists, page 16.

WHOLE TOWN IMMERSED

In Russia, in A. D. 988, the only baptism was immersion. By order of Vladimir the Great, on that date, the whole city of Kieff was immersed. While no Baptists would condone such wholesale immersions as scriptural baptisms, without proof of the conversions of those immersed, which we doubt, yet it shows that immersion was the way of baptizing in that early day. We quote from Baptist Encyclopedia, page 654.

"The proclamation stated that 'whosoever, on the morrow, should not repair to the river (Dnieper), whether rich or poor, he should hold for his enemy . . . Some stood in the water up to their necks, others up to their breasts, holding their young children in their arms . . . In this baptism thousands were immersed.' " Cited by Cathcart from Mouravieff's History of the Church of Russia.

RIVER BAPTISMS, BEDE'S ECCLESIASTICAL HISTORY

"This distinguished Christian, the first English historan, died in A. D. 735. His Church History gives an account of the conversion of the 'Angles, Jutes, and Saxons,' his English fathers. In it, he says, 'Paulinus, coming with the king and queen of the Northumbrians to the royal countryseat of Adgfrin (Yeverin, in Glendale), stayed there with them thirty-six days, fully occupied in catechising and baptizing, during which days, from morning till night, he did nothing else but instruct the people resorting from all the villages and places in Christ's saving Word, and then instructed **they were washed** (abulere) **in the river Glen,** which was nearby, with the water of absolution . . . Paulinius, like John and the Jordan, used the flowing river for his font.' "—Cited by Dr. Cathcart, Baptist Encyclopedia, page 991.

CHAPTER VII

THE LORD'S SUPPER—BAPTISTS CALLED "CLOSE COMMUNIONISTS"

INTRODUCTION

As an introduction to this brief study of the Lord's Supper we quote from the gifted writings of Dr. John T. Christian in his book, "Close Communion."

"The Baptists are strict communionists and are likely to remain such. We want to be just as close as the Word of God. If we have prospered as a people, it is because we have rigidly adhered to the Word of God. Whenever we turn aside from the well-trodden path for mere sentimentality or transient popularity, the day of our power or usefulness is gone. We are compelled to search for the old paths, and when we have found them to walk in them. Despite all criticism and abuse we have prospered as strict communionists. The reason is not far away. In the face of all clamor we have adhered to God's Word and God has greatly honored us. What we have done in the past we will do in the future. There is neither argument nor wisdom in open communion. It is based upon mere sentiment, and that a false sentiment. We are strict communionists and we are going to remain strict."

The above was written more than sixty years ago. Since then many who call themselves Baptists have departed from the **"faith once delivered to the saints,"** and have joined protestant sects in their practice of "open communion." However, orthodox Baptists still cling to this New Testament ordinance as it was delivered. We believe, with Dr. Christian, they will continue to do so.

The belief of Baptists on this important ordinance has probably given rise to more misunderstanding, and has occasioned more criticism, than any other doctrine which we hold. We have been called "narrow," bigoted, ignorant and selfish. Much of this abuse of Baptists would be dispelled if they were correctly understood. We hope to set forth in this study what we believe, and why.

* * * *

Religious contemporaries have said many hard things about Baptists for their belief and practice of what they call "close" communion. As a matter of fact many of our accusers are "closer" than we are.

We are told that it is the Lord's Table, and, therefore, we should let everyone who wants to eat with us do so. The very fact, however, that it is the Lord's Table makes it imperative that we guard it.

Jesus not only placed this ordinance in the true church but He gave us many instructions about how to keep it. The Supper is the Lord's and He has given it to His church (every Scriptural church) to hold inviolate, as His custodian of it. We have no right to invite to it any except those that the Scriptures themselves allow. There are many restrictions placed around this sacred table and we shall study them in the following pages of this book.

We shall show later that our position with reference to this ordinance depends largely upon our doctrine of Scriptural baptism. But this is not all; it rests, too, upon our doctrine of the church—and some other things. Baptists believe that only baptized believers can scripturally observe this ordinance. And we hold that, to be scripturally baptized, one must be a believer (thus a person old enough to believe) and be immersed by a true Missionary Baptist Church. "Baptism" then, by whatever act it is performed —pouring, or sprinkling of water, or immersion in water —by any other so-called church is not valid, and this person is not scripturally prepared for the Lord's Supper. But on the question of baptism being essential we note:

Robert Hall, the most celebrated of all "open Communion" advocates, perhaps, says: "We certainly make no scruple of informing a Pedobaptist candidate that we consider him as unbaptized, and disdain all concealment upon the subject."

Dr. Wall, in his "History of Infant Baptism," says: "No church ever gave the communion to any persons before they were baptized. Among all the absurdities that were ever held, none ever maintained that any person should partake of the communion before they were baptized." And Wall was a Pedobaptist.

Doddridge: "It is certain that Christians in general have always been spoken of by the most ancient fathers, as baptized persons. And it is also certain that, as far as our knowledge of primitive antiquity extends, no unbaptized person received the Lord's Supper."—**Miscellaneous Works**, p. 510.

Dr. Hibbard, a Methodist: "It is but just to remark, that in one principle the Baptist and the Pedobaptist churches agree. They both agree in rejecting from communion at the table of the Lord, and in denying the rights of church fellowship to all who have not been baptized.

"Valid baptism they consider as essential to constitute visible church membership. This, also, we hold. The only question then that here divides us is, what is essential to valid baptism? The Baptists, in passing a sweeping sentence of disfranchisement upon all other Christian churches, have only acted upon a principle held in common with all other churches, viz,: that baptism is essential to church membership . . . of course, they must be their own judges as to what baptism is. It is evident that, according to our views we can admit them to our communion; but with their views of baptism, it is equally evident, they can never reciprocate the courtesy; and the charge of **close communion** is no more applicable to the Baptists than to us; inasmuch as the question of church-membership is determined by as liberal principles as it is with any other

Protestant churches—so far, I mean, as the present subject is concerned, i. e., it is determined by valid baptism." Christian Baptism, pp. 171, 175, as quoted by Pendleton.

So, Dr. Hibbard, a Methodist, explodes the idea that Baptists are "narrow" or bigoted, because they do not invite non-Baptists to the Lord's Supper.

We are said to "unchristianize" all those whom we do not invite to eat with us. By this they mean, of course, that we say they are not Christians. The idea of baptismal regeneration or church salvation is behind this conclusion. And this idea is a false one. As a matter of fact, Baptists do not necessarily mean that those they do not invite are unsaved. The Lord's Supper is a church ordinance, set in a scriptural church, and there are scriptural ways of entering into that church which they must certainly enter to get to the Supper. Baptists are not "close Communionists" in the sense we are said to be. We might say that we are close on baptism, but that is not the **whole** truth. The real truth is we are "close" on the question of the church, **what it is and who it is.** The whole proposition of Baptists' belief and practice on the Lord's Supper is predicated on this premise.

We have seen that a Methodist absolves us from the charge of bigotry for our practice concerning the Ordinance. Now we refer you to an Episcopalian:

"The close communion of Baptist churches is but the necessary sequence of the fundamental idea out of which their existence has grown. No Christian church would willingly receive to its communion even the humblest and truest believer in Christ who had not been baptized. With Baptists, immersion only is baptism, and they therefore of necessity exclude from the Lord's table all who have not been immersed. It is an essential part of their system—the legitimate carrying out the creed."—Episcopal Recorder.

If space would permit we could show that many who criticize us for "close communion" are "closer" than we are. Baptists do not have two classes of members, the laity and the ministry, when it comes to eating the Lord's Supper as many of our "liberal" friends have. We eat and drink together, and at the same table and time.

We are reminded that the Bible says for a man to examine himself, meaning that we have no business interfering with any one who might want to eat with us, though he be a member of another denomination, a member of another "church" and, himself a person who does not believe many of the doctrines which we teach.

Under another topic I have explained this Scripture in detail. It is an admonition to a CHURCH, a New Testament church, a body of members that believed and practiced the same doctrines. The purpose of examination was a personal appraisal of one's own self as to the PURPOSE and MANNER he was observing this ordinance in HIS OWN CHURCH. It has no reference to communicants of various and sundry "churches" holding to all kinds of conflicting doctrines.

There are many functions of worship in which Baptists can associate with their fellow Christians of other faiths. We can give thanks together, can sing together, pray together, testify together with those whom we believe to be sincerely converted.

When it comes to community projects that are worthwhile from a standpoint of morals and ethics, Missionary Baptists have never been derelict. On the broad principles of human rights and social uplift we join hands with all. But on the principles of the church and its ordinances we ask our freedom. **"We ought to obey God rather than man."**

Our strictness has not been deterrent to our growth. There are some who think that if we would throw down the bars and open our arms to everybody regardless of what they believe, that we would sweep the world. The answer to that is that those who have done that have failed. We have Christian fellowship for all the saved. But we have CHURCH fellowship for only those who adhere to true doctrine.

It is interesting to note the words of a Presbyterian, Dr. J. L. Withrow. He says of the Baptists and their "narrow practices": "Furthermore, in their favor it is to be said, they have proved, beyond peradventure, that narrow church doors and severe communion conditions do not bar people out of the Christian church. Against creeds and communion bars there is ceaseless outcry from some quarters. The Baptists have no chaptered creed, but their unwritten creed, as England's unwritten constitution, is more insurmountable than the Thirty Nine Articles of Episcopacy, or the ponderous chapters of the Westminister Confession.

"Against chaptered creeds the complaints are so urgent that Congregationalists have recently made a new one—you may safely offer a dollar for every new convert which has been captured by that new creed who otherwise would not have been secured. And now the Presbyterians are wasting a heap of hard-earned money (contributed, much of it, by God's poor for better purposes), and are stirring bad blood between the brethren in an attempt to smooth off and sweeten up their creed. The claim is that we keep people out of the church, and candidates out of the ministry with such strict conditions as now exist. It sounds like arrogant nonsense in presence of the fact that the Baptist Church is the strictest church we have; and yet it is growing—not as a weed, but as the Word of God is promised to grow.

"There is no church, so far as we know, into which it is more difficult to enter than the Baptist through theological, ecclesiastical and ceremonial conditions. And yet there are throngs pressing through its narrow threshold. Whoever cares to study this subject of easy and exacting conditions of church membership, asking which is the most likely to secure accessions to the fellowship of professing Christians, should compare the history of the Baptist church with that of the liberal churches, so-called." As quoted by Dr. J. T. Christian in "Close Communion."

As Missionary Baptists, let us hold the fort. We have nothing to lose but all to gain.

ACCOUNTS OF THE FIRST SUPPER

Three of the Recording Evangelists give an account of the institution of the Lord's Supper. We quote them.

Matthew 26:26-30, "And as they were eating, Jesus took

bread, and blessed it, and brake it, and gave it to the disciples, and said, Take, eat; this is my body.

And he took the cup, and gave thanks, and gave it to them, saying, Drink ye all of it;

For this is my blood of the New Testament, which is shed for many for the remission of sins.

But I say unto you, I will not drink henceforth of this fruit of the vine, until that day when I drink it new with you in my Father's kingdom.

And when they had sung an hymn, they went out into the Mount of Olives."

Mark 14:22-26, "And as they did eat, Jesus took bread, and blessed, and brake it, and gave to them, and said, Take, eat; this is my body.

And He took the cup, and when He had given thanks, He gave it to them: and they all drank of it.

And He said unto them, This is my blood of the New Testament, which is shed for many.

Verily I say unto you, I will drink no more of the fruit of the vine, until that day that I drink it new in the Kingdom of God.

And when they had sung an hymn, they went out into the Mount of Olives."

Luke 22:19-20, "And He took bread, and gave thanks, and brake it, and gave unto them, saying, This is my body which is given for you: this do in remembrance of me.

Likewise also the cup after supper, saying, This cup is the new testament in my blood, which is shed for you."

PAUL'S ACCOUNT TO THE CORINTHIANS

The Apostle Paul had much to say to the church at Corinth about the Lord's Supper. We here recite it inasmuch as we shall have occasion to refer to it in this study.

I Corinthians 11:18-34, "For first of all, when ye come together in the church, I hear that there be divisions among you; and I partly believe it.

For there must be also heresies among you, that they which are approved may be made manifest among you.

When ye come together therefore into one place, this is not to eat the Lord's Supper.

For in eating every one taketh before other his own supper; and one is hungry and another drunken.

What? Have ye not houses to eat and to drink in? or despise ye the church of God, and shame them that have not? What shall I say unto you? shall I praise you in this? I praise you not.

For I have received of the Lord that which also I delivered unto you. That the Lord Jesus the same night in which He was betrayed took bread:

And when He had given thanks, He brake it, and said, Take, eat; this is my body, which is broken for you: this do in remembrance of me.

After the same manner also He took the cup, when He had supped, saying, This cup is the New Testament in my blood; this do ye, as oft as ye drink it, in remembrance of me.

> For as often as ye eat this bread, and drink this cup, ye do show the Lord's death till He come.
> Therefore whosoever shall eat this bread, and drink this cup of the Lord, unworthily, shall be guilty of the body and blood of the Lord.
> But let a man examine himself, and so let him eat of that bread, and drink of that cup.
> For he that eateth and drinketh unworthily, eateth and drinketh damnation to himself, not discerning the Lord's body.
> For this cause many are weak and sickly among you, and many sleep.
> For if we would judge ourselves, we should not be judged.
> But when we are judged, we are chastened of the Lord, that we should not be condemned with the world.
> Wherefore, my brethren, when ye come together to eat, tarry one for another.
> And if any man hunger, let him eat at home; that ye come not together unto condemnation. And the rest will I set in order when I come."

ONE OF TWO ORDINANCES

Our Saviour gave only two ordinances to the church, baptism and the Lord's Supper. These were to continue to the end of the age. Neither was to be substituted at any time, nor changed in any way, by any kind of church or synod's decree. The churches in New Testament times had only these two, and the true churches of their succession through all the centuries have had only the two. Baptists hold only to the two.

Christ not only fully constituted His church during His personal ministry but He set in it everything it was to need until the end of the age. All of the churches, all of the ministers and for that matter, all of the angels gathered in one place at the same time would be without any authority whatsoever to discontinue either of these ordinances or change them in any form. They are ordinances given by the Saviour Himself to His own church, the church He has **"purchased with His own blood,"** Acts 20:28.

NOT A SACRAMENT

It is a mistake to call the Lord's Supper a **sacrament**. The Roman and Greek Catholics teach that there are seven sacraments in the church. They are: baptism, confirmation, the eucharist (by this they mean the Lord's Supper), penance, extreme unction, holy orders and matrimony.

Of course there is not even one verse of Scripture that mentions any of these except two—baptism and the Lord's Supper. And they have perverted both of these.

Webster defines **sacrament** thusly: "In theology, an outward and visible sign of inward and spiritual grace; more particularly, a solemn religious ceremony enjoined by Christ, the head of the Christian church, to be observed by His followers, by which their special relation to Him is created, or their obligations to Him are renewed and ratified."

Sacrament, therefore, means a sign of grace, and according to Webster, renews, ratifies or even CREATES a relationship to Christ. Nothing can be farther from the truth as far as the purpose of the Lord's Supper is concerned. Of course the Lord will bless us in obeying His command that we observe this most important ordinance, as He always blesses the obedient in other things. But to say that the Lord's Supper, by whatever name you call it, brings either salvation, justification, sanctification, sonship with God, or other relationships by its observance is unscriptural.

It does not unlock the storehouse of grace. Grace operates upon an individual to bring salvation when that individual repents of his sins and believes in the Lord Jesus Christ. Grace must operate in salvation before we are qualified to approach the Lord's Supper. The ordinance is not a saving ordinance. It has but one purpose and that is to memorialize the death of Christ. We are saved by grace, Ephesians 2:8.

J. M. Frost said: "The Lord's Supper, like baptism, is not a saving ordinance. It has no mysterious or mystical power of saving people. Indeed, like its companion ordinance, it is intended for people who have already experienced the saving grace of God through faith in the Lord Jesus Christ. For others it has no meaning or value. But while having no saving efficacy it does have marvelous meaning and significance as a memorial. It bears testimony to an objective fact, viz.: the suffering and death of the Son of God for our sins, and not to subjective experiences except as awakened and influenced in the human soul by this memorial service.

"The Supper does not carry so much in itself as baptism carries; it is not so many sided as that ordinance in its pictorial representation; and yet, what it does carry it carries it with clearness and tremendous power; it has always had a richness of sentiment in its administration never possessed by the other ordinance. It is the memorial of a death, a vicarious death on account of sin, of atonement made for sin through the blood of the Lamb of God which taketh away the sin of the world. The bread and wine are in no sense a sacrifice, but in beautiful and powerful fashion symbolize the greatest of all sacrifices—the sacrificial death of the Lord Jesus Christ.

"It is of immense importance that the Lord's Supper be cleared of all the fictitious and factitious notions which have accumulated about it through the centuries, and be held to the one single purpose of a memorial service. This gives the ordinance real meaning, emphasizes its one definite purpose, brings it out into the clear sunlight so as to be seen as it was seen and observed on that sad night, when in the upper chamber Jesus said: **"Do this in remembrance of me."** This view is the background for all else concerning the ordinance, and creates every other value which it possesses, and makes its observance full of rich and blessed experience."

NOT COMMUNION WITH ONE ANOTHER

It is not a Communion service, if we mean by it that we commune with one another in observing the Lord's Supper. There is a sense, certainly, in which we, in some mysterious way, commune with the body and blood of the Lord. Dr. J. E. Cobb, in his "New Church Manual for Baptist Churches" has this to say: "There are those who speak of it as a 'communion service,' meaning usually that, in some mysterious way, we commune with the saints. But it is not in reference to each other that we observe the supper, but it is in reference to the Lord's death.

"There is a sense in which it is a 'communion service,'

but it should be remembered that it is not a communion with each other as brethren and sisters. I Corinthians 10:16, **'The cup of blessing which we bless, is it not a communion of the blood of Christ? The bread which we break, is it not a communion of the body of Christ?'**

"So, it is a communion of the body and blood of Christ, and not with each other as brethren and sisters."

Much of the criticism which has been leveled against Baptists would be stopped if the proper design of the Lord's Supper were understood. It is not a sign of love to one another, nor a rite testifying of our appreciation for each other. It is purely and exclusively a MEMORIAL Supper, **"showing forth the Lord's death till He comes again."**

Dr. J. M. Pendleton in his Church Manual says: "Some will perhaps say, that in the Lord's Supper we express our Christian fellowship for our fellow communicants. This is done only in indirect and incidental manner. Our communion, according to Paul, is the communion of the body and blood of Christ. It is a solemn celebration of His atoning death."

CHAPTER VIII

A PERPETUAL ORDINANCE

The Lord's Supper was placed in the church by the Head of the Church, Jesus Himself, on the very night of His betrayal, and at the conclusion of the Passover feast which He kept with His fellow Jew-disciples in the upper room in Jerusalem.

This Memorial Supper was to be observed perpetually through the Christian age. Note this: **"For as often as ye eat this bread, and drink this cup, ye do show the Lord's death till He come,"** I Corinthians 11:26. Observe that the Lord is coming again. Hundreds of scriptures teach us this all-important truth. In fact, this is our hope. Observe that we are commanded to **"eat this bread and drink this cup till He come."**

Jesus has not yet come the second time. And until He does come we are to observe this memorial feast. For almost two thousand years the churches of the Lord Jesus have been keeping this ordinance **"as delivered."** They have kept it not because it points to the Lord's coming, but in memory of what He did in dying for our sins when He was here the first time. We are simply to do this until His second coming that while we wait, we may ever be mindful of His sacrificial death on the Cross. It is just as necessary to observe the ordinance now as it was in the apostolic age and for the same purpose and in the same way and manner.

We quote from Melvill in his reference to I Corinthians 11:26: "An explicit declaration that there is in the Lord's Supper such a manifestation of the crucifixion of Jesus as will serve to set forth that event UNTIL HIS SECOND APPEARING." Melvin's Thoughts, p. 240.

The Presbyterian Confession of faith, chapter 29, Section 1, says: "The Lord's Supper is to be observed in His church UNTO THE END OF THE WORLD."

Albert Barnes, in his Notes on I Corinthians 11:26 says: "TILL HE COME; till he return to judge the world. This demonstrates that it was designed that this ordinance should be perpetuated and observed to the end of time. In every generation, therefore, and in every place where there are Christians, it is to be observed until the Son of God shall return; and the necessity of its observance shall cease only when the whole body of the redeemed shall be permitted to see their Lord, and there shall be no need of those emblems to remind them of Him, for all shall see Him as he is."

Those who actually saw Jesus die that day on the cross must have been struck with awe. It must have been a most graphic experience. To the day of their death they must have been continually reminded by their memory of that gruesome sight so that they never forgot it. However, only a comparable few saw Him nailed to the cross, saw Him writhe in agony and pain, saw the blood as it trickled down His sacred body, or heard Him cry, **"It is finished."** And they soon died, leaving the world without an eye witness.

Millions have been saved through that death of Jesus as assuredly as were the then followers of Jesus. Those of us today are removed in years almost two millenniums from His crucifixion, and human memory is faulty and humanity itself is corrupt. Satan, the flesh, and a wicked world-order, conspire to cause us to forget the importance of Christ's death. But it is all-important that we remember whence flowed our redemption. The Lord's Supper was God's way of reminding us through the years that **"He died for our sins according to the Scriptures,"** I Corinthians 1:3.

A CHURCH ORDINANCE

If all could understand that the Lord's Supper is a church ordinance, specifically and exclusively a church ordinance, it would clear up much confusion and do away with much criticism of the Baptist position regarding it.

The ordinance was not given to the saved generically;

that is, to the family of God, as such. It was not given to a denomination of Christians as such. It was not given to the ministry as such. It was given originally to a church, a New Testament church, the church at Jerusalem.

There was only one church in existence at the time the Lord's Supper was set in the church, nor was there another for several years afterwards. It must, therefore, have been given to a local and visible body in church capacity.

The Supper can only be observed in local church worship. It cannot be observed by an assembly of messengers representing several churches in the capacity of an association. The emblems of the Lord's Supper cannot be carried to the homes of people. The local church must be assembled together in **"one place."**

Dr. J. R. Graves says: "The Lord's Supper is **a** church ordinance and, as such, can only be observed by a church, as such, and by a person in the church of which he is a member . . . There is no denominational ordinance of divine appointment—because such a thing as a denomination, in the sense of an organized body, embracing all the churches of a province or nation, was unknown in the first ages. I have denominated the Lord's Supper a denominational ordinance whenever it is opened to the members of any and all Baptist churches present. We do not allow a brother not a member, in however good standing, the right to vote in our conventions, associations, presbyteries, councils, or church conferences, but we do confer upon him the rights of a member, without knowledge of his character, when we observe the Lord's Supper, the most sacred of all ordinances."—The Lord's Supper a Church Ordinance, pages 5, 6.

He is saying that the Lord's Supper was given to a local church and that only members of that local church can observe the Supper together.

The Lord's Supper is not a mere social ordinance. This is far from the purpose of it. There are many restrictions placed around this ordinance which we will presently note.

Dr. Graves further says: "But, the essential qualities of a church ordinance are: 1. That it is a rite, the duty of perpetuating which is committed to local visible churches, as such. 2. The qualifications of its recipients must be decided by the members of the churches as such. 3. Any rite which symbolizes church relations can only be participated in by members of the church celebrating, and is pre-eminently a church ordinance.

"A church act or privilege is one that can be transacted or enjoyed by the constituent members of one particular church. Voting upon all questions relating to the choice of officers, the fellowship and government of the church, is a church privilege, or act, which, from the very nature and constitution of a gospel church, belongs to the members of that particular church alone, and cannot be extended beyond its limits without peril to its very existence."

We believe the above sets forth the truth. Baptist churches being local, visible, separate and distinct from other church-units, being also self governing and autonomous, and clothed with disciplinary powers, and charged to keep the "ordinances as delivered" (I Corinthians 11:23) makes it unreasonable to conclude that we are to eat with those not subject to the discipline of that particular church. Where the discipline of a local church ends there must also end the offer of the emblems of the Supper.

That the Lord's Supper was given to churches as such we note the following scriptures:

"I have received of the Lord that which I also delivered unto you," I Corinthians 11:23.

The YOU here means the CHURCH at Corinth. It was not given here to the ministry or any other group.

"Therefore, brethren, stand fast, and hold the traditions which ye have been taught, whether by word or our epistle," II Thessalonians 2:15.

By tradition here he means all those instructions and ordinances which had been previously taught them. And this was to the CHURCH AT Thessalonica.

It was to the CHURCH at Corinth that Paul said:

I Corinthians 11:2, "Now I praise you, brethren, that ye remember me in all things, and keep the ordinances, as I delivered them to you."

We quote from Dr. W. W. Gardner: "Hence, we see that

the Baptists and others agree as to the nature of the Lord's Supper. All agree, (1) that it is an ordinance of the New Testament instituted by Jesus Christ; (2) that it is a positive ordinance, established by positive law; (3) that it is a church ordinance, and, as such, involves and expresses church fellowship; (4) that it is a commemorative ordinance; (5) that it is an ordinance of frequent occurrence; and (6) that it is a perpetual ordinance."—Church Communion, p. 35.

We quote from Professor Curtis: "We consider the Lord's Supper, then, as a symbol of CHURCH relations. When we say this, we mean that there is a fellowship in **church** relations, professed with those Christians with whom we visibly celebrate. We desire to show that this is the true view of the Lord's Supper. **'When ye come together therefore into one place,'** says the apostle, **'this is not to eat the Lord's Supper. For in eating every one taketh before other, etc. . . . Wherefore, my brethren, when ye come together to eat, tarry one for another,'** I Corinthians 11:20, 21, 33.

"The apostle here clearly alludes to it as the **universally current opinion,** that the Lord's Supper was a **church** ordinance, so far as this, that it was completely celebrated in one place, **by one church.**"

Again: "Thus, then, it is clear (i.e., from I Corinthians 11) that the Lord's Supper is given in charge to those visible churches of Christ, in the midst of which He has promised to walk and dwell (Revelation 2:2). To each of these it belongs to celebrate it as **one family.**"—Progress of Baptist Principles, p. 307.

Again we quote from Dr. Richard Fuller: "As the passover was a meal for each family only, so the Supper is a family repast, for the **members of that particular church in which the table is spread.** This is so plain in our minds, hearts and consciences, that there is never any discussion about it."—Baptism and Communion.

Curtis, again: "There is sufficient proof to convince a close student of church history of the first three centuries, that in the very early ages, the Lord's Supper was regarded as strictly a **"church ordinance."**—Communion p. 88.

Spencer: "How, then, did invitations originate? The answer is plain. **They originated with perversion of the ordinance.** When the ordinance came to take the place of Christ, the churches began to invite to it, as they had formerly invited to Christ. Hence in Romish churches today you hear plenty of invitations to ordinances, but none to Christ." —Invitations to the Supper.

The above words of Spencer show how important it is that we ever keep the proper DESIGN of the Lord's Supper. It is easy to drift into ceremonialism, and ceremonialism can easily become a substitute for Christ if men are to follow their own human concepts. We must stay close to the instructions of Jesus concerning the Lord's Supper. Baptists do this.

Dr. J. M. Frost says: "The Lord's Supper is a church ordinance for church administration to church members. This is one of the universals of Christian belief and practice. Moses built the tabernacle and set the Holy of Holies far within; Solomon built the Temple, both working after a divine pattern, and set the Holy of Holies within, and far aloft by steps and stairway, as a dwelling place for the Schechinah; Christ built His church and set His Holy Supper within—far within. Not in the house, of course, but within the church organization, an essential part of its organic structure and organic life, and necessarily for the observance of church members."—The Memorial Supper.

RESTRICTED TO BELIEVERS

The Lord's Supper is for believers only. The Lord deals with us as individuals. One is not commanded to observe the Lord's Supper until he is saved. The design of the Lord's Supper is to remember the death of the Saviour. It would be inconsistent for one to celebrate something he did not believe in or did not appreciate.

In what we call "The Great Commission," given to the church by the Lord Jesus in Matthew 28:20, Jesus set forth an order. We are to lead people to Jesus, then to baptize them and teach them "to observe all things." Among the "all things" is the Lord's Supper. First, be saved; second, be baptized; third, observe His commandments, including the Lord's Supper.

All of those present at the first Supper were disciples, were believers, were saved; unless Judas was present, which we think not. He was present at the Passover feast immediately preceding but had gone out by the time the Lord instituted His Supper for the coming church age. The Passover supper was a feast of, and for, the Jews in commemoration of the deliverance from Egypt. Judas was a Jew and, though unsaved, like many millions of other unsaved Jews through the centuries, was present. It celebrated a national deliverance and Judas was a Jewish national. If there are those who claim that Judas did partake of the Supper we will not argue; it proves nothing either way. He at least was a professed disciple and until this moment only Jesus Himself knew he was unsaved.

There is not one verse of Scripture which authorizes one not a believer to eat the Lord's Supper. There is not one example of such. It is purely for the saved, for those who have availed themselves of the death of Christ in the salvation of their souls. Baptists, however, are not by themselves in this position.

The requirement that one must be saved is the first restriction that the Lord has placed around His table. But how is one saved? Perhaps it will not be out of place here to set forth the simple plan of salvation.

We have already shown that the Lord's Supper does not save; nor does any other ordinance. The Bible is very plain on this most important matter.

First of all we must understand that we are BY NATURE sinners. We are not sinners because we have sinned but we have sinned because we are naturally sinners. Note this Scripture:

> "And you hath he quickened, who were dead in trespasses and sins; Wherein in time past ye walked according to the course of this world, according to the prince of the power of the air, the spirit that now worketh in the children of disobedience: Among whom also we all had our conversation in times past in the lusts of our flesh, fulfilling the desires of the

> flesh and of the mind; and were by nature the children of wrath, even as others," Ephesians 2:1-3.

Here we find that we are BY NATURE the children of wrath. But here is another Scripture which tells us something about us before we are saved:

> "The heart is deceitful above all things, and desperately wicked; who can know it?" Jeremiah 17:9.

And this: we are children of the devil until we are saved and born into the family of God and made His children.

> "Ye are of your father the devil, and the lusts of your father ye will do," John 8:44. Too, Paul says, "We have all sinned and come short of the glory of God."

It is evident that we all are sinners. There is absolutely nothing we can do to atone for our sins. But **there is a remedy** for sin. It is in the blessed death of Jesus, the very death that the Lord's Supper is designed to keep in our memory. Listen to these Scriptures, and if you are not saved, trust Jesus and be made God's child. Then you can approach the Lord's table, other conditions being met.

The Philippian jailer asked Paul how to be saved. Here is his question and also Paul's answer: **"Sirs, what must I do to be saved? And they said, Believe on the Lord Jesus Christ, and thou shalt be saved, and thy house,"** Acts 16:30-31.

We are saved by believing in Christ for it was He who died for our sins, the death which we remember in the Lord's Supper. It is the blood of Christ that atones for our sins.

> Acts 10:43, "To him give all the prophets witness, that through his name whosoever believeth in him shall receive remission of sins."
>
> John 3:18, "He that believeth on him is not condemned; but he that believeth not is condemned already."
>
> Ephesians 1:7, "In whom we have redemption through his blood, the forgiveness of sins, according to the riches of his grace."

It is this blood that we remember when we drink of the cup in the Lord's Supper. However, it is not the cup of which we drink that saves but the actual blood of Christ that was shed on the cross.

When we speak of faith we also speak of repentance.

The word repentance is found many times, such as:

> **"And the times of this ignorance God winked at; but now commandeth all men everywhere to repent," Acts 17:30.**
>
> **"I tell you, Nay; but, except ye repent, ye shall likewise perish," Luke 13:3.**

Faith and repentance are inseparable. You cannot truly repent without believing nor can you believe without repenting. Repent and believe, become a saved person through the blood of the cross. Keep the Lord's Supper in memory of that blessed death.

I will sing of my Redeemer,
    And His wondrous love to me;
On the cruel cross He suffered,
    From the curse to set me free.
I will tell the wondrous story,
    How my lost estate to save,
In His boundless love and mercy,
    He the ransom freely gave.
Sing, Oh, sing of my Redeemer,
    With His blood He purchased me;
On the cross He sealed my pardon,
    Paid the debt and set me free.

CHAPTER IX

RESTRICTED TO THE BAPTIZED

Almost every denomination agrees with the Baptists that one must be baptized to be qualified to eat the Lord's Supper. As to what constitutes baptism, however, they are often very far apart.

No where in the Scriptures do we find either a precept or example of taking the Lord's supper without first being baptized. We have already shown that one must be saved to partake of the Supper. He also must be scripturally baptized. This makes two restrictions the Lord has placed around the ordinance.

In the Commission given the church in Matthew 28:20 Jesus put both salvation and baptism before the Lord's Supper, the Supper being included in the **"all things whatsoever I have commanded you."**

All of the ones present at the institution of the Supper in the upper room had been baptized. Robert Hall, one of the foremost defenders of "open communion" admitted that these were baptized. He says: "It is almost certain that some, probably the most of them, had been baptized by John"—Works, Vol. 1, page 303. To be an apostle one had to company the disciples from John's baptism, Acts 1:21-22.

In the Gospel of John at least four of the disciples were declared to be the disciples of John the Baptist, John 1:36-40. Then, Jesus also made and baptized disciples, through His disciples, John 4:1.

The Supper being a church ordinance, to be observed by a church, and no one being considered a church member who has not been baptized, necessarily means that one must be baptized before eating the Lord's Supper. The church at Corinth was a group of baptized believers, and they ate the Lord's Supper. Nothing is said about any unbaptized persons being present.

A forceful argument is drawn from I Corinthians 10:1-4 as to the order of the two ordinances, Baptism and the Lord's Supper. We quote:

> "Moreover, brethren, I would not that ye should be ignorant, how that all our fathers were under the cloud, and all passed through the sea; and were all baptized unto Moses in the cloud and in the sea; And did all eat the same spiritual meat; And did all drink the same spiritual drink."

This experience of the Israelites in crossing the Red Sea is very typical of Christ and our Christian experience. First the Israelites had been called out, delivered by the blood of the paschal lamb sprinkled on the houses. We have been called, and we have been saved by the blood of the Lamb, Christ. The Israelites were led by the cloud by day and pillar of fire by night to the Red Sea where they were baptized in the cloud and in the sea. So, the Holy Spirit leads us to the waters of Christian baptism.

The Israelites being walled in on both sides by water, the ground under them and the cloud capped over them, were buried, submerged. This is the meaning of baptism. But they were baptized unto MOSES, not Christ. Yet, they were a delivered people, free from the taskmasters of Egypt and turned loose in the wilderness for a pilgrimage. They ate the same spiritual meat and drank the same spiritual drink, and that was Christ. The eating and the drinking was AFTER their baptism in the cloud and in the sea. They ate and drank by their faith in the coming Messiah.

When, after baptism, we eat and drink at the Lord's Supper, we are following this order. Jesus said, in handing the disciples the bread, **"This is my body;"** and the cup, **"This is my blood."** He certainly did not mean that it was the actual flesh and blood of His body, only these emblems were representative. Yet, in the symbolic sense they ate and drank of Him by faith as did the Israelites centuries before. But note the order, first the baptism and then the supper.

TESTIMONY OF SOME OTHERS

The Greek and Latin writers of old are quite plain upon the relative position of baptism and the Lord's Supper. We will let some of them speak.

Hippolytus, in the beginning of the third century, in a fragment preserved of his works, makes baptism precede the Lord's Supper.

Cyril of Jerusalem, 347, says: "After the baptism followed the holy communion, of which all the newly baptized were partakers."

Jerome; the most learned of them all, in A. D. 400, says: "Catechumens cannot communicate at the Lord's table, being unbaptized."—Patrologiae, Vol. 22, p. 658.

Augustine, in 400 A. D. "Of which certainly they cannot partake unless they are baptized."

The Didache says: "But let no one eat or drink of your eucharist, except those baptized into the name of the Lord." Didache, C. IX, Sec. 5.

Bede, A. D. 613, says: "If you will be baptized into the salutary fountain as your father was, you may also partake of the Lord's Supper as he did; but if you despise the former, ye cannot in any wise receive the latter."—Eccl. Hist., lib. 11, cau. 5, Patrologiae, Vol. 95.

Theophylact A. D. 1100, says: "No unbaptized person partakes of the Lord's Supper." (On Matthew 14.)

We coud fill page after page with quotations showing that all through the centuries, from the days of Christ until now, baptism always preceded the Lord's Supper just as Baptists practice today.

BUT WHAT IS BAPTISM

We must consider it here also to show what kind of baptism is required as a condition for taking the Lord's Supper.

As we have heretofore said, just about every denomination agrees with us that Baptism is necessary for the Lord's Supper. But Baptists and others differ widely as to what is Scriptural baptism.

To be scripturally baptized we must first be saved. Jesus enjoined the church to make disciples first, then baptize them. So, to have Scriptural baptism, we must have a Scriptural subject—a saved person.

One must be baptized by the authority of a scriptural New Testament Church, and by a qualified administrator. Baptists believe that only orthodox Missionary Baptist churches are New Testament churches, and therefore, scriptural churches. This means that we do not consider any one "baptized" by a Catholic or Protestant "church" as having Scriptural baptism, even though he or she was dipped or immersed. Baptists contend that only dipping or immersion is baptism. But immersion or dipping is not the only necessary thing for Scriptural baptism. It must be by the proper authority.

It is plain, therefore, that we cannot admit persons of heretical groups, though called churches, to the Lord's Supper with us for several reasons, one of them being that we do not consider them baptized. Other reasons will be given elsewhere. But let it be thoroughly understood that, while we do not invite them to Supper with us, we do not mean by this that we necessarily consider them unsaved. But something more than being saved is required. The Lord's Supper is a church ordinance, and we do not consider their organizations churches of the New Testament order.

The authority to issue passports is in the State Department. Suppose I should issue one. It might be the same size book, the same language and the same everything except the signature and seal. Valid? Certainly not. And only the church that Jesus built has the authority to baptize. But some one says, Baptists unchristianize others. This is not true. Baptism does not save, the church does not, nor does the Lord's supper save. Salvation is by grace through faith in the Lord Jesus Christ, and every individual who repents toward God and believes in Jesus Christ is saved. To be saved is one thing, to be Scripturally baptized and belong to the true church is another thing.

Mosheim says: "Neither those doing penance, nor those

not yet baptized, were allowed to be present at the celebration of this ordinance." Ecc. Hist. Vol 1, p. 189.

Neander: "At this celebration, as may be easily concluded, no one could be present who was not a member of the Christian church, and incorporated into it by the rite of baptism." Church Hist. Vol. 1, p. 271.

We could quote them page after page; Congregationalists, Methodists, Presbyterians, Catholics, et cetera. They all agree that baptism precedes the Lord's Supper.

We give one more Scripture text:

Acts 2:41-42, "Then they that gladly received his word were baptized; and the same day there were added unto them about three thousand souls. And they continued stedfastly in the apostles' doctrine and fellowship, and IN BREAKING OF BREAD, and in prayers."

RESTRICTED TO CHURCHES

The Lord's Supper being a church ordinance it is confined to members of churches. Again, there is no precept or example in the New Testament where a non-church member ate the Lord's Supper.

This is another reason why we cannot invite our friends and neighbors of other faiths to the Supper. We do not think they are members of churches of the Lord Jesus Christ. We do not necessarily mean that they are not good people, but we do mean that they are not members of a New Testament church and we have no alternative in the matter. **"We ought to obey God rather than men,"** Peter.

It is the writer's firm conviction that we cannot invite people of even other Missionary Baptist churches, though we hold them to be Scriptural and orthodox. Only members of a particular church can observe the Lord's Supper together. It is purely a church ordinance and it is not designed as a fellowship service. In short, it is more than a Christian ordinance, it is a church ordinance.

By drawing the line at our own church door steps we at once destroy the criticism that is leveled against us by Pedobaptists and others for our practice of "close Communion." We can show that we do the same thing for those of our own faith, and that by our "closeness" we do not necessarily "unchristianize" others, as they put it.

One Baptist Church is an orthodox and Scriptural New Testament church. So is a neighboring church. But both are separate and independent of each other. Each, under Christ, attends to its own business in all matters; worship, preaching, baptizing, and in matters of discipline. The Scriptures enjoin certain standards for the Lord's Supper observance. One of the churches may be lax in discipline. In permitting a member of the loose church to take the Supper with it the other church could very well unknowingly admit an unqualified person to the table. A church may offer the elements of the Supper only so far as its discipline extends. This is both scriptural and reasonable.

Jesus established His church during His personal ministry here on the earth. He did this in Person, taking the material that had been prepared by John the Baptist as had been foretold He would do long years before.

One must be a member of a church like that first established to be qualified to eat at the Lord's Table. We mean he must be a member of the church that has Jesus only as its Head, one that holds the same doctrines the first church held. That church must be more than just an **organization**, it must be an organism—a body with **Life**, and that **Life** must be Christ. It is not enough to just "belong" to some religious group called a church. One must be a member of the Church of Jesus Christ. What is a church? It can be defined briefly as a group of baptized believers associated together in the faith and fellowship of the Gospel. By the term **believer** we mean one who has been convicted of his personal sins, has repented toward God and has believed in Jesus the Christ for salvation. By **scripturally baptized** we mean one who has believed in Christ, been saved, therefore, and has been immersed in water by the authority of a New Testament church by a properly authorized administrator.

 Acts 2:47, "And the Lord added to the church daily such as should be saved."

The following is from the pen of John William Dean:

"Every Christian should join the church because of the safeguard that the organization throws around him in its leader, **Jesus.** The God-headship of Jesus gives the church the wisdom of Divine guidance. The constituent elements of the church are God, Jesus Christ, the Holy Spirit, and Christians. These factors, which constitute the church as an organization, make up an organization in which no person can afford to deprive himself of membership. Any person should be willing to strive hard to meet the conditions that Jesus imposed, so that he might have the high privilege of church membership.

"No church should, indiscriminately, grant the privilege of membership. Only when the privilege of church membership has been extended beyond the Scriptural limitations, has the church not been an inviting institution. When Jesus said, 'I will build My Church,' He immediately said;

> Matthew 16:19, "And I will give unto thee the keys of the kingdom of heaven; and whatsoever thou shalt bind on earth shall be bound in heaven; and whatsoever thou shalt loose on earth shall be loosed in heaven."

"No person has a right to membership in the church of Jesus Christ except those who, through the proper functioning of the church of Jesus, are bound in heaven; are 'Heirs of God, and joint-heirs with Christ,' Romans 8:17; have made their **'Calling and election sure,'** II Peter 1:10; and know that they **'Have passed from death unto life,'** I John 3:17"—The Lord's Supper.

Jesus, keep me near the cross,
    There a precious fountain
Free to all a healing stream,
    Flows from Calvary's mountain.
Near the cross, a trembling soul,
    Love and mercy found me;
There the bright and morning star
    Sheds its beams around me.

RESTRICTED TO THE SOUND IN THE FAITH

We have noted that one must be a believer, must be baptized and must be a member of a New Testament church to properly observe the ordinance of the Lord's Supper. There are other conditions.

The Scriptures authorize us to withhold the Supper from those who are heretical.

When the church was growing in Jerusalem and thousands were being added it is said of them that they continued **STEDFASTLY IN THE APOSTLES' DOCTRINE, and fellowship, and in BREAKING OF BREAD, and in prayers,** Acts 2:42.

We cannot take the Supper with heretics, whoever they may be. This forever bars us from "open communion," for, regardless of who is right in doctrine, our friends who differ with us, or ourselves, we cannot share the ordinance together. One is a heretic, and we sin in any case. This should be very plain.

Listen to Paul as he wrote to the church at Corinth, I Corinthians 11:18-20.

> "For first of all, when ye come together in the church, I hear that there be divisions among you; and I partly believe it. For there must also be heresies among you, that they which are approved may be made manifest among you. When ye come together therefore into one place, this is not to eat the Lord's Supper."

Paul here specifically forbade them to eat the Lord's Supper when they came together into one place (the church) because there were heresies among them. If we eat today with those who believe that salvation is in part or wholly by works, those who believe in sprinkling as baptism, those who believe in "falling from grace," baptismal regeneration, episcopal church government and hundreds of other human innovations, we violate the sacred ordinance which was included by our Lord in the "faith once delivered to the saints." We show ourselves derelict as custodians of the ordinance committed to our trust, and for our observance as it "was delivered."

On the question of doctrinal soundness as a qualification for the Lord's Supper, we further note.

To the church at Thessalonica Paul said:

> "Therefore, brethren, stand fast, and hold the traditions which ye have been taught, whether by word or our epistle," II Thessalonians 2:15.

The "traditions" which they had been taught by word or letter certainly embraced all the instructions and ordinances. The church was admonished to closely guard them. And in New Testament times they did this very thing.

To the church at Colosse he also said:

> "Though I be absent in the flesh, yet am I with you in the spirit, joying and beholding your ORDER, and the stedfastness of your faith in Christ. As ye have received Christ Jesus the Lord, so walk ye in Him. Beware lest any man spoil you through philosophy and vain deceit, after the traditions of men, after the rudiments of the world, and not after Christ," Colossians 2:5-6, 8.

We are often tempted to sin and we often yield. But in our lives we can strive to daily be better Christians. And we can be sound doctrinally. By intense study of the Word we can know what the doctrines are.

> "Study to show thyself approved unto God, a workman that needeth not to be ashamed, rightly dividing the word of truth," II Timothy 2:15.
>
> "If thou put the brethren in remembrance of these things, thou shalt be a good minister of Jesus Christ, nourished up in the words of faith and of good doctrine," I Timothy 4:6.
>
> "All scripture is given by inspiration of God, and is profitable for doctrine, for reproof, for correction, for instruction in righteousness: That the man of God may be perfect, throughly furnished unto all good works," II Timothy 3:16-17.

Leaven is a symbol of evil and false doctrine, Jesus Himself being witness. A church with heretical members is therefore leavened to just that extent. A church should be unified in both doctrine and practice, and only then can it function properly as a church, either in worship (and this includes the ordinances) or in its work of testifying to the unsaved. Note this Scripture:

> "Then Jesus said unto them, Take heed and beware of the leaven of the Pharisees and of the Sadducees . . . How is it that ye do not understand that I spake it not to you concerning bread, that ye should beware of the leaven of the Pharisees and of the Sadducees? Then understood they how that he bade them not beware of the leaven of bread, but of the DOCTRINE of the Pharisees and of the Sadducees," Matthew 16:6, 11-12.

A church is very much in disorder that has members who believe sundry doctrines subversive of the real truth. One who believes in salvation, either partially or wholly by works, has no place in a Baptist church. Reliance upon works makes null the doctrine of grace. Paul said, **"A little** leaven leaventh the whole lump," Galatians 5:9. He also said, "If by grace, then is it no more of works; otherwise grace is no more grace. But if it be of works, then is it no more grace; otherwise work is no more work," Romans 11:6.

> "Beloved, when I gave all diligence to write unto you of the common salvation, it was needful for me to write unto you, and exhort you that ye should earnestly contend for the faith which was once delivered unto the saints," Jude 3.

A church should be at oneness in all matters of faith and conduct. To achieve this end there must necessarily be discipline, and this kind of a church will not be popular. But this is the only kind of a church that can fittingly eat the Lord's Supper, and the only kind that will have power with God.

CHAPTER X

RESTRICTED AS TO ELEMENTS

Jesus Himself prescribed the very elements to be used in the Supper that is designed to remind us of His death. These two are: Bread and the "fruit of the vine." We shall now study these two substances which are so fittingly used.

The specification of one thing is the exclusion of another; therefore, when Our Saviour names bread we are not to use vegetables or flesh; when He says, "fruit of the vine" we are not to use colored water, apple cider or any other substitute.

BREAD ONE OF TWO EMBLEMS

It is fitting that bread be the emblem used to represent the body of Christ broken for us. He said He was the "bread from heaven." We quote from His own lips:

> "Jesus said unto them, Verily, verily, I say unto you, Moses gave you not that bread from heaven, but my Father giveth you the true bread from heaven.
> For the bread of God is he which cometh down from heaven, and giveth life unto the world. Then said they unto him, Lord, evermore give us this bread.
> And Jesus said unto them, I am the bread of life; he that cometh to me shall never hunger; and he that believeth on me shall never thirst . . .
> The Jews then murmured at him, because he said, I am the bread which came down from heaven . . .
> Your fathers did eat manna in the wilderness, and are dead.
> This is the bread which cometh down from heaven, that a man may eat thereof, and not die. I am that living bread which came down from heaven: if any man eat of this bread, he shall live forever: and the bread that I will give is my flesh, which I will give for the life of the world.
> The Jews therefore strove among themselves, saying, How can this man give us his flesh to eat?
> Jesus said unto them, Verily, verily, I say unto you, Except

> ye eat the flesh of the Son of man, and drink his blood, ye have no life in you.
> Whoso eateth my flesh, and drinketh my blood, hath eternal life; and I will raise him up at the last day.
> For my flesh is meat indeed, and my blood is drink indeed.
> He that eateth my flesh, and drinketh my blood, dwelleth in me, and I in him.
> As the living Father hath sent me, and I live by the Father: so he that eateth me, even he shall live by me.
> This is that bread which came down from Heaven: not as your fathers did eat manna, and are dead: he that eateth of this bread shall live forever." See John, the sixth chapter.

Of course Jesus did not mean they were to eat the material, literal flesh; nor drink His literal, material blood. He simply meant that by faith in Him we are to appropriate the sacrificial sufferings and death of Christ, and all the doctrines of grace that hang upon them, to our hearts in a most effective and personal manner to the needs of our souls. By His flesh and blood, He means for us to understand His words, His doctrines.

We quote from "What Is It to Eat and Drink Unworthily," by Dr. J. R. Graves: "The reader should bear in mind that in all the passages in which Christ speaks of His **body, flesh,** and **blood,** given for the **life** of the world, He does not mean His literal flesh and blood, but the '**words**'—**doctrine**—He taught them; in a word, the plan of salvation consummated by His vicarious sufferings in that body of our flesh, and by His blood shed for the remission of sins. It is by apprehending and cordially receiving the great truths represented to our minds by these expressive symbols that we eat the flesh and drink the blood of Christ, so that He becomes life eternal to us. A few passages will make this very clear to every mind."

Dr. Graves gives a literal translation of the following Scriptures:

> "Whoso abideth not in the doctrine of Christ hath not God. He that abideth in the doctrine of Christ hath both the Father and the Son," II John 9.
> "For that life which I now live in the flesh I am living by that faith of that God and Christ who loved me, even to the delivering himself up on my behalf," Galatians 2:20.

UNLEAVENED BREAD

We believe that the bread Jesus used in the first Supper was unleavened bread; that is, bread without any fermenting substance such as yeast. The Lord's Supper was instituted at the end of the passover feast which Jesus had kept with His fellow-Jews in the upper room the night of His betrayal. He had directed Peter and John to see that the Passover was properly prepared, Luke 22:8, and they had done so.

We are told that "He took bread," evidently some of the bread they had used in the passover supper. And this bread was unleavened bread, Exodus 12:15. No one was permitted to use anything less than unleavened bread on penalty of death or exclusion.

The passover of the Jews was a feast designed to remind that nation annually that God was their entire salvation from Egypt, and God alone. The Lord's Supper is designed, as we shall show later, to keep us reminded that our personal salvation from sin is entirely predicated upon the doctrine of the cross. Paul said, **"God forbid that I should glory, save in the Cross of the Lord Jesus Christ,"** Galatians 6:14. Of course, Paul meant by the Cross the doctrine of blood atonement, and all the doctrines of grace.

Bread, symbolizing the sinless body of Christ, must therefore be free of leaven, as leaven is a type of evil. It is always used in this sense, when used symbolically. To keep this in mind will make clear the parable of the meal and leaven in Matthew 13:33.

Only unleavened bread, therefore, can properly symbolize the perfect and sinless body of Christ. The body of Christ was begotten by God the Father. Note,

> **"And the angel answered and said unto her, The Holy Ghost shall come upon thee, and the power of the Highest shall overshadow thee: therefore also that holy thing which shall be born of thee shall be called the Son of God," Luke 1:35.**

That "thing" that was born was holy and that "thing" was the infant Jesus. And this holy state and this Son-relationship was kept by Him through life. Indeed, even today that very body that was born to Mary still exists though now in the presence of God, sitting at the right hand of the Father, Hebrews 1:3. **Of course He is now in His glory.**

Note further:

"For even hereunto were ye called: because Christ also suffered for us, leaving us an example, that ye should follow his steps; Who did no sin, neither was guile found in his mouth: Who, when he was reviled, reviled not again; when he suffered, he threatened not; but committed himself to him that judgeth righteously:

Who his own self bare our sins in his own body on the tree, that we, being dead to sins, should live unto righteousness: by whose stripes ye were healed," I Peter 2:21-24.

"Which of you convinceth me of sin?" John 8:46.

But surely we will not need to argue the point of Christ's complete righteousness.

Leaven is used to denominate false doctrine. In the parable of Matthew 13:33, referred to above, it is said that a woman **hid leaven** in three measures of meal. The whole of it was leavened. This represents false doctrines that false teachers and preachers began early to sow in Christendom. It has kept up its evil permeating work until we have the great harvest of heresy everywhere about us today.

We have said that the emblems in the Lord's Supper, the bread and the fruit of the vine, represent the body and blood of the Lord. And so they do. But we have also shown that, when Jesus said these were His flesh and His blood which we should eat and drink, He certainly did not mean that we literally eat and drink His body and blood.

In eating and drinking at the Lord's Supper we are mindful of His sufferings and subsequent death. This, in the thinking of this writer, is the ONE thing He meant the Supper for. He believes this ordinance should be stripped of everything else. It is absolutely a Memorial ordinance. The death of Christ is the basis of all the doctrines of grace by which we are saved.

Christ's doctrines are pure. They are without leaven, or the least particle of the false. Bread, which symbolizes these, must be unleavened. Let us note these truths:

"The words of the Lord are pure words; as silver tried in a furnace of earth, purified seven times," Psalm 12:6.

"The words that I speak unto you, they are spirit and they are life," John 6:63.

"The law of the Lord is perfect, converting the soul," Psalm 19:7.

The Apostle Paul was jealous for the real gospel of Christ. Notice what he said about it to the Galatians:

"I marvel that ye are so soon removed from him that called you into the grace of Christ unto another gospel; Which is not another; but there be some that trouble you, and would pervert the gospel of Christ.

But though we, or an angel from heaven, preach any other gospel unto you than that which we have preached unto you, let him be accursed," Galatians 1:6-8.

Bread used as an emblem of the doctrine of the grace of God whereby only we are saved, must be unleavened bread, free of putrefying elements. To use "soda crackers" or any other commercial product, is reprehensible.

When I survey the wondrous cross,
    On which the Prince of glory died,
My richest gain I count but loss,
    And pour contempt on all my pride.
Forbid it, Lord! that I should boast,
    Save in the death of Christ my God:
All the vain things that charm me most,
    I sacrifice them to His blood.
See, from His head, His hands, His feet,
    Sorrow and love flow mingled down;
Did e'er such love and sorrow meet,
    Or thorns compose so rich a crown?
Were the whole realm of nature mine,
    That were a present far too small;
Love so amazing so divine,
    Demands my soul, my life, my all.

THE FRUIT OF THE VINE

As bread was to represent the body of Christ, the cup, rather the content of the cup, represents His blood which was poured out for us.

There has been much controversy as to whether pure grape juice, the "fruit of the vine," is permissible or whether it must be fermented wine. Dr. Graves goes to great length to prove the latter. We do not have either the space or knowledge to go into this subject so far. It might be argued that, since the bread must be unleavened, the element emblematic of His blood must also be free of impurities. Though this be granted there is still the question whether pure grape juice is not pure. Man combines elements to make bread. But God Himself makes grape juice. The blood of the grape, if unmixed by us, is a pure fruit of the vine. However, we shall not be dogmatic on this question.

I quote from Dr. J. E. Cobb: "There have been strong contentions as to whether 'the cup,' that is, the element of drink, should be fermented wine or grape juice. The Lord spoke of the 'fruit of the vine,' and it will, no doubt, never be definitely determined whether or not this was fermented or unfermented. It is not the purpose of the author of this treatise to enter into a discussion of this phase of the subject, more than to say that it is his candid opinion that either pure grape wine or pure grape juice will answer the purpose of the element to be used; however, it may be said here, that it is likely very difficult to obtain absolutely pure grape wine. Most wines that might be called grape wines are, more than likely, sweetened with cane or maple sugar, hence there would be an element of leaven, even in so called grape wine. In order to have pure grape wine it is necessary that pure grape sugar be used in making the wine. The writer thinks this matter should not be urged to the extent of provoking contentions and divisions among the membership of a church. There is no positive command, so far as the writer has found to use fermented wine; Jesus stipulated only the "fruit of the vine," and certainly pure grape juice will answer this specification.

"No church, however, is privileged to substitute any other element in the place of this 'fruit of the vine.' "—A New Manual for Baptist Churches p. 119.

This element symbolizes the blood of Christ. It is amazing, when you notice carefully, how much is said about the place of the blood of Christ in the redemption of our souls. We cannot possibly give more importance to the doctrine of the blood of Jesus than it deserves.

Modernism discounts the blood of Christ. It has become not only neglected in many pulpits but it is made the target of vicious attacks by many who call themselves ministers of Christ. Of course, they are not Christ's ministers, if they deny the blood of Christ in its atoning work.

Jesus shed His blood for us. But we drink of it yet when we appropriate its efficacy to our souls by faith in Him. We symbolically drink of it when we drink the "fruit of the vine" in the Lord's Supper.

Many of our old gospel songs set forth in their lyrics the doctrine of blood atonement for sin. "There is a Fountain filled with blood, drawn from Immanuel's veins"; "There's power in the blood," and many, many more. They all tell the true story of the Cross. When we take out the blood we make of no effect the gospel. In fact, there can be no saving gospel without the blood of Christ.

The blood of the grape comes from a vine. Jesus said of Himself, **"I am the vine, ye are the branches,"** John 15:5. It is the blood of the True Vine (John 15:1) that hides us from our sins.

In the deliverance of the Israelites from Egypt, the blood of a lamb was sprinkled on the door posts and lintels of the houses and all who believed the Lord and did this were saved when the death angel passed over that night (Exodus 12:21-23). This was all indicative of the plan of personal salvation.

"For even Christ our Passover is sacrificed for us," I Corinthians 5:7.

To show the place of the blood of Christ in our redemption we ask our readers to give careful attention to the following Scriptures, and let me strongly admonish each one to ponder these forever in his heart.

> "Take heed therefore unto yourselves, and to all the flock, over the which the Holy Ghost hath made you overseers, to feed the church of God which **HE HATH PURCHASED WITH HIS OWN BLOOD,**" Acts 20:28.
>
> "And, having made peace through the blood of his cross, by him to reconcile all things unto himself; by him, I say, whether they be things in earth, or things in heaven," Colossians 1:20.
>
> "Neither by the blood of goats and calves, **BUT BY HIS OWN BLOOD** he entered in once into the holy place, having obtained eternal redemption for us. For if the blood of bulls and goats, and the ashes of an heifer sprinkling the unclean, sanctifieth to the purifying of the flesh: How much more

shall the **BLOOD OF CHRIST, who through the eternal Spirit offered himself without spot to God, purge your consciences from dead works to serve the living God?"** Hebrews 9:12-14.
"BUT WITH THE PRECIOUS BLOOD OF CHRIST, as of a lamb without blemish and without spot," I Peter 1:19.
"AND THE BLOOD OF JESUS CHRIST his Son cleanseth us from all sin," I John 1:7.

The elements of bread and "fruit of the vine" used in the Lord's Supper remain the same through the whole service. The Roman Catholics teach that at a given point in the ceremony of their eucharist, the bread is turned into the actual flesh of Jesus and the content of the cup is turned into the actual blood of Christ. This false doctrine is called transubstantiation. There are some others who believe, or say they do, as the Lutherans, that the actual flesh of Jesus and the actual blood of Jesus is **present** in the elements. This is called consubstantiation. Of course, both are absurd. These false ideas are based on the perversions of our Lord's meaning when He said, **"Take, eat; this is my body,"** and **"This cup is the New Testament in my blood."** Jesus simply meant by these words that the bread represents His flesh and the cup represents His blood.

RESTRICTED TO THE ORDERLY IN CONDUCT

The Lord's Supper is a very sacred ordinance. Jesus has guarded it by many restrictions, as we have seen and will see. To eat and to drink at the table of the Lord flippiantly or aimlessly and unworthily is to bring certain judgments.

Though one be a believer, a member of the church and Scripturally baptized, all this is not enough. The Scriptures are very explicit and tell us that those who are not Godly in life are not to profane the table with their presence.

We have shown that leaven is used by our Lord to describe heresy and unsound doctrines. It is likewise used to demonstrate an impious state and personal sins. One member who is immoral in his conduct leavens the whole church with his immorality. Let us consider a case just like that in the church at Corinth and what the Apostle Paul said about it. We set the whole context before you so as to better present this matter.

> "It is reported commonly that there is fornication among you, and such fornication as is not so much as named among the Gentiles, that one should have his father's wife.
>
> And ye are puffed up, and have not rather mourned, that he that hath done this deed might be taken away from among you.
>
> For I verily, as absent in body, but present in spirit, have judged already, as though I were present, concerning him that hath so done this deed.
>
> In the name of our Lord Jesus Christ, when ye are gathered together, and my spirit, with the power of our Lord Jesus Christ.
>
> To deliver such an one unto Satan for the destruction of the flesh, that the spirit may be saved in the day of the Lord Jesus.
>
> Your glorying is not good. KNOW YE NOT THAT A LITTLE LEAVEN LEAVENETH THE WHOLE LUMP?
>
> Purge out therefore the old leaven, that ye may be a new lump, as ye are unleavened. For even Christ our passover is sacrificed for us:
>
> Therefore let us keep the feast, not with old leaven, neither with the leaven of malice and wickedness; but with the unleavened bread of sincerity and truth.
>
> I wrote unto you in an epistle not to keep company with fornicators: Yet not altogether with the fornicators of this world, or with the covetous, or extortioners, or with idolaters; for then must ye needs go out of the world.
>
> But now I have written unto you not to keep company, if any man that is called a brother be a fornicator, or covetous, or an idolater, or a railer, a drunkard, or an extortioner; WITH SUCH AN ONE NO NOT TO EAT. For what have I to do to judge them also that are without: do not ye judge them that are within? But them that are without God judgeth. Therefore put away from among yourselves that wicked person."—Fifth chapter of First Corinthians.

We learn from the above that the church at Corinth was not to eat the Lord's Supper with the man who is mentioned as a fornicator. But there are some other sins mentioned also. If one is a drunkard, a railer, or is covetous, he should not be allowed to eat the Lord's Supper. And the church that allows such in its membership is leavened. Is there not oftentimes even malice in churches? It, also, is called leaven.

RESTRICTED AS TO ORDER

It is plain that Jesus first took bread, and, when they had eaten, He took and offered the cup. So, in our observance of the Lord's Supper the bread should be served first, then the cup.

We believe it the duty of the ordained ministry to

administer the Lord's Supper. It seems a general rule in our churches for the pastor to deliver the elements to the deacons for the actual serving to the members. While we find no specific example for this and no precept commanding it, we think it perfectly proper. However, the bread should be broken by the minister in charge.

It is the opinion of this writer that the pastor should prepare his people for this sacred ordinance before the Supper is undertaken. Perhaps a sermon along the line of its design or a short talk detailing the purpose and outlining the qualifications, etc. Certainly the church should be made very mindful of Christ's sufferings, His death and what it all means to a believer.

While I will not go into a discussion of it here I, too, believe that there should be but one loaf when the officiating minister takes charge; that he should call to prayer, break into pieces, and then serve. Personally, I prefer the membership to take the small piece of bread when it is passed but to hold it until all have been served and then, at the signal of the minister, all eat together.

It seems to me also fitting that there be but one original vessel of "the fruit of the vine." The Minister should pour out into as many vessels as are required. Some seem to think that individual glasses are unscriptural. I do not believe they are, if the above course is followed.

CHAPTER XI

RESTRICTED TO LOCAL CHURCH

Should a member of one Missionary Baptist church sit at the Lord's table in a sister church? In the opinion of this writer, no.

It is not a matter of training with him, either. In fact, I have only recently come to this conclusion. In pastoring churches nearly fifty years I have only pastored two that restricted the Supper to their own membership.

I realize that there is a widespread practice of inter-Baptist church communion. I have, however, through the years seen the pendulum swing towards the practice of local church observance. Of course, custom proves nothing, otherwise anything could be proved. We must go deeper than what somebody does to determine the right way to do things.

If every Baptist church withheld the emblems of the Lord's Supper from every one except her own members it would answer the "open communionists" in their tirade against Baptists for their restricted Supper as nothing else would do. But of course this is not the reason we should do it. The fact that more Baptist churches are practicing local church observance now, does not mean that until late years only have any done so. I believe that only in modern times, comparably, did they begin the practice of inviting members of sister churches to the table with them, and the farther back we go towards the Apostolic age the more we find Baptists keeping the table to each local church.

There is neither precept nor example in the New Testament for interchurch communion. We have repeatedly emphasized that the Lord's Supper is a CHURCH ordinance. It was given to a church, the church at Jerusalem. There was not another church in existence for several years. It is, then, a church ordinance.

It might be argued that Baptism is a church ordinance and we recognize the Baptism of a sister church. It is true, we do. However, the very nature of the ordinance of baptism admits of only one act, whereas the Lord's Supper is to be observed "till He comes again." The ordinances are different in purpose, form, elements and frequency. One is for the world to see and the other for the church itself.

The Scriptures are plain as to disciplinary powers being given the local church. Paul admonishes us not to eat with persons who are disorderly. The injunction is plain. And remember that the church is entrusted with this ordinance and is responsible for its violation so far as it is possible for it to guard it.

Every one knows that many churches have members who are very worldly, and even immoral, and nothing is done about it. For many, church discipline is a "lost art." There is no doubt that unsaved people form a very great percentage of the church membership in some places. Then, it is the experience of this writer that the churches hold in their membership many people who are far from being sound in the faith. Some hold many heretical notions. Of course churches should discipline these by proper teaching or exclusion. But it is a fact that many times they do not.

We are far too lax. Modernism has easy access to our orthodox churches through the door of church letters. It is entirely possible for one to get into an orthodox church by letter from an unorthodox one, there being many "ministers" and "churches" that are practically infidel.

By the practice of inter-church observance of the Lord's Supper it would be very easy for one who is immoral in life and heretical in doctrine to be invited to the table. It is only reasonable to conclude that our invitation should extend only so far as our discipline reaches. Otherwise we could even find ourselves eating with even the unbaptized.

We do not permit members of a sister church to vote

in our conferences. Each church is a unit in itself, separate and apart from every other church. It is responsible for its own deeds, and not another.

We quote from Dr. A. P. Williams: "He (a regular Baptist) has a right to the Communion in the church of which he has been added; but nowhere else."—Lord's Supper, p. 93.

Dr. Arnold, of Madison University, N. Y., says "Such a principle is in our judgment incompatible, alike with the independence and the responsibility of churches—with their independence, because it takes from them the right to judge of the qualifications of those whom they receive to their highest privileges; and with their responsibility, because it deprives them of the power to guard the table of the Lord against the approach of the unworthy."—Prerequisites to Communion, p. 62—as quoted by Graves.

Dr. Gardner says: "A member of one Baptist church has no more right to claim the privilege of voting in another Baptist church, than has a Campbellite, Methodist, or Presbyterian. The same is equally true of Communion at the Lord's table, which is a church act, and the appointed token, not of Christian or denominational, but of the church fellowship subsisting between communicants at the same table. Hence it follows that a member of one Baptist church has no more right, **as a right,** to claim communion in another Baptist church, than he has to claim the right of voting, for both are equally **church acts** and **church privileges.** The Lord's Supper being a **church** ordinance, as all admit, and every church being required to exercise discipline over all its communicants, it necessarily follows that no church can scripturally, (and it is certain that it cannot unscripturally) extend its communion beyond the limits of its discipline. And this, in fact, settles the question of church Communion, and restricts the Lord's Supper to the **members of each particular church."**—Communion pp 18, 19. Dr. Gardner refers us to the following for further study: Curtis, Paxton, Adkins, Harvey, Pendleton, and Hovey.

Let us always remember that the Lord's Supper is not

just a Christian Memorial but it is a CHURCH ordinance and given to separate and independent churches.

It is a fact that the Scriptures themselves warn us against eating with the immoral. But how are we to know when we invite those whom we do not know, when they come from churches on their own recommendation from other churches? Paul says:

> "But now I have written unto you not to keep company, if any man that is **CALLED A BROTHER** be a fornicator, or covetous, or an idolater, or a railer, or a drunkard, or an extortioner; with such a one, no, not to eat. For what have I to do to judge them also that are without. Do not **YE JUDGE THEM THAT ARE WITHIN**," I Corinthians 5:11-12.

We are warned not to observe the Lord's Supper when there are divisions and heresies in the church. It is our candid opinion that few churches are in position to observe this sacred ordinance. If not, however, they should immediately set about to put the church in order.

You will note that in Paul's admonition he mentions **a railer**. What is **a railer?** Webster said: "One who scoffs, insults, censures, or reproaches with opprobrious language." In eating and drinking with those of other churches we might very often eat and drink with these very persons. Usually this kind are the more bold and forward and love to pretend and push in. We are simply stating facts, facts that should cause us to be very careful whom we invite to the Lord's Supper. It is usually this kind that causes the confusion that Paul warns us against having with us at the table of the Lord.

I now quote from our own Dr. John T. Christian: "The reasoning is conclusive. By participating at the Lord's table together we declare ourselves to be partners, and members of the same organization, or church, and mutually responsible for the right administration of the Supper. Only members of the one body, the church, can join in the participation, since no others can be partners in this matter." Paul's reasoning is to the point. He says: "**The cup of blessing which we bless, is it not a communion of the blood of Christ? The bread which we break, is it not a communion of the body of Christ? Seeing that we who are many, are** one bread and one body: for we all partake of that one bread. Behold Israel after the flesh: have not they which eat the sacrifices communion with the altar, What say I then? That a thing sacrificed to idols is anything, or that an idol is anything? But I say, that the things which the Gentiles sacrifice, they sacrifice to devils, and not to God; and I would not that ye should have communion with devils. Ye cannot drink the cup of the Lord, and the cup of devils: ye cannot partake of the table of the Lord, and of the table of devils," I Corinthians 10:16-21, American Revised Version.

There is to be ONE loaf, representing ONE body, not elements from many bodies, or many churches.

From an Orthodox Creed, 1678: "And no unbaptized, unbelieving, or open profane, or wicked heretical person, ought to be admitted to this ordinance to profane it."

But if we admit those whom we know nothing of simply because they say they belong to sister churches, and knowing that many churches have that kind of people in them, are we not laying ourselves liable?

The safe thing, therefore, is for each local church to admit to the Lord's table only those within her gates, and no farther than her discipline extends.

We shall close this topic with the following quotations:

"The first deduction I make from this passage (I Corinthians 5:9), is, that the celebration of the Lord's Supper can not extend beyond the limits of church discipline. Suppose it does. Then the offender, without a satisfactory reformation, may go and join some organization, claiming to be a follower of Christ; and, at the very next communion season, when the usual general invitation is given, present himself, and the church thus having to eat with him would violate the command of Christ. The only way to avoid such guilt, such trouble (for cases of this kind sometimes occur), is carefully to restrict the communicants to those within the limits of church discipline. From this deduction it follows, that communion is a sign of church fellowship; and, consequently, **intercommunion is unscriptural.**"—Savage.

Gardner says: "Such intercommunion (i. e., without membership) among Baptists is not only without Scripture warrant, but does much harm, and no real good. The practice, therefore, is unscriptural and of evil tendency; and, doubtless, will be abandoned by all our churches as soon as they reflect properly upon the subject, and can overcome the force of habit and prejudice." p. 204, **Church Communion.**

Dr. Graves argues, and I believe well, that inasmuch as the church partaking of the Lord's Supper is one body, there should be one loaf or one piece, whatever its shape, originally, and to be divided just before eating. I here give some quotations from his "What Is It to Eat and Drink Unworthily," in which he quotes some others.

Knapp: "While we all eat of one and the same bread (a portion of which is broken for each), we profess to be all members of one body."—Christian Theology.

Dr. Adam Clarke, a Methodist, "the original would be better translated thus: Because there is one bread or loaf, we who are many are one body. As only one loaf was used at the passover, and those who partook of it were considered one religious body (family) so we who partake of the Eucharistical bread and wine in commemoration of the sacrificial death of Christ are one spiritual society."

Albert Barnes: I Corinthians 10:17, "Are one bread, one loaf, one cake. That is, we are united, or are one. There is evident allusion here to the fact, that the loaf or cake was composed of many separate grains of wheat, or portions of flour united in one; or, that, as one loaf was broken and partaken by all, it was implied that they were all one. We are all one society . . . and one body, one society."

Dr. William C. Buck: "That it was the design of the Lord to signify, in the use of this ordinance, the unity of each church as one body, is distinctly asserted by the apostle; for he assures us that "one bread" is the symbol of "one body"; and he further teaches us that "we," the apostles, break the "one bread"—loaf—and bless the "one cup," and we have proof as clear as a ray of light from Heaven, that they copied, with punctilious exactitude, the pattern set them by the Messiah. We may therefore consider this a settled principle in the practical philosophy of this rite."—Page 456, the Philosophy of Religion.

The Lord's Supper being a church ordinance it is best observed with as little ostentation as possible. Unlike the other ordinance, baptism, the Lord's supper is designed purely for the church. Baptism publicly declares to the world our new found faith, our death to sin and new life in Christ.

When I was just a lad of a boy, I remember in the old home church, far out in the country, the second Sunday in May was a high day for all around. On that day people came to spend the day. There was, sometimes, a Sunday school, and always a sermon in the morning. Then "dinner on the ground" and about two hours of visitation. They talked about their crops and other things. In the afternoon they "washed feet" and observed the Lord's Supper. They meant well, but they did wrong. It was a sort of high day of celebration, visitation and business.

There were only a very few present when the Lord established His Supper. Jesus' mother was not present. There must have been many others in Jerusalem who were baptized believers at that time, but they were not there.

At the close of the Lord's Supper nothing should be said or done that would detract from meditation on the design of the Supper. At the first Supper they "sang an hymn and went out." This practice is well for us.

As to the frequency of observing the Ordinance there is no specific directive in the Scriptures. Paul said to the Corinthians: **"For as often as ye eat this bread, and drink this cup, ye do show the Lord's death till He come."**

There is no command to observe it every Sunday. Certainly, on the other hand, it is wrong to habitually neglect it. There are various customs among the churches with reference to the frequency they set this memorable supper. Many churches do it annually, some semi-annually; others quarterly. Some have no set time, and some have not done so for years. It is a shame the way some churches that call themselves churches of the Lord Jesus Christ, and who claim much for their "orthodoxy," neglect this very sacred and tender ordinance. No wonder that some of them have judgments piled up a plenty.

Perhaps the Lord designedly commanded no specific time frequency lest it become a mere meaningless ceremony observed for the sake of ceremony and without discernment of His death. The design is more important than any regularity of frequency.

RESTRICTED AS TO DESIGN

We come now to the most important thing of all, the very design of this Supper. What is it for? What's its purpose? Why did Jesus set it in the church and guard it so jealously? There was only one primary reason for it, and that is very plainly taught by the Scriptures. He has not left us in ignorance as to why He wants it observed.

When an architect designs a building, he specifies as to size, rooms and materials used so as best to accommodate the purpose for which it is to be used. For example, a building designed for a home is far different from one to be used for a factory or business office. Jesus is the Great Architect, and He has designed the Lord's Supper to serve ONE purpose. That purpose is, as we have seen so many times already, to remind us of His death and all that death means to His people.

But why should we be reminded? In the first place, we are humans and heirs to human frailty. We are naturally prone to forget even our greatest benefactors. It is easy to remember, the flesh always prompting, of injuries done us, either fanciful or real, but we are so forgetful of the good that others do for us.

The greatest thing that was ever done for us is when Jesus gave His life a ransom for us.

> "For there is one God, and one mediator between God and men, the man Christ Jesus; Who gave himself a ransom for all, to be testified in due time," I Timothy 2:5-6.

The Supper is designed to remind us of His love that prompted the death which it commemorates:

> "For God so loved the world that he gave his only begotten Son that whosoever believeth in him should not perish but have everlasting life," John 3:16.

The Twenty-second Psalm should be memorized. It sets forth the sufferings of Christ.

The Supper is designed to remind us of His sacrifice, that He gave up even His life for us.

>"But this man, after he had offered one sacrifice for sins for ever, sat down on the right hand of God," Hebrews 10:12.

It is designed to remind us of His writhing agony and pain; His rejection among men, His being forsaken of the Father in His trying hour: **"My God, My God, why hast thou forsaken Me?"**; His blood poured out; His intense thirst and, finally, death itself in its most horrible form. And, before His death, He was subjected to most embarrassing insults and shame.

We can close this topic no better than to call to your mind the following Scripture: for this is what the Supper is designed to cause us to remember.

>"And when they were come to the place, which is called Calvary, there they crucified him, and the malefactors, one on the right hand, and the other on the left . . . And it was about the sixth hour, and there was a darkness over all the earth until the ninth hour. And the sun was darkened, and the veil of the temple was rent in the midst. And when Jesus had cried with a loud voice, he said, Father, into thy hands I commend my spirit; and having said thus, he gave up the ghost," Luke 23:33, 44-46.

>"And as they came out, they found a man of Cyrene, Simon by name: him they compelled to bear his cross.
>
>And when they were come unto a place called Golgotha, that is to say, a place of a skull,
>
>They gave him vinegar to drink mingled with gall; and when he had tasted thereof, he would not drink.
>
>And they crucified him, and parted his garments, casting lots: that it might be fulfilled which was spoken by the prophet, They parted my garment among them, and upon my vesture did they cast lots," Matthew 27:32-35.

Jesus designed the Lord's Supper in all of its details. There was to be one loaf of bread to symbolize the one body, the local church, that was to celebrate the Supper. This loaf was composed of many grain elements that had been brought together in the process of baking. The members of the church are symbolized by the grain-elements, all of the same kind, as the flour is that of kindred grain and moulded together in the loaf. The local church membership should be alike in faith and practice. They should be bound together in Christian love and fellowship.

Acts 2:42, **"And they continued stedfastly in the apostles' doctrine and fellowship, and in breaking of bread, and in prayers."**

The church is the mystical body of Christ (Ephesians 5:30-32). Our human body is composed of members. When one member suffers all suffer with it. The whole body is affected. Church members should love each other so much, and be bound so closely together, that, when one member has a misfortune, all the other members are grieved; and, when one member enjoys good, all the members rejoice with it. We have already shown that the church is ONE body and as such takes the Lord's Supper. Jesus therefore specified ONE loaf before it is broken and distributed to those who eat.

The bread was designed to represent His body, "which is broken for you." He designed that as we eat this bread it reminds us of Him and His death "Till he come."

He designed that the bread be unleavened so as to properly represent His sinlessness; and also the purity of the doctrine, His words, which are spirit and life.

He designed that the fruit of the vine be used in symbolizing His blood shed for us. **"This is my blood of the New Testament which is shed for you."** He designed that we remember that blood as it alone can atone for our sins.

Jesus was the Word of Life, says John: **"That which was from the beginning, which we have heard, which we have seen with our eyes, which we have looked upon, and our hands have handled, of the Word of life,"** I John 1:1.

There is a fountain filled with blood,
    Drawn from Immanuel's veins,
And sinners, plunged beneath that flood
    Lose all their guilty stains.
Dear dying Lamb, Thy precious blood
    Shall never lose its power,
Till all the ransomed church of God,
    Be saved to sin no more.
The dying thief rejoiced to see
    That fountain in his day;
And there may I, though vile as He,

Wash all my sins away.
E'r since by faith I saw the stream
  Thy flowing wounds supply,
Redeeming love has been my theme,
  And shall be till I die.
When this poor lisping, stammering tongue
  Lies silent in the grave,
Then in a nobler, sweeter song,
  I'll sing Thy power to save.

SHOULD EXAMINE OURSELVES

"Open Communionists" of all creeds continually remind us that the Bible says, **"Let a man examine himself, and so let him eat."** They say we have no right to say whether a man should eat or not eat the Lord's Supper.

The Bible does most emphatically say that we should examine ourselves. But whom did Paul say this to? Now, note well! It was to a New Testament church, all were members of that same church, the church at Corinth. They were not only members of the same church, they were all believers, and all baptized believers. So Paul is not saying this to the world, not even to so-called Christendom.

These church members, these Christians, these baptized believers at Corinth, were not told, therefore, to examine themselves to ascertain if they were saved, were baptized or were church members. They had met all these requirements. The purpose of this self-examination was something else.

The church at Corinth, while a New Testament church, was one in very bad order. Paul accused them of several wrongs and reprimanded them very severely. Read the fifth and sixth chapters of his first letter to this church. Among other irregular things, they were turning the Lord's Supper into a picnic affair. Some even got drunk, others paraded their plenty to eat, which they brought, while the poor dropped their heads in want.

But let us observe this whole account, and note carefully every word.

"For first of all, when ye come together in the church, I hear that there be divisions among you; and I partly believe it.

For there must be also heresies among you, that they which are approved may be made manifest among you.

When ye come together therefore into one place this is not to eat the Lord's supper.

For in eating every one taketh before other his own supper: and one is hungry, and another is drunken.

What? have ye not houses to eat and drink in? or despise ye the church of God, and shame them that have not? What shall I say to you? shall I praise you in this? I praise you not.

For I have received of the Lord Jesus that which also I delivered unto you, That the Lord Jesus the same night in which he was betrayed took bread:

And when he had given thanks, he brake it, and said, Take, eat: this is my body, which is broken for you: this do in remembrance of me.

And after the same manner also he took the cup, when he had supped, saying, This cup is the New Testament in my blood: this do ye, as oft as ye drink it in remembrance of me.

For as often as ye eat this bread, and drink this cup, ye do shew the Lord's death till he come.

Wherefore whosoever shall eat this bread, and drink this cup of the Lord, unworthily, shall be guilty of the body and blood of the Lord.

But let a man examine himself, and so let him eat of that bread, and drink of that cup.

For he that eateth and drinketh unworthily, eateth and drinketh damnation to himself, not discerning the Lord's body.

For this cause many are weak and sickly among you, and many sleep.

For if we would judge ourselves, we should not be judged.

But when we are judged, we are chastened of the Lord, that we should not be condemned with the world.

Wherefore, my brethren, when ye come together to eat, tarry one for another.

If any man hunger let him eat at home; that ye come not together unto condemnation. And the rest will I set in order when I come," I Corinthians 11:18-34.

Many of the members of the church at Corinth were guilty of eating and drinking "unworthily," and it is very plain in what way. "Unworthily" is an adverb. It does not say **unworthy.** None of us are worthy, even to be saved. We are saved by grace. We have shown that the Lord wants us to keep the Supper for one purpose, and that purpose is to let it remind of His death. But these Corinthians were doing so for reasons other than remembering the Lord's death. Some did because they were hungry or thirsty. Paul rebuked them and asked if they did not have homes in which to eat and drink. He also rebuked them for selfishness and a "show off" spirit before those who were poor. They had missed the whole purpose of the supper.

And what happened? Paul tells them that their sinful perversion of the ordinance was the cause of many of them being sick. And some had even died. Why the illness? and why the deaths? The reason is very apparent and is specifically named by Paul. They did not discern the Lord's body.

In order to avoid this penalty, this chastening, Paul admonishes them, in approaching the Lord's Supper, to examine themselves. Why the examination? Simply to see if they were eating and drinking in discernment and in memory of the death of the Lord, or whether for any other reason. That is why the admonition, "Let a man examine himself and so let him eat." A good man can even take this Supper unworthily.

A SURE JUDGMENT

The Corinthians had treated the Lord's Supper as an ordinary feast and had brought upon themselves swift judgment. In the above Scripture, Paul says that if we would judge ourselves, in other words see that we are doing right, it would not be necessary for God to judge us. And how severe His judgment can be! Some of the Corinthians He had killed; that is, they had died a natural death of the body. This does not mean that their souls were lost. He had chastened others with illness in order that they might not be condemned with the world. We should be thankful that God chastens rather than count us in with the world and its terrible judgments.

The Bible teaches chastening, or judgment, for the saved here in this life. When Paul said damnation in the above, he meant condemnation to themselves. And the judgment was to suffering and even death of the body, but not damnation of the soul.

That the Lord chastens His children, note the following:

> "And ye have forgotten the exhortation which speaketh unto you as unto children, My son, despise not thou the chastening of the Lord, nor faint when thou art rebuked of him:
> For whom the Lord loveth he chasteneth, and scourgeth every son whom he receiveth.

> If ye endure chastening, God dealeth with you as with sons; for what son is he whom the father chasteneth not? But if ye be without chastisement, whereof all are partakers, then are ye bastards and not sons," Hebrews 12:5-8.

The Lord's Supper is a church ordinance. It is a very sacred ordinance and has a specific design. There are many scriptural restrictions, as we have learned. It is a positive ordinance and should be observed, but only in the manner prescribed by the Scriptures. There are severe penalties in violating it.

THE SERIOUSNESS OF EATING UNWORTHILY

Paul tells us that we are guilty of the body and blood of the Lord when we eat and drink unworthily. Ominous words indeed! What do they mean, Guilty of body and blood of the Lord? Here are some opinions, as quoted by Graves.

Grotius renders it: "He does the same thing as if he should slay Christ."

Bretechneider: "Injuring by crime the body of Christ."

Bloomfield; "He shall be guilty respecting the body—i. e., guilty of profaning symbols of the body and blood of Christ, and consequently amenable to the punishment due to such an abuse of the highest means of grace."

Rosemuller: "He shall be punished for such a deed as if he had rejected Christ himself with ignominy."

Barnes: "The obvious and literal sense is evidently that they should, by such conduct, be involved in the sin of putting the Lord Jesus to death."

On the Communion question, Dr. Cathcart says "This practice (open Communion) is of comparably modern origin, and its history presents little to commend it. It seems to have been a natural outgrowth of persecuting times, when the people of God were few in number and were compelled to worship in secret places; and when the preservation of the fundamentals of divine truth made men blind to grave errors that were regarded as not soul destroying.

"In the first half of the Seventeenth century it made its appearance in England. John Bunyan was its ablest defender, and the church of which he was the honored pastor illustrates the natural tendencies of the system by its progress backward, in adopting infant sprinkling and the Congregational denomination.

"Open Communion refers to fellowship at the Lord's Table, and it has three forms,—a mixed membership; occasional communion by the unbaptized in a church whose entire membership is immersed; and two churches in the same building, meeting **together** for ordinary worship, but celebrating the Lord's Supper at separate times. The first was Bunyan's, the second is followed by Spurgeon, the third was the plan adopted by Robert Hall in Leisecter . . .

"In this country the mixed membership form of open communion had a very extensive trial, not in regular Baptist churches nor in regular Baptist Associations."—Baptist Encyclopaedia.

RESTRICTED COMMUNION IN PAST AGES

We have shown conclusively from the Scriptures that the Lord's Supper is restricted. As with other Baptist doctrines, this has been practiced in past centuries.

The Llantrisaint church, Wales, split over the Communion question in 1639. Those believing in mixed communion withdrew and organized another church in this place. The following is from Davis' History of Welsh Baptists, page 85.

"Llantrisaint church was first formed at Llanfaches, on the principle of mixed communion, by Mr. Wroth, assisted by Mr. Jesse of London, in the year 1639. In 1645, the Baptists separated themselves, and formed into a distinct church at Llantrisaint, and had for their minister, one David Davis, and others to assist."

Davis also says that there were but few ministers who preached mixed communion, page 95. He also says that the Reformers believed in mixed communion but the Baptists did not, page 20. Davis mentions several other instances.

CHAPTER XII

BAPTISTS AND EDUCATION

Baptists have ever been friends to education. The Welsh Baptists had a college in the sixth century.

We quote from Ford's, The Origin of Baptists, page 67:
"A council or convention was afterward held between Austin and Welsh preachers, at which the latter declared that they would do nothing without a full representation from their churches. Finally the Britons refused to enter into any terms of agreement with Austin. (Austin was a Catholic monk sent to Briton.) Well, then, said the haughty priest, as you will not have us as friends, you shall, as foes, and experience the vengeance of the Saxons."

"His threat was carried out. **The college** at Bangor was destroyed; the preachers were massacred, and over two thousand of these primitive Christians in Hereford were sacrificed to the demon of apostasy."

Baptists of America have ever been friends to true education. The Philadelphia Association, the first in America, established an academy in Hopewell, N. J., in 1756. This school declined when the Brown University was begun in Providence, R. I., in 1764.

Hamilton Theological Seminary was established in New York in 1819, and Madison University in the same city in 1846. A school was established in Rochester, N. Y., in 1850.

Colby University was started in Waterville, Maine, in 1820.

The Columbian College, later the Columbian University, was opened in 1822 in Washington, D. C. A medical school was provided with it at its beginning.

The Newton Theological Institution, Massachusetts, was founded in 1825. Dozens of others were founded in this century. In 1884, in the United States, there were 60 academies, thirty-three colleges, and eight theological seminaries. Another was a German Seminary.

The North American Baptist Association owns and maintains a Seminary in Jacksonville, Texas. Dr. Gerald D. Kellar is president at this time, Dr. W. J. Dorman, Dean. It was established in 1956.

There are several colleges on a state level in the North American Baptist Association.

At this present time we have Jacksonville Baptist College, Jacksonville, Texas, Curtis Carroll, president; W. C. Lacy, Dean.

Central Baptist College, Conway, Arkansas, A. R. Reddin, president; Wassell L. Burgess, Dean.

Southeastern College, Laurel, Mississippi, Jasper Fails, Dean.

Midwestern, Oklahoma City, Randall Reddin, president.

The Columbia Baptist Bible School, Magnolia, Arkansas, was begun in 1936, largely through the effort of Eld. E. B. Jones. It is sponsored by the Columbia Baptist Association and has trained many for Christian service. It is still operating.

John Clarke Baptist Academy, Battle Creek, Michigan, is the youngest school, starting in 1962. Harold Cosby is president; V. E. Gibson, Dean.

It appears that the first college in modern England was founded in Bristol, England.

"The Bristol Academy was the first seminary of any kind among the English Baptists; Rhode Island College, with the Americans. These nurseries of education have now become somewhat numerous, and are rapidly increasing."
—A General History of the Baptist Denomination in America by David Benedict.

BAPTIST INSTITUTIONS OF LEARNING, UNITED STATES

The following tables taken from Baptist Encylopaedia, pages 678, 679.
(To 1881)

NAME	FOUNDED	PRESIDENT	LOCATION
Brown University	1764	E. G. Robinson	Providence, R. I.
Madison University	1819	E. Dodge	Hamilton, N. Y.
Colby University	1820	Henry E. Robins	Waterville, Maine
Columbian University	1821	J. C. Welling	Washington, D. C.
Shurtleff College	1827	A. A. Kendrick	Upper Alton, Ill.
Georgetown College	1829	R. M. Dudley	Georgetown, Ky.
Denison University	1831	Alfred Owen	Granville, Ohio
Franklin College	1834	W. T. Scott	Franklin, Ind.
Wake Forest College	1834	T. H. Prichard	Wake Forest, N. C.
Mercer University	1838	A. J. Battle	Macon, Ga.
Richmond College	1832	B. Puryear	Richmon, Va.
Howard College	1843	J. T. Murfee	Marion, Ala.
Baylor University	1845	W. C. Crane	Independence, Texas
University at Lewisburg	1846	D. J. Hill	Lewisburg, Pa.
William Jewell College	1849	W. R. Rothwell	Liberty, Mo.
University of Rochester	1850	M. B. Anderson	Rochester, N. Y.
Mississippi College	1850	W. S. Webb	Clinton, Miss.
Carson College	1850	N. B. Goforth	Mosey Creek, Tenn.
Furman University	1857	J. C. Furman	Greenville, S. C.

NAME	FOUNDED	PRESIDENT	LOCATION
Central University	1852	L. A. Dunn	Pella, Iowa
Kalamazoo College	1855	Kendall Brooks	Kalamazoo, Mich.
Bethel College	1856	Leslie Waggener	Russellville, Ky.
University of Chicago	1859	Galusha Anderson	Chicago, Ill.
McMinnville College	1858	G. C. Burchett	McMinnville, Ore.
Waco University	1861	R. C. Burleson	Waco, Texas
Vassar College	1861	S. L. Caldwell	Poughkeepsie, N. Y.
University of Demoines	1865	J. A. Nash	Des Moines, Iowa
La Grange College	1859	J. F. Cook	La Grange, Mo.
Monongahela College	1867	H. K. Craig	Jefferson, Mo. (Greene Co.)
California College	1871	U. Gregory	Vacaville, Calif.
Southwestern Baptist University	1874	G. W. Jarmon	Jackson, Tenn.

Theological Institutions

NAME	FOUNDED	PRESIDENT	LOCATION
Hamilton Theological Seminary	1819	E. Dodge	Hamilton, N. Y.
Newton Theological Institution	1825	Alvah Hovey	Newton Centre, Mass.
Rochester Theological Seminary	1851	A. H. Strong	Rochester, N. Y.
Southern Baptist Theological Seminary	1858	Jas. O. Boyce	Louisville, My.
Shurtleff Theological Department	1862	A. A. Kendrick	Upper Alton, Ill.
Baptist Union Theological Seminary	1867	G. W. Northrup	Morgan Park, Ill.
Crozer Theological Seminary	1868	H. G. Westen	Upland, Pa.
Vardeman School Theo.	1868	W. R. Rothwell	Liberty, Mo.

Academies, Seminaries, and Female Institutions.

NAME	FOUNDED	PRESIDENT	LOCATION
Alabama Central, Female College	1857	A. K. Yancey, Jr.	Tuscaloosa, Ala.
Atlanta Baptist Seminary	1870	J. T. Roberts	Atlanta, Ga.
Baptist Female College	1855	John F. Lanneau	Lexington, Mo.
Bardstown M. & F. College	1842	H. J. Greenwell	Bardston, Ky.
Baylor Female College	1846	J. H. Luther	Independence, Tex.
Benedict Institute	1870	H. J. Goodspeed	Columbia, S. C.
Bethel Female College	1852	J. W. Rust	Hopkinsville, Ky.
Broadus Female College	1871	E. J. Willis	Clarksburg, W. Va.
Burlington Colored Inst.	1852	E. F. Stearns	Burlington, Iowa
Cedar Valley Seminary	1863	A. Bush	Osage, Iowa
Central Female Institute	1853	Walter Hillman	Clinton, Miss.
Chowan Baptist F. Inst.	1848	A. McDowell	Murfreesborough, N. C.
Colby Academy	1836	James P. Dixon	New London, N. H.
Colgate Academy	1872	F. W. Towle	Hamilton, N. Y.
Connecticut Lit. Inst.	1833	Martin H. Smith	Suffield, Conn.
Cook Academy	1872	A. C. Hill	Havana, N. Y.
Georgetown Fem. Academy	1846	J. J. Rucker	Georgetown, Ky.
Georgie Female College	1850	P. F. Asbury	Madison, Ga.
Grand River College	1859	T. H. Storts	Edinburg, Mo.
Greenville Baptist Female College	1854	A. S. Townes	Greenville, S. C.
Hardin Female College	1873	A. W. Terrell	Mexico, Mo.

NAME	FOUNDED	PRESIDENT	LOCATION
Hollin's Institute	1841	Chas. L. Cooke	Botetourt Spgs., Va.
Howe Literary Inst.	1874	S. F. Holt	East St. Louis, Ill.
Judson Female Inst.	1839	L. R. Gwaltney	Marion, Ala.
Keystone Academy	1868	J. H. Harris	Factoryville, Pa.
Leland University	1870	Seth J. Axtell	New Orleans, La.
Lea Female College	1877	C. H. Otken	Simmit, Miss.
Mary Sharp College	1850	Z. C. Graves	Winchester, Tenn.
Minnesota Academy	1877	S. H. Baker	Owatonna, Minn.
Mt. Pleasant Inst.	1873	Leroy Stevens	Mt. Pleasant, Pa.
Nashville Institute	1865	D. W. Phillips	Nashville, Tenn.
Natchez Seminary	1877	Charles Ayer	Natchez, Miss.
Normal & Theological School	1878	H. Woodsmall	Selma, Ala.
Peddle Institute	1865	E. J. Avery	Hightstown, N. J.
Reid Institute	1862	C. A. Gilbert	Reidsburg, Pa.
Richmond Institute	1867	C. H. Corey	Richmond, Va.
Shaw University	1865	H. M. Tupper	Raleigh, N. C.
South Jersey Institute	1870	H. K. Trask	Bridgeton, N. J.
Stephen's Female College	1856	R. P. Rider	Columbia, Mo.
University Academy	1846	W. E. Martin	Lewisburg, Pa.
University Female Institute	1846	Jonathan Jones	Lewisburg, Pa.
Vermont Academy	1872	H. M. Willard	Saxton's River, Vt.
Wayland Seminary	1865	G. M. P. King	Washington, D. C.

NAME	FOUNDED	PRESIDENT	LOCATION
Wayland University	1855	N. E. Wood	Beaver Dam, Wis.
Worchester Academy	1834	Nath. Leavenworth	Worchester, Mass.
Wyoming Seminary	1867	M. Heath	Wyoming, Del.
Young Ladies Institute	1832	D. Shepardson	Granville, Ohio.

England, Wales and Scotland

NAME	FOUNDED	PRESIDENT	LOCATION
Bristol College	1720	F. W. Gotch	Bristol
Chilwell College (Gen. Bapt.)	1797	F. Goadley	Nottingham
Rawdon College	1804	T. G. Rooks	Rawdon, Yorkshire
Pontypool College	1807	W. M. Lewis	Pontypool, Wales
Regent's Park College	1810	Joseph Angus	London
Haverfordwest College	1839	Thomas Davies	Haverfordwest, Wales
Theol. Inst. Scotland	1856	James Culrose	Glascow
Pastor's College (Spurgeon)	1856	C. H. Spurgeon	London
Llangollen	1862	Hugh Jones	Llangollen, N. Wales
Manchester Bapt. Theol. Inst.	1866	Edward Parker	Brighton Grove, Manchester

CHAPTER XIII

BAPTISTS AND MISSIONS

The spirit of missions, mixed with martyr's blood, has carried the Gospel, at one time or another, into all the world.

The very nature of the gospel is missionary. All truly, born-again Christians are missionary in heart, howsoever they may be hindered in practice by the world. Our God in heaven is missionary, having sent His Son. Our Saviour is missionary, both by example and by orders to His church.

The whole duty of a church can be summed up in two words, worship and missions. Under the general theme of missions can be classed such worthy causes as Christian education, personal witnessing, publications and benevolence.

We are not left to wonder if we should be missionary, for this work is straightforwardly commanded in the Scriptures. A few passages are given.

"Go ye therefore, and teach all nations, baptizing them in the name of the Father, and of the Son, and of the Holy Ghost:
Teaching them to observe all things whatsoever I have commanded you: and, lo, I am with you alway, even unto the end of the world," Matthew 28:19-20.

"And He said unto them, Go ye into all the world, and preach the gospel to every creature," Mark 16:15.

"Then said Jesus to them again, Peace be unto you: as My Father hath sent me, even so send I you," John 20:21.

"And Saul was consenting unto his death. And at that time there was a great persecution against the church which was at Jerusalem; and they were all scattered abroad throughout the regions of Judaea and Samaria, except the apostles," Acts 8:1.

Each member went out carrying the gospel.

The last words of Jesus were missionary. Standing on the mount of Olives, near to Bethany, just before He ascended to heaven, He said:

> "But ye shall receive power, after that the Holy Ghost is come upon you: and ye shall be witnesses unto me both in Jerusalem, and in all Judaea, and in Samaria, and unto the uttermost part of the earth," Acts 1:8.

Paul was a great foreign missionary, sent especially to the Gentiles. Peter was also. He was sent to the Jews. Barnabas, Timothy, Luke—in fact, all whom Jesus had taught were missionary in spirit. By command and example, by parable and proverb, the Bible teaches missions.

To the Corinthians, Paul said:

> "For we stretch not ourselves beyond our measure, as though we reached not unto you: for we are come as far as to you also in preaching the Gospel of Christ:
> Not boasting of things without our measure, that is, of other men's labors; but having hope, when your faith is increased, that we may be enlarged by you according to our rule abundantly, to preach the gospel in the regions beyond you, and not to boast in another man's line of things made ready to our hand," II Corinthians 10:14-16.

Paul wanted to go beyond Corinth and preach in regions where the gospel was not known. He depended on them to help support him while he did so; after their faith was increased he had hope they would do this. He did not want to build on someone's foundation. He was a "brush-breaking" missionary. Paul, then, encouraged missions support by the Corinth church.

Paul preached wherever men were found, in Jewish synagogues, markets, streets, on shipboards and in prisons. Not being able always to be physically present, he wrote letters. He was every inch a missionary.

One has only to read of the various Christian groups, among whom Baptists in every century were found, to know that they were missionary. The Anabaptists, Waldenses, Lollards, Paulicians, and people by many other names, were all missionary. Their faith, mixed with their blood, led many of their persecutors to Christ. We have examples of the very executioners of Baptists being converted as they piled wood around them to burn them alive. The Welsh Baptists in the first century were missionary. Paul's converts in Rome, people led to Christ through his prison bars, were missionary in spirit and carried the light of truth back to England.

We have an account of an association in Wales in 1663, as follows:

"At this time (1663) the Baptists met at Llantrisaint. In the association held at Abergavmy, this church proposed to revive the **old plan** of supporting ministers in weak and destitute churches; which was for the strongest to help the weakest. Willian Thomas was appointed **home missionary** for six months, and received from Swansea five pounds; Llastrisaint, two pounds, ten shillings; Carmarthen, two pounds, ten shillings."—Davis History Welsh Baptists, page 31.

The Rise of "Hardshell" Baptists

This group was led by one Daniel Parker. We have the following from the Minutes of the Kentucky General Association, Oct. 20, 1837, page 11.

"The anti-missionary spirit owes its origin to the notorious Daniel Parker. He was the first person called Baptist that lent a hand to the infidel and papist in opposing the proclamation of the gospel to every creature." —Quoted by Ben M. Bogard, Baptist Waybook.

Then, there is the testimony of Parker himself:

"It makes me shudder when I think I am the first one (that I have any knowledge of) among the thousands of zealous religionists of America, that have ventured to draw the sword against this error, and to shoot at it and spare no arrows."—Quoted by Bogard from Daniel Parker's address, page 3.

It is therefore very clear that before Parker's time all Baptists were missionary Baptists. The people called "Hardshells," and called by themselves "Old School," were unknown before this time.

What happens to a people who are not missionary? This writer can remember during his early ministry seeing many hardshell churches. The membership of these churches were good people, as good as any. As a rule they were honest, good citizens, even exemplary, but they have become fewer and fewer. The anti-mission spirit is responsible.

A warning note: A mere profession of a missionary spirit will not save us today from the fate of the "Hardshell" Baptists; there must be action, if we are to make progress. Parker said it "made him shudder" to think of the "error" of missions. Surely, we have no Baptists among us with that notion. However, the lack of interest many seem to have in missions makes one wonder if we are as zealous as we should be.

Missions in Modern Times

In the early part of the eighteen hundreds there were several missionary societies formed, both Protestant and Baptist, in America, as well as England. It is beyond our purpose to enumerate them. To those wishing to pursue the subject further they can read, A History of American Baptist Missions, by Mirriam.

In 1792, a small group of Baptist ministers met in a private house in Kettering, England, and organized the Baptist Missionary Society. You will note that this was a group of ministers, and not churches. The voluntary offering was thirteen pounds, two shillings and six pence.

The first missionaries of this society were William Carey and John Thomas, M.D., who sailed for India, June 13, 1793. This first missionary couple was a minister and a doctor. In 1795, there was formed the London Missionary Society, composed by Independent and non-conformists of England. Soon after, there were others organized in England, Baptists, Protestant, and the church of England.

In 1810, the American Board of Commissioners for Foreign Missions had been formed in Boston, led by students in the Andover Theological Seminary. This was the first Independent American movement in foreign missions. Nine missionaries had sailed for India in February, 1812. Adoniram Judson and wife, Ann Hasseltine, and Samuel Newell and Harriett, his wife, sailed from Salem, Massachusetts, on the 19, while on the 24, Gordon Hall and Samuel Nott, with their wives, and Luther Rice, sailed from Philadelphia.

On the long journey, Judson on the "Caravan," and Rice on the "Harmony," reflected much as they read their Bibles. It is said that Judson, during his study at Andover Theological Seminary, in a discussion concerning baptism, the professor had appointed him to present the views of the Baptists. Judson was then a pedobaptist. He convinced himself of Baptist sentiments during the study, though for a time he again regained his pedobaptist views. But they were short lived.

Soon after Judson arrived in Calcutta he fully became a Baptist. Though Mrs. Judson was at first disturbed about her husband's views, being an independent student, she also soon became a Baptist. They both were baptized in Calcutta by William Ward, September 6, 1812.

The life story of the Judsons will stir anyone's heart to missions if he will only read it.

"OLD SCHOOL," "PRIMITIVE" OR ANTI-MISSION BAPTISTS

David Benedict says—

"These people generally claim the first two of these appellations as descriptive of their peculiar views, in opposition to those of the friends of benevolent efforts; the last is applied to them by their opponents. Most of them disown the name; while D. Parker and a few others freely admit it as the proper cognomen of their party.

"It is one thing to complain of the modus operandi in the collection of funds and the management of missionary affairs at home and abroad, and another to take a dead stand against what is properly denominated the effort system; which, as I understand the matter, is done by the great mass of our denomination who are implicated in these remarks.

"It will be seen, by those who follow my narrations through the States where all these communities exist, that I make no distinction between them and what are called the effort Baptists in my historical details. If I have been less full in my descriptions of their affairs, it is on account of the backwardness of the people, and because their history could not be obtained.

"Again: I have in no case made any reference to the character of Associations, as to the subject of missions, unless some facts in their history required it; and my aim, through all my narratives, has been to say as little as possible relative to the disputes in different sections of the country on this subject. My reasons for this course are as follows:

"1. It is a family difficulty, about which cool observers at a distance feel very different from those who have been immediately identified with it; and I am fully satisfied, that my readers generally will derive no pleasure nor profit from any lengthy details respecting it.

2. It has been my settled opinion, for a long time past, that the cause of missions has had but little to do in this business, so very slender is its hold on the minds of the great mass of our community in most parts of the country, however they are distinguished. This is shown by their doings for benevolent objects. The fact is, that personal altercations, rivalships, and jealousies, and local contests for influence and control, have done much to set brethren at variance with each other. The mission question is the ostensible, rather than the real cause of the trouble, in many places. New men and new measures have run faster than the old travelers were accustomed to go, and they have been disturbed at being left behind. A long catalogue of things of this kind might be mentioned. (This should be well noted, W. J. B.)

"But doctrinal matters have been at the bottom of all the troubles, and predestination has been the bone of contention. The anti-mission party, as near as I can learn, without any exception, are high or hyper-Calvinists, and are so tenacious of the old theory of particular atonement, and have so far run the system up to seed, as to persuade themselves that the efforts of modern times are wholly needless, and Arminianism is the bugbear which they profess to fear.

"3. The anti-mission movement must, of necessity, be a short-lived one. It has within itself the elements of its dissolution; and before my stereotyped pages could reach the different parts of the country, to say nothing of remoter regions, it will be among the things that are past and forgotten. Whole churches and associational confederacies are either sinking into oblivion or coming over to the side of evangelical efforts.

"4. I am mortified that any Baptists should assume an opposing attitude as to missionary operations and the kindred objects of benevolence; so much so, that the fact would not have been named in my work, had I not been compelled to do it, as a matter of historical veracity.

"5. Old School and Primitive Baptists are appellations so entirely out of place, that I cannot, even as a matter of courtesy, use them without adding, so called, or some such expression. I have seen so much of the missionary spirit among the old Anabaptists, Waldenses and other ancient sects; so vigorous and perpetual were the efforts of those Christians, whom we claim as Baptists, in the early, middle and later ages, to spread the gospel in all parts of the world, among all nations and languages where they could gain access, that it is plain that those who merely preach up predestination, and do nothing, have no claim to be called by their name."—A GENERAL HISTORY OF THE BAPTIST DENOMINATION IN AMERICA by David Benedict.

WALDENSES WERE MISSIONARY

More from Benedict—

"Nothing was more remarkable about the early Waldenses than their missionary spirit; and the same thing is true of all the people of that age and character. It was by sending out missionaries two by two on foot to visit their brethren dispersed in France, the north of Spain, Flanders, Croatia, Dalmatia and Italy, that they kept alive the little piety which existed in the world at that day. These missionaries knew where to find their brethren; they went to their houses, held little meetings, administered the ordinances, ordained deacons, and sustained the faith and hopes of the persecuted and tempted ones. It is said that these missionaries would go at periods from Cologne to Florence, and stay every night at the houses of their brethren. It is on account of the great number of missionaries which these little and poor churches in the valleys sustained, that we read of there being sometimes one hundred and forty or fifty ministers at the meetings of their synods. But few of these were needed at home; the most were engaged in the foreign work.

"It is also remarkable that almost all the men whom God raised up from time to time in France and other countries, for more than six hundred years before the Reformation, seem to have had more or less to do with the Waldenses—such as Peter Waldo, Peter Bruis, Henry of Toulouse, and Lollard, who labored with so much zeal to diffuse the truth in England, and who was burned at Cologne.

"But not only did the preachers go out from the valleys to proclaim the glorious gospel, but humble and pious pedlers, itinerating merchants, of whom there were many in the middle ages, scattered the truth by carrying some leaves of the Word of Life, or some MSs. tracts beneath their merchandize, which they engaged those whom they found favorably disposed to receive and read," Dr. Baird's Italy.—A General History of the Baptist Denomination in America by David Benedict.

HISTORIAN BENEDICT AND MISSIONS

"The farther down I go into the regions of aniquity, the more fully is the missionary character of all whom we denominate our sentimental brethren developed. Propagandism was their motto and their watch-word. They seldom went alone, but two and two was the order of their going out; and such was the ardor of their zeal in their hazardous vocations, that no ordinary obstacles could alarm their fears or impede their progress. As nothing of this kind appears among the opponents of the missionary enterprise, I cannot, with my views of duty as an honest historian, apply to them the terms in question, as I fully believe they misapprehend their own character in this matter. And, furthermore, as I do not wish for any controversy with them on this subject, I prefer to say but little about it.

"I have ascertained, for a certainty, that in most of the associational communities which are ranked on the anti-mission side, there are members not a few who are entirely dissatisfied with the restrictions which are imposed upon them by a few of their zealous leaders. Their sympathies are with their effort brethren; they would be glad to have matters otherwise in the churches in which they are located, and from which they are not prepared to separate, and are sorry that so much is said and written about a difficulty which time only can heal.

"So illiberal, anti-republican and anti-baptist; so frightfully oppressive; so tyrannical and over-bearing, are the principles and measures of many of the anti-mission party, relative to all the objects of benevolence, as exhibited in their public documents; and finally, such a stretch of power have they assumed over the members of churches where they have majorities, that, for the honor of the Baptist name, I could wish to place what little I say on this part of their discipline in some obscure corner, where but few of my readers would see it. I would prefer to wrap the whole story in obscurity, rather than emblazon it to the world."
—A General History of the Baptist Denomination in America by David Benedict.

AN EDITORIAL BY HALL

On the point of the "Hardshells" it is interesting to read an editorial by Dr. J. N. Hall in the American Baptist Flag, issue of January 16, 1902. It follows:

"They have a peculiar state of affairs among the Hardshells. One branch of them asserts that everything that takes place is foreordained of God, and could not be otherwise. But they complain bitterly because many are separating from them on account of this doctrine, when, if their doctrine be true, the separation is the Lord's will —and so is their complaining. This would make the Lord foreordain a separation between His own people, and foreordaining a whining complaint from them because He was doing things His own way, when they pretend to want them done that way. We are glad that such stuff is not chargeable to the Lord."

From Burkitt's History, page 92, we read:

"This association agreed to consider the business of itinerant preaching. A committee was appointed for that purpose, and after deliberation thereon reported as follows:

" 'That not only ordained preachers, but young gifts also be advised and called upon by the churches to which they belong, to engage in the work, not only amongst the churches, but in other places where it may appear necessary.' "

"Mr. Tillman, also, at this time was solemnly commended to the grace of God in proceeding to Cheshire on a Missionary or Evangelistic tour." (See History Hill Cliff Church, by James Kenworthy, pastor, p. 46.)

CHAPTER XIV

BAPTIST DISTINCTIVES

By whatever name present day orthodox Baptists were called in different ages since the Saviour called out His church there are some things they have ever contended for. And none of these have been any hurt to anyone else.

Baptists believe in something more than tolerance for the religious views and practices of others; they believe in liberty and freedom absolute. They ask only that they be allowed to pursue their own convictions as well. Baptists have never been the persecutors but have often and in many countries, even America, been the persecuted. It is ironical that the persecuted who left Europe in search of freedom of worship became the persecutors of others as soon as they landed on the shores of America. History is replete with cases of the persecution of Baptists in New England and elsewhere in the early days.

Baptists, by whatever name called through the years, have advocated the following principles:

1. A regenerate church membership.
2. Entire separation of church and state. For this they have suffered greatly.
3. The Bible alone as our only rule of faith and practice.
4. The immersion of believers only as scriptural baptism.
5. The Lord's Supper, an ordinance committed only to the care of the church, and to be administered only to baptized believers.

6. That civil and religious freedom is the right of man.

7. That salvation is solely without ordinance, rite or ritual, works, moral or otherwise; but by grace through faith, with no former, attending, or future sacraments necessary.

8. Jesus only as Head.

THE SCRIPTURES OUR ONLY RULE OF FAITH AND PRACTICE

Regardless of the antiquity of a doctrine, the age itself does not validate it. All notions are to be tried by the Bible and, no matter who had them, or when. If they do not agree with the Sacred Book, they should be discarded for what they are, the doctrines of men. If, because of finding something taught and believed during the first centuries, it be accepted, simply because of this antiquity, then baptismal regeneration, episcopacy of government, and many others heresies would be substantiated. For, in reading history, we can find all these in very early ages, but not so early as the Apostolic Age.

BAPTISTS AS SEEN BY OTHERS

Appleton's Encyclopedia, edited by George Ripley and Charles A. Dana, defines "Baptists" as follows:

"The Baptists, properly defined, are those who hold that baptism of Christian believers is of universal obligation, and practice accordingly. And they hold this, because they acknowledge no master but Christ; no rule of faith but His Word; no baptism but that which is preached and hallowed by personal piety; no church but that which is the body of Christ, pervaded, governed, and animated by His Spirit. Whatever diversities of opinion and usage are found among them, these are their common and characteristic principles; by these they are known and distinguished in every country, and in every age . . .

"On the subject of church communion, the Baptists generally agree with other denominations, that it is not proper before baptism. As they find no exception to this rule in the New Testament they do not feel authorized to invite those who are not, in their view, duly baptized to unite with them at the Lord's table, however highly they may esteem them. They profess in this limitation of church communion, that they do not judge the conscience of others, but seek to preserve their own. Open communion, as advocated by Robert Hall, in England, the Baptists of the United States regard as an anomaly. Yet, while holding these views, they claim to feel a cordial sympathy with other evangelical denominations, and rejoice to cooperate with them as far as possible, in the work of Christ . . .

"Their ministers preach the Gospel freely, with a warm application to the conscience, and to the heart. No denomination is more characterized by experimental piety. The evidence of its possession is always required of candidates for baptism . . . The Baptists, as will be evident from the above exposition of their principles, claim their origin from the ministry of Christ and His apostles . . .

"They further claim that all the true Christian churches of the first two centuries after Christ were founded and built upon the principles they profess; in proof of which they appeal to the high critical authorities in church history, Mosheim, Neander, Hagenbach, Jacobi, and Bunsen. They further claim to be able to trace their history in a succession of pure churches (cathara) essentially Baptist though under various names, from the third century down to the reformation. These churches, from the fifth century onward, were the subjects of systematic persecutions from the state churches, both in the East and in the West . . ."

In the opinion of Sir Isaac Newton, as reported by Whiston, "The Baptists are the only body of Christians that has not symbolized with the church of Rome."

AN ENEMY COMMENDS THEM

The following sentiments of one of their bitterest opposers embody all that need to be said under this head:

"Reinerius, an apostate and persecutor of the Waldenses, in the thirteenth century, writes, 'that amongst all sects none is more pernicious than that of the Poor of Lyons, for three reasons: 1st, Because it is the most

ancient; some aver their existence from the days of Sylvester—others from the very times of the apostles. 2nd, Because it is so universal; for there is scarcely a country into which this sect has not crept. 3rd, Because all others render themselves detestable by their blasphemies, but this has a great appearance of godliness; they living a righteous life before men, believing right concerning God, confessing all the articles of the creed, only hating the pope of Rome.' "
—History, Baptist Denomination by David Benedict.

ROBERT HALL ABOUT THE BAPTISTS

"A lamented writer (Robert Hall), who directed some of his greatest efforts of his massive intellect against Scriptural terms of Communion, was asked for a New Testament precedent for the course he advocated. 'You should not ask for one, Sir. You should not ask for one,' was his reply; 'they were all Baptists in those days, Sir; but a new case has arisen now.' "
—Footnote, page 14 of Baptist Pamphlets.

ALEXANDER CAMPBELL AND BAPTIST PERPETUITY

Alexander Campbell, the father of Campbellism and advocate of the baptismal heresy, was first a Baptist. In a debate with a Mr. Walker in 1820, he said:

"The members, then, of the first Christian church ever planted on earth, gladly received the Word BEFORE they were baptized, and upon the SAME day of their baptism were added to the church; and thence forward CONTINUED in the above practices. It is then incontrovertibly evident, that the FIRST Christian church planted on earth was, in respect of baptism, as now distinguished, a BAPTIST CHURCH; or a church composed of baptized believers. It is true, it is not called by Luke a Baptist church, for all the churches were imitators of this first church, and to have called it a Baptist church would have implied that there was a Pedo-baptist church too, which was a thing unknown in the apostolic age, as all ancient historians declare. . . . Thus I have shown, that even in England, the

Baptists have continued from the apostolic times to the present day, as also that there have been in every century advocates for Baptist principles."

FROM MOSHEIM, A LUTHERAN HISTORIAN

Mosheim, Vol. I, page 92, says: "The churches in those ancient times, were entirely independent; none of them subject to any foreign jurisdiction, but each governed by its own rules and its own laws. For though the churches founded by the apostles had this deference shown them, that they were consulted in difficult and doubtful cases; yet they had no judicial authority, no sort of supremacy over the others, nor the least right to enact laws for them. Nothing on the contrary, is more evident than the perfect equality that reigned among the primitive churches."

TESTIMONY OF GIBBONS

Gibbons' Roman Empire, Vol. I, page 555: "Such was the mild and equal constitution by which the Christians were governed for more than a hundred years after the death of the apostles. Every society formed within itself an independent republic; and although the most distant of these little states maintained a mutual, as well as friendly intercourse of letters and deputations, the Christian world was not yet conducted by any supreme authority or legislative assembly."

PHILLIP SCHAFF'S OPINION

"The excesses of a misguided faction have been charged upon the whole body. They were made responsible for the peasant's war and the Munster tragedy, although the great majority of them were quiet, orderly and peaceful citizens, and would rather suffer persecution than to do an act of violence."—Schaff in Quarterly Review, Vol. 12, No. 43.

A CATHOLIC CARDINAL SAYS—

Cardinal Hosious said:

"If the truth of religion were to be judged of by the readiness and cheerfulness which a man or any sect shows

in suffering, then the opinion and persuasion of no sect can be truer than that of the Ana-Baptists, since there has been none for these twelve hundred years past that have been more generally punished or that have more cheerfully and steadfastly undergone and even offered themselves to the most cruel kind of punishment than these people."
—Baptist Way Book, Ben M. Bogard.

BOOK TWO

BAPTISTS AND THEIR INFLUENCE UPON EARLY AMERICAN HISTORY

CHAPTER I

SOURCE OF AMERICAN BAPTISTS AND EARLY COLONIAL ACTIVITIES

American Baptists From Several Sources

"We trace our connection with the English Baptists.

Dr. John Clarke organized the first Baptist Church at Newport, Rhode Island in 1638. In the same year Hanserd Nollys gathered a Baptist church at Dover. In 1644, Gregory Dexter united with the Baptist church at Providence, Rhode Island, being a minister of the Baptist faith in England before his arrival. John Emblem, from England, became pastor in Boston in 1684. John Burrows came from the West of England as a Baptist preacher in 1711, and labored in Pennsylvania. Jasoer Mentz came from England in 1727 and settled in Virginia where he labored about 30 years in the ministry. The list of ministers who came to America could be extended if necessary.

The American Baptists are also descended from the Welsh Baptists. John Miles, with several Baptists, came from Swansea, Wales, in 1663, and organized a church in Massachusetts, from which many of the present churches are descended. Thomas Griffith from South Wales, emigrated with the church of which he was pastor, in the year 1701. They settled at first near Penepeck, Pennsylvania, and remained two years, and then at Welsh Tract, Pennsylvania, now Delaware. From this solid church has come a long line of American Baptist churches.

Morgan Edwards came from Wales to this country in 1761; Samuel Jones in 1686; Hugh Davis in 1710; Nathaniel Jenkens, in 1701; Griffith Able Morgan in 1711.

All these were Baptists before they left Wales, and they have a large succession in America. From these two lines—the English Baptists and the Welsh Baptists— came the Baptists of America.

The English Baptists did not originate with John Symth, for he was first an English churchman, and afterwards united with the Brownites, and died in Holland, and never had any connection with an English Baptist church. He did not practice immersion for baptism, but sprinkling. The English Baptists originated from the Netherlands. History shows that there were Baptists in the Netherlands long before Luther was born and Flanders was full of them in the year 1223. The Netherlanders were descended from the ancient Waldenses; and the Waldenses were direct descendants from the apostolic age. And through the Welsh Baptists, the American Baptists have an equally if not a more direct descent from the days of Christ."—**The Sumpter Discussion,** Dr. J. J. Poeter, page 179.

Baptists in the South and Liberty

Cook has this to say—

The Baptists in New England, and in other states north, fought long and well to secure liberty, civil and religious; but in Virginia, one of the grandest conflicts the world ever beheld, was begun, carried on and successfully ended, mainly through the heroic efforts of the Baptists. The Old Dominion was the battle field on which was waged the war for the civil and religious liberties of this country and of the world—not with English soldiers, but with misguided and intolerant churchmen.

The growth of the Virginia Baptists was so rapid and great that their strength encouraged them "to entertain serious hopes, not only of obtaining liberty of conscience, but of actually overturning the church establishment," from whence all their oppressions had arisen.

In May, 1774, several Baptist ministers in prison, among them David Tinsley, wrote letters to the General

Association then in session. The Association set apart two days for public fast and prayer, for their "poor blind persecutors," and for the release of their brethren.

In 1775, the whole denomination in Virginia, united in general association, to strive together for the overthrow of the state church, they determined to petition the political convention, and to circulate petitions all over the state for signatures, asking for the abolition of the established church, and equality before the law of all denominations in their rights and privileges. They also advised resistance to, and war for, independence from Great Britain.

"Baptists were, to a man, favorable to any revolution by which they could obtain freedom of religion." At one time they would have been satisfied with liberty of conscience, and cheerfully have paid their tithes for the support of the state church. But now, nothing less than the overthrow of all ecclesiastical distinctions would satisfy them. After great efforts they had obtained licenses to preach in certain places, but they wanted to be unmolested to preach the gospel to every creature.

Their meekness in suffering persecutions, and their faithfulness to Christ and truth, created the sentiment that helped them in the struggle for freedom. Their petition was presented to the Virginia political convention in May, 1776. "The address of the Baptists, was received and produced, specially that part relating to civil freedom, a profound impression. This Convention framed the famous bill of rights, the 16th article of which secures religious freedom. The same body instructed the Virginia delegates in Congress to vote for a declaration of independence.

"It has generally been held, that the action of the Virginia Convention was not only among the earliest movements in that direction, but exercised a potential influence in the action of Congress. But let it be remembered, to the honor of the Virginia Baptists of that day, that their action was a year prior to that of the Convention, and undoubtedly, exercised a potential influence in moving the Convention, and through the Convention the Congress.

Thus did the Virginia Baptists effect a mighty achievement for both civil and religious freedom."

The first republican legislature of Virginia met in October, 1776, and an act was passed exempting the different societies of dissenters from contributing to the support of the established church and its ministers, and removing the restraints of worship. The salaries of the Episcopal clergy were only suspended, however, and the question of the general assessment for the support of religion, was only postponed. One step forward was gained, at least, and the Baptists continued to petition.

In 1779, the salaries of the clergy of the establishment were taken away; the general assessment bill was defeated and the famous act for establishing religious freedom prepared by Thomas Jefferson was presented. Efforts were made in 1784, to restore in a measure the disestablished church. The general assessment bill permitting the taxation of the people for the support of religion, the tax collected to be distributed among the different denominations, was revived and postponed.

All other denominations as a whole, favored, advocated and petitioned for it, except the Baptists. They were the only ones who plainly remonstrated, says Semple. They stood alone in opposition to it. The General Committee remonstrated. To defeat the bill they resorted to petitions. Papers protesting against the bill were circulated everywhere by them, for signatures for presentation to the assembly. "When the assembly met, the table of the House of Delegates almost sunk under the weight of the accumulated copies of the memorial sent forward from the different counties, each with its long and dense column of subscribers. The fate of the assessment was sealed." Besides, Jefferson's act for the establishment of religious freedom, was at once passed.

The memorial and remonstrance against the assessment bill was drawn up by James Madison, afterwards president of the United States, at the instance, probably of the Baptists, whose friend he was, and presented to the general assembly. Semple says:—"For elegance of style, strength of reasoning, purity of principle, it has perhaps, seldom been equalled." "The defeat of the general assessment bill was due considerably," says the same author, "to the active opposition of the Baptists."

The Establishment after a long, and desperate struggle, was finally overthrown and all denominations and ministers stood equal before the law. Baptist ministers could now perform the ceremony of marriage, and Baptist people were no longer compelled to support Episcopal clergymen.

Dr. Hawks, the Episcopal church historian of Virginia says:—"The establishment was finally put down. The Baptists were the principal promoters in this work, and in truth, aided more than any other denomination, in its accomplishment."

Dr. Wm. Cathcart points out the fact, that the Baptists in Virginia took an important part in securing the adoption of the Federal Constitution by their own state. They have the honor through their own influence, more than any others, of having saved it to the state and country at large. Through the exertion and self sacrifice of a Baptist, John Leland, Virginia was led in her Convention to ratify the Federal Constitution.

During the absence of James Madison from Virginia on public business, John Leland was chosen a candidate for the place that Madison would have filled, if he had been at home, in the Convention that met in 1788 to ratify or reject the Federal Constitution. Madison, upon his return, spent half a day with Leland which resulted in the withdrawal of the latter in favor of the former. Leland threw all his influence which was great, in favor of Madison, who was sent to the Convention.

Patrick Henry was opposed to the New Constitution, because he thought it "squinted towards monarchy." He carried the people with him and could have defeated it in the Convention, but for the presence and powerful influence of Madison. The Honorable J. S. Barbour, of Virginia declares: "That the credit of adopting the Constitution of the United States, properly belongs to a Baptist clergyman, formerly of Virginia, named Leland: 'If, said he, 'Madison had not been in the Virginia Convention, the Constitution would not have been ratified, and as the approval of nine States was necessary to give effect to this instrument, and as Virginia was the ninth State, if it had been rejected by her, the Constitution would have failed, (the remaining States followed her example,) and it was through Elder Leland's influence that Mr. Madison was elected to that Convention. It is unquestionable that Mr. Madison was elected through the efforts and resignation of John Leland and it is all but certain, that that act gave our country its famous Constitution.'"

The sufferings of the Baptists and their struggles for liberty, helped to unify them. Henceforth, from 1787, we hear no more about "Separate" or "Regular" Baptists, simply the Baptists of Virginia.

The work of the Baptists in Virginia, was not, however, done. They had still another battle to fight in Congress for the overthrow of ecclesiastical establishments, and for securing constitutional liberty throughout the land. The danger was not past. Dr. Cathcart quotes Thomas Jefferson, who says: "There was a hope confidently cherished about A. D., 1780, that there might be a State Church throughout the United States, and this expectation was specially cherished by Episcopalians and Congregationalists."

John Adams believed in leaving the matter to the states, each state having its own establishment. This design, it was the work of Baptists to frustrate. They did not want the Constitution of the United States, nor of any state, to be made a religious creed, but they were determined to have religious liberty for themselves and all the world.

In 1787 the Federal Constitution was ratified by the requisite number of states, and became the law of the land. The next year the question arose among the Baptists of Virginia, whether it made sufficient provisions for religious liberty. It prohibited any religious test for a qualification for office, but it was their unanimous opinion that religious liberty was not sufficiently provided for.

Acting upon the advice of Mr. Madison, an address from the Baptists of the whole state was presented by them to President Washington, in August, 1789. It was written by John Leland, and set forth, that the religious rights of the Baptists were not secured by the Federal Constitution.

Washington replied, that he never would have signed that instrument, had he supposed it endangered the liberties of any religious society, and that he would at once, move for its amendment, since by it, religious freedom was rendered insecure.

Washington in his address at this time, pays this tribute to the patriotism of the Baptists: "While I recollect with satisfaction, that the religious society of which you are members, have been, throughout America, uniformly and almost unanimously, the fast friends of civil liberty, and the persevering promoters of our glorious Revolution, I cannot hesitate to believe that they will be the faithful supporters of a free, yet efficient general government."

As the result of this address, the next month, James Madison proposed in the House of Representatives, the first amendment to the Constitution of the United States. It met with violent opposition, at first, but was finally passed. It was also approved by two-thirds of the states, and became the law of the country.

"But suppose," says the distinguished author above quoted, "it had not been adopted; Massachusetts might have had a State Church today, and her citizens rotting in prison, because they could not conscientiously pay a church tax, and any State might have established the Episcopal Church, and then committed Baptists or other ministers to prison as they did in Virginia, down to the Revolution.

"And Congress might have decreed that the Catholic Church was the religious fold of the nation, and might have levied taxes to support her clergy, and made laws to give secular power to her cardinals, archbishops, bishops, and priests over her schools, religious opinions, and personal freedom. Without it, sacardotal tryanny might have destroyed all our liberties.

"The grandest feature of our Constitution is the first clause of the first amendment. The Baptists have always claimed that the credit of this amendment belongs, chiefly, to them. The Baptists asked it through Washington; the request commended itself to his judgment, and to the generous soul of Madison, and to the Baptists, beyond a doubt, belong the glory of engrafting its best article, on the noblest Constitution ever framed for the government of mankind."

Here is the amendment as it reads in **Story, on the Constitution**: "Congress shall make no law respecting an establishment of religion, or prohibiting the free exercise thereof; or abridging the freedom of speech, or of the press; or the right of the people peacefully to assemble, and to petition to the government for a redress of grievances."

This ought to have ended the struggle, but it was not till 1798, that all dissenters were practically put upon "perfect equality" with Episcopalians.

James Madison was one of the most enlightened statesmen of his day, and that he fully understood what the Baptists were contending for, the following from an unpublished address of Dr. J. C. Long, shows full well:

"James Madison was not a member of a Baptist church himself, though his brother, General Madison, was; but he took great interest in the Baptists, on account of their sufferings. When George Mason, in the Virginia political convention, of 1776, wrote, in the celebrated Bill of Rights, that all men should enjoy the fullest toleration in the exercise of religion, Madison said; 'No, write instead, all men are entitled to the free exercise of their religion, according to the dictates of their consciences.' And so it was written. What prompted one of the youngest members of that assembly to insist upon the change of a word? Where did he get his views? He did not find them in his books. His friends, the Baptists, taught them. Was it from them that he learned the true principles of religious freedom?"

The question has sometimes been asked; "Would the

Baptists become a State church, if the opportunity offered?" We answer; No, judging by their principles and their past actions. They have ever refused for themselves, what they have declared a wrong for others to receive. For instance, in Virginia in 1792, "the Baptists had members of great weight in civil society; their congregations had become more numerous than any other Christian sect." They doubtless controlled the government of Virginia, and yet they secured equal liberty there for all.

In Wales, the Baptist churches and ministers declined state support by taxation of the people, such as others received, which was offered them, though they were as poor as any. For one hundred and fifty years, the Baptists had the sole power and rule in Rhode Island, and the evil example of others around them, but, unmoved in their principles, they used their power for the good of all alike.

The utter failure of Baptist principles has been again and again foretold, but Baptists have stood the test of centuries, and they have, more than any others, given civil and religious freedom to the world. With the origin and perpetuity of American liberty they have had much to do. How appropriate, then, that a Baptist, S. F. Smith, D. D., should give to our country its national hymn:— "My country, 'tis of thee," etc. — Copied from COOK'S STORY OF THE BAPTISTS, Pages 242-251.

Baptists in the North, and Independence
(Cook's Story of the Baptists)

The Baptists have ever been ardent lovers of liberty, civil and religious. This characteristic has ever brought upon them persecution from tyrants and bigots. The Baptists of America were true to their principles, and the beginning of the conflict between England and her colonies, for independence, found the Baptists on the side of their oppressed countrymen, and there they stood until America was free. They are said to have been among ardent advocates of, and leaders in, the American Revolution. This is true of the Baptists, North as well as South, where they sowed the seed of freedom that was to produce such wonderful results in all the land.

Rev. Isaac Backus, says of their attitude during the Revolution: "No denomination in America have acted with more prudence and vigor than the Baptists. In the fall of 1778, our Legislature (Massachusetts) passed an act to debar inimical persons (Royalists) from returning into this State, wherein three hundred and eleven men were named as such; and our enemies are welcome to point out one Baptist among them if they can."

It was principle that arrayed the Baptists on the side of the colonists, for England had, more than once, shielded them from their persecuting neighbors. This is said in general of Massachusetts, but there are not wanting, noble instances of patriotic devotion throughout the northern states.

"The leaders, as well as the mass of Baptists, were engaged in the war on the side of the colonists. Their ministers went into the army, some as chaplains, others as officers, and others still as privates, and inspired greatly by their patriotism their fellow soldiers.

Among these may be mentioned Rev. Charles Thompson and Rev. Hezekiah Smith, D. D., of Massachusetts; Rev. Dr. Rogers of Philadelphia and Rev. David Jones of New Jersey. The descendants of the latter are now distinguished Baptists of Philadelphia. (The Hon. H. G. Jones, D. C. L., is a grandson.) He was a bold and invaluable man, and was as often in the front of the battle as among the wounded in the hospital.

Others entered the army west and south. Rev. John Gano, first pastor of the First Baptist Church, New York City, was granted leave of absence to enter the army as a chaplain. Washington says: "Baptist chaplains were among the most prominent and useful in the army," and Howe, "The Baptists were among the most strenuous supporters of liberty."

Dr. Cathcart gives interesting sketches of two well known Baptist laymen of Revolutionary times, Colonel Joab Houghton and John Brown, which we reproduce. "Colonel

Houghton was one of the first to advocate the calling of the New Jersey Provincial Congress that overthrew English rule there. One Sunday morning while he was worshipping in the Baptist meeting-house at Hopewell, New Jersey, of which he was a member, a messenger, all breathless, came in and whispered something in his ear."

The information was respecting the battles of Concord and Lexington. Dr. S. H. Cone, grandson of Colonel Houghton, thus describes the scene:

"Stilling the breathless messenger, he sat quietly through the services, and when they were ended, he passed out, and mounting the great stone block in front of the meeting-house, he beckoned to the people to stop, men and women paused to hear, curious to know what so unusual a sequel to the service of the day could mean.

"At the first words, a silence, still as death, fell over all. The Sabbath quiet of the hour and of the place, was deepened into a terrible solemnity. He told them all, the story of the cowardly murder at Lexington by the royal troups; the heroic vengeance following hard upon it; the retreat of Percy; the gathering of the children of the Pilgrims around the beleaguered hills of Boston; then pausing and looking over the silent throng he said slowly, 'Men of New Jersey, the red-coats are murdering our brethren of New England! Who follows me to Boston?' and every man of that audience stepped out into line and answered: 'I!' There was not a coward or a traitor in old Hopewell Baptist meeting-house that day.

Says Dr. Cathcart, commenting upon this scene: "The annals of the American Revolution cannot furnish in its long list of fearless deeds and glorious sacrifices, a grander spectacle than this Sunday scene in front of the Baptist church of Hopewell. Joab Houghton's integrity, honesty of purpose, and military capacity, must have been of an unusual order to have secured for his appeal, such a noble response. And the men who gave it must have been nurtured in the lap of liberty in childhood, and taught enthusiastic love for her principles in all subsequent years.

But this was the spirit of American Baptists in the Revolution."

The account of John Brown is equally interesting. He was of Providence, Rhode Island, and Brown University was named after his father, Nicholas. He was also appointed a committee of one to build the present church edifice of the First Baptist Church which he did at a cost of $25,000 in 1774. It excited the admiration and surprise of the English Baptists, and was the best the Baptists had in America. It was he who struck the first blow in the war of Independence.

It was as early as June, 1772. A British war vessel, the "Gaspee," ran ashore below Pawtuxet. Mr. Brown, who had a large fleet of merchant vessels, when he heard of it, ordered eight large boats to be placed in charge of Captain Abraham Whipple, who, with 64 armed men rowed for the "Gaspee." When they drew near the vessel, shots were exchanged and Lieut. Buddington of the "Gaspee" was wounded. "This was the first British blood spilt in the war for Independence." The crew of the "Gaspee" fled, and Captain Whipple blew her up.

"While the defence of the civil rights of America appeared a matter of great importance, our religious liberties were by no means to be neglected; and the contest concerning each, kept a pretty even pace through the war." In this double contest, no man was more prominent than Isaac Backus himself, who was a sufferer, as well as his noble mother, from oppressive laws. The town of Ashfield, Massachusetts was settled by Baptists. In 1770, a few Congregationalists built a meeting-house, called a minister, and taxed the Baptists for his support. The greatest part of his salary of $1,000 came from Baptists.

Because they refused to pay this burdensome tax, 398 acres of their land were seized, together with their homes, cattle, crops, and graveyards—constituting everything of many families, and sold to pay the tax. Thus they were despoiled and made homeless, and told to leave if they did not like it. The property was sold far below its value, and the Orthodox minister was one of the purchasers.

In 1774 the law of 1573, was renewed, Massachusetts requiring that certificates should be recorded in each parish where Baptists lived, in order to exempt them from the tax for the state church support, for a copy of which certificate, a charge of four pence was made. This afforded no relief. It was additional injustice. That is, they must buy a copy of the law giving them protection from unjust taxes. Backus says, "This was equal to three pence sterling, the same which was laid on a pound of tea, which brought on the American Revolution."

The Baptists, feeling that they needed protection against unjust laws imposed upon them by the colonists, as the colonists needed protection against England's tyranny, took measures to secure their rights. On the 14th of September, 1774, the Warren Association of Baptist churches, which first met in 1767, convened at Medfield, and sent the Rev. Isaac Backus to present a petition from them to the First Continental Congress, then assembled in Philadelphia.

In that address, they proclaimed the Baptist loyalty to the cause of the colonists, and set forth their sufferings, reciting the Ashfield outrage. While they were willing to unite in defence of the common rights with the colonists, they demanded equal civil and religious rights with them.

In that address they say: "As the Baptist churches in New England are most heartily concerned for the preservation and defence of the rights and privileges of this country, and are deeply affected by the encroachments upon the same which have been lately made by the British Parliament, and are willing to unite with our dear countrymen to pursue every prudent measure for relief, so we would beg leave to say, that as a distinct denomination of Protestants, we conceive that we have an equal claim to charter rights with the rest of our fellow subjects, and yet we have been denied the full and free enjoyment of those rights, as to the support of religious worship. Therefore we have sent unto you the reverend and beloved Mr. Isaac Backus to lay our case before you for our relief."

Mr. Backus was to seek the co-operation of the Philadelphia Association then in session. A large delegation was appointed by the association to aid this cause. Mr. Backus and the committee together with some influential members of the Society of Friends, in Philadelphia, who joined in the petition, met the Massachusetts delegates and some members of Congress from other states, and had a four-hour conference with them, in Carpenter's Hall, October 14, 1774.

John Adams, delegate from Massachusetts, and afterwards president of the United States, said, "They might as well expect a change in the Solar system, as to expect that we would give up our ecclesiastical establishment." He meant the support of the Congregational churches by taxation. Paine, another delegate said, "There was nothing of conscience in the matter; it was only a contending about a little money." Mr. Backus replied: "It is absolutely a point of conscience with me, for I cannot give in the certificates they require, without implicitly acknowledging that power in man which I believe belongs only to God."

The delegates then promised to do what they could for the relief of the Baptists. John Adams returned home and reported, that Mr. Backus had been to Philadelphia to try to break up the union of the colonies. It is well for us as a nation, that all the country's leaders had not the same contracted views of liberty.

The first blood spilt in the war for freedom by the American people was shed at Lexington and Concord, Massachusetts, April 19, 1775. On the 4th of July, 1776, the Declaration of Independence of the American colonies was pronounced in Philadelphia, and sent over the land. The old bell in Independence Hall, which was then rung, has the inscription upon it, "Proclaim liberty throughout the land to all the inhabitants thereof." But there was no liberty in that sound for Baptists, except in prophecy. Liberty came not then, either to the country or to the Baptists. The spirit of John Adams was not yet dead.

The Baptists had to contend with the colonists for a long time before liberty was a reality.

John Hart, of Hopewell, New Jersey, was a Baptist and a signer of the Declaration of Independence. He was a man of integrity and worth. He gave the grounds and built upon it, the meeting-house for the Baptists of this town, which still stands today. He represented New Jersey in the First Continental Congress, in 1774. He risked and lost everything—home and property, by putting his name to that instrument. English troops hunted him, and he had to flee for his life. One night he slept in a dog-house with the dog. At another time he was forced to leave the bed side of his dying wife.

His native state has honored him and has erected a granite monument to his memory, over his grave at Hopewell, with this inscription upon it: "Honor the Patriot's Grave." He was in 1776, elected speaker of the New Jersey House of Assembly, to which position he was elected for the third time.

While our Baptist brethren were fighting for the colonists, Massachusetts was making unjust laws against them. "In 1778, upon the organization of the independent government, laws against Baptists were incorporated with the State Bill of Rights, and in 1780, were adopted with the State Constitution. The people who had risen in their majesty and power, and hurled from their necks the yoke of British oppression, immediately turned to fasten a still more galling yoke upon the necks of their brethren."

In 1789, when the people of Massachusetts assembled to consider the propriety of adopting the Federal Constitution, it was in danger of not being adopted. If Massachusetts rejected it, probably it would fail of adoption in the other states. They turned toward Massachusetts to see what her action would be.

Dr. Wm. Cathcart points out, that it was mainly through the instrumentality of Baptists, and especially owing to the efforts of those eminent Baptist ministers, Drs. James Manning and Stillman that it was adopted and that glorious instrument saved. Isaac Backus voted for it.

In the midst of profound silence, at the request of John Hancock, president, Dr. James Manning led the Convention in an eloquent, appropriate, closing prayer.

Rev. Isaac Backus says, that ten years before this Convention, a noted Congregational minister had said to the rulers of Massachusetts: "Let the restraints of religion once be broken down as they infallibly would be by leaving the subject of public worship to the humors of the multitude, and we might well defy all human wisdom to support and preserve order and government in the state. Yet this same man, in the convention of 1788, wherein much was said against adopting a constitution of government which had no religious test in it, was then in favor of the constitution, and to promote the adoption of it he said; 'God alone is the God of conscience, and consequently attempts to erect human tribunals for the consciences of men are impious encroachments upon the prerogatives of God.'"

"Though," continues Mr. Backus, "many have imagined that such liberty favors infidelity, yet Christianity is in full favor of it; and the power of the gospel against all the powers of Rome, prevailed as far and farther than the Roman Empire extended, for two hundred years, and Christianity has never appeared in the world in its primitive purity and glory since infant baptism was brought in, and after it the sword of the magistrates to support religious teachers."

Even after our national independence was secured, and the Constitution, and its amendment were ratified by the independent states, the persecution of Baptists in New England continued contrary to law.

The church at Barnstable, founded in 1771, was in the years 1788-99, taxed for $150 for the support of the Congregational minister whom they did not have, and when they had their own pastor to maintain. The Warren Association protested in January, 1799-80 so strongly, that the oppression was stopped, but the money was not returned.

At Harwick, where Baptists had worshipped forty years in their own meeting-house, there was no Congregational minister. But in 1792 when the Baptist church was without a pastor, a Congregational minister was sent to the place. The Baptists treated him kindly, but still maintained their own worship. In 1794, however, the handful of Congregationalists taxed the Baptists for their minister, and in 1795, six men were seized, and five of them imprisoned for refusing to submit to their imposition. The Baptists sued for redress in the local court, which was granted, but their oppressors took it to the higher court, which decided unjustly against the Baptists, who were compelled to lose $500.

In 1779, a pious deacon of the same church wrote: "The collector of Harwick seized four or five bushels of my rye, and sold it for one dollar, and made me pay two dollars for costs. Again, he seized three tons of my hay and sold it for forty-nine shillings, and returned me five shillings and six pence. For all this I was taxed to their ministers but seven shillings and a penny."

In 1804, Isaac Backus wrote respecting the liberty the law allowed: "Yet Massachusetts and Connecticut act contrary to it to this day." And it was not till 1833, that Massachusetts erased from the statutes her obnoxious and oppressive law. Let Baptists be called bigots no more. Who can cast a stone at them?—COOK'S STORY OF THE BAPTISTS, Pages 229-240.

CHAPTER II

THE AMERICAN REVOLUTION AND THE BAPTISTS

The Revolution and the Baptists
William Cathcart, D. D.

When the Legislature of Massachusetts, in 1778, forbade the return of 311 public enemies to their government, the historian Backus, who was acquainted with the facts, declares that not one of them was a Baptist. (Church History, p. 196. Philadelphia.) In Sabine's "History of American Loyalists" (Tories), with its 3200 brief biographies, we find 46 clergymen of one denomination, 6 of another, 3 of another, and but 1 Baptist minister.

This was Morgan Edwards, a man of great genius and worth, who was born in the Old World, and who failed to honor the patriotism of the Baptists of his **native** country by adopting it. We can discover no layman in Sabine's list who was a Baptist. Christopher Sower, of Germantown, Pennsylvania, is represented by Sabine as a German Baptist minister and a Tory.

Sower was a printer and bookseller, and unbound Bibles belonging to him, because of his loyalty to King George, furnished cartridge-paper for the Continental troops at the battle of Germantown. Sower was not a Baptist, but a member of a respectable German community that had no relations with the Baptists.

In the work of the Tory exile, Judge Curwen, of Salem, Massachusetts, there are the names of 926 persons who fled from Boston with General Howe when he sailed for Halifax; there are also the names of many others who left their country by the persuasion of State laws, committees of safety, or their own just fears.

Among these are persons of all occupations, and of all positions in colonial society, 46 clergymen keeping them in company. In this singular work (Curwen's "Journal and Letters," Boston, 1864, written in England, while its author was living on British alms), in which are the names of many American Tories, the gossiping ex-judge treats of literature, war, politics, theatres, and **theology,** but no hint is given that one of the Tories mentioned in it was a Baptist. Nor can we learn from other sources that any of them inflicted such a disgrace upon us.

President John Adams, in some respects an enemy of the Baptists, gives our people credit for bringing Delaware from the gulf of Toryism to the platform of patriotism. And he charges the disloyalty of her people on "the missionaries of the English Episcopal Society for the Propagation of the Faith." (Life and Works, by Charles Francis Adams, vol. X. p. 812.)

George Washington, in his reply to the "Committee of the Virginia Baptist Churches," which expressed to him grave doubts about the security of religious liberty under the Constitution of the United States, just adopted, said, "I recollect with satisfaction that the religious society of which you are members has been throughout America, uniformly and almost unanimously, the firm friends of civil liberty, and the persevering promoters of our glorious Revolution." (Writings of George Washington, Sparks, vol. XII. 154-55, Boston.)

With such a testimony from the noblest patriot of the whole human race, we may well bless God for our religious ancestry, who were among the most active builders of our country's great temple of liberty.—BAPTIST ENCYCLOPEDIA By William Cathcart, D. D. p. 973.

The Relations of the Baptists to the American Revolution
Rev. Wm. Cathcart, D. D.

When William Pitt stated in the British House of Commons, May 30th, 1781, that "the American war was conceived in injustice and nurtured in folly, and that it exhibited the highest moral turpitude and depravity, and that England had nothing but victories over men struggling in the holy cause of liberty, or defeats which filled the land with mourning for the loss of dear and valuable relations slain in a detested and impious quarrel," and when, six months later, in the same assembly, and two days after Cornwallis' surrender at Yorktown had been published in England, the eloquent Fox adopted the words of Chatham, uttered at the beginning of the Revolution, and said: "Thank God that America has resisted the claims of the mother country!" and when Burke and others, in the same legislature, spoke words of kindred import, full of peril to themselves, they expressed the sentiments of the Dissenters of England, and especially of the Baptists.

When Robert Hall, the future eloquent preacher, was a little boy, he heard the Rev. John Ryland, of Northampton, a man of commanding influence among the Baptists, say to his father, "If I were Washington I would summon all the American officers, they should form a circle around me, and I would address them, and we would offer a libation in our own blood, and I would order one of them to bring a lancet and a punch-bowl, and we would bare our arms and be bled; and when the bowl was full, when we all had been bled, I would call on every man to consecrate himself to the work by dipping his sword into the bowl and entering into a solemn covenant engagement by oath, one to another, and we would swear by Him that sits upon the throne and liveth forever and ever, that we would never sheathe our swords while there was an English soldier in arms remaining in America."

Dr. Rippon, of London, in a letter to President Manning, of Rhode Island College, written in 1784, says: "I believe all our Baptist ministers in town, except two, and most of our brethren in the country were on the side of the Americans in the late dispute. We wept when the thirsty plains drank the blood of your departed heroes, and the shout of a king was amongst us when your well-fought battles were crowned with victory; and to this hour we believe that the independence of America will, for a while, secure the liberty of this country, but if that continent had been reduced, Britain would not have been long free."

This was the spirit of the British Baptists during the Revolution, whose representatives in Parliament, though of another creed, breathed defiance in the ears of the king's ministers.

Baptists set the American People an Impressive Example of Disobedience to Wicked Laws. When the Baptists in Virginia were "forbidden to preach the Gospel of the Son of God," they went about more zealously than ever proclaiming Jesus over the entire Old Dominion.

When threatened with imprisonment and scourging, they defied the fetters and the lash; and when they were placed in confinement with the worst criminals they proclaimed the Word of Life to the eager throngs that hung around the doors and windows of the jail, and through evil-disposed persons, in some instances, erected a wall around the doors and windows of the jail, and though ployed half-drunken outcasts to beat a drum, that the voices of our honored brethren might not be heard, still they continued to preach the glorious Gospel of Christ, and the Spirit, as in apostolic times, blessed the jail witnesses for Jesus. Nor would the offer of immediate liberty, on condition of silence for a year, open the cell and close the lips of these grand old preachers.

In New England they were frequently arrested for not paying taxes to support the Congregational clergy, and women were honored with this privilege as well as men. Their property was seized, and generally sold for a mere trifle to pay the church dues of their neighbors of the "Standing Order."

The sacred tax collectors at Sturbridge, according to an unimpeachable witness, "took pewter from the shelves, skillets, kettles, pot and warming-pans, workmen's tools and spinning-wheels; they drove away geese and swine and cows, and where there was but one it was not spared.

A brother, recently ordained, returned to Sturbridge for his family, when he was thrust into prison, and kept during the cold winter till some one paid his fine and released him. Mr. D. Fisk lost five pewter plates and a cow; J. Perry was robbed of the baby's cradle and a steer; J. Blunt's fireplace was rifled of andirons, shovel, and tongs, and A. Bloice, H. Fisk, John Streeter, Benjamin Robbins, Phenehas Collier, John Newel, Josiah Perry, Nathaniel Smith and John Cory and I. Barstow were plundered of spinning-wheels, household goods, cows and their liberty for a season."

This case is but a specimen of what was occurring all over New England, except in Rhode Island. But our fathers submitted to robbery and loathsome prisons with foul associates rather than render willing obedience to iniquitous laws.

In the East and in the South Baptist witnesses, from prison windows, and sometimes with scourged shoulders, and in a voice as holy as ever floated on the lips of martyrs, announced to multitudes of men that "Unrighteous laws were conspiracies against God and the best interests of our race, plots of the Evil One, to be met by exposure and stern resistance, disobedience to which was loyalty to Jehovah."

Bordering on Revolutionary days persecutions were more general than ever before, and the testimony of Baptists against the crime of obeying sinful laws was in the very air and floating on the sunbeams of every morning, and when George III resolved on taxation for the Colonies without representation, the example of the Baptists became contagious, and resistance to this despotical theory became the engrossing thought of the Colonists of America.

Rhode Island is a Good Example of the Relations of our Baptist Fathers to Liberty and the Revolution. Many of the noble sons of Rhode Island, in the "times that tried men's souls," were of other creeds, but a much larger number followed the people, the stream of whose denominational life you can trace through every age till you see it issue forth from the heart of the Great Teacher, stepping up out of the Jordan.

Morgan Edwards, a man of great historical learning,

who died in 1795, says; "The Baptists have always been more numerous than any other sect of Christians in Rhode Island, two-fifths of the inhabitants, at least, are reputed Baptists. The governors, deputy governors, judges, assemblymen, and officers, civil and military, are chiefly of that persuasion."

"The first work of the Rhode Islanders," says Edwards, "after their incorporation in 1644, was to make a law that 'Every man who submits peaceably to civil government in this Colony shall worship God according to the dictates of his own conscience without molestation.'"

Rhode Island, as early as 1764, foresaw the coming Revolutionary storm, and to secure cooperation among the colonists established a "Committee of Correspondence," whose special duty it was to stir them up to maintain their liberties with spirit and to concert methods for united effort.

On the 4th of May, 1776, just two months before the adoption of the "Declaration of Independence," Rhode Island withdrew from the sceptre of Great Britain, and repudiated every form of allegiance to George III.

Scarcely had the retreating troops of General Gage reached Boston from Concord and Lexington when the nearest Rhode Island towns had sent recruits to their Massachusetts brethren in arms; and the Legislature soon after voted 1,500 men to be sent to the scene of danger. The people of Newport removed forty pieces of artillery from the royal fort to a place of security, where they might be ready for the defense and not the destruction of patriots.

When the Declaration of Independence was proclaimed at Newport, East Greenwich, and Providence, it called forth the most enthusiastic outbursts of delight, and shouts for "Liberty o'er and o'er the globe."

A British historian says: "The Rhode Islanders were such ardent patriots that after the capture of the island of Rhode Island by Sir Peter Parker, it required a great body of men to be kept there, in perfect idleness, for three years, to retain them in subjection."

Governor Green, in a dispatch to Washington, in 1781,

says: "Sometimes every fencible man in the State, sometimes a third, and at other times a fourth part was called out upon duty." But the little State that had declared its independence when other Colonies were hesitating, and thirty-two days before the brave and patriotic Virginians had renounced allegiance to the English king, never halted for a moment in her courageous efforts. Her sons, with the blood of Roger Williams and his valiant friends in their veins, showed their American brethren that liberty was the sovereign of their hearts.

Before the Revolution, Rhode Island was the freest Colony in North America, or in the history of our race. Her Baptist founders had made their settlement a Republic complete in every development of liberty, even while under the nominal rule of a king; they created a government with which there could be no lawful interference by any power in the Old World or the New.

Rhode Island had no viceroy; before the Revolution the king had no veto on her laws. In March, 1663, it was enacted that "no tax should be imposed or required of the Colony but by the act of the General Assembly." In 1704, Mompesson, the chief justice of New York, wrote Lord Nottingham that "when he was in Rhode Island the people acted in all things as if they were outside the dominion of the crown."

Bancroft speaks of Rhode Island at the Revolution "as enjoying a form of government, under its charter, so thoroughly republican that no charge was required beyond a reunuciation of the king's name in the style of its public acts."

"Rhode Island," says her historian, Arnold, when the United States Constitution was adopted, "for more than a century and a half has enjoyed a freedom unknown to any of her compeers, and through more than half of that period her people had been involved with rival Colonies in a struggle for political existence and for the maintenance of those principles of civil and religious freedom which are now every where received in America."—(Rest is missing from my copy—W.J.B.) Christian Repository, May, 1876.

CHAPTER III

VIRGINIA AND THE GENERAL ASSEMBLY

A memorial and remonstrance against the general assessment, presented to the general assembly of Virginia, at the session for the year of our Lord one thousand seven hundred and eighty five. Drawn by James Madison, later President of the United States.

A memorial and remonstrance. To the honourable the general Assembly of the Commonwealth of Virginia. **(Old English spelling followed.—WJB.)**

We, the fubscribers, citizens of the faid commonwealth, having taken into ferious confideration a bill, printed by order of the laft feffion of general affembly, entitled "A bill eftablifhing a provifion for teachers of the chriftian religion;" and conceiving, that the fame, if finally armed with the fanctions of a law, will be a dangerous abufe of power; are bound as faithful members of a free ftate, to remonftrate againft it, and to declare the reafons by which we are determined. We remonftrate againft the faid bill:

Becaufe we hold it for a fundamental and unalienable truth, "that religion, or the duty which we owe to the Creator, and the manner of difcharging it, can be directed only by reafon and conviction, not by force or violence." The religion, then, of every man, muft be left to the conviction and confciences of every man; and it is the right of every man to exercife it, as thefe may dictate. This right is, in its nature, an unalienable right. It is unalienable; becaufe the opinions of men depending only on the evidence contemplated by their own minds, cannot follow the dictates of other men. It is unalienable, alfo; becaufe what is here a right towards man, is a duty towards the Creator. It is the duty of every man to render to the Creator such homage, and such only, as he believes to be acceptable to him. This duty is precedent, both in order of time, and in degree of obligation, to the claims of civil fociety. Before any man can be confidered as a member of civil fociety, he muft be confidered as a fubject of the Governor of the univerfe. And if a member of civil fociety, who enters into any fubordinate affociation, muft always do it with a refervation of his duty to the general authority; much more muft every man who becomes a member of any particular civil fociety, do it with a faving of his allegiance to the univerfal Sovereign. We maintain, therefore, that, in matters of religion, no man's right is abridged by the inftitution of civil fociety; and that religion is wholly exempt from its cognizance. True it is, that no other rule exifts, by which any queftion which may divide a fociety can be ultimately determined, but by the will of the majority. But it is alfo true that the majority may trefpafs on the rights of the minority.

Becaufe if religion be exempt from the authority of the fociety at large, ftill lefs can it be fubject to that of the legiflative body. The latter are but the creatures and vicegerents of the former. Their jurifdiction is both derivative and limited. It is limited with regard to the co-ordinate departments: more neceffarily, it is limited with regard to the conftituents. The prefervation of a free government requires, not merely that the metes and bounds which feparate each department of power, be invariably maintained; but more efpecially, that neither of them be fuffered to overleap the great barrier which defends the rights of the people. The rulers who are guilty of fuch an encroachment, exceed the commiffion from which they derive their authority, and are tyrants. The people who fubmit to it, are governed by laws made neither by themfelves, nor by an authority derived from them, and are flaves.

Becaufe it is proper to take alarm, at the firft experiment on our liberties. We hold this prudent jealoufy, to be the firft duty of citizens, and one of the noblest characteriftics of the late revolution. The free-men of America did not wait until ufurped power had ftrengthened itfelf by exercife, and entangled the queftion in precedents. They faw all the confequences in the principle, and they avoided the confequences by denying the principle. We revere this leffon too much, foon to forget it. Who does not fee that the fame authority which can eftablifh chriftianity in exclufion of all other religions, may eftablifh, with the fame eafe, any particular fect of chriftians, in exclufion of all other fects? That the fame authority which can force a citizen to contribute three pence only of his property, for the fupport of any one eftablifhment, may force him to conform to any other eftablifhment, in all cafes whatfoever.

Becaufe the bill violates that equality which ought to be the bafis of every law; and which is more indifpenfable, in proportion as the validity or expediency of any law is more liable to be impeached. "If all men are, by nature, equally free and independent," all men are to be confidered as entering into fociety on equal conditions, as relinquifhing no more and therefore retaining no lefs, one than another, of their natural rights: above all, are they to be confidered as retaining an "**equal** title to the free exercife of religion according to the dictates of confcience." Whilft we affert for ourfelves a freedom to embrace, to profefs, and obferve the religion which we believe to be of divine origin; we cannot deny an equal freedom to thofe whofe minds have not yet yielded to the evidence which has convinced us. If this freedom be abufed, it is an offence againft God, not againft man. To God, therefore, and not to man, muft an account of it be rendered.

As the bill violates equality, by fubjecting fome to peculiar burdens; fo it violates the fame principle by granting to others, peculiar exemptions. Are the Quakers and Menonifts the only fects who think a compulfive fupport of their religions unneceffary and unwarrantable? Can their piety alone be entrufted with the care of public worfhip? Ought their religions to be endowed, above all others, with extraordinary privileges, by which profelytes may be enticed from all others? We think too favourably of the juftice and good fenfe of thefe denominations, to believe, that they either covet preeminences over their fellow citizens, or that they will be feduced by them from the common oppofition to the meafure.

Becaufe the bill implies, either that the civil magiftrate is a competent judge of religious truths, or that he may employ religion as an engine of civil policy. The firft is an arrogant pretenfion, falfified by the extraordinary opinion of rulers, in all ages, and throughout the world; the fecond, an unhallowed perverfion of the means of salvation.

Becaufe the eftablifhment propofed by the bill is not requifite for the fupport of the chriftian religion. To fay that it is, is a contradiction to the chriftian religion itfelf; for every page of it difavows a dependence on the power of this world; it is a contradiction to fact, for it is known that this religion both exifted and flourifhed, not only without the fupport of human laws, but in fpite of every oppofition from them; and not only during the period of miraculous aid, but long after it had been left to its own evidence and the ordinary care of Providence: nay, it is a contradiction in terms; for a religion not invented by human policy, muft have preexifted and been fupported, before it was eftablifhed by human policy; it is moreover to weaken in thofe who profefs this religion a pious confidence in its innate excellence and the patronage of its Author; and to fofter in thofe who ftill reject it, a fufpicion that its friends are too confcious of its fallacies, to truft it to its own merits.

Becaufe experience witneffes that ecclefiaftical eftablifhments, inftead of maintaining the purity and efficacy of religion, have had a contrary operation. During almoft fifteen centuries has the legal eftablifhments, of chriftianity been on trial. What have been its fruits? more or lefs in all places, pride and indolence in the clergy; ignorance and fervility in the laity; in both, fuperftition, bigotry, and perfecution. Enquire of the teachers of chriftianity for the ages in which it appeared in its greateft luftre? thofe of every fect point to the ages prior to its incorporation with civil policy. Propofe a reftoration of this primitive ftate, in which its teachers depended on the voluntary rewards of their flocks, many of them predict its downfall. On which fide ought their testimony to have greateft weight, when for, or when againft their intereft?

Becaufe the eftablifhment in queftion, is not neceffary for the fupport of civil government. If it be urged as neceffary for the fupport of civil government, only as it is a means of fupporting religion; and it be not neceffary for the latter purpofe, it cannot be neceffary for the former. If religion be not within the cognizance of civil government, how can its legal eftablifhment be faid to be neceffary to civil government? What influence in fact have ecclefiaftical eftablifhments had on civil fociety? In fome inftances they have been feen to exact a fpiritual tyranny on the ruins of the civil authority; in more inftances have they been feen upholding the thrones of political tyranny; in no inftance have they been the guardians of the liberties of the people. Rulers who wifhed to fubvert the public liberty, may have found an eftablifhed clergy convenient auxiliaries. A juft government inftituted to fecure and perpetuate it, needs them not. Such a government will be beft fupported by protecting every citizen in the enjoyment of his religion, with the fame equal hand which protects his perfon and his property; by neither invading the equal rights of any fect, nor fuffering any fect to invade thofe of another.

Becaufe the propofed eftablifhment is a departure from that generous policy, which, offering an afylum to the perfecuted and oppreffed of every nation and religion, promifed to luftre to our country, and an acceffion to the number of its citizens. What a melancholy mark is the bill of fudden degeneracy? Inftead of holding forth an afylum to the perfecuted, it is itfelf a signal of perfection. It degrades from the equal rank of citizens all thofe whofe opinions in religion do not bend to thofe of the legiflative authority. Diftant as it may be, in its prefent form, from the inquifition, it differs from it only in degree: the one is the firft ftep, the other the laft, in the career of intolerance.

The magnanimous fuffered under the cruel fcourge in foreign regions, muft view the bill as a beacon on our coaft, warning him to feek other haven, where liberty and philanthropy in their dues extent may offer a more certain repofe from his troubles.

Becaufe it will have a like tendency to banifh our citizens. The allurements prefented by other fituations, are every day thinning their number. To fuperadd a frefh motive to emigration, by revoking the liberty which they now enjoy, would be the fame fpecies of folly, which had difhonored and depopulated flourifhing kingdoms.

Because it will deftroy that moderation and harmony, which the forbearance of our laws to intermeddle with religion has produced among its feveral fects. Torrents of blood have been fpilt in the old world, by vain attempts of the fecular arm to extinguifh religious difcord by profcribing all differences in religious opinion. Time has at length revealed the true remedy. Every relaxation of narrow and rigorous policy, wherever is has been tried, has been found to affuage the difeafe. The American Theatre has exhibited proofs, that equal and complete liberty, if it does not wholly eradicate it, fufficiently deftroy its malignant influence on the health and prosperity of the ftate. If with the falutary effects of this fyftem under our own eyes, we begin to contract the bounds of religious freedom, we know no name that will too feverely reproach our folly. At leaft let warning be taken at the firft fruits of the threatened innovation. The very appearance of the bill has transformed that "christian forbearance, love, and charity," which of late mutually prevailed into animofities and jealousies which may not foon be appeafed. What mifchiefs may not be dreaded, fhould this enemy to the public quiet, be armed with the force of a law?

Because the policy of the bill is adverfe to the diffufion of the light of christianity. The firft wifh of thofe who ought to enjoy this precious gift ought to be, that it may be imparted to the whole race of mankind. Compare the number of thofe, who have as yet received it, with the number ftill remaining under the dominion of falfe religions, and how fmall is the former! Does the policy of the bill tend to leffen the difproportion? No; it at once difcourages thofe who are ftrangers to the light of truth, from coming into the regions of it: and countenances by example, the nations who continue in darkness, in fhutting out thofe who might convey it to them. Inftead of leveling as far as poffible every obftacle to the victorious progrefs of truth, and bill with an ignoble and unchristian timidity, would circumfcribe it, with a wall of defence against the encroachments of error.

Becaufe attempts to enforce by legal fanctions, acts, obnoxious, to fo great a proportion of citizens, tend to enervate the laws in general, and to flacken the bands of fociety. If it be difficult to execute any law, which is not generally deemed neceffary or falutary, what must be the cafe where it is deemed invalid and dangerous? And what may be the effect of fo striking an example of impotency in the government on its general authority?

Becaufe a meafure of fuch fingular magnitude and delicacy, ought not to be impofed, without the cleareft evidence that it is called for by a majority in this cafe may be determined, or its influence fecured. "The people of the refpecting counties are indeed requefted to fignify their opinion refpecting the adoption of the bill, to the next feffion of affembly." But the reprefentation muft be made equal, before the voice either of the reprefentatives or of the counties, will be that of the people. Our hope is that neither of the former, will after due consideration, efpoufe the dangerous principle of the bill. Should the event difappoint us, it will ftill leave us in full confidence, that a fair appeal to the latter will reverfe the fentence against our liberties.

Becaufe finally, "the equal right of every citizen to the free exercife of his religion according to the dictates of confcience," is held by the fame tenure with all our other rights. If we recur to its origin, it is equally the gift of nature; if we weigh its importance it cannot be lefs dear to us; if we confult the "Declaration of thofe rights which pertain to the good people of Virginia, as the bafis and foundation of government," it is enumerated with equal folemnity, or rather with ftudied emphafis. Either then we muft fay, that the will of the legiflature is the only meafure of their authority; and that, in the plenitude of this authority, they may fweep away all our fundamental rights; or, that they are bound to leave this particular right untouched and facred: either we muft fay that they may controul the freedom of the prefs; may abolish the trial by jury; may fwallow up the executive and judiciary powers of the ftate: nay, that they may annihilate our very right of fuffrage, and erect themfelves into an independent, and hereditary affembly; or we muft fay that they have no authority to enact into a law, the bill under consideration. We the fubfcribers fay, that the general affembly of this commonwealth have no fuch authority; and that no effort may be omitted on our part against fo dangerous a ufurpation, we oppose to it this Remonftrance, earneftly praying, by illuminating thofe to whom it is addreffed, may, on one hand, turn their councils from every act, which would affront his holy prerogative, or violate the truft committed to them; and on the other, guide them into every meafure which may eftablish more firmly the liberties, the prosperity, and the happinefs of this commonwealth.—Pages 435-444, HISTORY of the RISE AND PROGRESS of the BAPTISTS in VIRGINIA, by Robert B. Semple.

CHAPTER IV

SOME EXPERIENCES OF THE VIRGINIA BAPTISTS

Taken from the History of Virginia

The old English spelling is preserved in these excerpts.

Roanoke Association and Christian Education
(A Query Answered, 1803.)

Confiderable agitation of mind was excited at this feffion, in confequence of a query, introduced from a church in the county of Charlotte: Whether it was a maxim, firmly eftablifhed among the Baptifts, that "human learning is of no ufe."

This query arofe out of an illiberal affertion, contained in a letter from Mr. Rice, a presbyterian preacher of Charlotte, to the chairman of the committee of miffions; and which was publifhed in the Affembly's Miffionary Magazine of May, 1807. In which Mr. Rice declares, that, among the Baptifts of this neighbourhood, it is a maxim, very firmly eftablifhed, that human learning is of no ufe.

The Affociation took up the bufinefs, and appointed a committee of certain brethren, to anfwer and explain the fubject. The anfwer, which was ftrong and energetic, compofed by Mr. Kerr, was printed. No reply, or attempt to eftablifh the affertion, has been made by Mr. Rice, as yet.—Page 245, HISTORY of the RISE AND PROGRESS of the BAPTISTS IN VIRGINIA, by Robert B. Semple.

Roanoke Association on Authority of Ministers
(A Query Answered)

It is ftated in the minutes of this feffion, that in

the churches that compose the Roanoke Affociation, there are twenty five ordained, and five licenfed minifters. There are in all twenty nine churches; having on an average more than one preacher for each church. In this feffion the following query was introduced: Has a minifter of the gofpel any more power, in the government of a church, than an individual of the laity? Anfwered in the negative.

This decifion, muft doubtlefs, carry the principles of free government beyond all fcripture example; provided, by minifters of the gofpel, paftors of churches are intended. Nothing can be more clear, than that, through the whole tenor of the new teftament, they are recognized as having authority of fome sort. They are called rulers; and are promifed a reward if they rule well. They are called elders; alluding, no doubt, to elders under the Mofaic economy; who furely had authority in the nation.

Paul writes to the different churches in the language of authority; and advifes Timothy and Titus as minifters, whom he confiders as having power. It will then be asked, What kind of authority do they poffefs? To which it may be anfwered, They have a power fimilar to that of fathers: the authority of love. Hence, they are charged by Peter, not to lord it, over God's heritage: not to feel and act, as if they were lords and mafters. This fentiment, while it embraces the plain tenor of the word, is by no means repugnant to republican church-government; feeing paftors are chofen by the churches, and cannot, therefore, have any kind of power until given by them.

They are, therefore, reprefentatives of the churches, exercifing various branches of power, in the name and for the benefit of the church, and for the glory of God. If this were not the cafe, how could the paftor be refponfible for the ftanding of the church; as is evident, from the addreffes to the angels of the feven churches of Afia.—Page 224, HISTORY of the RISE AND PROGRESS of the BAPTISTS IN VIRGINIA, by Robert B. Semple.

Colored Ministers in Bluestone Association

It feems that the gofpel was firft carried into the

neighbourhood of Blueftone, by William Murphy and Philip Mulkey, about 1756. Their labours were very fuccefsful; and 1758 or 1759, they were fufficiently numerous to exercife the rights of a church. There were feveral white members, befides a large number of Blacks, belonging chiefly to the large eftate of Colonel Bird.

Many of thefe poor flaves became bright and fhining Chriftians. The breaking up of Bird's quarters, fcattered thefe Blacks into various parts. It did not rob them of their religion. It is faid, that through their labours in the different neighbourhoods into which they fell, many perfons were brought to the knowledge of the truth; and fome of them perfons of diftinction.—Page 222 and 223, HISTORY of the RISE AND PROGRESS of the BAPTISTS IN VIRGINIA, by Robert B. Semple.

Many Baptized by Colored Persons
(Allen's Creek Church)

The gofpel was carried here, about 1770; and many perfons embraced the truth, under the preaching of Mr. John Williams. They were united and happy, until Mr. Williams, in 1790, moved away. Being left deftitute of minifterial inftruction, and having a confiderable number of black people in their fociety, of whom there were fome preachers of talents; they commenced the adminiftration of the ordinances, without ordination.

They were perfecuted by one part of the community, and protected by others, equally refpectable. They increafed rapidly; fo that, in a few years, more than one hundred Blacks were baptized by them. Thefe branched out into different companies, or churches if they may be fo called. When Mr. Williams returned to the parts, he had no little difficulty in settling them into order. Many refufed to give up their independent ftate; but the moft orderly joined Mr. Williams: and he leaving it to the choice of thofe who had been baptized by the Blacks, to be rebaptized or not, moft chofe to be rebaptized.—Page 221 and 222, HISTORY of the RISE AND PROGRESS of the BAPTISTS IN VIRGINIA, by Robert B. Semple.

Lawsuit in an Association

Silas Hart, native of Pennfylvania, moved into the bounds of this church and became a member. He died and left by his will, to the Philadelphia affociation, property fufficient to yield an annuity of 50 pounds to be kept in the hands of truftees and applied to the education of young preachers. The Philadelphia affociation appointed the Rev'd David Jones to receive the money in their behalf; but upon application, the executors of Hart refufed to pay, upon the ground that the affociation was not incorporated, and confequently not known in law, or capable of maintaining an action.

David Jones commenced a fuit in chancery in Rockingham court, and in 1802 a decree was pronounced in favor of the executors. Jones appealed to the Staunton high court of chancery, when, in 1803, the decree was affirmed; he then appealed to the high court of appeals, where in 1807 the decree was finally affirmed.

Between the time of the decifion in the Staunton Chancery court and that in the court of appeals, the Philadelphia affociation became incorporated. This, taking place fubfequent to the commencement of the fuit, did not avail as to the fuit then depending. The court of appeals however, made a refervation in the decree, ftating that nothing done in this fuit fhould affect any other fuit which fhould be hereafter brought by the Baptift affociation, meeting in ordinary at Philadelphia: So that by reforting to another original action, the affociation will ultimately receive the money. This is certainly an important cafe to the Baptifts of Virginia. From the decifion above mentioned, it would feem doubtful whether any property holden by the Baptifts as a religious fociety is fafe.

It remains therefore for them hereafter to decide, whether it will be beft to fuffer their meeting houfes and other property to continue thus jeopardized, or to become incorporated. If their becoming incorporated would be a dangerous precedent, leading in any wife to religious oppreffion, it is better to remain as they are, for it would certainly be more wife to jeopardize property than principles. A fair and unprejudiced inveftigation of this fubject is defirable at this time, and would probably lead to beneficial effects.—Page 192 and 193, HISTORY of the RISE AND PROGRESS of the BAPTISTS IN VIRGINIA, by Robert B. Semple.

Church Rejected by Ketocton Association
(A Question of Ordination)

Mountponey, as will appear from the table, was conftituted 1774. Elder Saunders ferved them as a fupply, from a fhort time after their conftitution, until fome time in 1777. When the Rev. John Leland, from New England, came preaching among them, and became a member of Mount Poney Church. The church unanimoufly called him to the miniftration of the Word and ordinances, without ordination by the impofition of hands. This being contrary to the eftablifhed rule of the Ketocton Affociation, and indeed of the Baptists of Virginia generally, when the church fent her delegates to the next affociation they were rejected.—Page 177, HISTORY of the RISE AND PROGRESS of the BAPTISTS IN VIRGINIA, by Robert B. Semple.

Mr. Leland's free and jocund manners, have excited the fufpicions of fome, that he wanted ferious piety. His intimate friends, are confident that these are groundlefs fufpicions. They believe, that, among his other fingularities, he is fingularly pious. While in Virginia, he wrote feveral treatises, and was certainly very inftrumental in effecting the juft and falutary regulations concerning religion, in this ftate. He has been fimilarly employed fince his removal to New England. He has always been a zealous advocate for republican government.

Baptist Women Present a Present to Thomas Jefferson

When Mr. Jefferson was raised to the Presidential chair, the ladies of Mr. Leland's congregation, made a cheese of immense fize,* and fent it by Mr. Leland, as a present to Mr. Jefferfon. This affair made no little noise in the United States.

*It was said to have had in it 1400 lb. of curd, and to have weighed 900 weight when taken from the press. The enemies of Jefferson called it the Mammouth Cheese: they also wrote poems and vented much wit upon the occafion. It was, however, received by the President with pleasure, and viewed by the impartial as a singular pledge of patriotism.—Page 158 and 159, HISTORY of the RISE AND PROGRESS of the BAPTISTS IN VIRGINIA, by Robert B. Semple.

Minister Runs Away From Officers

This church, Guinea's Bridge, so called from its vicinity to a bridge of that name, is a church of high-ftanding, having a number of pious and worthy members. The gofpel was preached here, in its power and purity, at an early date after the rife of the Baptifts. This place was not without its perfecutors alfo. At one time, feveral preachers were apprehended, by virtue of a warrant from a magiftrate; Among them was Joseph Craig; remarkable for his eccentric manners. On their way to the magiftrate's houfe, Mr. Craig thinking it **no dishonour to cheat the devil**, as he termed it, flipped off the horse, and took to the bufhes. They hunted him with dogs, but Asahel like, being light of foot, he made good his retreat.—Page 156, HISTORY of the RISE AND PROGRESS of the BAPTISTS IN VIRGINIA, by Robert B. Semple.

Had Their Unworthies, Too

It was in this church that Thomas Bridges, now a prisoner in the Penitentiary for horfe-ftealing, was baptized in '88. Bridges began to preach soon after he was baptized; but being very illiterate, and of obfcure parentage, he was not much noticed in his own neighbourhood. He was, however, fo far encouraged by the church, as to obtain ordination: having from his youth, a propenfity to lying, he was detected in this mean practice, after he commenced preaching. The church, however, admitting his excufes, did not exclude him.

Feeling restless under these charges, he asked and obtained a letter of difmiffion from the church. He now travelled off into Loudon, and the adjacent counties, where he became confiderably popular as a preacher. He certainly had fome talents. He was fluent in his delivery, and for his education, fpoke in handsome language. His memory was exceedingly retentive, and he had, after becoming a preacher, read a good deal. He had alfo a large ftock of that kind of wit, which pleafes without profiting; but, in point of judgment, he was probably as deficient as ever man was. His opinions upon fubjects, that he had often studied and discuffed, were always incorrect; upon others, he was a mere child. After all, it is not likely that Bridges would ever become fo entirely abandoned, had he not unfortunately married a wife with a confiderable estate; by which, his fpirits being elevated far above their common level, he lost all the stock of prudence he previously poffeffed.

Not accustomed to the management of property to any tolerable extent, he foon, very foon, fpent what he had gotten by marriage. Still retaining the relifh for his new fphere of action; but having lost all lawful refources, he strangely reforted to the fhocking alternative of stealing horfes. For which, being condemned in 1803, he was confined in the Penitentiary, where he is now.—Pages 155 and 156, HISTORY of the RISE AND PROGRESS of the BAPTISTS IN VIRGINIA, by Robert B. Semple.

Goshen Association About Assessments

In Bethel church, one of the conftituents of this affociation, a rule had been formed, by a large majority, compelling each perfon, under the penalty of the displeafure of the church, to contribute towards her expences, according to what he was worth. This rule gave great umbrage, not only to a minority in the church, but to other churches likewise. At this affociation, a query was introduced in the following words:

"Does the association approbate a church that raises money, by affeffing her members?"

Which received the following solution:

"We do not approbate the method of raising money by affeffments, upon the principle of its not being fanctioned by new teftament examples, and the general principles of the Baptifts, and because of the unhappy confequences, which may refult from such a practice."—Page 148, HISTORY of the RISE AND PROGRESS of the BAPTISTS IN VIRGINIA, by Robert B. Semple.

Dover Association Received Colored Churches

Thif church, Williamfburg, if compofed almoft, if not altogether, of people of colour. Mofef, a black man, firft preached among them, and waf often taken up and whipped, for holding meetingf. Afterwardf Gowan, who called himfelf Gowan Pamphlet, moved from Middlefex, where he had been preaching for fome time; he became popular among the blackf, and began to baptize, as well af to preach.

It feems, the affociation had advifed that no perfon of colour fhould be allowed to preach, on the pain of excommunication; againft thif regulation, many of the blackf were rebelliouf, and continued ftill to hold meetingf. Some were excluded, and among thif number waf Gowan, juft mentioned.

Continuing ftill to preach and many profeffing faith under his miniftry, not being in connexion with any church himself, he formed a kind of church out of fome who had been baptized, who, fitting with him, received such as offered themfelves; Gowan baptized them, and was moreover appointed their paftor; fome of them knowing how to write, a church-book was kept; they increafed to a large number; fo that in the year 1791, when the Dover affociation was holden in Mathews county, they petitioned for admittance into the affociation, ftating their number to be about five hundred. The affociation received them, fo far, af to appoint perfonf to vifit them and fet thingf in order. Thefe, making a favourable report, they were received, and have affociated ever fince. A few yearf fince, Gowan died.—Pages 114 and 115, HISTORY of the

RISE AND PROGRESS of the BAPTISTS IN VIRGINIA, by Robert B. Semple.

Charles City

In this church there ufed to be and ftill are, a great number of blackf. For fome caufe, they were forbidden to preach; upon which they fet up a kind of independence, and went on not only to preach, but to baptize. It all, however, ended in confufion.—Page 112, HISTORY of the RISE AND PROGRESS of the BAPTISTS IN VIRGINIA, by Robert B. Semple.

Feet Washing in Dover Association
(Query Answered)

October 13th, 1798.—The next affociation met at Mathews meeting houfe, Mathews county, according to appointment. The letters did not detail any thing very interefting. The bufineff was altogether local, except as to the following.

Query. What is the opinion of the affociation, concerning wafhing the faints feet?

Answer. We do not confider the wafhing of feet, an ordinance of the gofpel, but an act of entertainment, and being a fervile act, appears to have been enjoined by Chrift, to be obferved by his difciples, as a token of humility, and may include any other act, ufually performed by fervants.—Page 99, HISTORY of the RISE AND PROGRESS of the BAPTISTS IN VIRGINIA, by Robert B. Semple.

On Baptism by Unordained Person, Dover Association
(A Query Answered)

A matter which had produced confiderable confufion in fome parts of the affociation, was now confidered, viz: Whether baptism was valid when adminiftered by an unordained perfon. To which the affociation replied: That, in cafes where the ordinance had been adminiftered, in a folemn and religious manner, that it might be confidered as valid, and that perfons fo baptized, might be admitted as members of a church, upon hearing and approving their experience . . .

In November, 1786, they met at Ground Squirrel meeting houfe, in Hanover county. Wm. Webber was chofen moderator, and Reuben Ford, Clerk.

The only bufinefs of general application tranfacted at this feffion, was the folution of the following query:

"How is ordination legally performed?"

Answer.—"A presbytery of minifters are fully empowered, to ordain any faithful man properly recommended, whom they fhall judge able to teach others; and that minifters fhall be fubject to minifters, with regard to their call to the miniftery, and the doctrine they preach. The church where the minifter is a member, fhall take cognizance of his moral character."

This decifion, though founded in reafon and fcripture, gave umbrage to fome, who indulged ftrong jealoufies refpecting minifterial influence, and who held, that a call from a church was fufficient ordination. In conference of this oppofition, the fubject was again introduced into the Dover Affociation, in the year 1792: to our hiftory of which, the reader is referred.—Pages 92-93, HISTORY of the RISE AND PROGRESS of the BAPTISTS IN VIRGINIA, by Robert B. Semple.

Dover Association on Matter of Ordination
(A Query Answered)

Among other bufinefs of lefs note, the fubject of the ordination of elders or church-officers, was taken up at this affociation. A queftion had been agitated for fome years, whether ordination ought to be by imposition of the hands of a presbytery, or plurality of elders (the mode commonly practised in Virginia), or, whether a solemn call from a church was not sufficient.

On the part of the advocates of ordination, without the impofition of hands, it was argued, that churches were acknowledged to be independent, but if they could not obtain the full fervices of a minifter, unlefs he had been previously examined and ordained by a presbytery, their independence was fo far destroyed; that churches were better judges, what gifts would fuit them, than presbyteries could be; that the impofition of hands mentioned in the fcripture, was with a view to miraculous, and not common gifts; and laftly, that it had the appearance, of being governed too much, by forms.

To thefe arguments, it was anfwered, that the new teftament did furely fanction the practice of laying on of hands, in fome cafes, where miraculous confequences did enfue: that, although the impofition of hands was a form, yet it was a fignificant form, ufed in all ages of the Chriftian church, for the purpofe of confecrating, or fetting afide perfons for holy offices: that baptifm and the Lord's supper were alfo external forms, but being fignificant, and fanctioned by the word of infpiration, they were owned and bleffed to the church: that it was true that churches were, and ought to be independent, to a proper extent; but this independence did not authorise them to ordain officers, contrary to revelation, unless they were independent of God also: that no minister or deacon, was imposed upon them but by their own consent: that although a church might judge better than a presbytery what fuited her, it was not reafonable that thofe who had not exercifed a public gift, fhould be fo competent to judge of public gifts thofe who had.

After the fubject had been inveftigated for years, at different times, and in different ways, it was finally decided in this affociation, in favor of the impofition of hands. After this, very little was ever said about it.—Page 97, HISTORY of the RISE AND PROGRESS of the BAPTISTS IN VIRGINIA, by Robert B. Semple.

Sends Paper to President Thomas Jefferson, 1808

The general meeting took up the following bufinefs: The propriety of offering an address to Mr. Thomas Jefferson, Prefident of the United States, who, having ferved his country faithfully for many years, was now about to retire from public life. The address was unanimously voted, and fent on; to which the President returned an immediate anfwer.—Page 88, HISTORY of the RISE AND PROGRESS of the BAPTISTS IN VIRGINIA, by Robert B. Semple.

Virginia Baptists and Slavery

The propriety of hereditary flavery, was alfo taken up at this feffion, and after fome time employed in the confideration of the fubject, the following refolution was offered by Mr. Leland, and adopted:

Resolved, That flavery is a violent deprivation of the rights of nature, and inconfiftent with a republican government, and therefore recommend it to our brethren, to make ufe of every legal meafure to extirpate this horrid evil from the land; and pray Almighty God that our honorable legislature may have it in their power to proclaim the great Jubilee, confiftent with the principles of good polity.—Page 70, HISTORY of the RISE AND PROGRESS of the BAPTISTS IN VIRGINIA, by Robert B. Semple.

Virginia Baptists and Strict Communion

Accordingly, on the 24th of November, 1781, they, by mutual confent, formed themfelves into a gofpel church called Greenbrier. They had a written church covenant, which they placed in the front of their church book. Mr. Alderfon of courfe, was their paftor.

The next fpring (1782) they appointed a communion, or in other words, the adminiftration of the Lord's fupper. Numbers came forward and requefted the privilege of communing with them; to whom the church replied, as might be expected, that none were admitted to the communion, except they were previoufly baptized, upon a profeffion of vital faith, and had yielded themfelves as members of the church. When they heard this, many of them changed their tone and became enemies.—page 330, A HISTORY of the RISE AND PROGRESS of the BAPTISTS IN VIRGINIA, by Robert B. Semple.

CHAPTER V

BAPTISTS AND THE RELIGIOUS AMENDMENT TO THE CONSTITUTION OF THE UNITED STATES

William Cathcart, D. D.

The first amendment to the United States Constitution was adopted in 1789, the year it went into operation. It reads, "Congress shall make no law respecting an establishment of religion, or prohibiting the free exercise thereof; or abridging the freedom of speech or of the press; or the right of the people peaceably to assemble, and to petition the government for the redress of grievances." The first clause of this amendment occupies properly its prominent place in that addition to the Constitution. Freedom of conscience was in legal bondage in 1789, and its friends had too much cause to be alarmed for its safety.

Had the amendment not been adopted, Massachusetts might have had her State church today, and her citizens rotting in prison because they could not conscientiously pay a church-tax; and any State might have established the Episcopal Church and then committed Baptists or other ministers to prison, as Virginia did down to the Revolution. And Congress might have levied taxes to support her clergy, and made laws to give secular power to her cardinals, archbishops, bishops, and priests over our schools, religious opinions, and personal freedom.

With the amendment we have been educated to practice universal religious freedom; without it, sacerdotal tyranny might have destroyed all our liberty. The grandest feature of our Constitution is the first clause of the first amendment. The Baptists have justly claimed that the credit for this amendment belongs chiefly to them. It is in strict accordance with their time-honored maxim, "The major part shall rule in civil things only."

Where else could it have come from? In the Revolution, and for a few years after, there were two great centers of political influence in our country, around which the other States moved with more or less interest,—Massachusetts and Virginia. Freedom of conscience could not come from Massachusetts; she was wedded to a State religion in 1789, which defied any divorcing agency to create a separation.

Just ten years before, she adopted her new constitution with an article in it giving legal support to Congregational ministers, as in good old Puritan times. And this tie only perished in 1834. Writing to Benjamin Kent, John Adams says, "I am for the most liberal toleration of all denominations, but I hope Congress will never meddle with religion further than to say their own prayers . . . **Let every colony have its own religion without molestation."** That is, from Congress; he wished every colony to have its own **established** church without molestation, if it desired such an institution.

He unjustly charged Israel Pemberton, a Quaker, whom, with the Baptists and other Friends, the Massachusetts delegates met during the session of the first Continental Congress, with an effort to destroy the union and labors of Congress, because he pled for the release of Baptists and Quakers imprisoned in Massachusetts for not paying the ministers' tax, and for the repeal of their oppressive laws.

And John Adams actually argued that it was against the consciences of the people of his State to make any change in their laws about religion, even though others might have to suffer in their estates or in their personal freedom to satisfy Mr. Adams and his **conscientious** friends. And he declared that they might as well think they could change the movements of the heavenly bodies as alter the religious laws of Massachusetts.

This was the spirit of New England when the first

amendment was proposed, except in Rhode Island, and among the Baptists, and the little community of Quakers outside of it. Thomas Jefferson, writing to Dr. Rush, says, "There was a hope confidently cherished about A.D. 1800, that there might be a State church throughout the United States, and this expectation was specially cherished by Episcopalians and Congregationalists." This was the sentiment of not a few New England Pedobaptists, and the hope of the remains of the Episcopal Church in the South. Massachusetts and her allies had no love for the first amendment, and, according to Backus, Massachusetts **did not** adopt it.

It came from Virginia, and chiefly from Baptists of the Old Dominion. The "mother of Presidents" was the mother of the glorious amendments. In 1776 the first republican Legislature of Virginia convened, and after a violent contest, daily renewed, from the 11th of October to the 5th of December, the **acts of Parliament** were repealed which rendered any form of worship criminal.

Dissenters were exempted from all taxes to support the clergy, and the laws were **suspended** which compelled Episcopalians to support their own church. But it was the pressure of Dissenters without that forced this legislation on the Assembly, for a majority of the members were Episcopalians. While this act relieved Baptists, the unrepealed common law still punished with dismissal from all offices for the first offense, those who denied the Divine existence, or the Trinity, or the truth of Christianity; and for the second, the transgressor should be rendered incapable of suing or of acting as guardian, administrator, or executor, or of receiving a legacy, and, in addition, should be imprisoned for three years.

These persecuting laws were not repealed till 1785. The tithe law, after being agitated frequently in every session, and annually suspended, was repealed in 1779. The Presbyterians and Baptists were the outside powers that swept away the State church of Virginia.

After tithes ceased to be collected, a scheme, known as the "assessment," was extensively discussed in Virginia by Episcopalians and others. The assessment required every citizen to pay tithes to support his minister, no matter what his creed. The Episcopalians warmly advocated the assessment. The united clergy of the Presbyterian Church petitioned for it, though many of their people disliked and denounced it.

Patrick Henry aided it with all the power of his eloquence. Richard Henry Lee, the most polished orator in the country, John Marshall, the future chief justice of the United States, and George Washington himself advocated it. The Baptists directed their whole forces against it, and poured petitions into the Legislature for its rejection.

After expending every effort, the friends of the assessment were defeated, and it was finally rejected in 1785, and all the laws punishing opinions repealed. This was a work of great magnitude. The Episcopalians, the Methodists, the Presbyterian clergy, and the eloquence and influence of some of the greatest men the United States ever had, or will have, were overcome by the Baptists, Jefferson and Madison, their two noble allies, and some Presbyterian and other laymen.

Semple truly says, "The inhibition of the general assessment may, in a considerable degree, be ascribed to the opposition made to it by the Baptists. They were the only sect which plainly remonstrated against it. Of some others it is said that the laity and ministry were at variance upon the subject, so as to paralyze their exertions for or against the bill."

Nor need any one dream that Jefferson and Madison could have carried this measure by their genius and influence. They were opposed by many men whose transcendent services, or unequaled oratory, or wealth, position, financial interests, or intense prejudices, would have enabled them easily to resist their unsupported assaults. Like a couple of first-class engineers on a "tender," with a train attached, but no locomotive, would Jefferson and Madison have appeared without the Baptists. They furnished the locomotive for these skillful engineers, which drew the train of religious liberty through every persecuting enactment in the penal code of Virginia.

In 1790, just one year after the adoption of the amendment, Dr. Samuel Jones, of Pennsylvania, states that there were 202 Baptist churches in Virginia. Semple, the historian of the Virginia Baptists, says that, in 1792, "The Baptists had members of great weight in civil society; their congregations became more numerous than those of any other Christian sect." The Baptists out-numbered all the denominations in Virginia, in all probability, in 1789, and they far surpassed them in the burning enthusiasm which persecution engenders, and to them chiefly was Virginia indebted for her complete deliverance from persecuting enactments.

In 1789, a few months after Washington became President, "The Committee of the United Baptist Churches of Virginia" presented him an address written by John Leland, marked by felicity of expression and great admiration for Washington, in which they informed him that their religious rights were not protected by the new Constitution. The President replied that he would never have signed that instrument had he supposed that it endangered the religious liberty of any denomination, and if he could imagine even now that the government could be so administered as to render freedom of worship insecure for any religious society, he would immediately take steps to erect barriers against the horrors of spiritual tyranny.

Large numbers were anxious about the new Constitution, and it had many open enemies. The Baptists who presented this address **controlled the government of Virginia, and they were the warmest friends of liberty in America.** They would suffer anything for their principles, and, as they suspect the new Constitution, it must be amended to embrace their soul liberty and secure their hearty support.

A few weeks later, James Madison, the special friend of Washington, who aided him five months before in composing his first inaugural address to congress, rises in the House of Representatives and proposes the religious amendment demanded by the Baptists, with other emendations, and declares that "a great number of their constituents were dissatisfied with the Constitution, among whom were many respectable for their talents and their patriotism, and **respectable for the jealousy which they feel for their liberty**" (religious). This language applied to his Virginia Baptist friends and their co-religionists over the land. He pressed his scheme amidst violent opposition, and Congress passed it. Two-thirds of the State Legislatures approved of it, and it became a part of the Constitution.

Denominationally, no community asked for this change in the Constitution but the Baptists. The Quakers would no doubt have petitioned for it if they had thought of it, but they did not. John Adams and the Congregationalists did not desire it; the Episcopalians did not wish for it. It went too far for most Presbyterians in Revolutionary times, or in our own days, when we hear so much especially from them, about putting the divine name in the Constitution. The Baptists asked it through Washington. The request commended itself to his judgment and to the generous soul of Madison, and to the Baptists, beyond a doubt, belongs the glory of engrafting its best enactment on the noblest Constitution ever framed for the government of mankind.

—BAPTIST ENCYCLOPEDIA, Edited by William Cathcart, D. D.

H. T. Besse (himself not a Baptist), in his Church History says, page 175, "The article on religious liberty found in the amendment of our national constitution, in 1789, is largely due to the effort of the Baptists."

CHAPTER VI

SOME OF THE OLDEST BAPTIST CHURCHES IN AMERICA

This list is taken from Mr. Benedict's History. The reader will note that he has listed Providence, Rhode Island (Roger William's group). However, later in life this historian changed his mind about this. See elsewhere in this book proof that Roger Williams, though holding some Baptist sentiments, was never a Baptist. We do not disparage this good man, for he held with Baptists the idea of absolute freedom of conscience.

Providence, Rhode Island	1639
First, Newport	1644

(It has been shown in this book that John Clarke organized the First Baptist church, Newport, in 1638. WJB.)

Second, Newport	1656
First, Swansea, Massachusetts	1663
First, Boston, Massachusetts	1665
North Kingston, Rhode Island	1665
Seventh Day, Newport, Rhode Island	1671
South Kingston, Rhode Island	1680
Tiverton, Rhode Island	1685
Smithfield, Rhode Island	1706
Middleton, New Jersey	1688
Lower Dublin, Pennsylvania	1689
Piscataway, New Jersey	1689
Charleston, South Carolina	1690
Cohansey, New Jersey	1691
Second, Swansea, Massachusetts	1693
First, Philadelphia, Pennsylvania	1698

Welsh Tract, Delaware	1701
Groton, Connecticut	1705
Seventh Day, Piscataway, New Jersey	1707
Hopkinton, Rhode Island	1708
Great Valley, Pennsylvania	1711
Cape May, New Jersey	1712
Hopewell, New Jersey	1715
Brandywine, Pennsylvania	1715
Montgomery, Pennsylvania	1719
New York City,	1724

(This has reference to the old church of General, or Armenian Baptists, out of which the present church arose.)

Scituate, Rhode Island	1725
Warwick, Rhode Island	1725
Richmond, Rhode Island	1725
French Creek, Pennsylvania	1726
New London, Connecticut	1726
Indian Town, Maine	1730
Cumberland, Rhode Island	1732
Rehoboth, Massachusetts	1732
Shiloh, New Jersey	1734
South Brimfield, Massachusetts	1736
Welsh Neck, South Carolina	1738
Leicester, Massachusetts	1738
Southington, Connecticut	1738
W. Springfield, Connecticut	1740
King Wood, New Jersey	1742
Second, Boston, Massachusetts	1743
N. Stonington, Connecticut	1743
Colchester, Connecticut	1743
East Greenwich, Rhode Island	1743
Euhaw Creek, South Carolina	1745
Heights Town, New Jersey	1745
South Hampton, Pennslyvania	1746
Scotch Plains, New Jersey	1747
King Street, Connecticut	1747
Oyster Bay, New York	1748
Sturbridge, Massachusetts	1749
Bellingham, Massachusetts	1750

Killingby, Connecticut 1750
Westerly, Rhode Island 1750
Exeter, Rhode Island 1750
Thompson, Connecticut 1750

A considerable number of these old churches were of the General Baptist order.

Summary of American Baptists in 1790

(Quoted by Mr. Benedict from John Asplund's first Register.)

STATES	Churches	Ord. Min.	Lic. Min.	Members
New Hampshire	32	23	17	1732
Massachusetts	107	95	31	7116
Rhode Island	38	37	36	3502
Connecticut	55	44	21	3214
Vermont	34	28	15	1610
New York	57	53	30	3987
New Jersey	26	20	9	2279
Pennsylvania	28	26	7	1231
Delaware	7	9	1	409
Maryland	12	8	3	776
Virginia	207	157	109	20157
Kentucky	42	40	21	3105
Western Territory	1			30
North Carolina	94	86	76	7742
Deceded Territory (Now Tenn.)	18	15	6	889
South Carolina	68	48	28	4012
Georgia	42	33	39	3184
Nova Scotia	4			
Total	872	722	449	64975

Rev. I. M. Allen, in his Triennial Register of the Baptists for 1830, makes the statistics as follows, for the U. S. and British possessions in America.

Associations	Churches	Min. Ord.	Min. Lic.	Members
372	2142	4075	966	517,523

These include the Freewill, Seventh Day, and Six

Principle Baptists, and also those in Canada and West Indies Islands.

First Sermon West of the Mississippi

In 1796, Elder James Kerr, a Baptist minister of Mercer county, Kentucky, traveled on horse-back, accompanied by his wife through the "Northwestern Territory," to the province of Upper Louisiana, now called Missouri. His daughter had married Alexander Clarke, and had moved to a place about fourteen miles from St. Louis.

While at his daughter's house, his wife died, and was interred in the grave-yard of the old "Village la Robert," now Brodgeton. It was at this place, on the sad occasion of his wife's funeral, that Elder Kerr preached the first sermon from anti-Romanist lips ever preached west of the Father of Waters. "In October, 1870," writes his grand-son, "I conversed with an old lady in St. Louis county who was present on that occasion." (Texas Baptist, January 6th.) Elder Kerr settled six miles west of St. Charles and continued to preach and to gather little churches until his death, which occurred in 1811.—Ford's Christian Repository, May, 1876.

CHAPTER VII

THE NEW HAMPSHIRE AND THE PHILADELPHIA CONFESSIONS OF FAITH

The New Hampshire Declaration of Faith

I. Of the Scriptures.—We believe that the holy Bible was written by men divinely inspired, and is a perfect treasure of heavenly instruction; that it has God for its author, salvation for its end, and truth without any mixture of error for its matter; that it reveals the principles by which God will judge us, and therefore is, and shall remain to the end of the world, the true center of Christian union, and the supreme standard by which all human conduct, creeds, and opinions should be tried.

II. Of the True God.—We believe that there is one, and only one, living and true God, an infinite, intelligent Spirit, whose name is Jehovah, the Maker and Supreme Ruler of heaven and earth, inexpressibly glorious in holiness, and worthy of all possible honor, confidence, and love; that in the unity of the Godhead there are three persons,—Father, the Son, and the Holy Ghost,—equal in every divine perfection, and executing distinct but harmonious offices in the great work of redemption.

III. Of the Fall of Man.—We believe that man was created in holiness, under the law of his Maker; but by voluntary transgression fell from that holy and happy state; in consequence of which all mankind are now sinners, not by constraint but choice; being by nature utterly void of that holiness required by the law of God; positively inclined to evil; and therefore under just condemnation to eternal ruin, without defense or excuse.

IV. Of the Way of Salvation.—We believe that the salvation of sinners is wholly of grace; through the mediatorial offices of the Son of God; who by the appointment of the Father, freely took upon Him our nature, yet without sin; honored the divine law by His personal obedience, and by His death made a full atonement for our sins; that having risen from the dead, He is now enthroned in heaven; and uniting in His wonderful person the tenderest sympathies with divine perfections, He is every way qualified to be a suitable, a compassionate, and an all-sufficient Saviour.

V. Of Justification.—We believe that the great gospel blessing which Christ secures to such as believe in Him, is justification; that justification includes the pardon of sin, and the promise of eternal life on principles of righteousness; that it is bestowed, not in consideration of any works of righteousness which we have done, but solely through faith in the Redeemer's blood; by virtue of which faith His perfect righteousness is freely imputed to us of God: that it brings us into a state of most blessed peace and favor with God, and secures every other blessing needful for time and eternity.

VI. Of the Freeness of Salvation.—We believe that the blessings of salvation are made free to all by the gospel; that it is the immediate duty of all to accept them by a cordial, penitent, and obedient faith; and that nothing prevents the salvation of the greatest sinner on earth but his own determined depravity and voluntary rejection of the gospel; which rejection involves him in an aggravated condemnation.

VII. Of Grace in Regeneration.—We believe that in order to be saved sinners must be regenerated, or born again; that regeneration consists in giving a holy disposition to the mind; that it is effected in a manner above our comprehension by the power of the Holy Spirit, in connection with divine truth, so as to secure our voluntary obedience to the gospel; and that its proper evidence appears in the holy fruits of repentance, and faith, and newness of life.

VIII. Of Repentance and Faith.—We believe that repentance and faith are sacred duties, and also inseparable graces, wrought in our souls by the regenerating Spirit of God; whereby, being deeply convinced of our guilt, danger, and helplessness, and of the way of salvation by Christ, we turn to God with unfeigned contrition, confession, and supplication for mercy; at the same time heartily receiving the Lord Jesus Christ as our Prophet, Priest, and King, and relying on Him alone as the only and all-sufficient Saviour.

IX. Of God's Purpose of Grace.—We believe that election is the eternal purpose of God, according to which He graciously regenerates, sanctifies, and saves sinners, that being perfectly consistent with the free agency of man, it comprehends all the means in connection with the end; that it is a most glorious display of God's sovereign goodness, being infinitely free, wise, holy, and unchangeable; that it utterly excludes boasting, and promotes humility, love, prayer, praise, trust in God, and active imitation of His free mercy; that it encourages the use of means in the highest degree; that it may be ascertained by its effects in all who truly believe the gospel; that it is the foundation of Christian assurance; and that to ascertain it with regard to ourselves demands and deserves the utmost diligence.

X. Of Sanctification.—We believe that sanctification is the process by which, according to the will of God, we are made partakers of His holiness, that it is a progressive work; that it is begun in regeneration; and that it is carried on in the hearts of believers by the presence and power of the Holy Spirit, the Sealer and Comforter, in the continual use of the appointed means—especially, the

Word of God, self-examination, self-denial, watchfulness, and prayer.

XI. Of the Perseverance of Saints.—We believe that such only are real believers as endure unto the end; that their persevering attachment to Christ is the grand mark which distinguishes them from superficial professors; that a special providence watches over their welfare; and they are kept by the power of God through faith unto salvation.

XII. Of the Harmony of the Law and the Gospel.—We believe that the law of God is the eternal and unchangeable rule of his moral government; that it is holy, just, and good; and that the inability which the Scriptures ascribe to fallen men to fulfill its precepts, arises entirely from their love of sin; to deliver them from which, and to restore them through a mediator to unfeigned obedience to the holy law, is one great end of the gospel, and of the means of grace connected with the establishment of the visible church.

XIII. Of a Gospel Church.—We believe that a visible church of Christ is a congregation of baptized believers, associated by covenant in the faith and fellowship of the gospel; observing the ordinances of Christ; governed by His laws; and exercising the gifts, rights, and privileges invested in them by His Word; that its only scriptural officers are bishops or pastors, and deacons whose qualifications, claims, and duties are defined in the epistles to Timothy and Titus.

XIV. Of Baptism and the Lord's Supper.—We believe that Christian baptism is the immersion in water of a believer, into the name of the Father, and Son, and Holy Ghost; to show forth, in a solemn and beautiful emblem, our faith in the crucified, buried, and risen Saviour, with its effect, in our death to sin and resurrection to a new life; that it is prerequisite to the privileges of a church relation; and to the Lord's Supper, in which the members of the church by the sacred use of bread and wine, are to commemorate together the dying love of Christ; preceded always by solemn self-examination.

XV. Of the Christian Sabbath.—We believe that the first day of the week is the Lord's day, or Christian Sabbath; and is to be kept sacred to religious purposes, by abstaining from all secular labor and sinful recreations; by the devout observance of all the means of grace, both private and public; and by preparation for that rest that remaineth for the people of God.

XVI. Of Civil Government.—We believe that civil government is of divine appointment, for the interests and good order of human society; and that magistrates are to be prayed for, conscientiously honored, and obeyed; except only in things opposed to the will of our Lord Jesus Christ, who is the only Lord of the conscience, and the Prince of the kings of the earth.

XVII. Of the Righteous and the Wicked.—We believe that there is a radical and essential difference between the righteous and the wicked; that such only as through faith are justified in the name of the Lord Jesus, and sanctified by the Spirit of our God, are truly righteous in His esteem; while all such as continue in impenitence and unbelief are in His sight wicked, and under the curse; and this distinction holds among men both in and after death.

XVIII. Of the World to Come.—We believe that the end of this world is approaching; that at the last day, Christ will descend from heaven, and raise the dead from the grave to final retribution; that a solemn separation will then take place; that the wicked will be adjudged to endless punishment, and the righteous to endless joy; and that this judgment will fix forever the final state of men in heaven or hell, on principles of righteousness.

The Philadelphia Confession of Faith

Put forth by the Elders and Brethren of many Congregations of Christians (Baptized upon Profeffion of their Faith) in London and the Country. Adopted by the Baptift Association met at Philadelphia, Sept. 25, 1742. The Sixth Edition. To which are added, Two Articles viz. Of impofition of Hands, and Singing of Pfalms in Publick Worfhip. Also A Short Treatife of Church Difcipline. With the Heart Man believeth unto Righteoufnefs, and with the Mouth Confeffion is made unto Salvation, Rom. 10:20. Search the Scriptures, John 5:39. Philadelphia: Printed by B. Franklin, M,DCC,XLIII.

I. Of the Holy Scriptures.—1. The Holy Scripture is the only sufficient, certain, and infallible rule of all-saving knowledge, faith, and obedience; although the light of nature, and the works of creation and providence do so far manifest the goodness, wisdom, and power of God as to leave men unexcusable; yet are they not sufficient to give that knowledge of God and His will which is necessary unto salvation. Therefore it pleased the Lord at sundry times, and in divers manners, to reveal Himself, and to declare that His will unto His church; and afterward, for the better preserving and propagating of the truth, and for the more sure establishment and comfort of the church against the corruption of the flesh, and the malice of Satan and of the world, to commit the same wholly unto writing; which maketh the Holy Scriptures to be most necessary, those former ways of God's revealing His will unto His people being now ceased.

2. Under the name of Holy Scripture, or the Word of God written, are now contained all the books of the Old and New Testament, which are these:

Of the Old Testament,—Genesis, Exodus, Leviticus, Numbers, Deuteronomy, Joshua, Judges, Ruth, I Samuel, II Samuel, I Kings, II Kings, I Chronicles, II Chronicles, Ezra, Nehemiah, Esther, Job, Psalms, Proverbs, Ecclesiastes, The Song of Songs, Isaiah, Jeremiah, Lamentations, Ezekiel, Daniel, Hosea, Joel, Amos, Obadiah, Jonah, Micah,

Nahum, Habakkuk, Zephaniah, Haggai, Zechariah, Malachi.

Of the New Testament, Matthew, Mark, Luke, John, The Acts of the Apostles, Paul's Epistle to the Romans, I Corinthians, II Corinthians, Galatians, Ephesians, Philippians, Colossians, I Thessalonians, II Thessalonians, I Timothy, II Timothy, to Titus, to Philemon, the Epistle to the Hebrews, the Epistle of James, the first and second Epistles of Peter, the first, second, and third Epistles of John, the Epistle of Jude, the Revelation. All which are given by the inspiration of God to be the rule of faith and life.

3. The books commonly called Apocrypha, not being of divine inspiration, are no part of the canon (or rule) of the Scripture, and therefore are of no authority to the church of God, nor to be any otherwise approved, or made use of, than other human writings.

4. The authority of the Holy Scriptures, for which it ought to be believed, dependeth not upon the testimony of any man or church, but wholly upon God (who is Truth itself), the author thereof; therefore it is to be received, because it is the Word of God.

5. We may be moved and induced by the testimony of the church of God to an high and reverent esteem of the Holy Scriptures; and the heavenliness of the matter, the efficacy of the doctrine, and the majesty of the style, the consent of all the parts, the scope of the whole (which is to give all glory to God), the full discovery it makes of the only way of man's salvation, and many other incomparable excellencies, and entire perfections thereof, are arguments whereby it doth abundantly evidence itself to be the Word of God; yet, notwithstanding our full persuasion, and assurance of the infallible truth, and divine authority thereof, is from the inward work of the Holy Spirit, bearing witness by and with the Word in our hearts.

6. The whole counsel of God concerning all things necessary for his own glory, man's salvation, faith and life, is either expressly set down, or necessarily contained in the Holy Scripture; unto which nothing is at any time to be added, whether by new revelation of the Spirit or traditions of men.

Nevertheless, we acknowledge the inward illumination of the Spirit of God to be necessary for the saving understanding of such things as are revealed in the Word, and that there are some circumstances concerning the worship of God and government of the church common to human actions and societies, which are to be ordered by the light of nature and Christian prudence, according to the general rules of the Word, which are always to be observed.

7. All things in Scripture are not alike plain in themselves, nor alike clear unto all, yet those things which are necessary to be known, believed, and observed for salvation, are so clearly propounded and opened in some place of Scripture or other, that not only the learned, but the unlearned, in a due use of ordinary means, may attain to a sufficient understanding of them.

8. The Old Testament in Hebrew (which was the native language of the people of God of old), and the New Testament in Greek, which (at the time of writing it) was most generally known to the nations, being immediately inspired by God, and, by his singular care and providence, kept pure in all ages, are thereafter authentical; so as in all controversies of religion the church is finally to appeal unto them. But because these original tongues are not known to all the people of God who have a right unto, and interest in, the Scriptures, and are commanded, in the fear of God, to read and search them, therefore they are to be translated into the vulgar language of every nation unto which they come, that the Word of God, dwelling plentifully in all, they may worship Him in an acceptable manner, and, through patience and comfort of the Scriptures, may hope.

9. The infallible rule of interpretation of Scripture is the Scripture itself: and therefore, when there is a question about the true and full sense of any Scripture (which is not manifold, but one), it must be searched by other places that speak more clearly.

10. The supreme judge by which all controversies of religion are to be determined, and all decrees of councils, opinions of ancient writers, doctrines of men, and private spirits are to be examined, and in whose sentence we are

to rest, can be no other but the Holy Scripture delivered by the Spirit, into which Scripture, so delivered, our faith is finally resolved.

II. Of God and of the Holy Trinity.—1. The Lord our God is but one only living and true God; whose subsistence is in and of Himself, infinite in being and perfection, whose essence cannot be comprehended by any but Himself; a most pure Spirit, invisible, without body, parts, or passions, who only hath immortality, dwelling in the light which no man can approach unto, who is immutable, immense, eternal, incomprehensible, almighty, every way infinite, most holy, most wise, most free, most absolute, working all things according to the counsel of His own immutable and most righteous will for His own glory, most loving, gracious, merciful, long-suffering, abundant in goodness and truth, forgiving iniquity, transgression, and sin, the rewarder of them that diligently seek Him, and withal most just, and terrible in His judgments, hating all sin, and will by no means clear the guilty.

2. God having all life, glory, goodness, blessedness, in and of Himself, is alone in, and unto Himself all-sufficient, not standing in need of any creature which He hath made, not deriving any glory from them, but only manifesting His own glory in, by, unto, and upon them, He is the alone fountain of all being, of Whom, through Whom, and to Whom are all things, and He hath most sovereign dominion over all creatures, to do by them, for them, or upon them, whatsoever Himself pleaseth; in His sight all things are open and manifest, His knowledge is infinite, infallible, and independent upon the creature, so as nothing is to Him contingent or uncertain; He is most holy in all His counsels, in all His works, and in all His commands; to Him is due from angels and men whatsoever worship, service, or obedience, as creatures they owe unto the Creator, and whatever He is further pleased to require of them.

3. In this Divine and Infinite Being there are three subsistences, the Father, the Word (or Son), and Holy

Spirit, of one substance, power, and eternity, each having the whole divine essence, yet the essence undivided; the Father is of none neither begotten, nor proceeding; the Son is eternally begotten of the Father; the Holy Spirit proceeding from the Father and the Son, all infinite, without beginning, therefore but one God, who is not to be divided in nature and being, but distinguished by several peculiar relative properties and personal relations; which doctrine of the Trinity is the foundation of all our communion with God, and our comfortable dependence on Him.

III. Of God's Decree.—1. God hath decreed in Himself from all eternity, by the most wise and holy counsel of His own will, freely and unchangeably, all things whatsoever comes to pass; yet so as thereby is God neither the author of sin, nor hath fellowship with any therein, nor is violence offered to the will of the creature, nor yet is the liberty of contingency of second causes taken away, but rather established, in which appears His wisdom in disposing all things, and power and faithfulness in accomplishing His decree.

2. Although God knoweth whatsoever may or can come to pass upon all supposed conditions, yet hath He not decreed anything because He foresaw it as future, or as that which would come to pass upon such conditions.

3. By the decree of God, for the manifestation of His glory, some men and angels are predestinated or foreordained to eternal life, through Jesus Christ, to the praise of His glorious grace; others being left to act in their sin to their just condemnation, to the praise of His glorious justice.

4. These angels and men thus predestinated and foreordained are particularly and unchangeably designed; and their number so certain and definite, that it cannot be either increased or diminished.

5. Those of mankind that are predestinated to life, God, before the foundation of the world was laid, according to His eternal and immutable purpose, and the secret counsel and good pleasure of his will, hath chosen in Christ unto

everlasting glory, out of His mere free grace and love; without any other thing in the creature as a condition or cause moving Him thereunto.

6. As God hath appointed the elect unto glory, so He hath by the eternal and most free purpose of His will foreordained all the means thereunto, wherefore they who are elected, being fallen in Adam, are redeemed by Christ, are effectually called unto faith in Christ, by His Spirit working in due season, are justified, adopted, sanctified, and kept by His power through faith unto salvation; neither are any other redeemed by Christ, or effectually called, justified, adopted, sanctified, and saved, but the elect only.

7. The doctrine of His high mystery of predestination is to be handled with special prudence and care; that men attending the will of God revealed in His Word, and yielding obedience thereunto, may, from the certainty of their effectual vocation, be assured of their eternal election; so shall this doctrine afford matter of praise, reverence, and admiration of God, and of humility, diligence, and abundant consolation to all that sincerely obey the gospel.

IV. Of Creation.—1. In the beginning it pleased God the Father, Son and Holy Spirit, for the manifestation of the glory of His eternal power, wisdom, and goodness, to create or make the world, and all things therein, whether visible or invisible, in the space of six days, and all very good.

2. After God had made all other creatures He created man, male and female, with reasonable and immortal souls, rendering them fit unto that life to God for which they were created, being made after the image of God, in knowledge, righteousness, and true holiness; having the law of God written in their hearts, and power to fulfill it; and yet under a possibility of transgressing, being left to the liberty of their own will, which was subject to change.

3. Besides the law written in their hearts, they received a command not to eat of the tree of knowledge of good and evil; which, whilst they kept, they were happy

in their communion with God, and had dominion over the creatures.

V. Of Divine Providence.—1. God, the good creator of all things, in His infinite power and wisdom, doth uphold, direct, dispose, and govern all creatures and things, from the greatest even to the least, by His most wise and holy providence, to the end for which they were created, according unto His infallible foreknowledge, and the free and immutable counsel of His own will, to the praise of the glory of His wisdom, power, justice, infinite goodness, and mercy.

2. Although in relation to the foreknowledge and decree of God, the first cause, all things come to pass immutably and infallibly; so that there is not anything befalls any by chance, or without His providence; yet, by the same providence, He ordered them to fall out according to the nature of second causes, either necessarily, freely, or contingently.

3. God in His ordinary providence maketh use of means; yet is free to work without, above, and against them, at His pleasure.

4. The almighty power, unsearchable wisdom, and infinite goodness of God so far manifest themselves in His providence, that His determinate counsel extendeth itself even to the first fall, and all other sinful actions both of angels and men (and that not by a bare permission), which also He most wisely and powerfully boundeth, and otherwise ordereth and governeth in a manifold dispensation, to His most holy ends; yet so as the sinfulness of their acts proceedeth only from the creatures, and not from God, who, being most holy and righteous, neither is nor can be the author or approver of sin.

5. The most wise, righteous, and gracious God doth oftentimes leave for a season His own children to manifold temptations and the corruptions of their own hearts, to chastise them for their former sins or to discover unto them the hidden strength of corruption and deceitfulness of their hearts, that they may be humbled, and to raise

them to a more close and constant dependence for their support upon Himself, and to make them more watchful against all future occasions of sin, and for other just and holy ends.

So that whatsoever befalls any of His elect is by His appointment, for His glory, and their good.

6. As for those wicked and ungodly men, whom God as a righteous judge, for former sin, doth blind and harden; from them He not only withholdeth His grace, whereby they might have been enlightened in their understanding and wrought upon in their hearts, but sometimes also withdraweth the gifts which they had, and exposeth them to such objects as their corruptions make occasion of sin; and withal gives them over to their own lusts and temptations of the world, and the power of Satan, whereby it comes to pass that they harden themselves, even under those means which God useth for the softening of others.

7. As the providence of God doth in general reach to all creatures, so, after a more special manner, it taketh care of His church, and disposeth of all things to the good thereof.

VI. Of the Fall of Man, Sin, and the Punishment Thereof.—1. Although God created man upright and perfect, and gave him a righteous law which had been unto life, had he kept it, and threatened death upon the breach thereof; yet he did not long abide in this honor. Satan, using the subtility of the serpent to seduce Eve, then by her seducing Adam, who, without any compulsion, did willfully transgress the law of their creation and the command given unto them in eating the forbidden fruit; which God was pleased according to His wise and holy counsel to permit, having purposed to order it to His own glory.

2. Our first parents, by this sin, fell from their original righteousness and communion with God, and we in them, whereby death came upon all; all becoming dead in sin and wholly defiled in all the faculties and parts of soul and body.

3. They being the root, and, by God's appointment, standing in the room and stead of all mankind; the guilt of the sin was imputed, and corrupted nature conveyed to all their posterity, descending from them by ordinary generation, being now conceived in sin, and by nature children of wrath, the servants of sin, the subjects of death, and all other miseries, spiritual, temporal, and eternal, unless the Lord Jesus set them free.

4. From this original corruption, whereby we are utterly indisposed, disabled, and made opposite to all good, and wholly inclined to all evil, do proceed all actual transgressions.

5. This corruption of nature, during this life, doth remain in those that are regenerated; and, although it be through Christ pardoned and mortified, yet both itself and the first motions, thereof are truly and properly sin.

VII. Of God's Covenant.—1. The distance between God and the creature is so great, that although reasonable creatures do owe obedience unto Him as their Creator, yet they could never have attained the reward of life but by some voluntary condescension on God's part, which He hath been pleased to express by way of covenant.

2. Moreover, man having brought himself under the curse of the law by his fall, it pleased the Lord to make a covenant of grace, wherein He freely offereth unto sinners life and salvation by Jesus Christ, requiring of them faith in Him, that they might be saved; and promising to give unto all those that are ordained unto eternal life His holy Spirit, to make them willing and able to believe.

3. This covenant is revealed in the gospel, first of all to Adam in the promise of salvation by the seed of the woman, and afterward by farther steps, until the full discovery thereof was completed in the New Testament; and it is founded in that eternal covenant transaction that was between the Father and the Son about the redemption of the elect; and it is alone by the grace of this covenant that all of the posterity of fallen Adam, that ever were saved, did obtain life and blessed immortality; man being

now utterly incapable of acceptance with God upon those terms on which Adam stood in his state of innocency.

VIII. Of Christ the Mediator.—1. It pleased God, in His eternal purpose, to choose and ordain the Lord Jesus, His only and begotten Son, according to the covenant made between them both, to be the Mediator between God and man; the prophet, priest, and king; head and Saviour of His church, the heir of all things, and judge of the world; unto Whom He did from all eternity give a people to be His seed, and to be by Him in time redeemed, called, justified, sanctified, and glorified.

2. The Son of God, the second person in the Holy Trinity, being very and eternal God, the brightness of the Father's glory, of one substance, and equal with Him; who made the world, who upholdeth and governeth all things He hath made; did, when the fullness of time was come, take upon Him man's nature, with all the essential properties and common infirmities thereof, yet without sin; being conceived by the Holy Spirit in the womb of the Virgin Mary, the Holy Spirit coming down upon her, and the power of the Most High overshadowing her, and so was made of a woman, of the tribe of Judah, of the seed of Abraham and David, according to the Scriptures: so that two whole, perfect, and distinct natures were inseparably joined together in one person, without conversion, composition, or confusion; which person is very God and very man, yet one Christ, the only Mediator between God and man.

3. The Lord Jesus in His human nature thus united to the divine, in the person of the Son, was sanctified and anointed with the Holy Spirit above measure; having in Him all the treasures of wisdom and knowledge; in whom it pleased the Father that all fullness should dwell; to the end that, being holy, harmless, undefiled, and full of grace and truth, He might be thoroughly furnished to execute the office of a Mediator and Surety; which office He took not upon Himself, but was thereunto called by His Father; who also put all power and judgment in His hand, and gave Him commandment to execute the same.

4. This office the Lord Jesus did most willingly undertake, which that He might discharge, He was made under the law, and did perfectly fulfill it, and underwent the punishment due to us, which we should have borne and suffered, being made sin and a curse for us; enduring most grievous sorrows in His soul and most painful sufferings in His body; was crucified and died, and remained in the state of the dead, yet saw no corruption; on the third day He arose from the dead, with the same body in which He suffered, with which He also ascended into heaven; and there sitteth on the right hand of His Father making intercession; and shall return to judge men and angels at the end of the world.

5. The Lord Jesus, by His perfect obedience and sacrifice of Himself, which He through the eternal Spirit once offered up unto God, hath fully satisfied the justice of God, procured reconciliation, and purchased an everlasting inheritance in the kingdom of heaven for all those whom the Father hath given unto Him.

6. Although the price of redemption was not actually paid by Christ till after His incarnation, yet the virtue, efficacy, and benefit thereof was communicated to the elect in all ages successively from the beginning of the world, in and by those promises, types, and sacrifices wherein He was revealed and signified to be the seed of the woman which should bruise the serpent's head; and the Lamb slain from the foundation of the world, being the same yesterday, and today, and forever.

7. Christ, in the work of mediation, acteth according to both natures, by each nature doing that which is proper to itself; yet by reason of the unity of the person, that which is proper to one nature is sometimes in Scripture attributed to the person denominated by the other nature.

8. To all those for whom Christ hath obtained eternal redemption He doth certainly and effectually apply and communicate the same; making intercession for them; uniting them to Himself by His Spirit; revealing unto them, in and by the Word, the mystery of salvation; persuading them to believe and obey; governing their

hearts by His Word and Spirit, and overcoming all their enemies by His Almighty power and wisdom, in such manner and ways as are most consonant to His wonderful and unsearchable dispensation; and all of free and absolute grace, without any condition foreseen in them to procure it.

9. This office of Mediator between God and man is proper only to Christ, who is the Prophet, Priest, and King of the Church of God; and may not be either in whole, or any part thereof, transferred from Him to any other.

10. This number and order of offices is necessary; for, in respect of our ignorance, we stand in need of His prophetical office; and, in respect of our alienation from God and imperfection of the best of our services, we need His priestly office to reconcile us and present us acceptable unto God; and, in respect of our averseness and utter inability to return to God, and for our rescue and security from our spiritual adversaries, we need His kingly office to convince, subdue, draw, uphold, deliver, and preserve us to His heavenly kingdom.

IX. Of Free Will.—1. God has indued the will of man with that natural liberty and power of acting upon choice, that it is neither forced nor, by any necessity of nature, determined to do good or evil.

2. Man, in his state of innocency, had freedom and power to will and to do that which was good and well pleasing to God; but yet was mutable, so that he might fall from it.

3. Man, by his fall into a state of sin, hath wholly lost all ability of will to any spiritual good accompanying salvation; so as a natural man, being altogether averse from that good and dead in sin, is not able, by his own strength, to convert himself or to prepare himself thereunto.

4. When God converts a sinner, and translates him into the state of grace, He freeth him from his natural bondage under sin, and, by His grace alone, enables him freely to will and do that which is spiritually good; yet

so as that, by reason of his remaining corruptions, he doth not perfectly nor only will that which is good, but doth also will that which is evil.

5. The will of man is made perfectly and immutably free to good alone in the state of glory only.

X. Of Effectual Calling.—1. Those whom God had predestinated unto life, He is pleased, in His appointed and accepted time, effectually to call by His Word and Spirit out of that state of sin and death in which they are by nature to grace of salvation by Jesus Christ; enlightening their minds spiritually and savingly to understand the things of God; taking away their heart of stone and giving unto them an heart of flesh; renewing their wills, and, by His almighty power, determining them to that which is good, and effectually drawing them to Jesus Christ; yet so as they come most freely, being made willing by His grace.

2. This effectual call is of God's free and special grace alone, not from anything at all foreseen in man, nor from any power or agency in the creature co-working with His special grace; the creature being wholly passive therein, being dead in sins and trespasses, until, being quickened and renewed by the Holy Spirit, he is thereby enabled to answer this call, and to embrace the grace offered and conveyed in it, and that by no less power than that which raised up Christ from the dead.

3. Elect infants, dying in infancy, are regenerated and saved by Christ through the Spirit, who worketh when, and where, and how He pleaseth; so also are all other elect persons who are incapable of being outwardly called by the ministry of the Word.

4. Others not elected, although they may be called by the ministry of the Word, and may have some common operations of the Spirit, yet not being effectually drawn by the Father, they neither will nor can truly come to Christ, and therefore cannot be saved; much less can men that receive not the Christian religion be saved, be they ever so diligent to frame their lives according to the light of nature and the law of that religion they do profess.

XI. Of Justification.—1. Those whom God effectually calleth He also freely justifieth, not by infusing righteousness into them, but by pardoning their sins, and by accounting and accepting their persons as righteous; not for anything wrought in them or done by them, but for Christ's sake alone; not by imputing faith itself, the act of believing, or any other evangelical obedience to them, as their righteousness, but by imputing Christ's active obedience unto the whole law, and passive obedience in His death, for their whole and sole righteousness; they receiving and resting on Him and His righteousness by faith, which they have not of themselves: it is the gift of God.

2. Faith thus receiving and resting on Christ and His righteousness, is the alone instrument of justification; yet it is not alone in the person justified, but is ever accompanied with all other saving graces, and is no dead faith, but worketh by love.

3. Christ, by His obedience and death, did fully discharge the debt of all those that are justified; and did, by the sacrifice of Himself, in the blood of His cross, undergoing in their stead the penalty due unto them, make a proper, real, and full satisfaction to God's justice in their behalf; yet, inasmuch as He was given by the Father for them, and His obedience and satisfaction accepted in their stead, and both freely, not for anything in them, their justification is only of free grace, that both the exact justice and rich grace of God might be glorified in the justification of sinners.

4. God did, from all eternity, decree to justify all the elect, and Christ did, in the fullness of time, die for their sins, and rise again for their justification; nevertheless, they are not justified personally until the Holy Spirit doth, in due time, actually apply Christ unto them.

5. God doth continue to forgive the sins of those that are justified; and, although they can never fall from the state of justification, yet they may, by their sins, fall under God's fatherly displeasure; and, in that condition, they have not usually the light of His countenance restored unto them until they humble themselves, confess their sins,

beg pardon, and renew their faith and repentance.

6. The justification of believers under the Old Testament was, in all these respects, one and the same with the justification of believers under the New Testament.

XII. Of Adoption.—1. All those that are justified, God vouch-safed, in and for the sake of His only Son, Jesus Christ, to make partakers of the grace of adoption, by which they are taken into the number, and enjoy the liberties and privileges, of children of God; have His name put upon them; receive the spirit of adoption; have access to the throne of grace with boldness; are enabled to cry Abba, Father; are pitied, protected, provided for, and chastened by Him as a father; yet never cast off, but sealed to the day of redemption, and inherit the promises as heirs of everlasting salvation.

XIII. Of Sanctification.—1. They who are united to Christ, effectually called, and regenerated, having a new heart and a new spirit created in them, through the virtue of Christ's death and resurrection, are also further sanctified, really and personally, through the same virtue, by His Word and Spirit dwelling in them. The dominion of the whole body of sin is destroyed, and the several lusts thereof are more and more weakened and mortified; and they more and more quickened and strengthened in all saving graces, to the practice of all true holiness, without which no man shall see the Lord.

2. This sanctification is throughout, in the whole man, yet imperfect in this life; there abideth still some remnants of corruption in every part, whence ariseth a continual and irreconcilable war: the flesh lusting against the spirit and the spirit against the flesh.

3. In which war, although the remaining corruption for a time may much prevail, yet through the continual supply of strength from the sanctifying Spirit of Christ, the regenerate part doth overcome; and so the saints grow in grace, perfecting holiness in the fear of God, pressing after an heavenly life in evangelical obedience to all the

commands which Christ, as Head and King, in His Word hath prescribed to them.

XIV. Of Saving Faith.—1. The grace of faith, whereby the elect are enabled to believe to the saving of their souls, is the work of the Spirit of Christ in their hearts, and is ordinarily wrought by the ministry of the Word, by which also, and by the administration of Baptism, and the Lord's Supper, prayer, and other means appointed of God it is increased and strengthened.

2. By this faith, a Christian believeth to be true whatsoever is revealed in the Word for the authority of God Himself; and also apprehendeth an excellency therein above all other writings and all things in the world, as it bears forth the glory of God in His attributes, the excellency of Christ in His nature and offices, and the power and fullness of the Holy Spirit in His workings and operations; and so is enabled to cast his soul upon the truth thus believed, and also acted differently upon that which each particular passage thereof containeth; yielding obedience to the commands, trembling at the threatenings, and embracing the promises of God for this life and that which is to come; but the principal acts of saving faith hath immediate relation to Christ, accepting, receiving, and resting upon Him alone for justification, sanctification, and eternal life, by virtue of the covenant of grace.

3. This faith, although it be different in degrees, and may be weak or strong, yet it is in the least degree of it different in the kind or nature of it (as is all other saving grace) from the faith and common grace of temporary believers; and therefore, though it may be many times assailed and weakened, yet it gets the victory, growing up in many to the attainment of a full assurance through Christ, Who is both the author and finisher of our faith.

XV. Of Repentance Unto Life and Salvation.—1. Such of the elect as are converted at riper years, having sometimes lived in the state of nature, and therein served divers lusts and pleasure, God, in their effectual calling, giveth them repentance unto life.

2. Whereas there is none that doeth good and sinneth not, and the best of men may, through the power and deceitfulness of their corruption dwelling in them, with the prevalency of temptation, fall into greater sins and provocations, God hath, in the covenant of grace, mercifully provided that believers so sinning and falling be renewed through repentance unto salvation.

3. This saving repentance is an evangelical grace, whereby a person, being by the Holy Spirit made sensible of the manifold evils of his sin, doth, by faith in Christ, humble himself for it with godly sorrow, detestation of it, and self-abhorrency, praying for pardon and strength of grace, with a purpose of endeavor, by supplies of the Spirit, to walk before God unto all well-pleasing in all things.

4. As repentance is to be continued through the whole course of our lives, upon the account of the body of death and the motions thereof, so it is every man's duty to repent of his particular known sins, particularly.

5. Such is the provision which God hath made, through Christ in the covenant of grace, for the preservation of believers unto salvation, that, although there is no sin so small but it deserves damnation, yet there is no sin so great that it shall bring damnation on them that repent; which makes the constant preaching of repentance necessary.

XVI. Of Good Works.—1. Good works are only such as God hath commanded in his Holy Word, and not such as, without the warrant thereof, are devised by men out of blind zeal or upon any pretense of good intentions.

2. These good works, done in obedience to God's commandments, are the fruits and evidences of a true and lively faith; and by them believers manifest their thankfulness, strengthen their assurance, edify their brethren, adorn the profession of the gospel, stop the mouths of the adversaries, and glorify God, whose workmanship they are, created in Christ Jesus thereunto, that, having

their fruit unto holiness, they may have the end, eternal life.

3. Their ability to do good works is not at all of themselves, but wholly from the Spirit of Christ; and that they may be enabled thereunto, besides the graces they have already received, there is necessary an actual influence of the same Holy Spirit to work in them to will and to do his good pleasure; yet are they not hereupon to grow negligent, as if they were not bound to perform any duty, unless upon a special motion of the Spirit, but they ought to be diligent in stirring up the grace of God that is in them.

4. They who in their obedience attain to the greatest height which is possible in this life, are so far from being able to supererogate and to do more than God requires, as that they fall short of much which, in duty, they are bound to do.

5. We cannot, by our best works, merit pardon of sin or eternal life at the hand of God, by reason of the great disproportion that is between them and the glory to come, and the infinite distance that is between us and God, whom by them we can never profit nor satisfy for the debt of our former sins; but when we have done all we can, we have done but our duty and are unprofitable servants; and because, as they are good, they proceed from His Spirit, and, as they are wrought by us, they are defiled and mixed with so much weakness and imperfection, that they cannot endure the severity of God's judgment.

6. Yet notwithstanding the persons of believers being accepted through Christ, their good works also are accepted in Him, not as though they were in this life wholly unblamable and unreprovable in God's sight, but that He, looking upon them in His Son, is pleased to accept and reward that which is sincere, although accompanied with many weaknesses and imperfections.

7. Works done by ungenerate men, although for the matter of them they may be things which God commands, and of good use both to themselves and others; yet, because they proceed not from a heart purified by faith, nor are done in a right manner according to the Word, nor to a

right end, the glory of God, they are sinful and cannot please God, nor make a man meet to receive grace from God; and yet their neglect of them is more sinful and displeasing to God.

XVII. Of the Perseverance of the Saints.—1. Those whom God hath accepted in the Beloved, effectually called and sanctified by His Spirit and given the precious faith of His elect unto, can neither totally nor finally fall from the state of grace, but shall certainly persevere therein to the end and be eternally saved, seeing the gifts and callings of God are without repentance (whence He still begets and nourisheth in them faith, repentance, love, joy, hope, and all the graces of the Spirit to immortality), and, though many storms and floods arise and beat against them, yet they shall never be able to take them off that foundation and rock which by faith they are fastened upon; notwithstanding, through unbelief and the temptations of Satan, the sensible sight of the light and love of God may, for a time, be clouded and obscured from them, yet it is still the same, and they shall be sure to be kept by the power of God unto salvation, where they shall enjoy their purchased possession, they being engraven upon the palm of His hands, and their names having been written in the book of Life from all eternity.

2. This perseverance of the saints depends not upon their own free will, but upon the immutability of the decree of election, flowing from the free and unchangeable love of God, the Father, upon the efficacy of the merit and intercession of Jesus Christ and union with Him, the oath of God, the abiding of His Spirit, and the seed of God within them, and the nature of the covenant of grace; from all which ariseth also the certainty and infallibility thereof.

3. And though they may, through the temptation of Satan and of the world, the prevalency of corruption remaining in them, and the neglect of means of their preservation, fall into grievous sins, and for a time continue therein, whereby they incur God's displeasure and grieve His Holy

Spirit, come to have their graces and comforts impaired, have their hearts hardened and their consciences wounded, hurt and scandalize others, and bring temporal judgments upon themselves, yet they shall renew their repentance and be preserved, through faith in Christ Jesus, to the end.

XVIII. Of the Assurance of Grace and Salvation.—1. Although temporary believers and other unregenerate men may vainly deceive themselves with false hopes and carnal presumptions of being in the favor of God and state of salvation, which hope of theirs shall perish; yet such as truly believe in the Lord Jesus, and love Him in sincerity, endeavoring to walk in all good conscience before Him, may, in this life, be certainly assured that they are in the state of grace, and may rejoice in the hope of the glory of God, which hope shall never make them ashamed.

2. This certainly is not a bare conjectural and probable persuasion, grounded upon a fallible hope, but an infallible assurance of faith, founded on the blood and righteousness of Christ, revealed in the gospel; and also upon the inward evidence of those graces of the Spirit unto which promises are made, and on the testimony of the Spirit of adoption, witnessing with our spirits that we are the children of God, and, as a fruit thereof, keeping the heart both humble and holy.

3. This infallible assurance doth not so belong to the essence of faith but that a true believer may wait long, and conflict with many difficulties, before he be partaker of it; yet being enabled by the Spirit to know the things which are freely given him of God, he may, without extraordinary revelation, in the right use of means, attain thereunto; and therefore it is the duty of every one to give all diligence to make his calling and election sure, that thereby his heart may be enlarged in peace and joy in the Holy Spirit, in love and thankfulness to God, and in strength and cheerfulness in the duties of obedience, the proper fruits of this assurance: so far is it from inclining men to looseness.

4. True believers may have the assurance of their

salvation divers ways shaken, diminished, and intermitted; as by negligence in preserving of it, by falling into some special sin, which woundeth the conscience and grieveth the Spirit; by some sudden or vehement temptation; by God's withdrawing the light of his countenance and suffering even such as fear him to walk in darkness and to have no light; yet are they never destitute of the seed of God and life of faith, that love of Christ and the brethren, that sincerity of heart, and conscience of duty, out of which, by the operation of the Spirit, this assurance may in due time be revived, and by the which, in the mean time, they are preserved from utter despair.

XIX. Of the Law of God.—1. God gave to Adam a law of universal obedience written in his heart, and a particular precept of not eating the fruit of the tree of knowledge of good and evil; by which He bound him and all his posterity to personal, entire, exact, and perpetual obedience, promised life upon the fulfilling, and threatened death upon the breach of it, and indued him with power and ability to keep it.

2. The same law that was first written in the heart of man continued to be a perfect rule of righteousness after the fall, and delivered by God upon Mount Sinai, in ten commandments, and written in two tables, the four first containing our duty towards God, and the other six our duty to man.

3. Besides this law, commonly called moral, God was pleased to give to the people of Israel ceremonial laws, containing several typical ordinances, partly of worship, prefiguring Christ, His graces, actions, sufferings, and benefits, and partly holding forth divers instructions of moral duties, all which ceremonial laws, being appointed only to the time of reformation, are by Jesus Christ, the true Messiah and only Lawgiver, Who was furnished with power from the Father for that end, abrogated and taken away.

4. To them also He gave sundry judicial laws, which expired together with the state of that people, not obliging

any now by virtue of that institution—their general equity only being of moral use.

5. The moral law doth forever bind all, as well justified persons as others, to the obedience thereof, and that not only in regard to the matter contained in it, but also in respect of the authority of God, the Creator, who gave it; neither doth Christ in the gospel any way dissolve, but much strengthen this obligation.

6. Although true believers be not under the law, as a covenant of works, to be thereby justified or condemned, yet it is of great use to them, as well as to others, in that, as a rule of life, informing them of the will of God and their duty, it directs and binds them to walk accordingly; discovering also the sinful pollutions of their natures, hearts, and lives, so as, examining themselves thereby, they may come to further conviction of, humiliation for, and hatred against sin, together with a clearer sight of the need they have of Christ and the perfection of His obedience: it is likewise of use to the regenerate to restrain their corruptions, in that it forbids sin, and the threatenings of it serve to show what even their sins deserve, and what afflictions in this life they may expect for them, although freed from the curse and unallayed rigor thereof. These promises of it likewise show that God's approbation of obedience, and what blessings they may expect upon the performance thereof, though not as due to them by the law as a covenant of works; so as man's doing good and refraining from evil, because the law encourageth to the one, and deterreth from the other, is no evidence of his being under the law and not under grace.

7. Neither are the forementioned uses of the law contrary to the grace of the gospel, but do sweetly comply with it, the Spirit of Christ subduing and enabling the will of man to do that freely and cheerfully, which the will of God, revealed in the law, requireth to be done.

XX. Of the Gospel and the Extent of the Grace Thereof.—1. The covenant of works being broken by sin, and made unprofitable unto life, God was pleased to give forth the promise of Christ, the seed of the woman, as the means of calling the elect, and begetting in them faith and repentance; in this promise, the gospel, as to the substance of it, was revealed, and therein effectual for the conversion and salvation of sinners.

2. This promise of Christ, and salvation by Him, is revealed only by the Word of God; neither do the works of creation or providence, with the light of nature, make discovery of Christ or of grace by Him, so much as in a general or obscure way, much less that men, destitute of the revelation of Him by the promise or gospel, should be enabled thereby to attain saving faith or repentance.

3. The revelation of the gospel unto sinners, made in divers times and by sundry parts, with the addition of promises and precepts, for the obedience required therein, as to the nations and persons to whom it is granted, is merely of the sovereign will and good pleasure of God, not being annexed by virtue of any promise to the due improvement of men's natural abilities, by virtue of common light received without it, which none ever did make or can so do; and, therefore, in all ages the preaching of the gospel has been granted unto persons and nations, as to the extending or limiting of it, in great variety, according to the counsel of the will of God.

4. Although the gospel be the only outward means of revealing Christ and saving grace, and is, as such, abundantly sufficient thereunto; yet that men, who are dead in trespasses, may be born again, quickened, or regenerated, there is, moreover, necessary an effectual, insuperable work of the Holy Spirit upon the whole soul for the producing in them a new spiritual life, without which no other means will effect their conversion unto God.

XXI. Of Christian Liberty and Liberty of Conscience.—1. The liberty which Christ hath purchased for believers under the gospel consists in their freedom from the guilt of sin, the condemning wrath of God, and rigor and curse of the law, and in their being delivered from this present evil world, bondage to Satan, and dominion of sin, from the evil of afflictions, the fear and sting of death, the victory of the grave, and everlasting damnation; as also in their free access to God, and their yielding obedience unto Him, not out of slavish fear, but a childlike love and willing mind.

All which were common also to believers under the law for the substance of them; but, under the New Testament, the liberty of Christians is further enlarged in their freedom from the yoke of the ceremonial law, to which the Jewish church was subjected, and in greater boldness of access to the throne of grace, and in fuller communications of the free Spirit of God, than believers under the law did ordinarily partake of.

2. God alone is Lord of the conscience, and hath left it free from the doctrines and commandments of men, which are in anything contrary to his Word or not contained in it. So that, to believe such doctrines, or to obey such commands, out of conscience, is to betray true liberty of conscience; and the requiring of an implicit faith and absolute and blind obedience is to destroy liberty of conscience and reason also.

3. They who, upon pretense of Christian liberty, do practice any sin, or cherish any sinful lust, as they do thereby pervert the main design of the grace of the gospel to their own destruction, so they wholly destroy the end of Christian liberty; which is, that, being delivered out of the hands of all our enemies, we might serve the Lord without fear, in holiness and righteousness before him all the days of our lives.

XXII. Of Religious Worship and the Sabbath Day.— 1. The light of nature shows that there is a God who hath lordship and sovereignty over all; is just, good, and doeth good unto all; and is therefore to be feared, loved, praised, called upon, trusted in and served, with all the heart and all the soul, and with all the might. But the acceptable way of worshiping the true God is instituted by Himself, and so limited by His own revealed will that He may not be worshiped according to the imaginations and devices of men, or the suggestions of Satan, under any visible representations, or any other way not prescribed in the Holy Scriptures.

2. Religious worship is to be given to God, the Father, Son, and Holy Spirit, and to Him alone; not to angels, saints, or any other creatures; and, since the fall, not without a Mediator, nor in the mediation of any other but Christ alone.

3. Prayer and thankfulness being one special part of natural worship, is by God required of all men. But that it may be accepted, it is to be made in the name of the Son, by the help of the Spirit, according to His will; with understanding, reverence, humility, fervency, faith, love, and perseverance, and, with others, in a known tongue.

4. Prayer is to be made for things lawful, and for all sorts of men living, or that shall live hereafter; but not for the dead, nor for those of whom it may be known that they have sinned the sin unto death.

5. The reading of the Scriptures, preaching and hearing the Word of God, teaching and admonishing one another in psalms, hymns, and spiritual songs, singing with grace in our hearts to the Lord, as also the administration of baptism and the Lord's Supper, are all parts of religious worship of God, to be performed in obedience to Him with understanding, faith, reverence, and godly fear; moreover, solemn humiliation, with fastings and thanksgiving, upon special occasions, ought to be used in a holy and religious manner.

6. Neither prayer nor any other part of religious worship is now, under the gospel, tied unto or made more acceptable by any place in which it is performed or towards which it is directed; but God is to be worshiped everywhere in spirit and in truth; as in private families daily and in secret, each one by himself, so more solemnly in the public assemblies, which are not carelessly nor willfully to be neglected or forsaken, when God, by His Word or providence, calleth thereunto.

7. As it is the law of nature that in general a proportion of time, by God's appointment, be set apart for the

worship of God, so, by His Word, in a positive, moral, and perpetual commandment, binding all men in all ages, He hath particularly appointed one day in seven for a Sabbath to be kept holy unto Him, which, from the beginning of the world to the resurrection of Christ, was the last day of the week, and, from the resurrection of Christ, was changed into the first day of the week, which is called the Lord's day; and is to be continued to the end of the world as the Christian Sabbath, the observation of the last day of the week being abolished.

8. The Sabbath is then kept holy unto the Lord when men, after a due preparing of their hearts and ordering their common affairs aforehand, do not only observe a holy rest all the day from their works, words, and thoughts about their worldly employment and recreations, but also are taken up the whole time in public and private exercises of His worship, and in the duties of necessity and mercy.

XXIII. Of Singing of Psalms.—1. We believe that singing the praises of God is a holy ordinance of Christ, and not a part of natural religion or a moral duty only; but that it is brought under divine institution, it being enjoined on the churches of Christ to sing psalms, hymns, and spiritual songs; and that the whole church, in their public assemblies (as well as private Christians), ought to sing God's praises according to the best light they have received. Moreover, it was practiced in the great representative church by our Lord Jesus Christ with His disciples after He had instituted and celebrated the sacred ordinance of His holy supper as a commemorative token of redeeming love.

XXIV. Of Lawful Oaths and Vows.—1. A lawful oath is a part of religious worship, wherein the person swearing in truth, righteousness, and judgment solemnly calleth God to witness what he sweareth, and to judge him according to the truth or falseness thereof.

2. The name of God only is that by which men ought to swear, and therein it is to be used with all holy fear and reverence; therefore to swear vainly or rashly by that

glorious and dreadful name, or to swear at all by any other thing, is sinful and to be abhorred; yet, as in matter of weight and moment, for confirmation of truth and ending all strife, an oath is warranted by the Word of God, so a lawful oath, being imposed by lawful authority, in such matters ought to be taken.

3. Whosoever taketh an oath warranted by the Word of God ought duly to consider the weightiness of so solemn an act, and therein to avouch nothing but what he knoweth to be the truth; for that by rash, false, and vain oaths the Lord is provoked, and for them this land mourns.

4. An oath is to be taken in the plain and common sense of the words, without equivocation or mental reservation.

5. A vow, which is not to be made to any creature, but to God alone, is to be made and performed with all religious care and faithfulness; but popish monastical vows of perpetual single life, professed poverty, and regular obedience are so far from being degrees of higher perfection that they are superstitious and sinful snares in which no Christian may entangle himself.

XXV. Of the Civil Magistrate.—1. God, the supreme Lord and king of all the world, hath ordained civil magistrates to be under Him over the people, for His own glory and the public good, and to this end hath armed them with the power of the sword for defense and encouragement of them that do good and for the punishment of evil-doers.

2. It is lawful for Christians to accept and execute the office of a magistrate, when called thereunto; in the management whereof, as they ought especially to maintain justice and peace, according to the wholesome laws of each kingdom and commonwealth, so, for that end, they may lawfully now under the New Testament wage war upon just and necessary occasions.

3. Civil magistrates being set up by God for the ends aforesaid, subjection in all lawful things commanded by them ought to be yielded by us in the Lord, not only for

wrath but for conscience's sake; and we ought to make supplications and prayers for kings and all that are in authority, that, under them, we may live a quiet and peaceable life in all godliness and honesty.

XXVI. Of Marriage.—1. Marriage is to be between one man and one woman; neither is it lawful for any man to have more than one wife, nor for any woman to have more than one husband at the same time.

2. Marriage was ordained for the mutual help of husband and wife, for the increase of mankind with a legitimate issue, and for preventing of uncleanness.

3. It is lawful for all sorts of people to marry who are able with judgment to give their consent; yet it is the duty of Christians to marry in the Lord; and therefore such as profess the true religion should not marry with infidels or idolaters, neither should such as are godly be unequally yoked by marrying with such as are wicked in their life or maintain damnable heresy.

4. Marriage ought not to be within the degrees of consanguinity or affinity forbidden in the Word; nor can such incestuous marriage ever be made lawful by any law of man or consent of parties, so as those persons may live together as man and wife.

XXVII. Of the Church.—1. The catholic or universal church, which, with respect to the internal work of the Spirit and truth of grace, may be called invisible, consists of the whole number of the elect that have been, are, or shall be gathered into one under Christ, the head thereof, and is the spouse, the body, the fullness of Him that filleth all in all.

2. All persons, throughout the world, professing the faith of the gospel and obedience unto God by Christ according unto it, not destroying their own profession by any errors, everything the foundation, or unholiness of conversation, are and may be called visible saints; and of such ought all particular congregations to be constituted.

3. The purest churches under heaven are subject to mixture and error, and some have so degenerated as to

become no churches of Christ, but synagogues of Satan; nevertheless, Christ always hath had and ever shall have a kingdom in this world, to the end thereof, of such as believe in Him and make profession of His name.

4. The Lord Jesus Christ is the head of the church, in whom, by the appointment of the Father, all power for the calling, institution, order, or government of the church is invested in a supreme and sovereign manner; neither can the pope of Rome in any sense be head thereof, but is that Antichrist, that man of sin and son of perdition, that exalteth himself in the church against Christ and all that is called God, whom the Lord shall destroy with the brightness of His coming.

5. In the execution of this power wherewith He is so intrusted, the Lord Jesus calleth out of the world unto Himself, through the ministry of His Word by His Spirit, those that are given unto Him by His Father, that they may walk before Him in all the ways of obedience which He prescribeth to them in His Word. Those thus called He commandeth to walk together in particular societies or churches, for their mutual edification and the due performance of that public worship which He requireth of them in the world.

6. The members of these churches are saints by calling, visibly manifesting and evidencing in and by their profession and walking their obedience unto that call of Christ; and do willingly consent to walk together according to the appointment of Christ, giving up themselves to the Lord and to one another by the will of God, in professed subjection to the ordinances of the gospel.

7. To each of these churches thus gathered according to His mind, declared in His Word, He hath given all that power and authority which is any way needful for their carrying on that order in worship and discipline which He hath instituted for them to observe, with commands and rules for the due and right exerting and executing that power.

8. A particular church, gathered and completely organized according to the mind of Christ, consists of officers

and members; and the officers, appointed by Christ to be chosen and set apart by the church so called and gathered, for the peculiar administration of ordinances and execution of power or duty which He intrusts them with, or calls them to, to be continued to the end of the world, are bishops, or elders, and deacons.

9. The way appointed by Christ for the calling of any person, fitted and gifted by the Holy Spirit, unto the office of bishop, or elder, in a church, is that he be chosen thereunto by the common suffrage of the church itself, and solemnly set apart by fasting and prayer, with imposition of hands of the eldership of the church, if there be any before constituted therein; and of a deacon, that he be chosen by the like suffrage, and set apart by prayer and the like imposition of hands.

10. The work of pastors being constantly to attend the service of Christ in His churches, in the ministry of the Word, and prayer, with watching for their souls as they that must give an account to Him, it is incumbent on the churches to whom they minister not only to give them all due respect, but also to communicate to them of all their good things, according to their ability, so as they may have a comfortable supply, without being themselves entangled in secular affairs, and may also be capable of exercising hospitality towards others; and this is required by the law of nature and by the express order of our Lord Jesus, who hath ordained that they that preach the gospel should live of the gospel.

11. Although it be incumbent on the bishops or pastors of the churches to be instant in preaching the Word, by way of office, yet the work of preaching the Word is not so peculiarly confined to them but that others also gifted and fitted by the Holy Spirit for it, and approved and called by the church, may and ought to perform it.

12. As all believers are bound to join themselves to particular churches, when and where they have opportunity so to do, so all that are admitted unto the privileges of a church are also under the censures and government thereof, according to the rule of Christ.

13. No church members, upon any offense taken by them, having performed their duty required of them towards the person they are offended at, ought to disturb church order, or absent themselves from the assemblies of the church, or administration of any ordinance, upon the account of such offense at any of their fellow-members, but to wait upon Christ in further proceeding of the church.

14. As each church and all the members of it are bound to pray continually for the good and prosperity of all the churches of Christ in all places, and upon all occasions to further it, every one within the bounds of their places and callings, in the exercise of their gifts and graces, so the churches, when planted by the providence of God, so as they may enjoy opportunity and advantage for it, ought to hold communion among themselves for their peace, increase of love, and mutual edification.

15. Cases of difficulty or differences, either in point of doctrine or administration, wherein either the churches in general are concerned, or any one church, in their peace, union, and edification; or any member or members of any church are injured in or by any proceedings in censures not agreeable to truth and order; it is according to the mind of Christ that many churches, holding communion together, do, by their messengers, meet to consider and give their advice in or about the matter in difference, to be reported to all the churches concerned; howbeit these messengers assembled are not intrusted with any church power, properly so called; or with any jurisdiction over the churches themselves, to exercise any censures either over any churches or persons; or to impose their determination on the churches or offices.

XXVIII. Of the Communion of Saints.—1. All saints that are united to Jesus Christ, their head, by His Spirit and faith, although they are not made thereby one person with Him, have fellowship in His graces, sufferings, death, resurrection, and glory, and, being united to one another in love, they have communion in each other's gifts and graces, and are obliged to the performance of such duties, public and private, in an orderly way, as to conduce to their mutual good, both in the inward and outward man.

2. Saints by profession are bound to maintain a holy fellowship and communion in the worship of God, and in performing such other spiritual services as tend to their mutual edification; as also in relieving each other in outward things, according to their several abilities and necessities; which communion, according to the rule of the gospel, though especially to be exercised by them in the relations wherein they stand, whether in families or churches, yet as God offereth opportunity, is to be extended to all the household of faith, even all those who in every place call upon the name of the Lord Jesus; nevertheless, their communion one with another as saints doth not take away or infringe the title or property which each man hath in his goods and possessions.

XXIX. Of Baptism and the Lord's Supper.—1. Baptism and the Lord's Supper are ordinances of positive and sovereign institution, appointed by the Lord Jesus, the only Lawgiver, to be continued in His church to the end of the world.

2. These holy appointments are to be administered by those only who are qualified and thereunto called, according to the commission of Christ.

XXX. Of Baptism.—1. Baptism is an ordinance of the New Testament ordained by Jesus Christ, to be unto the party baptized a sign of his fellowship with Him in His death and resurrection; of his being engrafted into Him; of remission of sins; and of his giving up unto God, through Jesus Christ, to live and walk in newness of life.

2. Those who do actually profess repentance towards God, faith in, and obedience to our Lord Jesus, are the only proper subjects of this ordinance.

3. The outward element to be used in this ordinance is water, wherein the party is to be baptized, in the name of the Father, and of the Son, and of the Holy Spirit.

4. Immersion, or dipping of the person in water, is

necessary to the due administration of this ordinance.

XXXI. Of Laying on of Hands.—1. We believe that laying on of hands, with prayer, upon baptized believers, as such, is an ordinance of Christ, and ought to be submitted unto by all such persons that are admitted to partake of the Lord's Supper, and that the end of this ordinance is not for the extraordinary gifts of the Spirit, but for a farther reception of the Holy Spirit of promise, or for the addition of the graces of the Spirit, and the influences thereof to confirm, strengthen, and comfort them in Christ Jesus; it being ratified and established by the extraordinary gifts of the Spirit in the primitive times, to abide in the church, as meeting together on the first day of the week was, Acts ii. 1, that being the day of worship, or Christian Sabbath, under the gospel; and as preaching the Word was, Acts x. 44, and as baptism was. Matt. iii. 16, and prayer was, Acts iv. 31, and singing psalms, etc., was Acts xvi. 25, 26, so this of laying on of hands was, Acts viii. and xix.; for, as the whole gospel was confirmed by signs and wonders, and divers miracles and gifts of the Holy Ghost in general, so was every ordinance in like manner confirmed in particular.

XXXII. Of the Lord's Supper.—1. The Supper of the Lord Jesus was instituted by Him the same night wherein He was betrayed, to be observed in His churches unto the end of the world, for the perpetual remembrance and showing forth the sacrifice of Himself in His death, confirmation of the faith of believers in all the benefits thereof, their spiritual nourishment and growth in Him, their further engagement in and to all duties which they owe unto Him, and to be a bond and pledge of their communion with Him and with each other.

2. In this ordinance, Christ is not offered up to His Father, nor any real sacrifice made at all for remission of sin, of the quick or dead, but only a memorial of that One offering up of Himself by Himself upon the cross, once for all; and a spiritual obligation of all possible praise unto God for the same. So that the popish sacrifice of the mass,

as they call it, is most abominable, injurious to Christ's own only sacrifice, the alone propitiation for all the sins of the elect.

3. The Lord Jesus hath in this ordinance appointed His ministers to pray, and bless the elements of bread and wine, and thereby to set them apart from a common to a holy use, and to take and break the bread, to take the cup, and, they communicating also themselves, to give both to the communicants.

4. The denial of the cup to the people, worshiping the elements, the lifting them up or carrying them about for adoration, and reserving them for any pretended religious use, are all contrary to the nature of this ordinance and to the institution of Christ.

5. The outward elements of this ordinance, duly set apart to the uses ordained by Christ, have such relation to Him crucified as that truly, although in terms used figuratively, they are sometimes called by the name of the things they represent, to wit, the body and blood of Christ, albeit in substance and nature they still remain truly and only bread and wine, as they were before.

6. The doctrine which maintains a change of the substance of bread and wine into the substance of Christ's body and blood, commonly called transubstantiation, by consecration of a priest, or by any other way, is repugnant, not to Scripture alone, but even to common sense and reason, overthroweth the nature of the ordinance, and hath been and is the cause of manifold superstitions, yea, of gross idolatries.

7. Worthy receivers, outwardly partaking of the visible elements in this ordinance, do then also inwardly, by faith really and indeed, yet not carnally and corporeally, but spiritually, receive and feed upon Christ crucified and all the benefits of His death; the body and blood of Christ being then not corporeally or carnally, but spiritually present to the faith of believers in that ordinance, as the elements themselves are to their outward senses.

8. All ignorant and ungodly persons, as they are unfit to enjoy communion with Christ, so are they unworthy of

the Lord's table, and cannot, without great sin against him, while they remain such, partake of these holy mysteries, or be admitted thereunto; yea, whosoever shall receive unworthily, are guilty of the body and blood of the Lord, eating and drinking judgment to themselves.

XXXIII. Of the State of Man After Death and of the Resurrection of the Dead.—1. The bodies of men after death return to dust and see corruption; but their souls, which neither die nor sleep, having an immortal subsistence, immediately return to God who gave them; the souls of the righteous, being then made perfect in holiness, are received into paradise, where they are with Christ, and behold the face of God, in light and glory, waiting for the full redemption of their bodies; and the souls of the wicked are cast into hell, where they remain in torment and utter darkness, reserved to the judgment of the great day; besides these two places for souls separated from their bodies, the Scripture acknowledgeth none.

2. At the last day, such of the saints as are found alive shall not sleep but be changed, and all the dead shall be raised up with the self-same bodies, and none other; although with different qualities, which shall be united again to their souls forever.

3. The bodies of the unjust shall, by the power of Christ, be raised to dishonor; the bodies of the just, by His Spirit, unto honor, and be made conformable to His own glorious body.

XXXIV. Of the Last Judgment.—1. God hath appointed a day wherein He will judge the world in righteousness by Jesus Christ, to whom all power and judgment is given of the Father; in which day not only the apostate angels shall be judged, but likewise all persons that have lived upon the earth shall appear before the tribunal of Christ to give an account of their thoughts, words, and deeds, and to receive according to what they have done in the body, whether good or evil.

2. The end of God's appointing this day is for the manifestation of the glory of His mercy in the eternal

salvation of the elect; and of His justice in the eternal damnation of the reprobate, who are wicked and disobedient; for then shall the righteous go into everlasting life, and receive that fullness of joy and glory with everlasting reward in the presence of the Lord; but the wicked, who know not God, and obey not the gospel of Jesus Christ, shall be cast into eternal torments, and punished with everlasting destruction from the presence of the Lord and from the glory of His power.

3. As Christ would have us to be certainly persuaded that there shall be a day of judgment, both to deter all men from sin and for the greater consolation of the godly in their adversity, so will He have that day unknown to men, that they may shake off all carnal security, and be always watchful, because they know not at what hour the Lord will come, and may ever be prepared to say, Come, Lord Jesus, come quickly. Amen.

Influence of the Philadelphia Confession of Faith.

William Cathcart, D. D.

The London Confession of 1689 was the basis of our great American Articles of Faith, and its composition and history are worthy of our careful consideration.

It was adopted "by the ministers and messengers of upwards of one hundred baptized congregations in England and Wales, denying Arminianism." Thirty-seven ministers signed it on behalf of the represented churches.

The sessions of the Assembly which framed it were held from the 3rd to the 12th of September, 1689.

The Confession of the Westminster Assembly—the creed of all British and American Presbyterians—was published in 1647; the Savoy Confession, containing the faith of English Congregationalists, was issued in 1658. The Baptist Assembly gave their religious beliefs to the world in 1689. This was not the first Baptist deliverance on the most momentous questions.

It was styled by its authors, "A Confession of Faith put forth by the Elders and Brethren of Many Congregations of Christians Baptized upon Profession of their Faith, in London and the Country, with an Appendix concerning Baptism." The authors of the Confession say that in the numerous instances in which they were agreed with the Westminster Confession, they used the same language to describe their religious principles.

The Appendix to the London Confession occupies 16 octavo pages, and the Articles 52. The former is a vigorous attack on infant baptism, apparently designed to give help to the brethren in defending the clause of Article XXIX., which defines the subjects of baptism as believers. Dr. Rippon gives the Minutes of the London Assembly which adopted the Confession. These include the topics discussed, the residences of the signatory ministers, and the Articles, but not the Appendix. In addition to his "Narrative of the Proceedings of the General Assembly," as the London Convention was called, Rippon issued a pamphlet edition of the Articles without the Appendix, with an advertisement of his Register on the Cover. Crosby does not give it in his Confession of 1689. No one ever questioned the right of either to drop the Appendix. It was not one of the Articles, but chiefly a mere argument in favor of one of them.

The Appendix has this statement: "The known principle and state of the consciences of divers of us that have agreed in this Confession is such that **we cannot hold church communion with any other than baptized believers, and churches constituted of such;** yet some others of us have a greater liberty and freedom in our spirits that way." This refers to the admission of unbaptized persons to the Lord's Table by some churches, and their rejection by others.

Within a few years, an effort has been made in this country to prove that our Baptist fathers of the Philadelphia, and other early Associations, practiced "open communion" because of this item in the Appendix of the London Confession. The learned "strict communion" author of "Historical Vindications" has contributed to this error, by making the grave mistake that the Appendix was

Article XXXIII. of **The Philadelphia Confession of Faith.** And he gives as his authorities for this extraordinary statement the **Hanserd Knollys Society's** copy of the Confession of 1689, and the Pittsburg edition of The Philadelphia Confession of Faith. In the former, it is not placed as an **Article,** but as an **Appendix.** In the latter, it is not to be found in any form. It **never appeared in any edition of The Philadelphia Confession of Faith,** from Benjamin Franklin's first issue down to the last copy sent forth from the press. And this could have been easily learned from the title page. In the end of the title in the Hanserd Knollys Society's copy of the Confession of 1689 are the words, **"With an Appendix concerning Baptism."** The portion of the title covering the Appendix, and the Appendix itself, cannot be found in any copy of our oldest American Baptist creed. That the honored writer acted in good faith in this part of his valuable work, I have no doubt; but that he was led astray himself, and that he has drawn others into a grave mistake, I am absolutely certain.

The Appendix admits that "open communion" existed among the English Baptists. It does not assert the truth of it; the "strict communion" members of the body which adopted the Confession would tolerate nothing of that nature. And as **no such practice existed in the Philadelphia Association when its Confession was adopted, or at any other period in its history,** such an admission would have been destitute of a fragment of truth. The Cohansie Church, in 1740, sent a query to the Philadelphia Association, asking if a pious Pedobaptist, who declined to have his children baptized, might come to the Lord's Table without being baptized; and they wished also to know from the Association if the refusal of such a request would not betray a want of charity. The Association unanimously decided that the man should be refused a place at the Lord's Table in the Cohansie church, and that such action showed no lack of charity. Their action, and their reasons for it, read: "Given to vote, and passed, all in the negative. Nemine contradicente. Reasons annexed. First. It is not for want of charity that we thus answer. Our practice shows the contrary; for we baptize none but such as, in the judgment of charity, have grace, being baptized; but it is because we find, in the Commission, that no unbaptized persons are to be admitted to church communion. Matt. XXVIII. 19, 20; Mark XVI. 16. Compare Acts II, 41; I Cor. XII, 13. Second. Because it is the church's duty to maintain the ordinances as they are delivered to us in the Scripture. II Thess. II, 15; I Cor. XI 2; Isa. VIII. 20. Third. Because we cannot see it agreeable, in any respect, for the procuring that unity, unfeigned love, and undisturbed peace, which are required, and ought to be in and among Christian communities. I Cor. I:10; Eph. IV:3."

This wise decision, supported by solid reasons, shows, that two years before the formal adoption of the Confession of 1689, as the greater portion of the Philadelphia Confession of Faith, the Philadelphia Association was unanimously opposed to an "open communion" proposition. Thirty-three years after the Association was formed, and while the Confession of 1689 was "owned" as a Baptist creed, without the special adoption which it afterwards received, one of the oldest churches in the Association would not admit a pious Pedobaptist to the Lord's Supper without consulting the Association. And that body voted as a unit against the practice.

The declaration of the orthodox London brethren, in reference to themselves, could have been used by the Philadelphia Association about all its churches, at any period in its past history: "The known principle and state of the consciences of us all is such that we cannot hold communion with any other than baptized believers, and churches constituted of such." And hence the truth required the exclusion of the Appendix from the Confession of the Philadelphia Association.

The London Confession of 1689, in Article XXVI., section 6, says, "The members of these churches are saints by calling,—and do willingly consent to walk together according to the appointment of Christ, giving up themselves to the Lord and one to another, by the will of God, in professed subjection to the ordinances of the gospel." And in Article XXVIII., section 1, it says, "Baptism and the Lord's Supper are ordinances of positive and sovereign institution, appointed by the Lord Jesus, the only Law-giver, to be continued in His church to the end of the world." And in Article XXIX., section 2, it says, "Those who do actually profess repentance towards God, faith in and obedience to our Lord Jesus, are the only proper subjects of this ordinance"; and in section 4, "Immersion, or dipping the person in water, is necessary to the due administration of this ordinance."

In Article XXX., "On the Lord's Supper," there is no clause giving the unbaptized authority to come to the Lord's Table. Their existence in connection with this institution is not noticed by a single word. And as the Articles declare that the members of the churches which adopted them lived in "professed subjection to the ordinances of the gospel"; that baptism and the Lord's Supper were "ordinances appointed by the Lord Jesus, to be continued in His church to the end of the world"; and that repentance, faith and immersion are necessary to baptism, the Articles describe orderly believers only, who lived in professed subjection to the ordinances of the gospel. There is not a word in them which the strictest Baptist on earth might not heartily receive. The men who avow that "The known principle and state of the consciences of divers of us, that have agreed in this Confession, is such, that we cannot hold church communion with any other than baptized believers and churches constituted of such"—men like Hansert Knollys and William Kiffin—were the last men to sign a Confession favoring "open communion." The Philadelphia Association, while avowing the most stringent "close communion" doctrines in 1740, owned, in a general way, the Confession of 1689. The Charleston Association, S. C., adopted the London Articles, and imported two hundred copies of them; and yet was restricted in its communion. In 1802, in answer to a question in reference to the consistency of Baptists inviting pious

Pedobaptists to the Lord's Table, that body replied, "We cannot but say it does not appear to be consistent with gospel order." In England and America, church, individuals, and Associations, with clear minds, with hearts full of love for the truth, and with a tenacious attachment to "restricted communion," have held with veneration the Articles of 1689. The Article, "On the Lord's Supper," needs safeguards, and the Philadelphia Confession of Faith furnishes them.

The Philadelphia Confession of Faith is not the London Creed of 1689.

Almost every writer on this question falls into the mistake of supposing that it is, and he proceeds to prophesy evils, if he is a scriptural communionist, or he begins forthwith to whip us with the supposed **liberal** scourge of our fathers, if he is a free communionist. The London Creed has thirty-two Articles, and an Appendix; The Philadelphia has thirty-four, and, instead of an Appendix, it has "A Treatise of Discipline," which was held in as great regard as the Confession for many years. Thirty-two of the thirty-four Articles in the Philadelphia Confession are taken from the English fathers of 1689. One of the two new Articles is on Singing in the Worship of God,—a practice which it commends as a divine ordinance. This Article would have entirely changed the character of the Confession of 1689 to some of the churches that adopted it; for they looked with horror upon such a custom. But in Article XXXI., in the new Confession, **"On Laying on of Hands,"** the Lord's Supper receives its appropriate safeguards. In section 1 we read, "We believe that laying on of hands, with prayer, **upon baptized believers, as such,** is an ordinance of Christ, and ought to be submitted unto **by all such persons that are admitted to the Lord's Supper."**

According to the compilers of this Article, no man should come to the Lord's Table without baptism and the imposition of hands. It has been declared, with an air of victory, that the Philadelphia Confession of Faith requires no ceremonial qualification before approaching the Lord's Table. This jubilant spirit is the result of carelessness in examining the venerable Confession: "All such persons that are admitted to partake of the Lord's Supper" should be baptized believers, who have received the imposition of hands, with prayer. So that two ceremonial prerequisites to the Lord's Supper—Baptism and the laying on of hands—are demanded by the Philadelphia Confession of Faith.

THE PHILADELPHIA CONFESSION OF FAITH, and not the English Confession of 1689, was the BASIS ON WHICH NEARLY ALL THE ORIGINAL ASSOCIATIONS OF THIS COUNTRY WERE FOUNDED.

In 1742, the Philadelphia Association adopted the Confession which bears its name. Some deny that the Association ever formally adopted it; or if it did they assert that we know nothing of the time when such action took place. This statement is based upon a certain amount of recognition which the London Articles undoubtedly received in the Philadelphia Association before 1742; and also upon the fact that the Association simply voted to "reprint" the London Confession. When a publishing house resolves to reprint an English work now it adopts it; it makes the work its own. The Confession of 1689, in 1742 had never been printed in America; the Philadelphia Association voted to reprint it, that is, to adopt its Articles; and they also added two Articles to it, and A Treatise on Discipline. And every copy printed since Benjamin Franklin's first edition appeared in 1743, bears on its title-page, "Adopted by the Philadelphia Association, Sept. 25th, 1742." This statement on the title-page would have been true. The Warren Association makes the same record about the date of its adoption; Morgan Edwards gives 1742 as the date of its adoption, on page 5 of his "Materials towards the History of the Baptist, etc.," published in Philadelphia, 1770, and the act cannot be reasonably doubted, nor the date called in question.

The Kehukee Association, founded in 1765, adopted the Philadelphia Confession. The Warren Association of Rhode Island, organized 1767, adopted the same Confession. The general Association of Virginia received the Philadelphia Confession in 1783 with explanations, none of which favored "open communion." The Elkhorn Association of Kentucky, formed in 1785, adopted the Philadelphia Confession. The Charleston Association of South Carolina was established by Oliver Hart in 1751, fresh from the Philadelphia Association, and full of admiration for its principles and its usefulness. It adopted the Articles of 1689, and a Treatise on Discipline, prepared by Oliver Hart, and Brethren Pelot, Morgan Edwards, and David Williams. This Association, though not adopting the Philadelphia Confession, followed its spirit and plan, and it practiced "restricted communion."

There was not one of the original Baptist Associations of this country that invited the unbaptized to the Lord's Table. Once we have seen the statement rashly made, and Asplund given as its authority, that there was one early Baptist Association that held "open communion,"—evidently referring to the Groton Conference, Connecticut. But the writer omitted to state that Asplund gave an account, in the same list of Associations, of Six Principle Baptists, Free-Will Baptists, and Seventh-Day Baptists. The "open communion" body of which he speaks was not composed of Regular Baptists, nor were the Seventh-Day brethren named by Asplund as members of our denomination. They did not assume the name of an Association,—they called themselves the Groton Conference. And Asplund says that " they keep no correspondence,"—that is they were not recognized as Regular Baptists. They neither enjoyed, nor were they entitled to, such recognition.

Asplund mentions several other early Baptist Associations that adopted THE CONFESSION OF FAITH,—that is, the Philadelphia. But further reference to this question is needless. Nearly all the original Associations of America adopted the Philadelphia Confession of Faith; and not one of these bodies held "open communion." There were "open communionists" outside of our organizations, when our early Associations sprang into life,—especially in New England, whose erring judgments soon learned the way of the Lord more perfectly, and they united with Regular Baptist communities.

If the Philadelphia Confession of Faith had been accepted in England, as the legitimate successor of the confession of 1689, the Strict Baptists of Norwich would never, by a just legal decision, have been deprived of their church edifice for the advantage of "open communionists."

The Philadelphia Association never had an "open communion" church in its fellowship; and it has repeatedly declared the practice to be unscriptural. Its Confession of Faith as adopted in 1742 **never was repealed or modified in any of its parts. The latest edition is an exact reprint of the first,** and "open communion" cannot even find a shelter in it.

OTHER CONFESSIONS. — In 1611 a church of English Baptists, residing in Holland, adopted a Confession of Faith, prepared most probably by Thomas Helwys, their pastor. Not many months after the Confession was published they returned to their native country and settled in London. The Confession has twenty-six articles, and though most of them are thoroughly sound, others are Arminian, and show clearly that those who framed them were troubled by a defective knowledge of New Testament teachings.

The Confession of Faith of 1644, was adopted by seven London churches. It is the first Calvinistical creed published by our English brethren. It has fifty articles. The first name which appears on the Confession is that of illustrious William Kiffin. The twenty-first article reads, "Jesus Christ did purchase salvation for the elect that God gave unto Him. These only have interest in Him, and fellowship with Him, for whom He makes intercession to His Father, and to them alone doth God by His Spirit apply this redemption; also the free gift of eternal life is given to them and none else." The thirty-ninth article is, "Baptism is an ordinance of the New Testament, given by Christ, to be dispensed upon persons professing faith, or that are made disciples, who, upon profession of faith, ought to be baptized, and after to partake of the Lord's Supper."

An "Appendix" to this Confession of Faith, written by Benjamin Cox, and printed in 1646, has twenty-two articles, a part of the twentieth of which reads, "The apostles first baptized disciples, and then admitted them to the use of the Supper; we, therefore, do not admit any to the use of the Supper, nor communicate with any in the use of this ordinance but disciples baptized, lest we should have fellowship with them in their doing contrary to order."

The "Confession of Faith of Several Churches of Christ in the County of Somerset," and of some churches in adjacent counties, in England, was issued in 1656. It was signed by the representatives of sixteen churches, and it was probably written by Thomas Collier, who was ordained in 1655 to the "office of general superintendent and messenger to all the associated churches." The Confession has forty-six articles; it is Calvinistic, Baptistic, and consequently, thoroughly Scriptural.

The London Confession of Faith was signed in the English metropolis in 1660. It was prepared by members of the General (Arminian) Baptists churches. On some disputed questions it is nearer the truth than the Confession of 1611, but this statement does not apply to its representation of the doctrine of final perseverance. It has twenty-five articles. This Confession was "owned and approved by more than twenty thousand persons."

"An Orthodox Creed," published in London in 1678, gives another view of the doctrines of the General Baptists. It has fifty articles, and it is remarkable for its Calvinistic tone, though it came from a body professedly Arminian. Its mode of describing election, providence, free will, and final perseverance is in the main scriptural. The extent of the atonement is the only question about which it differed from the opinions of our Orthodox brethren of that day.

The Confession of 1689 was "put forth by the elders and brethren of many congregations of Christians, baptized (immersed) upon profession of their faith, in London and the country." It has thirty-two articles, and "an appendix concerning baptism." It is in many respects the best compilation of Christian belief ever published. After dropping its lengthy appendix, and inserting two new articles, it became, in 1742, "The Philadelphia Confession of Faith," and it was adopted by most of the early Baptist Associations of this country. (See article on The Philadelphia Confession of Faith.)

The New Hampshire Confession of Faith was written by the late Dr. J. Newton Brown while laboring in the State whose name it bears. It was prepared with a view "to pending controversies with the Free-Will Baptists, who are numerous there." Dr. Cutting says, "It has been sometimes criticized as aiming at the difficult task of preserving the stern orthodoxy of the fathers of the denomination, while at the same time it softens the terms in which that orthodoxy is expressed, in order to remove the objections of neighboring opponents." (Historical Vindication, p. 105.) We have unlimited faith in the goodness and sanctity of the late Dr. Brown, but we very much prefer the Philadelphia Confession of Faith, so dear to our fathers, to the New Hampshire Creed.—Baptist Encyclopaedia, by William Cathcart, D. D., pp. 264-268.

BOOK THREE

ORIGIN OF OTHERS WHO HELD BAPTIST PRINCIPLES

(Alphabetically Arranged)

THE ALBIGENSES

William Cathcart, D. D., and Others

The Albigenses received this name from the town of Albi, in France, in and around which many of them lived. The Albigenses were called Cathari, Paterines, Publicans, Paulicians, Good Men, Bogomiles, and they were known by other names. They were not Waldenses. They were Paulicians, either directly from the East, or converted through the instrumentality of those who came from the earlier homes of that people.

The Paulicians were summoned into existence by the Spirit of God about A.D. 660. Their founder was named Constantine. The reading of a New Testament, left him by a stranger, brought him to the Saviour. He soon gathered a church, and his converts speedily collected others. Armenia was the scene of his labors. They were denounced as Manicheans, though they justly denied the charge.

They increased rapidly, and in process of time persecution scattered them. In the ninth century many of them were in Thrace, Bulgaria, and Bosnia; and, later still, they became very numerous in these new fields, especially in Bosnia. Indeed, such a host had they become that in 1238 Coloman, the brother of the king of Hungary, entered Bosnia to destroy the heretics. Gregory IX congratulated him upon his success, but lived to learn that the Bogomiles were still a multitude.

A second crusade led to further butchery, but the blood of martyrs was still the seed of the church, and they continued a powerful body until the conquest of their country by the Turks, in 1463. There was direct communication between these Bogomiles and the Albigenses in

France. Matthew Paris tells us that the heretic Albigenses in the provinces of Bulgaria, Crotia, and Dalmatia elected Bartholomew as their pope, that Albigenses came to him from all quarters for information on doubtful matters, and that he had a vicar who was born in Carcassone, and who lived near Thoulouse.

At an early period the Paulicians entered Italy and established powerful communities, especially in Milan. They spread over France, Germany, and other countries. In the eleventh century they were to be found in almost every quarter of Europe. St. Bernard, in the twelfth century, says of them: "If you interrogate them about their faith nothing can be more Christian, if you examine into their conversation nothing can be more blameless, and what they say they confirm by their deeds. As for what regards life and manners, they attack no one, they circumvent no one, they defraud no one."

Reineruis Saccho belonged to the Cathari (not the Waldenses, he was never a member of that community) for seventeen years. He was afterwards a Romish inquisitor, and he describes his old friends and the Waldenses, in 1254, in these words: "Heretics are distinguished by their manners and their words, for they are sedate and modest in their manners. They have no pride in clothes, for they wear such as are neither costly nor mean.

They do not carry on business in order to avoid falsehoods, oaths, and frauds, but only live by labor as workmen. Their teachers also are shoemakers and weavers. They do not multiply riches, but are content with what is necessary, and they are chaste, especially the Leonists. They are also temperate in meat and drink.

They do not go to taverns, dances, or other vanities." The Leonists were the followers of Peter Waldo, of Lyons, the Waldenses, as distinguished from his own old sect, the Albigenses. Reinerius then proceeds to charge these men who shun business to avoid falsehoods with hypocrisy.

No body of men could receive a better character than St. Bernard and the inquisitor give these enemies of the Church of Rome, and no community could be more wickedly abused by the same men than these identical heretics. For some centuries the Albigenses figure universally in history as externally the purest and best of men, and secretly as guilty of horrible crimes, such as the pagans charged upon the early Christians.

Reinerius mentions several causes for the spread of heresy. His second is that all the men and women, small and great, day and night, do not cease to learn, and they are continually engaged in teaching what they have acquired themselves. His third cause for the existence and spread of heresy is the translation and circulation of the Old and New Testaments into the vulgar tongue.

These they learned themselves and taught to others. Reinerius was acquainted with a rustic layman who repeated the whole book of Job, and with many who knew perfectly the entire New Testament. He gives an account of many schools of the heretics, the existence of which he learned in the trials of the Inquisition.

Assuredly these friends of light and of a Bible circulated everywhere were worthy of the curses and tortures of men like Reinerius and lordly bigots like St. Bernard. In a council held at Thoulouse in 1229 the Scriptures in the language of the people were first prohibited. The Albigenses surviving the horrid massacre of the Pope's murderous crusaders were forbidden to have the "books of the Old or New Testament, unless a Psalter, a **Breviary,** and a **Rosary,** and they forbade the translation in the vulgar tongue." No doubt many of the members of the council supposed that the Breviary and Rosary were inspired as well as the Psalter.

Reinerius gives a catalogue of the doctrines of the Cathari, which corresponds with the list of heresies charged against them for two hundred years before he wrote by popes, bishops, and ecclesiastical gatherings, the substance of which has no claim upon our credulity, though some of the forms of expression may have been used by certain of these venerable worthies.

Reinerius says that the Cathari had 16 churches, the church of the Albanenses, or of Sansano, of Contorezo, of

Bagnolenses, or of Bagnolo, of Vincenza, or of the Marquisate, of Florence, of the Valley of Spoleto, of France, of Thoulouse, of Cahors, of Albi, of Sclavonia, of the Latins at Constantinople, of the Greeks in the same city, of Philadelphia, of Bulgaria, and of Dugranicia.

He says, "They all derive their origin from the two last." That is, they are all Paulicians, originally from Armenia. He says that "the churches number 4000 Cathari, of both sexes, in all the world, but believers innumerable." By churches we are to understand communities of the Perfect devoted to ministerial and missionary labor. The Believers in the time of Reinerius were counted by millions.

Upon **infant baptism** the Albigenses had very decided opinions. A council held in Thoulouse in 1119, undoubtedly referring to them, condemns and expels from the church of God those who put on the appearance of religion and condemned the sacrament of the body and the blood of the Lord and the **Baptism of children.**

At a meeting of "archbishops, bishops, and other pious men" at Thoulouse, in 1176, the Albigenses were condemned on various pretexts. Roger De Hoveden, a learned Englishman, who commenced to write his "Annals" in 1189, gives a lengthy account of this meeting. He says that Gilbert, bishop of Lyons, by command of the bishop of Albi and his assessors, condemned these persons as heretics; and the third reason, according to Hoveden, given by Gilbert for his sentence was that they would not save children by baptism.

He also preserves a "Letter of Peter, titular of St. Chrysogonus, Cardinal, Priest, and Legate of the Apostolic See," written in 1178, in which, speaking of the Albigenses, he says, "Others stoutly maintained to their faces that they had heard from them that baptism was of no use to infants." Collier gives the meaning of Hoveden correctly when he represents him as stating, in reference to the Albigenses, "These heretics refused to own infant baptism."

Evervinus, in a letter to St. Bernard, speaking evidently of Albigenses, in Cologne, in 1147, and consequently before the conversion of Peter Waldo, says, "They do not believe infant baptism, alleging that place of the gospel, 'Whosoever shall believe and be baptized shall be saved.'"

Eckbert, in 1160, in his work against the Cathari, written in thirteen discourses, says in the first, "They say that baptism profits nothing to children who are baptized, for they cannot seek baptism by themselves, because they can make no profession of faith."

The Paulicians received their name because they were specially the disciples of the Apostle Paul. They were established as a denomination by a gift of the Scriptures to their founder, through which he received Christ, became a mighty teacher, and gathered not converts simply, but churches.

At the great trial in Thoulouse in 1176 they would not accept anything as an authority but the New Testament. Throughout their wide-spread fields of toil from Armenia to Britain, and from one end of Europe to the other, and throughout the nine hundred years of their heroic sufferings and astonishing success, they have always shown supreme regard for the Word of God. If these men, coming from the original cradle of our race, journeying through Thrace, Bulgaria, Bosnia, Italy, France, and Germany, and visiting even Britain, were not Baptists, they were very like them.

If all the wicked slanders about them were discarded it would most probably be found that some of them had little in common with us, but that the majority, while redundant and deficient in some things as measured by Baptist doctrines, were substantially on our platform. This position about the Paulicians of the East is ably defended by Dr. L. P. Brockett in "The Bogomils." — BAPTIST ENCYCLOPEDIA by William Cathcart, D.D. pp. 18-21.

William Crosby says, in Scenes From Christian History, 1852, page 176: "In fact, from the beginning, there were everywhere Protestants,—men, that is, who never gave the pope any power over their Christianity." Again, page 177, "The inhabitants of the Alps had never cared for the pope. The people of mountains are apt to breathe free. A like heresy extended in the beautiful regions of the South of France. Innocent the Third, therefore, organized a crusade against the heretical Albigenses, so called from Albi, their chief seat in the region, who **from the earliest times** had disregarded the power of his chair."

Our enemies have written much in their effort to discredit all groups who would not follow Rome. All their accusation can be answered, even though most of the history we have comes from our enemies. Not only did Catholicism destroy lives but they destroyed any records they could get hold of that would commend those that disagreed with their dogmas. We quote:

"Mr. Hume had a much more correct view of the character of the Albigenses, and it is singular that Mr. Gifford should have overlooked it. The following is the passage to which I refer. 'The Pope (Innocent 3rd) published a crusade against the Albigenses, a species of enthusiasts in the south of France, whom **he denominated heretics, because,** like other enthusiasts, **they neglected the rights of the church, and opposed the power and influence of the clergy.**

'The people from all parts of Europe, moved by their superstition and their passion for wars and adventures, flocked to his standard. Simon de Montfort, the general of the crusade, acquired to himself a sovereignty in these provinces. The count of Toulouse, who protected, or perhaps only tolerated the Albigenses, was stripped of his dominions. And these sectaries themselves, though THE MOST INNOCENT AND INOFFENSIVE OF MANKIND, were exterminated with all the circumstances of extreme violence and barbarity.'—**History of England,** vol. II ch. XI.

Nothing can be more just than this account of the Albigenses, provided we allow Mr. Hume his own definition of the term "enthusiasts"—a term which he uniformly employs to denote all those who believe the Bible to be the word of God, and who receive it as the rule of their faith and practice. I may further add, that the reader will find his account of the Albigenses to be perfectly consonant to all that is related to them in the following pages.— HISTORY OF CHRISTIAN CHURCH, by William Jones, PREFACE, page IV.

ORIGIN OF THE ANABAPTISTS
David Benedict

"Before the rise of Luther and Calvin there lay concealed in almost all the countries of Europe, particularly in Bohemia, Moravia, Switzerland and Germany, many persons who adhered tenaciously to the spiritual nature of the kingdom of Christ. And that this kingdom should be inaccessible to the wicked and unrighteous, and exempt from all human institutions,"—and infant baptism among the rest. (quoting Mosheim—WJB)

We see that this main peculiarity of the ancient anabaptists respecting this spiritual kingdom, is twice inserted in the foregoing selections. The author repeats it with emphasis, declares it was the true source of all the peculiarities of this ancient and wide-spread community, and again and again denounces it as a fanatical opinion. This he does with entire self-complacency, as if such an idea had never been thought of before in any part of the world by any but visionaries and enthusiasts. This is not so strange in a doctor of the Lutheran church, which, in the old countries at least, like all other national hierarchies, is made up of a motley mixture, without any such discrimination of character as the Baptists have always prescribed.

The extensive spread of this people corroborates the statement made by other writers, that their missionaries could go the whole length of Germany at an early period, and lodge every night with their friends.

The history of the Anabaptists is hid in the remote

depths of antiquity, and is, of consequence, extremely difficult to be ascertained.

Were we not acquainted with the author of this statement, we should think it was made to Baptist order, so perfectly does it correspond with the facts of the case,—uttered, too, by a pedobaptist writer who had dug very deep into the history of antiquity, and whose prejudices, moreover, were unusually strong against the community whose affairs he describes.

Many questions have been raised for a number of centuries past, as to the denominational character of "the Waldenses, the Petrobrussians, the Wickliffites, the Hussites, the Henricians, and other ancient sects;" but here all is made plain, and they are all set over to the Baptist side; and this great historian concedes that they are not entirely mistaken when they boast of their descent from these **witnesses of the truth** in times of universal darkness and supersitition.

Dr. Mosheim does not practice any concealment or disguise as to the baptismal character of the great body of dissenters "in the remote depths of antiquity, in almost all the countries of Europe."

We must now go back nearly five hundred years, and give an account of those German anabaptists, as related by Evervinus, an old Catholic writer, in a letter from him to the famous St. Bernard, a little before the year 1140.

"There have lately been some heretics discovered among us near Cologne, of whom some have with satisfaction returned again to the church. One that was a bishop among them, and his companions, openly opposed us in the assembly of the clergy and laity, the lord archbishop himself being present, with many of the nobility, maintained their heresy from the words of Christ and His apostles. But finding that they made no impression, they desired that a day might be fixed upon which they might bring along with them men skilful in their faith, promising to return to the church, provided their teachers were not able to answer their opponents; but that otherwise they would rather die than depart from their judgment. Upon this declaration, having been admonished to repent for three days, **they were seized by the people in their excess of zeal, and burnt to death;** and what is most astonishing, they came to the stake and endured the torments of the flames not only with patience, but even with joy. In this case, O, Holy Father, (he addresses the pope—WJB) were I present with you, I should be glad to ask you how these members of Satan could persist in their heresy with such constancy and courage as is rarely to be found among the most religious in the faith of Christ.

"Their heresy is this:—They say that the church is only among themselves, because they alone follow the ways of Christ and imitate the apostles, not seeking secular gains, possessing no property, following the pattern of Christ, who was Himself perfectly poor, nor permitting His disciples to possess anything[1].

"They do not hold the baptism of infants, alleging that passage of the gospel, 'He that believeth and is baptized shall be saved.' They place no confidence in the intercession of saints; and all things observed in the church, which have not been established by Christ Himself or His apostles, they call superstitious.

"I must inform you, also, that those of them who have returned to our church, tell us, that **they had great numbers of their persuasion scattered almost everywhere, and that amongst them were many of our clergy and monks.** And as for those who were burnt, they, in the defense they made for themselves, told us that his heresy had been concealed from the time of the martyrs; and that it had existed in Greece and other countries.

"The letter of Evervinus had all the effect upon Bernard that he could desire... He is extremely offended with them for deriding the Catholics because they baptized infants, and prayed for the dead, and asserted purgatory; condemned their scrupulous refusal to swear at all—which, according to him, was one of their peculiarities—upbraids them with their secrecy in the observance of their religious

[1] "We shall see reason hereafter to believe that in this particular Evervinus misrepresented them."—**Jones.**

rites, not considering the necessity which persecution imposed upon them . . . They are increased to great multitudes throughout all countries, to the great danger of the church; for their words eat like a canker, and, like a flying leprosy, runs every way, infecting the precious members of Christ. These, in our Germany, we call them Cathari, in Flanders they call them Piphles; in France, Tisserands, from the art of weaving, because numbers of them are of that occupation."

"In 1223," says Mr. Orchard, "an innumerable multitude of heretics were burned alive throughout Germany; this was by the combined operations of the crusades and the inquisition."

Mr. Jones has followed the history of this same kind of people, and finds them numerous, throughout the twelfth century, in the neighborhood of Cologne, and also in Flanders, the south of France, Savoy and Milan.

My limits will not permit me to give even detached accounts of the persecutions which they continually endured, and which scattered them abroad into other countries.

About 1510 the German anabaptists passed in shoals into Holland and the Netherlands, and, in the course of time, amalgamated with the Dutch baptists.

Some farther accounts of the anabaptists, and of all who lay concealed in all parts of Europe, will be given in my next chapter, when we come to speak of the Reformation, and of their high expectations on the first announcement of this great movement, and their sad disappointment at the secular and imperfect manner in which it was conducted.

So great has been the lapse of time, and so many have been the changes in the world in all respects since the great struggles of the reformation commenced, and so generally do all—who do not sympathize with Rome—applaud in the gross all that pertains to that stupendous revolution, which gave such a different current to the affairs of most part of Europe, that we, at the present time, have but a faint conception of the disappointment which these old veterans in the cause of spiritual religion must have experienced.

Although the reformers theorized well, and promised to throw off all the errors and traditions of the old system, and build their churches upon the gospel model, yet it was soon discovered by these people that "the plan of Luther and his associates was much beneath the sublimity of their views," and that instead of taking the scriptures alone for their only guide, as they at first had promised to do, that some of the worst features of the church, whose jurisdiction they had adjured, were to be preserved; that the new churches, instead of being formed of spiritual members, were to be composed of a motley mixture of materials, and all to be guided, directed and defended by the secular power. Under these circumstances it is not at all surprising that they became deeply dissatisfied, "and consequently undertook a more perfect reformation, and proposed to found a church entirely spiritual and truly divine."

Those of these old and faithful witnesses for the truth who dared to venture out from their obscure retreats, made their advances to the new converts from the catholic church with openness and freedom; but when they ascertained that the adulterous union of church and state was to suffer no divorcement, that infant baptism, after being divested of its multitudinous appendages, was not only to be continued, but defended at all hazards, and that anabaptism, or the simple act of baptizing anew those whose former baptism had been premature or imperfect, was to be "looked upon as among the most intolerable and flagitious heresies," and not only those who dared thus to administer the rite, but all who became the subjects of their administrations, of whatever sex or condition, were doomed to suffer from the anathemas of the church, and all the cruel appliances of the secular power.

When all these things are considered, we may begin to discover the causes of the disappointment to which we have alluded.

They were well apprised of the fact that a portion of the reformers, at least, had a prodigious struggle in their efforts to reconcile their testimony and their practice on the subject of infant baptism, and that this old, time-honored error hung for a while in an equivocal position; they also soon learnt, to their sorrow, that right or wrong, a large majority of the new doctors had decided that it must and should be maintained.

Mennonites

Having carried the history of the German anabaptists thus far, as my information of them after the time of Menno was very limited, I left the article unfinished, until more knowledge of them should be acquired. I had very little expectation, however, of gaining anything more than detached passages from different writers, statistical tables, etc., and I had intended to insert what little I should say of them, under this head. But, as a good Providence has so favored my efforts, that by the aid of the old Dutch Martyrology I am able to go into the interior of their history more fully than of any party of Baptists except those of England and this country, I shall carry forward the article, and give them a place among the reformers, where they properly belong.—Mr. David Benedict's treatment of Historian Mosheim's account. See General History of the Baptist Denomination, page 49.

THE DONATISTS

William Cathcart, D. D.

In North Africa, during the fierce persecution of Dioclesian, many Christians courted a violent death. These persons, without the accusation, would confess to the possession of the Holy Scriptures, and on their refusal to surrender them, they were immediately imprisoned and frequently executed. While they were in confinement they were visited by throngs of disciples, who bestowed upon them valuable gifts and showed them the highest honor.

Mensurius, bishop of Carthage, disapproved of all voluntary martyrdom, and took steps to hinder such bloodshed. And if he had gone no farther in this direction he would have deserved the commendation of all good men. But by zealous Christians in North Africa he was regarded as unfriendly to compulsory martyrdom, and to the manifestations of tender regard shown to the victims of tyranny. And by some he was supposed to be capable of a gross deception to preserve his own life, or to secure the safety of his friends.

When a church at Carthage was about to be searched for copies of the Bible, he had them concealed in a safe place, and the writings of heretics substituted for them. This removal was an act of Christian Faithfulness, but the works which he put in the church in their stead were apparently intended to deceive the heathen officers. Mensurius seems to us to have been too prudent a man for a Christian bishop in the harsh times in which he lived. In his own day his conduct created a most unfavorable opinion of his religious courage and faithfulness among multitudes of the Saviour's servants in his country.

Secundus, primate of Numidia, wrote to Mensurius, giving utterance to censures about his conduct, and glorifying the men who perished rather than surrender their Bibles. Caecilian was the archdeacon of the bishop of Carthage, and was known to enjoy his confidence and share his opinions.

Mensurius, returning from a visit to Rome, became ill, and died in the year 311. Caecilian was appointed his successor, and immediately the whole opposition of the enemies of his predecessor was directed to him. In his own city a rich widow of great influence, and her numerous friends, assailed him; a synod of seventy Numidian bishops excommunicated him for receiving ordination from a **traditor** (one who had delivered up the Bible to be burned to save his life); and another bishop was elected to take charge of the church of Carthage. The Donatist community was then launched upon the sea of its stormy life.

Bishop Donatus, after whom the new denomination was

named, was a man of great eloquence, as unbending as Martin Luther, as fiery as the great Scotch Reformer, whose principles were dearer to him than life, and who was governed by unwearied energy. Under his guidance the Donatists spread all over the Roman dominions on the African coast, and for a time threatened the supremacy of the older Christian community.

But persecution laid its heavy hand upon their personal liberty, their church property, and their lives. Again and again this old and crushing argument was applied to the Donatists, and still they survived for centuries. Their hardships secured the sympathy of numerous bands of armed marauders called Circumcelliones, men who suffered severely from the authorities sustained by the persecuting church, "free lance" warriors who cared nothing for religion, but had a wholesome hatred of tyrants.

These men fought desperately for the oppressed Donatists. Julian the Apostate took their side when he ascended the throne of the Caesars, and showed much interest in their welfare, as unbelievers in modern times have frequently shown sympathy with persecuted communities in Christian lands.

There were a few Donatist churches outside of Africa, but the denomination was almost confined to that continent. They suffered less from the Vandals than their former oppressors, but the power of these conquerors was very injurious to them; and the victorious Saracens destroyed the remaining churches of this grand old community.

The Donatists were determined to have only godly members in their churches. In this particular they were immeasurably superior to the Church Universal (Catholic), even as represented by the great Augustine of Hippo. Their teachings on this question are in perfect harmony with our own. They regarded the Church Universal as having forfeited her Christian character by her inconsistencies and iniquities, and they refused to recognize her ordinances and ministry.

Hence they gave the triple immersion a second time to those who had received it in the great corrupt church.

Their government was not episcopal in the modern sense. Mosheim is right in representing them as having at one time 400 bishops. The Roman population on the North African coast would not have required twenty diocesan bishops to care for their spiritual wants.

Every town, in all probability, had its bishop, and if there were two or more congregations, these formed but one church, whose services were in charge of one minister and his assistants. These church leaders were largely under the control of the people to whom they ministered. The Donatists held boldly the doctrine that the church and the state were entirely distinct bodies. Early in their denominational life, Constantine the Great, for the first time in earthly history, had united the church to the Roman government, and speedily the Donatists arose to denounce the union as unhallowed, and as forbidden by the highest authority in the Christian Church.

No Baptist in modern times brands the accursed union between church and state with more appropriate condemnations than did his ancient Donatist brother. Their faith on this question is well expressed in their familiar saying, "What has the emperor to do with the church?" Soul liberty lived in their day.

It is extremely probable that they did not practice the baptism of unconscious babes,—at least in the early part of their history. It is often urged that Augustine, their bitter enemy, would not fail to bring this charge against them if they had rejected his favorite rite. His works now extant do not **directly** bring such an accusation against them, and it is concluded that they followed his own usage.

This argument would have great weight if it were proved that all the Catholics of Africa baptized unconscious babes. But there is no evidence of such universal observance. Outside of Africa, in the fourth century, the baptism of an unconscious babe was a rare occurrence. Though born in it of pious parents, Augustine himself was not baptized till he was thirty-three years of age. His works are bristling with weapons to defend infant baptism; they are the arsenal from which its modern defenders have procured their most effective arms, and if the custom had been universally accepted, he would have seen no cause to keep up such a warfare in its defense.

The frequency with which Augustine treats of infant baptism is striking evidence that its observance in his day and country was often called in question, and that had he directly pointed out this defect in the observances of the Donatists he would have been quickly reminded that he had better remove the oppostion to infant baptism from his own people before he assailed it among the Donatists.

This fact would account for the supposed silence of Augustine on this question. The second canon of the Council of Carthage, where the principles of Augustine were supreme, "Declares an anathema against such as deny that children ought to be baptized as soon as they are born." —Du Pin, I. 635. Dublin.

If this curse is against the Donatists, it shows that they did not practice the infant rite; if it is against other Africans, it gives a good reason why Augustine should be cautious in bringing charges against the Donatists on this account. Augustine wrote a work "on Baptism, Against the Donatists," in which, speaking of infant baptism, he says, "And if **any one seek divine authority** in this matter, although, what the whole church holds, not as instituted by councils, but as a thing always observed, is rightly held to have been handed down by apostolical authority." (Et si quisquam in hac re auctoritatem divinam quaret.—Patrol. Lat., vol. xlii. p. 174, Migne. Parisiis.)

This book is expressly written against the views of baptism held by the Donatists; it was designed to correct their errors on that subject. And he clearly admits that some of them doubted the divine authority of infant baptism, and he proceeds to establish it by an argument from circumcision.

Augustine was a powerful controversialist; to have charged the Donatists directly with heresy for rejecting infant baptism would have been an accusation against many in his own church, and he prudently assails his enemies on this point, as if only some of them regarded infant baptism as a mere human invention; and he boastfully and ignorantly, or falsely, speaks of it as always observed by the whole church, while one of his own African councils pronounces a curse upon those who "denied that children ought to be baptized as soon as they are born."—BAPTIST ENCYCLOPEDIA, page 341, by William Cathcart, D. D.

THE DUTCH BAPTISTS

Edward T. Hiscox, D. D.

The Baptists of Holland have a history that reaches back to a very remote period, if not to the apostolic age, as some confidently assert. And this antiquity is conceded by historians who have no sympathy with their denominational sentiments.

MOSHEIM, in his church history, says: "The true origin of that sect which acquired the name Anabaptists, is hid in the remote depths of antiquity, and is consequently extremely difficult to be ascertained."

ZWINGLE, the Swiss reformer, contemporary with Luther, declares: "The institution of Anabaptism is no novelty, but for thirteen hundred years has caused great disturbance in the church." Thirteen hundred years before his time would have carried it back to within two centuries of the death of Christ.

Dr. DERMONT, Chaplain to the king of Holland, and Dr. YPEIJ, Professor of theology at Groningen, a few years since received a royal commission to prepare a history of the Reformed Dutch Church. That history, prepared under royal sanction, and officially published, contains the following manly and generous testimony to the antiquity and orthodoxy of the Dutch Baptists. "We have now seen that the Baptists, who were formerly called Anabaptists, and in later times Mennonites, were the original Waldenses, and have long in the history of the church received the honor of that origin. On this account, the Baptists may be considered the only Christian community which has stood since the apostles, and as a Christian society, which has preserved pure the doctrines of the gospel through all ages."

MOSHEIM says of the persecutions of this people in the sixteenth century: "Vast numbers of these people, in nearly all the countries of Europe, would rather perish miserably by drowning, hanging, burning, or decapitation, than renounce the opinions they had embraced." And their innocency he vindicates thus: "It is indeed true that many Anabaptists were put to death, not as being bad citizens, or injurious members of civil society, but as being incurable heretics, who were condemned by the old canon laws. For the error of adult baptism was in that age looked upon as a horrible offence." That was their only crime.

This testimony is all the more welcome, because it comes from those who have no ecclesiastical sympathies with Baptists, but who, in fidelity to history, bear honest testimony to the truth which history teaches. The circumstances under which their evidence was produced, give it additional force.

CARD. HOSSIUS, chairman of the council at Trent, says: "If the truth of religion were to be judged of by the readiness and cheerfulness which a man of any sect shows in suffering, then the opinions and persuasions of no sect can be truer or surer, than those of the Anabaptists; since there have been none, for these twelve hundred years past, that have been more grievously punished." Many thousands of the Dutch Baptists, called Anabaptists, and Mennonists, miserably perished by the hands of their cruel persecutors, for no crime but their refusal to conform to established churches.—BAPTIST SHORT METHOD, by Rev. Edward T. Hiscox, D. D., pages 193-197.

ENGLISH BAPTISTS
(Davis' History)

"The Gospel message went out from Jerusalem in the days of the Apostles to remote parts of the world with great speed. We find them in England in the first century. The following is taken from Davis' History of the Welsh Baptists.

"About fifty years before the birth of our Saviour, the Romans invaded the British Isle, in the reign of the Welsh king, Cassibellan; but having failed, in consequence of other and more important wars, to conquer the Welsh nation, made peace with them, and dwelt among them many years. During that period many of the Welsh soldiers joined the Roman army, and many families from Wales visited Rome; among whom there was a certain woman of the name of Claudia, who was married to a man named Pudens. (Paul mentioned a man by that name in Rome in his letter to Timothy, II Timothy 4:21—WJB.)

"At the same time, Paul was sent a prisoner to Rome, and preached there in his own hired house, for the space of two years, about the year of our Lord 63. Pudens, and Claudia his wife, who belonged to Caesar's household, under the blessing of God on Paul's preaching, were brought to the knowledge of the truth as it is in Jesus, and made a profession of the Christian religion.

"These, together with other Welshmen, among the Roman soldiers, who had tasted that the Lord was gracious, exerted themselves on the behalf of their countrymen in Wales, who were at that time vile idolaters.

"Whether any of the Apostles ever preached in Britain cannot be proved, and though it is generally believed that Joseph of Arimathea was first that preached the gospel in that part of the world, we must confess that we are not positive on that subject. The fact, we believe, is this: The Welsh lady, Claudia, and others, who were converted under Paul's preaching ministry in Rome, carried the precious seed with them, and scattered it on the hills and valleys of Wales; and since that time, many thousands have reaped a most glorious harvest.

"They told their countrymen around, what a dear Saviour they had found; they pointed to His redeeming blood, as the only way whereby they might come to God.

"The Welsh can truly say: if by the transgression of

a woman sin came into the world, it was through the instrumentality of a woman, even painted Claudia, that the glorious news of the gospel reached their ears, and they felt it to be mighty through God, to pull down the strong holds of darkness.

"How rapidly did the mighty gospel of Christ fly abroad! The very year 63, when Paul, a prisoner, was preaching to a few individuals, in his own hired house in Rome, the seed sown there is growing in the Isle of Britain. We have nothing of importance to communicate respecting the Welsh Baptists, from this period to the year 180, when two ministers by the names of Faganus and Damicanus, who were born in Wales, but were born again in Rome, and there becoming eminent ministers of the gospel, were sent from Rome to assist their brethren in Wales. In the same year, Lucius, the Welsh king, and the first king of the world who embraced the Christian religion, was baptized.

"Faganus and Domicanus were two faithful witnesses, bearing testimony to the truth, and were remarkably successful in winning souls to Christ. Through their instrumentality, the light of the gospel burst forth from the isle of Anglesea to the isle of Thanet, like the sun in the morning after the dark night of Druidism; the glorious light of the gospel dispelled the shades of ignorance and error, in which the seed of Gomer had been enveloped from generation to generation.

"Fired with a sacred zeal for the cause of Christ, and the welfare of immortal souls, our Welsh apostles followed the superstitions and cruelties of paganism to their most secret chambers, and exposed them in their native deformity.

"It is true they had not to stretch on the rack, neither had they to endure the flames; yet they had to encounter with pagan ignorance, and much opposition from Beelzebub, the prince of darkness.

"Though the gospel had been preached in the island since the year 63; yet, as God had not departed from his general way of disseminating his truth among the children of men, by beginning with small things in order to obtain great things, hitherto it had been the day of small things with our forefathers, the inhabitants of the ends of the earth. But now Zion's tent was enlarged, and the curtain of her habitation stretched forth; she broke forth on the right hand and on the left; kings became nursing fathers and queens nursing mothers. Behold king Lucius, not only embracing the religion of Christ himself, but finding the means of propagating the gospel very inadequate, sending a most earnest request to Eleutherus, for additional help. Here the Macedonian cry vibrated from the Welsh throne at Carludd, as well as from the Welsh cabin at the foot of Caderidris or Plimlimon.

"About the year 300, the Welsh Baptists suffered most terrible and bloody persecution, which was the tenth pagan persecution under the reign of Dioclesian. Alban had the pain, and honor, to be the first martyr on the British shore. Next to him were Aaron and Julius, renowned men, who lived at Carleon, South Wales. The number of persons, meeting houses, and books, that were burnt at that time, is too horrid to relate; but, however, they were not all consumed by the flames. Religion, yes, pure religion, the religion of Christ and his apostles, was yet alive. Here, as well as in many other places, the blood of the martyrs proved to be the seed of the church."—Davis' History of the Welsh Baptists, pages 7-9.

The English Baptists

Edward T. Hiscox

At what time the Baptists appeared in England in definite denominational form, it is impossible to say. But from the **twelfth** to the **seventeenth** century, many of them suffered cruel persecutions, and death by burning, drowning, and beheading, beside many other, and sometimes most inhuman tortures.

And this they suffered both from Papists and Protestants, condemned by both civil and ecclesiastical tribunals, only because they persisted in worshipping God according to the dictates of their consciences, and because they would not submit their religious faith and worship to the dictates of popes and princes. In 1538, royal edicts were issued against them, and several were burnt at the stake in Smithfield.

BRANDE writes that: "In the year 1538, thirty-one Baptists, that fled from England, were put to death at Delft, in Holland; the men were beheaded, and the women were drowned." What crime had they committed to merit such treatment as this?

BP. LATIMER declares that: "The Baptists that were burnt in different parts of the kingdom, went to death intrepidly, and without any fear," during the time of Henry VIII.

Under the rule of the Popish Mary, they suffered perhaps no more than under that of the Protestant Elizabeth. During the reign of the latter, a congregation of Baptists was discovered in London, whereupon several were banished, twenty-seven imprisoned, and two burnt at Smithfield.

DR. FEATLEY, one of their bitter enemies, wrote of them, in 1633: "This sect, among others, hath so far presumed upon the patience of the state, that it hath held weekly conventicles, re-baptizing hundreds of men and women together in the twilight, in rivulets, and in some arms of the Thames, and elsewhere, dipping them all over head and ears. It hath printed divers pamphlets in defence of their heresy; yea, and challenged some of our preachers to disputation."

BAILEY wrote, in 1639, that: "Under the shadow of independency, they have lifted up their heads, and increased their numbers above all sects in the land. They have forty-six churches in and about London. They are a people very fond of religious liberty, and very unwilling to be brought under bondage of the judgment of others."

The first book published in the English language on the subject of baptism, was translated from the Dutch, and bears date, 1618. From this time they multiplied rapidly through all parts of the kingdom. The first regularly organized church among them, known as such in England, dates from 1607, and was formed in London by a Mr. Smyth, previously a clergyman of the established church.

In 1689, the Particular Baptists, so called, held a convention in London, in which more than one hundred congregations were represented, and which issued a confession of faith, still in use and highly esteemed.

The last Baptist martyr in England was Edward Wightman, of Burton upon Trent, condemned by the Bishop of Conventry, and burnt at Litchfield, April 11, 1612.— BAPTIST SHORT METHOD, by Rev. Edward T. Hiscox, D. D., pages 197-201.

John Bunyan a Baptist

John Marsh

He was the son of a tinker, born 1628. In early life, he was infamous for the most daring impiety. Thrice was he snatched from the jaws of death; but the divine mercies he only abused to sin. Fortunately he married the daughter of a pious man, whose only portion was two books, "The Practice of Piety," and "The Plain Man's Pathway to Heaven."

These books brought conversion to his heart; and submitting himself to God, he entered into the communion of the Baptist Church, at Bedford, in his 27th year, and soon became an active and powerful preacher of the gospel. He established himself at Bedford, and was active in forming numerous churches around him. At the restoration, he was siezed and thrown into prison, where he lay twelve years.

But there he was not idle. He maintained himself and family, by making long tagged thread laces; and there wrote that most wonderful book, "The Pilgrim's Progress." After he regained his liberty, he traveled through England, to comfort and establish his brethren. A meeting house was built for him at Bedford; but he often preached in London, where he attracted vast crowds. He died August 31, 1688, aged 60 years. He was a man of deep humility and gentleness. His industry is to be seen in his two folio volumes.

His Pilgrim's Progress has been translated into various languages, and has been printed more times than any book excepting the Bible. Until the middle of the 18th century, the Baptists never admitted psalmody into their worship, considering it a human ordinance. It was then introduced by some, and a violent controversy ensued.—EPITOME OF GENERAL ECCL. HISTORY, by Rev. John Marsh.

(Bunyan, however, was an open communionist. W.J.B.)

English Baptists Descended From the German Baptists

D. B. Ray

We now come to the direct question—"Where did the English Baptists originate?" Historians admit that persons holding Baptist views, have existed in various parts of England and Wales from very early times. This may be seen from the proclamations and edicts of kings against the hated "Anabaptists." The same is shown by Davis, in his History of the Welsh Baptists; and by Crosby, Orchard, and Evans, in their histories of English Baptists.

It is an egregious mistake to suppose that the English Baptists had their rise since the Reformation of the sixteenth century. But, owing to the fierce and continued persecutions waged against them, they were accustomed, as much as possible, to conceal themselves from public view.

They frequently met in private houses, or barns, and even in the thick forest in the dead of night, for the worship of God; but whenever they were detected by the vigilance of Papal spies, they were seized and delivered over to the vengeance of the secular arm. And from the fact that all their books and records were diligently sought and burned by their enemies, we have but little material for history, except the prejudiced statements and edicts of their enemies. We are, however, able to furnish many instances of emigration of German Baptists to England in these early times. Many of the early Baptists of England were called Lollards.

Mr. Crosby, the historian, says: "In the time of King **Edward** the Second, about the year 1315, **Walter Lollard, a German** preacher, a man of great renown among the **Waldenses,** came into England; he spread their doctrines very much in these parts, so that afterward they went by the name of **Lollards."**

That these Lollards were Baptists, who had their descent through the German Baptists, from the ancient Waldenses, is shown by Mr. Orchard. "The Lollards' Tower," in which these witnesses for Christ suffered, still stands in London, as a monument of Papal cruelty toward these ancient English Baptists.

Of the Baptists of England, "Bishop **Burnet** says: 'At this (Anno 1549) there were many **Anabaptists** in several parts of **England.** They were generally **Germans,** whom the revolutions there had forced to change their scats.'" In this we have the testimony of Burnet, that the early English Baptists, called Anabaptists, were from Germany, and were numerous, long before the John Smith affair, in Holland.

In the year 1538, King Henry VIII., issued a proclamation against the **Anabaptists** (Baptists) and others; and in the same year, Archbishop Cranmer received a commission "to inquire after Anabaptists, to proceed against them, to restore the penitent, to burn their books, and to deliver the obstinate to the secular arm."

And of this time, "Mr. Fuller tells us, 'that in this year a match being made by the Lord Cromwell's contrivance, between King **Henry** and the Lady **Anne of Cleve. Dutchmen** flocked faster than formerly into **England,** and soon after began to broach their strange opinions, being branded with the general name of **Anabaptists.** These Anabaptists,' he adds, 'for the main, are but **Donatists,** new dipt; and this year their name first appears in our **English** Chronicles. I read,' says he, 'that four **Anabaptists,** three men and one woman, all **Dutch,** bare faggots at **Paul's** cross; and three days after, a man and a woman of their **sect,** were burnt in Smithfield.'"

This is the testimony of Thomas Fuller, a historian of the Church of England, that Dutch Baptists (Anabaptists) flocked into England in the year 1538, in the reign of Henry VIII., long before the time of John Smith.

But we have still more direct testimony concerning the succession of the more modern English Baptists, from whom the Baptists of America descended. In the year 1633 a large number of Pedobaptists, belonging to the Independents, became convinced of the correctness of Baptist principles. They were puzzled at first as to the best method of obtaining valid baptism. They appointed one of their number, Richard Blunt, to visit Holland and there receive baptism from a church which was known to be in the regular succession from the ancient Waldenses. Mr. Crosby introduces the testimony of William Kiffin as follows: "This agrees with an account given of the matter in an ancient manuscript, said to be written by **Mr. William Kiffin,** who lived in those times, and was a leader among those of that persuasion.

"This relates, that several sober and pious persons belonging to the congregations of the **dissenters** about **London,** were convinced that **believers** were the only proper subjects of **baptism,** and that it ought to be administered by **immersion** or **dipping** the whole body into the water, in resemblance of a **burial** and **resurrection,** according to Colos. ii: 12, and Rom. vi: 4.

"That they often met together to pray and confer about this matter, and consult what methods they should take to enjoy this ordinance in its primitive purity: That they could not be satisfied about any **administrator** in **England** to begin this practice; because, though some in this nation rejected the **baptism** of **infants,** yet they had not, as they knew of, revived the ancient custom of **immersion.**

"But, hearing that some in the **Netherlands** practiced

it, they agreed to send over one Mr. Richard Blunt, who understood the **Dutch** language: That he went accordingly, carrying letters of recommendation with him, and was kindly received both by the church there, and Mr. **John Batte,** their teacher: That upon his return he baptized Mr. **Samuel Blacklock,** a minister, and these two baptized the rest of their company, whose names are in the manuscript to the number of fifty-three.

"So that those who followed this **scheme** did not receive their **baptism** from the aforesaid Mr. **Smith,** or his congregation at **Amsterdam,** it being an ancient congregation of foreign **Baptists** in the low **countries** to whom they sent."

Here we have the undisputed historic fact, that the Baptists of London were so careful to obtain valid baptism that they delegated Richard Blunt, formerly a Pedobaptist minister, to visit a regular Baptist church, at Amsterdam, in Holland, which belonged to the old Waldensean succession.

And after the baptism of Richard Blunt by John Batte, by the authority of said church, he returned to London and baptized Samuel Blacklock, and they baptized the rest of the company, to the number of fifty-three members; and thus was formed a Baptist church, which was afterward recognized as a Particular Baptist church. And from this influential church has flown the stream of succession down to the present time.

We have now seen that the English Baptists, instead of originating with John Smith, have descended from the Dutch and German Baptists, who descended from the ancient Waldenses. In following up the succession of Baptists, we have found them in England, suffering almost incredible hardships and persecutions under the bloody reigns of James and his father, Charles II.

In these fearful times it was no light matter to become a Baptist. It involved the renunciation of the grandeur and honors of the world, and to become the objects of Papal and Protestant cruelties. They were the faithful martyrs who were hunted down by the blood-hounds, in human form, of the established Church, as though they had been wild beasts.

And about this time many of them, fleeing from persecution, emigrated to America. And, also, we have seen that, in the time of Henry VIII., and in more remote periods, the Dutch Baptists bore witness for Christ in England at the sacrifice of their lives.

And it has been shown that companies of Dutch Baptists flocked into England, from time to time, and propagated their principles long before the London Dissenters embraced Baptist principles, and sent Richard Blunt to the continent to receive baptism.

But it is not our purpose to attempt to follow up all the chains of succession which connect the English Baptists with the old Waldensean Baptists of Germany. At the present, I am only tracing the most direct line which connects the English with the German Baptists.

And for the present we take our leave of the English Baptists; and from the British Isles, cross the North Sea to the Netherlands. And here we find the Baptists, with the same heaven-born principles, amidst the frowning monarchies and despotisms of continental Europe, bearing the same unflinching testimony for religious liberty which they have borne in England and America. It will be remembered that in the term **German Baptists,** we include the Dutch Baptists also. As already intimated, many of the German Baptists had, from time to time, emigrated to England; but they were so sorely persecuted that they were sometimes driven to other countries, or compelled to secrete themselves from the view of the public.

For long years, it was the policy of the English Baptists to avoid, as much as possible, the notice of the authorities of government; and in order to do this, they studiously avoided any communications with the Pedobaptists of all classes; because the Protestants were almost as bitter in their persecutions against the English Baptists as were the Catholics.

Taking this view of the condition of the Baptists of England at this time, it is no wonder that these Pedobaptists were not well posted in the affairs of the Baptists of England. Their want of knowledge on this point, is no evidence that there were no true Baptists in England at this time. Though some of the English Baptist historians were of the opinion that the sending to the continent to get valid baptism was unnecessary, yet it was their duty to do this, if they knew of no Scriptural administrator nearer.

No one can plead the authority of the Scriptures for "alien" baptisms. It is certainly much safer to be guided by the example of Jesus Christ and the apostles, in this as all other matters of religious duty.—BAPTIST SUCCESSION by D. B. Ray, pp. 84-90.

THE GERMAN BAPTISTS

The German Baptists Did Not Originate With the Munster Riot
D. B. Ray

It appears that in every age, from the time of Christ the Baptist denomination has been made the scape-goat to bear the sins of the world. Almost every crime known to earth, has been laid to their charge. They are considered the enemies of governments, ringleaders of sedition and revolution, and obstinate and incurable heretics. It has been supposed that earthquakes, wars, famines, and pestilences, have been sent upon the human family on account of the crimes of the Baptists. And it is now gravely stated, by a certain class of "charitable" writers, who have not the power, as did their fathers, to imprison and burn Baptists, that **the Baptist denomination originated with the Munster riot in Germany, about the year 1525.** And this class of men are generally very clamorous about Baptist "Close Communion." But did the Baptists originate with the madmen of Munster? Upon an investigation of the history of the Munster affair, the following facts are developed:

1. The Munster rebellion did not arise from any

religious, or denominational, opinions whatever, but in order to resist the oppressions of the despotic governments of Germany. Of the miserable condition of this wretched people, Mr. Robinson, the historian, says: "The condition of the peasants in Germany, in the year twenty-four (1524), was deplorable, if there be anything to deplore in a deprivation of most of the rights and liberties of rational creatures. The feudal system, that execration in the eyes of every being that merits the name of man, had been established in early ages in Germany, in all its rigor and horror. It had been planted with a sword reeking with human gore, in the night of barbarism, when cannibals drank the warm blood of one enemy out of the skull of another, and it had shot its venomous fibers every way, rioted itself in every transaction; in religion, in law, in diversions, in everything secular and sacred, so that the wretched rustics had only one prospect for themselves and all their posterity—one horrid prospect of everlasting slavery."

And of the effort of this unfortunate people to break the iron yoke of tyranny, the author of the Religious Encyclopedia says: "Munzer, and his associates, in the year 1525, put themselves at the head of a numerous army, and declared war against all laws, governments, and magistrates of every kind, under the chimerical pretext that Christ himself was now to take the reins of all governments into His hands: but this seditious crowd was routed and dispersed by the Elector of Saxony, and other Princes, and Munzer, their leader, put to death." The same author adds: "It must be acknowledged that the true rise of the insurrections of this period ought not to be attributed to religious opinions."

2. The prime movers of the Munster riot were Pedobaptists.

Mr. Benedict says: "It is certain that the disturbances in the very city of Munster, were begun by a Pedobaptist minister, of the Lutheran persuasion, whose name was Bernard Rotman, or Rothman; that he was assisted in his endeavors by other ministers of the same persuasion; and that they began to stir up tumults, that is, teach revolutionary principles, a year before the Anabaptist 'ringleaders,' as they are called, visited the place. These things the Papists knew, and they failed not to improve them to their own advantage. They uniformly insisted that Luther's doctrine led to rebellion, that his disciples were the prime movers of the insurrections, and they also asserted that a hundred and thirty thousand Lutherans perished in the rustic war."

3. If the testimony of their enemies is entitled to credit the Munsterites, in their practices, very much resemble the Mormons of our day. And it would be as legitimate to charge the Baptists with the Mormon abominations, as with the excesses of the frenzied German peasants of the sixteenth century.

4. The most of these insurgents were of no religion. They entered the rebellion as men driven to desperation, in order to gain their independence. But it is freely admitted that some Catholics, some Lutherans, and some socalled Anabaptists, were engaged in this struggle for freedom.

5. These deluded fanatics were finally destroyed in battle.

Of their destruction Mr. Orchard says: "These oppressed men were consequently met by their lords with a sword, instead of redress; being defeated, they were slaughtered and reproached—the invariable results and concomitants of defeat; Munzer, their friend and chief, was put to death.

6. It is extremely unjust, therefore, to censure the Baptist denomination for the improprieties of some of its members who were, or many have been, seduced into fanaticism and turbulence. Of the unjustness of these aspersions, Mr. Evans says: "Historians of a certain class, and partisan writers, have been fond of designating as 'Anabaptists,' and gathering around us all those elements of social disorder and fearful profligacy which the scenes

of Munster, and the mad vagaries of Stork and his brethren, ever suggest. Hard have they labored to identify us with these men. We are not careful to answer them in this matter.

The men that shrunk not from the severe privations of the jail, and the more terrible punishment of the stake, were not affected much by a name. It answered the purpose of their adversaries for a time; but they were blind to the logical consequences of their own position.

They forgot, in the fullness of their malice, the retribution to which they were exposing themselves. To trace the sad events which resulted from the efforts to secure social freedom, to the doctrines that the individual consciousness of God's claim on man's affections, and that the Christian profession is only made by an immersion of the individual in water, 'in the name of the Father, of the Son, and of the Holy Ghost'; is only to lay open their own system to the most crushing retort.

It were just as easy to demonstrate that the world has been the vast theater on which Pedobaptists have perpetrated crimes at which humanity shudders, and over which piety and virtue must weep, as that the Anabaptists, as a body, were found steeped in crime and reveling in lust."

Thus it is shown by Mr. Evans that if the Baptists are liable to censure, simply because some of the Munster fanatics rejected infant baptism, then, on the same principles, the Pedobaptists are chargeable with all the crimes committed by their Catholic ancestors. For instance, who instituted the Inquisition? Pedobaptists. Who preached up the crusades against the ancient Waldenses? Pedobaptists. Who are guilty of the blood of sixty millions of the saints for conscience sake? Pedobaptists.

But these things are passed over lightly by our accusers; and because some deluded Anabaptists of Germany joined in a death struggle for liberty, the Baptists, as a denomination, are stigmatized as originating the Munster riot! The injustice of these charges is shown by Mr. D'Anvers, as follows: "That take it for granted, that things were so as to matter of fact, that many Anabaptists did prove so horribly **wicked,** as **Spanhemius, Sleidan, Osiander,** and others do report, yet how unreasonable and uncharitable would it be to render all this people, either in those times or since, to be such persons also; and to judge an error in the principle from the error in conversation of some that have professed it; for by the same rule may not the purest state of the church, both in the Old and New Testament, be censured and judged; who had their **Chora's, Judas'** and **Diotrephes',** among them?

But that others that owned that principle, were men of another spirit, both in that as well as former and latter times, you have most ample and authentic testimony from their greatest enemies."

But in no sense can it be stated that the Baptists originated with the Munster rebellion. It would be as legitimate for future historians to contend that the American Baptists organized with the Mormon movement as for one to affirm that the German Baptists started with the Munster movement. It will be seen that the German Baptists existed under the name of Anabaptists long before this unhappy affair.

Mr. Brown, editor of the **Religious Encyclopedia** says: "It is but justice to observe, also, that the Baptists in Holland, England, and the United States, are to be considered as entirely distinct from those seditious and fanatical individuals above mentioned, as they profess an equal aversion to all principles of rebellion on the one hand, and of enthusiasm on the other.—**Buck's Theol. Dictionary; Milner's Church History; Robinson's Eccl. Researches; Encyclopedia America; Benedict's History of the Baptists.**"

These writers are too candid to associate the Baptists with the Munster riot. D'Aubigne, an eminent Pedobaptist historian, says: "On one point it seems necessary to guard against misapprehension. Some persons imagine that the (Munster) Anabaptists of the times of the Reformation, and the Baptists of our day, are the same. But they are as different as possible." This is the testimony of the learned historian, who declares that the Baptists are as **different as possible** from the Munster Anabaptists.

Again: we have the testimony of the Royal Encyclopedia, as quoted by Mr. Graves in the Tri-Lemma. Mr. Graves says: "This great work, by William H. Hall Esq., with other learned, ingenious gentlemen, was begun in London, in 1788, and completed in three large folio volumes. In the article 'Anabaptists,' after recounting the excesses of Muntzer, Matthias, Borkholdt, and others, during the sixteenth century, in Germany, the Encyclopedia proceeds: 'It is to be remarked that the Baptists, or Mennonites, in England and Holland are to be considered in a very different light from the enthusiasts we have been describing; and it appears equally uncandid and invidious to trace up their distinguished sentiments, as some of their adversaries have done, to those obnoxious characters, and then to stop, in order, as it were, to associate with it the ideas of turbulence and fanaticism, with which it certainly has no natural connection.

Their coincidence with some of those oppressed and infatuated people, in denying baptism to infants, is acknowledged by the Baptists, but they disavow the practice which the appellation of Anabaptist implies; and their doctrines seem referable to a more ancient and respectable origin. They appear supported by history in considering themselves the descendants of the Waldenses, who were so grievously oppressed and persecuted by the despotic heads of the Romish hierarchy.' "

Reader, take notice: the authors of the Royal Encyclopedia are positive in their statement that the **Baptists have no connection** with the Munster mob; but, on the contrary, they affirm that **their doctrines seem referable to a more ancient and respectable origin.** No one now, except an extremely wicked or ignorant man, will, in the face of these historic facts, presume to affirm that the Baptists originated with the Munster affair.

Again, Mr. Benedict, speaking of the true Baptists of these times, says: "Their peace principles, and those on oaths, capital punishment, etc., were the same before the rustic war as afterward; and may be traced down, through the history of the Waldenses and other evangelical parties, 'to the remote depths of antiquity.' Menno was, indeed, a distinguished teacher among the Anabaptists during the whole of his ministry; but Mosheim's account of his gathering up the fragments of the society after their dispersion, and re-organizing them upon new and better principles, is not at all sustained by anything that appears in their own relations. They were the same people in policy and practice before Menno came among them as afterward.

We see them almost daily on trial in the criminal courts; and never were a people so uniform, and I may say so dauntless, in their religious professions, as were the German Anabaptists for the century and a half now under review. The charges against them seemed to have been destroyed by the inquisitors, and their answers were uniform as to matters of fact, and always mild and explicit; and, as to the men of Munster or Amsterdam—for the scenes at both places were often referred to—they uniformly answered: **'These were not our brethren—we have no fellowship with such men. The men of Munster were among yourselves,'** or of your party. **They did not admit, or even intimate, that they went off from them, or were ever in their connection.**

But they bitterly complained of having to suffer for the faults of others that they knew nothing about, **because some of them agreed with them in rejecting infant baptism."** It may be proper to observe here, that the term **Mennonites** has, in history, been applied to different classes of religionists. Menno himself, and the most of the Mennonites of his day, were strict Baptists in their religious views; but the modern Mennonites are wholly different: They practice pouring for baptism. When I use the term Mennonites, in this work, as synonymous with Baptists, I refer to the true Baptist Mennonites of old.—BAPTIST SUCCESSION by D. B. Ray, pp. 91-99.

THE HENRICIANS
William Cathcart, D. D.

Henry, a monk in the first half of the twelfth century, became a great preacher. He was endowed with extraordinary powers of persuasion, and with a glowing earnestness that swept away the greatest obstacles that mere human power could banish, and he had the grace of God in his heart. He denounced prayers for the dead, the invocation of saints, the vices of the clergy, the superstitions of the church, and the licentiousness of the age, and he set an example of the sternest morality. He was a master-spirit in talents, and a heaven-aided hero, a John Knox, born in another clime, but nourished upon the same all-powerful grace.

When he visited the city of Mans the inferior clergy became his followers, and the people gave him and his doctrine their hearts, and they refused to attend the consecrated mummeries of the popish churches, and mocked the higher clergy who clung to them. In fact, their lives were endangered by the triumph of Henry's doctrines. The rich and the poor gave him their confidence and their money, and when Hildebert, their bishop, returned, after an absence covering the entire period of Henry's visit, he was received with contempt and his blessing with ridicule. Henry's great arsenal was the Bible, and all opposition melted away before it.

He retired from Mans and went to Provence, and the same remarkable results attended his ministry; persons of all ranks received his blessed doctrines and forsook the foolish superstitions of Rome and the churches in which they occupied the most important positions. At and around Thoulouse his labors seem to have created the greatest indignation and alarm among the few faithful friends of Romanism, and Catholics in the most distant parts of France heard of his overwhelming influence and his triumphant heresy with great fear. In every direction for many miles around he preached Christ, and at last Pope Eugene III. sent a cardinal to overthrow the heretic and his errors. He wisely took with him, in 1147, the celebrated St. Bernard. This abbot had the earnestness and the temper of Richard Baxter, whom he resembled in some respects. He was a more eloquent man, and he was probably the most noted and popular ecclesiastic in Europe. He speaks significantly of the state of things which he found in Henry's field: "The churches (Catholic) are without people, the people without priests, the priests without due reverence, and, in short, Christians are without Christ; the churches were regarded as synagogues, the sanctuary of God was not held to be sacred, and the sacraments were not reckoned to be holy, festive days lost their solemnity, men died in their sins, souls were snatched away everywhere to the dread tribunal, alas! neither reconciled by repentance nor fortified by the holy communion. The life of Christ was closed to the little children of Christians, whilst the grace of baptism was refused, nor were they permitted to approach salvation, although the Saviour lovingly proclaims before them, and says, 'Suffer the little children to come to me.'"

Elsewhere, St. Bernard, speaking of Henry and other heretics, says, "They mock us because we baptize infants, because we pray for the dead, because we seek the aid of (glorified) saints." That Henry had a great multitude of adherents is beyond a doubt, and that he was a Bible Christian is absolutely certain, and that he and his followers rejected infant baptism is the testimony of St. Bernard and of all other writers who have taken notice of the Henricians and their founders. We incline to the opinion of Neander that Henry was not a Petrobrusian. We are satisfied that he and his disciples were independent witnesses for Jesus raised up by the Spirit and Word of God. The Henricians were Baptists, and their founder perished in prison.—BAPTIST ENCYCLOPEDIA by William Cathcart, D.D., pg. 518.

THE MENNONITES
(Mosheim)

"The true origin of that sect which acquired the denomination of Anabaptists, by their administering anew the rite of baptism to those who came over to their communion, and derived that of Mennonites, from the famous man, to whom they owe the greatest part of their present felicity, is hid in the remote depths of antiquity, and is, of consequence, extremely difficult to be ascertained.

This uncertainty will not appear surprising, when it is considered, that this sect started up, all of a sudden, in several countries, at the same point of time, under leaders of different talents and different intentions, and at the very period when the first contests of the reformers with the Roman pontiffs drew the attention of the world, and employed the pens of the learned, in such a manner, as to render all other objects and incidents almost matters of indifference.

The modern Mennonites not only consider themselves as the descendants of the Waldenses, who were so grievously oppressed and persecuted by the despotic heads of the Roman church, but pretend, moreover, to be the purest offspring of these respectable sufferers, being equally averse to all principles of rebellion, on the one hand, and all suggestions of fanaticism on the other. Their adversaries, on the contrary, represent them as the descendants of those turbulent and furious Anabaptists, who, in the sixteenth century, involved Germany, Holland, Switzerland, and more especially the province of Westphalia, in such scenes of blood, perplexity, and distress; and allege, that, terrified by the dreadful fate of their associates, and also influenced by the moderate counsels and wise injunctions of Mennon, they abandoned the ferocity of their primitive enthusiasm, and were gradually brought to a better mind. After having examined these two different accounts of the origin of the Anabaptists with the utmost attention and impartiality, I have found that neither of them are exactly comfortable to truth.

It may be observed in the first place, that the Mennonites are not entirely mistaken when they boast of their descent from the Waldenses, Petrobrusians, and other ancient sects, who are usually considered as **witnesses of the truth,** in the times of universal darkness and superstition. Before the rise of Luther and Calvin, there lay concealed, in almost all the countries of Europe, particularly in Bohemia, Moravia, Switzerland, and Germany, many persons who adhered tenaciously to the following doctrine, which the Waldenses, Wickliffites, and Hussites had maintained, some in a more disguised, and others in a more open and public manner, viz: "That the kingdom of Christ, or the visible church He had established upon earth, was an assembly of true and real saints, and ought therefore to be inaccessible to the wicked and unrighteous, and also exempt from all those institutions, which human prudence suggests, to oppose the progress of iniquity, or to correct and reform transgressors."—Mosheim, Vol. 3, page 320.

THE MONTANISTS

G. H. Orchard

"Towards the conclusion of the second century, one Montanus, who lived in a Phrygian village called Pepuza, undertook a mission to restore Christianity to its native simplicity. One class of professors being at the period carried away with Egyptian symbols, while others made up a system of religion from philosophic notions, oriental customs, and a portion of the gospel; apparently prompted this humble individual to attempt a reformation, or rather a restoration of the primitive order of things.

"Being destitute of classical lore himself, he required it not in others who were willing to further his designs. He was decidedly hostile to those ministers, who with the new system, emanated from Alexandria. He was very successful in his labor of love, since his views and doctrines spread abroad, and were received through Asia, Africa, and in part of Europe.

"His doctrine and discipline, though severe, gained him the esteem of many who were not of the lowest order. Some ladies of opulence aided Montanus with their services and their fortunes. We noticed the inquiries made of Tertullian, by females in this Christian community, respecting minor baptism, and of Tertullian seceding from the Catholic church in Carthage, and his uniting with the Montanists, on the grounds of purity of communion.

"From Tertullian's works, his views and arguments in support of their doctrines, with the nature of their discipline, can be ascertained. He formed in his own city a separate congregation, which continued for two hundred years. Agrippinus its first pastor, with Tertullian, admitted members by examination and baptism, but all such as joined the Montanists from other communities were rebaptized.

"A name often appears in church history, which it will be necessary for us to mention and illustrate. A physician, named Manes, embraced Christianity, and taught others the views he adopted. It is plain he had many followers in this, and in the following centuries. An endless variety of tales are told of this man, and his adherents, who were called after him, **Manicheans** which name became a kind of warning **Merimo** to all the orthodox.

"Their enemies being the recorders of their creed and discipline, deserve little credit, as in this case, with others already mentioned, their interested accusers confounded all Dissenters with the profligates and the enthusiasts, and most state clergy have pursued the same path and spirit. This class of orientals was unconnected with all hierarchies, and consisted of innumerable churches in different countries.

"Though errors were probably mixed up with this new system, one circumstance is favorable to these people, that of their enumeration by early Catholic writers, with the Messalians, Novatianists, Donatists, and Paulicians, whose memories and creeds have been rescued from undeserved reproach. We do not expect perfection in any body of Christians, but taking dissenters in every age, they have been found preferable in their knowledge of doctrines, and their practice of morals, to any community in national forms; while it is easy to discover these only have maintained civil and religious freedom, I Corinthians vii. 23, in their native dignity.

"These people accounted for the origin of evil as many had done before them, supposing it to arise out of physical or natural imperfections. They rejected the Old Testament, (as a rule to Christians, of which more hereafter).

"The leading errors in the African churches arose from their adopting the Old Testament rites, which probably occasioned these Christians with others to reject its precepts.

"Their morals were rigidly severe, their worship simple but mixed with oriental visions. Their doctrines were a mixture of national superstitions with the tenets of Christianity. Their exact views are probably not ascertained, and the reproaches heaped upon all nonconformists, leave us room to exercise charity in their case and creed.

"Their congregations, like those of the English dissenters, were divided into hearers and members, whom they called **auditors** and **elect.** They refused oaths, remonstrated against penal sanctions, and denied the authority of magistrates over conscience. Dr. Mosheim has demonstrated that they did administer baptism to those who desired it, but not without the candidates' consent, and that they did not baptise infants: which is further evident by those books published against dissenters; wherein are shown that all parties administered baptism, single or trine, and all re-baptized.

"The Manichean reproach has been charged on the Paulicians and Albigenses, since these people have been rescued from the stigma of palpable and damnable errors, we doubt not had similar investigation been pursued by unprejudiced men; a similar result would have ensued to a considerable extent, respecting the Manicheans."— History of Foreign Baptists by G. H. Orchard.

Edward Burton, in his History of the Christian church,

says, "Calumnies were spread against them in later times, as if they practiced some horrid and mysterious cruelties in their religious meetings; but **there is no reason to think that such stories had any foundation in truth.**"—Page 229.

Augustus Neander says in his Memorials of Christ's Life, "This mental tendency was opposed to many erroneous elements which had already disturbed the pure Christian consciousness, and Montanism, on many points, **advocated the interests of the primitive Christian truth in its conflict with such errors.**"—Page 49.

THE NOVATIANS

(Ray's Baptist Succession)

The Churches Called "Novatian Churches" Did Not Originate With Novatian

"Let no man deceive you by any means: for that day shall not come, except there come a falling away first, and that man of sin be revealed, the son of perdition," II Thess. 2:3.

The mystery of iniquity had begun his work of death even in the time of Paul's ministry. Corruptions were introduced into the early churches at a very early period. This was in fulfillment of predictions of Christ and the apostles, that false prophets should arise and deceive many, and, if possible, deceive the very elect. And that grievous wolves will appear among the flock, or Church of Christ, and that even church members would arise speaking perverse things to draw disciples after them.

Historians and theologians have been accustomed to appeal to the practice of the Christians of the second and third centuries, as of almost equal authority with the word of God itself. This is the fatal mistake which has aided to inundate the world with Catholic superstitions.

Concerning the records of the ancient church, the learned Isaac Taylor says: "If at any time, or in any particular instance, the authority of the ancient church is to be urged upon the modern church, then surely there is a pertinence in turning to the apostolic prophesies of perversions, corruptions, apostacies, quickly to spring within the sacred inclosure itself, which meet us at the threshold, and seem to bring us under a most solemn obligation to look to it, amid the fervors of an indiscriminate reverence, we seize for imitation the very things which the apostles foresaw and forewarned the church of as fatal errors."—Taylor's Ancient Chris., p. 47.

This timely warning of this eminent author points out to us the danger of embracing errors because of their antiquity. While the flood of corruptions was pouring upon the ancient churches, and many were being overwhelmed by it, God had faithful witnesses all the time to withstand this tide of error, and contend earnestly for the faith delivered to the saints.

And prominently among these witnesses the Novatians appear, bearing their unflinching testimony for Christ. As to Novatian himself, he is so fearfully misrepresented by his enemies that it is somewhat difficult to give a correct account of him. He was a presbyter, or elder, in the church at Rome before the rise of the Roman Catholic Church. Cornelius, the rival and implacable enemy of Novatian, was elected bishop, or pastor, of the church at Rome in the year two hundred and fifty-one.

He represents Novatian as having been "baptized in his sick bed, by aspersion." However this may be, it does not affect the standing of the Novatian churches, for it will be seen that the Novatians did not receive their origin or baptism from Novatian. All candid historians admit that Novatian was grossly misrepresented by Cornelius. Novatian was a man eminent for stern piety, learning and eloquence.

Dupin, the Catholic historian, says of him: "This author has abundance of wit, knowledge and eloquence; his style is pure, clean, and polite; his expressions choice, his thoughts natural, and his way of reasoning just: he is full of citations of texts of Scripture that are always to the purpose: and besides, there is a great deal of order and method in those treatises of his we now have; and he never speaks but with a world of candor and moderation."—Dup., vol. IV, p. 1.

Robinson, the historian, says: "The history of Novatian is long, and, like that of all others in his condition, beclouded with fables and slander. The character of the man ought no more to be taken from Cyprian than his ought from the Pagans, who, by punning on his name, called him Coprian, or the Scavenger."—Eccl. Res., p. 126.

The case, in brief, was this: Novatian was an elder in the church at Rome. He was a man of extensive learning, and held the same doctrine as the church did, and published several treatises in defense of what he believed. His address was eloquent and insinuating, and his morals were irreproachable. He saw, with extreme pain, the intolerable depravity of the church.

Christians, within the space of a very few years were caressed by one emperor, and persecuted by another. In seasons of prosperity, many rushed into the church for base purposes. In times of adversity they denied the faith and ran back to idolatry again. When the squall was over, away they came again to the church, with all their vices, to deprave others by their example.

The bishops, fond of proselytes, encouraged all this, and transferred the attention of Christians from the old confederacy for virtue, to vain shows at Easter, and a thousand other Jewish ceremonies, adulterated, too, with paganism. On the death of Bishop Fabian, Cornelius, a brother elder, and a vehement partisan for taking in the multitude, was put in nomination. Novatian opposed him; but as Cornelius carried his election, and he saw no prospect of reformation, but, on the contrary, a tide of immorality pouring into the church, he withdrew, and a great many with him.

Cornelius, irritated by Cyprian, who was just in the same condition, through the remonstrances of virtuous men at Carthage, and who was exasperated beyond measure with one of his elders named Novatus, who had quitted

Carthage and had gone to Rome to espouse the cause of Novatian, called a council, and got a sentence of excommunication passed against Novatian.

In the end, Novatian formed a church and was elected bishop. Great numbers followed his example, and all over the empire Puritan churches were constituted, and flourished through the succeeding two hundred years. Afterward, when penal laws obliged them to lurk in corners, and worship God in private, they were distinguished by a variety of names, and a succession of them continued till the Reformation.

Thus we see that Novatian made a noble stand against the growing corruptions in the church at Rome, which resulted in the division of the church and the formation of another, over which Novatian was elected pastor.

It is not known that Novatian aided in the formation of any other church than this. He only organized, and was pastor of a church at Rome. Laxity of discipline, especially the reception of those who had lapsed into idolatry, had greatly disturbed the churches in the cities. And when Novatian made his stand for virtue and church discipline, "great numbers followed his example, and all over the empire Puritan churches were constituted."

So we discover that Novatian had nothing more to do with the organization of the Novatian churches throughout the empire than the force of example. And, as in all such cases, no doubt, when the line of separation was drawn, some churches sided with the popular party, while others were numbered with those called Novatian. And, as to the case of Novatian himself, his lack of baptism, if the charge be correct, would no more affect the succession of the Novatians than the lack of baptism upon the part of a few "Baptist" ministers who have received "alien immersion."

Again, Mr. Robinson says: "They say Novatian was the first anti-pope; and yet there was, at that time, no pope in the modern sense of the word. They call Novatian the author of the heresy of Puritanism; yet they know Tertullian had quitted the church near fifty years before for the same reason, and Privatus, who was an old man in the time of Novatian, had, with several more, repeatedly remonstrated against the alterations taking place, and, as they could get no redress, had dissented and formed separate congregations.

They tax Novatian with being the parent of an innumerable multitude of congregations of Puritans all over the empire; and yet he had no other influence over any, than what his good example gave him. People saw everywhere the same cause of complaint, and groaned for relief, and when one man made a stand for virtue, the crisis had arrived—people saw the propriety of the cure, and applied the same means to their own relief."—Robinson's Eccl. Res., p. 127.

Thus it is clearly made out that Novatian was not the founder of the churches called by his name.—BAPTIST SUCCESSION by D. B. Ray, pages 154-158.

Origin of the Novatians
D. B. Ray

We have already shown, upon good authority, that the Waldenses were descended from the Novatians, and observed the same faith and practice; or, in other words, the same class of Christians who were called Novatians in Italy, were called Waldenses in the valleys of the Alps.

As the modern denominations lay no claim to any historic connection with the Novatians, it will not require much labor to show their Baptist character and connection with the apostolic churches.

The Novatian period extends from about the middle of the third century to the middle of the fifth—about two hundred years.

It is not to be understood that the Novatians began and ended with these periods; but that the witnesses for Christ, in the Roman empire, were called Novatians during the period named. They did not call themselves Novatians at the first, but this name was given by their enemies as a term of reproach.

What is termed by historians the Novatian rupture,

did not take place on account of a difference in doctrine, so far as the church ordinances were concerned, but on account of the growing corruptions in some of the churches, in consequence of the lax discipline in the reception of apostates.

When historians use the term Catholic Church with reference to these times—about the third century—they have no allusion to what is now called the Roman Catholic Church; for at that time no such church existed. But in the use of the term Catholic, they only intended to refer to the church in general. And it was this party, which claimed to be the Catholic, orthodox, or general church, in the third century, that in after times grew to be the Romish Church.

Concerning the cause which led to the division called the Novatian rupture, Mr. Orchard remarks: "When Decius came to the throne, in 249, he required, by edicts, all persons in the empire to confirm to Pagan worship. Forty years' toleration had greatly increased professors, and they were found in every department of the government. They had been so long unaccustomed to trials, that the lives of many were unsuited to suffering. Decius' edicts rent asunder the churches; multitudes apostatized, and many were martyred. In two years the trial abated, when many apostates applied for restoration to Christian fellowship, and sanctioned their application by letters written by some eminent Christians who had been martyrs during the persecution. The flagrancy of some apostates occasioned an opposition to their re-admission."—Orch. Ch. His., vol. I, p. 52.

This slack discipline has been the curse of the churches, more or less, in every age. No church can prosper which has not vital action sufficient to throw off the corrupt or foreign matter. For some time before the "Novatian rupture" there had been a growing tendency in some churches toward ministerial usurpation; and the leaven of the mystery of iniquity was at work, which finally produced Anti-christ in his full proportions. The time for the "falling away," spoken of by Paul, had now fully come. For it matters not which party is in the majority when a separation occurs, it is always true that the party which departs from the faith has fallen away.

It is generally admitted by historians, whether Catholic or Protestant, that the Catholic party departed from the simplicity of the Gospel, at least in point of morals. And it appears that, previous to the separation, many persons had deplored the growing corruptions in some of the churches; and they hailed with delight the earliest opportunity of bearing testimony for Christ by rejecting from their fellowship those individuals and churches which had departed from the simplicity of the faith.

Gieseler, in his Ecclesiastical History, gives the following account of the Novatians: "The Presbyter Novatian, at Rome, was dissatisfied with the choice of the Bishop Cornelius (A.D. 251), on account of his lenity toward the Lapsi. In the controversy which now ensued, Novatian, chiefly supported by the Presbyter Novatus, of Carthage, returned to the old principle, that those who had once fallen from the faith could in no case be received again. The church being divided by this schism, Novatian was chosen bishop by the one party in opposition to Cornelius. Though the other bishops, and especially Cyprian at Carthage, and Dionysius at Alexandria, were on the side of Cornelius, great numbers in all parts joined the stricter party."—Gies. Eccl. His., vol. I, p. 163.

This very important testimony from Gieseler, the learned German historian, shows that, after the division of the church at Rome, Novatian was chosen pastor or bishop of the stricter party; and when the division extended throughout the empire, "great numbers in all parts joined the stricter party."

And this establishes the fact that these great numbers in all parts did not originate with Novatian. But their origin is with the apostolic churches. And even the church in Rome, over which Novatian was pastor, did not receive its baptism nor origin from him. But this church derived its origin from the original apostolic church at Rome to whom Paul addressed his letter to the Romans. In fact, the Novatian party were that part of the original church at Rome, founded by the apostles, which preserved the purity of discipline and worship against the growing apostacy which sided with Cornelius.

And this firm stand of the Novatians at Rome for virtue, furnished an example for others. Orchard remarks that: "On account of the church's severity of discipline, the example was followed by many, and churches of this order flourished in the greatest part of those provinces which had received the Gospel."—Orch. Ch. His., vol. I, p. 55.

Therefore, instead of Novatian being the founder of this class of Christians, he only bore testimony, with others, in favor of the purity of discipline which had been preserved from the time of the apostles.

To show that Novatian did not act alone in his early stand for virtue and truth, we here insert a statement from Neander, as follows: "As his principles are so clearly to be explained from the sternness of his Christian character, and as he was acting, in this instance, in the spirit of a whole party of the church existing at that time, there is the less need to resort to an explanation, deduced from an external cause, which is supported by no historical proof."—Neand. His. Chr. Rel. & Ch., p. 143.

This statement of Neander was made in refutation of the charge that Novatian received his principles from the Stoic philosophy. And it shows that, instead of his being the originator of these principles, he only acted in concert with "a whole party of the church," which existed before the "Novatian rupture."

And it is evident that if the Novatians had no just claims to be regarded as the primitive church, they would not have dared, in the face of such powerful and bitter enemies, to claim to be the only Church of Christ on earth. Upon this point, Neander remarks: "The controversy with the party of Novatian turned upon two general points:

1. On the principles of penitence.
2. On what constitutes the idea of the essence of a true church."—Neand. Ch. His., p. 145.

In regard to the first point, which Neander calls

"penitence"—owing to the fearful corruptions which resulted from the indiscriminate reception of those who had apostatized into paganism and idolatry—the Novatians refused to restore such heinous offenders to church fellowship; but they did not deny that such might obtain forgiveness from God.

And in regard to the second point of difference between the Novatians and the popular party, which involved the church question, Neander has the following:

"As far as concerns the second point in dispute, the notion of the church, Novatian held the following opinion: As the mark of purity and holiness is one of the essential marks of a true church, every church which, neglecting the right use of church discipline, suffers those who have violated their baptismal vow by great sins to remain in the midst of her, or to receive them into her again, ceases thereby to be a true church, and loses all the rights and advantages of such a church. The Novatianists, therefore, as they claimed to be the only unstained, pure church, called themselves oi katharoi, 'the pure.'"

Since it is allowed on all hands that even the enemies of the Novatians did not charge them with impurity in doctrine or discipline, but only with schism, and that the Catholic party were corrupt in discipline, the claim of the Novatians ought, therefore, to be conceded to them, that they were the pure, uncorrupted apostolic church.

On this claim the editor of the Religious Encyclopedia remarks: "Novatians; a numerous body of Protestant dissenters from the church of Rome, in the third century, who, notwithstanding the representations of their adversaries, have some just claims to be regarded as the pure, uncorrupted, and apostolic Church of Christ. They called themselves Cathari—that is, the pure; but they received their name of Novatians from their adversaries, after their distinguished leader Novatian, who, in the year 251, was ordained the pastor of a church in the city of Rome, which maintained no fellowship with the (so-called) Catholic party."—Religious Encyc., p. 877.

This distinguished author affirms that the Novatians

have "just claims to be regarded as the pure, uncorrupted and apostolic Church of Christ." This unites the Baptist history to the apostolic churches of Jesus Christ in the first century.

After a thorough examination on this point, Orchard, the historian, makes the following statement concerning the Novatians: "The churches thus formed upon a plan of strict communion and rigid discipline, obtained the reproach of PURITANS; they were the oldest body of Christian churches of which we have any account; and a succession of them, we shall prove, has continued to the present day. Novatian's example had a powerful influence, and Puritan churches rose in different parts in quick succession. So early as 254, these dissenters are complained of as having infected France with their doctrines, which will aid us in the Albigensean churches, where the same severity of discipline is traced and reprobated."—Orch. His. Bapt., vol. I, p. 55.

Yes, no doubt, the Novatians were descendants of, and formed part of, the oldest body of Christian churches, which were established by Christ and the apostles. And Mr. Cramp, in his late history, has the following: "We may safely infer that they abstained from compliance with the innovation, and that the Novatian churches were what are now called Baptist churches, adhering to the apostolic and primitive practice."

Notwithstanding all the false and bitter charges of their enemies, the proof is positive, that the Novatians, in every element of church organization, were Baptists, and descended from the primitive apostolic churches.

It should be observed that the Donatists in Africa, in the fourth century, are generally admitted to be the same class of Christians with the Novatians.

When the division occurred at Carthage, similar to that at Rome, that party which adhered to the purity of church discipline and primitive practice in the administration of the ordinances, were called Donatists.

Cryspin, the French historian, affirms that they hold together in the following things:

"First: For purity of church members, by asserting that none ought to be admitted into churches but such as were visibly true believers and real saints.

Secondly: For the purity of church discipline, as the application of church-censures, and keeping out such as had apostatized or scandalously sinned.

Thirdly: They both agreed in asserting the power, rights, and privileges of particular churches, against anti-Christian encroachments of presbyters, bishops, and synods.

Fourthly: That they baptized again those whose first baptism they had ground to doubt."—D'Anvers on Baptism, p. 223.

The foregoing, as found in D'Anvers on Baptism, exhibits the fact that the Donatists were but the Novatians of Africa. And although they were called by different names on different continents, yet they were one and the same class of Christians, who were the successors of the original churches that withstood the mighty flood of corruptions which beat upon the Church of Christ in the third, fourth, and fifth centuries.

And that the Novatians adhered to the primitive principles of the first century, is admitted by Mr. Waddington, in his History of the Church. In speaking of the Novatians, whom he dignifies with the title "Sectaries," he remarks: "And those rigid principles which had characterized and sanctified the church in the first century were abandoned to the profession of schismatic sectaries in the third."—History of the Church, p. 70.

This very important statement of George Waddington, the learned Episcopal historian, establishes two important points:

1. That the Novatians, called Sectaries by their enemies, "PRESERVED THOSE RIGID PRINCIPLES WHICH HAD CHARACTERIZED AND SANCTIFIED THE CHURCH IN THE FIRST CENTURY."

2. That the Catholic, or orthodox party, "ABANDONED" THESE PRINCIPLES "TO THE PROFESSION OF SCHISMATIC SECTARIES IN THE THIRD" CENTURY.

Therefore, as the Catholics, or orthodox, were the party which abandoned the primitive principles of Christianity, they were undoubtedly the party that fell away or apostatized from the truth. But, on the other hand, as the Novatians were the party which maintained the primitive principles of Christianity, they must be regarded as the original church, in spite of the pompous pretentions of the so-called Catholics.

While it is an admitted fact that the term Novatians, which was applied to the early witnesses for Christ, was derived from Novatian, yet it is not true that he was their founder, or that the church of which he was pastor was the first church in the separation from the popular religion. There were other churches before this, independent of the so-called orthodox, which bore the same testimony for the original principles.

I here call attention to a statement from Robinson, introduced in the former section, as follows: "They say Novatian was the first anti-pope in the modern sense of the word. They call Novatian the author of the heresy of Puritanism; and yet they know that Tertullian had quitted the church near fifty years before for the same reason; and Privatus, who was an old man in the time of Novatian, had, with several more, repeatedly remonstrated against the alterations taking place, and as they could get no redress, had dissented, and formed separate congregations. They tax Novatian with being parent of an innumerable multitude of congregations of Puritans all over the empire; and yet he had no other influence over any than what his good example gave him. People saw every-where the same cause of complaint, and groaned for relief; and when one man made a stand for virtue, the crisis had arrived—people saw the propriety of the cure, and applied the same means to their own relief."

Thus we discover that even before the time of Novatian, there existed "separate congregations" which bore testimony against the corruptions of the popular party. It is a fact, conceded by all historians, that the primitive churches, with few exceptions, down to the time of Novatian, preserved the church ordinances as they were originally delivered by inspiration.

The corruptions had respect mainly to the lax discipline which prevailed, especially in the city churches. In other words, all parties acknowledge that the main body of the early churches, prior to the middle of the third century, were true churches of Christ, and that they had their origin from Christ and the apostles. And as it has been fully shown, upon good authority, that the Novatians had their origin from these primitive churches, therefore their succession reaches back through the primitive churches to Christ and the apostles.

In regard to these early Baptist churches, Mr. Robinson remarks, that "during the first three centuries, Christian congregations, all over the East, subsisted in separate, independent bodies, unsupported by Government, and consequently without any secular power over one another. All this time they were baptized (Baptist) churches, and though all the fathers of the first four ages down to Jerome were of Greece, Syria, and Africa; and though they give great numbers of histories of the baptism of adults, yet there is not one record of the baptism of a child till the year 370, when Galates, the dying son of the Emperor Valens, was baptized, by order of a monarch who swore he would not be contradicted."

It was the custom of the old English writers to use the word baptized where we use the word baptist. So we have the historic fact, stated in the foregoing, that these early churches were Baptist churches.

From the shores of America we have followed the footprints of the Baptist denomination back through England, Holland, and Germany, to the valleys of Piedmont, and thence to Italy and the land of Judea, in the apostolic age. In our examinations we find no flaw or break in the chain of our denominational succession. But it is admitted that our ancestors were called by different names in different ages of the world. We now find ourselves connected with the primitive churches of the first and second centuries. And it is admitted by all that these churches bore the apostolic character. They were modeled after the original church founded by Christ himself at Jerusalem.

In making out the chain of our succession, we have not embraced all, in different parts, who bore the Baptist character; but we only designed to present the most direct line of our connection with the apostolic churches without the introduction of a great many names.

Thus we have reached the fountain-head of that mighty stream of Scriptural churches flowing down from Jerusalem through the desert gloom of more than eighteen centuries, and watering the famishing world with the pure Gospel of the River of Life. Here is found the light-house of the world, erected upon the Rock of Eternal Ages, casting its beams of heavenly light far over the stormy seas, while gross darkness enveloped the world, and the multitudes were wondering after the Beast.

Notwithstanding we have traced our denominational line of succession directly up to the apostolical age, yet this would avail us nothing if we are found destitute of the peculiar characteristics which distinguished the apostolic churches.—BAPTIST SUCCESSION By D. B. Ray, pages 159-170.

THE PAULICIANS

William Jones

While the Christian world, as it has been the fashion to call it, was thus sunk into an awful state of superstition —at a moment when "darkness seemed to cover the earth, and gross darkness the People"—it is pleasing to contemplate a ray of celestial light darting across the gloom. About the year 660, a new sect arose in the east, under the name of **Paulicians**[1], which is justly entitled to our attention.

In Mananalis, an obscure town in the vicinity of Somosata, a person of the name of Constantine entered at his house a deacon, who, having been a prisoner among the

Mahometans, was returning from Syria, whither he had been carried away captive. From this passing stranger Constantine received the precious gift of the New Testament in its original language, which, even at this early period, was so concealed from the vulgar, that Peter Siculus, to whom we owe most of our information on the history of the Paulicians, tells us, the first scruples of a Catholic, when he was advised to read the bible, was, "it is not lawful for us profane persons to read those sacred writings, but for the priests only."

Indeed the gross ignorance which pervaded Europe at that time, rendered the generality of the people incapable of reading that or any other book; but even those of the laity who could read, were dissuaded by their religious guides from meddling with the Bible. Constantine, however, made the best use of the deacon's present—he studied his New Testament with unwearied assiduity—and more particularly the writings of the apostle Paul, from which he at length endeavoured to deduce a system of doctrine and worship. "He investigated the creed of primitive Christianity," says Gibbon, "and whatever might be the success, a protestant reader will applaud the spirit of the inquiry."[1]

The knowledge to which Constantine himself was, under the divine blessing, enabled to attain, he gladly communicated to others around him, and a Christian church was collected. In a little time several individuals arose among them qualified for the work of the ministry; and several other churches were collected throughout Armenia and Cappadocia. It appears, from the whole of their history, to have been a leading object with Constantine and his

---

[1] It is much to be regretted, that of this class of Christians, all our information is derived through the medium of their enemies. The two original sources of intelligence concerning them are Photius, b. i. Contra Manichaeos; and Siculus' Hist. Manicheor, and from them Mosheim and Gibbon have deduced their account of the Paulicians. The latter writer has entered far more fully into the subject than the former, and, what is singular enough, he has displayed more candour! I have collected from these two modern authors the concise account given above, and have aimed at impartiality.

brethren, to restore, as far as possible, the profession of Christianity to all its primitive simplicity.

Their public appearance soon attracted the notice of the Catholic party, who immediately branded them with the opprobrious appellation of Manichaeans; but "they sincerely condemned the memory and opinions of the Manichaean sect, and complained of the injustice which impressed that invidious name on them." There is reason, therefore, to think they voluntarily adopted the name of Paulicians, and that they derived it from the name of the great apostle of the Gentiles. Constantine now assumed or received the name of Sylvanus, and others of his fellow labourers were called Titus, Timothy, Tychicus, & c. and as the churches arose and were formed in different places, they were named after those apostolic churches to which Paul originally addressed his inspired writings, without any regard to the name of the city or town in which they assembled for worship.

The labours of Constantine—Sylvanus, were crowned with much success. Pontius and Cappadocia, regions once renowned for Christian piety, were again blessed with a diffusion of the light of divine truth. He himself resided in the neighbourhood of Colonia in Pontus, and their congregations, in process of time, were diffused over the provinces of Asia Minor, to the westward of the Euphrates. "The Paulician teachers," says Gibbon, "were distinguished only by their scriptural names, by the modest title of fellow-pilgrims; by the austerity of their lives, their zeal and knowledge, and the credit of some extraordinary gift of the Holy Spirit. But they were incapable of desiring, or at least of obtaining, the wealth and honours of the Catholic prelacy. Such antichristian pride they strongly censured."

Roused by the growing importance of this sect, the Greek emperors began to persecute the Paulicians with the most sanguinary severity; and the scenes of Galerius and Maximin were reacted under the Christian forms and names. "To their excellent deeds," says the bigoted Peter Siculus, "the divine and orthodox emperors added this virtue, that they ordered the Montanists and Manichaeans (by which epithets they chose to stigmatize the Paulicians) to be capitally punished, and their books, wherever found, to be committed to the flames; also that if any person was found to have secreted them, he was to be put to death, and his goods confiscated."

A Greek officer, armed with legal and military powers, appeared at Colonia, to strike the shepherd, and, if possible, reclaim the lost sheep to the Catholic fold. "By a refinement of cruelty, Simeon (the officer) placed the unfortunate Sylvanus before a line of his disciples, who were commanded, as the price of their own pardon, and the proof of their repentance to massacre their spiritual father. They turned aside from the impious office; the stones dropt from their filial hands, and of the whole number, only one executioner could be found; a new David, as he is styled by the Catholics, who boldly overthrew the giant of heresy."

This apostate, whose name was Justus, stoned to death the father of the Paulicians, who had now laboured among them twenty-seven years. The treacherous Justus betrayed many others, probably of the pastors and teachers, who fared the fate of their venerable leader; while Simeon himself, struck with the evidences of divine grace apparent in the sufferers, embraced at length the faith which he came to destroy—renounced his station, resigned his honours and fortunes, became a zealous preacher among the Paulicians, and at last sealed his testimony with his blood.[1]

During a period of one hundred and fifty years, these Christian churches seem to have been almost incessantly subjected to persecution, which they supported with Christian meekness and patience; and, if the acts of their martyrdom, their preaching, and their lives, were distinctly recorded, I see no reason to doubt, that we should find in them the genuine successors of the Christians of the two first centuries.

And in this, as well as former instances, the blood of the martyrs was the seed of the church. A succession

[1] "Thrice hail, ye happy shepherds of the fold,
By tortures unsubdued, unbribed by gold;
In your high scorn of honours, honoured most,
Ye chose the martyr's, not the prelate's post."

of teachers and churches arose; and a person named Sergius, who had laboured among them in the ministry of the gospel thirty-seven years, is acknowledged, even by their vilest calumniators, to have been a most exemplary Christian. Their persecution had, however, some intermissions, until at length Theodora, the Greek empress, exerted herself against them, beyond all her predecessors. She sent inquisitors throughout all Asia Minor, in search of these sectaries, and is computed to have killed by the gibbet, by fire, and by the sword, A HUNDRED THOUSAND PERSONS. Such was the state of things at the commencement of the ninth century."—THE HISTORY OF THE CHRISTIAN CHURCH by William Jones, pp. 239-241.

THE PETROBRUSIANS

William Cathcart, D. D.

Peter de Bruys was the Catholic priest of an obscure parish in France, he became a preacher of the gospel. How he unlearned the gospel of the Seven Hills and was instructed in that of Calvary we cannot tell, but he was educated in both directions. Many Romanists, like Staupitz of Fenelon, have received the saving knowledge of Jesus and retained their connection with the papal church; but Peter abhorred popery.

He taught that baptism was of no advantage to infants, and that only believers should receive it, and he gave a new baptism to all his converts; he condemned the use of churches and altars, no doubt for the idolatry practiced in them; he denied that the body and blood of Christ are to be found in the bread and wine of the Supper, and he taught that the elements on the Lord's table are but signs of Christ's flesh and blood; he asserted that the offerings, prayers, and good works of the living could not profit the dead, that their state was fixed for eternity the moment they left the earth; like the English Baptists of the seventeenth century, and like the Quakers of our day, he believed that it was wrong to sing the praises of God in worship; and he rejected the adoration of crosses, and destroyed them wherever he found them.

It is said that on a Good-Friday the Petrobrusians once gathered a great multitude of their brethren, who brought with them all the crosses they could find, and that they made a large fire of them, on which they cooked meat, and gave it to the vast assemblage. This is told as an illustration of their blasphemous profanity. Their crucifixes, and along with them probably the images of the saints, were the idols they had been taught to worship, and when their eyes were opened they destroyed them, just as the converted heathen will now destroy their false gods. Hezekiah did a good thing in destroying the serpent of brass, which in the wilderness had miraculous powers of healing, when the Israelites began to worship it as a god.

Peter's preaching was with great power; his words and his influence swept over great masses of men, bending their hearts and intellects before their resistless might. "In Provence," says Du Pin, "there was nothing else to be seen but Christians rebaptized, churches profaned or destroyed, altars pulled down, and crosses burned. The laws of the church were publicly violated, the priests beaten, abused, and forced to marry, and all the most sacred ceremonies of the church abolished."

Peter de Bruys commenced his ministry about 1125, and such was his success that in a few years in the places about the mouth of the Rhone, in the plain country about Thoulouse, and particularly in the city itself, and in many parts of "the province of Gascoigne" he led great throngs of men and women to Jesus, and overthrew the entire authority of popes, bishops, and priests.

Had the life of this illustrious man been spared the Reformation probably would have occurred four hundred years earlier under Peter de Bruys instead of Martin Luther, and the Protestant nations of the earth would not have had a deliverance from four centuries of priestly profligacy and widespread soul destruction, but they would have entered upon a godly life with a far more Scriptural creed than grand old Luther, still in a considerable measure wedded to Romish sacramentalism, was fitted to give them.

Peter and his followers were decided Baptists, and like ourselves they gave a fresh baptism to all their converts. They reckoned that they were not believers when first immersed in the Catholic Church, and that as Scripture baptism required faith in its candidates, which they did not possess, they regarded them as wholly unbaptized; and for the same reason they repudiated the idea that they re-baptized them, confidently asserting that because of the lack of faith they had never been baptized.—BAPTIST ENCYCLOPEDIA by William Cathcart, D. D., pp. 911, 912.

ORIGIN OF THE SEPARATE BAPTISTS

Robert B. Semple

The Baptists of Virginia originated from three sources. The first were emigrants from England, who about the year 1714, settled in the south east parts of the state.

About 1743, another party came from Maryland, and formed a settlement in the north west.

Each of these will be treated of in their proper places.

A third party, from New England, having acted the most distinguished part, first demands our attention.

By the preaching of Mr. Whitefield through New England, a great work of God broke out in that country, distinguished by the name of the **New-light-stir.** All who joined in it were called **Newlights.** Many preachers of the established order, became active in the work . . . Their success was so great, that numbers of the parish clergy, who were opposed to the revival, were apprehensive that they should be deserted by all their hearers. They therefore not only refused them the use of their meeting houses, but actually procured the passage of a law to confine all preachers to their own parishes . . . This opposition did not affect the intended object . . . The hearts of the people being touched by a heavenly flame, could no longer relish the dry parish service, conducted, for the most part, as they thought, by a set of graceless mercenaries.

The **New-light-stir** being extensive, a great number were converted to the Lord . . . These, conceiving that the parish congregations, a few excepted, were far from the purity of the gospel, determined to form a society to themselves. Accordingly they embodied many churches . . . Into these none were admitted, who did not profess vital religion. Having thus separated themselves from the established churches, they were denominated **Separates.** Their church government, was entirely upon the plan of **Independents,** the power being in the hands of the church. They permitted unlearned men to preach, provided they manifested such gifts as indicated future usefulness. They were **Pedo-baptists** in principle, but did not reject any of their members, who chose to submit to believer's baptism.

The **Separates** first took their rise, or rather their name, about the year 1744. They increased very fast for several years. About a year after they were organized into a distinct society, they were joined by Shubal Stearns, who becoming a preacher, laboured among them until 1751, when forming acquaintance with some of the Baptists, he was convinced of the duty of believer's Baptism. Being a good man, to know his duty, was sufficient to induce him to perform it. The same year in which he was baptised he was ordained, and took the pastoral care of a church. Mr. Stearns and most of the **Separates,** had strong faith in the immediate teachings of the spirit.

They believed that to those who sought him earnestly, God often gave evident tokens of His will. That such indications of the divine pleasure, partaking of the nature of inspiration, were above, though not contrary to reason, and that following these, still leaning in every step, upon the same wisdom and power by which they were first actuated, they would inevitably be led, to the accomplishment of the two great objects of a Christian's life, the glory of God and the salvation of men.

Mr. Stearns, listening to some of these instructions

of heaven, conceived himself called upon by the Almighty to move far to the westward, to execute a great and extensive work. Incited by his impressions, in the year 1754, he and a few of his members took their leave of N. England. They halted first at Opeckon, in Berkeley county, Virginia, where he found a Baptist church under the care of the Rev. John Garrard, who received him kindly.

Here also he met his brother in law, the Rev. Daniel Marshall, just returned from his mission among the Indians, and who after his arrival at this place had become a Baptist. They joined companies and settled for a while on Cacapon in Hampshire county, about 30 miles from Winchester. Here, not meeting with his expected success, he felt restless. Some of his friends had moved to North Carolina, he received letters from these, informing him, that preaching was greatly desired by the people of that country: That in some instances they had rode 40 miles to hear one sermon.

He and his party once more got under way, and travelling about 200 miles came to Sandy Creek, in Guilford county, N. Carolina. Here he took up his permanent residence. Soon after his arrival, **viz,** Nov. 22, 1755, he and his companions, to the number of 16, were constituted into a church called **Sandy Creek,** and to which Mr. Stearns was appointed pastor. In this little church in the wilderness, there were, besides the pastor, two other preachers, **viz.** Joseph Breed and Daniel Marshall, neither of whom was ordained.

Thus organized, they began their work, kindling a fire which soon began to burn brightly indeed, spreading in a few years over Virginia, North and South Carolina and Georgia.

The subsequent events, seem completely to have verified Mr. Stearns' impressions, concerning a great work of God in the West.—HISTORY of the RISE AND PROGRESS of the BAPTISTS IN VIRGINIA, by Robert B. Semple, chapter I, pages 1-3.

Another Account of the Origin of the Separate Baptists

William Cathcart, D. D.

When George Whitefield preached in New England, as elsewhere, many were converted to God; and as in the State Congregational churches religion was in a very low condition, the new disciples were regarded as a strange element, except by those in them, ministers or laymen, who had been blessed with new hearts.

These persons for a time were called Newlights; but, as their treatment by the old religious communities was cold and sometimes unfriendly, and as the truth was frequently neither loved nor preached in the churches of the "standing order," the Newlights established religious services of their own, and in process of time they organized churches, into which only regenerated members were received.

These communities were first established about 1744, and they were pious Congregational churches, as distinguished from the formal legalized bodies of the State. Baptists and Pedobaptists were often found in the Separate churches. Isaac Backus and Shubal Stearns were ministers among them. This union, however, was not permanent.

The Baptists did not care to see a child sprinkled in a church to which they belonged, and the Congregationalists were not happy when one of their believing brethren was immersed. Open communion, instead of fostering charity, promoted discord, and ultimately either the Baptists or the Congregationalists withdrew from the church which they had formed and organized another on the basis of the truth as they held it.

Mr. Stearns was ordained among the Separates; and after he had been immersed and ordained as a Baptist minister, impressed with what seemed to him the call of God to remove far to the West to perform a great work for his Master, he and a few of his members, in 1754, departed from Connecticut.

He stopped on the way before he reached the home selected for him by the providence of God, Sandy Creek,

Guilford Co., N. C., when, on Nov. 22, 1755, he and his companions formed a church of sixteen members.

The first Separate church in Virginia was constituted in 1760, with Dutton Lane as its pastor. Daniel Marshall, Dutton Lane, and Col. Samuel Harriss enjoyed extraordinary success in their ministrations, converts came to Christ in throngs, churches were constituted, Associations were formed, the first of which was established among the Separates in North Carolina in 1758.

In 1770 there were but two Separate churches in Virginia north of the James River, and about four south of it; in 1774 there were thirty south and twenty-four north of it that sent letters to the Association, and there were probably several others not yet identified with the Association. The ministers traveled extensively and preached everywhere. Messrs. Harriss and Read baptized 75 at one time on a preaching tour, and in one of their journeys they immersed 200.

Sometimes the floor of the house where the meeting was held was covered with persons struck down with conviction of sin, and frequently the ministers were raised up at night to point weeping penitents to Jesus. A torrent of saving grace descended on Virginia, North Carolina, and other States through the labors of the Separate Baptists, which has never been exceeded in saving power in one section of country since the Saviour ascended into heaven.

The separate Baptists did not lay so much stress upon an educated ministry as their Regular brethren; they were unwilling for a time to be bound by any creed, and finally, only with explanations, accepted the Philadelphia Confession of Faith on Aug. 10, 1787, as one of the terms of a union with the Regular Baptists, consummated at that time, after which the Baptists of the Old Dominion were known as the United Baptist churches of Virginia.

The Separate Baptists had some leaders who were strongly inclined to Arminianism, though generally they were sound on the doctrines of grace; and they were for a time regarded by their Regular brethren as somewhat loose, and lacking in order in their religious meetings.

We heartily approve of the old Calvinism of the Regular Baptists of Virginia, and as heartily commend the holy fervor and boundless zeal of their Separate brethren. United, they have planted churches all over Virginia, swept out of existence the union between Church and State, and secured through James Madison and George Washington the religious amendment to the United States Constitution.

The Separate Baptists had for a time a distinct and vigorous existence in several other States besides Virginia, and whenever they were found they were the most aggressive and successful body of Christians ever known in our country. No effort or sacrifice stood in their way where souls were to be saved or Christ's truth honored.

The Separate Baptists were divinely prepared agents, exactly suited to the people among whom they labored to accomplish a gigantic work for God and for the Baptist denomination in the Southern and Southwestern States of this country; and whatever may have been their deficiencies as compared to their Regular brethren of their own day, or to the Baptists of our times, they are worthy of grateful and everlasting remembrance by their present successors and by the Saviour's friends of every name.

Long since the chasm between them and the Regular Baptists has been bridged, and the two bodies everywhere are now one in name and in religious principles.—THE BAPTIST ENCYCLOPEDIA By: William Cathcart, D.D. pp. 1041, 1042.

THE WELSH BAPTISTS

In no country have the principles of our faith as Baptists been more generally understood and more bravely defended than in the little principality of Wales. It is commonly believed that all through the dark reign of popery in the seclusions of her valleys and in the fastnesses of her mountains there were those who preserved the ancient purity of doctrine and worship.

The general quickening of religious thought, which

was one of the distinguishing features of the Reformation, was, however, the beneficent agency in facilitating their emergence into the clear light of historic recognition. The earnest study of the sacred oracles at this time caused numbers of the most learned and God-fearing of the sons of the Established Church to declare themselves converts to the Baptist faith.

Such men as Penry, Wroth, Erbury, and Vavasor Powell became leaders of mighty influence. They suffered much for the principles which they professed and preached. Vavasor Powell was a preacher of extraordinary power. Fluent in both Welsh and English, and withal enriched with a cultivated mind, he reached all classes and commanded all hearts. He was immured in about thirteen prisons, in one of which he died on the 27th of September, 1670.

The ministry of these distinguished Reformers and others of the same type was abundantly fruitful, in spite of the most persistent opposition from every form of worldly power. The seed sprinkled with tears and blood could not fail to grow and flourish. Churches sprang into existence in different parts of the land, and the waters of many a rural stream bore witness to the joyful obedience of hundreds who had been brought to the knowledge of the truth.

The first churches in Wales after the Reformation were missionary centres of wide-reaching activity. In addition to one or more pastors they separated by immense distances, and that at a time when roads were frequently impassable, there was scarcely a village or neighborhood throughout the length and breadth of the land where the gospel of salvation was not occasionally preached. It is said that Christmas Evans traversed Wales forty times from north to south, preaching the gospel, in the course of his fruitful ministry.

Every renowned preacher of the past century gave a large portion of his time to evangelistic work. The religious status of the Welsh people is largely attributable to this liberal diffusion of stimulating and enlightening thought. The rugged heroes of the past century, who with self-sacrificing devotion exposed themselves to every form of indignity and to all the rigors of a variable climate that they might make known the saving truths of the gospel, are worthy of being held in everlasting remembrance.

The influence which the Welsh Baptists have exerted upon the religious thought and life of this country demands special recognition. They have contributed more than any other people who have sought a home in this Western world to the spread of our principles, and to the integrity of our denominational life. Much of the formative work in Rhode Island, New Jersey, Virginia, New York, Delaware, and Pennsylvania was done by them. The first Baptist church in this country was established in Providence, R. I., by a Welshman.[1] The first Baptist church in what is now the State of Massachusetts was founded by a Welshman.

The first Baptist church now in Pennsylvania, the mother of the Philadelphia Association and of many churches in Pennsylvania and New Jersey, kept its records in the Welsh language for many years, and its first Bible, which is treasured by the American Baptist Historical Society, was in Welsh. The Welsh Tract church, which was the first holding our faith in Delaware, and for many years a most influential community, was formed in Wales, came out of this country as a body, and, after remaining a short time at Lower Dublin, settled permanently in Delaware.

There is not a State in the Union where Welshmen have not had an honored part in furthering Baptist interests. In many instances they have given direction and energy to our denominational life when as yet it could hardly be said to have an organized existence.

In not a few neighborhoods, in addition to those already mentioned, where our name is now a power and blessing, they were the fearless pioneers. The superstructure of our Baptist faith owes much of its present strength and

[1] Mr. Cathcart here asserts an opinion generally held in his day; however, we have shown elsewhere in this volume that Roger Williams, to whom he refers, was never a Baptist, though he did hold some Baptist sentiments. He was not scripturally baptized, and the church he organized in Providence, died after 4 months. The first Baptist Church in Rhode Island, and in America, was organized in Newport, R. I., in 1638. W.J.B.

grandeur to the solid foundation-work in which they had so large a share.

Roger Williams, the fearless champion of civil and religious liberty, whose teaching and example did so much to introduce into the Constitution of this country its distinguishing excellence; John Miles, who exerted such a powerful influence upon Baptist progress in the early days of our history; Dr. Samuel Jones, of Lower Dublin, and the venerable Isaac Eaton, first master of Hopewell Academy; Abel Morgan and Morgan Edwards, distinguished as writers and preachers; David Thomas, the veteran preacher of Virginia and Kentucky; David Jones, Horatio Gates Jones, and John Williams, of New York, all men of might in their day, were Welshmen or the immediate descendants of Welshmen.

There are in Wales at the present time nearly 500 Baptist churches, with a membership aggregating between 60,000 and 70,000. The practice of restricted communion is universal save in a few English churches in the large centres of population.—BAPTIST ENCYCLOPEDIA by William Cathcart, D. D., pp. 1229, 1230.

THE WALDENSES

William Jones

Towards the middle of the twelfth century, a small society of these **Puritans,** as they were called by some, or **Waldenses,** as they are termed by others, or **Paulicians,** as they are denominated by our old monkish historian, William of Neuberg, made their appearance in England. This latter writer, speaking of them, says, "They came originally from Gascoyne, where, **being as numerous as the sand of the sea,** they sorely infested both France, Italy, Spain and England."

The following is the account given by Dr. Henry, in his history of Great Britain, vol. viii. p. 338, oct. ed., of this emigrating party, which, in substance, corresponds with what is said of them by Raphin, Collier, Lyttleton, and other of our writers.

"A company, consisting of about thirty men and women, who spoke the German language, appeared in England at this time, (1159,) and soon attracted the attention of government by the singularity of their religious practices and opinions. It is indeed very difficult to discover with certainty what their opinions were, because they are recorded only by our monkish historians, who speak of them with much asperity.

They were apprehended and brought before a council of the clergy at Oxford. Being interrogated about their religion, their teacher, named Gerard, a man of learning, answered in their name, that they were Christians, and believed the doctrines of the apostles. Upon a more particular inquiry, it was found that they denied several of the received doctrines of the church, such as purgatory, prayers for the dead, and the invocation of saints; and refusing to abandon these damnable heresies, as they were called, they were condemned as incorrigible heretics, and delivered to the secular arm to be punished.

The king (Henry II.), at the instigation of the clergy, commanded them to be branded with a red hot iron on their forehead, to be whipped through the streets of Oxford, and, having their clothes cut short by their girdles, to be turned into the open fields, all persons being forbidden to afford them any shelter or relief under the severest penalties.

This cruel sentence was executed in its utmost rigour; and, it being the depth of winter, all these unhappy persons perished with cold and hunger. These seem to have been the first who suffered death in Britain for the vague and variable crime of heresy, and it would have been much to the honor of the country if they had been the last."

There is an account of the punishing of these Waldenses, in the ARCHAEOLOGIA, vol. ix. p. 292-305, written by the Rev. Mr. Denne, of Wilmington; from which I shall here give a short extract by way of supplement to the preceding narrative. "These persons," says he, "having been believers of the essential doctrines of Christianity, (as is admitted by the bishops,) and as it may be inferred from the silence of the historian, that these sectaries were in their manners inoffensive, nothing but the evil spirit of persecution could have prompted their judges to deliver them up to the civil magistrate.

It was the more culpable in the prelates, because there was so little ground for an alarm of their propagating with success their peculiar tenets. For though they seem to have resided for some time in England, they only converted one woman of inferior rank, and she was so slightly attached to them, that she was soon prevailed on to recant and forsake their society. And as they were not disturbers of the public peace, it is some-what strange that the king, whose disposition was humane, should think those people merited branding and exile.

But it was during the contest between Henry and Becket, in support of the just rights of the crown, that this occurrence happened; and his hard usage of these foreigners has been attributed to an unwillingness of affording a pretext to the pope and his adherents to charge them with profaneness, or an inattention to the cause of religion.

By the council of Tours, held in 1163, princes were exhorted and directed to imprison all heretics within their dominions, and to confiscate their effects. Of this injunction Henry could not be ignorant, and he might be actuated by it to treat the delinquents with more rigour than he otherwise would have done." Mr. Denne has fixed the sitting of the council at Oxford in the year 1166.

But the **Cathari,** or Puritans, were not the only sect which during the twelfth century, appeared in opposition to the superstition of the church of Rome. About the year 1110, in the south of France, in the provinces of Languedoc and Provence, appeared Peter de Bruys, preaching the gospel of the kingdom of heaven, and exerting the most laudable efforts to reform the abuses and remove the superstitions which disfigured the beautiful simplicity of the gospel worship.

His labours were crowned with abundant success. He converted a great number of persons to the faith of Christ, and after a most indefatigable ministry of twenty years continuance, he was burnt at St. Files, a city of Languedoc, in France, in the year 1130, by an enraged populace, instigated by the clergy, who apprehended their traffic to be in danger from this new and interpid reformer.

His followers were called Petrobrusians; but of his doctrinal sentiments, the following are those alone which we can be sure of at this remote period—That the ordinance of baptism was to be administered only to adults—that it was a piece of idle superstition to build and dedicate churches to the service of God, who in worship has a peculiar respect to a state of the heart, and who cannot be worshipped with temples made by hands—that crucifixes were objects of superstition, and ought to be destroyed—that in the Lord's supper the real body and blood of Christ were not exhibited, but only represented in the way of symbol or figure—and lastly, that the oblations, prayers, and good works of the living, could in no respect be beneficial to the dead.—HISTORY OF CHRISTIAN CHURCH, by William Jones, page 275-277.

Were the Waldensians Pedobaptists?—

Vindication of Jones, the Historian.

S. H. Ford

We place in permanent form the vindication of Jones the historian, from the charges of falsehood made by Drs. Miller and Rice. We give in full the language of the latter: "Jones has, in one instance, actually changed the language of the document from which he quotes, in order to conceal the fact that the Waldenses were Pedobaptists!

In Perrin, B. 1, ch. 5, we have the following quotation from Vecebium' Oration of the Waldenses: 'King Louis XII, having been informed by the enemies of the Waldenses dwelling in Provence, of many grievous crimes which were imposed upon them, sent to make inquisition in those places, the Lord Adam Fumee, Master of Requests, and a Doctor of Sorbon called Parui, who was his Confessor.

They visited all their parishes and temples, and found neither images, nor so much as the least show of any ornaments belonging to their masses and ceremonies of the church of Rome, much less any such crimes as were imposed upon them; but rather that they kept their Sabbaths duly, causing their children to be baptized according to the order of the primitive church, teaching them the articles of the Christian faith and the commandments of God.'

Now Jones quotes this precise statement from Perrin, referring to the chapter; but instead of the words—'causing their children to be baptized'—he writes these words—'Observed the ordinance of baptism, according to the primitive church.' A bolder falsification of a historical record I never saw."

Now the fact in regard to the quotation is this: The story of Louis XII sending persons to inquire into the tenets and deportment of the Waldenses in Provence is found in an Oration on the Waldenses by Vesembecius. Upon this oration, for the facts in the case, both Perrin and Jones profess to rely. Perrin does not quote literally, but condenses in his own language the story in the oration.

Jones follows Perrin, and never departs materially from his language, except where fidelity to the original compelled him. Hence his reference is properly given—"Vesembecius' Oration on the Waldenses, in Perrin, ch. 5." He does not say, as in Perrin. He clearly means, that the facts are derived from the oration, and the language mainly from Perrin. The whole question turns upon properly adjusting a discrepancy between the two historians as to what the commissioners reported of baptism among the Waldenses of Provence. According to Perrin the report was, "that they kept their Sabbath duly, causing their children to be baptized according to the order of the primitive church."

Jones says the report was, that they "observed the ordinance of baptism according to the primitive church." The question then is, which author is sustained by Vecembecius, upon whom they both professedly rely? Neither of them had a right to state any fact in the premises not fully authorized by the oration; and Jones would have been grossly criminal, if, in using the abridgment of Perrin, he had followed it away from any material fact stated by Vesembecius. The language of the oration is: "That men were baptized—the articles of faith and the ten commandments were taught—the Lord's day observed—the Word of God preached, and no shew of wickedness or fornication to be perceived amongst them: but that they found not any images in their churches, nor ornaments belonging to the mass."

The discussion of Pope and Maguire has been before the public for forty-nine years. The quotation by Pope made directly from the original in Dublin University Library, unquestioned by Maguire, an eminent Romanist, is unchallenged. On this oration or the paragraph which we have given, Perrin and Jones based their statements. Now which was correct? Perrin or Jones? The commissioner reported, "That (homines Baptizari) men, people, were baptized—not children. Was not Jones correct in saying (without quoting the words of Perrin), "They observed the ordinances of baptism according to the primitive church"? Who then falsified the record? Some one gave to homines (adults) the meaning of children. Perrin wrote in French; either he or his translator into English has done this deed; but Jones is vindicated and the charge of falsifying history rests on the advocates of infant baptism. This vindication, in substance, was given by us in the Western Recorder twenty years ago. It is re-produced by request.—S. H. Ford, Christian Repository, May 1876.

Three Confessions of Faith

William Jones

Confession of Faith of the Waldenses

1. We believe and firmly maintain all that is contained in the twelve articles of the symbol, commonly called the apostles' creed, and we regard as heretical whatever is inconsistent with the said twelve articles.

2. We believe that there is one God—the Father, Son, and Holy Spirit.

3. We acknowledge for sacred canonical scriptures the books of the Holy Bible. (Here follows the title of each, exactly conformable to our received canon, but which it is deemed, on that account, quite unnecessary to particularize.)

4. The books above mentioned teach us—That there is one God, almighty, unbounded in wisdom, and infinite in goodness; and who, in his goodness, has made all things. For he created Adam after his own image and likeness. But through the enmity of the devil and his own disobedience, Adam fell, sin entered into the world, and we became transgressors in and by Adam.

5. That Christ had been promised to the fathers who received the law, to the end that, knowing their sin by the law, and their unrighteousness and insufficiency, they might desire the coming of Christ to make satisfaction for their sins, and to accomplish the law by himself.

6. That at the time appointed of the Father, Christ was born—a time when iniquity every where abounded, to make it manifest that it was not for the sake of any good in ourselves, for all were sinners, but that He, who is true, might display His grace and mercy towards us.

7. That Christ is our life, and truth, and peace, and righteousness—our shepherd and advocate, our sacrifice and priest, Who died for the salvation of all who should believe, and rose again for their justification.

8. And we also firmly believe, that there is no other mediator, or advocate with God the Father, but Jesus

Christ. And as to the Virgin Mary, she was holy, humble, and full of grace; and this we also believe concerning all other saints, namely, that they are waiting in heaven for the resurrection of their bodies at the day of judgment.

9. We also believe, that, after this life, there are but two places—one for those that are saved, the other for the damned, which (two) we call paradise and hell, wholly denying that imaginary purgatory of Antichrist, invented in opposition to the truth.

10. Moreover, we have ever regarded all the inventions of men (in the affairs of religion) as an unspeakable abomination before God; such as the festival days and vigils of saints, and what is called holy water, the abstaining from flesh on certain days, and such like things, but above all the masses.

11. We hold in abhorrence all human inventions, as proceeding from Antichrist, which produce distress, and are prejudicial to the liberty of the mind.

12. We consider the Sacraments as signs of holy things, or as the visible emblems of invisible blessings. We regard it as proper and even necessary, that believers use these symbols or visible forms when it can be done. Notwithstanding which, we maintain that believers may be saved without these signs, when they have neither place nor opportunity of observing them.

13. We acknowledge no sacraments (as of divine appointment) but baptism and the Lord's supper.

14. We honour the secular power, with subjection, obedience, promptitude, and payment.

The Second Confession of Faith

The Centuriators of Madgeburgh, in their History of the Christian Church, under the twelfth century, recite from an old manuscript the following epitome of the opinions of the Waldenses of that age.

In articles of faith the authority of the Holy Scripture is the highest; and for that reason it is the standard of judging; so that whatsoever doth not agree with the Word of God, is deservedly to be rejected and avoided.

The decrees of fathers and councils are (only) so far to be approved as they agree with the Word of God.

The reading and knowledge of the Holy Scriptures is open to, and is necessary for all men, the laity as well as the clergy; and moreover the writings of the prophets and apostles are to be read rather than the comments of men.

The sacraments of the church of Christ are two, baptism and the Lord's supper: and in the latter, Christ has instituted the receiving in both kinds, both for priests and people.

Masses are impious; and it is madness to say masses for the dead.

Purgatory is the invention of men; for they who believe go into eternal life; they who believe not, into eternal damnation.

The invoking and worshipping of dead saints is idolatry.

The church of Rome is the Whore of Babylon.

We must not obey the pope and bishops, because they are the wolves of the church of Christ.

The pope hath not the primacy over all the churches of Christ; neither hath he the power of both swords.

That is the church of Christ, which hears the pure doctrine of Christ, and observes the ordinances instituted by him, in whatsoever places it exists.

Vows of celibacy are the inventions of men, and productive of uncleanness.

So many orders (of the clergy) so many marks of the beast.

Monkery is a filthy carcass.

So many superstitious dedications of churches, commemorations of the dead, benedictions of creatures, pilgrimages; so many forced fastings, so many superfluous festivals, those perpetual bellowings, (alluding to the practice of chanting) and the observations of various other ceremonies, manifestly obstructing the teaching and learning of the word, are DIABOLICAL INVENTIONS.

The marriage of priests is both lawful and necessary.

About the time of the Reformation, the Waldenses who resided in the south of France, and who of course were subjects of the French king, were persecuted with the most sanguinary severity, particularly those resident in the country of Provence. In the year 1540, the parliament of Aix, the chief judicature of the province, passed a law that "they should all of them promiscuously be destroyed, that their houses should be pulled down, the town of Merindole be levelled with the ground, all the trees cut down, and the country adjacent converted into a desert."

Voltaire, speaking of this cruel decree, says, "The Waldenses, terrified at this sentence, sent a deputation to cardinal Sadoletus, bishop of Carpentras, who at that time was in his diocese. This illustrious scholar, this true philosopher, this humane and compassionate prelate, received them with great goodness, and interceded in their behalf, and the execution of the sentence was for a time suspended." The sentence, nevertheless, was executed in all its rigour five years afterwards, as will be related in a future section. In the preceding year, however, (1544) as we are informed by Sleiden, in his history of the reformation, p. 347, the Waldenses, to remove the prejudices that were entertained against them, and to manifest their innocence, transmitted to the king, in writing, the following confession of their faith.

The Third Confession of Faith

1. We believe that there is but one God, who is a Spirit—the Creator of all things—the Father of all, who is above all, and through all, and in us all; who is to be worshipped in spirit and in truth—upon whom we are continually dependent, and to whom we ascribe praise for our life, food, raiment, health, sickness, prosperity, and adversity. We love Him as the source of all goodness; and reverence Him as that sublime being, who searches the reins and trieth the hearts of the children of men.

2. We believe that Jesus Christ is the Son and image

of the Father—that in Him all the fulness of the Godhead dwells, and that by Him alone we know the Father. He is our Mediator and Advocate; nor is there any other name given under heaven by which we can be saved. In His name alone we call upon the Father, using no other prayers than those contained in the Holy Scriptures, or such as are in substance agreeable thereunto.

3. We believe in the Holy Spirit as the Comforter, proceeding from the Father, and from the Son; by whose inspiration we are taught to pray; being by Him renewed in the spirit of our minds; who creates us anew unto good works, and from whom we receive the knowledge of the truth.

4. We believe that there is one holy church, comprising the whole assembly of the elect and faithful, that have existed from the beginning of the world, or that shall be to the end thereof. Of this church the Lord Jesus Christ is the head—it is governed by His word and guided by the Holy Spirit. In the church it behooves all Christians to have fellowship. For her He (Christ) prays incessantly, and His prayer for it is most acceptable to God, without which indeed there could be no salvation.

5. We hold that the ministers of the church ought to be unblameable both in life and doctrine; and if found otherwise, that they ought to be deposed from their office, and others substituted in their stead; and that no person ought to presume to take that honour unto himself but he who is called of God as was Aaron—that the duties of such are to feed the flock of God, not for filthy lucre's sake, or as having dominion over God's heritage, but as being examples to the flock, in word, in conversation, in charity, in faith, and in chastity.

6. We acknowledge, that kings, princes, and governors, are the appointed and established ministers of God, whom we are bound to obey (in all lawful and civil concerns). For they bear the sword for the defence of the innocent, and the punishment of evil doers; for which reason we are bound to honour and pay them tribute. From this power and authority, no man can exempt himself, as is

manifest from the example of the Lord Jesus Christ, who voluntarily paid tribute, not taking upon Himself any jurisdiction of temporal power.

7. We believe that in the ordinance of baptism the water is the visible and external sign which represents to us that which, by virtue of God's invisible operation, is within us—namely, the renovation of our minds, and the mortification of our members through (the faith) Jesus Christ. And by this ordinance we are received into the holy congregation of God's people, previously professing and declaring our faith and change of life.

8. We hold that the Lord's supper is a commemoration of, and thanksgiving for, the benefits which we have received by His sufferings and death—and that it is to be received in faith and love—examining ourselves, that so we may eat of that bread and drink of that cup, as it is written in the Holy Scriptures.

9. We maintain that marriage was instituted of God —that it is holy and honourable, and ought to be forbidden to none, provided there be no obstacle from the divine word.

10. We contend, that all those in whom the fear of God dwells, will thereby be led to please Him, and to abound in the good works (of the gospel) which God hath before ordained that we should walk in them—which are love, joy, peace, patience, kindness, goodness, gentleness, sobriety, and the other good works enforced in the Holy Scriptures.

11. On the other hand, we confess that we consider it to be our duty to beware of false teachers, whose object is to divert the minds of men from the true worship of God, and to lead them to place their confidence in the creatures, as well as to depart from the good works of the gospel, and to regard the inventions of men.

12. We take the Old and the New Testament for the rule of our life, and we agree with the general confession of faith contained in (what is usually termed) the apostles' creed.—Jones' Church History.

(In the main these sentiments are what Baptists believe today. There are some variations, which might be expected in the circumstances. But these published statements of belief certainly prove that in times of darkest Romanism and sinister heresy, and during times of persecution as cruel as the evil nature of man could invent, there were a people who held tenaciously to the main principles we hold today, even in the light of martyr fires.—W.J.B.)

Another Testimony of the Virtue of the Waldenses

(Edward's History of Redemption)

The profound and amiable President Edwards bears the following testimony to the religious character of the Waldenses, and other dissenting parties from the church of Rome.

"In every age of this dark time, there appeared particular persons in all parts of Christendom, who bore a testimony against the corruptions and tyranny of the church of Rome. There is no age of antichrist, even in the darkest time of all, but ecclesiastical historians mention a great many by name who manifested an abhorrence of the pope and his idolatrous worship, and plead for the ancient purity of doctrine and worship.

God was pleased to maintain an uninterrupted succession of witnesses, through the whole time, in Germany, France, Britain, and other countries, as historians demonstrate and mention them by name, and give an account of the testimony which they held. Many of them were private persons and many of them ministers, and some magistrates and persons of great distinction. And there were numbers in every age who were persecuted and put to death for their testimony.

"Besides these particular persons dispersed here and there, there was a certain people called the Waldenses, who lived separate from the rest of the world, who kept themselves pure, and constantly bore a testimony against the church of Rome, through all this dark time.

The place where they dwelt was the Vaudois, or the five valleys of Piedmont, a very mountainous country between Italy and France. The place where they lived was compassed with those exceeding high mountains called the Alps, which were almost impassable. The passage over these mountainous desert countries was so difficut, that the valleys where this people dwelt was almost inaccessible.

There this people lived for many ages, as it were, alone, where in a state of separation from all the world, having very little to do with any other people, they served God in the ancient purity of His worship, and never submitted to the church of Rome. This place in this desert, mountainous country, probably was the place especially meant in Revelation xii 6, as the place prepared of God for the woman, that they should feed her there during the reign of antichrist.

"Some of the popish writers themselves own that that people never submitted to the church of Rome. One of the popish writers, speaking of the Waldenses, says the heresy of the Waldenses is the oldest heresy in the world. It is supposed that this people first betook themselves to this desert, secret place among the mountains to hide themselves from the severity of the heathen persecutions, which were before Constantine the Great, and thus the woman fled into the wilderness from the face of the serpent, Rev. xii 6; and so ver. 14. 'And to the woman were given two wings of a great eagle, that she might fly into the wilderness into her place, where she is nourished for a time and times and half a time from the face of the serpent.' And the people being settled there, their prosperity continued there from age to age afterwards; and being, as it were, by natural walls as well as by God's grace, separated from the rest of the world, never partook of the overflowing corruption."—Edward's History of Redemption, pp. 293, 294—quoted by David Benedict.

Persecutions of the Waldenses

Thomas Armitage

The crusade of Simon of Montfort so utterly destroyed them that Sismondi says: 'Simon stamped out not only a people but a literature.' Dominic, the father of the Inquisition, persecuted them with a high hand. From A.D. 1160-1500 their fortunes varied from the greatest prosperity to the depths of misery; alternating from an ardent zeal against the Romish Church to a cowing dread and a wretched compromise on the part of many with the doctrines of Rome, very similar to the Old Catholic movement of our times.

The most dreadful of all their persecutions began in 1560, when many of their villages were deserted. The old, the feeble, women and children, fled to the forests, the rocks, the highest peaks of the mountains. Untrained peasants were obliged to form themselves into small brigades. Tottering old men and boys organized themselves into guards and sentinels, and accomplished immortal exploits by their skill and fortitude against veteran invaders.

Possibly it had been better had they earlier invoked the spirit of men, who, in defense of their holiest rights to serve God, must measure swords with the incarnate fiends and craven bigots who dare to oppose them, on the ground that to thrash a coward is to challenge his respect.

The horrible Inquisition was formed for the express purpose of planting an iron foot upon the throat of the most hallowed rights of man. It never was suppressed till organized force chastised it; and the same treatment might have cowed its devilishness much sooner, both to the honor of God and man.

This tribunal of infernal origin clothed certain monks with limitless power to torture Waldensians and lead them to execution without legal forms or the rights of trial. And that power was plied upon these inoffensive people in those extremes which nothing can inflame but sanctimonious infernalism.

Many of them were frozen to death, others were cast

from high precipices and dashed to pieces. Some were driven into caverns, and by filling the mouths of their caves with fagots were suffocated. Others were hanged in cold blood, ripped open and disemboweled, pierced with prongs, drowned, racked limb from limb till death relieved them; were stabbed, worried by dogs, burned, or crucified with their heads downward.

Fox relates one case in which four hundred mothers who had taken refuge in the Cave of Castelluzzo, some 2,000 feet above the valley, entered by a projecting craig, were smothered with their infants in their arms. And all the time that this gentle blood was flowing, that sanctified beauty known as Innocent III. drank it in like nectar of Paradise.

Of the Waldensians and other murdered sheep of Christ, he said: 'They are like Samson's foxes. They appear to be different, but their tails are tied together.'

The blood-thirst of the Dominicans earned for them the stigma of 'Domini Canes,' or the 'Lord's Dogs.' The very sentences which they pronounced in mockery of trial and justice were a Satanic compound of formality and heartlessness, sanctimony and avarice, obsequiousness and arrogance. At the conclusion of a session of the Inquisition, held in Switzerland, 1430, the following decree was published:

'In the name of God, Amen. We, Brother Ulrich of Torrente, of the Dominican order at Lausanne, and with full apostolic authority, Inquisitor of heretical iniquity, in the diocese of Lausanne; and John de Columpnis, Licentiate and especially appointed to this work by the venerable father in Christ, Lord William of Challant, Bishop of Lausanne, have directed by the pure process of the Inquisition that you, Peter Sager, born at Montrich, now sixty years old, thirty years and more ago forswore the Waldensian heresy in the city of Bern, but since then have returned to that perverse faith, as a dog to his vomit, and held and done many things detestable and vile against the most holy and venerable Roman Church.

You have stubbornly asserted that there is no purgatory, but only heaven and hell; that masses, intercessions and alms for the souls of the departed are of no avail; and there are many other things proved against you in your trial, that show that you have fallen back into heresy. O grief! Therefore after consideration, and investigation, and mature consideration, and weighing of evidence; and after consulting the statutes, both of divine and human law, and arming ourselves with the revered sign of the Holy Cross, we declare: In the name of the Father, Son, and Holy Ghost, Amen;—That our decision may proceed from the presence of God and our eyes behold justice, turning neither to the right nor to the left, but fixed only on God and on the Holy Scriptures, we make known as our final sentence from this seat of judgment, that you, Peter Sager, are and have been a heretic, treacherously recreant to your oath of recantation.

As a relapsed heretic, we commit you to the arm of the secular power. However, we entreat the secular authorities to execute the sentence of death more mildly than the canonical statutes require, particularly as to the mutilation of the members of the body. We further decree, that all and every property that belongs to you, Peter, is confiscated, and after being divided into three parts, the first part shall go to the government, the second to the officers of the Inquisition, and the third to pay the expenses of the trial.

Costs of a Burning

Some of the town expenses attending the execution of Peter are found in the town records, as follows: 'Paid to Master Garnaucie for burning Peter Sager, 20 shillings; for cords and stake, 10 shillings; for the pains of the executioner, 28 shillings; special watchmen during the execution in the city, 17 shillings, 6 pfennigs; in the citadel, 9 sols; for the beadles, 14 shillings.' The fuel must have cost a large amount, as twelve wagon loads were used.

Side by side with this fiendish record stand these two charges: 'Twenty-eight measures of wine for the dance at the court-house, in honor of the Count of Zil.—cauldron, in which Casper Antoine, of Milan, was boiled.' Have Waldensian blood and purity ever been avenged?—History of the Baptists, Thomas Armitage, pages 310-312.

Cathcart's Account of the Waldenses

The Waldenses are the most interesting people in Europe. Their history reaches back to the period when popes gathered armies without difficulty to desolate prosperous Albigensian regions of what is now the French republic, when the Bible was almost an unknown book, and when the intellect and liberties of Europe were in shackles, except in the cast of heretical heroes, who were treated as outlaws by the banded priests and tyrants of the Old World. We speak of this people with reverence, and think of their long records of fidelity and suffering with tender affection.

There is nothing reliable about the Waldenses before the time of Peter Waldo, of Lyons. It is likely that in their celebrated valleys a people who hated Romish errors, and loved the atoning Saviour, lived from the time of Claude, bishop of Turin, in the ninth century. It is possible that such a community may have served God in these secluded retreats from a much earlier period. But we have no clear testimony on this question.

Peter Waldo, a wealthy citizen of Lyons, was converted about 1160, by a sudden death which occurred at a public meeting which he attended. He had an extraordinary desire to see the Word of God in a good translation, and for this purpose he employed Stephen de Ansa and Bernard Ydros to prepare him such a work in the Romance language. He first procured the gospels, and then by degrees the entire Bible. He also had a collection of choice sayings prepared from the early fathers, on faith and practice.

Filled with the hope of heaven, he distributed his property among the poor and scattered copies of his Bible around, and converts rewarded his zeal and rejoiced the angels. The archbishop of Lyons denounced Waldo and his efforts, but the seal of Christ was upon the enterprise, and the gospel leaven worked mightily. He was compelled to leave Lyons, and many of his adherents followed him.

He entered Dauphiny, where his labors resulted in a great harvest of converts; by persecution he was driven into Picardy, where the gospel as the saving power of God produced the same heart-changing fruits; from France his disciples pressed into Italy, and the Piedmontese mountains, where the Protestant bishop of Turin three centuries before had sowed the seed of the blessed gospel, gave them a comparatively secure refuge from armed superstition; from France the reformer of Lyons proceeded to Germany, where his usual reception awaited him from the common people, and from the priests and rulers.

Some fifty years after the death of Waldo there were multitudes of heretics in the districts of the Rhine and elsewhere in the fatherland of Luther. At Triers "there were," says Neander, "three schools of the heretics; there seem to have been various sects it is true; but the spread of German versions of the Bible, and the doctrine of the universal priesthood (of Christians), are certainly marks which indicate the Waldenses."

Waldo finally retired to Bohemia, where he led throngs of men to Jesus, who contained to uphold the banner of the Cross for generations. Altogether the Waldensian movement was a manifest work of God, and its triumphant progress gave the papacy the heaviest blows and the greatest fears.

The Waldenses were not Albigenses, Kathari, or Paterines. They lived frequently in the same regions, and held many things in common with them, but they had a different origin and birthplace, and came into existence hundreds of years later.

The Waldenses were persecuted with atrocious cruelty, and hosts of them were wickedly put to death.

They have no writings older than the end of the twelfth century. "The Treatise on Antichrist" and "The

Noble Lesson" are supposed to have been published at the close of the twelfth century.

Their theology in most features is like the Protestant system of the present day, and it is a perfect contrast to the scheme of Rome.

On baptism the Waldenses were divided. There is reason to believe that some of them practiced infant baptism. It is not unlikely that some of them were Quakers about baptism and the Lord's Supper. The inquisitor, Reinerius Saccho, is the chief authority about the Waldenses, to whom he did not belong, and the Albigenses, with whom he was a member for seventeen years; he states about the Waldenses that "they say a man is then first baptized when he is received into their sect. **Some of them hold that baptism is of no use to little children, because they are not yet actually able to believe**" (Quidam eorum BAPTISMUM PARVULIS NON VALERE TRADUNT, eo quod nondum actualiter credere possunt).—Allix's "Churches of Piedmont," p. 206. Oxford, 1821.

The celebrated Du Pin gives Reinerius the weight of his great learning and truthfulness as he quotes his statement, "And first about baptism they say, that the preliminary admonition is worth nothing; **that the washing of infants is of no avail to them; that the sureties do not understand what they answer to the priest.**"—II. 482. Dublin. There is no reasonable ground for doubting that for a long period the Baptists were respectably represented among the "Poor of Lyons," the "Leonists," the "Waldenses."

The Waldenses loved the Scriptures, could repeat entire books with ease, sometimes the whole New Testament, and were extremely anxious to circulate Bibles, and to read them to men. Reinerius, the apostate and papal inquisitor, gives the well-known representation of the Waldensian peddler, who, after selling articles to ladies in splendid homes, tells them about a richer jewel, which, if the situation is favorable, he presents; and they see and speedily hear the Scriptures read and expounded. The business of the traveling merchant is undertaken only to make known the teachings of the Bible. According to the testimony of their greatest enemies they were humble, truthful, self-sacrificing Bible Christians.

In 1530, according to Du Pin, the Waldenses united with the Reformers, and were persuaded to renounce certain peculiarities which heretofore they held, and to receive doctrines which till then had been foreign to their creed. This new arrangment harmonized the reformations of the twelfth and sixteenth centuries, and probably removed Baptist doctrines from the valleys of Piedmont. This ancient community is now Presbyterian, and had its delegate in the recent Pan-Presbyterian Council in Philadelphia. —BAPTIST ENCYCLOPEDIA by William Cathcart.

Remarks of Mr. Jones

These are the closing remarks of Mr. Jones in the preface to the fifth edition of his history of the Waldenses, in 1825.

These remarks were made with special reference to Mr. Gilly's narrative, Ec., and give the following summary view of the character of this people.

"In the first place they were dissenters—protestant dissenters—dissenters upon principle, not only from the church of Rome, but also from all national establishments of religion. They existed by mere toleration from the civil government; they acknowledged no earthly potentate as head of the church; they absolutely protested against everything of the kind.

They had no Book of Common Prayer, no Liturgy, no Thirty-nine Articles to guard them from error, heresy or schism. They had no reverend gentleman, no privileged order of clergymen, paid or pensioned for discharging the pastoral office among them.

They paid particular respect to the Lord's words;— 'Be ye not called Rabbi, for one is your master even Christ, and all ye are brethren; call no man your father upon earth, for one is your Father which is in heaven; neither be ye called masters, for one is your master even Christ; but he that is greatest among you shall be your servant.'

They brought up their children in the nurture and admonition of the Lord; but they neither sprinkled nor immersed them, under notion of administering christian baptism.—They were, in a word, so many distinct churches of Antipedobaptists."—A General History of the Baptist Denomination in America—by David Benedict.

Later Waldenses Were Heretical

D. B. Ray

When we refer to the Waldenses as Baptists we mean the ancient Waldenses before the Reformation. As a matter of fact many of them merged into the reformed churches during and following the reformation and began to practice sprinkling and adopted the episcopal form of church government. But the original Waldenses, for many centuries, were baptistic in the main doctrines. We submit these quotations to show that historians have recognized the difference between the **ancient** and the **modern** Waldenses. We quote from Ray's Baptist Succession, as he quotes from others and makes comment.

"Mr. Robinson, the historian, says: 'They (ancient Waldenses) are also distinguished from the latter Vaudois, and the reformed churches, by not using any liturgy; by not compelling faith; by condemning parochial churches; by not taking oaths; by allowing every person, even women, to teach; by not practicing infant baptism; by not admitting godfathers; by rejecting all sacerdotal habits; by denying all ecclesiastical orders of priesthood, Papal and Episcopal; by not bearing arms, and by their abhorrence of every species of persecution.'

"How wide the ecclesiastical gulf between the ancient Waldenses—who patiently suffered the loss af all things, even to life itself, rather than shed the blood of others—and these modern pedobaptist Waldenses, who established themselves by cruel war and bloody revenge! . . .

"No one who is not prompted by sectarian motives,

will associate these warlike Waldenses with the ancient suffering witnesses for Christ, called Waldenses.

"It is also a well known fact in history, that the ancient Waldenses formly resisted every form of state religion. But these pedobaptist Waldenses were incorporated into national churches, and their ministers finally enrolled among the state clergy of the empire.

"It was about the year 1532 that the Pedobaptist Waldenses, in connection with George Moril and Peter Mason, united with the reformers under Luther and Calvin. And this class of Waldenses were classed by the Catholics with the Lutherans . . .

"Concerning the distinction between the ancient and Modern Waldenses, Mr. Benedict remarks (page 77); 'For a number of the first centuries their discipline partook of the freedom and simplicity of the Baptists, and was more free to the teaching of females, and the brotherhood generally, than many of our churches would now admit. By degrees they were moulded into Presbyterian measures, and the end, that portion of them which still survived in the ancient valley, adopted in substance the Episcopal form of church government.'

"The author of the Encyclopedia of Religious Knowledge (page 1149) remarks that: 'It is necessary here that we distinguish between the ancient and the modern Waldenses. It appears, from all the accounts we gather of them before the reformation, that their principles and practice were more pure and Scriptural than since that period." See Ray's Baptist Succession, pages 126-128.

ORCHARD'S LINE OF SUCCESSION

Mr Orchard has taken pains to group together, under one head, the names of the different sects, and follows down the dates of the origin or existence of those who are implicated in this statement for 1200 years, for the Pichards and Waldenses in 1450, to the Novatianists in 250. Although nearly all the facts and authorities may be found interwoven in the preceding narrative, yet, as the recapitulation will assist the reader to go over the whole at one glance, I have condensed his article, and present it in the following manner:

Names of the Parties	Date	Authorities
Waldenses and Picards	1450	Wall
Hussites	1420	Crosby and Ivemy
Waldo and his followers	1176	Jones
Waldenses and Albigenses	1150	Collier
Arnoldists	1140	Bellarmine
Henricians	1135	Wall
Petrobrusians	1110	Wall
Berengarians	1049	Mezaeray
Gundulphians	1025	Jortin
Paterines	945	Jones
Vaudois in France and Spain	714	Robinson
Paulicians	653	Gibbon, Allix
Donatists	311	Mosheim
Novatianists	250	Brit. Ency.

This is one line of the Baptist succession.—**Foreign Baptists,** p. 336, quoted by Benedict.

HISTORIAN BENEDICT SUMMARIZES

I will now give a brief review of the different parties whose history I have in part related.

Montanists—This party arose towards the close of the second century, in Phrygia, and continued for a member of centuries. With them the famous Tertullian united, about 200.

Novatianists broke off from the church of Rome in 250, and in a few centuries spread over a great part of the Roman empire, and in the end were absorbed in new seceding parties.

The **Donatists** began their operations at Carthage, in Africa, a little after 300; they spread extensively in that country, and continued until after the seventh century.

The **Paulicians** arose within the bounds of the Greek church about the middle of the seventh century; they spread far and wide in many parts of Europe, and continued till the eleventh century, when they amalgamated with the Waldenses and other sects.

The **Paterines** began in Italy in the 10th century. They spread extensively in that kingdom, also in Poland, Bohemia, France, Ec., and were finally absorbed, in the thirteenth century, in the great body of the Waldenses.

Waldenses and **Albigenses.**—The history of these people forms the most prominent article in this portion of my history. They became more publicly known under Peter Waldo, who became one of their distinguished leaders about 1165, but of the people who afterwards bore this name, most emphatically will the remark of Mosheim apply, that their origin is "hid in the remote depths of antiquity."

Of the **German anabaptists** nothing need to be said as to their denominational character; their name is their voucher for their dipping propensities, which runs back to a period so remote that the profoundest researches into antiquity cannot ascertain their origin.

The other parties, of which some accounts will be given, viz. the followers of Peter de Bruis, Henry, Huss, Wickliffe, Ec., as well as of Waldo, all held to the same principles as those of an earlier date.

Thus we see the different companies lapped over each other, and covered the whole ground; and notwithstanding all the persecutions, gibbets and flames, to which they were exposed,—the interdicts, banishments and exile, which were their never-ceasing portion, they continued in great numbers up to the time of the Reformation.

Accounts of Eminent Reformers and Evangelical Parties Of Which but Very Brief Sketches can be Given.

Berengarius arose in France in 1050; he was a person of great learning and talents, and advanced in honors in the church of Rome until he became an archbishop. His first attack on the corruptions of this church was against the doctrine of transubstantiation, or as it was called, the real presence.

His contest with the pope was long and severe. He recanted and burned his books, and then returned to his former course. He began the work of reformation when young. He was at different periods denounced and caressed by the Roman pontiffs, but in the end died in peace, at the age of 80, after having been a preacher 50 years.

In the language of Mosheim, notwithstanding his versatility of mind, he left behind him in the midst of the people a deep impression of his extraordinary sanctity; and his followers were as numerous as his fame was illustrious. They were called Gospellers for one hundred years, and many of them suffered death for their opinions.

Bellarmine says, "The Berengarians admitted only adults to baptism, which error the anabaptists embraced"; and Mezeray declares Berengarius to have been the head of the sacramentarians or anabaptists.

Peter de Bruis and the Petrobrussians.—The famous man from whom this party took its name arose in the south of France, about 1110. Some account of them has already been given. These people are ranked by Mosheim among the anabaptists.

Henry of Toulouse and the Henricians.—Henry appears as a reformer, about 1116. He is said to have been a disciple of Peter de Bruis. He had been a monk and a hermit. He began his evangelical career in Switzerland, and died in prison at Rheims, in 1158. "All we know of him," says Jones, "is that he rejected infant baptism; censured with severity the licentious manner of the clergy," Ec.

Arnold of Brescia and the Arnoldists.—This man appears as a reformer about 1137. Mr. Jones has some hesitation about adding him to the list of reformers, on account of the great political changes which historians have generally ascribed to him in the heart of Rome. His countrymen regarded him as the apostle of religious liberty, and all except catholics agree in ascribing to him a good character and sound principles. He fell a victim to the Roman power in 1155.

Leonists, or poor men of Lyons.—This is but another name for the Waldenses, and was given to them from the city of Lyons, from which Waldo originated. This name very often occurs among old catholic writers, and always with severe denunciations and bitter complaints. This is the party which one of them asserted could trace their history till near or quite to the apostolic age.

Cathari, or Puritans.—The first is from the Greek, and conveys the same idea as the other in English. Different parties at different periods have had this character applied to them by way of reproach; but as with us, so in former centuries, in process of time it would gain a standing among denominational names, and was adopted by the parties themselves, the same as methodist, newlight, anabaptist, Ec.

Hussites, so named from John Huss, a famous reformer of Bohemia, where he was born of parents of affluent circumstances, in 1373. He was a man of learning and talents. He appeared in the character of a reformer in 1407, and suffered martyrdom in 1415. The Hussites became a very numerous body of dissenters in different parts of Europe, and as we have seen already, were classed by Mosheim in the list of anabaptists.

Jerome of Prague was the companion of Huss in labors and sufferings, and was committed to the flames soon after him. The Hussites prevailed in Hungary and Silesia, though his followers were most numerous in those cities of Germany that lay on the Rhine, especially at Cologne.

Picards, Pighards and Beghards.—All these names appear to have had the same origin, but were pronounced differently in different countries, in conformity to the language of each. Such is the testimony of Dr. Wall, who furthermore says, that such as came over to their church must be baptized anew, in mere water—of course they were anabaptists.

According to Orchard, the name of Picards was first applied to the followers of Waldo in Bohemia, who came principally from Picardy in France. For many ages it was the common appellation of the Waldenses in this kingdom, but it often occurs in many other countries.

Lollards and Wickliffites, so called from Walter Lollard and John Wickliffe, who were distinguished reformers in the fourteenth century. Lollard is represented by Mosheim to have been a Dutchman. Wickliffe was a native of England, where these two parties prevailed much, as we shall see when we come to the history of that country. The Wickliffites, as we have seen by Mosheim's account, was one of the principal branches of the anabaptists. The baptists claim the disciples of these men, as, in my opinion, they may justly do, as distinguished advocates of their principles, long before the rise of Luther and Calvin.

Lollard was burnt at Cologne, 1320.

Wickliffe died in peace, 1384; but forty years afterwards, by a decree of the council of Constance, his books and his bones were committed to the flames on account of his heretical opinions.—A GENERAL HISTORY OF BAPTIST DENOMINATION By David Benedict, Page 51.

SAINT PATRICK HELD THE LEADING DOCTRINES OF THE BAPTISTS

"St. Patrick rejected all canons, creeds, and councils—The Nicene creed—Columbanus and a remarkable canon—Contempt of Irish missionaries for canons—The Bible is Patrick's code of laws—His love for it—Ancient Irish eulogy of it—Religious liberty for pagans and others—Patrick as a foreign missionary—His teaching ultimately sends out swarms of missionaries to heathen lands.

"Baptists have always refused to surrender the independence of their churches, even to their own Associations. They reject all ecclesiastical authority, with its canons, creeds, and synods, except the Holy Scriptures, with their laws for the government of lives and churches.

St. Patrick stood on the same ground. He rejected the creed of the council of Nice, a celebrated synod, which convened in A. D. 325. He made a creed for himself, which will be found in the second chapter of His "Confession," in this volume. In it he treats chiefly of the Godhead, and its Trinity of equal persons. The Nicene creed is devoted to the same mysterious and exalted subjects; but it is not Patrick's creed. We have before us the Nicene creed preserved by Socrates, and also the copy of Theodoret, the one born again about A. D. 380, and the other about 387.

We have also the creed of Constantinople, adopted A.D. 381, an enlargement of the Nicene, and passing under its name in the Episcopal church and elsewhere. Patrick's creed differs widely from the Nicene, and more extensively from the creed of Constantinople. Nor can the supposition that Patrick intended to write the Nicene creed, but quoted from memory instead of a written text, account for the serious differences between the two creeds.

Patrick never calls his the Nicene creed, and this is a remarkable omission. If he had intended it for the venerable document of Nice, notwithstanding its variations; he should have given its name to it. His "Confession," in which he placed it, was intended as a defense. The council of Nice was the most honored synod that ever assembled, and its name attached to his creed would have given it and him a valuable orthodox character.

But Patrick recognized no authority in creeds however venerable, nor in councils, though composed of several hundred of the highest ecclesiastics, and many of the most saintly men alive. He never quotes any canons, and he never took part in making any, notwithstanding the pretended canons of forgers. So abhorrent to the apostle of Ireland was the dospotism of councils, canons, and creeds, that he did not designate as a creed that portion of his "Confession," which, by its terms and theme has been called by some his "creed."

Nor does he invite any special attention to the creed-like section of his "Confession"; it stands with the same claims to respect as the account of his conversion, of his missionary call to Ireland, of his strong desire to save men, or of God's frequent answers to his prayers.

Patrick wrote his "Confession," as he states, late in life, and not long before his death; what he does not describe as a creed, because it was not intended to possess either the power or the name of a creed in his day, though we call it Patrick's creed, is in his "Confession"; so that, during his entire ministry of fifty or sixty years prior to the writing of the "Confession," Patrick had no creed either for himself or his churches. In that document he imposes no creed upon his followers; he and they were as free from councils, and their canons and creeds, as the apostles and their churches, or as modern Baptists.

Tirechan, who wrote in the seventh century, and from whose documents we learn so much of interest, declares that Patrick ordained four hundred and fifty bishops in Hibernia. This was a violation of the fourth canon of the council of Nice, which required at least three bishops to consecrate a new member of their order. This canon is still binding in the Protestant Episcopal church.

And in the Methodist church, its spirit still survives; the bishop-elect is required to have the hands of three bishops laid upon him, or "at least of one bishop and two elders," or, in extreme cases, the hands of three elders. But Patrick ordained his own bishops without Scruple. He paid no attention to canons.

In the latter half of the sixth century, when Kentigern was to be ordained bishop of the Strathclyde Britons, whose country was formerly Roman territory, in which the canons of Nice were binding, according to Ussher, an Irish bishop, when requested, crossed the sea, and unaided, consecrated Kentigern; he, like Patrick, was no respecter of canons.

In the end of the sixth century, Columbanus, a Hibernian, went to the continent as a missionary, prompted by the great success of Columba among the Picts. Annoyed in his mission on account of his observance of Easter at the Irish time, he appealed to Boniface IV. for permission to keep it at the customary time of his country without reproach, and he urged his application because the second canon of the council of Constantinople, in A. D. 381, decreed that: "The churches of God among the barbarians, must be administered according to the customs of the fathers which have prevailed."

The word "barbarians," to an ancient Roman, meant generally foreigners, a nation, like the Irish, never subject to the Romans. The interpretation of this canon by Columbanus, if accepted, would have largely freed the Irish

Christians from the ever threatening tyranny of councils. For the customs of the fathers, which prevailed in Hibernia, and still bore sway there, Patrick and his missionaries were to set aside all councils with their canons and creeds.

Columbanus himself knew that there was no biblical authority for councils, canons, and creeds, and his appeal to the canon of Constantinople shows that when he was at home he cast aside the whole system, as this canon would have allowed, if the Roman empire still existed.

The English Boniface, the Romish apostle of Germany, writes about Clement, an Irish missionary in his field: "He resisted the Catholic church; rejected the canons of the churches of Christ; refuted the works and opinions of the holy fathers, Jerome, Augustine, and Gregory; and he regarded with contempt the laws of councils."

These Irish ministers, instructed by Patrick's teaching, and many others like them, held, with the apostle of Ireland, that no councils, canons, or creeds, have any scriptural dominion over Christ's churches. Modern Baptists unite with St. Patrick in cherishing this doctrine.

His sole authority to rule churches or Christians is the Bible. He never appeals to any other. In his "Confession," and "Letter to Coroticus," Dr. Wright, with each page, has printed the Scriptures quoted or alluded to; and they number one hundred and thirteen. He has done the same thing with the hymn called "The Deer's Cry," and in it the references are thirty-two. Considering the small size of these works, the number of allusions to or quotations from the Divine word are very remarkable. Promises, commands, prohibitions, heart exercises, prayers, the condition of men around, these and many other things stir up Patrick to quote Scripture.

In the "Leber Brecc Homily on St. Patrick," written in the thirteenth century, we have either an ancient sketch from Patrick's own pen of the Bible, or else the exact echoes of his teaching about the Book of books. It says:

"One of the noble gifts of the Holy Spirit is the Divine Scripture whereby every ignorance is enlightened, every earthly distress is comforted, every spiritual light is kindled, and every weakness is strengthened. For it is through the Holy Scripture that heresies and schisms are cast forth from the church. In it is found perfect counsel and fitting instruction by each and every grade in the church. For the Divine Scripture is a mother and a gentle nurse to all the faithful ones who meditate upon it and consider it, and who are nurtured until they are chosen sons of God through its counsel."

These were Patrick's sentiments, whether or not he penned the words originally. In the Bible he saw everything to bless the soul and rule the church, and outside of it nothing ecclesiastical or secular to exercise lordship over Christ's people. He could apply the words of Chillingworth to himself and his converts: "The Bible, I say the Bible only, is the religion" of Patrick and his Christian Hibernians, to guide their souls and rule their religious communities. In this, Patrick was a Baptist.

There is reason for believing that Patrick taught that no good citizen should be punished for his irreligious or pagan opinions. This doctrine is in harmony with his whole converted life. St. Patrick's mother is said to have been a sister of St. Martin, the celebrated bishop of Tours. Ninian, a countryman of St. Patrick, built a church for the southern Picts bearing his name. Dr. M'Lauchlan says, "He became famous in the Celtic churches." No man in his day was better known or more highly esteemed all over western Europe. When Priscillian and his friends were condemned to death for heresy, Martin declared it to be an unheard-of thing that an ecclesiastical matter should be judged by a secular court on principles of the civil war; and he entreated Maximus to spare the lives of the unfortunate men, but they were beheaded. This event created a great sensation, speedily known for that age, even in Britain and Ireland. The course of Martin was applauded. St. Patrick, through Gallic friends, and probably relatives, who sent money and helpers for his mission, heard of it, and in his warm-hearted way denounced secular penalties for erroneous religious opinions; and that for ages made the

Hibernian churches the freest in the world; religious opinions, except in times of ungovernable excitement, could not be punished by secular penalties.

Columba and Columbanus followed Patrick's example in becoming foreign missionaries, the first to leave Ireland to preach abroad, and they followed his doctrine of liberty of conscience. In A. D. 575, there was held at Drumceatt, about twenty miles from Londonderry, Ireland, a great national convention. It was composed of the chief men of Ireland in civil and in ecclesiastical life, with immense numbers of retainers. The convention continued fourteen months, and was under arms during its whole existence.

It granted independence to the Irish Dalriada kingdom of Scotland the great object for which it met. When it was unanimously agreed at the convention to put the bards to death as adverse to the Christian religion, Columba alone plead for them. They opposed his mission in Caledonia at every step, yet he could not slay or hurt them for paganism.

And such was the eloquence and power of the appeal and the influence of the advocate, that the bards were saved. Full of gratitude for their deliverance, the bards issued a poem, composed by Dallan Forgaill, poet laureate of Ireland at that time, in honor of Columba, which is still in existence.

Columba's treatment of the bards showed Christian generosity, conformity to the Saviour's will, and attachment to the famous doctrine of Roger Williams.

When Columbanus, who was born in Ireland in A. D. 543, was prosecuting a successful mission in France, the envy of neighboring bishops led them to summon him before their synod to punish him, ostensibly for keeping Easter at the Irish instead of the Romish time. He sent a letter in reply, declining their request, and telling them that "He desired only that every one might keep his own custom, and follow his own tradition."

According to Columbanus these bishops had no right to dictate to him in any religious act, and punish him for not conforming to their views as they were planning to do; neither had he or any one else authority to inflict civil penalties upon the religious opinions or acts of others unless they were criminal. St. Patrick, Columba, and Columbanus, stood upon the Baptist platform of liberty of conscience.

Patrick was remarkable as a missionary. When he sailed for Ireland to preach the gospel, that country had many British slaves engaged in the lowest occupations and suffering the greatest hardships. His old master waited to seize him and enslave him again. Petty wars, piracy, tyranny, and idolatry were rampant all over the island; but the intrepid Patrick, in the name of Jesus, fearlessly entered upon his work and pursued it for half a century or more, until all Ireland was nominally Christian, though its entire people were not converted.

He presents his missionary plan in his "Confession" when he writes: "Therefore, it is necessary to spread our nets so that a large multitude and throng may be taken for God." There never was a foreign missionary whose heart embraced a wider field, and whose labors among pagan barbarians were more successful in the conversion of souls; among whom he planted such a missionary spirit as led them to complete his unfinished work in Ireland, and to send missionaries to Caledonia to the pagon Anglo-Saxons, and in unparalleled numbers to many other Europen nations. The denomination of Carey and Judson may justly claim Patrick, the illustrious foreign missionary, as holding all their leading doctrines, and as being substantially a Baptist.
—THE ANCIENT BRITISH AND IRISH CHURCHES By William Cathcart, D. D., pages 158-164.

Note: Whether Patrick was a full Baptist, or not, it is certain that he held many of their sentiments, and it is equally certain that he was not a modern catholic. But Catholics are opportunists and know how to make any sort of claim that gives them an advantage. W.J.B.

Of Saint Patrick, Dr. William Cathcart says: "Patrick, Saint, the Apostle of Ireland, was of Scotch birth. His proper name was Succathus; the name by which we designate him is of Latin origin; **Patricius** means noble, illustrious; it was a surname and a title of honor at the same time given to him by his grateful admirers.

"Patrick was wild and wicked until his sixteenth year, when he remembered the God of his fathers and repented him of his sins, and enlisted in the divine service. There is no ground for doubting but that he preached the gospel of repentance and faith in Ireland, and that his ministrations were attended by overwhelming success. There are accounts extant of a number of his baptisms, but they are **immersions** . . . We have strong reasons for regarding St. Patrick as a Baptist Missionary, and beyond contradiction his baptism was immersion."—Baptist Encyclopaedia, page 886.

IN THE VALLEYS OF THE PIEDMONT

The Antiquity of the Evangelical Churches in the Valleys Of Piemont, From the Days of Christ and His Apostles, Down to the Present Age.

(Author's note: the above is the heading of article appearing in a book, written in 1658, by Samuel Moreland and entitled The Churches of The Valleys of the Piemont. This man was Commissionar extraordinary to the people of the above named valleys of the king of Britain, Ireland and Scotland, as he himself testifies. He was perfectly familiar and sympathetic with, these ancient people in their cruel sufferings. The book contains documents with signatures and attestations of notary publics. He publishes documents and tells where the originals are to be found. This book was recently republished by Baptist Sunday School Committee, Texarkana, Arkansas, where it is available. It gives a graphic account of these people for many hundreds of years. We recommend that it be purchased and read. It is hard to read on account of the old English spelling. In the following article, which we here publish from it, we have converted to modern spelling for greater ease in reading. The name of these valleys is spelled in this Book **Piemont.** In modern times it is **Piedmont.** Original punctuation is preserved, as is his use of capitals—W.J.B.)

"The fore-going Chapter presents to the Readers eye, the beautiful Situation of the Valleys of Piemont, with the great abundance of Fruits which the Earth there brings forth, both for the necessity and convenience of the body: This gives him as pleasant a prospect of the heavenly situation of those Evangelical Churches, together with the spiritual and divine Fruits of Faith, Hope, and Patience; which were long since planted by Christ and His Apostles, and cultivated by their Successors in following Generations, down to this present Age.

True it is, That a great part of the most ancient Records, and Authentic Pieces, treating of, and discovering the Antiquity of those Churches, have been industriously sought after, and committed to the flames, by their bloody Persecutors, in the Years 1559, and 1560, that so the truth of their affairs might lie forever smother'd under those ashes, and be buried in perpetual silence; nevertheless God has been so gracious to his Church, both in preserving, as it were by miracle, many Authentic Pieces relating to this particular, compiled and written by the ancient Inhabitants in their own proper Language, as also by suffering even the most eminent and bitter of their Adversaries, ever and anon unwarily to let fall many remarkable passages to this purpose, in those very Writings which they composed expressly against them; That by the help of these two Mediums, it will be easy to produce such Arguments for the antiquity of that Religion, which both they and we at this day profess, as are sufficient to convince any sober person, who does not wilfully shut his eyes against a noon-day truth.

But before we fall directly upon this point, it will be necessary to premise this, namely, that it is a truth generally received by all those who profess to be versed in Ecclesiastical History, that before the year 800, the differences between the Catholics and Reformed Churches (excepting some few clouds of Ceremonies which were yet no bigger than a man's hand) did not all publicly appear, (at least, so as to be established by General Councils or decrees) in any part of Italy. As for the first 500 years,

Bishop Fewel will undertake, that not any one clear sentence can be produced out of any one Father or Council for the Papists against the Protestants. And therefore we may take the generality of the Fathers and Writers in those Ages to be on our side, in all points then controverted and now maintained by us against Rome. So that the main of the Quere will fall upon the 2 next Centuries, which was a period most barren of Authors, and of those few that wrote Italy had but a small proportion, yet we may instance in one or two of note. Gregory the first entitled the Great, who died A. D. 605. (besides his detesting and rejecting the title of Occumenical Bishop, which was the next year after his death, claimed by Boniface the third, consented to by Phocas the Emperor, and confirmed by a Council at Rome A. D. 607) is ours in very many points against the present Church of Rome, some whereof Illyricus in his Catalogus Testium hath collected, and more might be gathered, had not the Papists so abominably corrupted him, as Dr. Thomas James in his Bellum Gregorianum hath made to appear in some hundreds of places. Also Paulinus Bishop of Aquileia in the year 790, held the truth in many of the controverted points, as appears out of the same Illyricus. In the year 794, the Synod of Franckfort, at which were present many Italian Bishops, condemned the second Nicene Council for decreeing Image-worship (though Binius and others would fain evade it) for confirmation whereof there are cited Aventinus 1. 4. Aimonius 1. 4. c. 85. Hincmarus in Ludg. Episcop. c. 20. Abb. Urspergensis, whole testimonies are related by Hospinian de Origine Imaginum, c. 10. printed Tiguri 1603, and partly by Vignier in his Recuel de 1' Histoire de 1' Eglise, ad An. 794.

These things being premised, in the first place therefore it may be affirmed, That these Churches of the Valleys of Piemont remained united with the other Christian Churches, and particularly with that of Rome, so long as it retained the true Religion, which was planted throughout all Italy, by the Apostles, their Disciples, and Successors. But when as the Church of Rome began to corrupt itself, and would by no means be persuaded to retain the purity of that Apostolical Doctrine and Divine worship, then those of the Valleys began to separate themselves from them, and to come out from amongst them, that so they might not be partakers of their sins, nor receive of their plagues. And thus is evident by divers very ancient Manuscripts, long since laid up and preserved in the Valley of Pragela, which do directly strike at and oppose the Errors of the Church of Rome. Among these Manuscripts there are three very considerable: The first is intitled, Qual cosa sia Anticrist? that is to say, What thing is Antichrist? which was written in the year 1120. The second was written (as is supposed much about the same time, Entitled, Purgatori Soima, that is to say, The Cause of our separation from the Church of Rome. These Manuscripts are not only made mention of by that famous and learned Mr. Paul Perrin in his History Des Vandois; but likewise avered by Mr. Thomas Tronchin the chief Minister of Geneva, (a person of known probity and learning,) whose formal Attestation is here inserted.

The Attestation of Mr. Thomas Tronchin, the chief Minister of Geneva, a person of known probity and learning, concerning certain Manuscripts touching the ancient Doctrine and Worship of the Evangelical Churches in the Valleys of Piemont, inserted in Mr. Paul Perrin's History.

The true Original of which Attestation, is to be seen, together with the rest of the Original Papers and Pieces of this present History, in the public Library of the famous University of Cambridge.

I whose Name is here under-written, Minister of the Holy Gospel, and Divinity Professor at Geneva, do attest, that Sieur Jean Paul Perrin coming into this City to print the History of the Waldenses and Albigenses by him compiled, did then communicate to me that his Work, and divers Original Manuscripts, out of which he had extracted the ancient Doctrine and Discipline of those People, which Manuscripts I then saw and persued, in faith whereof I have given this present Attestation, to the end that it may serve and bear witness to the truth, when and where ever

there shall be occasion. Made at Geneva, Nov. 19, 1656.
THO: TRONCHIN.

Now then I say, These Churches of the Valleys of Piemont, separating from the Church of Rome, do not upon this account either begin or cease to be the true Church of God; but rather did hereby manifest their perseverance in that ancient Doctrine of Christ and his Apostles, from which the Church of Rome was now departed. Even as the Jewish Church of old separated itself from the ten idolatrous Tribes; and so, the faithful Jews believing in Jesus Christ, and retaining the ancient Doctrine of the Patriarchs and Prophets, when they were persecuted by the High Priests of the unbelieving Jews, separated themselves from them; But yet neither did the one or the other by this separation lose their ancient right of succession; nay, on the contrary, they did hereby retain the safe in its first channel, and primitive purity.

In the second place, and in confirmation of the former, the Ecclesiastical History that treats of Charles the Great and his Followers, tells us, That both that Emperor and the Western Churches did jointly strive and use their utmost endeavor in the Council held at Franckfort in the Year 794. to have drawn Pope Adrian and the Church of Rome out of that Gulf of Superstition, into which it had precipitated itself, by persuading them to imbrace the true Doctrine of Christ and his Apostles. Moreover, that one of the chief Counsellors of the said Emperor, (by name Claudius Archbishop of Turin, and consequently of the Valleys of Piemont) was exceeding active, and did very much stickle in this business. This Claudius was one of the most learned and renowned Worthies of his Age, he was one of the chief Founders of the Academy of Paris, (as the Bishop de Meaux in his Preface to the books of Charles the Great touching Images, abundantly testifies.) And about the Year of our Lord 815, the Emperor Louis Le Debonair Son of Charles the Great, preferred him to the Archishoprick of Turin, that so he might furnish his Diocess with the Doctrine devoted Italic & plebi, to the people of Italy: the which he in truth did with all his might, (as his famous Adversary Jonas Aurelianensis confesseth) as well by frequent Writings, as by painful and constant preaching to, and instructing the Flock committed to his charge: for, indeed, this holy man finding that he was not able to withstand that mighty torrent of the Romish Superstitions in other parts, imployed all his endeavours, to preserve his own Dioceses from being infected with those idolatrous principles; and to this end he ceased not to instruct his people by all ways and means, That they ought not to run to Rome for the pardon of their sins, nor have recourse to the Saints or their Relics; That the Church is not founded upon St. Peter, much less upon the Pope, but upon the Doctrine of the Apostles; That they ought not to worship images, nor so much as have them in their Churches. And this he observed throughout his whole Dioceses, as is confessed by the above said Jonas Aurelianensis, in a Book that he wrote expressly against him, in the Year 820. The same is likewise reported by Bellarmine, from whence I conclude, (and it is exceeding remarkable as to the proof of the matter in hand) that the same Belief which was publicly taught and professed in those Valleys of Piemont in the Year 820. was the very same that is at this day professed and owned by the Reformed Churches; that is to say, the true, ancient and Evangelical Doctrine. To this I shall add, that not the most bitter Adversaries of this Claudius Arch-bishop of Turin, were ever able to lay to his charge any fundamental Error, for as much as he always retained Fidei Catholic & Regulam the Rule of the Catholic Faith; and did not express any opposition, save only against the (pretended) Traditions Ecclesiasticas, Ecclesiastic Traditions. These are Jonas Aurelianensis his own expressions, yet in the mean time he dexterously gives himself the Lie, for that Calumny of Arrianism wherewith in other parts of his Writings he had unjustly branded that worthy Bishop and his Disciples, merely for their not complying with the idolatrous and superstitious inventions of the Church of Rome. And this is all likewise that Rainerius Saccon has to object against the Waldenses, who succeeded this Arch-bishop and his

Disciples; For saith he, All other Sects render themselves horrible, by reason of their Blasphemies against God himself, but on the contrary, this hath great appearance of piety, for as much as they live justly in the sight of men; they believe well, as concerning God, in all things, and hold all the Articles of the Creed; there is only one thing against them, that is, they hate and blaspheme the Church of Rome, and hereby they easily gain credit and belief among the people. In like manner Samuel de Cassini a Frier of the Franciscan Order, writing against the Waldenses, inhabiting the Valleys of Piemont, declares plainly in the beginning of his Book, intitled, Vittoria Trionsale, printed at Coni Cum privilegio, in the Year 1510, That all the (pretended) Errors of those Waldenses consisted in this, that they denied the Church of Rome to be the holy Mother Church, and would not obey her Traditions. As touching other points, he confesseth, that the Waldenses did acknowledge the Christian Church, Whereof likewise he reckons and esteems them as true members.

By this then, say they, first, it plainly appears, that the Inhabitants of those Valleys have professed and taught the safe Evangelical Doctrine which they now own, before the Dukes of Savoy had any possession of Piemont; and therefore he has no justifiable pretext to deprive them of their ancient Liberties and Privileges, upon the account of Religion.

Again it is as manifest, and necessarily follows, that the Waldenses who escaped the Massacres in France, in the Year 1165. and came from thence into the Valleys of Piemont, were not the first Founders of that Religion, but rather that they joined themselves to those their faithful Brothers, for the better fortifying and mutual edification of each others Faith, just as those other Waldenses did, who having recourse to Bohemia, closed with the faithful Professors of the Greek Church there, who had retained the ancient and true Religion, (not the Papal, as Stranchi Reip. Bohem. testifies). Neither is it at all probable, that it could be otherwise; for the Waldenses knew right well, that the seat of their chief Adversary was in

Italy; and therefore they would not have been so void of all sense and common prudence, as to have undertaken so long and tedious a Journey over the Alps, had they not been well assured that the Natives of those Valleys who professed the same Religion with them, would receive and embrace them as their Brethren. D'Aubigno a very judicious Historian seems to be clearly of this opinion. And Mr. Perrin amongst his older Manuscripts makes mention of a certain Epistle of the Waldenses, inscribed, La Epistola al sereissimo Rey Lancelau, a li Ducs, Barons, a li plus veil del Regne, Lo petit tropel deli Christians appella per fals nom salsament P. O. V. That is to say, an Epistle to the most serene King Lancelau, the Dukes, Barons, and most ancient Nobilitie of the Realm. The little troop of Christians falsely called by the name of poor people of Lions, or Waldenses. By which it is most evident, that they had not their original from the said Waldo, but their Adversaries, to make the world believe, that their Religion was but a Novelty, or a thing of yesterday. Thus those who escaped the Massacres in France, were by the popish party sirnamed either according to the places where they inhabited, or the chief of their Leaders; for example, from Waldo a Citizen of Lyons, they were named Waldenses, and from the Country of Albie, Albigenses. And because those who did adhere to the doctrine of Waldo came out of Lyons, naked and stript of all their Goods and Estates, they were in derision, styled, The Poor of Lyons. In Dauphine they were nick named in mockery Chaignards. And for as much as part of them went over the Alps, they were called Tramontani. In England they were known by the name of Lollards, from one Lollard who was one of their chief instructors in that Isle. In Provence they were usually termed Siccars, from a vulgar word then in use, which signified Cut-purses. In Italy they had given them the title of Fraticelli, or Men of the Brotherhood, because they lived together like Brethren. In Germany they were named Gazares, a word which signifies execrable, and wicked in the highest degree. In Flanders they went under the name of Turlepins, that is to say, Men inhabiting with, or companions of Wolves, because those poor people were ofttimes constrained in the heat of persecution, to inhabit in Woods and Deserts, amongst wild and savage beasts. Sometimes to render them more execrable, their Adversaries borrowed the names of several ancient Heretics to brand them with. Thus for as much as they made profession of purity in their life and Doctrine, they were called Cathares, that is, Puritans. And because they denied the Host which the Priest holds up at Mass, to be God, they were called Arrians, as those who denied the Divinity of the eternal Son of God. And because they maintained that the Authority of the Kings and Emperors of the World, did not depend upon the Jurisdiction of the Pope, they were called Manichsi, as men asserting two first principles. And for such like cause as these they were sirnamed Gnostiques, Cataphrygians, Adamites, and Apostolics. Yea sometimes their Adversaries were outragious, Matthew Paris calls them Ribaux, that is, Rogues, Rascals, Scoundrels, Varlets, or Base Fellows. The Authour of the Tresor des Histoires, calls them Bougres, that is, Buggerers or Sodomites. Rubis reports, that the word Sorcerer was in those days expressed by the term Valdensis.

Now the lapse of time between Claudius Arch-bishop of Turin, and Waldo, does not at all hinder the continual Succession of those Churches and that Religion, no more than those dark Intervals which were in the Church before and after the Deluge, those Intervals of the Egyptian Bondage, the Judges, the Babylonion Captivity, and the like in after ages, did hinder or interrupt the continual Succession of the Jewish Religion; no more than the Sun or Moon do cease to be, when their light is eclipsed or withdrawn from the eye by the interposition of other Bodies; no more than the Rivers, Po, the Rhene, or Guadiana in Spain, do lose their continual current, because for some time they run under ground or among the Rocks, and appear not; so for the Church of God, though sometimes it has not been so visible to the eye of men, it hath notwithstanding continued in a constant uninterrupted succession through all ages and Generations. Thus the good

Prophet Elijah in his days thought he had been left alone, but yet God had reserved at that very time seven thousand souls of the very same principles and profession with himself.

Although this be a truth that is by many thought sufficient of it self against the fiercest objections of the gain-saying Adversaries, yet I shall proceed a step further, and make bold to allege moreover, that Marc. Aurelio Priour of Lucerna in his Narratione del Introduttione de gl' Heretici nelle Valle di Piemonte, printed at Turin, Anno Dom 1632. with approbation and privilege, confesses that it continued to the ninth and tenth Century, which is the very interval between the said Claudius and Peter Waldo, or rather the retreat of certain of his Disciples into the said Valleys. For the said Rorenco testifies in express terms pag. 16. Nel non e decimo fecolo continuarono 1' heresie antecedenti, that is, The above said Heresy continued throughout the ninth and tenth Centuries. And to remove all scruples, that this Doctrine which he calls Heresy, (as S. Paul speaks Acts 24:14. and which the Enemies of the Christian Religion call Heresies) continued in the Valleys of Piemont, the same Rorenco in his Historical observations printed at Turin, 1649. with approbation, and dedicated to the Duke himself, confesseth page 3. That the said Claudius Arch-bishop of Turin, (and consequently of the Valleys, which were within that Diocese) maintained this very Doctrine in the ninth Century. Wherefore seeing the Succession of the Evangelical Religion is manifest from the time of the Apostles to that of Claudius Arch-bishop of Turin, which was in the eighth Century, and that his Doctrine continued in the ninth and tenth Centuries; and that in the begining of the eleventh Century the Waldenses or Disciples of Peter Waldo came into the Valleys to reside with their Brethren, where they have professed and taught the same ever since; The professors of the Reformed Religion may clap their hands in token of an absolute Triumph forever against all the Disciples of the Church of Rome, and say, that they are now able manifestly and undeniably to prove and make good the continual Succession of their Religion from the days of Christ and His Apostles down to this present Age.

In the second place, the faithful people of the Valleys in the Year 1535. being at that time possessed of their ancient Histories and Manuscripts, testifying the Antiquity of their Churches, which were afterwards consumed to ashes by their Persecutors in the Years 1559. and 1560. caused to be printed at their own proper cost and charges the first French Bible that was ever put forth, or came to light, and that for the benefit of the Evangelical Churches where this Language was in use, and dedicated the same to God himself by the Pen of their Interpreter Robert Olivetan, in the Preface of the said Bible; which was a Piece most solemnly consecrated, and speaking as it were to God himself, wherein they mention, that they have always had the full enjoyment of that heavenly Truth contained in the holy Scriptures, ever since they were enriched with the same by the Apostles themselves. And for as much as it is a Piece so exceeding rare, and to be found in very few places of the World, I have here inserted the same at length, in the original Language, and their own words as followeth.—Book I, chapter 3.

BOOK FOUR

ASSOCIATIONS OF CHURCHES

CHAPTER I

THE NATURE OF AN ASSOCIATION OF CHURCHES

Churches can associate together in Scriptural enterprises, such as missions, education, publications and benevolence. But, while churches may associate, they cannot federate into one unit, with a common governing head.

The unit of membership in a scriptural association must be the local, visible church. No individual is a member of an association except by his relationship to a local church. Thus, while an association is composed of church-units, such an association never meets except by means of messengers elected by the local churches.

A Scriptural association must have equal representation of the churches. It matters not if the number be one, three or a dozen, so long as each church, regardless of size, have the same number of messengers. A church with only a few members is as much a church, and has as much authority, as another with many members. We must keep in mind that the New Testament idea of a church is a local, visible, autonomous and democratic body; few, or many members.

The only guarantee for the safety of this rule is for the church to confine its messengers to its own members. It must be clear that if church number one elects its full number of messengers to an association and church number two elects other members of church number one to represent it, then we have one church with more members representing than the other churches.

Paul was sent out as missionary by the church at

Antioch (Acts 13:16), but other churches associated together in his support. See II Corinthians 11:1, 8.

In Paul's day the churches associated together in benevolence. "And we have sent with him the brother, whose praise is in the gospel throughout all the churches; and not that only, but who was also chosen of the churches to travel with us with this grace which is administered by us to the glory of the same Lord, and declaration of your ready mind," II Corinthians 8:18-19.

Associations through the years

There were associations in the second century. See Orchard, page 110. And there were associations among the Paterines in Italy in the third century. See Orchard, page 146. There were associations in Greece in the third century, Orchard, page 29.

There were associations in Wales before the Reformation. We have the following quotation from Davis' History of the Welsh Baptists: **"We find him (H. Vaughn) in the first association formed in Wales since the Reformation, held at Abergavenny, Monmouthshire, on 14, 15 days of August, 1653."**

So there were associations before and after the Reformation, in Wales. There were a large number of associations among the Welsh Baptists in the seventeenth century.

In America there were literally scores of associations in many states during the eighteen hundreds. We could, if space permitted, catalogue the names, places and states. We must be satisfied with a few tables. We list elsewhere a summary, taken from Asplund's Register of Associations in North America previous to the year 1800. They are quoted from Ford's Christian Repository.

The oldest Baptist Association in America was the Philadelphia, organized in 1707. The next was the Charleston Association, organized in 1751. The Charleston was followed by the Sandy Creek in North Carolina in 1758. The Warren Association in Rhode Island and Massachusetts was formed in 1767. There were four associations in Vermont before 1796. The Boston Association was formed in 1812 and later divided into four.

If the reader will refer to Benedict's History of the Baptists he will find listed detailed information about many others of the eighteenth and nineteenth centuries. We list the above just to show that Baptists have long worked in associations.

We learn what we were not surprised to find that there were differences then, as has always been the case, on some points—inter-church communion, even open communion sometimes; laying on of hands of all the baptized, etc. There were some for and some against. But, in the main, they were exactly as we today.

We also find that they were missionary, even though occasionally someone would hold the opposite view.

E. F. Merriam, in his History of American Baptist Missions, says there were 2417 Baptist churches in America in 1812. A large number of these churches worked together in associations that were organized in the late seventeen hundreds.

CHAPTER II

ENGLISH ASSOCIATIONS

Particular Baptist Associations, England

Here is a quote from Thomas Armilage—

When we come to trace the effects of Toleration on the English Baptists, after it was procured, we see at once the paralyzing result of false doctrine, and their decline in spiritual power. This is nowhere more distinctly visible than in their Associations and General Assemblies. The insidious leaven of centralization had even worked itself into the later notions of Smyth, and the fifth charge on which Morton and Helwys expelled him in Holland was his teaching, "that an elder in one church is an elder of all the churches in the world."

A tinge of interchurch authority crept into the Confession of the eight churches, 1643, in these words: "Although the particular congregations be distinct and several bodies . . . they are to have counsel and **keep** one of another, if necessity require it, as members of one body in the common faith, under Christ their head."

The paternal principle of Associations was laid down here, with a slight margin for its abuse also. An Association was formed in 1653, when the Somerset Churches, with those of Wilts, Devon, Gloucester and Dorset, met at Wells, "on the sixteenth and seventeenth days of the month."

This body of Particular Baptists published the "Somerset Confession" in 1656, which is not to be confounded with the "Somerset Confession" issued by the General

Baptists in 1691. The Midland Association of Particular Baptists was formed in 1655, at Warwick, but was reconstructed in 1690, and still exists; (1889) its original record books, however, are lost.

The Associations very early encroached on the rights of the churches. Adam Taylor describes their business thus: 1. The reformation of inconsistent and immoral conduct, in ministers and private christians; 2. The suppression of heresy; 3. Reconciling of differences between members and churches; 4. Giving advice in difficult cases to individuals and churches; 5. Proposing plans of usefulness; 6. Recommending cases requiring pecuniary support; 7. Devising means to spread the Gospel in the world at large, but especially in their own churches.

The first four of these would not be tolerated amongst us, and the desire for a stronger bond than that of mutual love soon brought them into serious trouble. The General Baptists experienced this, first, by establishing a "General Assembly," it is not certain at what precise date, but before 1671. It met only on "emergent occasions," on an average, once in two years. Article XXXIX of the "Orthodox Creed" claims that it had "divine authority, and is the best means under heaven to preserve unity, to prevent heresy, and superintendence among, or in any congregation whatsoever, within the limits of jurisdiction." Appeals were made to this assembly "in case any injustice be done, or heresy and schism is countenanced in any particular congregation of Christ, . . . and such General Assemblies have lawful powers to hear and determine, and also to excommunicate." Here, the independent polity of Baptist Church was merged into a form of presbytery, and its disastrous effects soon became apparent.

The first "General Assembly" of the Particular Baptists was held in 1689, on a call from the London Churches, signed by Kiffin, Knollys and Keach, with three others. The request was for a "general meeting here in London of two principal brethren, of every church of the same faith with us, in every county respectively." This body is merely what is now known as an "Association", and it "disclaimed all manner of superiority or superintendency over the churches," on the ground, that it had "no authority or power to prescribe or impose anything upon the faith and practice of any of the Churches of Christ, their whole intendment being to be helpers together of one another, by way of counsel and advice."

At its fourth meeting in May, 1692, there were one hundred and seven associated Churches, and the Assembly voted: "That no Churches make appeals to them to determine matters of faith or fact; but propose or query for advice." At this time, The General Baptists had fallen into great trouble by making their Assembly a court of appeals, and the Particular Baptists resolved to take warning and escape that fate. For some cause, which does not appear, the London Churches dropped out of the Assembly after 1694, but the country Churches continued to meet, down to 1730, and the records of their meetings are still preserved.—History of the Baptists, by Thomas Armitage, pages 557-559.—Published 1889.

See also Baptist Encyclopaedia, page 374.

Other Associations in England

Benedict has this to say—

In the year 1650, the Baptist churches began to form themselves into associations; and three years afterwards, an epistolary correspondence was opened, including the English, Scotch Irish, and Welsh churches. During the commonwealth, they were distinguished in various ways. Some of their ministers, possessing university honors, preached in parish churches; and some of their members, as Sir Henry Vane, and General Harrison, occupied high posts under the government.

The name of the mighty Milton, too, is connected with that period. Amidst the changes which followed, much suffering was endured, but great glory resulted from the exhibition of Christian principles. Amongst the conspicuous objects of the times under consideration, we have to notice the character and sufferings of Thomas de Laun, Benj.

Keach, and John Bunyan, immortal names—illustrious men of the Baptist denomination.—Copied from BENEDICT'S HISTORY, Page 304.

London Association

John Marsh writes:

At the revolution in 1688, the Baptists, with the other dissenters, gained a legal toleration; and in the next year, delegates from upwards of an hundred churches met in London to inquire into the state of the churches, and adopt measures for their prosperity. By this assembly was published the confession of faith, known as the century confession. It continued its annual sessions a few years. At this period there were in England and Wales about 300 churches, though many of them were small and without pastors.

Their increase in the last century was small. Of the Particular Baptists, there were in 1768, 217 churches; in 1790, 312; in 1798, 361. In Wales, there were about 80 churches. In Ireland, but 8 or 10. In Scotland, but a few, and these have been Sandemanians, who have had no fellowship with the English Baptists. The general Baptists have about an hundred churches in Great Britain. They are generally Arminian and Unitarian.

In 1793, the Particular Baptists formed a missionary society, and sent Messrs. Thomas, Carey, and Marshman, to India, who, under God, have done wonders.

The assembly of 1689, laid the foundation of a Baptist academy, at Bristol, for the education of ministers. This has been very flourishing. Another was founded near London, in 1810.—Taken from EPITOME OF GENERAL ECCL. HISTORY By Rev. John Marsh.

CHAPTER III

EARLY AMERICAN ASSOCIATIONS

Hiscox's Account of Early American Churches

With the increase of population, Baptists rapidly increased and widely spread over the country. Edwards' Tables give one hundred and thirty-seven as the number of their churches in 1768. According to Asplund's Register, in 1790 they had eight hundred and seventy-two churches; seven hundred and twenty-two ordained, and four hundred and forty-nine unordained ministers; with sixty-four thousand nine hundred and seventy-five church members. According to Benedict's History, in 1812 there were two thousand six hundred and thirty-three churches; two thousand one hundred and forty-two ordained ministers; one hundred and eleven associations; two hundred and four thousand one hundred and eighty-five church members.

Allen's Triennial Register gives, for 1836, three hundred and seventy-two associations; seven thousand two hundred and ninety-nine churches; four thousand and seventy-five ordained, and nine hundred and sixty-six unordained ministers; five hundred and seventeen thousand five hundred and twenty-three church members, including the small denominations of Seventh Day, Six Principle, and Free-Will Baptists.

According to the American Baptist Year Book, in 1868, there were of regular Baptists in the United States, six hundred and thirty associations; thirteen thousand three hundred and fifty-five churches; eight thousand five hundred and seventy-four ordained ministers; one million one hundred and nine thousand nine hundred and twenty-six church members; total in America, including the British provinces, six hundred and forty-six associations; thirteen thousand nine hundred and sixteen churches; eight thousand nine hundred and thirty-one ordained ministers; one million one hundred and forty-nine thousand nine hundred and ninety-two church members. These figures must be below the facts, since full returns are never reported.—BAPTIST SHORT METHOD, by Rev. Edward T. Hiscox, D. D., pages 201-206.

Virginia Associations

The following table will furnish a general view of the state of the Virginia Associations, to 1810.

Names of Associations	When constituted	Present no. of Churches	Present no. of Members
General Association	1760		
General Committee	1783		
General Meeting of Correspondence	1800		
Dover Association	1783	37	9628
Orange	1783		
Goshen	1791	19	2650
Albemarle	1791	9	1037
Culpepper	1791	18	1353
Middle District	1783	8	1329
Appomattox	1804	16	2114
Meherrin	1804	16	980
Roanoke	1788	30	2510
Strawberry	1766	24	1728
New River	1793	9	348
Holston	1788	10 in V.	591
Mountain	1799	3 in V.	190
Accomack	1808	7	891
Ketocton	1765	32	2061
Greenbrier	1807	7	356
Union	1804	13	262
Red Stone	1776	7 in.V.	344
Portsmouth	1790	20	2170
Mayo*	1798		
Totals		287	30,548

*The accounts from Mayo are not come to hand; of course this association must be left almost blank.

—History of Baptists By Robert B. Semple, page 445.

CHAPTER IV

THE NUMBER OF ASSOCIATIONS INCREASE

English and American Associations

It appears that in England an association of Baptist churches was organized in Somersetshire and adjacent counties in 1653. Later, because of the inconvenience of travel there were several smaller bodies. The first general meeting representing the nation was held in 1689, and was composed of delegates from over an hundred churches scattered over England and Wales.

It gave sanction to the statement of principles, with additions, of the Philadelphia Confession of faith. The association disclaimed all **"power to prescribe or impose anything upon the faith or the practice of any of the churches of Christ."** It further stipulated, that, **"whatever is determined by us in any case shall not be binding upon any one church till the consent of that one church be first had."**

The Philadelphia Association was formerly established in 1707. However, meetings were held in less formality from 1688. In 1707 they had regular messengers from Lower Dublin, Middletown, Cohansie, Piscataqua, and Welsh Tract, five churches composing the association. In 1880 there were 1005 associations in the United States.

It will be seen that the Baptists of the Philadelphia Association were not modern Convention Baptists, as the local churches were in control, just as the churches of the North American Baptist Association are today.

Oldest American Baptist Associations

This account is taken from Baptist Encyclopaedia by William Cathcart, page 47.

The Philadelphia Association, 1707
The Charleston Association, South Carolina, 1751
The Sandy Creek Association, North Carolina, 1758
The Kehukee Association, North Carolina, 1765
The Ketocton Association, Virginia, 1766
The Warren Association, Rhode Island, 1767
The Stonington Association, Connecticut, 1772
The Red Stone Association, Pennsylvania, 1776
The New Hempshire Association, New Hampshire, 1776
The Shaftesbury Association, Vermont, 1781
The Woodstock Association, Vermont, 1783
The Georgia Association, Georgia, 1784
The Holston Association, Tennessee, 1786
The Bowdoinham Association, Maine, 1787
The Vermont Association, Vermont, 1787

A Period of Unrest

During the period from 1890 to 1900 there was much dissatisfaction with the conventions, both on state level and in the Southern Baptist Convention. There was a number of grievances publicized in the papers concerning the leadership in these organizations. Among them were, centralization, misuse of funds, violations of church sovereignty, discrimination and others. This writer has learned from personal observation, however, that it is very easy to criticise and unjustly make judgment.

I firmly believe that much of the controversy through this period was based, as it usually is, on personalities. However, there is no doubt that there was some justification. I have read papers published in the early nineteen hundreds and am somewhat acquainted with the controversy. I have observed that some were of a mind to find fault just for the sake of it. I have read the writings of the renowned J. N. Hall, one of the ablest debaters of his time, where he bitterly attacked the idea of smallpox vaccination.

During this period and for many years there was much effort made in missions by the "direct, gospel missionaries." Many of the churches, association in principle, supported these men for the reason that they were not willing to longer support the Convention. There is no doubt that much good was done by these "directors." However, these men were foes of an association such as we have in the associations of today. They had no objections to associations merely as times of visitation and fellowship. If they were alive today, including Dr. Hall, it is my opinion they would fight us as hard as they did the convention of their day.

But there was much truth in the allegations of heresy in leadership that caused many churches in many states to become concerned. While they believed in association, they also believed in equality of representation and church sovereignty. For this reason the state associations of Arkansas and Texas, and the General Association in which churches in several states cooperated, were organized. The first in 1902, the second in 1900 and the latter in 1905.

CHAPTER V

THE NORTH AMERICAN BAPTIST ASSOCIATION

This association was organized in the sanctuary of the Temple Baptist Church, 2400 Wright Avenue, in Little Rock, Arkansas, on May 25, 26, 1950. There were 465 churches represented by 822 messengers. Many visitors also attended. Sixteen states were represented. They were: Alabama, Arizona, Arkansas, Florida, Idaho, Kansas, Louisiana, Michigan, Mississippi, Missouri, New Mexico, Oklahoma, Oregon, Tennessee, Texas and Washington.

These churches until 1950 were members of the American Baptist Association which was organized in 1924. For several years there had been much dissatisfaction over several matters, chiefly the question of messenger representation in the associational meetings.

This formative meeting was called for by the Park Place Baptist Church, Little Rock, Dr. D. N. Jackson, pastor, and Temple Baptist Church, W. J. Burgess, pastor. The call for this meeting was occasioned by events at the American Baptist Association in Lakeland, Florida, in the previous March. Some churches engaged in the practice of electing members of another church as their messengers, thus enabling a church to have more than the three the association's constitution allowed. The church being the unit of membership, it is apparent that this was unequal representation.

At a meeting of the association in Temple Church in Little Rock in 1949 the matter was referred back to the churches in the form of a proposed amendment providing that a messenger must be a member of the church he is sent to represent. The amendment was to be voted on at the following session in Lakeland, Florida. The proposed amendment was never allowed to be voted on. This caused the final rupture, though it was evident that a large majority of the churches had adopted the amendment in their local conferences. Letters from the churches so stating were never allowed to be read.

The Lakeside Night Meeting

After it was apparent the officers in charge would not permit the vote, and after the Wednesday night session, hundreds of messengers, together with many sympathizing visitors, gathered by the side of Lake Mirror a short way from the auditorium to consider further moves.

The writer was chairman of this meeting, and the first speaker being Dr. D. N. Jackson; and there were many others. Elsewhere in Dr. Jackson's account of this meeting is given a resolution that was written by Dr. D. N. Jackson and adopted by the group. It must be emphasized that no association was organized at this mass meeting. In fact, a provision of the resolution adopted plainly stated that any organization must be called for by some church. The writer invited the formative meeting, after the event of the next day, to be held in Temple Church. Immediately upon returning home, and on the following Sunday, the matter was placed before the Temple church and it voted to invite such meeting. So did Dr. Jackson and the Park Place Church, Little Rock.

The Formal Organization

The formal organization took place in the auditorium of the Temple Baptist Church, Little Rock.

Preliminary services were held on the evening of May 24, at which time Elder C. A. Darst, St. Louis, delivered the sermon. About 9 A.M. the following day, the auditorium was filled and the meeting was called to order by Eld. W. J. Burgess, pastor of the Temple Church. Both the Temple Church and the Park Place Church, Dr. D. N.

Jackson, pastor, had officially invited this meeting. W. J. Burgess was elected temporary chairman.

The congregation being too large for even the new and large auditorium (seating 1000) the congregation was divided for the preaching hour. Eld. T. Sherron Jackson was selected to preach in the old auditorium which adjoined the new. Eld. Harley L. Groom preached in the new auditorium.

Previous to the sermons, however, a motion prevailed that 21 men be selected to draft a Statement of Principles. In the afternoon session this Statement of Principles and Doctrinal Statement was adopted. (It is given elsewhere.)

Permanent organization resulted in the election of Dr. Gerald D. Kellar President. Assistants elected were Dr. J. E. Cobb and Eld. J. W. Duggar. Previously elected as temporary clerks were: M. E. Childers, E. T. Burgess and Gerald Parsons. These three were made permanent clerks. Dr. W. J. Dorman was elected to preach at the evening session in the new auditorium and Bro. J. W. Duggar in the old auditorium. (Eld. Jeff D. Welch was elected Secretary of Missions. Brother Welch died before the next meeting. Brother Welch did a magnificent work during the few months he was permitted to serve.)

At the Friday morning session a Publications Committee was elected. A motion carried to accept the invitation of Jacksonville Baptist College, Jacksonville, Texas, to elect a committee to confer with the trustees of Jacksonville College for the purpose of making Jacksonville Seminary a project of this association and that the Education Committee of this association be that committee.

The Committee on Education consisted of: Glen Fox, Luke Wadley, J. W. McCrackin, L. T. Simmons, D. N. Jackson, W. J. Dorman, J. W. Pope, W. E. Nunn, C. O. Strong, Alfred Jones, J. J. Johnson, C. C. Bishop, Roy McClure, M. H. Works, Ralph Brand, D. R. Raper, Tom Netherton, A. J. Schell, C. D. Barton, Johnnie Womack, R. R. Anderson, J. B. Pruitt, R. R. Stracener, R. N. Davis, J. G. Murry and C. C. Winters, honorary.

Dr. J. E. Cobb was elected Editor of Publications.

Walter Griffin was elected Secretary-treasurer of Publications. Date for next annual meeting was set for Wednesday following the second Sunday in March and the place chosen was Laurel, Mississippi. Dr. D. N. Jackson was chosen to preach the annual sermon and Eld. W. R. Speer was named as alternate. Report of Missionary Committee was adopted. Missionary Committee: W. R. Speer, chairman; L. D. McClung, M. N. Gregson, Jesse Burns, John Lee, S. F. Cruz, J. B. Vickery, J. E. James, W. S. Gordon, L. S. Walker, W. B. Duncan, James Hoover, E. B. Jones, Jodie Newton, Gordon Reddin, D. C. Dunson, Harry Darst, Walter Griffin, Elton Stewart, J. D. Hankins, G. C. Fielden, Ollie Parker, G. E. Jones, Robert Ford, Olin Wade.

Motion to elect L. H. Raney as writer and special editor to work with Dr. J. E. Cobb on Publications Committee. Motion that Publications Committee, together with Secretary-treasurer of Publications, determine the location for Publications business. Salary for Secretary of Missions was set at $250.00 monthly, plus traveling expenses.

Friday afternoon session. Eld. C. A. Darst elected chairman of Publications Committee. Salary of Secretary of Publications to be same as Secretary of Missions.

Publications Committee: J. F. McClain, G. C. Stockstill, Errol Williams, H. G. Burch, Mark Wells, A. R. Reddin, Jack Welch, Ady J. Smith, J. H. Gibson, Harold Brunson, L. H. Raney, H. F. Gunn, R. G. Holland, R. P. Campbell, C. A. Darst, August Holden.

L. H. Raney of Waxahachie, Texas, was elected to assist the editor and manager of publications with special writings.

The 1951 session was held March 14, 15 in Civic Center in Laurel, Mississippi. Dr. Gerald D. Kellar, president; Dr. C. C. Winters and J. W. Duggar chosen vice presidents. E. T. Burgess, M. E. Childers and Gerald Parsons elected recording secretaries. Dr. D. N. Jackson preached the annual message at the morning hour. W. R. Speer brought the message at the evening service.

Brother Jeff D. Welch, first Secretary of Missions, having been claimed by death during the year, Mrs. Welch had cared for the work until this session. W. J. Burgess was elected Secretary of Missions, which place he has filled until this date (1963). Walter Griffin was re-elected Manager of Publications and Dr. J. E. Cobb was re-elected Editor of Publications.

The Publications report covered less than a year, yet it showed a sales figure $24,564.32. Plans were adopted to expand this part of the work.

In the department of missions the report showed $38,351.65 had been received from the churches during the year. Interstate missionaries during the year were, Gordon Thompson, H. F. Gunn, J. W. Miller, T. L. Duren. Earl Kinney and E. C. Endicott. All these brethren had served the American Baptist Association but came with the North American Baptist Association in the separation the previous year.

Another missionary of the old American Baptist Association, and who identified himself with the North American Baptist Association, was Harold Morris. During the year he became the first foreign missionary of the latter association, going to Brasil in December of 1950. He is still at date of this writing a missionary of the association.

At the 1952 session Walter Griffin announced his desire to retire from the office of Secretary-manager of Publications to return to the pastorate. T. O. Tollett of Texarkana, a layman and business man, was elected to this important position. He is at this writing still leading in a very successful manner. He is one of our best and most devoted business men.

The 1953 session met in Little Rock. At this meeting Dr. J. E. Cobb, Editor of Publications, asked that he be relieved of this responsibility. D. O. Silvey, Texarkana, was elected to succeed him in this very important position. He has continued in this place until now and has been a very devoted and capable servant.

Foreign Publications. The Publications Department of the association has expanded its work to foreign fields. For several years a modern printing establishment has been owned and operated by our missionaries in Brasil. This extension of publications is under the direction of Manager T. O. Tollett of the home offices. **The Grafica,** as it is known in the Portuguese, is used to publish Sunday school literature, Baptist Training Service literature, tracts, booklets, and even larger books, in the Portuguese language for use, not only in Brasil, but in Portuguese-speaking countries in Europe and Africa.

From the formation of the association in 1950 to the present (1963) we can only give a summary of activities.

The work of Publications has had a phenominal growth. At first located in a small rented building the need for more room was apparent in a matter of months. A modern bookstore has taken its place among the leading stores of the city. The publications offices are in the same building. Another is maintained in Texarkana where the editor of the publications works.

Literature for all ages and departments of Sunday schools is published, as is also literature for training classes of all ages. Study books, magazines and helps are prepared for any need of the churches. Starting with nothing in 1950, the association now has one of the largest literature and book concerns in the category of association Baptists. The bookstore, besides furnishing a local trade, has a very wide mail-order business. Literature is now sold to more than 1500 churches.

Starting in a rented building the need was soon seen for larger quarters. In 1955 some property at 716 Main Street was purchased and a modern building erected. This building is now far too small. More property becoming available in 1963 it was purchased at a very high price. The association now owns in one block, 128 feet on Main Street, Little Rock. Plans are to erect a very large building in the near future, a building that will house all departments of the association.

From a very few missionaries the first year, the association now has missionaries in several foreign countries as well as several on the home field. The association has missionaries in Brasil, Mexico, Costa Rica, Portugal, Cape Verde Islands, Japan, Formosa, Nicaragua and France.

The Missions Office initiated a new venture to solve one of its hardest problems, that of housing for missions, in 1962. It had a trailer built that could open to a width of 24 feet and fold to ten for travel. This mobile missions unit was the first of its kind among any group. It is very modern with carpeted floors, central heating and cooling, rest rooms. Fully furnished with all needed facilities, it can be hauled to any location and set up in a matter of hours. There are now several of these in use.

The association has also pioneered in providing for funds on a revolving basis with which mission churches can buy property. This department has been very successful the past few years and enables young and weak congregations to get started in building projects.

The association has also a department known as the Baptist Building Savings, Incorporated. Sherman Harmon is the Executive Director of this concern. It enables churches to float bonds with which to build or enlarge their plants. This department was inaugurated in 1962. All profits go into the Revolving Loan Fund and this has been a great boon to the Interstate work the past few months.

At the 1954 session in Amarillo, Texas, the association created the office of Assistant Secretary of Missions. At the 1955 session held in Jackson, Mississippi, Richard L. Walters was elected to this work. He did a great work but at the end of the year asked to be allowed to return to the pastorate of a church he had organized on the mission field during the year. Craig Branham was nominated by the Secretary of Missions and was elected. He has continued to this date in this position and has been invaluable. This addition to the missions office had become necessary because of the growth of the mission work.

Another department of the association is that of Research and Public Relations. This has been and still is a valuable asset in making known our principles and acquainting our own people with each other, gathering statistics and publishing them in booklet form. Dr. D. N. Jackson was chosen for this work and is still the Director. Later, Leon Gaylor was added as assistant. Both have done a great service.

The association established a Theological Seminary in Jacksonville, Texas, in 1956. Dr. G. D. Kellar was chosen president and is still in this position. The seminary has a very attractive location and very modern buildings, including administration, library and housing accommodations. This institution is widely recognized for its fundamental and orthodox teaching. Already many graduates have gone out to lead in various fields of Christian service. It is under the direct supervision, as is all other departments, of the association.

In addition to the colleges and the seminary in the States, the association maintains a seminary in Brasil. A modern dormitory was built some years ago in a village near Campinas. This school has been a blessing in training nationals, especially young men, in Christian doctrines. It is supervised by the missionaries of the association in Brasil, Missionary John Elliott, president; Rufus Crawford and Marvin Henson at the present time. The school was originally founded by Missionary Harold Morris, the first missionary of the association, to go to Brasil.

A seminary was established, with the help of Missionary Harold Morris and Missionary Carol Thompson, by the Portugal Association this year (1963). It is located in Lisbon.

Publications and Missions Receipts 1950-1963

(North American Baptist Association)

	MISSIONS	PUBLICATIONS
1951	$ 38,351.65 (Eight Months)	$ 26,726.74
1952	$ 58,665.37	$ 56,996.48
1953	$ 83,769.38	$ 78,351.48
1954	$107,368.82	$102,989.76
1955	$106,360.67	$121,274.90
1956	$130,647.05	$137,956.30
1957	$150,400.16	$154,480.47

1958	$176,871.29 (15 months)	$214,801.79
1959	$126,854.78 (9 months)	$157,494.18
1960	$212,826.94	$224,764.00
1961	$223,143.18	$231,960.00
1962	$227,444.03	$261,191.92
1963	$253,730.26	$278,044.00
1964	$313,946.70	$296,546.86

Summary Statistics of North American Baptist Association

	1959	1960	1961
No. state associations	15	16	16
No local or district associations	78	78	78
No. churches (reporting statistics)	1,169	1,179	1,200
Total membership on church rolls	134,067	140,102	143,964
Estimated active membership (70% of total membership)	93,844	98,071	100,775
Total paid pastors	$2,083,508	$2,169,018	$2,344,022
Total all local causes (salaries, building & repairs, etc.)	$4,564,609	$4,954,759	$5,108,433
Total outside causes (missions education, benevolence, etc.)	$ 723,799	$ 750,894	$ 789,572
Grand total all causes	$5,288,388	$5,705,643	$5,907,005
Per capita giving all causes	56.35	58.18	58.62
Per capita giving to all mission causes	7.71	7.66	7.92

	1959	1960	1961
Average N.A.B.A. Church Membership (on roll)	114	119	120
Estimated active membership (70% no. on church roll)	80	83	84
Paid pastor	$1,782	$1,834	$1,953

Paid all local causes (salaries
building & repairs, etc) $3,904 $4,203 $4,257
Paid all outside causes (missions,
education, benevolence) $619 $637 $665
Grand total all causes $4523 $4,839 $4,923

Membership Range of N.A.B.A. Churches
    58% of the churches have less than 100 membership.
    28% of the churches have between 100-200 membership.
    9.3% of the churches have between 200-300 membership.
    3.5% of the churches have between 300-500 membership.
    1.2% of the churches have over 500 membership.

Percentage of (Full, ½ or ¼) Time Churches in the N.A.B.A.
    90% of the churches have full-time pastors.
    6% of the churches have half-time pastors.
    4% of the churches have fourth-time pastors.

Number of Local or District Associations in Each State

Arkansas	17
California	2
Florida	1
Kansas	2
Louisiana	3
Mississippi	10
Missouri	6
New Mexico	2
Oklahoma	5
Texas	30
Total	78

No. District Associations (Covering more than one state) 3

No. of State Associations 16
    Total local, district & state associations 97

States with Churches but no Organized Associations Within the State
    Alaska, Colorado, Georgia, Idaho, Indiana, Kentucky, Nebraska, North Carolina, Ohio, Virginia and Washington.

District Associations Covering More Than one State
   Gulf Coast Association (Florida, Alabama and Georgia)
   Great Lakes Association (Michigan, Illinois and Indiana)
   Northwestern Association (Idaho, Oregon and Washington)

Note: We have several local associations that have churches located in more than one state . . . for example Harmony Association in Arkansas.

Facts About N.A.B.A. Churches

The churches of N.A.B.A. have 108 missionaries serving on the local, state, interstate and foreign fields.

5% of the churches paid their pastors more than $5,000 salary in 1961.

Total membership gain for 1961 was only 3,862.

—Directory and Handbook, North American Baptist Association, 1963-64.

Missions Personnel and Their Fields, 1963

Interstate. Gordon Thompson, California; Homer Gunn, Illinois; Arlis East, Tennessee; John Boland, North Carolina, Eugene Gambill, Arizona; Phillip Misenheimer, Florida; Wilbur Wright, Alaska and George Stockstill, Mississippi.

Brasil. John W. Elliott, Mr. and Mrs. Rufus Crawford, Mr. and Mrs. Marvin Henson, Mr. and Mrs. Harold Morris, and Mr. and Mrs. Carol Thompson. At this time the Morris family is on leave in the States. These are all American missionaries. A national missionary is Elias Felix Vasconcelos. Besides, there are several other native workers in the grafica of the Association.

Mexico. Mr. and Mrs. Paul Robinson, Americans, are missionaries-elect to Mexico but not yet on the field. Nationals are: Pablo Valero Herrera, Monterrey; Fernando Fabian, Mexico City; Alfonso Quiroz, Veracruz; David Cervantes, Salinas Cruz. Several others are being supported by some churches through the Missions Office.

Japan. Mr. and Mrs. Z. T. Rankin, Hachioji City, Americans. Nationals are, Ichiro Noshiro and Shigeo Oyama.

Formosa. Mr. and Mrs. Jack Bateman and Mr. and Mrs. Dale Thornton, Taipei, Americans. Peter Li, a national.

Cape Verde Islands. Manuel Ramos, a national.

Costa Rica. Mr. and Mrs. Duane Heflin, Americans. Working in San Jose.

Portugal. Mr. and Mrs. Carol Thompson, Americans, at first missionaries to Brasil, transfered to Portugal but at this writing are having to leave. Will probably be working in France when this is published. National missionaries in Portugal are: J. L. Oliveira, Antonio Pego, Jaime Nipo, Horacio Cipriano, Luis Lourenco and Agostinho Matos.

Mr. and Mrs. Jack Courtney, another American couple, are missionaries-elect to Portugal. Not yet on field.

France. Missionary Harold Morris and Missionary Luis Lourenco of Portugal established a mission in France in 1963. If association agrees in its next meeting the Morris family will probably go to France to work.

West Indies. Mr. and Mrs. Eugene Thurman, Americans, are working in St. Johns, Antigua.

Nicaragua. Mr. and Mrs. Paul Robinson now making plans to open a new field in Nicaragua.

Doctrinal Statement
North American Baptist Association

The churches of this Association heartily subscribe to and agree to defend and promulgate the historic Missionary Baptist Faith and Practice, the interpretation of which is tersely stated as follows:

1. The Trinity of God.
2. The infallible and plenary verbal inspiration of the Scriptures.
3. The Biblical account of creation.
4. The personality of Satan.
5. Hereditary and total depravity of man in his natural state involving his fall in Adam.

6. The virgin birth and deity of Jesus Christ.
7. Christ's blood atonement for fallen man.
8. His bodily resurrection and ascension back to His Father.
9. The person and work of the Holy Spirit.
10. Justification before God by faith without any admixture of works.
11. Separation of God's children from the world.
12. Water baptism (immersion) to be administered to believers only and by Divine authority as given to Missionary Baptist churches.
13. The Lord's Supper a church ordinance to be administered to baptized believers only and in Scriptural church capacity.
14. Eternal security of the believer.
15. The establishment of a visible church by Christ Himself during His personal ministry on earth.
16. World wide missions according to the Great Commission which Christ gave His Church (Matthew 28:19-20).
17. The perpetuity of Missionary Baptist churches from Christ's day on earth until His second coming.
18. The right of scriptural churches to be held as equal units in their associated capacities, with equal rights and privileges for all.
19. The subjection of all scriptural associational assemblies and their committees to the will of the churches, so that they shall forever remain as servants of the churches originating them.
20. The separation of the Lord's church from all so-called churches or church alliances which advocate, practice, or uphold heresies and other human innovations which are not in harmony with the word of God. Open communion, alien baptism, pulpit affiliation with heretical churches, modernism, and all kindred evils arising from these practices are unscriptural.
21. The only valid baptism is that administered by the authority of a scriptural Missionary Baptist church. Any so-called Baptist church which knowingly receives

alien baptism, habitually practices this or other evils as those listed in statement 20 cannot be a scriptural Baptist church, nor can its ordinances remain valid.
22. The personal, bodily and imminent return of Christ to earth.
23. The bodily resurrection of the dead.
24. The reality of heaven, involving Divine assurance of eternal happiness for the redeemed of God.
25. The reality of Hell, involving everlasting punishment of the incorrigible wicked.

NOTE: The following statements are not to be binding upon the churches already affiliated with this association, nor to require adoption by churches petitioning this body for privileges of cooperation, nor to be a test of fellowship between brethren of churches. However, they do express the preponderance of opinion among the churches of the North American Baptist Association:
1. We believe in the premillennial return of Christ to earth, after which He shall literally reign in peace upon the earth for a thousand years, Revelation 20:4-6.
2. We believe the Scriptures to teach two resurrections: the first of the righteous at Christ's coming; the second of the wicked dead at the close of the thousand year reign, I Thessalonians 4:13-17; Revelation 20:4-6, 12-15.

Womens Missionary Auxiliary

The 1953 annual session of the North American Baptist Association met in Little Rock in the auditorium of the Temple Baptist Church.

Some weeks previously a call had been made for all women's auxiliaries of the churches composing the association to send messengers for the purpose of organization of a national auxiliary. They met at 10 A.M.

Mrs. Oliver Forbes of Texas made a motion that a National Women's Auxiliary be organized. Mrs. E. J. Banks was elected chairman and Mrs. D. L. Wadley and Mrs. Coleman were elected recording secretaries. A motion was made by Mrs. John Duggar that permanent organization be effected. Permanent officers thus elected were: president, Mrs. John W. Duggar; first vice, Mrs. E. J. Banks; second vice president, Mrs. Z. W. Swafford; third vice president, Mrs. Ady J. Smith. Mrs. Bert Coffee and Mrs. Douglas Laird were chosen recording secretaries. Mrs. L. L. Collins, Sr. was named corresponding secretary; Mrs. Ralph Brand, reporter.

The newly formed national auxiliary began missions work immediately, voting in this session to send a missionary to some foreign field that the association might designate. There were 100 local auxiliaries represented by 210 messengers.

From the organization of the national auxiliary until this date it has been very active in missionary enterprises. It has built a church building in the Cape Verde Islands, built one in Mexico, bought several thousand dollars worth of property in Japan for our missions in Japan and Formosa (where it is now building a church building), and many other projects costing many thousands of dollars.

The present corresponding secretary is Mrs. E. J. Banks, a position she has held several years.

State Associations Affiliated
With the North American Baptist Association

(Date of Organization)

Alabama State Association, December 12, 1951

Arizona State Association, May 30, 1953

Arkansas Missionary Baptist Association, November 14, 15, 1950

Baptist Missionary Association of California, September, 1954

Baptist Missionary Association of Louisiana, November 5, 1952

Baptist Missionary Association of New Mexico, February 14, 1955

Baptist Missionary Association of Texas, July 6, 1900

Florida State Association, 1955

Illinois State Association, August 22, 1959
Kansas State Association, January 23, 1959
Michigan State Association, August 21, 1943
Mississippi State Association, 1806, (originally)
Missouri State Association, November 14, 1928
Oklahoma State Association, 1951
Tennessee State Association, August 24, 1957

There are several other state and regional associations but I do not have the exact dates and places of organization. I had intended to give a brief history of these associations but two things prevented. First, lack of space; second, the difficulty in obtaining information.—W.J.B.

BOOK FIVE

PERSECUTIONS IN ALL CENTURIES

Readings in Baptist History—Graphic Accounts of How Our Baptist People Have Suffered Through the Ages

Introduction—We can only mention a few of the tens of thousands of martyr deaths, occasioned by both Catholics and Protestants on Baptists through the centuries.

Baptists have been known by many different names since the personal ministry of Christ. We do not say that everyone of every group through which our ancestry runs was worthy of the cause with which they were identified.

Take the people called Baptists today, what a varied group they comprise. Yet, amid these we find one true strain of orthodoxy. So it was through the dark ages when a people of common heritage and doctrines were called by such names as Montanists, Albigenses, Waldenses, Paulicians, and many other names. A people called by one name in a given country, or valley retreat, or mountain fastness, were the same people called by another name in another place. Communication was difficult and scarce, contact seldom.

Persecuting groups during the first century were the unbelieving Jews; then the pagan powers. When popes gained ascendency, the Catholics, taking the sword from pagan hands, wielded it without mercy! When the powers of the Catholic hierarchy were shaken and protestantism arose, the Episcopal church followed the steps of her mother. Nor is she, of the protestant clan, the only one that did so. Other protestant sects, both in Europe and in America did likewise. Baptists have been always the persecuted, but never the persecutors.

The so-called reformers themselves killed Baptists freely.

The following are quotes from various historians which give evidence of persecutions in each one of the twenty centuries. Many others could be given.

CENTURY ONE

One has only to read the Gospels and the Acts of the Apostles to learn of persecutions during the first century—John the Baptist, then Stephen. Indeed, all of the Apostles, save John; and he was sent into exile to Patmos.

Saul (Paul) consented to the death of Stephen, but becoming a Christian later, he himself was a martyr in Nero's persecution, Acts 7:54-60. Then, the whole church at Jerusalem was persecuted and were scattered abroad.

"And Saul was consenting unto his death. And at that time there was a great persecution against the church which was at Jerusalem: and they were all scattered abroad throughout the regions of Judaea and Samaria, except the apostles," Acts 1:8.

Since the New Testament is the best evidence, we leave the reader to pursue its pages for more details of Christian sufferings in this century.

When the infant church of Jesus Christ was born it was laid in a cradle of thorns. It was in the world, but not of it. The Gospel traveled far during the first century and much of its spread was due to the persecutions in its native land.

From the following quotation it will be seen that the enemies of the Christians began early to make ridiculously false charges against them in order to cover their own evil persecutions. Such has been Satan's policy from the beginning. So, we start with Nero at Rome. But alas, it does not end there. It is seen to this day.

"Under these circumstances, it is no wonder that Nero should select the Christians as a sacrifice to the Roman people, and endeavor to transfer to this hated sect the guilt of which he was so strongly suspected, that of having caused and enjoyed the fire which had nearly desolated Rome.

"With this in view, he inflicted upon them the most exquisite tortures, attended with every circumstance of the most refined cruelty. Some were crucified; others impaled; some were thrown to wild beasts, and others wrapped in garments dipped in pitch and other combustibles, and burned as torches in the gardens of Nero and other parts of the city by night.

"He was far, however, from obtaining the object of his hopes and expectations; and the virtues of the Christians, their zeal for the truth, and their constancy in suffering, must have considerably contributed to the respectability of their sect, and their tenets more generally known."—M. Reuter, A Concise History of the Christian church, pages 23, 24.

"Domitian, in his temper and disposition, inherited all the savage cruelty of the Monster Nero. Yet he spared the Christians in a considerable degree, until about the year 95, when several were put to death, and others banished, on account of their religion, both in Rome and throughout all the provinces. Among those put to death was his own cousin and colleague in the consulship, Fabius Clemens; and, among the banished, the wife and niece of the latter, both named Flaviae Domitillae. At this time the Apostle John was banished to the island of Patmos, from whence he wrote his epistles to the seven churches in Asia. He is said to have survived the persecution of Domitian, though it is uncertain how long; and to have died at Ephesus in the reign of Nerva or Trajan, at which city he was buried. The crime alleged against the Christians at this period, and which drew down upon them the cruel hand of persecution, was that of **atheism,** by which it is to be understood, that they refused to throw a grain of incense on the altars of the heathen deities."—History of the Christian Church, Jones, page 115.

CENTURY TWO

The chief victim we mention for this century is Polycarp. He was a disciple of the Apostle John. We quote from William Jones.

The churches of Asia appear to have suffered dreadfully at this period. Polycarp was pastor of the church in Smyrna, an office which he had held for more than eighty years, and which he had filled up with honour of himself, to the edification of his Christian brethren, and the glory of his divine Master. It only remained for him now to seal his testimony with his blood. The eminence of his station soon marked him out as the victim of popular fury.

The cry of the multitude against Polycarp was, "This is the doctor of Asia, the father of the Christians, the subverter of our gods, who teaches many that they must not perform the sacred rites, nor worship our deities. **Away with these Atheists."**

The philosophy of the emperor could not teach him, that this pretended Atheism was a real virtue, which deserved to be encouraged and propagated amongst mankind. Here reason and philosophy failed him; and his blind attachment to the gods of his country caused him to shed much blood, and to become the destroyer of the saints of the living God.

The friends of Polycarp, anxious for his safety, prevailed on him to withdraw himself from public view, and to retire to a neighbouring village, which he did, continuing with a few of his brethren, day and night, in prayer to God, for the tranquillity of all the churches. The most diligent search was, in the mean time, made for him without effect. But when his enemies proceeded to put some of his brethren to the torture, with the view of compelling them to betray him, he could no longer be prevailed upon to remain concealed. "The will of the Lord be done," was his pious ejaculation; on uttering which he made a voluntary surrender of himself to his persecutors, saluted them with a cheerful countenance, and invited them to refresh themselves at his table, only soliciting from them on his own behalf one hour for prayer.

They granted his request, and his devotions were prolonged to double the period, with such sweetness and savour, that all who heard him were struck with admiration, several of the soldiers repenting that they were employed against "so venerable an old man." His prayer being ended, they set him on an ass, and conveyed him towards the city, being met on the road by Herod, the Irenarch, (a kind of justice of the peace) and his father Nicetes, who were the chief agents in this persecution. Many efforts were tried to shake his constancy, and induce him to abjure his profession; at one time he was threatened by the proconsul with the fury of wild beasts. "Call for them," said Polycarp, "it does not become us to turn from good to evil." "Seeing you make so light of wild beasts," said the magistrate, "I will tame you with the more terrible punishment of fire." But Polycarp bravely replied, "You threaten me with a fire that is quickly extinguished, but are ignorant of the eternal fire of God's judgment, reserved for the wicked in the other world. But why do you delay? Order what punishment you please." Thus finding him impenetrable both to the arts of seduction and the dread of punishment, the fire was commanded to be lighted, and the body of this venerable father burnt to ashes, in the year 166.—HISTORY OF CHRISTIAN CHURCH, by William Jones, page 128-129.

More Pagan Persecutions

By William Jones

Melito was, at this period, pastor of the neighbouring church of Sardis. As the rage of persecution grew more violent, he drew up an apology for the Christians, which he presented to the emperor (A.D. 170) about the tenth year of his reign, a fragment of which is still preserved in Eusebius. He complains of it as an almost unheard of thing, that pious men were now persecuted, and greatly distressed by new decrees throughout Asia; that most impudent informers, who were greedy of other people's substance, took occasion, from the imperial edicts, to plunder others, who were entirely innocent. He then humbly beseeches the emperor that he would vouchsafe to examine the things charged on the Christians, and stop the persecution, by revoking the edict, published against them; and reminds him, that the Christian religion was so far from being destructive to the Roman empire, as its enemies suggested, that the latter was much enlarged since the propagation thereof.

In the same year that Polycarp was put to death (166), Justin Martyr drew up a second apology, which he addressed to the emperor Antoninus, and to the senate of Rome. He states the case of his Christian brethren, complains of the unrighteousness and cruelty with which they were every where treated, in being punished merely because they were Christians, without being accused of any crimes; answers the usual objections against them, and desires no greater favour than that the world might be really acquainted with their case. His appeal seems to have produced no impression upon those to whom it was addressed. Justin and six of his companions were seized and carried before Rusticus, the praefect of the city of Rome, where many attempts were made to persuade them to obey the gods and comply with the emperor's edicts. Their exhortations had no effect. "No man," says Justin, "who is in his right mind, can desert truth to embrace error and impiety." And when threatened, that unless they complied they should be tortured without mercy, "Dispatch us as soon as you please," said the disciples, "for we are Christians, and cannot sacrifice to idols." On saying which the governor pronounced the following sentence, "that they should be first scourged and then beheaded, according to law," which was immediately carried into effect.

The history of the reign of this philosophic emperor abounds with similar instances of unrelenting cruelty on the part of the magistracy, and of patient suffering for Christ's sake on that of His disciples. Justin Martyr, in the account he gives us of the martyrdom of Ptolemaeus, assures us, that the only question asked him was, "Are you a Christian?" and upon his confessing that he was one, he was immediately put to death. Lucius was also put to death for making the same confession, and for asking Urbicus the praefect why he condemned Ptolemy, who was neither convicted of adultery, rape, murder, theft, robbery, nor of any other crime, but merely for owning himself to be a Christian. Hence it is sufficiently manifest, that it was the mere name of a Christian that was still made a capital offence, and that while these inhuman proceedings were sanctioned by an emperor who made great pretensions to reason and philosophy, they were carried on for the purpose of supporting a system of superstition and idolatory repugnant to every principle of reason and truth. These cruelties were exercised on persons of the most virtuous characters, for their adherence to the worship of the one true God, the first principle of all true religion.

How precious, in those times especially, must have been the consolatory sayings of Jesus Christ; and what but an unshaken confidence in his almighty power and faithfulness could have supported the hearts of his people in such trying circumstances?

Towards the close of the reign of this emperor (A. D. 177,) the flame of persecution reached a country, which had hitherto afforded no materials for ecclesiastical history, viz. the kingdom of France, in those days called Gallia. By whom, or by what means, the light of the glorious gospel was first conveyed into that country, we have no certain information; for the first intelligence that we have of the fact itself, arises from the account of a dreadful persecution which came upon the churches of Vienne and Lyons, two cities lying contiguous to each other in that province. Vienne was an ancient Roman colony: Lyons was more modern; and of this latter church the presbyters or elders were Pothinus and Iraeneus. "Whoever (says Milner) casts his eye on the map of France, and sees the situation of Lyons, at present the largest and most populous city in the kingdom, except Paris, may observe how favourable the confluence of the Rhine and the Soane, on which it stands, is for the purposes of commerce. The navigation of the Mediterranean, in all probability was conducted by the merchants of Lyons and Smyrna, and hence the easy introduction of the gospel from the latter place, and from the other Asiatic churches, is apparent."

That it was in some way as this Christianity was first planted there, seems probable also from this circumstance, that not only the names of Pothinus and Iraeneus, the pastors of the church at Lyons, are Grecians, but that also the names of several other distinguished persons in these churches, prove them to have been Greek extraction. And when we reflect upon the cruel persecutions by which the friends of Jesus had been harassed, both in Greece and Asia Minor, it seems not unreasonable to expect that they should seek an asylum from the storm in those cities. The churches, too, though they appear to have been but recently planted, were evidently very numerous, at the time this terrible persecution overtook them. When the violence of the storm had in some measure subsided, a pretty copious account of it was drawn up, as is supposed, by Iraeneus, in the form of a epistle from the churches of Vienne and Lyons to the brethren in Asia and Phrygia. We are indebted to Eusebius for preserving it from oblivion, in his Ecclesiastical History, and I incline to the judgment of Dr. Lardner, when he pronounces it the finest thing of the kind in all antiquity."

Eusebius gives it as a specimen of what was transacted in other places; and that the reader may have some notion of the savage rage with which this persecution was carried on, not only with the connivance, but with the knowledge and approbation of this philosophic emperor, I shall give a copious abridgement of the account. The epistle opens with the following simple address—

"The servants of Christ, sojourneying in Vienne and Lyons in France, to the brethren in Asia propria and Phrygia, who have the same faith and hope of redemption with us; peace and grace, and glory, from God the Father and Christ Jesus our Lord." They then declare themselves unable to express the greatness of the affliction which the saints in those cities had recently sustained, or the intense animosity of the heathen against them. Christians were absolutely prohibited from appearing in any house, except their own, in baths, in the market, or in any public place whatever. "The first assault came from the people at large—shouts, blows, the dragging of their bodies, the plundering of their goods, casting of stones, with all the indignities that may be expected from a fierce and outrageous multitude—these were magnanimously sustained. Being then led into the forum by the tribune and the magistrates, they were examined before all the people whether they were Christians; and on pleading guilty, were shut up in prison until the arrival of the governor." Before him they were at length brought, and "he treated us," say they, "with great savageness of manners."

Vettius Epigathus, one of their brethren, a young man full of charity both to God and man—of exemplary conduct—a man ever unwearied in acts of beneficence, was rousted at beholding such a manifest perversion of justice, and boldly demanding to be heard in behalf of the brethren, pledging himself to prove that there was nothing atheistic or impious among them. "He was a person of quality"—but however equitable his demand was, it only served to excite the clamour of the mob, and to irritate the governor, who merely asked him if he was a Christian, which he confessed in the most open manner, and for which he was immediately executed. Others imitated his confidence and zeal, and suffered with the same alacrity of mind. In process of time, ten of their number lapsed, "whose case," say they, "filled us with great and immeasurable sorrow." This appears to have much dejected the churches, and to have spread a general alarm, "not that we dreaded the torment," say they, "with which we were threatened, but because we looked forward unto the end, and feared the danger of apostacy." The vilest calumnies were propagated against them at this time—they were accused of eating human flesh, and of various or imagined, and such as ought not to be believed of mankind." The rabble became incensed against them, even unto madness—and the ties of blood, affinity or friendship, seem to have been wholly disregarded. "Now it was," say they, "that our Lord's word was fulfilled—'the time will come when whosoever killeth you will think that he doeth God service.'" The martyrs sustained tortures which exceed the powers of description. "The whole fury of the multitude, the governor, and the soldiers was spent in a particular manner on Sanctus, a deacon of the church of Vienne, and on Maturus, a late convert indeed, but a magnanimous wrestler in spiritual things; and on Attalus of Pergamus, a man who had been the pillar and support of our church; and on Blandina, a female, who was most barbarously tortured from morning to night, with the intent of extorting from her a confession which should criminate her brethren; but it was an evident refreshment, support, and an annihilation of all her pains to say, 'I am a Christian, and no evil is committed among us.'"

The most barbarous indignities were inflicted upon Sanctus the deacon, to extort from him something injurious to the gospel, which he sustained in a manner more than human; and such was the firmness with which he resisted the most intense sufferings, that to every question which was put to him by his tormentors, he had uniformly one reply, "I am a Christian." This provoked the executioners so much, that they applied red hot plates of iron to the tenderest parts of his body, till he was one wound, and scarcely retained the appearance of the human form. Having left him a few days in this ulcerated condition, they hoped to make him more exquisitely sensible to fresh tortures. But the renewal of these while he was dreadfully swelled, was found to have the effect of reducing him to his former shape, and restoring him to the use of his limbs. Biblias, a female, was one of those who had swerved from her profession at the commencement of the persecution. She was now pitched upon as being one who was likely to accuse the Christians; and the more effectually to extort from her that confession which they wished her to make, this weak and timorous creature was put to the torture. The fact which was pressed upon her to acknowledge was, that the Christians ate their children. "In her torture she recovered herself," it is said, "and awoke as out of a sleep, and in answer to their interrogations, 'How can we eat infants—we, to whom it is not lawful to eat the blood of beasts.'" She now recovered her fortitude, avowed her Christianity, and "was added to the army of martyrs." . . . The populace becoming clamorous to have the Christians thrown to the wild beasts in the amphitheatre, that favorite spectacle was at length provided for them, on this occasion, and Maturus, Sanctus, Blandina, and Attalus, were brought out for this purpose. But previous to the wild beasts being produced, Maturus and Sanctus were put to their torture in the amphitheatre, as if it had not been applied to them before; and everything that an enraged multitude called for having been tried upon them, they were at last roasted in an iron chair, till they sent forth the offensive effluvia of burnt flesh. Upon Sanctus, however, the only effect produced was a declaration of his former confession that he was a Christian; and at length death terminated his sufferings.

Blandina was then produced, and on being fastened to a stake, a wild beast was let loose upon her; but this she bore with the greatest composure; and, by her prayers, encouraged others to bear with fortitude whatsoever might befall them: but as the wild beast did not meddle with her, she was remanded back to prison.

At length Attalus was loudly called for; and he was accordingly led round the amphitheatre, with a board held before him, on which was inscribed, **This Is Attalus the Christian.** It appearing, however, that he was a Roman citizen, the president remanded him to prison, until the emperor's pleasure should be known concerning him, and others who were in the same predicament. In this respite they so encouraged many who had hitherto declined this glorious combat, as it was justly called, that great numbers voluntarily declared themselves Christians.

The emperor's answer was, that they who confessed themselves to be Christians should be put to death; but that those who denied it should be set at liberty. Upon this, a public assembly was convened, attended by a vast concourse of people, before whom the confessors were produced, when such of them as were found to be Roman citizens were beheaded, and the rest thrown to the wild beasts. But to the astonishment of all present, many who had previously renounced their Christianity, and were now produced only to be set at liberty, revoked their recantation, and, declaring themselves Christians, suffered with the rest. These had been greatly encouraged so to do, by Alexander, a Phrygian, who had shown himself particularly solicitous for the perseverance of the brethren.

The multitude became greatly enraged at this; and Alexander being called before the tribunal, and confessing himself a Christian, he was sentenced to be thrown to the wild beasts; and on the following day he was produced in the amphitheatre for that purpose, together with Attalus, whom the people had insisted upon being brought out once more. Previous to their exposure to the wild beasts they were subjected to a variety of tortures, and at last run through with a sword. During all this, Alexander said nothing, but evinced the greatest firmness of mind. And, when Attalus was placed in the iron chair, he only said, in allusion to the vulgar charge against the Christians of those days, of murdering and eating infants, "this, which is your own practice, is to devour men; we neither eat men, nor practice any other wickedness."

On the last day of the show, Blandina was again produced, together with a young man of the name of Ponticus, about fifteen years of age, who had been brought out daily to be a spectator of the sufferings of others. This youth, being required to acknowledge the heathen deities, and refusing to do so, the multitude had no compassion for either of them, but subjected them to the whole circle of tortures, till Ponticus expired in them; and Blandina, having been scourged, and placed in the hot iron chair, was put in a net, and exposed to a bull; and after being tossed for a time by the furious animal, she was at length dispatched with a sword. The spectators acknowledged that they had never known any female bear the torture with such fortitude.

When this scene was over, the multitude continued to show their rage by abusing the dead bodies of the Christians. Those who had been suffocated in prison were thrown to the dogs, and watched day and night, lest their friends should bury them. The same was done with the bodies that were unconsumed by the fire; that had been mangled or burned, with the heads only of some, and the trunks of others. Even in this horrid state the heathens insulted them, by asking where was their God, and what their religion had done for them. The mangled carcasses having been exposed in this manner for six days, were then burned; and being reduced to ashes, the latter were cast into the river to disappoint them, as was fondly imagined, of their hopes of a resurrection. From what was done in this place, says Eusebius, we may form an estimate of what was transacted in others.

The prisons were now glutted with the multitude of the Christians—they were thrust into the darkest and most loathsome cells, and numbers were suffocated; even "young men who had been lately seized, and whose bodies had been unercised with sufferings, unequal to the severity of the confinement, expired." Pothinus, one of the elders of the church at Lyons, upwards of ninety years of age, though very infirm and asthmatic, was dragged before the tribunal; "his body," says the narrative, "worn out indeed with age and disease, yet he retained a soul through which Christ might triumph." After being grossly ill-treated by the soldiers and the rabble, who unmercifully dragged him about, insulting him in the vilest manner, without the least respect to his age, pelting with whatever came first to hand, and everyone looking upon himself as deficient in zeal if he did not insult him in some way or other; he was thrown into prison, and after languishing two days, expired.—History of the Christian Church, William Jones, pages 129-135.

Christianity Widespread in Second Century

Tertullian, of Carthage, who flourished about the middle of the second century, and wrote probably not more than twenty years after Irenaeus, gives a larger account, and mentions Britain by name. Quoting the words of David, Psalm 19:4, as applicable to the apostles, "Their line is gone out through all the earth, and their words to the end of the world." "In whom," says he, "have all the nations of the earth believed, but in Christ? Not only Parthians, and Medes, and Elamites, and the dwellers in Mesopotamia, and in Judea, and Cappadocia, in Pontus and Asia, Phrygia and Pamphylia, in Egypt, and in the parts of Lybia and Cyrene, and strangers at Rome, Jews and proselytes, and the other nations; but also the boundaries of the Spaniards, all the different nations of the Gauls, and those parts of Britain which were inaccessible to the Romans, are become subject to Christ."

He goes on to say, after enumerating other nations, "In all which the name of Christ reigns, because he is now come; before whom doors of brass fly open, and bars of iron are snapt asunder; that is, these hearts once possessed by the devil, by faith in Christ are set open." — THE WELSH BAPTISTS by J. Davis, page 176-177.

CENTURY THREE

Jones says—

When the persecution arose under the emperor Decius, or rather, as is expressed by a late writer, "when the gates of hell were once more opened, and merciless executioners were let loose upon the defenceless churches, who deluged the earth with blood" (A.D. 249), Cyprian was presbyter of the church of Carthage, having been ordained the preceding year.

He was soon marked out as a victim to imperial fury, but he prudently fled from Carthage, in consequence of which he was proscribed, and his effects were seized. He has been censured by some persons as a deserter of his flock; but the firmness and Christian piety with which he afterwards (under the reign of Valerian, A. D. 258,) laid down his life, afford a presumption that he had not retired for want of courage.

His works, which consist of a collection of his epistles, eighty-three in number, and several tracts, contain much information respecting the state of Christianity at that period, at the same time that they display a benevolent and pious mind, and evince much of the character of the Christian pastor, in the affectionate solicitude with which he watched over his flock. The letters which he wrote during his retirement, give a distressing picture of the effects which had been produced upon the churches by that state of tranquillity and exemption from suffering, which, with little interruption, they had enjoyed from the death of Severus, in 211, to the reign of Decius, in 249,—a period of about forty years.—HISTORY OF CHRISTIAN CHURCH, by William Jones, page 151.

"Decius began his reign by one of the most sanguinary persecutions that ever opposed the church. The Christians throughout the empire were driven from their habitations, dragged to execution like common malefactors, and subjected to the most exquisite tortures. Great numbers betook themselves to the mountains and deserts, choosing rather to live among wild beasts than wild human beings mad with religious fanaticism."—A Pictorial History of Ancient Rome, By S. G. Goodrich, page 233.

We again quote from Jones, his history I have before me—W.J.B.

"After Perpetua had entered the theater among the wild beasts, singing praises to God, the execution is thus reported: Perpetua and Felicitus were first enclosed in a net and then exposed to a wild cow. But this struck the spectators with horror, as the former was a delicate woman, and the breasts of the latter were streaming with milk after her delivery. They were therefore recalled and exposed in a common loose dress.

Perpetua was first tossed by the beast and being thrown down, she had the presence of mind to compose her dress as she lay on the ground. Then rising and seeing Felicitus much more torn than herself, she gave her hand, and assisted her to rise; and for sometime they both stood together near the gate of the amphiteater. Thither Perpetua sent for her brother, and exhorted him to continue firm in the faith, to love his fellow Christians, and not to be discouraged by her suffering.

Being in a mangled condition, they were now taken to the usual place of execution, to be dispatched with a sword, but the populace requesting that they should be moved to another place, where the execution might be seen to more advantage, they got up of their own accord to go thither; then, having given each other the kiss of charity, they quietly resigned themselves to their fate."— Jones Church History, page 145.

We could quote page after page of persecution by Pagan Rome during this period. When Papal Rome came to power sometime later, it snatched the sword and continued the tortures.

We could multiply cases like the above.

The Donatists were very prominent in North Africa during this time and they were especially the target of the persecutors. The so-called "Christian emperor" Constantine, supposedly converted to Christianity, also put Donatists to death. The Donatists were Baptists under another name.

For persecutions in Wales in this century, see Davis History of the Welsh Baptists, page 18.

The writer had the privilege of exploring the catacombs in North Africa several years ago. They stretch for several miles, some twenty feet under ground, and in all directions.

These catacombs are only a few miles from the Mediterranean Sea where it washes the shore of the city of Sousse, and only a few miles from the ancient city of Carthage, the queen-city of its day. In this old city were many Christians who lived in these underground homes. Dying, they were buried there. They worshipped there. All this was to escape the cruel persecution.

These were our Baptist brothers. Some ten thousands made their homes in the catacombs. There are some chapel rooms where they went to worship. Originally, there are rich mosaics covering the walls and ceilings. For the most part these have been stolen away. Some are in a museum in Sousse, and some in other places. On the walls can still be seen figures of various things such as fishes and sheep. One is that of a man with a lamb on his shoulder. Along the walls, too, are vaults dug into their sides where they buried their dead. Some times a stone marker is in front of the cavity. I noticed one place where a small child had been laid. Though its body had long since decayed, there still remained the imprint in the chalk-like clay of its hands and feet.

North Africa was covered with Christian churches in this early age. Today, there are scarcely any. Mohammedanism has devastated all. Many of the staunchest Christian defenders of early times lived and wrought in this part of the dark continent.—W.J.B.

Suffering Baptists in the Third Century

Eusebius gives the following account—

Why should I now mention the names of others, or number the multitude of men, or picture the various torments of the admirable martyrs of Christ; some of whom were slain with the axe, as in Arabia; some had their limbs fractured, as in Cappadocia; and some were suspended by the feet, and a little raised from the ground, with their heads downward, were suffocated with the ascending smoke of a gentle fire kindled below, as was done to those in Mesopotamia; some were mutilated by having their noses, ears, and hands cut off, and the rest of their limbs, and parts of their body cut to pieces, as was the case at Alexandria?

Why should we revive the recollection of those at Antioch, who were roasted on grates of fire, not to kill immediately, but torture them with a lingering punishment? Others, again, rather resolved to thrust their arm into the fire, than touch the unholy sacrifice; some shrinking from the trial, sooner than be taken and fall into the hands of their enemies, cast themselves headlong from the lofty houses, considering death an advantage compared with the malignity of these impious persecutors.

A certain holy and admirable female, admirable for her virtue, and illustrious above all at Antioch for her wealth, family, and reputation, had educated her two daughters, who were now in the bloom of life, noted for their beauty, in the principles of piety. As they had excited great envy among many, every measure was tried to trace them in their concealment; but when it was discovered called to Antioch. They were now caught in the toils of the soldiery.

The mother, therefore, being at a loss for herself and daughters, knowing what dreadful outrages they would suffer from the men, represented their situation to them, and, above all, the threatened violation of their chastity, an evil more to be dreaded than any other, to which neither she nor they should even listen for a moment. At the same time declaring, that to surrender their souls to the slavery of demons was worse than death and destruction. From all these, she suggested there was only one way to be delivered, to betake themselves to the aid of Christ. After this, all agreeing the same thing, and having requested the guards a little time to retire on the way, they decently adjusted their garments, and cast themselves into the flowing river. These, then, destroyed themselves.

Another pair of virgins at this same Antioch, distinguished for piety, and truly sisters in all respects, illustrious in family, wealth, youth, and beauty, but no less so for their serious minds, their pious deportment, and their admirable zeal, as if the earth could not bear such excellence, were ordered by the worshippers of demons to be thrown into the sea. Such were the facts that occurred at Antioch.

Others at Pontus, endured torments that are too horrible to relate. Some had their fingers pierced with sharp reeds thrust under their nails. Others, having masses of melted lead, bubbling and boiling with heat, poured down their backs, and roasted, especially in the most sensitive parts of the body.

Others, also, endured insufferable torments on their bowels and other parts, such as decency forbids to describe, which those generous and equitable judges, with a view to display their own cruely, devised as some pre-eminence in wisdom, worthy their ambition. Thus constantly inventing new tortures, they vied with one another, as if there were prizes proposed in the contest, who should invent the greatest cruelties.

But as to the last of these calamities, when the judges now had despaired of inventing any thing more effectual, and were weary with slaughter, and had surfeited themselves with shedding of blood, they then applied themselves to what they considered kindness and humanity, so that they seemed disposed to exercise no further cruelty against us.

For said they, the cities should not be polluted with blood any more, and the government of the sovereigns which was so kind and merciful toward all, should not be defamed for excessive cruelty: it was more proper that the benefits afforded by their humane and imperial majesties, should be extended to all, and that we should no longer be punished with death. For we were liberated from this punishment by the great clemency of the emperors.

After this, therefore, they were ordered only to tear out our eyes, to deprive us of one of our legs. Such was their kindness, and such the lightest kind of punishment against us; so that in consequence of this humanity of theirs it was impossible to tell the great and incalculable number of those that had their right eye dug out with the sword first, and after this seared with a red hot iron; those too, whose left foot was maimed with a searing iron; after these, those who in different provinces were condemned to the copper mines, not so much for the service as for the contumely and misery they should endure.

Many, also, endured conflicts of other kinds, which it would be impossible to detail; for their noble fortitude surpasses all power of description. In this the magnanimous confessors of Christ that shone conspicuous throughout the whole world, every where struck the beholders with astonishment, and presented the obvious proofs of our Saviour's divine interposition in their own persons. And hence, to mention each by name, would be at least a long and tedious work, not to say impossible.—Eusebius' Ecclesiastical History.

CENTURY FOUR
Those Who Were in the Palace
Eusebius continues—

But of all those who were celebrated, or admired for their courage, whether among Greeks or barbarians, these times produced noble and illustrious martyrs, in the case of Dorotheus and his associates, domestics, in the imperial palace. These though honoured with the highest dignity by their masters, and treated by them with not less affection than their own children, esteemed the reproaches and trials in the cause of religion, as of much more real value than the glory and luxuries of life; and even the various kinds of death that were invented against them were preferred to these, when they came into competition with religion.

We shall give an account of the end of one, leaving it for our readers to conjecture what must have been the character of the sufferings inflicted on the others. He was led into the middle of the aforesaid city, before those emperors already mentioned. He was then commanded to sacrifice, but as he refused, he was ordered to be stripped and lifted on high, and to be scourged with rods over his whole body, until he should be subdued in his resolution, and forced to do what he was commanded.

But as he was unmoveable amid all these sufferings, his bones already appearing bared of the flesh, they mixed vinegar with salt, and poured it upon the mangled parts of the body. But as he bore these tortures, a gridiron and fire was produced, and the remnants of his body, like pieces of meat for roasting and eating, were placed in the fire, not at once, so that he might not expire soon, but taken by little and little, whilst his torturers were not permitted to let him alone, unless after these sufferings he breathed his last before they had completed their task.

He, however, persevered in his purpose, and gave up his life victorious in the midst of his tortures. Such was the martyrdom of one of the imperial domestics, worthy in reality of his name, for he was called Peter. But we shall perceive in the course of our narration, in which we shall study briefly, that the martyrdoms of the rest were in no respect inferior to this. We shall only state of Doroteus, and Gorgonius, with many others of the imperial freedmen, that after various sufferings, they were destroyed by the halter, and bore away the prize of a heavenly victory. At this time also, Anthimus, then bishop of the church of Nicomedia, was beheaded for his confession of Christ, and to him were added a multitude of believers that thronged around him.

I know not how it happened, but there was a fire that broke out in the imperial palace at Nicomedia, in these days, which, by a false suspicion reported abroad, was attributed to our brethren as the authors; in consequence of which, whole families of the pious here were slain in masses at the imperial command, some with the sword, some also with fire.

Then it is said that men and women, with a certain divine and inexpressible alacrity, rushed into the fire. But the populace binding another number upon planks, threw them into the depths of the sea. But the imperial domestics, also, who after death had been committed to the earth with proper burial, their legal masters thought necessary to have dug up again from their sepulchres, and likewise cast into the sea, lest any, reasoning like themselves, should worship them in their graves, as if they were gods. And such, then, was the complexion of things in the commencement of the persecution at Nicomedia.

But, ere long, as there were some in the region called Melitina, and others, again, in Syria, that attempted to usurp the government, it was commanded, by an imperial edict, that the heads of the churches every where should be thrust into prison and bonds. And the spectacle of affairs after these events exceeds all description. Innumerable multitudes were imprisoned in every place, and the dungeons, formerly destined for murderers and the vilest criminals, were then filled with bishops, and presbyters, and deacons, readers and exorcists, so that there was no room left for those condemned for crime.

But when the former edict was followed by another,

in which it was ordered that the prisoners should be permitted to have their liberty if they sacrificed, but persisting, they should be punished with the most excruciating tortures, who could tell the number of those martyrs in every province, and particularly in Mauritania, Thebais, and Egypt, that suffered death for their religion? From the last place, especially, many went to other cities and provinces, and became illustrious for their martyrdom.—Eusebius' ECCLESIASTICAL HISTORY, pp. 323-325.

"All the Christians were apprehended and imprisoned; and Galerius privately ordered the imperial palace to be set on fire that the Christians might be charged as the incendiaries, and a plausible pretence given for carrying on the persecution with the greatest severities. A general sacrifice was commenced, which occasioned various martyrdoms. No distinction was made of age or sex; the name of Christian was so obnoxious to the pagans that all indiscriminately fell sacrifices to their opinions.

Many houses were set on fire, and whole Christian families perished in the flames; and others had stones fastened about their necks, and being tied together, were driven into the sea. The persecution became general in all the Roman provinces, but more particularly in the East; and as it lasted ten years, it is impossible to ascertain the number martyred, or to enumerate the various modes of martyrdom.

Racks, scourges, swords, daggers, crosses, poison, and famine, were made use of in various parts to dispatch the Christians; and invention was exhausted to devise tortures against such as had no crime, but thinking differently from the votaries of superstition.

A city of Phrygia, consisting entirely of Christians, was burnt, and all the inhabitants perished in the flames. Tired with slaughter, at length, several governors of provinces represented to the imperial court, the impropriety of such conduct. Hence many were respited from execution, but, though they were not put to death, as much as possible was done to render their lives miserable, many of them having their ears cut off, their noses slit, their right eyes put out, their limbs rendered useless by dreadful dislocations, and their flesh seared in conspicuous places with red-hot irons."—Fox's Book of Martyrs, page 25.

Constantine the Great
By S. G. Goodrich

1. Constantine, now master of Rome, removed the great source of the calamities which had befallen that city, by disbanding the Praetorian Guards. He restored the authority of the senate and magistrates, recalled all those who had been banished by Maxentius, and dismissed the whole tribe of spies and informers. He revoked the edicts which had been issued against the Christians, and paid great respect to the bishops and clergy.

2. In the mean time, by the death of Galerius, and the overthrow of Maximian, his associate, the empire of the east had passed into the hands of Licinius, who was a zealous champion of paganism. These rivals were soon engaged in a struggle for the superiority; but at length Licinius, being defeated in two severe battles, was taken prisoner at Nicomedia and put to death, A.D. 324.

3. Constantine became thus sole master of the Roman empire. During his reign the controversies in the church led to the convocations of the celebrated Council of Nice, A.D. 325, in which the doctrine of the trinity was fixed and defined, the heresy of Arius condemned and the spiritual supremacy of the emperor virtually acknowledged. When the labors of this assembly terminated, Constantine returned to the western provinces, and paid a visit to Rome, where he was received in a manner by no means flattering.

4. The populace loaded him with insults and execrations for abandoning the religion of his forefathers. His rage at this insulting treatment is said to have greatly influenced him in removing the seat of government from Rome to Byzantium. At the same time he was harassed by domestic troubles. Instigated by the Empress Fausta, he put his eldest son, the virtuous Crispus, to death, without a trial, and when too late he discovered his error, he caused Fausta and her accomplices to be slain.

5. These horrid deeds aggravated his unpopularity among the Romans; but he no longer regarded their displeasure, having finally resolved to give a new capital to the empire. For this purpose he made choice of Byzantium on the Thracian Bosphorus, a place with a magnificent harbor, open to the commerce of the Black Sea and the Mediterranean.

6. Here Constantine built a new city, A.D. 330, on a plain rising gently from the water, and commanding the strait which serves as the communication between two great seas. Enormous sums were spent in embellishing the new metropolis, which was divided into fourteen regions, and adorned with a capitol, amphitheatre, splendid palaces, churches, and other public buildings.

7. This city received the name of Constantinople; and its long prosperity, and the invincible resistance which it offered to its barbarian aggressors for a thousand years, show how admirably sagacious was the choice of its founder.

8. The removal of the seat of government completed the change in the Roman constitution, which had been commenced in the reign of Dioclesian; it became a simple despotism, with more of a political than of a military character. After he had fixed his residence in the new capital, Constantine adopted oriental manners.

9. He affected the gorgeous attire of the Persian monarchs, decorated his head with false hair of different colors, and with a diadem covered with pearls and gems. He substituted flowing robes of silk, embroidered with flowers, for the austere garb of Rome, or the unadorned purple of the first emperors. He filled his palace with spies and parasites, and lavished the wealth of the empire upon stately architecture.

10. Under Constantine, Christianity became the established religion of the empire; yet the emperor himself was hardly a Christian. Up to the age of forty he had continued to make a public profession of paganism, although he had long favored the Christians. His devotion was divided between Jesus and Apollo, and he adorned the

temples of the pagan gods, and the altars of the new faith, with equal offerings.

11. But as he advanced in age, his confidence in the Christians increased, and he gave up to them the education of his children. When he felt the attacks of the disease which terminated his life, at the age of sixty-three, he was formally received into the church and baptized. He expired at Nicomedia, A.D. 337.—HISTORY OF ANCIENT ROME by S. G. Goodrich, pages 243-244.

Constantine Orders Donatists Killed

Constantine appointed this controversy to be examined by the bishop of Rome, assisted by three others; and the result of their deliberations was favourable to Caecilianus. Felix of Aptungus was not less fortunate; his cause was examined by the proconsul of Africa, and by his decision he was absolved.

But the restoration of the degraded bishop was not calculated to satisfy the minds of his adversaries, who, headed by Donatus, an African bishop, fomented fresh discontents, and occasioned the emperor (Constantine) to convene a council at Arles, where they were again condemned. Their dissatisfaction still continued; and two years afterward, Constantine, to whom the different parties had consented to refer their cause, approved the consecration of Caecilianus. The resentment and contumely with which the Donatists received this decision, added to their former behaviour, so much exasperated the emperor, that he deprived them of their churches, banished the seditious bishops, and even condemned to death some of the party. This violent, and perhaps imprudent resentment, was not calculated to produce peace.—A CONCISE HISTORY OF THE CHURCH by Martin Ruter, D.D., page 80.

Let one read the above and decide for himself if Constantine was a Christian. As for this writer, he does not believe it. When one human being deliberately persecutes another human being (and more often the persecuted is a far better man than the persecutor) it is prima facie evidence that he is not a Christian. There is no excuse for such. W.J.B.

CENTURY FIVE

G. H. Orchard says—

In the fourth Latern council, canons were made to banish them as heretics, and these canons were supported by an edict in 413, issued by emperors Theodosius and Honorius, declaring that all persons rebaptized, and the rebaptizers, should be both punished with death.

Accordingly, Albanus, a zealous minister with others, was punished with death, for rebaptizing. The edict was probably obtained by Augustine, who could endure no rival, nor would he bear with any who questioned the virtue of his rites, or the sanctity of his brethren, or the soundness of the Catholic creed; and these points being disputed by the Novatianists and Donatists, two powerful and extensive bodies of dissidents in Italy and Africa, they were consequently made to feel the weight of his influence. These combined modes of oppression led the faithful to abandon the cities, and seek retreats in the country, which they did, particularly in the valleys of Piedmont, the inhabitants of which began to be called Waldenses.—A Concise History of Foreign Baptists, by Orchard, Thirteenth edition, pages 60-61.

More could be cited for this century if space permitted. Baptists then were as Baptists now, they rebaptized all those who they considered not scripturally baptized. Certainly no "church" that has its roots in Catholicism, even if through the Reformers, has a scriptural baptism. W.J.B.

Catholic Relic Worship in Fifth Century
William Jones

In the beginning of the fifth century, Vigilantius, a learned and eminent presbyter of a Christian church, took up his pen to oppose those growing superstitions. His book, which unfortunately is now lost, was directed against the institution of monks—the celibacy of the clergy,—

praying for the dead and to the martyrs—adoring their relics—celebrating their vigils—and lighting up candles to them after the manner of the Pagans.

Jerome, esteemed luminary of the Catholic church, who was a most zealous advocate for all these superstitious rites, undertook the task of refuting Vigilantius, whom he politely styles 'a most blasphemous heretic,' comparing him to the Hydra, to Cerberus, the Centaurs, Ec., and considers him only as the organ of the daemon. He, however, furnishes us with all the particular articles of his heresy, in the words of Vigilantius himself, which are as follows:

"That the honours paid to the rotten bones and dust of the saints and martyrs, by adoring, kissing, wrapping them up in silk and vessels of gold, lodging them in their churches, and lighting up wax candles before them, after the manner of the heathen, were the ensigns of idolatry. That the celibacy of the clergy was a heresy, and their vows of chastity the seminary of lewdness. That to pray to the dead, or to desire the prayers of the dead, was superstitious; for that the souls of the departed saints and martyrs were at rest in some particular place, whence they could not remove themselves with pleasure, so as to be present every where to the prayers of their votaries; that the sepulchres of the martyrs ought not to be worshipped, nor their fasts and vigils to be observed; and lastly, that the signs and wonders said to be wrought by their relics and at their sepulchres, served to no good end or purpose of religion."
—Jones History of Christian Church, page 203.

Ridiculous Superstition

Towards the close of the sixth century, the Greek Empress made a pressing application to Pope Gregory I. for the body of the apostle Paul, to be placed in the church at Constantinople, which had then recently been erected in honour of that apostle. Gregory wrote to her in reply, that she had solicited what he durst not grant; for, said he, "the bodies of the apostles Paul and Peter are so terrible by their miracles, that there is reason to apprehend danger, even in approaching to pray to them. My predecessor wanted to make some alteration on a silver ornament on the body of St. Peter, at the distance of fifteen feet, when an awful vision appeared to him, which was followed by his death. I myself wished to repair somewhat about the body of St. Paul, and with a view to that had occasion to dig a little near his sepulchre: when in digging, the superior of the place raising some bones apparently unconnected with the sacred tomb, had a dismal vision after it, and suddenly died.

"In like manner, the workmen and the monks, not knowing precisely the grave of St. Lawrence, accidentally opened it; and having seen the body, though they did not touch it, died in ten days. Wherefore, madam, the Romans, in granting relics, do not touch the saints' bodies: they only put a little linen in a box, which they place near them: after some time they withdraw it, and deposite the box and linen solemnly in the church which they mean to dedicate.

This linen performs as many miracles as if they had transported the real body. In the time of Pope Leo, some Greeks, doubting the virtue of such relics, he took a pair of scissors, as we are assured, and cutting the linen, forthwith the blood flowed from it."

He, however, tells the Empress that he would endeavour to send her a few grains of the chain which had been on Paul's neck and hands, and which had been found peculiarly efficacious, provided they succeeded, which was not always the case, in filing them off.

This may suffice for giving the reader some idea of the deplorable state to which the "holy catholic church" was reduced in the fifth centuries of the Christian era— and I therefore quit the subject, to pass on to affairs of a different description.—HISTORY OF THE CHRISTIAN CHURCH by William Jones, page 205.

CENTURY SIX

Orchard's History of Foreign Baptists, page 101 says: "The Donatists still, however, remained a separate body, possessed their churches, and defended themselves against the reproach of their enemies. They industriously tried every means to resuscitate their interests; but the hostility of the rising pope, Gregory, operated considerably on society, to their prejudice. This pope wrote to two African bishops, requiring them to exert themselves in every possible way, to suppress the Donatists.

"Marked out for vengeance, and realizing opposition and persecution in every form, they disappeared. It is presumed these people, "of whom the world was not worthy," emigrated to Spain and Italy, or mingled with the pagans in the interior, and worshipped the Redeemer as opportunity offered. From their conduct in assembling in caves and dens of mountains to worship, they obtained the name of Montenses, that is, mountaineers."

CENTURY SEVEN

The Paterines, Bogomilians, Paulicians, Anabaptists, and others with other names, were essentially Baptists. In this century there were persecutions. Again, we go to Orchard, page 134, History of Foreign Baptists, 13th edition. We quote—

A Greek officer named Simeon, armed with legal and military authority, appeared at Coronia to strike the shepherd, Sylvanus, and to reclaim, if possible, the lost sheep. By a refinement of cruelty, this minister of justice placed the unfortunate Sylvanus before a line of his disciples, who were commanded, as a price of their pardon, and as a proof of their penitence, to stone their spiritual father. The affectionate flock turned aside from this impious office; the stones dropped from their filial hands; and of the whole number, only one executioner could be found.

This apostate, Justus, after putting Sylvanus to death gained by some means admittance into communion, and again deceived and betrayed his unsuspecting brethren; and as many as were treachously ascertained and could be collected, were massed together into an immense pile, and by order of the emperor, consumed to ashes. Simeon, the officer, struck with astonishment at the readiness with which the Paulicians could die for their religion, examined their arguments, and became himself a convert, renounced his honors and fortune, and three years afterwards went to Cobossam and became the successor of Constantine Sylvanus, a zealous preacher among the Paulicians, and at last sealed his testimony with his blood.

CENTURY EIGHT

It would appear that there was some relenting by the persecuting powers during the eighth century. However, it must be remembered that we have but little history passed on to us by our Baptist progenitors. Not only have they been misrepresented and falsely accused but every document favorable has been destroyed that could possibly be confiscated.

But we do have account of suffering in even this century. It is fair to presume that if we had the facts there would be more bloody pages of history. Here again Orchard is quoted—

"From the blood and ashes of the first Paulician victims, a succession of teachers and congregations repeatedly arose. The Greeks, to subdue them, made use of both arguments and arms, with all the terror of penal laws, without effecting their object."—Orchard's History of the Foreign Baptists, Thirteenth Edition, page 135.

CENTURY NINE

The policy of falsely charging true believers with crime continued in this century. This is an old trick of Satan, and is used even today. In spite of this, however, the Paulicians continued, though persecuted, to grow. According to the following account one hundred thousand of them were put to death—

"The power and influence of these dissidents were found to be so great as to suggest the policy of allowing them to return to their own habitations, and dwelling there in tranquility. The severest persecution experienced by them was encouraged by the empress Theodora, A.D. 815.

"Her decrees were severe, but the cruelty with which they were put into execution by her officers was horrible beyond expression. Mountains and hills were covered with inhabitants. Her sanguinary inquisitors explored cities and mountains in lesser Asia. After confiscating the goods and property of **one hundred thousand of these people,** the owners to that number were put to death in the most barbarous manner, and made to expire slowly under a variety of the most exquisite tortures.

The flatterers of the empress boast of having extirpated in nine years that number of Paulicians. Many of them were scattered abroad, particularly in Bulgaria."—Orchard's History of the Foreign Baptists, Thirteenth Edition, page 137.

It will be remembered that these Paulicians were Baptists.—Benedict, page 15.

The Paulicians, though they held some errors, bore witness against the errors of the seventh and eighth centuries . . . But no man so powerfully stemmed the torrent of superstition as Claudius, bishop of Turin. He opposed the supremacy of the pope, the doctrine of merit and transubstantiation, and the worship of images, preached the pure doctrines of the Gospel, and laid the foundations of those churches, which, long after, flourished in the valleys of the Piedmont. He was a bright light, in an age of great darkness.

In Germany, Goteschalcus bore witness to the doctrines of predestination and grace; defended them with great ability; was heard with deep attention, but was publicly condemned, whipped, and confined in a loathsome dungeon until he died, A.D. 869.—Epitome of General Eccl. History, John Marsh, **Page 243.**

CENTURY TEN

During the reign of John Zimicus, they (Paulicians) gained considerable strength, and during the tenth century, they spread themselves abroad throughout different provinces. From Bulgaria they removed into Italy, and spreading themselves from thence through the other provinces of Europe, "they became extremely troublesome to the Roman pontiffs upon many occasions."

Here the history of the interesting people rests, so far as it respects the Levant; but we shall give a slight statement of their migratory movements in order to make our future sections illustrative of these people, though under different names.

From Italy, says Mosheim, "the Paulicians sent colonies into almost all the other provinces of Europe, and formed gradually a considerable number of religious assemblies, who adhered to their doctrine, and who realized every opposition and indignities from the popes."—Orchard's History of Foreign Baptists, Thirteenth Edition, page 138, quoted directly from his works.

Ford quotes from Henry's History of Great Britain, thusly:

A company of about thirty men and women attracted the attention of the Government by the singularity of their religious practices and opinions. They were apprehended and brought before the Council of the clergy at Oxford. Being interrogated about their religion, their teacher, named Gerard, a man of learning, announced in their name, that they were Christians, and believed the doctrines of the apostles. Upon a more particular inquiry, it was found that they denied several of the received doctrines of the church, and, refusing to abandon their damnable heresies, they were condemned as incorrigible heretics, and delivered to the secular arm to be punished.

The King (Henry II) at the instigation of the clergy, commanded them to be branded with a red hot iron on their foreheads, whipped through the streets of Oxford, and having their clothes cut short at their girdles, to be turned into the open fields, all persons being forbidden to afford them any shelter or relief under the severest penalties. This cruel sentence was executed with the utmost rigor, and, it being the depth of winter, all these unhappy persons were pressed with cold and hunger.

CENTURY ELEVEN

We quote again directly from Orchard's History of Foreign Baptists, 13th Edition, page 147. I also have before me as I write the old edition, volume one. Quote—

During the kingdom of the Goths and Lombards, the Antibaptists, as the Catholics called them, had their share of churches and baptisteries, during which time they hold no communion with any hierarchy. After the ruin of these kingdoms, laws were issued by the emperors, to deprive the dissenters of baptismal churches and to secure them to the Catholic clergy. Consequently the brethren worshipped in private houses, under different names. Each of the houses where they met seemed to be occupied by one of the brethren: they were marked so as to be known only among themselves; and though they differed in some things, yet there was perfect agreement in all those points mentioned above.

One of the things mentioned they agreed on was their rejection of infant baptism, just as do Baptists today. W.J.B.

Marsh states—

The eleventh century differed little from the tenth. It was almost equally sunk in wickedness and ignorance. The pope reigned with absolute and awful sway. **But there were some pious people in France,** who ventured to deny the doctrine of transubstantiation, and the propriety of praying to martyrs and confessors. **Thirteen of them were burnt alive, A.D. 1017.**—Epitome of Eccl. History, John Marsh, Page 244.

CENTURY TWELVE

"Arnold maintained his station above ten years, while two popes, either trembled in the Vatican, or wandered as exiles in the adjacent cities" (Roman History, ch. 69—cited by Orchard). The wound appeared "unto death," but the pope having mustered his troops, and placing himself at their head, soon became possessed of his official dignity. Arnold's friends were numerous, but a sword was no weapon in the article of his faith.

In 1155, this noble champion was seized, crucified and burnt. His ashes were strewn into the river. "The clergy triumphed in his death; with his ashes his sect dispersed; his memory still lives in the minds of the Romans."—Orchard's History of Foreign Baptists, 13th Edition, page 151. See also Epitome of Eccl. History, Marsh, page 244.

There are some revolting cases in history of this period which we will not detail here. See Wall's History, Pt. 2, page 379.

Arnold was a Baptist in sentiment. He was called a heretic by the Catholics. See C. A. Jones' History of the Church, pages 35, 45. C. A. Jones is a different Jones from William Jones who wrote History of the Christian Church, which we also quote several times.

"In France alone, above a million were slain for their adherence to the truth. In Germany and Flanders, too, they were persecuted with peculiar severity. The monks were urged by the popes to treat them worse than they treated the Saracens. In the castle of Menerbe on the frontiers of Spain, 140 persons of both sexes were burned alive. Persecutions often drove the Waldenses to the top of the Alps in the dead of Winter, where they perished. One hundred and eighty infants were one time found dead there in their cradles. Four hundred little children were suffocated in a cave in the valley of Loyse, where they had been placed for safety. Often did this unhappy people change masters, and every new sovereign seemed anxious to commend himself to the pope, by exterminating them with fire and sword."—Epitome of Eccl. History, John Marsh, page 246.

The Decree of Pope Lucius II. Against Heretics, A.D. 1181

The Decree of Idlefonsus, A.D. 1194
From Jones' History

To abolish the malignity of divers heresies which are lately sprung up in most parts of the world, it is but fitting that the power committed to the church should be awakened, that by the concurring assistance of the Imperial strength, both the insolence and mal-pertness of the heretics in their false designs may be crushed, and the truth of Catholic simplicity, shining forth in the holy church, may demonstrate her pure and free from the execrableness of their false doctrines.

Wherefore we, being supported by the presence and power of our most dear son, Frederic, the most illustrious emperor of the Romans, always increaser of the empire, with the common advice and counsel of our brethren, and other partriarchs, archbishops, and many princes, who from several parts of the world are met together, do set themselves against these heretics, who have not different names from the several false doctrines they profess, by the sanction of this present general decree, and by our apostolical authority, according to the tenor of these presents, we condemn all manner of heresy, by what name soever it may be denominated.

More particularly, we declare all Catharists, Paterines, and those who call themselves "the poor of Lyons," the Passigines, Josephists, Arnoldists, to lie under a perpetual anathema. And because some, under a form of godliness, but denying the power thereof, as the apostle saith, assume to themselves the authority of preaching; whereas the same apostle saith, "How shall they preach except they be sent?"—we therefore conclude under the same sentence of a perpetual anathema, all those who, either being forbid or not sent, do, notwithstanding, presume to preach publicly or privately, without any authority received either from the Apostolic See, or from the bishops of their respective dioceses: As also all those who are not afraid to hold or teach any opinions concerning the sacrament of the body and blood of our Lord Jesus Christ, baptism, the remission of sins, matrimony, or any other sacraments of the church, differing from what the holy church of Rome doth preach and observe: And generally all those whom the same church of Rome, or the several bishops in their diocesses, with the advice of their clergy, or the clergy themselves, in case of a vacancy of the See, with the advice, if need be, of neighbouring bishops, shall judge to be heretics.

And we likewise declare all entertainers and defenders of the said heretics, and those that have shewed any favour or given countenance to them, thereby strengthening them in their heresy, whether they be called comforted, believers, or perfect, or with whatsoever superstitious name they disguise themselves, to be liable to the same sentence.

And though it sometimes happens that the severity of ecclesiastical discipline, necessary to the coercion of sin, is condemned by those who do not understand the virtue of it, we notwithstanding by these presents decree, That whosoever shall be notoriously convicted of these errors, if a clergyman, or one that endeavours to conceal himself under any religious order, he shall be immediately deprived of all prerogative of the church orders, and so being divested of all office and benefice, be delivered to the secular power to be punished according to demerit, unless immediately upon his being detected he voluntarily returns to the truth of the Catholic faith, and publicly abjures his errors, at the discretion of the bishop of the diocess, and makes suitable satisfaction.

And as for a layman who shall be found guilty either publicly or privately of any of the aforesaid crimes, unless by abjuring his heresy and making satisfaction he immediately return to the orthodox faith, we decree him to be left to the sentence of the secular judge to receive condign punishment according to the quality of the offence.

And as to those who are taken notice of by the church as **suspected** of heresy, unless at the command of the bishop they give full evidence of their innocence, according to the degree of suspicion against them and the quality of their persons, they shall be liable to the same sentence.

But those who after having abjured their errors, or cleared themselves upon examination to their bishop, if they be found to have relapsed into their adjured heresy—We decree that without any further hearing they be forthwith delivered up to the secular power and their goods confiscated to the use of the church.

And we further decree, That this excommunication, in which our will is that all heretics be included, shall be repeated and renewed by all patriarchs, archbishops, and bishops, in all the chief festivals and on any public solemnity, or upon any other occasion to the glory of God and the putting a stop to all heretical pravity: ordering by our apostolic authority, that if any bishop be found wanting or slow herein, he be suspended for three years from his episcopal dignity and administration.

Furthermore, with the counsel and advice of bishops, and intimation of the emperor and princes of the empire, we do add, That every archbishop or bishop, either in his own person or by his archdeacon, or by other honest and fit persons, shall once or twice in the year visit the parish in which it is reported that heretics dwell, and there cause two or three men of good credit, or, if need be, the whole neighbourhood, to swear that if they know of any heretics there, or any that frequent private meetings, or that differ from the common conversation of mankind, either in life or manners, they will signify the same to the bishop or archdeacon: the bishop also or archdeacon shall summon before them the parties accused, who, unless they at their discretion, according to the custom of the country, do clear themselves of the guilt laid to their charge; or if, after having so cleared themselves, they relapse again to their former unbelief, they shall be punished at the bishop's discretion. And if any of them, by a damnable superstition, shall refuse to swear, that alone shall suffice to convict them of being heretics and liable to the punishments before mentioned.

We ordain further, That all earls, barons, governors, and consuls of cities and other places, in pursuance of the commonition of the respective archbishops and bishops, shall promise upon oath, that in all these particlars, whenever they are required so to do, they will powerfully and effectually assist the church against heretics and their accomplices; and endeavour faithfully, according to their office and power, to execute the ecclesiastical and imperial statutes concerning the matters herein mentioned.

But if any of them shall refuse to observe this, they shall be deprived of their honours and charges, and be rendered incapable of receiving others; and, moreover, be involved in the sentence of excommunication, and their goods be confiscated to the use of the church. And if any city shall refuse to yield obedience to these Decretal Constitutions, or that, contrary to the episcopal commonition, they shall neglect to punish opposers, we ordain the same to be deprived of the episcopal dignity.

We likewise decree, That all favourers of heretics, as men stigmatized with perpetual infamy, shall be incapable of being attorneys, or witnesses, or of bearing any public office whatsoever. And as for those who are exempt from the law of diocesan jurisdiction, as being immediately under the jurisdiction of the Apostolic See; nevertheless, as to these constitutions against heretics, we will, That they be subject to the judgment of the archbishop and bishops, and that in this case they yield obedience to them, as to the delegates of the Apostolic See, the immunity of their privileges notwithstanding."

Ildefonsus, king of Arragon, also testified his zeal against the Waldenses, by an edict published in the year 1194, from the tenour of which we are authorized to infer, that the doctrine of Waldo had not only found its way into Spain, but that it had got such footing there as to create no little alarm, and call forth the determined interference of the government. The following is a copy of this severe edict, as given by Pegna, in his notes on the "Directory of the Inquisitors."

Ildefonsus, by the grace of God, King of Arragon, Earl of Barcelona, Marquis of Provence, to all archbishops, **bishops, and other prelates of the church of God,** earls, viscounts, knights, and all people of his kingdom, or belonging to his dominions, wideth health, and the sound observance of the Christian Religion.

Forasmuch as it hath pleased God to set us over His people, it is but fit and just, that according to our might we should be continually solicitous for the welfare and defence of the same; wherefore we, in imitation of our ancestors, and in obedience to the canons which determine and ordain heretics, as persons cast out from the sight of God and all Catholics, to be condemned and persecuted every where, do command and charge, that the Waldenses, Inzabbati, who otherwise are called the "poor of Lyons," and all other heretics who cannot be numbered, being excommunicated from the holy church, adversaries to the cross of Christ, violaters and corrupters of the Christian religion, and the avowed enemies of us and our kingdom, to depart out of our kingdom and all our dominions.

Whosoever, therefore, from this day forward shall presume to receive the said Waldenses, and the Inzabbati, or any other heretics of whatsoever profession, into their houses, or to be present at their pernicious sermons, or to afford them meat, or any other favour, shall thereby incur the indignation of Almighty God, as well as ours, and have his goods confiscated, without the remedy of an appeal, and be punished as if he were actually guilty of high treason.

And we strictly charge and command, that this our edict and perpetual constitution, be publicly read on the Lord's days by the bishops and other rectors of churches, in all the cities, castles, and towns of our kingdom and throughout all our dominions: and that the same be observed by vicars, bailiffs, justices, Ec. and all the people in general; and that the aforesaid punishment be inflicted on all transgressors.

We further will, That if any person, noble or ignoble, shall in any part of our dominions find any of these wicked wretches, who shall be known to have had three days' notice of this our edict, and that do not forthwith depart, but rather are obstinately found staying or lingering; let such know that if they shall any way plaque, despitefully use or distress them, wounding unto death and maiming them only excepted, he will in so doing perform nothing but what will be very grateful and pleasing to us, and shall be so far from fearing to incur any penalty thereby, that he may be sure rather to deserve our favour.

Furthermore, we give these wicked miscreants respite, though that may seem somewhat contrary to reason and our duty, till the day after All Saints' day: but that all those who either shall not be gone by that time, or at least preparing for their departure, shall be spoiled, beaten, cudgelled, and shamefully ill-treated.—THE HISTORY OF THE CHRISTIAN CHURCH by William Jones, pp. 306-309.

CENTURY THIRTEEN

Slaughter of the Albigenses

The crusade against the Albigenses had hitherto been conducted by an ecclesiastic, the Abbe de Cisteaux; but having been prolonged beyond the period at first calculated upon, and the entire reduction of the heretics being found not quite so easy a task as was first expected, the supreme command was now vested in the hands of Simon, Earl of Montfort, a person of some military talents, but of a fierce and ungovernable temper. He was appointed governor of the whole country, both of what had been already conquered, and what should be conquered in future. This nobleman, under the mask of piety and zeal for religion, gratified a relentless and covetous disposition. He plundered, assassinated, and committed to the flames, the poor Albigenses, without regard to character, sex or age. Dazzled by his success, he set no bounds to his rapacious cruelty; and encouraged by the papal legate, he insolently proposed that the Earl of Toulouse should absolutely surrender to him all the castles and territories as conquered by the catholic army. Raymond refused, and appealed to Philip, king of France, his lord paramount. The haughty count, however, began to execute his threats, and laid siege to the castle of Minerba, (or Minerva,) a place strongly fortified by nature, in the territory of Narbonne, on the confines of Spain. "This place," says he, "is of all others the most exercrable, because no mass has been sung in it for thirty years"—a remark which gives us a striking idea of the number of the Waldenses; the very worship of popery, it seems, was expelled from the place. On the surrender of the castle, which was defended by Raymond, Earl of Termes, and compelled to capitulate for want of water, they exerted all their influence to induce him to recant his religion and turn Catholic; but finding him inflexible, they shut him up in a close prison, where he soon after died. They then seized his wife, sister, and virgin daughter, with other females of distinguished rank, all of whom they laboured to convert, both by flattery and frowns, by fair speeches and cruel threats; but finding that nothing could prevail upon them to recant, they made a large fire, into which they were all thrown and consumed to ashes.

After the castle had been taken, the Earl of Montfort caused the Abbe de Vaux, a friar, to preach to the inhabitants, exhorting them to acknowledge the pope and church of Rome; but they interrupted him, exclaiming, "We will not renounce our religion; you labour to no purpose, for neither life nor death shall induce us to abandon our profession." On this the Earl and the legate commanded a hundred and eighty men and women to be committed to the flames! These went, it is said, with cheerfulness, blessing God that he was pleased to confer on them the honour of dying for his sake; at the same time warning the Earl of Montfort that he would one day pay dear for his cruelties towards them. All who witnessed their constancy and courage were astonished.—History of the Christian Church, by William Jones, page 370.

We quote from two more noted historians.

"In 1210, the Paterines had become so numerous and so odious to the state clergy, that the old bishop of Ferrara obtained an edict of the emperor Otho IV for the suppression of them; but this measure extended only to that city. In five years after, Pope Innocent III of bloody celebrity, held a council at the Lateran, and denounced anathemas against heretics of every description. Dr. Wall declares that the council did enforce infant baptism on the dissenters, as heretics taught it was of no purpose to baptize children. (Wall was a defender of infant baptism and he here admits that baby baptism was **enforced.** W.J.B.)

In this council, the Milanese were censured for sheltering the Paterines. After a variety of efforts to suppress them, the cruel policy of the court of Rome extended its sanguinary measures over Italy. In 1220, Honorius III procured an edict of Frederick II which extended over all the imperial cities, as had been the case some years over the south of France, and the effects of the pontiff's anger was soon felt by the deniers of the infant rite. The edicts were every way proper to excite horror, and which rendered the most illustrious piety and virtue incapable of saving from the most cruel death such as had the misfortune, says Mosheim, to be agreeable to the inquisitors. No alternative of escaping those human monsters presented itself but that of flight.—Orchard's History of Foreign Baptists, Thirteenth Edition, page 155.

For further information about the cruelties of this age let the reader refer to Jones' History of the Christian Church, pages 306-309—

"During the whole course of this century," (the thirteenth,) says Mosheim, "the Roman pontiffs carried on the most barbarous and inhuman persecutions against those whom they branded with the denomination of heretics, i.e. against all those who called their pretended authority and jurisdiction in question, or taught doctrines different from those which were adopted and propagated by the church of Rome.

"For the sects of the Catharists, Waldenses, Petrobrussians, Ec., gathered strength from day to day, spread imperceptibly throughout all Europe, assembled numerous congregations in Italy, France, Spain and Germany, and formed, by degrees, such a powerful party as rendered them formidable to the Roman pontiffs, and menaced the papal jurisdiction with a fatal revolution.

"To the ancient sects new factions were added, which, though they differed from each other in various respects, yet were all unanimously agreed in this one point, viz. 'That the public and established religion was a motley system of errors and superstition; and that the dominion which the popes had usurped over Christians, as also the authority they exercised in religious matters, were unlawful and tyrannical.'

"Such were the notions propagated by the sectaries, who refuted the superstitions and impostures of the times by argument drawn from the Holy Scriptures, and whose declamations against the power, the opulence, and the vices of the pontiffs and clergy were extremely agreeable to many princes and civil magistrates, who groaned under the usurpations of the sacred order. The pontiffs, therefore, considered themselves as obliged to have recourse to new and extraordinary methods of defeating and subduing enemies, who, both by their number and their rank, were every way proper to fill them with terror."

Ford quotes from—A General History of the Baptist Denomination in America by David Benedict.

CENTURY FOURTEEN

All Bohemian writers state that the Picards or Waldenses settled early in this kingdom, and that these people baptized and rebaptized such persons as joined their churches, and that they had always done so. They are said in the 14th century to have numbered 80,000 in the kingdom . . . by the banishment of these two noblemen, the voice of reform at court was silenced; ignorance, profligacy, and vice prevailed among all orders of men in the national church; the inquisition was introduced to enforce uniformity in matters of religion. (What is the goal of the Ecumenicalists?—W.J.B.)

The consequence was, that multitudes withdrew themselves from the public places of worship, and followed the dictates of their own conscience, by worshipping God in private homes, woods, and caves. Here they were persecuted, dragooned, drowned, and killed; and thus matters went on, until Huss and Perome of Prague appeared.—Orchard, page 236.

Jones says—They fled to one of the highest mountains of the Alps with their wives and children . . . Their inhuman invaders, whose feet were swift to shed blood, pursued them in their flight until night came on, and slew great numbers of them before they could reach the mountain . . . Fourscore of their infants deprived of life, many of their mothers also lying dead by their sides.

CENTURY FIFTEEN

Two of the more noted martyrs, John Huss and Jerome, were put to death during this century. Baptists in that day were often called Hussites after Huss.

Orchard says, page 238: "Huss was excommunicated by the pope for contumacy, and all his followers were involved in the same censure. He, however, realized protection for some time from the king, queen, and nobility of Bohemia; but in 1415, he was shamefully betrayed, and afterwards tried for heresy, convicted, and burnt."

Orchard goes on to say: "It is difficult to say what his religious views were. His sermons were full of anabaptist (not ANTIbaptist) errors, as they were called, and many of his followers became Baptists. His views found a prepared people in Bohemia, in the persons of the Waldenses, Picards, or Beghards, of which party he has often been considered the head.

"Huss and Jerome were tried by the same council, and afterwards burnt by their order. Huss suffered, July, 1415. He sustained his sentence with the most heroic fortitude, praying for his persecutors. The dread of suffering at first intimidated Jerome, which caused the sentence to be delayed. His enemies took advantage of those symptoms, in hopes of gaining him over; but he recovered his wonted vigor, and avowed his sentiments in the most open manner, and supported them with increasing confidence to the last. He expired in the flames, singing, "This soul of mine, in flames of fire, O Christ, I offer Thee."

William Jones states—

Through this whole oration he shewed a most amazing strength of memory. (Jerome) had been confined almost a year in a dungeon: the severity of which usage he complained of, but in the language of a great and good man. In this horrid place he was deprived of books and paper. Yet, notwithstanding this, and the constant anxiety which must have hung over him, he was at no more loss for proper authorities and quotations, than if he had spent the intermediate time at leisure in his study.

His voice was sweet, distinct, and full: his action every way the most proper, either to express indignation, or to raise pity; though he made no affected application to the passions of his audience. Firm and intrepid, he stood before the council, collected in himself; and not only contemning, but seeming even desirous of death. The greatest character in ancient story could not possibly go beyond him. If there is any justice in history, this man will be admired by all posterity. I speak not of his errors: let these rest with him. What I admired was his learning, his eloquence, and amazing acuteness. God knows whether these things were not the ground-work of his ruin.

Two days were allowed him for reflection; during which time many persons of consequence, and particularly my lord cardinal of Florence, endeavored to bring to a better mind. But persisting obstinately in his errors, he was condemned as a heretic.

With a cheerful countenance, and more than stoical constancy, he met his fate; fearing neither death itself, nor the horrible form in which it appeared. When he came to the place, he pulled off his upper garment, and made a short prayer at the stake; to which he was soon bound with wet cords and an iron chain, and inclosed as high as the breast in faggots.

Observing the executioner about to set fire to the wood behind his back, he cried out, "Bring the torch hither. Perform thy office before my face. Had I feared death, I might have avoided it."

As the wood began to blaze, he sang a hymn, which the violence of the flame scarce interrupted.

Thus died this prodigious man. The epithet is not extravagant. Whatever his life may have been, his death, without doubt, is a noble lesson of philosophy. — THE HISTORY OF THE CHRISTIAN CHURCH By William Jones, page 408.

Driven From Bohemia

We quote from Ford's History, page 34, of the cruel edict of the emperor in driving the Anabaptists out of Bohemia, the very region where both Paul and Titus had preached—

Their destruction was planned and brutally executed. An edict for their banishment was obtained for the Emperor, and Protestant and Catholic rejoiced in its enforcement. About forty thousand Baptists were proscribed. His majesty in the edict, expresses his astonishment at the number of Anabaptists, and his horror at their principal error, which was, that they would submit to no human authority on matters of religion. The edict was published just three weeks before the harvest and vintage came on, that these poor people might not be able to carry away the produce of their toil. Their lands were to be forfeited to the emperor, and they banished to beggary. And three weeks after the proclamation of the edict, death would be inflicted on any of them found in the borders of the country. And thus is the scene described:

It was autumn, the prospect and the pride of husbandmen. Heaven had smiled on their honest labors. Their fields stood thick with corn; and the sun and the dew were improving every moment to give them their last polish. The yellow ears waved an homage to their owners; and the wind, whistling through the stems and the russet herbage, softly said, **Put in the sickle, the harvest is come.** Their luxuriant vine leaves, too, hung aloft by the tendrils, mantling over the clustering grapes, like watchful parents over their tender offspring; but all were fenced by an imperial edict, and it was instant death to approach. Without leaving one murmur upon record, in solemn, silent submission to the power that governs the universe and causes all things to work together for good to His creatures they packed up and departed. In several hundred carriages they conveyed their sick, the innocent infants sucking at the breasts of their mothers who had newly lain-in, and their decrepit parents, whose work was done, and whose silvery locks told every beholder that they wanted only the favour of a grave. At the borders they filed off, some to Hungary, others to Transylvania, some to Wallachia, others to Poland and Sach-hel—greater, far greater for their virtue, than Ferdinand for all his titles and for all his glory.—Carafa, page 133, quoted by Robinson in Researches, as quoted by Ford.

The Inquisition—Spain

From Duruy's General History of the World, Volume 2, page 300, we read—

The Inquisition. The Power of Royalty. The population of the Peninsula (Spain, Granada) then presented a singular mixture of Mussulmans, Jews, and Christians. Isabella (the queen) and Ferdinand (king) decided to bring dissenters to a common religious faith by persuasion, and above all by terror.

With this intent they had already instituted that tribunal of melancholy fame, the Holy Office or Inquisition, intended to enforce obedience to "the properly constituted authorities, divine and secular." It was established in Castile about 1480, and in Aragon four years later. Between January and November, 1481, in Seville alone the inquisitors sent to torture 298 Christian proselytes, accused of judaizing in secret, and 2000 in the provinces of Cadiz and Seville. In 1492 (the year of Columbus's voyage) they expelled the Jews, of whom 800,000 departed from Spain. In 1499 they deprived the Moors of the religious liberty which the treaty of Granada had guaranteed. Torquemada, the first grand inquisitor, alone condemned 8800 persons to the flames.

Thus, we get another picture of Ferdinand and Isabella, the benefactors of Columbus. W.J.B.

CENTURY SIXTEEN

This was the century of the great reformation. For more than a thousand years the world, black with popish rule had enshrouded the nations. Only the little candles of truth in the hands of the Baptists, known by various names as elsewhere mentioned, shined to fulfill the Lord's promise, **"And I say also unto thee, That thou art Peter, and upon this rock I will build my church; and the gates of hell shall not prevail against it,"** Matthew 16:18.

As Satan, for his cause, overstepped his effort in crucifying Christ; Rome, with its moral and political corruptions and its cruel persecutions of the innocent, lost—by the Providence of God—its hold on governments.

The sun of soul freedom began to rise on the earth. The human instruments used by the Lord are well known to readers of history. Luther, Huss, Jerome, Wickliff, Zwingle, Melancthon and many others. We must remember, however, that these men, for the most part, were yet not free from all Catholicism; indeed, some of them despised the Baptists of that day much as did those who remained in the "church." But they were used by the Lord to break the chains that had held captive the souls of millions for centuries.

Despite the break of light this century also had its persecutions. Ray's Baptist Succession, page 376, says:

"In the early part of the Sixteenth century the most cruel persecution continued to be urged against the Waldenses in the South of France; and in 1585 John Weiner led the Catholic forces against the Waldenses in Province, France, and among other horrible cruelties, this inhuman wretch shut up about forty women in a barn full of hay and straw, and then set it on fire; and after that, the poor creatures, having attempted in vain to smother the fire with their clothes, which for that end they had pulled off, betook themselves to the great window, at which hay is commonly pitched into the barn, with an intention to leap out from thence, but were keep in with pikes and spears, so that all of them perished in the flames."—Baptist Succession, page 376.

Wife and Children See Husband and Father Burn

"The first martyr was John Rogers. He had been a fellow laborer of Tyndall and Coverdale, in translating the Bible, and was now prebendary of St. Paul. He had a wife and ten children with whom he wished to speak, but was not permitted. He was burned at Smithfield, February 4, 1555. His wife, with her ten children, one hanging at the breast, was a spectator of the scene."—EPITOME OF GENERAL ECCL. HISTORY By Rev. John Marsh, page 335.

Sentence Against Quirius Pieters, in 1545

"Whereas, Quirius Pieters, a native of Groeningen, has joined the unbelief and heresy of the anabaptists; having been re-baptized nearly six years ago, by Menno Simon, a teacher of said sect, and whereas, he maintains pernicious views in regard to the sacraments of the holy church, and besides has led others into the same belief and error, persuading them thereto, which is contrary to edica of their imperial majesties, our gracious lords, and furthermore, remains obstinate in said unbelief; therefore, my lords, the council, having heard the charges preferred by the bailiff against the said Quirius Pieters, and fully considered the defendant's answer and confession, and all the circumstances of the case, have sentenced said Quirius to be burnt by the executioner, and further, declare his property to be confiscated to the imperial treasury. Pronounced the 16th of April, in the presence of the whole court, by Sir Henry Dirks, burgomaster. Quirius Pieters was in consequence of this executed the same day." (N. N. Martyrs' Mirror, pages 402-3.)—Footnote, BENEDICT'S HISTORY, page 129.

Sentence of Anna Heyndriks, Surnamed Vlaster

"Whereas, Anna, daughter of Heyndriks, or Anna de Vlaster, formerly a citizen of this place, prisoner for the time being, has been unmindful of her soul's salvation, and of the obedience which she owed to our mother, the holy church, and your royal majesty, as her natural lord and prince, and has, moreover, despised the ordinances of the holy church, so much so, that she has not been for six or seven years at confession, or at the holy, reverend sacrament, but went to the meetings of the cursed sect of Mennonites or anabaptists, so that they have even held secret meetings, or assemblies at her house; and, moreover, three years ago she denied the baptism she received in her infancy from the holy church; departed from it and became re-baptized; and also received the breaking of bread after the manner of the sect of Mennonites, and married her present husband by night, at a county seat, after the manner of the Mennonites.

"And further still, as during her imprisonment, she was persuaded, and at different times exhorted by the alderman, and by several ecclesiasticals to abandon said cursed sect; yet she refused to comply, and still persists in her obstinacy, so she (the prisoner) by virtue of the foregoing, has committed human and divine treason, inasmuch as the peace and prosperity of the country is disturbed by said sect, as shown by the decrees of your majesty thereof treating, which crime, as an example to others, ought not to go unpunished;

"Therefore the lords of the court, after hearing the accusation of my Lord, the bailiff, and seeing her confession, and considering her stubbornness and obstinacy, have sentenced her, and by virtue of these presents, do sentence her to be burnt according to the decrees of your majesty; they further declare all her estate confiscated for the benefit of his royal majesty. Done before the court, the 10th November, A.D. 1571, in the presence of the alderman, and with the advice of all the burgomasters. Witness, W. Pieters, Town Clerk.

"She was racked the 27th of Oct., A.D. 1571, by virtue of the sentence of the alderman, as appears from the protocol of her confession."

"Copied from the records at Amsterdam." "Martyr's Mirror, p. 790."—Footnote, BENEDICT'S HISTORY, page 129.

Denied a Few Moments to Pray

Benedict gives the following as a footnote—

"Maeyken Wauters, an amiable young lady, begged the executioner to allow her a few moments to pray to God for assistance in her greatest need. But the unfeeling wretch, with insulting blasphemy, replied, 'Pray to our lords the magistrates, and believe with us in the Roman church,' Ec. and soon she was plunged from the bridge into the fatal stream below."—Martyrs' Mirror, p. 993.

In many cases the heretic hunters would rush into the houses of lonely and unprotected women, and drag them away to prison from their crying children, without giving them any time to adjust their household affairs. In but rare cases did they see their families again, unless among the spectators at the place of their execution.

A very affecting incident of this kind of muffling is given in the case of Mary Ken Wens, who was burnt Oct. 6, 1573. Her oldest son, Adrian, took with him a younger brother of three years old, to the place of execution. This heroic lad of but 15, after the people had dispersed, hunted among the ashes till he found the screw with which his mother's tongue was made fast, which was preserved in the family. "In 1659," says our author, "several of the relatives of this martyress resided among them," —Martyrs' Mirror, p. 892.

This class of men, in those times, was a kind of privileged order, and managed things much in their own way. The business of legalized murder was a very popular and lucrative vocation. They killed the heretics by the head the same as butchers do their cattle, and with rare exceptions they were as unfeeling and unceremonious. Those to be burnt were generally strangled first. The work of beheading was done sword in hand, and often with revolting cruelty.

Two men who were employed as Trappers of two different classes of offenders, had the following singular conversation with each other. The one whose business it was to hunt real rogues told what a strong force he was obliged to take with him for fear of being killed; the heretic hunter replied, that he had no fear of going alone, for his business was altogether with good men.—Footnote, BENEDICT'S HISTORY, pages 122-123.

Another Burned at Stake

Again from Benedict's footnotes, quoting from Martyr's Mirror—

"Joss Kind, who was burnt at the stake in 1553, at Kortryk, in Flanders, was a notable example of this kind. He and his opponents spoke to each other with as much freedom as if they had been engaged in a public debate under the license of the government, which cases were by no means uncommon.

They accused him of being led astray by Menno Simon, David Joris, Adam Pastor and other famous teachers among the anabaptists at that time. But he retorted upon them that their church was the false one, and his the true. They pressed him hard to inform them who baptized him, but this he would not do. Infant baptism, the sacrament of the altar, and the whole round of catholic doctrines came under discussion. As to who baptized him, and who were witnesses or sponsors, as they called them, his answer was, 'I will not tell you, though you tear me into pieces. You may put me into a bag and drown me by night, so that no one will see it, or throw me into the fire.' He told them plainly that they did not understand the Scriptures, which was very plain from their false quotations. Again and again he exclaimed, 'Go away from me, for you are not sent from God. Away, away from me, and do not come to me again. Depart from me you devils.'

"He accused them of falsehood and simony, of being enemies of the cross of Christ, of fighting against God, etc. After two or three hours of this kind of running fight, the inquisitors went to their homes, and the condemned anabaptist was delivered into the hands of the executioner." (Article appeared in Martyr's Mirror, pp. 465-470.)—Footnote, BENEDICT'S HISTORY, page 127.

Robert Smith, The Martyr

The following is one account, of many millions, had we the records, of how Baptists suffered the martyr's fire—

Smith, Robert, the Martyr, was in the employment of Sir Thomas, provost of Eton College in 1555. Then he came to the Windsor College, where he had a clerkship of ten pounds a year. He was tall and slender in stature, very active in his labors, and invested with great powers of mind.

The ferocious Bonner, bloody Mary's principal inquisitor in murdering the saints of Jesus, met in him an intellectual giant, who could expose his sophistries in a moment and defy his rage. When he found Christ precious to his soul he was filled with a flowing enthusiasm and a fearless courage which made him despise danger and death. He was deprived of his clerkship by Mary's visitors and brought to Newgate by command of the Council.

He was led in due time before Bonner, and we give a few of the questions and answers of his examination:

BONNER. "How long is it since you confessed to any priest?"

SMITH. "Never since I had years of discretion. For I never saw it needful, neither was I commanded of God to show my faults to any of that sinful number whom you call priests."

BONNER. "How long is it since you received the sacrament of the altar?"

SMITH. "I never received the same since I had years of discretion, nor ever will by God's grace; neither do I esteem the same in any point, because it hath not God's ordinance, neither in name, nor in other usage, but rather is set up to mock God."

BONNER. "You must be burned."

SMITH. "You shall do no more to me than you have done to better men than either of us. But think not thereby to quench the Spirit of God, or make your case good; for your sore is too well seen to be healed so privily with blood. For even the very children have all your deeds in derision; so that although you patch up one place with authority, yet shall it break out in forty to your shame."

BONNER. "I believe, I tell thee, that if they (infants) die before they be baptized, they be damned."

SMITH. "You shall never be saved by that belief. But I pray you, my Lord, show me, are we saved by water, or by Christ?"

BONNER. "By both."

SMITH. "Then the water died for our sins; and so must ye say that the water hath life, and it being our servant and created before us, is our Saviour. This, my lord, is a good doctrine, is it not." (Acts and Monuments, V 11. pp. 348, 352. London, 1838.)

The protracted examination of this great man shows a marvelous acuteness of mind and lofty heroism in danger. He was given to the flames at Uxbridge, and out of their midst he discoursed to the spectators. When black with smoke and almost roasted, drawn into a shapeless mass, and regarded as dead, he suddenly rose up before the people, lifting the stumps of his arms, and clapping the same together, he told them of his triumphant joys, and then, bending down over the fire, his spirit soared away to the everlasting glories of heaven.—Baptist Encyclopedia, page 1071.

A Peek at Popery in Luther's Day
(Indulgences sold)

Marsh gives this record—

While he (Luther) was filling the highly important station to which Providence had raised him, with great credit to himself, and his country, and gaining more and more knowledge of the fundamental doctrines of the Gospel, John Tetzel appeared, in the year 1517, in the neighborhood of Wittemburg, selling indulgences. To this office that bold Dominican inquisitor had been delegated by Albert, Archbishop of Mentz, to whom the indulgences had been sent by Leo X.

Had Tetzel been of a mild and timid spirit, the reformation might have been delayed another century; but he was a man of uncommon boldness and impudence, just calculated to rouse the indignation of Luther. He was indeed a veteran in the traffic. Ten years before he had collected 2000 florins in the space of two days; and he boasted that by his indulgences, he had saved more souls from hell than ever St. Peter converted by his preaching.

The following was one of his abominable articles of traffic: "May our Lord Jesus Christ have mercy upon thee, and absolve thee by the merits of his most holy passion. And I, by His authority, that of the apostles Peter and Paul, and of the most holy pope, granted and committed to me in these parts, do absolve thee first, from all ecclesiastical censures, in whatever manner they have been incured, and then from all the sins, transgressions and excesses, how enormous soever they may be, even such as are reserved for the cognizance of the Holy See, and as far as the keys of the church extend; I remit to thee all the punishment which thou deservest in purgatory on their account; and I restore thee to the holy sacraments of the church, to the unity of the faithful, and to the innocence and purity which thou possessed at baptism; so that when thou diest, the gates of punishment shall be shut, and the gates of the paradise of delight shall be opened; and if thou shalt die at present, this grace shall remain in full force when thou art at the point of death. In the name of the Father, and of the Son, and of the Holy Ghost."

Another related to the deliverance of departed friends from the fires of purgatory; and such was the grossness of this man, that he would publicly say, "The moment the money tinkles in the chest, your father's soul mounts out of purgatory."

The prices of these indulgences varied according to the circumstances and crimes of the purchasers. For the better sale of them, whole districts of country were farmed out to the highest bidders. These were often men of the most licentious characters, who, after they had quieted the consciences of thousands in sin, spent their nights in riot and voluptuousness. John Tetzel was a common adulterer.—Epitome of Eccl. History, John Marsh, page 262.

In a footnote, he quotes from Milner: "In the year 1709, the privateers of Bristol took a galleon, in which they found 500 bales of bulls, for indulgences, and 16 reams were in a bale. So that they reckon the whole came to 3,840,000, averaging in price, from 20 pence to eleven pounds. In Spain, the king had the profits. In Portugal, the king and pope go shares."

Footnote, page 263, Epitome Eccl. History by Marsh.

CENTURY SEVENTEEN

Massacre of Waldenses, 1655

Quoted by Wm. Jones

"A brief Narrative of those horrible Cruelties which were exercised against the Waldenses, in the late Massacre, in April, 1655."

Brethren and Fathers!

Our tears are no more tears of water, but of blood, which not only obscure our sight, but oppress our very hearts. Our pen is guided by a trembling hand, and our minds distracted by such unexpected alarms, that we are incapable of framing a letter which shall correspond with our wishes, or the strangeness of our desolations. In this respect, therefore, we plead your excuse, and that you would endeavour to collect our meaning from what we would impart to you.

Whatever reports may have been circulated concerning our obstinacy in refusing to have recourse to his royal highness for a redress of our heavy grievances and molestations, you cannot but know that we have never desisted from writing supplicatory letters, or presenting our humble requests, by the hands of our deputies, and that they were sent and referred, sometimes to the council de propaganda fide, at other times to the Marquis of Pionessa, and that the three last times they were positively rejected, and refused so much as an audience, under the pretext that they had no credentials nor instructions which should authorise them to promise or accept, on the behalf of their respective churches, whatever it might please his highness to grant or bestow upon them. And by the instigation and contrivance of the Roman clergy, there was secretly placed in ambush an army of six thousand men, who, animated and encouraged thereto by the personal presence and active exertions of the Marquis of Pionessa, fell suddenly and in a most violent manner, upon the inhabitants of S. Giovanni and La Terre.

This army, having once entered and got a footing, was soon augmented by the addition of a multitude of the neighbouring inhabitants throughout all Piedmont, who, hearing that we were given up as a prey to the plunderers, fell upon the poor people with impetuous fury. To all those were added an incalculable number of persons that had been outlawed, prisoners, and other offenders, who expected thereby to have saved their souls and filled their purses. And the better to effect their purposes, the inhabitants were compelled to receive five or six regiments of the French army, besides some Irish, to whom, it is reported, our country was promised, with several troops of vagabond persons, under the pretext of coming into the vallies for fresh quarters.

This great multitude, by virtue of a licence from the Marquis of Pionessa, instigated by the monks, and enticed and conducted by our wicked and unnatural neighbours, attacked us with such violence on every side, especially in Angrogne, Villaro, and Bobio; and in a manner so horribly treacherous, that in an instant all was one entire scene of confusion, and the inhabitants, after a fruitless skirmish to defend themselves, were compelled to flee for their lives, with their wives and children; and that not merely the inhabitants of the plain, but those of the mountains also. Nor was all their diligence sufficient to prevent the destruction of a very considerable number of them. For, in many places, such as Villaro and Bobio, they were so hemmed in on every side, the army having seized on the fort of Mareburg, and by that means blocked up the avenue, that there remained no possibility of escape, and nothing remained for them but to be massacred and put to death. In one place they mercilessly tortured not less than an hundred and fifty women and their children, chopping off the heads of some, and dashing the brains of others against the rocks. And in regard to those whom they took prisoners, from fifteen years old and upwards, who refused to go to mass, they hanged some, and nailed others to the trees by the feet, with their heads downwards. It is reported that they carried some persons of note prisoners to Turin, viz. our poor brother and pastor, Mr. Gros, with some part of his family. In short, there is neither cattle nor provisions of any kind left in the valley of Lucerne;—it is but too evident that all is lost, since there are some whole districts, especially S. Giovanni and La Torre, where the business of setting fire to our churches and houses was so dexterously managed, by a Franciscan friar and a certain priest, that they left not so much as one of either unburnt. In these desolations, the mother has been bereft of her dear child—the husband of his affectionate wife! Those who were once the richest amongst us, are reduced to the necessity of begging their bread, while others still remain weltering in their own blood, and deprived of all the comforts of life. And as to the churches in S. Martino and other places, who, on all former occasions, have been a sanctuary to the persecuted, they have themselves now been summoned to quit their dwellings, and every soul of them to depart, and that instantaneously and without respite, under pain of being put to death. Nor is there any mercy to be expected by any of them who are found within the dominions of his royal highness.

The pretext which is alleged for justifying these horrid proceedings is, that we are rebels against the orders of his highness, for not having brought the whole city of Geneva within the walls of Mary Magdalene church; or, in plainer terms, for not having performed an utter impossibility, in departing, in a moment, from our houses and homes in Bubbiana, Lucerne, Fenile, Bricheras, La

Torre, S. Giovanni, and S. Secondo; and also, for having renewed our repeated supplications to his royal highness to commiserate our situation, who, while on the one hand he promised us to make no innovations in our lot, on the other hand refused us permission to depart peaceably out of his dominions, for which we have often entreated him, in case he would not allow us to continue and enjoy the liberty of our consciences, as his predecessors had always done. True it is, that the Marquis of Pionessa adduced another reason, and we have the original copy of his writing in our possession, which is, that it was his royal highness' pleasure to abase us and humble our pride, for endeavouring to shroud ourselves and take sanctuary, under the protection of foreign princes and states.

To conclude, our beautiful and flourishing churches are utterly lost, and that without remedy, unless our God work miracles for us. Their time is come, and our measure is full! O have pity upon the desolations of Jerusalem, and be grieved for the afflictions of Joseph. Shew forth your compassions, and let your bowels yearn in behalf of so many thousands of poor souls, who are reduced to a morsel of bread, for following the Lamb whithersoever He goeth. We recommend our pastors, with their scattered and dispersed flocks, to your fervent Christian prayers, and rest in haste,

Your brethren in the Lord.

April 27, 1655.

Jones continues—

The reader may collect from this letter some general notion of the tenor of the proceedings that were at that time carried on against the Waldenses in Piedmont; and they appear to have been extended progressively throughout almost the whole country. But if Credit is to be given to the statements of our countryman, Sir Samuel Morland, who in the very same year was sent by the English government to administer pecuniary assistance to these afflicted people,—if any regard is due to the attestations which he has produced from persons who were spectators of the dreadful work of carnage, it is but a faint impression of the scene which can be derived from that letter. The representation given us by Sir Samuel, and further corroborated by Leger, in his General History of the Churches of Piedmont, beggars all description for atrocity. Nor, if the infernal regions had been disembowelled of their inhabitants, and the whole let loose among the vallies of Piedmont, could we have expected the perpetration of greater enormities. The bare report of them spread amazement throughout all the Protestant states of Europe, as we shall presently see; and the principal actors in this deep tragedy found it necessary to aim at extricating their characters from the odium which attached to it. In particular, the Marquis of Pionessa laboured to cast the blame upon certain officers of his army, which induced one of them not only to give up the command of the regiment, but actually to draw up an affidavit, which he attested with his own hand, and got it further corroborated by the testimony of two of his brother officers, in vindication of his conduct in that affair. Sir Samuel Morland obtained possession of the original document, which he deposited in the University of Cambridge, along with an infinite number of other interesting manuscripts relating to this subject, and it appears of sufficient importance to be submitted to the reader's consideration.

"I, Sieur Du Petit Bourg, first captain of the regiment of Groncy, who also commanded the same, having received direction from prince Thomas to join the Marquis of Pionessa, who was then at La Torre, and to receive his orders—when I was upon the eve of departure, the ambassador sent for me, and desired me to speak to M. de Pionessa, and to use my endeavours to accommodate the troubles which had happened among those of the religion (of the Waldenses) in the vallies of Piedmont. In order to which I addressed myself to the Marquis, earnestly entreating him that he would give way, and allow me to undertake an accommodation, which I supposed I might have been able to effect. But he repeatedly refused my request, in defiance of all the endeavours I could possibly use to persuade him. And instead of the least mitigation of matters, which could be produced by any consideration that I could lay before him, I was witness to many acts of violence and extreme cruelties exercised by the banditti and soldiers of Piedmont, upon all sorts of persons, of every age, sex and condition, whom I myself saw massacred, dismembered, hung up; females violated, and numerous other horrid atrocities committed. And so far is it from being true that the whole was done by virtue of the orders that were issued by me, as falsely stated in a certain Narrative, printed in French and Italian, that I beheld the same with horror and regret. And whereas it is said in the same Narrative, that the Marquis of Pionessa commanded me to treat them peaceably, without hostility, and in the best manner I possibly could, the event clearly demonstrated that the orders he gave were altogether of a contrary tendency, since it is most certain that without distinction of those who resisted, from those who made no resistance, they were used with all sorts of inhumanity—their houses burnt, their goods plundered, and when prisoners were brought before the Marquis of Pionessa, I was a witness to his issuing orders to give them no quarters at all, assigning as a reason, that his highness was resolved to have none of that religion in any of his dominions.

"And as to what he protests in the same declaration, namely, that no hurt was done to any except during the fight, nor the least outrage committed upon any unoffending and helpless persons, I do assert, and will maintain, that such is not the truth, having seen with my own eyes several men killed in cold blood, and also women, aged persons, and children, miserably murdered.

"And with regard to the manner in which they put themselves in possession of the valley of Angrogne, to pillage, and entirely burn the same, it was done with great ease. For, excepting six or seven persons, who, seeing there would be no mercy shewn them, made some shew of resistance, the rest were dispersed without difficulty, the peasants consulting how to flee, rather than how to fight the enemy. In short, I absolutely deny and protest, as in the presence of God, that none of those cruelties were executed by my order; but, on the contrary, seeing that I could not procure a remedy, I was constrained to retire and quit the command of the regiment, not liking to be present at such wicked transactions.

Done at Pignerol, November 27th, 1655."

Du Petit Bourg.

—History of the Christian Church, by William Jones. pp. 479-483.

In this late century we find Baptists suffering in France whose soil had through the years been reddened by Baptist blood. The following account is taken from Orchard's History, page 292—

In 1685, October 8, the edict of Nantz was repealed, by which act no toleration could be allowed to dissenters from the Catholic church. Fifteen days were allowed to Protestant ministers to leave the kingdom; two millions of persons were condemned by this instrument, and banished from their native soil. This cruel instrument ruined the Protestant churches, and freed France and other kingdoms from the witness of the truth. If any remained, it was at the peril of life and liberty; yet some braved the danger, and worshipped unseen and unheard by malicious foes. Pious females, shrouded by the night, bent their way amidst darkness and danger toward the spot assigned for their religious services—a dark lantern guided their perilous steps; arrived at their temple, amidst the rocks, two walking-sticks hastily struck in the ground, and covered with a black silk apron of the female auditors, formed what they called the pulpit of the desert.

To such an assembly how eloquent must have appeared the lessons of that preacher, who braved death at every word he uttered, how impressive that service, the attending of which incurred the penalty of fetters for life. These were the glorious days of Baptists in France; these were her proudest triumph, she could then boast of valor of which the world was not worthy, her martyrs then bore testimony to their faith at the fatal tree, or were chained for life to the oar of the galleys; and women, with the same noble feelings, in the same sacred cause, shrank not from perpetual imprisonment in the gloomy tower that overhangs the shores of the Mediterranean.

The most horrid scenes of violence and bloodshed were exhibited from 1660 to 1690, among the Waldenses, whom the papists persecuted with relentless fury.—Epitome of Eccl. History, John March, page 322.

Minutes of a Persecuted Church

The Broadmead Church, Bristol, England, was founded in this century, 1640. There is a good account in Cook's Story of the Baptists, pages 152-155. We give a few extracts from the records of the church—

January 29, 1682. The church met at four different places. Many of them went in the afternoon on Durdham Down and got into a cave of rock toward Clifton, where Brother Thomas Whinnell preached to them.

March 12. Met in the fields by Barton Hundred, and Mr. Samuel Buttall, of Plymouth, preached in the forenoon, and Brother Whinnell in the evening. It was thought there were near a thousand persons in the morning.

July 2. Our pastor preached in another place in the wood. Our friends took much pains, in the rain, because many informers were ordered out to search; and we were in peace, though there were near twenty men and boys in search.

July 6. Brother Frowns, first, and Brother Whinnell, after, preached under a tree, it being very rainy.

January 21, 1683. We met at eight in the morning and though there were seven on horseback, and twenty on foot, to seek after us, we escaped, having broken up at ten.

"March. This week about one hundred and fifty dissenters were convicted by our recorder, on the statutes of 23rd. Elizabeth, for 20 pounds per month, for not coming to church. (This was equal to about one hundred dollars.)

March 25. Mr. Fownes, though very ill, went to the meetings in the woods; but after three quarters of an hour, we were surrounded by horse and foot, the former in ambush. Mr. Fownes was arrested and sent to Gloucester jail for six months.

November 14. A day of prayer, having some hours together in the wood between London and Sodbury Road; the enemy came upon us unaware and seized about eight persons; but the brethren escaped to admiration. The bushes were of great service to us. A number of the sisters were taken, and were closely questioned, but refused to tell who their preacher was, so they were let go.

December 30. Being a hard frost and snow on the ground, we met in the wood, and though we stood in the snow, the sun shone upon us, and we were in peace.

October 10, 1684. New Mayor and Sheriff being chosen, James Twyford, sheriff, threatens to find out our little meetings, and he would be like death, spare none.

On the 29 of November, 1685, our pastor, Brother Fownes, died in Gloucester jail, having been kept there for two years and about nine months a prisoner, unjustly and maliciously, for the testimony of Jesus and preaching the Gospel.—Dr. Cramp, in The Story of the Baptists, by Cook.

"One Dr. Leighton, a Puritan, was condemned in the Star Chamber, at Laud's instigation, for publishing an appeal to the Parliament against prelacy. When sentence was pronounced, the archbishop pulled off his cap and gave thanks. This is his own cool record of its execution: 'Nov. 6, 1. He was severely whipped before he was set in the pillory. 2. Being set in the pillory, he had one of his ears cut off. 3. One side of his nose was slit up. 4. He was branded on the cheek with a red-hot iron, with the letters S.S. On that day, sen'night, his sores upon his back, ears, nose, and face, not being cured, he was whipped again at the pillory in Cheapside, cutting off the other ear, slitting the other side of his nose, and branding the other cheek.' He was then imprisoned with peculiar severity for about eleven years, and when released by the Parliament, he could neither hear, see, nor walk."—Epitome of Gen. Eccl. History by Marsh, 6 Edition, 1841, page 348-349.

Whipped and Branded

"They also whipped a minister of the word, took him out into the country as far as Burgundy, who there marked him with a branding iron, and let him go among the French; but as he could not speak their language, he had to wander three days before he could get his wound dressed, and obtain any refreshment; so that when they stripped him in order to bind up his burn, the matter ran down over his back, as was related to me by a brother who assisted in dressing the wound.

"Thus they act with great violence, and will not relinquish their design till they have driven this harmless people entirely from the country. It appears, moreover, that nothing can be effected in favor of the oppressed brethren —for, not only the friends at Amsterdam and elsewhere have labored for several years in this cause, so that petitions have been presented by the lords of Holland, and particularly those of Amsterdam, and by other respectable persons to the authorities here; but, moreover, Adolf de Vrede, was sent here as an express in the year 1660, but he accomplished but very little for the advantage of our friends. Hence, I cannot see that we can effect anything that would tend to the relief of our oppressed brethren. We will have to wait in patience for the issue which the Lord our God may grant them." (Article appeared in Martyrs' Mirror, page 1022.) — Footnote, BENEDICT HISTORY, page 120.

Persecution in American Colonies

We quote here from Robert Semple—

Our ancestors, being chiefly emigrants from England, brought with them all that religious intolerance which had so long prevailed in the mother country. Thus we see, that the first care of our early legislatures was to provide for the church of England, as established by the act of parliament. By the first act of 1623, it is provided that, in every plantation, or settlement, there shall be a house or room set apart for the worship of God. But, it soon appears that this worship was only to be according to the canons of the church of England, to which a strict uniformity was enjoined.

A person absenting himself from divine service, on a Sunday, without a reasonable excuse, forfeited a pound of tobacco; and he that absented himself a month, forfeited 50 lbs. Any minister who was absent from his church above two months in a year, forfeited half his salary; and he who absented himself four months forfeited the whole.

Whoever disparaged a minister, whereby the minds of his parishioners might be alienated, was compelled to pay 500 lbs. of tobacco, and ask the minister's pardon publicly in the congregation. No man was permitted to dispose of any of his tobacco, till the minister was satisfied, under the penalty of forfeiting double his part of the minister's salary.

The first allowance made to the ministers was ten lb. of tobacco and a bushel of corn for each tithable; and every labouring person, of what quality or condition soever, was bound to contribute. In the year 1631, the assembly granted to the ministers, besides the former allowance of ten pounds of tobacco and a bushel of corn, the 20th calf, the 20th kid, and 20th pig. This was the first introduction of tithes, properly so called, in Virginia. But it did not continue long; for, in 1633, the law was repealed.

To preserve the "purity of doctrine, and unity of the church," it was enacted in 1643, that all ministers should be conformable to the orders and constitutions of the church of England, and that no others be permitted to teach or preach publicly or privately. It was further provided, that the governor and council should take care that all nonconformists, departed the colony with all conveniency.—History of the Rise and Progress of the Baptists in Virginia, Robert B. Semple, 1810.

"Several Anabaptists spread in Massachusetts, and contemned the civil and ecclesiastical authorities. A severe law was passed against them in 1644. An adherence to their principles was punished by banishment. So little did the puritans understand the rights, for which they themselves had contended."—Epitome of Eccl. History, John Marsh, page 381.

Edict of the Duke of Savoy, 1686

Edict of the Duke of Savoy, for the extirpation of the Waldenses, January 31, 1686.
Victor Amadeus, by the grace of God, Duke of Savoy and of Piedmont, and King of Cyprus.

Political as well as Christian prudence, advises us very often to neglect, in some manner, the ulcers that are not yet in a condition to be healed, and that might be made worse by a precipitate cure. This conduct has been observed as well in other monarchies, as by our serene predecessors, who in truth had never any other design, than to rescue their subjects professing the pretended Reformed Religion, out of the darkness of heresy, which by an unhappy vicissitude, and a fatal corruption of these times, had passed from the very centre of the vallies of Lucerne, into the very heart of Piedmont.

Nevertheless, by reason of the succours which the zealots of that religion received from foreign countries, this holy work could not be brought to the end we so much desired; insomuch that not having been able to purge our country of this poison, we did reduce them to, and shut them up in the vallies of Lucerne, of Angrone, of St. Martin, of Ceruse, of St. Bartholomew, of Roccapiata, and of Parustin; and by way of toleration, we did suffer them to exercise there their false religion, in the limits before prescribed them, according to the juncture of times, till it should please God Almighty to give us a favorable opportunity of bringing back those misled souls into the bosom of the Holy and only Catholic, Apostolic, and Romish religion.

Yet time has discovered how much it was necessary to cut off the numerous heads of this hydra, since the said heretics, instead of answering this favour with a deep submission, and with a sincere acknowledgment of this kind toleration, have very often made bold to be disobedient, to a scandal, and to rise against their own Sovereign.

And because at present the principal cause of this said toleration is now removed by the zeal and piety of the glorious monarch of France, who has brought back to the true faith his neighbouring heretics; we think the particular graces we have received from his Divine Majesty, and which we enjoy still, would accuse us of the greatest ingratitude, if by our negligence we should let slip the opportunity of executing this work, according to the intention of our glorious predecessors.

It is for this, and several urgent reasons, that by virtue of this present Edict, with our full knowledge, and by our absolute power, as also by the advice of our council, we have declared and ordered, and do declare and order by these presents, to our subjects of the pretended Reformed Religion, to desist for the future from all the exercise of the said religion.

And we do prohibit them further, after the publishing of this Edict, from holding any assemblies or conventicles, in any place or particular house, to exercise the said religion, under what title, pretext, or occasion whatsoever, under pain of their lives and confiscation of their goods. And we ordain also, that the past pretended toleration be of no effect, under what colour or pretence whatsoever.

Our will is also, that all the churches, granges, and houses, in which at present the said religion is exercised, shall be razed to the ground; and also all other places in which for the future such assemblies shall be held, to the prejudice of what the precedent articles contain; and this is to be executed, though the owners of such places are ignorant thereof.

And we command accordingly all ecclesiastics, ministers, and schoolmasters, of the said pretended Reformed Religion, who in one fortnight after the publishing this present Edict, do not effectually embrace the Catholic religion, shall retreat out of our territories after the said term be past, under pain of death, and confiscation of their goods; with express command, and under the same punishment, not to make, within the said time, or before their departure, any sermon, exhortation, or any other act of the said religion.

And furthermore, we forbid, under the said punishment, and the forfeiture of our favour, all those that make profession of the pretended Reformed Religion, to keep for the future any public or private school; it being our intention, that from this very time their children shall be instructed by Catholic schoolmasters.

And concerning the ministers who within the said time shall embrace the Catholic Religion, our will and pleasure is, that during their lives, and after they are dead, their widows, as long as they shall live unmarried, shall enjoy the said exemptions and immunities which they enjoyed heretofore, during the exercise of their charge.

And our will is over and above, that to the said ecclesiastics who shall be made converts in the said manner, there shall be paid during their life a pension one third part larger than the salary was which they enjoyed in quality of being ministers of the said religion; and that after their death their widows enjoy one half of the said pension as long as they shall continue unmarried.

And concerning the children that shall be born by father and mother of the said pretended Reformed Religion, our intention is that after the publishing this present Edict, they shall be baptized by the priests of the parish that are already, or that shall be established for the future in the said vallies; to this purpose, we command their fathers and mothers to send or bring them to the churches under pain of being sent five years to the gallies for their fathers, and whipping for their mothers; and moreover the said children shall be brought up in the said Catholic, Apostolic, and Roman Religion.

And we command expressly all judges, bailiffs, gaolers, and other officers, to see these presents duly executed. And we do confirm also the Edict we have published the 4th of November past, concerning the subjects of His Most Christian Majesty that make profession of the pretended Reformed Religion, and that are to be found in our territories, and that have left their merchandises, money, or other effects behind them; and concerning the other foreigners of the said Religion, who, to the prejudice of some of our predecessors' Edicts, have established themselves in the vallies, without their consent in writing, comprehending therein their offspring that are born there; we command, that in case, within one fortnight after the publishing this present Edict, they do not declare to be willing to embrace the Catholic, Apostolic, and Roman Religion, they shall be obliged, if the said term be past, to retreat out of our territories, under pain of death, and confiscation of their goods.

And though lawfully, by virtue of the said Edicts, the goods which the said foreigners have acquired in our territories ought to be confiscated for our royal treasury; nevertheless we are willing in this case to shew our accustomed clemency, and to give them leave to sell their said goods (if they please) within the said term, and to dispose of the same as they think convenient; yet upon these conditions, that the selling the immovable goods shall only be made in favour of the Catholics; but in case they shall find no buyer, they shall be looked upon as sold, and united to our dominions under a reasonable price.

Finally, we command all the magistrates established by us, ministers of state, officers, judges, and all others whom it concerns, to see this present Edict inviolably observed; and so to order the same, that the council of Piedmont may enroll it, and give their full approbation of what is contained therein.

Moreover, our will is, that the publishing hereof made in the accustomed places, and in the ordinary manner, shall have the same virtue as if it had been made known to every particular person; and that there be the same observance paid to the copy hereof, printed by Sinibal our printer, as to this my original itself; for this is our Will. Given at Turin, Jan. 31, 1686. By his Royal Highness' Command. VICTOR AMADEUS.—THE HISTORY OF THE CHRISTIAN CHURCH By William Jones.

CENTURY EIGHTEEN

When church and state unite there is always the seed of persecution, waiting a favorable sun to sprout.

For persecution in this century we do not have to go to Europe or England. We find it here on our own soil. Episcopalians and others joined with civil powers. We cannot, in this short space, give but a few instances of Baptists being persecuted. Some cases are mentioned elsewhere in this book.

During the last century Roger Williams, though not a Baptist, did believe in soul liberty. For this he was banished from Massachusetts. Baptists were jailed in Virginia.

We give the following account, in the old English as my authority writes it—

The firft inftance of actual imprifonment, we believe, that ever took place in Virginia, was in the county of Spottfyvania. On the fourth of June, 1768, John Waller, Lewis Craig, James Childs, and others, were feized by the fheriff, and haled before three magistrastes, who ftood in the meeting houfe yard, and who bound them in the penalty of one thousand pounds, to appear at court two days after. At court they were arraigned as difturbers of the peace; on their trial, they were vehemently accufed, by a certain lawyer, who faid to the court, "May it pleafe your worfhips, these men are great difturbers of the peace, they cannot meet a man upon the road, but they muft ram a text of fcripture down his throat." (They were missionary—WJB.)

Mr. Waller made his own, and his brethren's defence fo ingeniously, that they were fomewhat puzzled to know how to difpofe of them. They offered to releafe them, if they would promife to preach no more in the county, for a year and a day. This they refufed; and, therefore, were fent into clofe jail. As they were moving on, from the court houfe to the prifon through the ftreets of Fredericksburg, they fung the hymn, "Broad is the Road that leads to death."—Rise and Progress of the Baptists of Virginia, Semple.

Patrick Henry, a Friend

Ford gives this record of Patrick Henry—

Patrick Henry was a young lawyer when Joseph Craig and Aaron Bledsoe were hailed into Virginia court for **Preaching the Gospel of the Son of God in the Colony of Virginia.** He came into the courtroom as the charge was being read by the clerk. He rode horseback some 60 miles, after hearing of the two men being arrested. He was a friend to Baptists. The following is the first part of his address to the court:

"May it please your worships: I think I heard read by the prosecutor as I entered this house the paper I now hold in my hand. If I have rightly understood, the king's attorney of this colony has framed an indictment for the purpose of arraigning, and punishing by imprisonment, three inoffensive persons before the bar of this Court, for a crime of magnitude—as disturbers of the peace. May it please the Court, what did I hear read? Did I hear it distinctly, or was it a mistake of my own? Did I hear an expression as if a crime, that these men, whom your worships are about to try for a misdemeanor, are charged with—what?"—and continuing in a low, solemn, heavy tone, "For preaching the Gospel of the Son of God!"

Pausing, amid the most profound silence and breathless astonishment, he slowly waved the paper three times around his head, when, lifting his hands and eyes to heaven, with peculiar and impressive energy he exclaimed, "Great God!" The exclamation—the action—the burst of feeling from the audience, were all over-powering.—The Origin of the Baptists, Ford, page 5.

Patrick Henry was not a Baptist, but his brother, General Henry, was, and a member of a Virginia Baptist church. Many times did Patrick Henry go to the defense of Baptists in the courts of Virginia.

CENTURY NINETEEN

For a change we go to the far East. Adoniram and Anne Judson sailed for Burma February 19, 1812, arriving in Calcutta June 17th. They were Congregationalists when they left New York. They had time for much study on the long voyage and were convinced by the Scriptures that Baptists were right. They were the first American foreign missionaries, and landed as Baptists.

It was seven years before they had their first convert. Theirs is a graphic story. Everyone should read it. But we give the following account of their persecution—

On the 8th of June, just as we were preparing for dinner, in rushed an officer, holding a black book, with a dozen Burmans, accompanied by one, whom, from his spotted face, we knew to be an executioner and a 'son of the prison.'

'Where is the teacher?' was the first inquiry. Mr. Judson presented himself. 'You are called by the king,' said the officer—a form of speech always used when about to arrest a criminal. The spotted man instantly seized Mr. Judson, threw him on the floor, and produced the small cord, the instrument of torture. I caught hold of his arm (Mrs. Judson writing). 'Stay,' said I: 'I will give you money.' 'Take her, too,' said the officer, 'she also is a foreigner.' Mr. Judson, with an imploring look, begged that they would let me remain till further orders. The scene was shocking beyond description. The whole neighborhood had collected, and the hardened executioner, with a kind of hellish joy, drew tight the cords, bound Mr. Judson, and dragged him off, I knew not whither. In vain I begged and entreated the spotted face to take the silver and loosen the ropes; but he spurned the offers and immediately departed. When a few rods from the house, the unfeeling wretches again threw their prisoner on the ground and drew the cords still tighter, so as almost to prevent respiration.

Mr. Judson was committed to the 'death prison,' while his tender wife spent a night af almost indescribable anguish. 'A guard of ten ruffians' was placed around the house, who tried to force an entrance into it, and spent the night in dreadful carousing and almost diabolical language. But the anguish of that night was to be prolonged and intensified for months. Both husband and wife were doomed to suffer terrible indignities and cruelties before relaese came.

With all the white prisoners, Mr. Judson was confined in the death-prison, with three pairs of fetters each, and fastened to a long pole to prevent them moving. Mrs. Judson, after affecting her own release, was hardly permitted to alleviate the sufferings of her husband. But with true womanly fidelity, she attended upon all the prisoners, as far as she was allowed, by paying a fee to the keepers, preparing their food, and encouraging them. In the midst of these trials, her little daughter Maria was born to the lonely woman. For seven long months this bitter imprisonment continued. Mrs. Judson often walked from the prison to her house, two miles distant, after nine o'clock at night, alone, fatigued and anxious. More than once, as Mrs. Judson afterwards learned, the execution of the captives had been ordered.—Story of the Baptists, Cooke, page 332.

Above is an example of sufferings foreign missionaries sometimes have to endure. In this case, the British army arrived in time to free Bro. Judson.—W. J. B.

CENTURY TWENTY

Missionaries Assailed by Mob

Dear Brother Burgess:

"My tongue also shall talk of thy righteousness all the day long; for they are confounded, for they are brought unto shame, that seek my hurt."

These words of the Psalmist were literally fulfilled in our lives and experiences these last two days.

We had planned a revival meeting in the village of Arrifana to start Monday night, December 3rd. According to plan, we were there at the appointed hour. We found the house already nearly full awaiting to hear the Word of the Lord. Lois played the accordion for several minutes while others came. Brother Nipo led the song service as usual. I read my text, John, chapter one, and my subject was: The Word Became Flesh.

At the beginning, all was calm except for cat-calling in the distance that sounded like Indians in the Wild West, but as I began to prove from the Scriptures that Jesus was and is God made flesh to redeem us from our sins, the devil decided to take over and stop it. It became increasingly hard to preach over the noise of the mob that was now at the door. I did not finish my sermon. Brother Nipo came up to the front and said: "Let me take over, and you go call the police to handle this crowd."

I went out into that dark village street to face one of the wildest most fanatical mobs that I have ever seen. There is nothing worse than religious fanatics. They were filled with new wine and armed with cowbells and clubs and were using the most blasphemous language possible to their very limited vocabulary. Only the Lord knows what would have happened if the Portuguese State Police had not arrived and scattered the mob with their billyclubs.

The police, themselves, were not in sympathy with us, but they had to maintain law and order. The local Justice of the Peace was the chief promoter of the riot, of course, backed by the Catholic padre.

One big man, a would-be big shot, came up to me with a club and said: "I'm 56 years old and half drunk, but I can still whip you." He wanted to fight, but I learned a long time ago where that if one doesn't want to, two don't fight. I looked at him and knew that physically I could handle him, but in the dark behind him, I could see the angry faces of many young men growling with diabolical groans.

I knew that I faced more than flesh and blood and that my only weapon was the Sword of the Lord hidden in my heart; so I decided to tell him about Jesus and his need for the Saviour. This only provoked his fury more, and he blurted out: "I don't need a saviour, I'm the saviour myself." Seeing that there was no point in preaching to him, I changed tactics.

I put my arm around him and said, "Did you know that I love you? In spite of all this, I love the Portuguese." At this, a smile came upon his face and he said, "Do you love me?" I replied, "Yes." He stuck out his hand, shook hands with me, and walked away. The mob followed him. It was only the Lord who delivered us and once again He showed that love is more powerful than hate.

While I was facing the mob outside, Lois was able to calm those inside with soft music, and Brother Nipo preached to them about the persecutions of Paul. I did not finish my sermon, but as we left we promised to return the next night at the same hour. The people promised to be there.

Last night we returned for the second night of the revival thinking that because of what had happened the night before that we would have no trouble, but we underestimated the will-power of the devil. He was not so easily defeated. All went well at first, except for the cries in the distance, but we thought that surely they would stay at a distance this time. Lois played a number of hymns, then taught the children some choruses, including "With Christ in Your Life, The Storm Passes."

Bro. Nipo started the service. Brother Agostinho Matos and one of our preacher boys, Vitorino Araujo, had come with us. During the song service, Brother Nipo read 82 verses of the 119 Psalm. During this reading, all was calm, and at least they heard that much of the Word of the Lord, but this time I was not to finish reading my text.

The very minute I started reading in the Gospel of John, the mob took over. Brother Matos, who is an ex-policeman and a big man with a strong voice, came to the stand and asked me to let him take over and preach while I went out to face the mob. Brother Matos wasn't able to preach either. The night before had been mild in comparison to what I was now to face.

I had left Brother Vitorino, who is also an ex-soldier,

to watch the car, and in spite of this, they had punctured one of the tires and tried to stone us and the car. But happily, most of the stones missed the car, and none of them hit us; although some of them came pretty close.

The Lord gave holy-boldness, but even one time then when the stones were coming pretty thick, I was tempted to run for shelter. I tried to no avail to calm the mob, but they only became more furious. By this time, a group of fanatical women and girls had joined the mob, and there's nothing worse to face than a fanatical group of ignorant, devil controlled women who are dedicated to Mary and the Catholic Church.

Brother Vitorino and I faced the threats and insults of the mob alone until Brother Matos decided that he couldn't preach either and came out to join us. Brother Nipo closed the door so that those inside could not get out, nor those who were on the outside could get in. Lois played soft music to try to calm those who came for the service, but Brother Nipo did not attempt to preach.

Brother Matos thought that he would preach to the mob in the street, but they advanced furiously with one accord on him, and when he saw he could not resist, he joined them in their dancing and clapping hands, and it was almost funny. He thanked them for the great reception with which they were honoring us. He told them that it was an honor for the whole town to turn out to greet us.

A young man, that I did not recognize at the moment in the midst of the turmoil, showed up on a motorcycle and offered to go to the next town to call the police. I found out later that he was a member of the Rio Maior Church, who had come 28 kilometers on a motorcycle over dark, rough roads to attend the service.

Surely, the Lord sent him. When the mob saw the motorcycle take off, they were calm a little bit, and by this time they were divided among themselves—sometimes fighting one another, but never doing more than threatening us. It was a furious sight, and we didn't know what would happen the next minute.

A group of men and women who were against such

demonstrations gathered around me. They helped me change the tire while the mob paraded, shouted, cursed, bumped into me, and at times stoned the car. A new leader in uniform appeared on the scene and demanded that I leave the village without changing the tire, but finally after much difficulty, we got the spare tire on, and since the police had not come, Brother Matos wanted to go get them. We had now faced the mob for nearly an hour.

As we left, they jeered and stoned the car and shouted. About half-way to the next town, we met the bus, and the police were on it fully armed for combat. Brother Matos got on the bus with the police and told Vitorino and me to return alone so that the police would arrive on the bus by surprise. We returned. The mob, expecting the police, had backed away from the meeting place into the dark to see what the police would do, but we drove up near to them where they could see as I turned around that the police were not with me.

Seeing that the police were not in the car, they let out the war-cry, and with one accord marched on the car, throwing stones as they came and overjoyed that we did not have police protection. They made ready for the final victory over the "heretics," who were troubling their village. I did not know if I could hold out 'til the police came, but I got out and faced them as though they were my friends.

Just as the multitude approached me with clubs, and one fellow made like he had a gun or a knife, and all with anger on their faces thinking that we did not have police protection, and sure that this time they would finish us, the bus drove up and flashed the bright lights on the mob. For the first time I really saw them, so did the police, but they didn't pay any attention to the bus, because it was the bus that comes every night to the village.

Just as the leader, who had threatened, cursed, and ordered me time after after to leave, struck at me and nearly knocked me down, Brother Matos jumped off the bus and police-like knocked him down, and two armed policemen jumped off the bus, grabbed him, shook him, and ordered him into my car as a prisoner. The policemen then left me to watch him while they went through the village after the others.

The one who had been so brave only a few minutes before, was now as humble as a lamb. I reminded him that I had warned him what would happen if he didn't quit disturbing a religious service. He admitted that he had done wrong. He also admitted that he was serving another. He didn't call the priest's name, but we knew who his master was. I took the opportunity to preach Jesus to him and tell him that we loved him and desired his salvation and his well-being and that we were sorry that he had to be taken prisoner for disobeying the law of the land in order to obey a man. We pray that the Lord will save his soul.

The police, with Brother Matos, in the center of the village, warned the people not to take part in further demonstrations against us, because the Portuguese Constitution guarantees religious liberty to all and that the penalty for disturbing a religious service carries a minimum of two years in prison.—Harold Morris, Missionary, North American Baptist Association, 1962. This was in Portugal.

Persecution in New Guinea

"Anti-Christian atrocities that killed 80 Christians and razed 50 tribal villages apparently strengthened rather than dampened the consecration of New Guinea Baptists.

"The massacre of Dani Christians in the North Baliem Valley occurred on Sunday, September 30, and was led by two tribal chiefs who had harassed religious activities ever since Australian Baptist missionaries moved into the valley in 1956."—Baptist World, December 1962.

A SUMMATION OF THE CENTURIES

Methods of Torture and Death

William Jones gives the following summary—

I shall dismiss the subject by an extract from Dr. Chandler's History of Persecutions, relating to this period.

"The most excessive and outrageous barbarities," says he, "were made use of upon all who would not blaspheme Christ and offer incense to the imperial gods. They were publicly whipped—drawn by the heels through the streets of cities,—racked till every bone of their body was disjointed,—had their teeth beat out,—their noses, hands, and ears cut off,—sharp pointed spears run under their nails,—were tortured with melted lead thrown on their naked bodies,—had their eyes dug out,—their limbs cut off,—were condemned to the mines,—ground between stones,—stoned to death,—burnt alive,—buried alive—thrown headlong from the high buildings,—beheaded,—smothered in burning lime kilns,—run through the body with sharp spears,—destroyed with hunger, thirst and cold,—thrown to wild beasts,—broiled on gridirons with slow fires,—cast by heaps into the sea,—crucified, scraped to death with sharp shells,—torn in pieces by the bough of trees,—and, in a word, destroyed by all the various methods that the most diabolical subtlety and malice could devise."—HISTORY OF CHRISTIAN CHURCH, by William Jones, page 151.

BOOK SIX

PERSECUTION IN ALL COUNTRIES

CHAPTER I

ITALY—THE MORALS OF THE PERSECUTORS

Eusebius wrote the following about 300 A.D.—

Maxentius, the son of Maximian, who had established his government at Rome, in the commencement, pretended indeed, by a species of accommodation and flattery towards the Romans, that he was of our faith. He, therefore, commanded his subjects to desist from persecuting the Christians, pretending to piety with a view to appear much more and merciful than the former rulers.

But he by no means proved to be in his actions such as he was expected. He sunk into every kind of wickedness, leaving no impurity or licentiousness untouched; committing every species of adultery and fornication, separating wives from their lawful husbands, and after abusing these, sending them thus most shamefully violated back again to their husbands. And these things he perpetrated not upon mean and obscure individuals, but insulting more particulary the most prominent of those that were most distinguished in the senate.

Whilst he was thus dreaded by all, both people and magistrates, high and low were galled with a most grievous oppression; and though they bore this severe tyranny quietly, and without rebellion, it produced no relief from his murderous cruelty. On a certain very slight occasion, therefore, he gave up the people to be slaughtered by the praetorian guards, and thus multitudes of the Roman people were slain in the very heart of the city, not with the arrows and spears of Scythians or barbarians, but of their own fellow-citizens. It would be impossible to tell what slaughter was made of the senators merely for the sake of their wealth, thousands being destroyed on a variety of pretexts and fictitious crimes.

But when these evils had reached their greatest height, the tyrant was induced to resort to the mummery of magic. At one time he would cut open pregnant females, at another examining the bowels of new born babes; sometimes also slaughtering lions and performing any kind of execrable acts, to invoke the daemons, and to avert the impending war. For all his hope now was that victory would be secured to him by these means. It is impossible then to say, in what different ways this cruel tyrant oppressed his subjects, so that they were already reduced to such extreme want and scarcity, such as they say has never happened at Rome, or elsewhere in our time.

But Maximinus, who was sovereign of the east, as he had secretly formed an alliance with Maxentius, his true brother in wickedness at Rome, designed to conceal his designs as long as possible. But being at length detected, he suffered the deserved punishment. It was wonderful how nearly allied, and similar, rather how vastly beyond the tyranny of the Roman, were the cruelties and crimes of this tyrant.

The first of impostors and jugglers, were honoured by him with the highest rank. He became so extremely timorous and superstitious, and valued the delusion and supposed influence of daemons above all, so that he was hardly able to move his finger, one might say, or undertake any thing without soothsayers and oracles. Hence, also, he assailed us with a more violent and incessant persecution than those before him.

He ordered temples to be erected in every city, and those that had been demolished by time, he commanded in his zeal to be renewed. Priests of the idols he established in every place and city; and over these a high priest in every province, some one of those who had been particularly distinguished for his skill in the management of political affairs, adding a military guard. He granted to all his jugglers the same reverence as if they were the most pious and acceptable to the gods, freely bestowing on them governments, and the greatest privileges.

And from this time forth he began to vex, not merely a single city or region, but harassed all the provinces under him, by exactions of silver and gold and money, by the most oppressive seizures and confiscations of property, in different ways and on various pretexts. Despoiling the wealthy of the substance inherited from their fathers, he bestowed vast wealth, and heaps of money upon the flatterers around him. And he had now advanced to such a pitch of rashness, and was so addicted to intoxication, that, in his drunken frolics he was frequently deranged and deprived of his reason, like a madman; so that what he commanded when he was intoxicated, he afterwards regretted when he became sober.

But determined to leave no one his superior in surfeiting and gluttony, he presented himself a fit master of iniquity to the rulers and subjects around him. Initiating the soldiers, by luxury and intemperance, into every species of dissipation and revelling, encouraging the governors and generals, by rapacity and avarice, to proceed with their oppressions against their subjects, with almost the power of associate tyrants. Why should I mention the degrading and foul lust of the man? Or why mention his innumerable adulteries? There was not a city that he passed through in which he did not commit violence upon females. And in these he succeeded against all but the Christians. For they, despising death, valued his power but little.

The men bore fire, sword, and crucifixions, savage beasts, and the depths of the sea, the maiming of limbs, and searing with red hot iron, pricking and digging out the eyes, and the mutilations of the whole body. Also hunger, and mines, and prisons; and after all, they chose these sufferings for the sake of religion, rather than transfer that veneration and worship to idols which is due to God only.

The females, also, no less than the men, were strengthened by the doctrine of the divine word; so that some endured the same trials as the men, and bore away the same prizes of excellence. Some, when forced away, yielded up their lives rather than submit to the violation of their bodies.

The tyrant having fully gratified his lust on others at Alexandria, his unbridled passion was defeated by the heroic firmness of one female only, who was one of the most distinguished and illustrious at Alexandria, **and she was a Christian.** She was in other respects distinguished both for her wealth, and family, and condition, but esteemed all inferior to modesty.

Having frequently made attempts to bring her over to his purposes, though she was prepared to die, he could not destroy her, as his passion was stronger than his anger; but, punishing her with exile, he took away all her wealth. Many others, also, unable to bear even the threats of violation from the rulers of the heathen, submitted to every kind of torture, the rack and deadly punishment.

Admirable, indeed, were all these; but far above all most admirable, was that lady who was one of the most noble and modest of those whom Maxentius, in all respects like Maximinus, attempted to violate. For whom she understood that the minions of the tyrant in such matters, had burst into the house (for she was also a Christian), and that her husband, who was the perfect of Rome, had suffered them to carry her off, she requested but a little time, as if now for the purpose of adorning her body: she then entered her chamber, and when alone thrust a sword into her breast.

Thus, dying immediately, she indeed left her body to the conductors; but in her deeds, more effectually than any language, proclaims, to all who are now and will be hereafter, that virtue, **which prevails among Christians,** is the only invincible and imperishable possession. Such, then, was the flood of iniquity which rushed on at one and the same time, and which was wrought by the two tyrants that swayed the east and the west.

And who is there that examines the cause of these evils, that would be in doubt whether he should pronounce the persecution raised against us, proceeding from these as their cause? Especially as the confusion of the empire, which prevailed to a great extent, did not cease before the Christians received full liberty of conscience to profess their religion—THE ECCLESIASTICAL HISTORY, by EUSEBIUS, written about 300 A.D. and translated by Christian Frederick Cruse, 1850. Above taken from recent publication by Baker Book House, Grand Rapids 6, Mich.

CHAPTER II

NETHERLANDS, GERMANY, SWITZERLAND—ANABAPTIST MARTYRS

(Cook's Story of the Baptists, 1889)

There were many Anabaptists, who suffered for the Truth's sake at the hands of Papists and Protestants in the Netherlands, Germany and Switzerland. In the **Martyrs' Mirror,** and the **Baptist Martyrology,** there are hundreds of cases recorded.

In all of these places the persecutions were legalized both by civil enactment, and by ecclesiastical sanction. In Germany, the edict of King Ferdinand in 1527, death was the penalty for Anabaptism. The Emperor Charles V. caused them to be hunted down and put to death. In 1529, at the Diet of Spires, it was ordained that death should be visited upon every Anabaptist. There also met at Homberg in 1536, a Diet composed of the Reformers of Germany and their followers in church and state. Luther and Melancthon were among the number. That body sanctioned the punishment of Anabaptists, even by death, by the civil authorities.

At the beginning of the Reformation, the first to suffer martyrdom in Germany were Hans Koch, and Leonard Meyster, who were put to death at Augsburg in 1524. They were said to have been descendants of the Bohemian and Moravian Waldenses, and were placed at the head of the list of Anabaptist martyrs. Michael Satler, who had been a monk, was put to death in 1527, for uniting with the Anabaptists, and marrying a wife. He was executed in a most barbarous manner. His tongue was cut out, his flesh was torn with red hot pinchers and his body finally burned.

Leonard Schoener, a barefooted monk, growing disgusted with the hypocrisy and wantonness of the monastic orders, became an Anabaptist under the ministry of Hubmeyer. He was an educated man. Having preached throughout Bavaria, he was beheaded, and then burnt at Rottenburg, in 1528.

Hans Schloffer was tortured with great cruelty, and questioned by the priest upon the subject of infant baptism. He answered, "that we must first preach the Word, and baptize those only who hear, understand, and believe and receive it. This is true Christian baptism and no infant baptism. The Lord has nowhere commanded to baptize infants."

At Alzey there was a wholesale slaughter of Anabaptists in 1529. Three hundred and fifty were confined in prison and literally dealt out to the executioner like sheep to the slaughter, as fast as the executioner could dispatch them. In whose body, then, was the cruel soul of Nana Sahib? Those who were their turn to die, sang until the executioner came for them. It was at this same place—Alzey—that nine brethren and three sisters were imprisoned, and when they refused to renounce their faith, were put to death, the men by the sword and the women by drowning.

A sister came to comfort the female prisoners while they were yet in prison and exhorted them to be true and firm, despite their sufferings, and for the sake of the eternal joy to come to them. For this visit—for comforting and strengthening these suffering saints—she was burned to death.

Two young girls were arrested at Bamberg, shortly after their baptism, and after being cruelly tortured to make them recant, were burned to death. While going to the stake their tormentors put upon their heads, in derision, crowns of twisted straw, when one of the girls said to her companion; "Our Saviour wore a crown of thorns for us, and shall not we wear these harmless crowns for Him?

and, besides, we shall soon be crowned by Him with glorious crowns of gold."

Among many Christians condemned to be burned at Saltzburg, there was a young and beautiful girl of sixteen. Even the hearts of her persecutors were moved, and after vainly trying to persuade her to recant, the executioner took her in his arms to a trough for watering horses, that was near by, and thrusting her head under the water, held it there until she was dead.

Wolfgang Brand-Hueber was an Anabaptist preacher, who was put to death at Lintz. This was one hundred years before Roger Williams' celebrated proclamation of civil and religious liberty in Rhode Island, and yet this martyr expressed the same sentiments when he taught that obedience and submission should be rendered to magistrates in all things not contrary to God. And to this day, there is not full liberty in Germany for our brethren (1889).

The Anabaptists appeared in Switzerland in 1523. According to Erasmus, they were numerous there in 1529. (Cook quotes here from Orchard's History of Foreign Baptists, page 346.) They suffered there at the hands of the Reformed. The first decree against them imposing a fine, was passed by the senate at Zurich, one of the cantons, in 1525. In 1526, another decree was passed, making the penalty for Anabaptism—death. It forbade believer's baptism, and compelled the baptism of infants. And these laws were made with the full approbation of the reformers, who were intensely active in securing their execution. And yet, Bullinger, one of the reformers, testifies; "for the people said, 'Let others say what they will of the dippers, we see in them nothing but what is excellent, and hear from them nothing else but that we should not swear, or do wrong to any one, that every one ought to do what is right, that every one must live Godly and holy lives. We see no wickedness in them'" (Martyrology).

Still, for a long period, the persecutions continued throughout all Switzerland, which so far from checking Anabaptism, seemed to stimulate its growth. It was either, go to the reformed church, or die. They preferred death.

Here are a few instances of the many. Balthazar Hubmeyer was one of the most distinguished Anabaptists who felt the severity of the laws and the persecuting spirit of the Swiss reformers. Hubmeyer was a learned and eloquent Catholic priest, and was called Doctor, by the Romanists. He was born in Bavaria in 1480. In 1516, we find him preaching in the cathedral at Ratisbon to great crowds of people, at which time he began to take sides with the reformers, preaching against many Romish errors.

He soon fully embraced the Reformed doctrines and practices, and became the friend of the Swiss reformers, and with Zwingle, lived in the most intimate intercourse. He had translated the Gospel and the Epistles into the language of the German people, to whom he also now preached the Gospel. He came, finally, to regard infant baptism as a popular error and renounced it. After pleading in vain with his friend Zwingle, and his associates to do the same, he was baptized, with over one hundred others, by William Roubli.

Hubmeyer, himself, soon after baptized three hundred upon profession of their faith. He was seized and imprisoned at Zurich. It was said by his enemies that he recanted, but on one occasion when a large concourse of people were collected in the great church by the leaders, and Zwingle and his companions were there to hear the recantation, he disappointed them. They waited in breathless silence to hear him condemn Anabaptism. When he did break the silence with his voice, it was to reassert that infant baptism was without the authority of God. His voice was drowned in the uproar of the horrified people, and above the din was heard the voice of Zwingle. They had argued with him in prison, and (these Protestant reformers) had even applied the tortures of the rack, to convince him that he was wrong, but he would not deny the truth, so he was hurried back to prison.

It is said that he made a recantation afterwards, and was released from prison, but he was still confined to the city of Zurich, from which he soon escaped. He was not long allowed the liberty of preaching Christ, for he was again arrested, and taken to Vienna, where he was burned to death, March 10, 1528; and at the same time his devoted wife was drowned in the Danube, by the same unpitying hands. His last words were; "With joy I die that I may come to the Lamb of God, that taketh away the sin of the world." His wife urged him to constancy. He has left many writings to live after him.

Previous to the execution of Hubmeyer, Felix Mantz, a native of Zurich was drowned at that city. This was in 1527. Like Hubmeyer, he was at one time a friend of the Swiss reformers, but when he began to preach to crowds upon the unscripturalness of infant baptism and an unregenerated church membership, and to baptize believers, he was imprisoned by them. His last words were, "Into thy hands, O Lord, I commend my spirit."

Louis Hetzer was another intimate friend of Zwingle, until he adopted Anabaptist principles. He translated a portion of the Scriptures. He was beheaded at Constance in 1529. His death was glorious. Even his enemies were surprised at his calmness, his charity, his courage, his faith, and remarked, never was there such a death seen at Constance. Many more cases of oppression and cruelty could be related. The effort was to exterminate. Even as late as 1671, seven hundred persons, homeless and destitute, were driven out of Berne. Great was the suffering of old and young.

From Switzerland, the Anabaptists fled in great numbers to the Netherlands, to escape persecution. Previously (1510) great numbers passed into Holland and the Netherlands and coalesced with the Dutch Baptists. Papist and Protestants persecuted them as elsewhere (Orchard's History Foreign Baptists, page 330). The Emperor Charles V. (1535), his son and successor, Phillip II. of Spain (1556) issued their imperial bloody edicts, against them, and the terrible Spanish Inquisition was brought, at length, to help the magistrate to discover and punish the so-called heresy.

The Lord soon raised up for them, in the country of their adoption, a leader in Menno Simon, from whom they have been given the name of Mennonites, and by whose labors they were greatly increased in numbers. He was born in the year 1492, at Witmarsum, Friesland. He was, at first, a Catholic priest and preached in his native village, was a man of great ability, and, evidently, of extensive learning. He was then ignorant of the Scriptures, however, and knew nothing of experimental religion. When first awakened to the errors of popery, and upon searching, was unable to find infant baptism in the Scriptures; he went to Luther and to other reformers for conference, but they gave him no light. He united with an Anabaptist church in 1536, and retired from public life, but his brethren, recognizing his humility and talents, brought him forward as a leader and teacher among them. At their earnest solicitation, and his own feeling: "Woe is me, if I preach not the gospel," he gave himself up to the work of the Gospel ministry, knowing full well that bonds and imprisonments awaited him.

"From the commencement of his ministry among the German Anabaptists, to the end of his days, that is, during the space of twenty-five years, he traveled from one country to another, with wife and children, exercising his ministry under pressures and calamities of various kinds, that succeeded each other without interruption, and constantly exposed to the danger of falling a victim to the severity of the laws. East and West Friesland, together with the province of Groningen, were first visited by this zealous apostle of the Anabaptists; from thence he directed his course into Holland, Gelderland, Brabant, and Westphalia, continued it through the German provinces that lie on the coast of the Baltic sea, and penetrated as far as Lavonia. In all these places his ministerial labors were attended with remarkable success, and a large number of believers were added to the church. Hence, he is deservedly looked upon as the common chief of almost all the Anabaptists, and the parent of that body that still subsists under that denomination. The success of this missionary will not appear surprising to those who are acquainted with his character, his spirit and talents, and who have a just notion of the condition of the Anabaptists at the period of time now under consideration" (Moshiem).

The martyrdom of Sicke Snyder was the means of awakening Menno, himself. He was beheaded in Lewarden, in 1531. The constancy of this man to his views of believer's baptism, preferring even an ignominious death to renouncing his sentiments, led Menno to inquire into the subject of baptism. Menno could not find infant baptism in the Bible; and on consulting a minister of that persuasion, a concession was made that it had no foundation in the Bible. Not willing to yield, he consulted celebrated reformers, but all these he found to be at variance, as to the grounds of the practice, consequently he became confirmed that the Baptists were suffering for truth's sake. In studying the Word, convictions of sinfulness, and of his lost condition became deepened; and he found God required sincerity and decision. He now sought new spiritual friends, and found some with whom he, at first, privately associated, but afterwards became one of their community (Orchard, page 342).

In 1539, when pursued by enemies, Menno took refuge in the house of his friend and brother Tiaert Keynerts. Menno escaped but his friend was arrested. It was a capital offence to give shelter to a heretic, in those days. He was cruelly tortured to make him reveal where Menno was concealed, but he refused to tell, and died for his brother. In 1543, Menno was hunted through all West Friesland and a price was set on his head. Even malefactors and murderers were offered pardon, the freedom of the country, the favor of the emperor, and a hundred carlgulden to deliver him to the criminal judge. On one occasion, a traitor had promised, for a certain sum of money, to deliver him to his enemies. He tried to betray him at a meeting, but Menno escaped in a wonderful manner. Not long after, the traitor with an officer, and in search of Menno, passed him in a boat in a canal. The traitor said not a word, but let him pass on to some distance, and escape upon shore. Then he exclaimed, "The bird has escaped us." "Why," said the officer, "did you not inform us?" "I could not speak," said the man, "for my tongue was tied." Whereupon the officer, calling him a villian, severely punished him.

By the kind intervention of Providence, he was permitted to escape the vigilance of his pursuers and finally, to die in peace. A kind nobleman, the Lord of Fresenberg, Holstein, beholding the sufferings of the Anabaptists, and observing the true nobility of their character, invited them to settle upon his estates, where he would extend to them his protection. Many accepted his generous offer, and before long whole churches were living there in prosperity and peace. Here, Menno lived the latter part of his life, sending into the countries around the written word of life, and here he died, January 13, 1559.

Anneken Von de Hove was an Anabaptist and was buried alive at Brussels, in 1597. The high court, in company with some Jesuits, (members of the so-called Catholic Society of Jesus,) went with her to the hole dug outside the city. When they had covered her lower extremeties with earth, the Jesuits called upon her to recant. She refused to deny her Lord, so the work went on, they still calling upon her to renounce her faith, until they threw the earth upon her face, and heaped it over her head and finally with deadly hate stamped upon it with their feet.

The time came, however, when civil and religious liberty was granted the Anabaptists in the Netherlands. They found a friend in William, Prince of Orange, "the glorious founder of Belgic liberty" (Mosheim's history). "He resolutely stood out against all meddling with men's consciences, or inquiring into their thoughts. While smiting the Spanish Inquisition into the dust, he would have no Calvinistic Inquisition set up in its place. Earnestly a convert to the reformed religion, but hating and denouncing only what was corrupt in the ancient church, he would not force men, with fire and sword, to travel to heaven upon his own road."—Motley's Rise of the Dutch Republic, II. pages 362, 206.—Above taken from Cook's Story of the Baptists, pages 59-70.

CHAPTER III

ENGLAND—THE REFORMATION

John Marsh gives the following information—

The reformation in England, being little besides a transfer of supreme power from the Pope to the king, left the nation still groaning under the monstrous corruptions of popery; so that the history of this church presents a long and hard struggle between such as wished for a thorough reform, and the friends of the papacy. Henry VIII, was a monarch of violent passions. He had broken from the Pope; but he was determined to be Pope in his own dominions, and, whether right or wrong, would be obeyed. Fortunately for the cause of truth he elevated to the See of Canterbury, Thomas Cranmer, a man of great learning and sound judgment, of a calm temper and an honest heart; whose mind rapidly opened to the doctrines of the Bible, and which, for many years, he most ably defended.

The language of Wickliff's version of the New Testament, which had been made one hundred and fifty years antecedent to this period, had become obsolete and was moreover a prohibited book, so that the nation were really without the Scriptures. But one William Tyndall, impressed with the immense importance of a free circulation of the Bible, in the language of the day, retired, for security, to the continent, where he translated the New Testament into English. An edition was printed at Antwerp, with short comments, and sent to England, for distribution, in 1526. But its circulation was violently opposed by the papists, and prohibited by the bishops as infected with heresy; and Tonstel, bishop of London, had the edition privately purchased and publicly burnt at Cheapside. This event was far from being unfavorable; for with the money for which Tyndall sold his books, he was enabled to print, in 1534, a more correct version; and the very act of conflagration, excited great displeasure, and a spirit for reading the Scriptures, which nothing could suppress. Many who dispersed this hated book, and many who preached and avowed its doctrines, were brought before the bishop's courts, and condemned to the flames. Tyndall himself was villaincusly betrayed at Brussels; and first strangled at the stake and then burnt. He expired, praying, "Lord, open the king of England's eyes."

Cranmer, assisted by the new queen, Ann Boleyn, endeavored to stop the persecutions in England; but the king had written in defence of the Romish faith, and had too much pride to renounce his opinions, and was violently pressed to what he still believed to be duty, by the Duke of Norfolk, Gardiner, bishop of Winchester, and the greater part of the clergy.

Convinced that there could be no reformation without the Scriptures, Cranmer prevailed upon the king, in 1534, to order a translation of the Bible by some learned men, which should be printed and put into the hands of the people. It was a great point gained. The work was committed to nine eminent scholars; and when finished, was sent to Paris to be printed. The next year, Miles Coverdale, an associate of Tyndall, printed at Zurich the whole Bible in English; which immediately received the royal sanction, and was placed, by the king's orders, in every parish church in the kingdom. Cranmer's Bible was no sooner printed, than it was seized by the inquisitors and committed to the flames. The printers fled to London with the presses, and few copies that were saved, where it was re-printed and offered by royal decree for sale to all the king's subjects. But so small was the number of the people that could read, that the edition of only 600 copies was not wholly sold off in three years.

The royal decree exceedingly grieved the papal clergy;

but the people received the Bible with great joy. Multitudes continually flocked to the churches to hear portions of the Scriptures from those who could read. Cranmer's heart was filled with gladness at this "day of reformation," which he concluded was now risen in England since the light of God's word did shine over it without a cloud.

The next thing to which Cranmer directed his attention, was the suppression of the monasteries. These gave law to the learning and religion of the nation; and while they remained, ignorance and superstition would brood over the land. Henry at once coincided with the views of Cranmer, as the monks were all his enemies, and would not acknowledge his supremacy, and he could fill his empty coffers from their vast funds. In 1535, commenced their visitation; the object of which was to expose their iniquities. They were required to acknowledge the king's supremacy, and to pursue a holy course. In both they were condemned. Indeed their vices are not to be named. 375 of the lesser convents were dissolved. Henry acquired 10,000L. in plate and moveables, and a clear yearly revenue of 30,000L.; above 10,000 persons were cast upon the world. Pleased with the result, the profligate monarch proceeded to lay hands on the large religious houses; the people being quieted with the declaration, that they would never again be burdened with taxes, for the revenue obtained would support 40 earls, 60 barons, 8000 knights, and 40,000 soldiers; make provision for the poor, and support the preachers of the Gospel. All this might have been done, so immensely rich had the monks become, but Henry squandered the money among his favorites.

In the suppression of the monasteries, their relics were all brought forth, and made the objects of ridicule and scorn. Abominable frauds were exposed. A vial which was said to contain our Saviour's blood, which could be seen only by the righteous, and which had long been venerated, was exhibited and found to be thick and opaque on the side held to sinners, and transparent on the opposite. An image which has been a favorite object of pilgrimage, because it moved its head and feet, was taken to pieces, and its mechanism was exposed to the people in church, by the bishop of Rochester. The shrine of Becket was the most profitable in England. It received annually over 1000L. An immense sum at that age. Henry unsainted and unshrined him, and ordered his name to be struck from the calendar and his bones to be burnt.

The Pope could not now restrain his anger. Henry was excommunicated, and his kingdom laid under an interdict; but the days of John were passed away. Henry regarded it as the idle wind.

A rebellion broke out among the papists in England. A hundred thousand collected in Yorkshire, under one Aske, and called their march the pilgrimage of grace. This encouraged risings in other parts of the country. But they were suppressed by the royal armies.

The king had filled his coffers by exterminating monasteries, relics, and images,—but he adhered rigorously to transubstantiation, and committed to the flames such as denied it. In this, Cranmer, who had not as yet gained light, coincided with him. But in 1539, to his great grief, six popish articles, establishing transubstantiation, purgatory, the celibacy of priests and auricular confession, were enacted in Parliament, and the papal cause gained a temporary triumph. Five hundred persons were committed to prison, and numbers to the flames. Cranmer came near falling a sacrifice. The king suffered him to be summoned before the council to be tried for his life, but he had a secret affection for him, and he gave him his sealed ring to present to them, should they go to extremities. This alone saved him.

At this critical moment, Henry died, A.D. 1547, cursed by the papists and abhorred by the Protestants. He was succeeded by Edward VI.; a prince only nine years of age, but remarkably mature and eminently devoted to the service of God, and the cause of the reformation. He lived but six years from this time; but he did every thing that he was able to do in so short a period, for the deliverance of his dominions from the corruptions of popery, and to bring his subjects to the knowledge of the truth. His religious principles were Calvinistic. Geneva was acknowledged as a sister church; but he adhered to the Episcopal form which had been established. He had a liturgy prepared for the people, that prayers to the saints, and lying legends, might cease; articles of religion framed, corresponding to those of Calvin; all laws and canons requiring celibacy in the clergy, repealed; auricular confession abolished; and he invited eminent reformers from the continent, particularly Martyr, Bucer, Fagius and Ochinus, to reside in his dominions, that they might aid in enlightening his people. Farther he would have proceeded if he could. In his diary, he laments "that he could not restore the primitive discipline according to his heart's desire, because several of the bishops were unwilling to it."

In his reign the doctrine of transubstantiation was fully discussed, and renounced, by Cranmer, Ridley, and Latimer, the three principal reformers. But Cranmer still thought it right to burn for heretical opinions, and had Joan of Kent, a fanatical anabaptist, brought to the flames, though Edward signed the commission with tears, saying that the archbishop must answer for it. Van Paris, a Dutchman, was afterwards burnt for being an Arian.

The reformers made merciless destruction of the wealth of churches and monasteries, and in many cases exceedingly enriched themselves. The Catholics rose in many parts of the country, and threatened the entire subversion of the government, but were subdued. They had a warm friend in Mary, the sister of the king, who contrived to have mass in her house, and was a rallying point to all who were friendly to the old religion.

This violent Catholic succeeded her brother. It was a mysterious providence. Edward had willed the crown to the Lady Jane Grey, a Protestant; but Mary the lawful heir, was immediately received by the people. Her mind was superstitious and melancholy. She had always hated the reformed religion, and she was resolved to bring the nation back to the church of Rome.

On the 8th of August, 1553, king Edward was buried. Cranmer read the Protestant service; but he felt it to be the burial of the reformation. The Catholics throughout the kingdom, set up their forms of worship without waiting for a repeal of the laws of king Edward. Bonner, Gardiner and others, who had formerly been removed from the bishoprics, were restored. All preaching was prohibited except such as received the queen's license. The reformers were driven with great insolence from their pulpits. All the marriages of the clergy were declared null, and their children were pronounced illegitimate. Gardiner, bishop of Winchester, a man who would have held the first rank among the Spanish inquisitors, was made Lord chancellor. All the laws of king Edward relating to religion, were repealed; and the ancient service was re-established. The queen expressed her desire to the Pope that England might again be received as a faithful daughter of the church, and that Cardinal Pool might be sent from Rome with legatine power.

These various proceedings taught the reformers that they had nothing to expect but death, in its most horrid forms. Many of them fled into Scotland, Switzerland, and Germany. Cranmer was advised to escape, as it was supposed that he would be the first victim; but he refused, saying it ill became him to quit the station in which providence had placed him at an early period, he and Latimer were sent to the tower. He was greatly beloved, and it was feared by many, that violence toward him would arouse the people. But the queen and his relentless enemies were bent on his destruction. Gardiner, however, fearing that Pool would succeed him in office, protracted that event as long as possible.

To strengthen herself, Mary united in marriage with Philip, son of the Emperor Charles V., sent Elizabeth, her sister, afterward queen, to prison, and brought the Lady Jane Grey to the block. Jane was an eminently pious woman, of whom the world was not worthy. She rejoiced, she said, at her "approaching end, since nothing could be to her more welcome than to be delivered from that valley of misery, into that heavenly throne to which she was to be advanced." She repeated the fifty-first psalm, laid her head upon the block, and said, "Lord Jesus, into thy hand I commend my spirit."

To give the papal cause the appearance of justice and moderation, a public disputation was held at Oxford, in the spring of 1554, between the leading divines on both sides. Three questions were discussed, viz.; whether the natural body of Christ was really in the sacrament? Whether any other substance remained besides the body and blood of Christ? Whether, in the mass, there was a propitiatory sacrifice for the dead and living? Cranmer, Ridley, and Latimer, spoke for the reformed with great boldness and power. But they were declared vanquished, required to subscribe to the popish faith, and on refusal, were pronounced obstinate heretics, and excluded from the church.

In the succeeding summer, the bishops performed their visitations, and saw that the Catholic religion was fully established. Such priests as conformed, were anointed and clothed with priestly vestments. Above twelve thousand who refused, were ejected, and the most eminent were imprisoned. In November, sanguinary laws were passed in Parliament, and persecution began.

The first martyr was John Rogers. He had been a fellow laborer of Tyndall and Coverdale, in translating the Bible, and was now prebendary of S. Paul. He had a wife and ten children with whom he wished to speak, but was not permitted. He was burned at Smithfield, Feb. 4, 1555. His wife, with her ten children, one hanging at the breast, was a spectator of the scene.

The next was Lawrence Saunders. He was burnt at Coventry. He embraced the stake, exclaiming, "Welcome, cross of Christ! welcome, everlasting life!" The third was Hooper, bishop of Gloucester, the most laborious and popular preacher of the day. He had once fled from the persecution of Henry to Zurich, but returned on the accession of Edward. He had there imbibed some presbyterian principles, and refused to be consecrated in the episcopal vestments; but finally conformed. When he left Zurich, he anticipated martyrdom. "The last news of all," said he to his friends, "I shall not be able to write, for there where I shall take most pains, there you shall hear of me burned to ashes." He was again advised to flee, but refused. When he and Rogers were brought out of prison for examination, the sheriff found it difficult to conduct them through the streets, so great was the press to see them. They were men greatly beloved and respected. That the effect might be the greater, he was sent to his own diocess to be burnt there. On the 9th of February, he was bound to the stake. The fire consumed him but slowly. One hand was seen to drop off before he expired. His last words were, "Lord Jesus, receive my spirit." An immense crowd of people were witnesses of the horrid scene. He was the great father of the puritans.

The same day, Dr. Rowland Taylor was burnt at Hadley; and in the month of March, a number of others were burnt at Smithfield. The effect of these dreadful scenes was very different from what the papists expected. Gardiner supposed that two or three burnings would extirpate Protestantism from England. But the blood of the martyrs was again the seed of the church. The reformers stood firm to their cause, and glorified in their sufferings for Christ. The nation became exasperated. Philip openly disavowed them, and they were stopped for a time.

The prisons were crowded with the ablest and best men of England, and were, in fact, the best Christian schools and churches. There religious instruction was constantly imparted, and prayer and praise were offered.

In the month of June, the business of burning recommenced. The dead body of a robber who had on the scaffold uttered something true, was condemned and burnt. John Bradford, a preacher in London, was a distinguished victim. When in prison, a recantation was sent to him; and when he had heard it, he asked for his condemnation, pricked his hand and sprinkled upon the bill his blood, bidding them carry it to the bishop, and tell him he had already sealed it with his blood. "He endured the flame as a fresh gale of wind on a hot summer's day," and exclaimed in the fire, "Straight is the way, and narrow is the gate that leadeth to salvation, and few there be that find it." Through the months of July, August, and September, numbers were burnt at several places. Six were burnt in one fire in Canterbury. On the 16th of October, two distinguished victims were sacrificed at Oxford, Ridley and Latimer. The former was one of the most able and learned of English reformers; the latter was a man of great simplicity of character, of wit and boldness, who by his preaching had done more than almost any man to expose the follies of popery, and sustain the truth. When he was burnt, he was 84 years of age. He had suffered much from cold damps of his prison, and hard treatment, and had very decrepid appearance. He came before the council, "hat in hand, with a handkerchief bound round his head, and over it a night cap or two, with a great cap, such as townsmen used in those days, with two broad flaps to button under the chin. His dress was a gown of Bristol frieze, old and threadbare, fastened round the body with a penny leathern girdle; his Testament was suspended from his girdle by a leathern string, and his spectacles without a case, were hanging from his neck upon his breast." Ridley wrote several valuable epistles to his friends and countrymen during his imprisonment, which still remain. After his condemnation he was publicly degraded from his office. They were led out together to the place of death, which was near Baliol College. They embraced each other, and knelt and prayed. A short sermon was preached to mock them. And when the fire was brought, the venerable old man said, "Be of good courage, master Ridley, and play the man. We shall this day light such a candle, by God's grace, in England, as I trust shall never be put out." Bags of gun powder were tied about their bodies to hasten their death. Latimer soon yielded to the flames, but Ridley suffered a tedious martyrdom.

No sooner was the vengeance of the odious Gardiner glutted with the death of these excellent men, than he was called to give up his account. His last words were, "I have sinned with Peter, but I have not wept with Peter." Bonner had already been active in the bloody work, and was ready to continue it. Three were burnt at one stake in Canterbury, in November, and on the 18th of December, Philpot, archdeacon of Westminster, suffered at Smithfield. "I will pay my vows," said this excellent man, "in thee, O Smithfield." Sixty-seven had this year been burnt for their attachment to the Protestant cause.

But the great object of the queen's vengeance still remained. This was Cranmer. No sooner had this great and good man discerned the course which was to be taken, than he settled all his private affairs, that he might be prepared for the worst. His confinement was long, and no means were spared to convert him to the Romish faith. On September 12th, 1525, commissioners were sent by the queen to Oxford, to try him. Cranmer defended himself with meekness and learning. He was commanded to appear before the Pope at Rome in eighty days. This he said he would do if the queen would send him. But it was done in mockery; and before the term expired, he was degraded from his office. Clothed with vestments of rags and canvass, with a mock mitre and pall, he was publicly exhibited. The utmost efforts were again made to induce him to recant; and alas! Peter like, he finally yielded, and set his hand to a paper, renouncing the principles of the reformation, and acknowledging the authority or the papal church. The Catholics triumphed in his fall. But they had no idea of sparing his life. The queen could not forgive the man who advised to Henry's divorce from her mother. A writ was issued for burning, and he was brought to St. Marie's church and placed on a platform. Cole, provost of Eaton, preached a sermon in which he announced that Cranmer was to die, and magnified his conversion as the work of God, and assured him of the salvation of his soul. Cranmer discovered great confusion, and frequently shed floods of tears. When Cole had finished, he bade him disclose his faith. Cranmer prayed and addressed the people; repeated the apostles' creed, and declared his faith in the holy Scriptures. He then turned to that which troubled his conscience more than anything else, his recantation—declared it was drawn from him by the fear of death; had filled his soul with the deepest sorrow, and was most bitterly repented of; and that the hand which had done it should burn first in the fire. The papists were thrown into confusion, gnashed on him with their teeth, and drew him to the stake, where Ridley and Latimer had been burned. When the fire was kindling, he stretched forth his right hand to the flame, never moving it until it was burnt away. As the flames gathered around his body, he exclaimed often, "That unworthy hand—Lord Jesus, receive my spirit." Thus died one of the greatest promoters of the reformation, March 21st, 1556, in the 67th year of his age. But it was a martyrdom most injurious to the Romish cause. It was a direct breach of promise. The sympathy of thousands was awakened by his repentance, and his calm patient endurance of torment.

For two years more, the persecution continued with unabated fury. Bonner scorned to burn men singly and drove them in companies to the stake. The bodies of Bacer and Fagius were dug up, and with their books, were publicly burnt. But the reformers increased. They assembled together secretly for consultation and prayer. They afforded relief to those in prison, and buried the bodies of such as died there and were cast out in disgrace.

At length, to extirpate the hated religion entirely, the king and queen resolved upon the introduction of the Inquisition, with all its horrors. But England was happily preserved from this by the death of Mary, on the 17th of November, 1558.

The Irish Protestants escaped her vengeance through a singular providence. Their number had become great, through the energetic proceedings of George Brown, whom Henry VIII. had created archbishop of Dublin, and Mary had resolved to extirpate them by flame. But while her messenger was on his way with the bloody commission, the wife of an inkeeper, hearing him say that he had a commission which would lash the Protestants of Ireland, and being friendly to them, contrived to steal away his commission, and put in its place a pack of cards. When the commissioner arrived in Dublin, he opened his commission in presence of the public authorities, and, to his confusion, found nothing but the cards; and before he could get a renewal of the commission, the queen was dead, and God's people escaped. Queen Elizabeth was so pleased with the tale that she conferred upon the woman forty pounds a year for life.

No one can contemplate this dark period of England's history without feelings of horror at its bloody scenes, and gratitude for the blessings we enjoy. Two hundred and eighty-eight persons, including twenty clergymen, of whom five were bishops, were burnt alive; many were deprived of means of subsistence, imprisoned, tortured, scourged, placed in the most painful posture, until they expired under their accumulated sufferings. An immense amount of wealth was sacrificed, and the spirit and character of the nation was sunk very low. But it was a fiery trial, through which it seemed necessary for the nation to pass. She had given strength to the beast. Though reformed under Henry and Edward, she had not been weaned. This day of persecution made her heartily sick of popery. No one mourned the death of Mary. Every one hailed the accession of Elizabeth and the restoration of the Protestant religion.

Elizabeth had been singularly preserved from the merciless fangs of Gardiner and Bonner. She began to reign at the age of twenty-four, and governed England forty-five years, with an energy, sagacity, and prudence, of which few monarchs can boast. During her reign, Protestantism was firmly established in her dominions, and favored and supported by her in other parts of Europe.

On her way to London she was greeted by thousands, and as the bishops and clergy came around her to congratulate her, she smiled upon all, except Bonner, from whom she turned in indignation, as a man of blood. At her coronation, as she passed under a triumphal arch, an English Bible was let down into her hands, by a child representing truth, which she received with reverence, accounting it the most valuable gift that could be bestowed.

No sooner was her accession known, than all who had

fled into foreign countries returned. The papists had flattered themselves that they had at least extinguished the light of the reformation; but, to their astonishment, a great body of learned and pious men came forth, who in exile or concealment, had made themselves well acquainted with the word of God. Elizabeth filled the vacant Sees with Parker, Grindall, Cox, Sands, Jewel, Parkhurst, Pilkington, and others, who proved great ornaments to the British nation. She re-established kind Edward's service in all the churches, and forbade the priests to elevate the host at mass, but she would use no violence. Such papists as chose, she permitted to retire beyond the seas. Such as retired from the priest's office, she pensioned. Of these, the number was small; the papists thinking it better for their own cause to acknowledge the queen's supremacy, than refuse and quit the kingdom. Out of nine thousand and four hundred beneficed men, only fourteen bishops and one hundred and seventy-five others resigned their livings. The others remained in the church, "a miserable set of weather-cocks." The monks returned to secular life, and the nuns went to France and Spain. Bonner maintained his sullen temper, refused to submit to the queen, was committed to prison, where he died. Elizabeth was in favor of images in the churches, but so did the clergy oppose them, that she gave orders to have them all taken down. The Bible was translated anew, and published in 1571. The articles of religion received by king Edward, were revised and adopted, leaving the doctrine of the real presence untouched, and the English establishment was settled nearly upon its present form.—Epitome of General Ecclesiastical History, Marsh, 1841, 6th Edition.

CHAPTER IV

GERMANY AND FRANCE—
LUTHER AND OTHER REFORMERS

Martin Luther is generally looked upon as the man who first opposed the popes, and gave rise to the Reformation. However, before Luther there were men who raised their voices against the corruptions of the Catholic church. A few names stand out as leaders in the revolt that gave birth to the Reformation, and Luther is foremost.

It is to be observed that many of these men who broke with Rome did so on only a few points. Luther died with much Catholicism still in him. But these men did break the fetters of Catholicism which, until then, held men so hard. Immediately there sprang out from their hiding Baptists, by various names, who had been hunted, and when found, put to death. One historian says they sprang up at once in every country. The reason is obvious. They did not start then, they were already in existence. They merely came out of hiding.

Luther himself had no use for Baptists, even after he renounced Catholicism. He despised them. We quote from Orchard, pages 345-346:

"When some of Luther's assistants went into Moravia, they complained, that between Baptists and papists (note that Baptists were already on the scene—WJB) they were very much straightened, though they grew among them as lilies among thorns. The success and number of the Baptists 'exasperated him to the last degree,' and he became their enemy, notwithstanding all he had said in favor of dipping (while he contended with Catholics on the sufficiency of God's Word); but now he persecuted them under the name of re-dippers, re-baptizers or Anabaptists.

"One thing troubled Luther, and he took no pains to conceal it; that was a jealousy lest any competitor should step forward, and put in execution that plan of reformation which he had laid out; this was his foible; he fell out with Carolostadt, he disliked Calvin, he found fault with Zuinglius, who were all supported by great patrons, and he was angry beyond measure with the Baptists. His half measures, his national system, his using the Roman liturgy, his consubstantiation, his infant baptism, without Scripture or example, were disliked by the Baptists—yea, the Picards or Vaudois hated his system; **and he hated all other sects.**

"The violence of Luther sunk his cause into that of a party. The reformers differed as widely among themselves about the ordinances, as they did from others: and their spirit of contention subsided into acts of persecution and reproach. But Moshiem remarks 'there were certain sects and doctors against whom the zeal, vigilance, and severity of Catholics, Lutherans (and Mosheim was a Lutheran—WJB), and Calvinists were united. The objects of their common aversion were the Anabaptists."

See Orchard's History for authorities he cites for the above, pages, 345, 346.

"They came into contact with the reformers everywhere. And they were reviled and persecuted by them all—by Lutherans, and Episcopalians, and Puritans, and Presbyterians. Even the Romanists did not denounce them so bitterly as did Melancthon and Luther, Calvin, and Zwingle, and Knox, Cranmer, and Ridley and Latimer."—Dr. Winkler, quoted by Graves in Old Landmarkism, What Is It?, page 176.

We desist here, though more could be quoted.

From another historian we learn that John Calvin was a persecutor.

"Michael Servetus, a Spanish physician, who had written against the doctrine of the Trinity, came to Geneva in

1553. Calvin caused him to be apprehended and brought before the senate. Being condemned as a heretic, Servetus appealed to the four Swiss churches. They approved of the sentence, and he was burnt October 27. Calvin wished to have the mode of his execution changed, **but he thought the sentence should be capital** (death)"—Epitome of Eccl. History by John Marsh, page 321.

Thus it is seen that when the Baptists came from their hiding from the bloody hands of the Catholics they were smitten by another foe, the Reformers.

The conclusion is obvious. Baptists were before the Reformation, and they go back to Christ. Protestantism today is yet no friend to real Baptists. They are forming an hierarchy in the National Council of churches that will formulate another "Act of Uniformity."

Rivers of blood have been spilled because Baptists would not conform to somebody's ritual or "sacrament." Their denial of infant baptism, "high church," popish authority, and human innovations in worship, have sent them to all manner of deaths. Will we see such again? Evidence now says, yes.

Baptists were persecuted by the very people who fled to America to escape persecution. They brought the spirit of their persecutors with them and used them against Baptists in their new home. We could fill pages in relating incidents of mistreatment Baptists suffered in the colonies alone. Benedict says:"

"With the catholics it was, the mass, or the musket— The full sacraments of the church, or tortures, gibbets and flames, Conformity, or death.

"With the church of England, it was the prayer book, or the prison, the whole service of her rubric, or the severest penalties of its laws. Submission, or Smithfield (burning at stake).

"With the Puritans (the rulers—WJB) it was, the meeting-house worship, or the custody of the jailor, parish rites, or stakes, stripes and confiscations, the **seal of the covenant,** or the statute of exile."

We do not want to be misunderstood. We do not refer

to persons, but to denominations. The driving force of ecumenicalism of the National Council of Churches, and other such movements, will array all Protestantism as such against real Baptists. It is to be expected that many with the Baptist name will join the ecumenical movement, but real Baptists, the kind that have come down from the days of Christ, will not. We face persecution, both from the Catholics and Protestants in the not very distant future. Perhaps many will not agree with this statement. I only ask that you wait and see.

Luther Disavows the Anabaptists

"These scenes were deeply painful to Luther. 'Satan,' said he, 'rages; we have need of your prayers. The new sectarians called Anabaptists, increase in number, and display great external appearances of strictness of life, as also great boldness in death, whether they suffer by fire or water.'

"While he detested their tubulence and pitied their delusion, he knew that the papists looked upon them as his followers, and upon him as the grand culprit; and that such proceedings, such cries, as 'No tribute, all things in common, no magistrates,' must alarm every ruler in Christendom, and make each consider the extinction of Lutheranism as essential to his safety.

"Luther was no fanatic. He had an enlightened and noble spirit. 'We differ,' said he, 'from these fanatics not merely in the article of baptism, but also in the general reason which they give for rejecting the baptism of infants. It was, say they, a practice under the papacy. Now we do not argue in that manner. **We allow that in the papacy are many good things, and all those good things we have retained.'**"—EPITOME OF GENERAL ECCL. HISTORY, By John Marsh.

Luther's treatment of the Anabaptists

The following condensed article on this subject, I have selected from Mr. Orchard's work on Foreign Baptists.

"The tones of authority assumed by Luther, and his

magisterial conduct towards those who differed from him, made it evident that he would be head of the reformers. He and his colleagues had now to dispute their way with hosts of Baptists all over Germany, Saxony, Thuringia, Switzerland, and other kingdoms, for several years. Conferences on baptism were held in different kingdoms, which continued from 1516 to 1527. The support which the baptists had from Luther's writings, made the reformers' efforts of little effect.

"At Zurich, the senate warned the people to desist from the practice of re-baptizing, but all their warnings were in vain. The efforts to check the increase of Baptists being ineffectual, carnal measures were selected. The first edict against anabaptism was published at Zurich in 1525, in which there was a penalty of a silver mark set upon all such as should suffer themselves to be re-baptized, or should withhold baptism from their children. And it was further declared that those who openly opposed this order, should be yet more severely treated. This being insufficient to check immersion, the senate decreed, like Honorius, in 413, that all persons who professed anabaptism, or harbored the professors of the doctrine, should be punished with death by drowning.

"It had been death to refuse baptism, and now it was death to be baptized; such is the weathercock-certainty of state religion. In defiance of this law, the Baptists persevered in their regular discipline; and some ministers of learned celebrity realized the severity of the sentence. Many Baptists were drowned and burnt. These severe measures, which continued for years, had the consent of the reformers, which injured greatly the Lutheran cause. It was the cruel policy of papacy, inflicted by brethren.

"Wherever the Baptists settled, Luther played the part of universal bishop. He wrote to princes and senates to engage them to expel such dangerous men; but it was their refusing to own his authority, and admit his exposition of the Scriptures, which led him to preach and publish books against them, taxing them with disturbing the peace. We have recorded that the Baptists were the common objects of aversion to Catholics, Lutherans, and Calvinists, whose united zeal was directed to their destruction.

"So deeply were the prejudices interwoven with the state party, that the knights, on oath, were to declare their abhorrence of anabaptism. The sentiments of these people, and which were so disliked by statesmen, clergy and reformers, may be stated under five views, viz.: A love of civil liberty in opposition to magisterial dominion; an affirmation of the sufficiency and simplicity of revelation, in opposition to scholastic theology; a zeal for self-government, in opposition to clerical authority; a requisition of the reasonable service of a personal profession of Christianity rising out of man's own convictions, in opposition to the practice of force on infants—the whole of which they deemed superstition, or enthusiasm; and the indispensable necessity of virtue in every individual member of a Christian church, in distinction from all speculative creeds, all rites and ceremonies, and parochial divisions.

"These views, to the statesman, were adverse to his line of policy with his peasants; to the clergy they were offensive, since it placed every man on a level with the priesthood, and sanctioned one to instruct another; to the reformers they were objectionable, since they broke the national tie, and allowed all persons equal liberty to think, choose, and act in the affairs of the soul; thus these sentiments were the aversion of all.

"An edict issued by Frederick, at a later period, shows how unpalatable these views were. His majesty expressed his astonishment at the number of anabaptists, and his horror at the principal error which they embraced, which was, that according to the express declaration of the holy scriptures (I Cor. vii, 23), they were to submit to no human authority. He adds, that his conscience compelled him to proscribe them, and accordingly be banished them from his dominions of pain of death."—A GENERAL HISTORY OF BAPTIST DENOMINATION, By David Benedict, page 81.

Calvin Agrees to Persecution

"At Geneva, Calvin's doctrine of decrees was openly condemned by Castalio, master of the public school, and Jerome Bolsec, a French monk. Both were banished from the city. Michael Servetus, a Spanish physician, who had written against the doctrine of the Trinity, came to Geneva in 1553. Calvin caused him to be apprehended and brought before the Senate. Being condemned as a heretic, Servetus appealed to the four Swiss churches. They approved of the sentence, and he was burnt, Oct. 27.

Calvin wished to have the mode of his execution changed, but he thought the sentence should be capital. It was the opinion of the age that erroneous religious principles should be capitally punished by the civil magistrate. A miserable way of opposing and subduing error. The severity of Calvin's doctrine and discipline, (for he not only excommunicated all the flagitious from the church, but even had them punished by the magistrate and banished from the city,) roused the resentment and malignity of the libertines of Geneva, who gave him perpetual trouble."
—EPITOME OF GENERAL ECCL. HISTORY, By Rev. John Marsh, page 321.

More About Calvin

"At this juncture John Calvin arrived. He was a Frenchman from Noyon, who had just published a remarkable book, **The Christian Institutes,** wherein he condemned everything which did not seem to him prescribed by the Gospel, while Luther, less audacious, allowed everything to subsist which did not appear to him positively contrary to it. The eloquence, the austerity of Calvin's life, and his radical doctrines gave him in Geneva an authority which he used to convert that joyous city into a somber cloister, where every frivolous word or deed was punished as a crime. A poet was beheaded for his verses. Michael Servetus was burned for having thought otherwise concerning the Trinity than his spiritual director. But none the less, Geneva became the citadel, and as it were the sanctuary of the Calvinistic Reformation."—Duruy's General History of The

World, pages 323-324. See also Rishell's History Christioniay, pages 273, 356.

Even John Fox, author of Fox's Book of Martyrs, thought Baptists should be punished in some way, though not by death.—Cook's Story of The Baptists, page 82.

Luther Throws Inkstand

Martin Luther, while detained in the Wartburg castle in Thuringia, near Eisenach, claimed to have had a vision of the devil, at whom he threw his inkstand. It struck the wall, and the ink spots were formerly exhibited but later covered with plaster, it is said. See Rishell, in his note on page 352.

This is very crazy behaviour for one who is hailed as the great reformer, but it is consistent with his other inconsistencies.

Zwingli a Persecutor

Zwingli, another early reformer, Switzerland, was also a persecutor of Baptists. See Armitage's History of the Baptists, pages 338, 350.

CHAPTER V

BOHEMIA—PERSECUTIONS

(By John Fox)

The emperor Ferdinand, whose hatred to the Bohemian Protestants was without bounds, not thinking he had sufficiently oppressed them, instituted a high court of reformers, upon the plan of the Inquisition, with this difference, that the reformers were to remove from place to place, and always to be attended by a body of troops.

These reformers consisted chiefly of Jesuits, and from their decision, there was no appeal, by which it may be easily conjectured, that it was a dreadful tribunal indeed.

This bloody court, attended by a body of troops, made the tour of Bohemia, in which they seldom examined or saw a prisoner, suffering the soldiers to murder the Protestants as they pleased, and then to make a report of the matter to them afterward.

The first victim of their cruelty was an aged minister, whom they killed as he lay sick in his bed; the next day they robbed and murdered another, and soon after shot a third, as he was preaching in his pulpit.

A nobleman and clergyman, who resided in a Protestant village, hearing of the approach of the high court of reformers and the troops, fled from the place, and secreted themselves. The soldiers, however, on their arrival, seized upon a schoolmaster, asked him where the lord of that place and the minister were concealed, and where they had hidden their treasures. The schoolmaster replied that he could not answer either of the questions.

They then stripped him naked, bound him with cords, and beat him most unmercifully with cudgels. This cruelty not extorting any confession from him, they scorched him in various parts of his body; when, to gain a respite from his torments, he promised to show him where the treasures were hid. The soldiers gave ear to this with pleasure, and the schoolmaster led them to a ditch full of stones, saying, "Beneath these stones are the treasures ye seek for." Eager after money, they went to work, and soon removed those stones, but not finding what they sought after, they beat the schoolmaster to death, buried him in the ditch, and covered him with the very stones he had made them remove.

Some of the soldiers ravished the daughters of a worthy Protestant before his face, and then tortured him to death. A minister and his wife they tied back to back and burnt. Another minister they hung upon a cross beam, and making a fire under him, broiled him to death. A gentleman they hacked into small pieces, and they filled a young man's mouth with gunpowder, and setting fire to it, blew his head to pieces.

As their principal rage was directed against the clergy, they took a pious Protestant minister, and tormenting him daily for a month together, in the following manner, making their cruelty regular, systematic, and progressive.

They placed him amidst them, and made him the subject of their derision and mockery, during a whole day's entertainment, trying to exhaust his patience, but in vain, for he bore the whole with true Christian fortitude. They spit in his face, pulled his nose, and pinched him in most parts of his body. He was hunted like a wild beast, until ready to expire with fatigue.

They made him run the gauntlet between two ranks of them, each striking him with a twig. He was beat with their fists. He was beat with ropes. They scourged him with wires. He was beat with cudgels. They tied him up by the heels with his head downwards, until the blood started out of his nose, mouth, etc. They hung him by the right arm until it was dislocated, and then had it set again. The same was repeated with his left arm. Burning papers dipped in oil were placed between his fingers and toes. His flesh was torn with red-hot pinchers. He was put to the rack. They pulled off the nails of his right hand. The same repeated with his left hand. He was bastinadoed on his feet. A slit was made in his right ear. The same repeated on his left ear. His nose was slit. They whipped him through the town upon an ass. They made several incisions in his flesh. They pulled off the toe nails of his right foot. The same they repeated with his left foot.

He was tied up by the loins, and suspended for a considerable time. The teeth of his upper jaw were pulled out. The same was repeated with his lower jaw. Boiling lead was poured upon his fingers. The same was repeated with his toes. A knotted cord was twisted about his forehead in such a manner as to force out his eyes.

During the whole of these horrid cruelties, particular care was taken that his wounds should not mortify, and not to injure him mortally until the last day, when the forcing out of his eyes proved his death.—FOX'S BOOK OF MARTYRS, pages 151-153.

CHAPTER VI

FRANCE—THE GREAT SLAUGHTER OF THE PROTESTANTS

(Dr. Brewer's History of France.)

The Huguenot leaders entrapped (1571, 1572). Almost immediately after peace was concluded for the third time, Charles IX. married Elisabeth of Austria; and from that moment, a deep-laid plot was devised for lulling the suspicion of the Protestants, and cutting them off by treachery.

In order to carry out the plot the more effectively, Catherine proposed a marriage between her daughter Marguerite and Henri of Navarre, the acknowledged chief of the Protestant faction. All the principal Huguenots were invited to the nuptials: Jeanne D'Albret (Dal-bray), the dowager queen of Navarre and mother of the bridegroom; Henri de Conde, son of the famous prince de Conde assassinated at the battle of Jarnac; the sire de Coligny, lord High Admiral of France; and many others.

The great Catholic leaders were also present; Henri de Guise; his brother the duc de Mayenne (My-yenn); the old cardinal de Lorraine, his uncle; and, of course, the two princes of the blood, Henri duc d'Anjou, and Francois duc d'Alencon, the king's brothers.

Henri de Guise, son of duke Francois, was the most popular young nobleman of the time. He was only 21 years old, but was the favourite leader of the Catholic faction.

During the lifetime of the great duke he was styled the

prince de Joinville (Zjwoin-veel), and made his military debut at the siege of Orleans under his father, who died in his arms, ascribing his death to the admiral de Coligny (Co-leen-ye). (Francois duc de Guise was killed by Poltrot de Mere, but affirmed, in his dying moments, that Coligny counselled the deed.)

The fiery young duke took a solemn oath, on the battle-field, to avenge his father's "murder" upon the admiral and all his family; and to persecute with relentless zeal the whole Huguenot party.

Such were the discordant elements brought together on this occasion. Persons who hated each other with mortal hatred, but, for the once, put on the semblance of courtly politeness and social friendship.

Scarcely had Jeanne d'Albret (Dal-bray) reached the Louvre, when she was suddenly taken ill, and died. It was generally believed, that she had been poisoned by a pair of gloves, presented to her by queen Catherine. Her death, however, did not interrupt the wedding, which was duly solemnized on the 18th of November, 1572.

The bridegroom, now king of Navarre since his mother's death, was just 19 years of age. His eyes were sharp and penetrating, his hair black and cropped, his eye-brows thick, his nose aquiline, and his beard beginning to sprout.

The bride was barely 20; the most beautiful and best educated woman of Europe. Her hair was black, complexion brilliant, eyes shaded with long dark lashes, mouth small and rosy, neck and figure extremely graceful, and feet tiny as a child's. She could read Greek with ease, and converse fluently in Latin, Italian, Spanish, and Portuguese.

There was much apparent congruity in this match: both bride and bridegroom were of royal birth, about the same age, possessed of noble forms and mental qualities of a very superior order; yet was the alliance productive of happiness to neither.

Both felt themselves sacrificed to state policy, and neither loved the other. In fact, Marguerite was in love with Henri of Guise, a married man; and the bridegroom with

Madame de Sauve, a married woman in the suite of the queen-mother.

The wedding was followed by several fete days, during which the Catholics showed the Huguenots most marked attention; but, as the ceremonies commenced with the death of Jeanne d'Albret (Dal-bray), the bridegroom's mother, it was brought to a close by an attempt to assassinate the sire de Coligny (Co-leen-ye):

As the old admiral was returning from the Louvre one night to his hotel, he was shot at by a man, from behind a grated window. The assassin was a servant of duke Henri's, and had been appointed by his master to way-lay the aged Huguenot. He was not killed, though he was severely wounded. The shot had fractured his arm, and blown off two fingers.

Catherine de Medicis (Med-e-cee) and the king expressed great concern at this outrage, and even went in person to visit the wounded admiral at his hotel. It is thought, however, that the whole proceeding was only a part of the plot shortly about to be carried into execution.

Orders were immediately issued to close the city gates, and allow no one, without a pass, to leave the city. This was done, ostensibly, to prevent the escape of the assassin, but, in reality, to prevent the exit of the Huguenots.

In the meantime, a most minute account was brought to the king of the name and abode of every Protestant in Paris. Everything looked suspicious, and hundreds were admitted to the secret, but the Huguenots were without suspicion. For two more days, all remained quiet; but it was the lull before the storm.

(Jeanne d'Albret (1530-1572) mother of Henri IV, was the daughter and successor of Henri d'Albret king of Navarre and Bearn. She married Antoine de Bourbon duc de Vendome, and remained queen for ten years after her husband's death. Jeanne introduced into her kingdom the reformed religion, and was one of the chief supporters of the Huguenot party.)

MASSACRE OF ST. BARTHOLOMEW (24th August 1572). At midnight, on the 24th of August, a bell in the tower of the royal palace gave the signal for a general massacre of all the Protestants in the city. The Swiss guard, the city militia, and all others officially employed in this nefarious slaughter, were distinguished by a scarf on their left arm, and a white cross on their hat.

At the first stroke of the bell, Henri de Guise, with a band of assassins, rushed to the hotel of Coligny (Co-leen-ye). He was not in bed, but was engaged in prayer. "Are you Coligny?" asked one of the duke's German servants. "Yes," replied the admiral, "but honour these grey hairs, young man." The ruffian made no reply, but plunged his sword into the old man's body; while the other assassins coming up dispatched him, and threw his carcase into the streets.

The head of the venerable reformer was lopped off, and carried as a trophy to the queen-mother, who caused it to be embalmed, and sent as a present to the sovereign pontiff. The trunk, after being dragged through the streets by the frantic mob, was suspended to a gibbet at Montfaucon (Mon-fo-kong), over a slow fire.

The city was filled with assassins. The Huguenots rushed half-naked into the streets, and perished by thousands. The young monarch, stationed at an open window in the Louvre, "amused himself" by firing at those who sought, in their terror, to cross the river. The butchery was horrible. Women and infants, the sick and the infirm, all were cut down without mercy. For three days and three nights the hunters of blood ceased not; and no fewer than 6000 persons were massacred in the city of Paris alone.

In the meantime, the provinces were summoned to a similar butchery; and Meaux (Mo), Angers (Arn-zja), Bourges (Boor-zj), Lyons, Toulouse, Orleans, and Rouen (Roo-on'g), gained to themselves an unenviable notoriety by the zeal with which they obeyed the summons.

Other governors, however, refused to publish the murderous edict; amongst which were those of Bayonne, Macon (Mar-kon), Burgundy, Provence (Pro-varnce), Dauphine (Do-fe-nay), and Auvergne (O-vairn). The answer of the Commandment of Bayonne was truly heroic: "Sire," wrote he to the king, "your majesty has in this good city many a loyal subject, and many a brave soldier, but one executioner."

The number that perished in this national massacre has been estimated at 50,000, some indeed swell the number to 80,000. Henry of Navarre and prince Conde escaped only by consenting, for the once, to attend mass in the chápel royal.

Of the Protestant leaders who perished, the chief were the venerable Coligny, his son-in-law Teligny, the young La Rochefoucauld, Caumont de la Force, de Guerchy, Antoine de Clermont, the Marquis de Renel, Pardaillan, and the captain de Piles.

The day after that called St. Bartholomew, the king went in state to Notre-dame to assist in a Te Deum or solemn service of thanksgiving. All the bells of the city rang joyous peals; but the massacre was going on, and still were heard the shrieks of the dying or roar of burning houses.

On the third day, with an immense retinue of ladies and cavaliers in their gayest costumes, Charles went to Montgaucon to visit the gibbet, where the murdered body of Coligny (Co-leen-ye) was hanging. Nothing could exceed the splendour of the cortege, for the gaudy dresses, brought into fashion by **Francois I.**, still continued, and had not yet given way to the gloomy stinted robes of the third Henri.

In the procession, was Henri of Navarre and his beautiful bride, the king and his mother Catherine, the dukes of Anjou and Alencon, the Guises, and a vast cavalcade of ladies, pages, esquires, valets and common people, to the amount of 10,000.

From the gibbet hung a half-burnt blackened mass, bespattered with blood and dirt. The trunk was suspended by the heels, and the head was supplied by a whisp of straw twisted into a knot. "Fragrance, sweeter than a rose, Rises from our slaughtered foes," cried the king, in a silly doggerel, as he stood before the gibbet; and all the courtiers applauded with a laugh. He passed on; and every follower, as he went by, thought it a compliment to the king to indulge in some pleasantry, or to offer some insult.

The next proceeding in this frightful drama was for the king to go in person to the Paris **Parliment,** to boast in a set speech of what he had done. The grave magistrates and wise councillors heard him to the end, and then accorded him a vote of thanks for his "holy zeal."

In Rome, the news was received with unbounded enthusiasm. Gregory XIII. celebrated the event with bonfires. A state procession went to the church of St. Louis to assist in a grand Te Deum, and a year of jubilee was proclaimed, because "God had put it into the hearts of his faithful servants to purge the earth of heretics."—**Dr. Brewer's History of France** Pages 157-161, Eighth Edition, 1893.

CHAPTER VII

AMERICA—PERSECUTIONS IN THE COLONIES AND EARLY STATES

Colonies were Religio-Political States

Charles W. Rishell, History of Christianity from the German of Rudolph Sohm, says, "Prior to the Revolutionary War there had been colonies in which Christianity was established in the form of particular creeds and theories of church government. In New York, Maryland (after 1691), and Virginia, Christianity was established in the English church. The Plymouth colony and its offshoots were practically ecclesiastico-civil states in which Christianity was only free in the form peculiar to their Puritan founders."—Page 306

Rishell says further, "The first successful colony was settled at Jamestown, Virginia, 1607. PRIOR TO THIS, numerous attempts at Protestant colonization had been made, but none of them had proved successful. A colony of Huguenots on the St. James River was massacred by the Roman Catholics of St. Augustine under their desperate leader, Melendez, before the close of the sixteenth century." Page 309.

Seeds of Persecution

"On the 25 of August, 1630, on board the ship Arabella, before they landed, at the first meeting of the **Court of Assistants**, the first dangerous act was performed by the rulers of this incipient government, which led to innumberal evils, hardships, and privations to all who had the misfortune to dissent from the ruling powers in after time."

"The first question propounded was, **How shall the ministers be maintained?** "It was ordered, that houses be built for them with convenient speed at the **public charge,** and their salaries were established."—History of the Baptists, Benedict, page 368.

Virginia—Persecution of Baptists in America

(Baptist Encyclopedia—Cathcart.)

John Waller, Lewis Craig, and James Childs, three Baptist ministers, were arrested in Spottsylvania County, Virginia, "for preaching the gospel contrary to law," and while in prison they proclaimed the good news to listening throngs through the doors and windows of the jail.

In Middlesex and Caroline Counties, Virginia, many Baptist ministers were imprisoned for preaching; they were subjected to the treatment of common felons, and if possible to worse indignities. William Webber and Joseph Anthony were imprisoned in Chesterfield County, Virginia, for telling the story of the Cross. James Ireland suffered imprisonment in Virginia, and illegal and wicked efforts were made to kill him in jail because he was a herald of Calvary.

To keep the people from hearing the imprisoned preachers, walls were sometimes built around the jails in which they were confined, and half-drunken outcasts were hired to beat drums to drown their voices. When out of prison in the Old Dominion they were mobbed; while immersing converts men on horseback would ride into the water to create a disturbance.

They were often interrupted in their discourses and insulted, but they despised the jail, the lash, and the malicious jeers. When hunted like wild beasts, and denounced as wolves in sheep's clothing, they meekly replied, "That if they were wolves and their persecutors the true sheep, it was unaccountable that they should treat them with such cruelty; that wolves would destroy sheep, but that it was never known till then that sheep would prey upon wolves." (Semple's History of Virginia Baptists, p. 21.)

Cathcart says—

"In New England, outside of Rhode Island, our brethren were frequently arrested for not paying taxes to support the Congregational clergy. Women, too, had their rights recognized, and they were arrested and robbed to support the ministers of their neighbors. The sacred tax-gatherers took from the Baptists "pewter dishes, skillets, kettles, pots and warming-pans, workmen's tools, and spinning-wheels; they drove away geese and swine and cows, and when there was but one it was not spared.

"A brother recently ordained returned to Sturbridge, Massachuetts, for his family, when he was thrust into prison and kept during the cold winter, till some one paid his fine and secured his release. Mr. D. Fisk was robbed at Sturbridge of five pewter plates and a cow, J. Perry of the baby's cradle and a steer, J. Blunt of andirons, shovel, and tongs, and A. Bloice, H. Fisk, John Streeter, Benjamin Robbins, Phenehas Collier, John Newel, Josiah Perry, Nathaniel Smith, John Corry, and J. Barstow of spinning wheels, household goods, cows, and of their liberty for a season." Backus's Church History, ii. 94, 95. Newton.)

Sturbridge was but a specimen of what was taking place all over New England, and of the love cherished for our Baptist fathers by men who only differed from them about baptism. Early the persecution of Baptists was commenced in New England; Roger Williams was compelled to fly from Salem to escape illegal violence in 1635; the meeting-house of the First Baptist Church of Boston, in 1677, was closed by order of the General Court of Massachusetts, and after a little, when they ventured to use it again, the doors were nailed up and a paper fastened on them, which read, "All persons are to take notice that by order of the court the doors of this house are shut up, and that they are prohibited from holding any meeting therein or to open the doors thereof without license from authority till the General Court take further order, as they will answer the contrary at their peril." (Hildreth's History of the United States, i. 497-499. New York.)

The town of Ashfield, Massachusetts, was settled by Baptists, and when it had a few Congregational families in it they built a church, called a minister, and then laid a tax upon the land to meet the cost of the one and the support of the other. The Baptists refused to pay the church bills of their Puritan neighbors, and immediately the best portion of the cultivated land in the town was seized and sold for trifling sums to pay their iniquitous dues. The house and garden of one man were taken from him, and the young orchards, and meadows, and the cornfields of others.

The grave-yard of the Baptists was actually sold to liquidate the debts of a church with which they had nothing to do, and to support a minister with whom they did not intend to worship. These properties were sold in 1770 for L35.10, and they were worth L363.8. The Congregational minister was one of the purchasers. This was but the first payment, and two others were to follow. (Minutes of the Philadelphia Baptist Association for 1770, p. 160.) Such were some of the countless wrongs which our fathers suffered even in this land.—BAPTIST ENCYCLOPEDIA, pp. 907, 908, William Cathcart, D.D.

The Virginia Baptists

(Cook's Story of the Baptists)

The Baptists of the Old Dominion deserve special mention. During the first century of the colony, which was settled in 1607, the Baptists are not mentioned by name, but Morgan Edwards speaks of Baptists in North Carolina as early as 1695, who had gone there from Virginia to escape intolerant laws. Prof. J. C. Long, D.D., LL. D., of Crozer Theological Seminary, an eminent authority, says, that it is almost certain that there were no Baptist organizations in Virginia, as early as 1695; though there may have been individual Baptists; and that the laws were so stringently enforced in reference to conventicles, that had there been Baptist churches, we would have heard something about them.

Virginia was settled by cavaliers from England, who were loyalists devoted to their king; and churchmen wedded to the Episcopal Church. By their charter the Episcopal was the established religion of the colony. Departure from the church was treason against the state. Hence a struggle for liberty, civil and religious, was to be expected.

In 1611, Governor Dale ordered every man to come to the minister to be questioned as to his religious belief. The penalty for the first refusal was whipping; for the second, a double flogging, and a confession of the fault on Sabbath day before the congregation; and for the third offense, whipping daily until pardon was asked and the law complied with.

As early as 1643, a law was enacted, "to preserve purity of doctrine," forbidding any one to teach, or preach publicly or privately, who was not a minister of the Episcopal Church, and did not conform to its mode of worship. It was first banishment, and in 1661, imprisonment for nonconformity.

In 1673, a house of worship was commanded to be erected on every plantation, and the service to be Episcopal. Every body was required at attend church, or be heavily fined, and no one could sell his tobacco till his tax for the support of the Episcopal minister was paid.

Geo. B. Taylor, D.D., says; "Such laws prevailed from the settlement of Virginia, 1607, to the Revolution, 1775, except during the Protectorate. For this entire period, as Hening says; 'The religion of the Church was the religion of the ruling party in the State, and none other was tolerated.' These laws were vigorously enforced."

Dr. Taylor also says: "Specially the severe laws against those refusing to practice infant baptism, prove the existence of some who rejected that rite. The Quakers have been referred to; but they were never numerous in Virginia. The preamble to one of the acts, punishing those rejecting infant baptism, declared there were many, not merely neglecting (as careless persons might have done,) but refusing to have their children baptized. Moreover, such persons are further described as acting out of their averseness to the established religion, etc."

Rev. R. B. Semple says that there were three sources from which the Baptists of Virginia came; from England, Maryland, and New England. "The first were emigrants from England, who about the year 1714, settled in the southeast parts of the state," and formed, at that time, the first church organized in the state at Burleigh, Isle of Wight county. The church still exists under the name of Mill Swamp. They were Arminian in doctrine, but finally became Regular Baptists.

They appealed for a minister to their brethren in England, who ordained and sent them Robert Nordin, who remained their pastor till his death in 1725. Dr. J. C. Long remarks, that the inference to be drawn from the action of the Burleigh church in sending to England for a pastor is, that there were no ordained Baptist ministers in Virginia, or even in North Carolina at that time.

The Kehukee Association was formed in 1765, and the Portsmouth in May, 1791. The second company of Baptists of whom Semple speaks came into Virginia from Maryland, and from them arose what were then known as the Regular Baptists, in contradistinction to the Separates. These were not so numerous as the Separates, but were a large and respectable body of people.

Edward Hays and Thomas Yates, members of Sater's Baptist church in Maryland, came with a company and settled in Berkley county in 1743. They were soon followed by their minister, Henry Loveall, who preached to the people and baptized fifteen persons. The church was reorganized in 1751, by some ministers of the Philadelphia Association, with which body the church then united. Samuel Heton and John Garrard were successively pastors of the church.

While their brethren in other parts of the state were contending with hostile whites, they were defending themselves against savages. The country was then thinly inhabited and subject to the inroads of Indians, nevertheless the church grew in zeal and numbers. The Ketocton church was formed, probably, in 1756, and the association known by that name in 1766. About 1760 Rev. David Thomas, a "learned" Baptist minister, came from Pennsylvania first to Berkley, and then to Fauquier county, and formed and became pastor of the Broad Run church.

Among those whom he baptized were Daniel and William Fristoe, and Jeremiah Moore, so well known as able preachers of the word. Lewis Lunsford, "who in point of talents as a preacher, was never excelled," was born in Stafford county of indigent parents, and baptized by William Fristoe. Lunsford carried the standard of the cross far and wide, and planted it below Fredricksburg in the counties of the Northern Neck.

The most important company from which the Baptists of Virginia arose was, according to Semple, the "third party" and came from New England. They were called the "New Lights," and were under Shubael Stearns, their pastor. They first came to Opekon, Berkeley county, in 1754, where there was already a Baptist church with John Garrard as pastor. Here Stearns met his brother-in-law, Daniel Marshall, a missionary to the Indians, who had just become a Baptist.

They joined companies and went to Hampshire county, where hearing that the people of North Carolina were thirsting for the preaching of the gospel, to hear which some had been known to ride forty miles; they went a journey of two hundred miles to Sandy Creek, Guilford county, North Carolina, and there, November 22, 1755, constituted a church with sixteen members, of which Stearns became pastor.

"Thus organized," says Semple, "they began their work, kindling a fire which soon began to burn brightly indeed, spreading in a few years over Virginia, North and South Carolina and Georgia. . . . Into parts of Virginia, adjacent to the residence of this religious colony, the gospel had been quickly carried by Mr. Marshall. He had baptised several in some of his first visits. Among them was Dutton Lane, who shortly after his baptism, began to preach. A revival succeeded, and Mr. Marshall at one time baptized fifty-two persons.

"In August, 1760, a church was constituted under the pastoral care of the Rev. Dutton Lane. This was the first Separate Baptist church in Virginia, and thus, in some sense, the mother of all the rest. This church prospered under the ministry of Mr. Lane, aided by the occasional visits of Mr. Marshall and Mr. Stearns. They endured much persecution, but God prospered them, and delivered them out of the hands of all their enemies."

"In 1770," says Dr. J. C. Long, "there were but six Separate Baptist churches in all Virginia. In 1774, there were forty-four, so mightily grew the word of God."

The Separates or New Lights, and the Regular Baptists became, finally, one body, and were henceforth known in history as the Baptists of Virginia.

Speaking of their common sufferings for conscience' sake Dr. George B. Taylor, says: "Time would fail to tell of the persecutions they suffered legally, and under color of law, and at the hands of ruffians instigated, in some cases, by the gentry and parson.

Dr. Hawks, the Episcopalian historian, says: Cruelty taxed its ingenuity to devise new modes of punishment and annoyance. Our ministers were fined, pelted, imprisoned, poisoned and hunted with dogs; their congregations were assaulted and dispersed; the solemn ordinance of baptism was rudely interrupted, both administrators and candidates being plunged and held beneath the water till nearly dead; they suffered mock trials, and even in courts of justice were subjected to indignities not unlike those inflicted by the infamous Jefferys; nor were these cases few and confined to restricted localities, as some have seemed to think.

But these things could not prevent the progress of the truth. Those men of God were full of courage, and zeal, and love for the truth and for Jesus, and pity for perishing souls; and they went everywhere preaching the word, rejoicing that they were counted worthy to suffer for the name of Jesus, and gladly encountering, in the glades and mountains of what is now West Virginia, fatigue, cold and hunger."

Among the noble sufferers, was Samuel Harriss, styled "the apostle of Virginia"; and born in that state in 1724. He was a member of the legislature, colonel of militia, captain of Mayo Fort, commissary for the fort and army, judge of the court, sheriff, and church warden. He was a remarkable man, and became serious and melancholy without knowing why.

By reading and conversation, he discovered that he was a hopeless sinner, and that a sense of his guilt was the cause of his gloom of mind. He ventured to attend Baptist preaching, and obtained relief by faith in the Saviour. Semple thus graphically describes his conversion:

"On one of his routes to visit the forest in his official character, he called at a small house, where he understood there was to be Baptist preaching. The preachers were Joseph and William Murphy. Being rigged in his military dress he was not willing to appear in a conspicuous place. He seated himself behind a loom. God, nevertheless, found him out by his Spirit.

His convictions now sunk so deep, that he could no longer conceal them. He left his sword and other parts of his rigging, some in one place, and some in another. The arrows of the Almighty stuck fast in him, nor could he shake them off, until some time after. At a meeting when the congregation rose from prayer, Colonel Harriss was observed still on his knees, with his head and hands hanging over the bench. Some of the people went to his relief; and found him senseless.

When he came to himself, he smiled, and in all ecstacy of joy, exclaimed, Glory! Glory! Glory!" Daniel Marshall baptized him in 1758. From that time his life was one act of devotedness and zeal. Practising rigid economy in his house, he employed his whole surplus income in advancing the cause of religion.

At the time of his conversion, he was engaged in erecting a large mansion for the accommodation of his family, in a style suited to his rank and station; it was turned into a meeting-house, and he continued to reside in the old building. He began at once, like Paul, to preach. "There was scarcely any place in Virginia, where he did not sow the gospel seed. His excellency lay chiefly in his addressing the heart, and perhaps even Whitefield did not surpass him in this. When animated, himself, he seldom failed to animate his auditory.

Some have described him as pouring forth streams of celestial light, shining from his eyes, which whithersoever he turned his face would strike down hundreds at once. He was often called 'Boanerges.' " He died in 1794. "Shubael Stearns, Daniel Marshall, and Samuel Harriss were the principal founders of the Baptist interests in the South. They were the first three, and their names should be held in everlasting remembrance."

Col. Harriss' standing did not save him from persecution. Once he was arrested and carried into court, as a disturber of the peace. A Captain Williams, vehemently accused him as a vagabond, a heretic, and a mover of sedition everywhere. The court ordered that he should not preach in the country again for the space of twelve months; or be committed to prison. He told them that he lived two hundred miles away, and was not likely to disturb them again for a year, and was dismissed.

On his way home, having gone farther, he came again into Culpepper, where this happened, and attended a meeting. He presently rose and said; "I partly promised the devil, a few days past, at the court-house, that I would not preach in this country again in the term of a year. But the devil is a perfidious wretch, and covenants with him are not to be kept; and therefore I will preach.

He preached and was not molested. On another occasion, he was pulled down, while preaching, and dragged about sometimes by the hair of the head, and sometimes by the legs. At another time he was knocked down by a brutal fellow, while preaching. Having gone once to Hillsborough to preach to prisoners, he was locked in and kept for some time.

John Waller was born in Virginia in 1714. He was of an honorable family, "manifested a great talent for satirical wit," and was educated for the law, but gave way to his unbridled inclinations to vice, and became a gambler. His wickedness and profanity, obtained for him the infamous appellation of "Swearing Jack Waller."

It was frequently remarked, that there could be no deviltry among the people, unless he was at the head of it. Once he had three warrants served on him, at one time. Sometimes he was called the devil's adjutant to muster his troops. To these failings may be added his fury against Baptists. He was one of the grand jury that presented Louis Craig for preaching.

Craig addressed the jury thus; "I thank you gentlemen of the grand jury, for the honor you have done me. While I was wicked and injurious you took no notice of me, but since I have altered my course of life and endeavor to reform my neighbors, you concern yourselves much about me."

When Mr. Waller heard him speak in this manner, and observed the meekness of his spirit, he was convinced that Craig was possessed of something he had never seen in man before. He thought within himself, that he would be happy if he could be of the same religion as Mr. Craig. From that time he began to attend their meetings, and feeling himself to be a sinner, to call upon the name of the Lord. His convictions were so deep and pungent that he abstained for several months from all but necessary food, and was almost driven to despair.

But on his knees in prayer he, at last, found peace. He was baptized in 1767, began to preach at once, and was greatly blessed in his ministry. His death in 1802 was truly glorious, and while his pains appeared to be excruciating, yet no murmur was heard from his lips.

June 4, 1768, Waller, Louis Craig, and James Childs, were seized by the sheriff and brought before three magistrates, who stood in the meeting-house yard, and bound over to appear before court.

To the court the prosecuting attorney said:—"May it

please your courtships, these men are great disturbers of the peace, they can not meet a man upon the road, but they must ram a passage of Scripture down his throat." The authorities offered to release them upon condition that they would not preach. This they refused and were sent to jail. As they went through the street of Fredricksburg to prison they sang:—"Broad is the road that leads to death," etc.

Hon. John Blair, deputy-governor, became interested in their case and wrote of them to the attorney:—"Their petition was a matter of right, you may not molest these conscientious people, so long as they behave themselves as becometh pious Christians. I am told they administer the sacrament of the Lord's Supper near the manner we do, and differ in nothing from our churches, but in that of Baptism, and their renewing the ancient discipline, by which they have reformed some sinners and brought them to be truly penitent. Nay, if a man of them is idle and neglects to labor and provide for his family as he ought, he incurs their censures, which have had good effect. If this be their behavior, it were to be wished we had some of it among us."

The attorney paid no attention to the letter. They remained in jail forty-three days, and preached through the grated windows; the mob without trying in vain to keep the people from hearing.

William Webber and John Waller were once on a preaching tour, when a magistrate drew back his club to knock Webber down as he was preaching, but some one behind caught the club, and saved him. But as two sheriffs, the parson and a posse were at hand to aid him, he arrested Webber, Waller, James Greenwood and Robert Ware, and cast them into prison, because they refused to cease preaching.

"The prison swarmed with fleas. They borrowed a candle of the jailer, and, having sung the praises of that Redeemer whose cross they bore, and from whose hands they expected a crown in the end; having returned thanks that it was a prison, and not hell, that they were in; praying for themselves, their friends, their enemies, and their persecuters, they laid down to sleep." Next Sunday they preached to their friends who came to them in the prison and announced preaching for every Wednesday and Sunday. While preaching, their enemies often beat drums that they might not be heard. "It was not until after thirty days' close confinement and sixteen days in bonds, that they were set at liberty."

Sometimes the leading men of the state church would attend Baptist meetings to argue with the preachers as men of a baser sort used force, and would call them false prophets in sheep's clothing. "Waller and the other preachers boldly and readily replied, that if they were wolves in sheep's clothing and their opponents were the true sheep, it was quite unaccountable that they were persecuted and cast into prison: it was well known that wolves would destroy sheep, but never till then that sheep would prey upon wolves."

A FORWARD LOOK

Cook continues—

The Baptist General Association of Virginia, after existing in other forms and under other names from 1771, was organized as at present, June 9, 1823. At its grand jubilee meeting held in Richmond, May, 1873, Dr. J. L. M. Curry, during his masterly speech, showed a spoon used by Waller, while a prisoner for conscience' sake, and a brick from the foundation of the old jail at Urbana, Middlesex County, in which were imprisoned several Baptist preachers.

He asked that the brick might go into the foundation of the monument to be erected to the memory of these noble sufferers for Christ. He also held up the lock and key of the old Culpepper jail, where James Ireland, Elijah Craig, John Corbeley and Thomas Ammon, preachers, and Adam Banks and Thomas Maxfield, laymen, and John Delaney, were imprisoned. The latter, though not a member of the church, was arrested for allowing a prayer meeting to be held in his house, and the others for conducting it.

The Baptist church at Culpepper now stands on the site of the old jail. Preaching began there long before the meeting-house was erected. James Ireland, a godly and eminent man while in prison, though greatly enfeebled by cruelties, preached through the grated windows, to the people, who had gathered outside to hear him. This noble man dated his letters while in prison: "From my palace in Culpepper." This reminds us of these lines:
"And prisons would palaces prove,
If Jesus would dwell with me there."
He had much to endure during his confinement. Several attempts were made to murder him. They first put powder under the floor of his room to blow him up, then tried to suffocate him by filling his cell with the fumes of burning brimstone, and finally with the aid of a physician poisoned him; but his life was spared.

Persecution made Baptists shun publicity. "Still," says Dr. David Weston, "though overborne and suppressed for a hundred years, Baptist principles were secure in their own immortality, and were, even in Virginia, silently, unobtrusively, but effectively laying a foundation for subsequent glorious triumphs." When release from persecution finally came, then, as Dr. Howell beautifully says; "Church after church noiselessly arose like the shining out of the stars of evening, and sparkled like gems in the American firmament, which they were destined ere long to fill with radiance and beauty."

And now there are 215,604 Baptists in the State. Only two other States, Georgia and North Carolina, can boast a larger number. In Richmond, where the First church was formed in 1780, the Baptists out-numbered all other denominations combined.—Copied from COOK'S STORY OF THE BAPTISTS, Pages 214-228.

Georgia—First Colored Church

Benedict gives the following record—

The origin of this church was in the following manner. About the beginning of the American war, George Leile, sometimes called George Sharp, but more commonly called among his brethren and friends by the name of brother George, began to preach at Brampton and Yamacrew, near the city of Savannah. He had been converted about two years before the war, by the preaching of a Baptist minister in Burke county, whose name was Matthew Moore; by this minister he was baptized, and by the church of which he was pastor he was approbated to preach. His labors were attended with a blessing among the people of his own color on different plantations, many of them were brought, by his means, to a saving acquaintance with the gospel. When the country was evacuated by the British, George, with many others, removed from Georgia to Kingston, in the island of Jamaica. Here his labors were attended with great success, and by him a large church was soon raised up; in giving the history of which, we shall relate more at large the character and labors of this worthy man.

Such was the beginning of the first African church in Savannah, which, after having been the mother of others, now contains about 1200 members.

"Previous to George's departure for Jamaica, he came up to the city of Savannah from Tybee river, where departing vessels frequently lay ready for sea, and baptized Andrew Bryan and Hannah, his wife, and two other black women, whose names were Kate and Hager. These were the last labors of George Leile in this quarter. About nine months after his departure, Andrew began to exhort his black brethren and friends, and a few whites who assembled to hear him. Edward Davis, Esq., permitted him and his hearers to erect a rough wooden building on his land at Yamacraw, in the suburbs of Savannah. Of this building they were in a short time very artfully dispossessed. It appears that these poor defenseless slaves met with much opposition from the rude and merciless white people, who, under various pretences, interrupted their worship, and otherwise treated them in a barbarous manner. Andrew Bryan, and his brother Samson, who was converted about a year after him, were twice imprisoned, and they, with

about fifty others, without much ceremony, were severely whipped. Andrew was inhumanly cut, and bled abundantly; but, while under their lashes, he held up his hands and told his persecutors, that he rejoiced not only to be whipped but would freely suffer death for the cause of Christ! The chief-justices Henry Osbourne, James Habersham and David Montague, Esqs., the kind master of Andrew and Samson, interceded for his own servants, and the rest of the sufferers, and was much grieved at their punishment. The design of these unrighteous proceedings against these poor innocent people, was to stop their religious meetings. Their enemies pretended, that under a pretence of religion, they were plotting mischief and insurrections; but by well doing, they at length silenced and shamed their persecutors, and acquired a number of very respectable and influential advocates and patrons, who not only rescued them from the power of their enemies, but declared that such treatment as they had received would be condemned among barbarians. The chief-justice Osbourne then gave them liberty to continue their worship any time between sun-rising and sun-set; and the benevolent Jonathan Bryan told the magistrates that he would give them the liberty of his own house or barn, at a place called Brampton, about three miles from Savannah, and that they should not be interrupted in their worship. From this period, Andrew and Samson set up meetings at their master's barn, where they had little or no interruption for about two years."
—General History of Baptist Denomination in America, Benedict, page 740.

Maryland—Early Law Concerning Religion
Published By J. H. Grimes

"For as much as in a well governed and Christian Commonwealth, Matters concerning Religion and the Honour of God ought to be in the first place to be taken into serious consideration, and endeavored to be settled. Be it therefore Ordained and Enacted by the Right Honorable CAECILIUS Lord Baron of Baltimore, absolute Lord and Proprietary of this Province, with the Advice and Consent of the Upper and Lower House of this General Assembly, That whatsoever person or persons within this Province and the Islands thereunto belonging, shall from henceforth blaspheme GOD, that is, curse him; or shall deny our Saviour JESUS CHRIST to be the Son of God, or shall deny the Holy Trinity, the Father, Son and Holy Ghost or the Godhead of any of the said Three Persons of the Trinity, or the Unity of the Godhead, or shall use or utter any reproach speeches, words, or language, concerning the Holy Trinity, or any of the said three Persons thereof, shall be punished with death, and confiscation or forfeiture of all his or Lands and Goods to the Lord Proprietary and his Heirs,

"And be it also enacted by the Authority, and with the advice and assent aforesaid, That whatsoever person or persons shall from henceforth use or utter any reproachful words or speech concerning the blessed Virgin Mary, the Mother of our Saviour, or the holy Apostles, or Evangelists, or any of them shall in such case for the first Offense forfeit to the said Lord Proprietary and his Heirs, Lords and Proprietaries of this Province, the sum of Five pounds Sterling or the value thereof to be levied on the goods and chattels of every such person so offending; but in case such offender or offenders shall not then have goods and chattels sufficient for the satisfying of such forfeiture, or that the same be not otherwise speedily satisfied, that then such offender or offenders shall be publicly whipt, and be imprisoned during the pleasure of the Lord Proprietary, or the Lieutenant or Chief Governor of this Province for the time being; And that every such offender or offenders for every second offense shall forfeit Ten Pounds Sterling or the value thereof to be levied as aforesaid, or in case such offender or offenders shall not then have goods and chattels within this Province sufficient for that purpose, then to be publicly and severely whipt and imprisoned as before is expressed; and that every person or persons before mentioned, offending herein the third time shall for such third offense forfeit all his lands and goods, and be forever banished and expelled out of this Province."—American History by David S. Mussey, of Barnard College, Columbia University, New York, p. 56. Quoted by J. H. Grime in, Roman Catholicism, 1929.

Massachusetts—Law Against the Baptists
(From Benedict's History)

"Forasmuch as experience hath plentifully and often proved, that since the first rising of the Anabaptists, about one hundred years since, they have been incendiaries of commonwealths, and the infectors of persons in main matters of religion, and the troublers of churches in all places where they have been, and that they have held the baptizing of infants unlawful, have usually held other errors or heresies therewith, though they have (as other heretics used to do), concealed the same, till they spied out a fit advantage and opportunity to vent them, by way of question or scruple; and, whereas, divers of this kind, since our coming into New England, appeared among ourselves, some, whereof (as others before them), denied the ordinance of the magistracy, and the lawfulness of making war, and others the lawfulness of magistrates, and the inspection into any breach of the first table; which opinions, if they should be connived at by us, are like to be increased amongst us, and so must necessarily bring guilt upon us, infection and trouble to the churches, and hazard to the whole commonwealth; it is ordered and agreed, that if any person or persons within this jurisdiction shall either openly condemn or oppose the baptizing of infants, or go about secretly to seduce others from the approbation or use thereof, or shall purposely depart the congregation at the ministration of the ordinance, or shall deny the ordinance of magistracy, or their lawful right and authority to make war, or to punish the outward breaches of the first table, and shall appear to the court wilfully and obstinately to continue therein, after due time and means of conviction, every such person or persons shall be sentenced to banishment."

The following lengthy quote is from Benedict's history—

This was the first law which was made against the Baptists in Massachusetts. It was passed November 13, 1644, about two months after Mr. Williams landed in Boston, as above related. Two charges, which it contains, Mr. Backus acknowledges are true, viz: that the Baptists denied infant baptism and the ordinance of magistracy; or, as a Baptist would express it, the use of secular force in religious affairs; but all the other slanderous invectives he declares are utterly without foundation.

He furthermore asserts, that he had diligently searched all the books, records, and papers, which he could find on all sides, and could not find an instance then (1777) of any real Baptist in Massachusetts being convicted of, or suffering for any crime, except the denying of infant baptism, and the use of secular force in religious affairs.

If a Puritan Court in the seventeenth century, professing to be illuminated with the full blaze of the light of the Reformation, could thus defame the advocates for apostolic principles, will any think it strange if we suspect the frightful accounts which were given of them in darker ages by a set of monkish historians, who believed that fraud and falsehood were Christian virtues, if they could be made subservient to the good of the church?

Mr. Hubbard, one of their own historians, speaking of their making this law, says, "but with what success it is hard to say; all men being naturally inclined to pity them that suffer, Ec." The clergy doubtless had a hand in framing this shameful act, as they, at this time, were the secretaries and counselors of the legislature.

Mr. Backus' observations upon these measures, and the men by whom they were promoted, are very judicious. "Much (says he) has been said to exalt the characters of the good fathers of that day: I have no desire of detracting from any of their virtues; but the better the men were, the worse must be the principles that could ensnare them in such bad actions."

According to Hubbard, in the following year a petition came into the general court against this singular law, and also against one more singular still, which had been made some years before, forbidding any one to entertain strangers without a license from two magistrates. The traveling merchant in the town, as well as the wandering pilgrim in the wilderness, all fell under this prohibition. The men of business complained of it as hurtful to their trade, and a multitude of others as an encroachment on the rights of hospitality, which they were willing to exercise towards the houseless and benighted stranger, which might seek a shelter in the darkness of the night from the raging storm.

Although the magistrates might be far away, and far apart, their signatures must be had, before the threshhold of the remotest and humblest cottage could be passed.

So fearful were these bigoted puritans that some infectious Anabaptist, Quaker, churchman, or other contaminating heretic, should lead their people astray.

The Catholics went great lengths in laws of this kind, but such police regulations as this were probably never known in the most despotic countries.

Sufferings of Obadiah Holmes, John Clarke, and others.

We are now prepared to give an account of a scene of suffering peculiarly cruel and afflictive, and to see the Bloody Tenet literally exemplified.

We have already seen that there were some Baptists at Lynn, in 1640, when Lady Moody left the place, and it is probable that a little band remained there until the period now under consideration.

In July, 1651, Messrs. Clark, Holmes, and Crandal, "being the representatives of the church at Newport, upon the request of William Witter, of Lynn, arrived there, he being a brother in the church, who, by reason of his advanced age, could not undertake so great a journey as to visit the church." This account is found among the records of the ancient church at Newport. The circumstance of these men being representatives, leads us to infer that something was designed more than an ordinary visit.

Mr. Witter lived about two miles out of the town,

and the next day after his brethren arrived, being the Lord's day, they concluded to spend it in religious worship at this house. While Mr. Clark was preaching from Revelations 3:10,—"Because thou hast kept the word of my patience, I also will keep thee from the hour of temptation, which shall come upon all the world, to try them that dwell upon the earth," and illustrating what was meant by the hour of temptation and keeping the word with patience, "two constables (says he) came into the house, who, with their clamorous tongues, made an interruption in my discourse, and more uncivilly disturbed us than the old English bishops were wont to do, telling us that they were come with authority from the magistrate to apprehend us. I then desired to see the authority by which they thus proceeded whereupon they plucked forth their warrant, and one of them, with a trembling hand (as conscious he might have been better employed), read it to us; the substance whereof was as followeth:

"By virtue hereof, you are required to go to the house of William Witter, and so to search from house to house, for certain erroneous persons, being strangers, and them to apprehend, and in safe custody to keep, and to-morrow morning at eight o'clock to bring before me. Robert Bridges."

"When he had read the warrant, I told them—Friends, there shall not be, I trust, the least appearance of a resisting of that authority by which you come unto us; yet, I tell you that, by virtue hereof, you are not strictly tied; but, if you please, you may suffer us to make an end of what we have begun, so may you be witnesses either to or against the faith and order which we hold. To which they answered, they could not. Then said we, notwithstanding the warrant, or anything therein contained, you may.

They apprehended us and carried us away to the ale-house or ordinary, where at dinner one of them said unto us, Gentlemen, if you be free I will carry you to the meeting. To whom it was replied, Friend, had we been free thereunto we had prevented all this; nevertheless, we are in thy hand, and if thou wilt carry us to the meeting, thither will we go. To which he answered, Then will I carry you to the meeting. To this we replied, If thou forcast us into your assembly, then shall we be constrained to declare ourselves, that we cannot hold communion with them.

The constable answered, That is nothing to me, I have not power to command you to speak when you come there, or to be silent. To this I again replied, Since we have heard the word of salvation by Jesus Christ, we have been taught, as those that first trusted in Christ, to be obedient unto him both by word and deed; wherefore, if we be forced to your meeting, we shall declare our dissent from you both by word and gesture.

After all this, when he had consulted with the man of the house, he told us he would carry us to the meeting; so to their meeting we were brought, while they were at their prayers and uncovered; and at my first stepping over the threshold I unveiled myself, civilly saluted them, and turned into the seat I was appointed to, put on my hat again, and sat down, opened my book and fell to reading.

Mr. Bridges being troubled, commanded the constable to pluck off our hats, which he did, and where he laid mine, there I let it lie, until their prayers, singing, and preaching were over; after this I stood up and uttered myself in these words following: I desire as a stranger, to propose a few things to this congregation, hoping in the proposal thereof, I shall commend myself to your consciences, to be guided by that wisdom that is from above, which, being pure, is also peaceable, gentle, and easy to be entreated; and therewith made a stop, expecting that if the Prince of peace had been among them, I should have had a suitable answer of peace from them.

"Their pastor answered, we will have no objections against what is delivered.

"To which I answered, I am not about, at present, to make objections against what is delivered, but, as by my gesture at my coming into your assembly, I declared my dissent from you, so lest that should prove offensive unto some whom I would not offend, I would now by word of mouth declare the grounds, which are these: First, from consideration that we are strangers each to other, and so, strangers to each other's inward standing with respect to God, and so, cannot conjoin and act in faith: and what is not of faith, is sin.

And, in the second place, I could not judge that you are gathered together, and walk according to the visible order of our Lord. Which, when I had declared, Mr. Bridges told me I had done, and spoke that for which I must answer, and so commanded silence. When their meeting was done, the officers carried us again to the ordinary, where, being watched over that night as thieves and robbers, we were the next morning carried before Mr. Bridges, who made our mittimus, and sent us to the prison at Boston."

About a fortnight after, the court of assistants passed the following sentences against these persecuted men, viz.: that Mr. Clark should pay a fine of twenty pounds, Mr. Holmes of thirty, and Mr. Crandal of five, or be publicly whipped.

"They all refused to pay their fines, and were remanded back to prison. Some of Mr. Clark's friends paid his fine without his consent. Mr. Crandal was released upon his promise of appearing at their next court. But he was not informed of the time until it was over, and then they exacted his fine of the keeper of the prison. The only crime alleged against Mr. Crandal was, his being in company with his brethren.

But Mr. Holmes was kept in prison until September, and then the sentence of the law was executed upon him in the most cruel and unfeeling manner. In the course of the trial against these worthy men Mr. Clark defended himself and brethren with so much ability, that the court found themselves much embarrassed. 'At length (says Mr. Clark) the Governor stepped up and told us we had denied infant baptism, and being somewhat transported, told me I had deserved death, and said he would not have such trash brought into their jurisdiction; moreover, he said, 'You go up and down, and secretly insinuate into those that are weak; but you cannot maintain it before our ministers. You may try and dispute with them.' To this I had much to reply, but he commanded the jailer to take us away.

"So, the next morning, having so fair an opportunity, I made a motion to the court in these words following:—

"To the honorable Court assembled at Boston.

"Whereas it pleased this honored court yesterday, to condemn the faith and order which I hold and practise; and, after you had passed your sentence upon me for it, were pleased to express I could not maintain the same against your ministers, and thereupon publicly proffered me a dispute with them: be pleased, by these few lines, to understand I readily accept it and therefore desire you to appoint the time when, and the person with whom, in that public place where I was condemned, I might, with freedom, and without molestation of the civil power, dispute that point publicly, where, I doubt not, by the strength of Christ, to make it good out of his last will and testament, unto which nothing is to be added, nor from which nothing is to be diminished. Thus desiring the Father of Lights to shine forth, and by his power, to expel the darkness, I remain in your well-wisher, John Clark. "From the Prison, this 1st day, 6th mo., 1651.

"This motion, if granted, I desire might be subscribed by their Secretary's hand, as an act of the same court by which we were condemned."

This motion was presented, and, after much consultation, one of the magistrates informed Mr. Clark that a disputation was granted to be the next week. But, on the Monday following, the clergy held a consultation, and made no small stir about the matter; for, although they had easily foiled these injured men in a court of law, yet they might well anticipate some difficulty in the open field of argument, which they were absolutely afraid to enter—as will soon appear. Near the close of the day, the magistrates sent for Mr. Clark into their chamber, and inquired whether he would dispute upon the things contained in his sentence, Ec. "For," said they, "the court sentenced you, not for your judgment and conscience, but for matter-of-fact and practice."

To which Mr. Clark replied, "You say the court condemned me for matter-of-fact and practice;—be it so. I say that matter-of-fact and practice was but the manifestation of my judgment and conscience; and I make account, that man is void of judgment and conscience, with respect unto God, that hath not a fact and practice suitable thereunto.

"If the faith and order which I profess do stand by the word of God, then the faith and order which you profess must needs fall to the ground; and if the way you walk in remain, then the way that I walk in must vanish away—they cannot both stand together; to which they seemed to assent.

Therefore, I told them that, if they please to grant the motion under the Secretary's hand, I would draw up the faith and order which I hold, as the sum of that I did deliver in open court, in three or four conclusions; which conclusions I will stand by and defend until he whom you shall appoint, shall, by the word of God, remove me from them;—in case he shall remove me from them, then the disputation is at an end. But if not, then I desire like liberty, by the word of God, to oppose the faith and order which he and you profess, thereby to try whether I may be an instrument in the hand of God to remove you from the same.

They told me the motion was very fair, and the way like unto a disputant, saying, because the matter is weighty, and we desire that what can may be spoken, when the disputation shall be, therefore would we take a longer time. So I returned with my keeper to prison again, drew up the conclusion, which I was resolved, through the strength of Christ, to stand in defense of, and through the importunity of one of the magistrates, the next morning very early I showed them to him, having a promise I should have my motion for a dispute granted under the Secretary's hand."

Mr. Clark's resolutions were four in number, and contained the leading sentiments of the Baptists, which have been the same in every age respecting positive institutions, the subjects and mode of baptism, and gospel liberty and civil rights. But while he was making arrangements and preparing for a public dispute, his fine was paid, and he was released from prison.

Great expectations had been raised in Boston and its vicinity respecting this dispute, and many were anxious to hear it. And Mr. Clark, knowing that his adversaries would attribute the failure of it to him, immediately on his release drew up the following address:

"Whereas, through the indulgency of tender-hearted friends, without my consent, and contrary to my judgment, the sentence and condemnation of the court at Boston (as is reported) have been fully satisfied on my behalf, and thereupon a warrant hath been procured, by which I am secluded the place of my imprisonment, by reason whereof I see no other call for present but to my habitation, and to those near relations which God hath given me there; yet, lest the cause should hereby suffer, which I profess is Christ's, I would hereby signify, that if yet it shall please the honored magistrates, or General Court of this colony, to grant my former request under their Sectretary's hand, I shall cheerfully embrace it, and upon your motion shall through the help of God, come from the island to attend it, and hereunto I have subscribed my name, John Clark. 11th day, 6th mo., 1651.

This address was sent next morning to the magistrates, who were at the commencement at Cambridge, a short distance from Boston, and it was soon noised abroad that the motion was accepted and that Mr. Cotton was to be the disputant on the pedobaptist side. But in a day or two after, Mr. Clark received the following address from his timorous adversaries:

"Mr. John Clark,

"We conceive you have misrepresented the Governor's speech, in saying you were challenged to dispute with some of our elders; whereas it was plainly expressed, that if you would confer with any of them, they were able to satisfy you, neither were you able to maintain your practices to them by the word of God, all which we intended for your information and conviction privately; neither were you enjoined to what you were then counseled unto; nevertheless, if you are forward to dispute, and that you will move it yourself to the court or magistrates about Boston, we shall take order to appoint one, who will be ready to answer your motion, you keeping close to the questions to be propounded by yourself, and a moderator shall be appointed also to attend upon the service; and whereas you desire you might be free in your dispute, keeping close to the points to be disputed on, without incurring damage by the civil justice, observing what hath been before written, it is granted; the day may be agreed, if you yield the premises.

                        John Endicott, Governor
                        Thomas Dudley, Dep. Gov.
                        Richard Bellingham,
                        William Hibbins,
                        Increase Nowel

"11th day of the 6th mo., 1651".

This communication Mr. Clark answered in the following manner:—

"To the honored Governor of the Massachusetts, and the rest of that Honorable Society these present.
"Worthy Senators,

"I received a writing subscribed with five of your hands, by way of answer to a twice repeated motion of mine before you, which was grounded, as I conceive, sufficiently upon the Governor's words in open court, which writing of yours doth no way answer my expectation, nor yet that motion which I made; and whereas (waving that grounded motion) you are pleased to intimate that if I were forward to dispute, and would move it myself to the court, or magistrates about Boston, you would appoint one to answer my motion, Ec., be pleased to understand, that although I am not backward to maintain the faith and order of my Lord the King of saints, for which I have been sentenced, yet am I not in such a way so forward to dispute, or move therein, lest inconvenience should arise. I shall rather once more repeat my former motion, which, if it shall please the honored General Court to accept, and under their Secretary's hand shall grant a free dispute, without molestation or interruption, I shall be well satisfied therewith; that what is past I shall forget, and upon your motion shall attend it; thus desiring the Father of mercies, not to lay that evil to your charge, I remain your well-wisher, John Clark. "From prison, this 14th day, 6th month, 1651."

Thus ended Mr. Clark's chastisement and the Governor's challenge. The last communication which he had from his fearful opponents, was indeed signed by the heads of departments, but it was not made in official manner. Mr. Clark all along kept in view the law which had been made seven years before, which threatened so terribly any one who should oppose infant baptism. This was the reason of his requesting an order for the dispute in a legal form. But it was abundantly evident to him, as it will be to every impartial reader, that neither the great Mr. Cotton, nor any of his clerical brethren, dared to meet him in a verbal combat. Infant baptism was safe while defended by the sword of the magistrate, but they dared not risk it in the field of argument. Mr. Clark therefore left his adversaries in triumph; but poor Mr. Holmes was retained a prisoner, and in the end experienced the full weight of their cruel intolerance. An account of his sufferings is thus related by himself:

"Unto the well-beloved brethren, John Spillsbury, William Kiffin, and the rest that in London stand fast in the faith, and continue to walk steadfastly in that order of the gospel, which was once delivered unto the saints by Jesus Christ: Obadiah Holmes, an unworthy witness that Jesus is the Lord, and of late a prisoner for Jesus' sake, at Boston, sendeth greeting.

"Dearly-Beloved and Longed After,

"My heart's desire is to hear from you, and to hear that you grow in grace, and in the knowledge of our Lord and Saviour Jesus Christ, Ec.

"Not long after these troubles (at Rehoboth which he relates in the first part of this letter) I came upon occasion of business into the colony of the Massachusetts, with two other brethren, as brother Clark being one of the two can inform you, where we three were apprehended, carried to Boston, and so to the court, and were all sentenced; what they laid to my charge you may here read in my sentence; upon the pronouncing of which, as I went from the bar, I expressed myself in these words; I bless God I am counted worthy to suffer for the name of Jesus. Whereupon John Wilson (their pastor, as they call him) struck me before the judgment seat, and cursed me, saying, the curse of God or Jesus go with thee.

So we were carried to the prison, where not long after I was deprived of my two loving friends, at whose departure the adversary stept in, took hold of my spirit, and troubled me for the space of an hour, and then the Lord came in and sweetly relieved me, causing to look to himself, so was I stayed, and refreshed in the thoughts of my God; and although during the time of my imprisonment, the tempter was busy, yet it pleased God so to stand at my right hand, that the motions were but sudden, and so vanished away; and although there were that would have paid the money, if I would accept it, yet I durst not accept of deliverance in such a way, and therefore my answer to them was, that although I would acknowledge their love to a drop of cold water, yet I could not thank them for their money, if they should pay it. So the court drew near, and the night before I should suffer according to my sentence, it pleased God I rested and slept quietly; in the morning my friends came to visit me, desiring me to take the refreshment of wine and other comforts; but my resolution was not to drink wine nor strong drink that day, until my punishment was over; and the reason was, lest in case I had more strength, courage, and boldness, than ordinarily could be expected, the world should either say he is drunk with new wine, or else that the comfort and strength of the creature hath carried him through; but my course was this: I desired brother John Hazel to bear my friends company, and I betook myself to my chamber, where I might communicate with my God, commit myself to him, and beg strength from him.

I had no sooner sequestered myself, and come into my chamber, but satan lets fly at me, saying, Remember thyself, thy birth, breeding, and friends, thy wife, children, name and credit, but as this was sudden, so there came in sweetly from the Lord as sudden as answer, 'Tis for my Lord, I must not deny him before the sons of men (for that were to set men above him), but rather lose all, yea, wife, children, and mine own life also. To this the tempter replies, Oh, but that is the question, is it for him? and for him alone? is it not rather for thy own or some other's sake? thou hast so professed and practised, and now art loth to deny it; is not pride and self at the bottom? Surely this temptation was strong, and thereupon I made diligent search after the matter as formerly I had done."

Mr. Holmes proceeds in his narrative, and exhibits the strength of faith which bore him up in anticipation of the appalling scene which was before him.

"And when I heard the voice of my keeper come for me, even cheerfulness did come upon me, and taking my Testament in my hand, I went along with him to the place of execution, and after a common saluation there stood. There stood by also one of the **magistrates, by** name Increase Nowel, who for a while kept silent, and spoke not a word, and so did I, expecting the Governor's presence, but he came not. But after a while Mr. Nowel bade the executioner do his office. Then I desired to speak a few words, but Mr. Nowel answered, it is not now a time to speak.

Whereupon I took leave, and said, men, brethren, fathers, and countrymen, I beseech you give me leave to speak a few words, and the rather because here are many spectators to see me punished, and I am to seal with my blood, if God give me strength, that which I hold and practise in reference to the word of God, and the testimony of Jesus. That which I have to say in brief is this: although I confess I am no disputant, to dispute that point with any that shall come forth to withstand it. Mr. Nowel answered me, now was no time to dispute. Then said I, then I desire to give an account of the faith and order I hold, and this I desired three times, but in comes Mr. Flint, and saith to the executioner, Fellow, do thine office, for this fellow would but make a long speech to delude the people. So I being resolved to speak, told the people, that which I am to suffer for is the word of God, and testimony of Jesus Christ. No, saith Mr. Nowel, it is for your error, and going about to seduce the people. To which I replied, not for an error, for in all the time of my imprisonment, wherein I was left alone (my brethren being gone), which of all your ministers in all that time, came to convince me of an error; and when upon the Governor's words a motion was made for a public dispute, and upon fair terms so often renewed, and desired by hundreds, what was the reason it was not granted? Mr. Nowel told me, it was his fault that went away and would not dispute; but this the writings will clear at large.

"Still Mr. Flint calls to the man to do his office: so before, and in the time of his pulling off my clothes, I continued speaking, telling them, that I had so learned, that for all Boston I would not give my body into their hands thus to be bruised upon another account, yet upon this I would not give the hundredth part of a wampum peague to free it out of their hands, and that I made as much conscience of unbuttoning one button as I did of paying the 30 in reference thereunto.

"I told them, moreover, the Lord having manifested his love towards me, in giving me repentance towards God, and faith in Jesus Christ, and so to be baptized in water, by a messenger of Jesus, into the name of the Father, Son, and Holy Spirit, wherein I have fellowship with him in his death, burial and resurrection, I am now come to be baptized in afflictions by your hands, that so I may have further fellowship with my Lord, and am not ashamed of his sufferings, for by his stripes am I healed.

"And as the man began to lay the strokes upon my back, I said to the people, though my flesh should fail and my spirit should fail, yet my God would not fail. So it pleased the Lord to come in, and so to fill my heart and tongue as a vessel full, and with an audible voice I broke forth, praying unto the Lord not to lay this sin to their charge: and telling the people, that now I found he did not fail me, and therefore now I should trust him forever, who failed me not; for in truth as the strokes fell upon me, I had such a spiritual manifestation of God's presence, as the like thereof I never had nor felt, nor can with fleshly tongue express, and the outward pain was so removed from me, that indeed I am not able to declare it to you, it was so easy to me, that I could well bear it, yea, and in a manner, felt it not, although, it was grievous, as the spectators said, the man striking with all his strength (yea, spitting in his hands three times, as many affirmed) with a three corded whip, giving me therewith thirty strokes.

"When he had loosed me from the post, having joyfulness in my heart and cheerfulness in my countenance, as the spectators observed, I told the magistrates, you have struck me as with roses; and said moreover, although the Lord hath made it easy to me, yet I pray God it may not be laid to your charge. After this, many came to me rejoicing to see the power of the Lord manifested in weak flesh; but skilful flesh takes occasion hereby to bring others in trouble, informs the magistrates hereof, and so two more are apprehended as for contempt of authority; their names were John Hazel and John Spur, who came indeed and did shake me by the hand, but did use no words of contempt or reproach unto any."

In imitation of the persecutors of old, these New England puritans made it a capital offence for any one to show any sympathy to the victims of their severity, or to afford them any comfort or relief. (In a manuscript of Governor Joseph Jenks, written more than a hundred years ago, he says, "Mr. Holmes was whipt thirty stripes, and in such an unmerciful manner, that in many days, if not some weeks, he could take no rest but as he lay upon his knees and elbows, not being able to suffer any part of his body to touch the bed whereon he lay.")

"Now thus it hath pleased the Father of mercies so to dispose of the matter, that my bonds and imprisonments have been no hindrance to the gospel, for before my return, some submitted to the Lord and were baptized, and divers were put upon the way of inquiry. And now being advised to make my escape by night, because it was reported there were warrants forth for me, I departed; and the next day after, while I was on my journey, the constable came to search at the house where I lodged, so I escaped their hands, and was, by the good hands of my heavenly Father, brought home again to my near relations, my wife and eight children; the brethren of our town and Providence having taken pains to meet me four miles in the woods, where we rejoiced together in the Lord. Thus have I given you as briefly as I can, a true relation of things; wherefore my brethren, rejoice with me in the Lord, and give glory to him, for he is worthy, to whom be praise forevermore; to whom I commit you, and put up my earnest prayers for you, that by my late experience who have trusted in God, and have not been deceived, you may trust in him perfectly. Wherefore my dearly beloved brethren, trust in the Lord, and you shall not be ashamed nor confounded; so I also rest,

Yours in the bond of charity,
Obadiah Holmes."

Warrants were issued out against thirteen persons, whose only crime was showing some emotions of sympathy toward this innocent sufferer. Eleven of them escaped, and two only were apprehended; their names were John Spur, and John Hazel. Spur was probably the man who had been apprehended at Weymouth, Hazel was one of

Mr. Holmes' brethren at Rehoboth. Both of these men were to receive ten lashes, or pay forty shillings apiece. The latter they could not do with a clear conscience, and were therefore preparing for such another scourging as they had seen and pitied in their brother Holmes. But some, without their knowledge, paid their fines.

Mr. Backus has given an account of their trial, and the depositions which were preferred against them, in which nothing more was pretended than that they took Mr. Holmes by the hand when he came from the whipping-post, and blessed God for the strength and support he had given him. But this was "a heinous offence," and called for the vengeance of the civil arm. Mr. Hazel was upwards of sixty years old, and died a few days after he was released, before he reached home.

Mr. Clark went to England this same year, where he published a narrative of these transactions from which the preceding sketches have been selected.

These measures of intolerance and cruelty tended to promote rather than retard the Baptist cause.—BENEDICT'S HISTORY, pages 371-377.

BOOK SEVEN

APPENDIX—OR MISCELLANEOUS QUOTES

ITEM I

SEARCHING FOR BAPTISTS TO PUNISH

By David Benedict

Singular methods of detecting the heretics. The priests would sometimes carry a crucifix through the market, or wherever there was a concourse of people, and all who did not pay it reverence were marked as victims to be apprehended and examined; if a woman was heard singing a pious hymn, or a man was observed to ask a blessing at his meals at the inns or elsewhere where he might stop on a journey, or on business—in short, any indications of piety above the catholic standard, which was at that time extremely low, would excite suspicion and alarm.

Informers would run with the news to the minions of the hierarchy. In this way multitudes were arrested, and if they declined to swear themselves clear, their trials would go on. As these brethren were conscientiously opposed to oaths of all kinds, deplorable indeed was their condition. Again, if any one showed any kindness or sympathy towards the suffering martyrs in the prisons, the courts, or at the stake, they would run the risk of their liberty and life.

The great sufferings of the Martyrs previous to being put to death. Their imprisonments were generally long and distressing; they were often thrust into the most wretched and filthy places that could be selected, among vile malefactors, in doleful dungeons, deprived of every comfort, and exposed to every thing degrading and painful. But all these things were the beginning of their sorrows; but few of them escaped torture of all the painful varieties which the cruel inquisitors well knew how to inflict.

They were racked upon the wheel, suspended with cords, with heavy weights fastened to their limbs, screws and lashes, and all the tormenting contrivances of persecuting vengeance, with savage barbarity and in quick succession were dealt out to the poor defenseless anabaptists, without distinction of age or sex. Multitudes were thus crippled for life, had they been permitted to live.

And all these excruciating and agonizing pains were inflicted upon them, not to extort from them their religious faith, for this they freely confessed in the outset, but to make them disclose the names of their brethren—their places of abode—who baptized them—who were present at the time—where their meetings were held, Ec. And in addition to all the rest of their protracted trials, was the annoyance which they experienced from the never ending officiousness of the priests and monks, who came to them with their drivelling mummery in favor of the catholic faith, with an earnest solicitude for the salvation of their souls.

The very faulty character of these men was generally well understood by the sufferers, and excited in them an abhorrence and disgust which it required strong efforts to suppress, and some of the more resolute brethren would bear down upon them in a most plain and pointed manner.
—Copied from BENEDICT'S HISTORY, pages 126-127.

ITEM II

FROM THE FIRST CENTURY TO ABOUT THE TIME OF CONSTANTINE

By John Marsh

The history of the Church of Christ, from the close of the first century to the commencement of the fourth, is one of continual enlargement, but of gradual and deep declension in doctrine and holy practice; and of awful suffering from the fires of persecution. It was not, as it had been under the ancient dispensation, a distinct nation, governed by its own rulers and laws, appointed by God; but it was composed of a vast multitude, who lived in all parts of the Roman empire, who had been persuaded to renounce idolatry, and enlist under the banner of the Lord Jesus Christ; and who were united in small associations or churches—each enjoying the ministration of the Gospel and Christian ordinances from a stated Pastor.

Every year, converts to Christianity were prodigiously multiplied, until one of the Fathers could say, "We have filled all your towns, cities, islands, castles, boroughs, councils, camps, courts, palaces, senate, forum;" but we have no means of correctly ascertaining the exact time when the Gospel was carried to various distant nations, or who were, in all cases, the favored instruments of dissemination of the truth.

We have already seen with what amazing rapidity it spread during the ministry of the Apostles. But it is not like an art or a science, which mankind find useful to themselves, and which is no sooner known by one nation, than it is carefully sought for and possessed by every other. It must be carried to the world, and pressed upon their notice by those who possess it; and it will be carried by those only who are constrained by the love of Christ. Had the church retained her first zeal and love, not a nation or family would long have remained without the Gospel. But her love and zeal subsided, until few efforts were made to bring men to the acknowledgment of Christ, except for purposes of worldly ambition. It is certain, however, that Christ was known and worshipped as God, among the Franks, Germans, Spaniards, Celts, Britons, and throughout the East, before the close of the second century; and that, at the end of the period we are considering, Christianity became the acknowledged religion of the whole Roman empire.

As the church advanced in age, and became widely extended, the means of increase and strength were in some respects changed. The Apostolic office had ceased. The sacred canon being closed, prophets were no more. As the Gospel was received by different nations, among whom preachers were raised up, there was no farther use for the miraculous gift of tongues. And as it was essential that the world should be convinced by miracles that Christ and the first promulgators of truth only, were inspired from Heaven, the power of healing diseases and interrupting the established laws of nature, was soon withheld; at what exact period, has been the subject of much dispute, but is of little moment. One thing is certain, that men are converted by the Gospel, by evangelical truth, and not by miracles; and that, as far as true religion was spread, and men were gathered into the kingdom of God, it was by the preaching of Christ and Him crucified. This remained the standing means of salvation.

Copies of the sacred Scriptures were multiplied and circulated to as great an extent as they could be, in an age when the art of printing was unknown, and the mass of Christians were neither learned nor wealthy. The Latin versions were chiefly used, because that language was generally spoken throughout the Roman empire.

Most of the emperors who reigned in the second century, were of a mild and lenient character; and, under their administration, the churches enjoyed many seasons of tranquillity, though occasionally they were called to pass through the fire. Before the close of the first century, Nerva had granted toleration to the church, and restored the Christian exiles. But his successor, Trajan, renowned for his philosophic virtues, if he did not issue edicts against the Christians, suffered the populace to wreak their vengeance on them, and destroy them at their pleasure.

A violent persecution raged in Bithynia. Not knowing what course to pursue, Pliny, governor of the province, addressed a letter to the emperor, which, as it gives such an account of the Christians, as a heathen of intelligence and candor would form, and an official relation of the persecutions of the age, deserves, together with the answer of Trajan, a place in every ecclesiastical history. It was probably written in the year 106 or 107, soon after the death of the Apostle John.

Pliny to Trajan, Emperor.

"Health. It is my usual custom, Sir, to refer all things of which I harbor any doubt, to you. For who can better direct my judgment in its hesitation, or instruct my understanding in its ignorance? I never had the fortune to be present at any examination of Christians, before I came into this province. I am therefore at a loss to determine what is the usual object of inquiry or of punishment, and to what length either of them is to be carried.

It has also been with me a question very problematical: whether any distinction should be made between the young and the old, the tender and the robust; whether any room should be given for repentance, or the guilt of Christianity once incurred, is not to be expiated by the most unequivocal retraction; whether the name itself, abstracted from any flagitiousness of conduct, or the crimes connected with the name, be the object of punishment. In the mean time, this has been my method, with respect to those who were brought before me as Christians.

I asked them whether they were Christians. If they plead guilty, I interrogated them twice afresh, with a menace of capital punishment. In case of obstinate perseverance, I ordered them to be executed. For of this I had no doubt, whatever was the nature of their religion, that a sullen and obstinate inflexibility called for the vengeance of the magistrate. Some were infected with the same madness, whom on account of their citizenship, I reserved to be sent to Rome, to your tribunal. In the course of this business, informations pouring in as is usual when they are encouraged, more cases occurred. An anonymous libel was exhibited, with a catalogue of names of persons, who yet declared that they were not Christians then, nor ever had been; and they repeated after me an invocation of the gods and of your image, which, for this purpose, I had ordered to be brought with the images of the deities. They performed sacred rites with wine and frankincense, and execrated Christ, which, I am told, no Christian can ever be compelled to do. On this account, I dismissed them.

Others named by an informer, first affirmed, and then denied the charge of Christianity; declaring that they had been Christians, but had ceased to be so, some three years ago; others, still longer; some even twenty years ago. All of them worshipped your image, and the statues of the gods, and also execrated Christ.

And this was the account which they gave of the nature of the religion they once had professed, whether it deserves the name of crime or error, namely—that they were accustomed on a stated day to meet before daylight, and to repeat among themselves a hymn to Christ, as to a god, and to bind themselves by an oath, with an obligation of not committing any wickedness; but, on the contrary, of abstaining from thefts, robberies and adulteries; also of not violating their promise, or denying a pledge; after which it was their custom to separate, and to meet again at a promiscuous, harmless meal, from which last practice, however, they desisted, after the publication of my edict, in which, agreeably to your order, I forbade any societies of that sort.

On which account I judged it the more necessary to inquire, by torture, from two females, who were said to be deaconesses, what is the real truth. But nothing could I collect except a depraved and excessive superstition. Deferring therefore any farther investigation, I determined to consult you. For the number of culprits is so great, as to call for serious consultation.

"Many persons are informed against, of every age and of both sexes; and more still will be in the same situation. The contagion of the superstition hath spread, not only through cities, but even villages in the country. Not that I think it impossible to check and to correct it.

The success of my endeavors hitherto forbids such desponding thoughts; for the temples, once almost desolate, begin to be frequented, and the sacred solemnities, which had long been intermitted, are now attended afresh, and the sacrificial victims are now sold every where, which once could scarcely find a purchaser. Whence, I conclude that many might be reclaimed, were the hope of impunity on repentance absolutely confirmed."

Trajan to Pliny.

"You have done perfectly right, my dear Pliny, in the inquiry which you have made concerning Christians. For truly, no one general rule can be laid down, which will apply itself to all cases. These people must not be sought after. If they are brought before you and convicted, let them be capitally punished; yet with this restriction, that if any one renounce Christianity, and evidence his sincerity by supplicating our gods, however suspected he may be for the past, he shall obtain pardon for the future on his repentance. But anonymous libels ought, in no case, be attained to; for the precedent would be of the worst sort, and perfectly incongruous to the maxims of my government."

From this important correspondence, we learn that Christians were then very numerous;—that they every where worshipped Christ as God; that their morals were not only unimpeachable, but of an high character, and that, because of the spirit of Christianity, the heathen temples were almost desolate, and the sacrificial victims could scarce find a purchaser. This is the testimony, not of a Christian, but of a heathen governor.

Strange that such men as Trajan and Pliny should not have been allured by a religion which made such good men and peaceable citizens; or, at least, should not have withheld from them entirely the arm of persecution. But there is no coinsidence between the religion of a virtuous pagan, and the Gospel of Christ. The one fosters human pride; the other, humbles man in the dust; so that often the bitterest enemies of the cross, are those who have made the greatest attainments, as they themselves think, in the moral virtues.

The order of Trajan, however, was favorable to the Christians, as it forbade all search to be made after them and prohibited all anonymous libels and accusations, though it still left the door open for persecution and death.

From this correspondence also, and from the other historical records of the age, we learn that the Christians were looked upon with the utmost contempt. Pliny calls their religion a "depraved and excessive superstition," and views their attachment to the Gospel, as a sullen and obstinate inflexibility, demanding the vengeance of the magistrate. No epithets could be too debased to be heaped upon them. They were called atheists, magicians, haters of the light, self-murderers, eaters of human flesh; and were accused of unnatural crimes, which are not to be mentioned. But their accusers could bring nothing against them, excepting that they would not invoke the gods and execrate Christ; and when any apostates would do this, they were at once forgiven and admitted into favor, notwithstanding these charges of gross immorality.

Had we correct biographical notices of those who conversed with them, and survived the Apostles, we should, no doubt, find many among them who illustriously adorned the doctrine of God their Saviour. The writings only of Clement, who presided nine years over the Church of Rome, and whom Paul calls his fellow laborer, whose "name is in the book of life," have come down to us. He wrote an epistle to the Corinthians, at the close of the first century; which presents him as strongly attached to the fundamental doctrines of the Gospel, and animated by a truly apostolic spirit; and the Corinthians, as still possessing the faith, and hope, and charity of the Gospel, though tarnished, as in the days of Paul, with pride and a schismatical spirit.

The successor of James, in the pastoral office at Jerusalem, was Simeon. The church had fled to Pella, when the city was encompassed with the Roman armies; but it returned to Judea, about the beginning of Trajan's reign, after quiet was restored, and the city in some measure rebuilt. There Adrian found them worshipping in a small building upon Mount Zion, when he came to repair Jerusalem. Simeon lived to a great age. Being accused before Atticus, the Roman governor, he was scourged many days and then crucified A.D. 107.

In the same year, Ignatius, who presided in the church of Antioch, suffered martyrdom for the faith of Jesus. He had in his youth been a disciple of John, and had been intimately acquainted with Peter and Paul. Peter, it is said, laid hands on him when he was ordained to the pastoral office.

Having continued in the pastoral charge about forty-five years, he presented himself before Trajan on his way to the Parthian war, hoping to avert a storm which was then ready to burst on the Christians.

"What an impious spirit art thou," said Trajan, "both to transgress our commands, and to inveigle others into the same folly to their ruin!"

"Theophorus ought not to be called so," answered Ignatius, "forasmuch as all wicked spirits are departed from the servants of God. But if you call me impious because I am hostile to evil spirits, I own the charge in that respect. For I dissolve all their snares through Christ, the heavenly king."

Trajan, "Pray, who is Theophorus?"

Ignatius, "He who has Christ in his breast."

Trajan, "And thinkest thou not that gods reside in us also, who fight for us against our enemies?"

Ignatius, "You mistake in calling the demons of the nations by the name of gods. For there is only one God, who made heaven and earth, the sea and all that is in them; and one Jesus Christ, his only begotten Son, whose kingdom be my portion."

Trajan, "His kingdom, do you say, who was crucified under Pilate?"

Ignatius, "His, who crucified my sin with its author, and has put all the fraud and malice of Satan under the feet of those who carry him in their hearts."

Trajan, "Dost thou then carry him who was crucified with thee?"

Ignatius, "I do; for it is written, 'I dwell in them, and walk in them.'"

Then Trajan pronounced this sentence against him. "Since Ignatius confesses that he carries within himself him that was crucified, we command that he be carried, bound by soldiers, to great Rome, there to be thrown to the wild beasts for the entertainment of the people."

This excellent man, "full of faith and of the Holy Ghost," was hurried off to the place of suffering. On his way to Rome, he stopped at Smyrna to visit Polycarp. They had been fellow disciples of John. Their meeting was joyful. Seven epistles were written by him to as many churches before he reached the end of his journey. From these, which are still extant, though perhaps corrupted, we learn that the churches of Asia retained much evangelical purity, though they were often greatly perplexed by heresies, and borne down by persecution; that the Deity, manhood, and atonement of Christ, were doctrines unspeakably precious; and that an entire separation from all who deny the fundamental doctrines of Christianity, was the foundation of their long continued prosperity. When he came to Rome he was anxious for a speedy martydom, and had his wish granted, for he was immediately led into the amphitheatre and thrown to the wild beasts. His bones were carefully collected by his friends and carried to Antioch.

Trajan was succeeded by Adrian, A.D.117. This emperor was respectfully addressed by Quadratus and Aristides, two excellent Athenian Christians, in behalf of the churches; and by them he seems to have been induced to direct that the calumniators of Christians should not only not be heard, but should be punished; and that, if any were presented before the magistrates, they should be condemned only as it should appear that they had broken the laws. This was the most favorable decree that had ever been made relating to the followers of Christ.

During Adrian's reign, appeared a great imposter among the Jews, called Barchobebas, because he pretended to be the Star prophesied of by Balaam. Defeated in every way and reduced to the greatest extremities, the Jews received him with open arms. He came out in rebellion against the emperor, but was soon defeated and slain. In the conflict, however, the Christians were great sufferers; for the Jews, looking upon them as the authors of their calamities, everywhere inflicted upon them the greatest cruelties.

The next emperor, Antoninus Pius, was still more favorable to the Christians. In the third year of his reign, A.D. 140, Justin Martyr, a very able defender of the truth, presented him an apology for Christianity, which had no small influence on his mind. An edict issued by him, in consequence of complaints made from Asia of the Christians, as the cause of the earthquakes, speaks volumes in his praise, and in praise too, of the persecuted.

"THE EMPEROR TO THE COMMON COUNCIL OF ASIA."

"I am quite of opinion that the gods will take care to discover such persons. For it much more concerns them to punish those who refuse to worship them, than you, if they be able. But you harass and vex the Christians and accuse them of atheism and other crimes, which you can by no means prove. To them it appears an advantage to die for their religion; and they will gain their point, while they throw away their lives rather than comply with your injunctions. As to the earthquakes which have happened in past times, or lately, is it not proper to remind you of your own despondency, when they happen, and to desire you to compare your spirit with theirs and observe how serenely they confide in God! In such seasons you seem to be ignorant of the gods, and to neglect their worship.

"You live in the practical ignorance of the supreme God himself, and you harass and persecute to death those who do worship him. Concerning these same men, some others of the provincial governors wrote to our divine father Adrian, to whom he returned answer, 'That they should not be molested, unless they appeared to attempt something against the Roman government.' Many, also, have signified to me concerning these men, to whom I have returned an answer agreeable to the maxims of my father. But if any person will still persist in accusing the Christians merely as such—let the accused be acquitted, though he appear to be a Christian, and let the accuser be punished."

This was certainly no ordinary, and we are assured by Eusebius, it was no empty edict; for it was fully put in execution, and gave the church about twenty-three years of peace and prosperity. But such seasons she was liable to abuse; provoking against her the anger of heaven. From worldly mindedness and stupidity, however, she was **again soon roused** by the fires of persecution.

In the year 161, Pius was succeeded by Marcus Antoninus, a man of eminence in the schools of philosophy; whose meditations, humanity, and beneficence, have gained him the plaudits of succeeding generations, but whose pride and self importance made him scorn the doctrines of the cross; made him, for nineteen years, a bitter persecutor of the followers of the meek and lowly Jesus. Very able apologies were made for the Christians by Justin, Tatian, Athenagoras, Apollinaris, Theophilus, and Melito; but they were regarded by Marcus as a vain, obstinate, and evil-minded race, and left without relief, to the most cruel tortures. So much, however, were former edicts regarded, that none could be condemned unless some crime was brought against them; but the enraged heathen priests and corrupt judges found no difficulty in suborning false witnesses, and procuring the death of all who were brought before them.

In the year 163, the able apologist, Justin, slept in Jesus. He was educated a philosopher, and was, probably, the most learned man, who, from the days of the Apostles, had embraced Christianity. In early life he wandered through all the systems of philosophy in pursuit of God and happiness, but found no satisfactions. At length, he examined the Gospel, and found peace for his soul. To the cause of the Redeemer he consecrated his habits of study, and became its able supporter. His views of Christian doctrine were once, in the main, evangelical; but he was nearly ruined by a philosophizing spirit. Of those who denied the Deity of Christ, he thus expressed himself: "There are some who call themselves Christians, who confess him to be the Christ, but still maintain that he is a mere man only, with whom I agree not; neither do most of those who bear that name agree with them; because we are commanded by Christ himself not to obey the precepts of men, but His own injunctions, and those of the holy prophets. As for myself, I am too mean to say any thing becoming His infinite Deity." His apologies for Christianity are still extant, and are very valuable.

This learned and excellent man was imprisoned, whipped, and beheaded for the crime of being a Christian. We have his testimony to the interesting and important fact, that the churches in his time examined those they received, not only concerning their creed, but concerning a work of grace in their hearts.

But the most distinguished martyr of the age was Polycarp. This venerable man was the disciple of John,—was intimate with the apostles, and was ordained by them over the church of Smyrna. The learned Usher says, it is beyond all question, that he was the angel of the church of Smyrna, to whom the apocalyptical epistle was sent. If so, his martyrdom was there particularly predicted. For seventy years he had been a firm pillar in the church. Against the heretics of the age, especially the Docetae, who denied the humanity of Christ, rejected the Old Testament, and mutilated the New, he opposed himself with the greatest firmness. To Marcion, their chief, who one day called out to him, "Polycarp, own us;" "I do own thee," said he, "to be the first born of Satan." Ireneus informs us that he often heard from his lips an account of his conversations with John, and others who had seen our Lord, whose sayings he rehearsed.

This venerable man was brought to the tribunal in the hundredth year of his age. The proconsul told him to reproach Christ and he would release him. "Eighty and six years," said Polycarp, "have I served him, and he hath never wronged me, and how can I blaspheme my King who hath saved me?" "I have wild beasts," said the proconsul. "Call them," said the martyr. "I will tame your spirit by fire." "You threaten me with fire which burns for a moment and will be soon extinct; but you are ignorant of the future judgment, and of the fire of eternal punishment reserved for the ungodly. But why do you delay? Do what you please."

The fire being prepared, and he being bound, a distinguished sacrifice, clasped his hands, which were tied behind him, and said, "O Father of thy beloved and blessed Son, Jesus Christ, through whom we have attained a knowledge of thee, O God of angels and principalities, and of all creation, and of all the just who live in thy sight, I bless thee that thou hast counted me worthy of this day, and this hour, to receive my portion in the number of martyrs, in the cup of Christ, for the resurrection to eternal life, both of soul and body in the incorruption of the Holy Ghost, among whom may I be received before thee this day as a sacrifice well savored and acceptable, which thou the faithful and true God has prepared, promised beforehand, and fulfilled accordingly. Wherefore I praise thee for all these things, I glorify thee by the Eternal High Priest, thy well beloved Son, through whom with him in the Holy Spirit, be glory to thee, both now and forever. Amen."

Eleven brethren from Philadelphia suffered with him, A.D. 167. If the Lord Jesus Christ died as a mere martyr to the truth, how inferior was he in fortitude to his servant Polycarp! "O My Father," said He, "If it be possible, let this cup pass from me." But He was an atoning sacrifice called to bear His Father's wrath for our sins.

By the persecutions of Antoninus, our attention is here directed to a country hitherto unknown in ecclesiastical history. Flourishing churches had been planted in Vienne, and Lyons in France, then called Galia; probably by the churches of Asia. The account given by themselves of their sufferings, under Severus, the Roman governor, will be read with great interest by all who love to trace the children of God in their Christian warfare. It affords a very full account of the humility, meekness, patience, magnanimity and heavenly-mindedness of the martyrs; of the influences of the Holy Spirit; of the supports of religion, under the most excruciating sufferings, and must excite in every reader, a spirit of gratitude to God, for the inestimable blessings which we, in this age of light and liberty, are permitted to enjoy.—Epitome Gen. Eccl. History, John Marsh, pages 169-179.

ITEM III

FURNISHINGS OF JERUSALEM TEMPLE LOST AT SEA.

"The Vandals in their sacking of Rome loaded all the rich ornaments of the Capital on ships and sailed toward Africa. On this ship were many of the furnishing of the Temple in Jerusalem that Titus had carried from there to Rome in his destruction of Jerusalem in A.D. 70. The ship went down with all its cargo, in A.D. 455."—Goodrich's Pictoral History of Ancient Rome, page 261.

ITEM IV

STRONG CONCESSIONS FROM HARNACK'S HISTORY OF DOGMA

J. Lewis Smith, D.D.

Harnack says that the idea of the Catholic (not Roman) church sprung up in the third—third of the third century—about 280 A.D.

He says: "In the latter writings of Tertullian, dating from the reigns of Corocalla and Heliogabolas, he tells us that the bishop of Rome claimed for his office for the full authority of the apostolic office." This claim of the episcopal office was not found in any of Tertullians or Iremen's earlier writings. It is not found in the apostolic constitutions, compared about the end of the 3rd century.

It is completely unknown to Clement of Alexandria. On the origin of this claim of Rome, Harnack says (vol. 11 p. 73): "This notion lies at the basis of the exhortations of Ignatius (viz. every individual congregation is to be an image of the heavenly church). He knows nothing of an empiracle union of the different communities into one church guaranteed by any law or office."

On page 73 he says: "The bishop is of importance only for the individual community, and has nothing to do with the essence of the church, nor does Ignatius view the separate communities as united in any other way than by faith, charity and hope."

The expression "Catholic church" appears first in Ignatius.

Harnack says it does not express a new conception of

the church, which respects her as an empiracal commonwealth.

Only the individual, earthly communities exist empiracally and the universal, i.e., the whole church occupies the same position toward these as the bishops of the individual communities do toward the Lord," vol. 11, p. 74.

Again: "The earlier expressions for the whole of Christendom are: 'All the churches,' 'churches in every city,' 'The churches in the world,' 'The churches under heaven,' " p. 75.

In early times Catholic originally meant, he says, the same as orthodox. "The Catholic church which is in Smyrna" (Mart, Polyc. xvi 2 from Ignatius).

He says: "The independence of each individual community had a wide scope not only at the end of the second but also in the third century.

"Consequently the revolution which led to the Catholic church was a result of the situation of the communities in the world in general, and of the struggle with the Gnostics and Marcion in particular, and though it was a fatal error to identify the Catholic and Apostolic churches, this change did not take place without an exalting of the Christian spirit and an awakening of its self-consciousness.

"But there never was a time in history when the conception of the church, as nothing else than the visible communion of those holding the correct apostolic doctrine, was clearly grasped or exclusively emphasized," vol. 11, page 77.

On the "Invisible church" idea Harnack says (vol. 11 p. 83): "No one thought of the desperate idea of an invisible church; this notion would probably have brought about a lapse from pure Christianity far more rapidly than the idea of the Holy Catholic church."

If this idea of an invisible church would have brought about a lapse in the early centuries what will it do now? It is the pillar of modern Sectarianism. Without it the sects could not exist at all.

Iraneus, Clement, Tertullian and Origin knew nothing of an invisible church idea. In their day, Harnack says,

"It would have produced a lapse from Christianity."

Cyprian was the father of the idea of the church as an aristocratic governed state—governed by the bishop.

Stephen, Calixaus and Victor each, in a measure, claimed the primacy over all churches, new and old.

But Cyprian opposed Stephen and maintained that every bishop is responsible for his practice to God alone.

Firmillian Epis. 75, indirectly declared the succession of Peter, claimed by Stephen, to be of no importance, and flatly denied that the Roman church had preserved an apostolic tradition to that effect.

Harnack says that Clement of Rome was the first to compare the conductors of the public worship in Christian churches to priests and Levites, and the author of the Didacha was the first to liken the Christian prophets to the high priests, vol. 11, p. 128. Again, Harnack says: "It cannot, however, be shown that there were any Christian circles where the leaders were directly styled 'priests' before the last quarter of the second century," p. 128.

He says Hippolytus claimed high priesthood for the Bishops, and Origin justified the names "priests" and Levites, for those conducting Christian public service.

Cyprian, and the literature of the Greek churches immediately following him, give the pastors or bishops the title of priests.

On infant baptism, Harnack says: "Complete obscurity prevails as to the churches' adoption of the practice of child baptism, which, though it owes its origin to the idea of this ceremony being indispensable to salvation, it is nevertheless a proof that the superstitious view of baptism had increased.

"In the time of Iraneus and Tertullian child baptism had already become very general and was founded on Matthew 19:14.

"We have no testimony regarding it from earlier times; Clement of Alexandria does not yet assume it. Tertullian was against it vol. 11, p. 142.

"Child communion originated the same time as child baptism.

"We hear of it first in Cyprian's testimony 111:25, de laps. 25 vol. 11, p. 147."

From these clear testimonies of so clear and so great an historian as Prof. Harnack we draw the same conclusions we have been led to draw from many another church historian.

1. That the "Catholic" or "universal church" idea is a thing of man's devising and sprang up in the latter part of the 3rd century.

2. The idea of the bishop claiming to hold his office as a succession from the apostolic office is not found in the earlier writings of Iraneus or Tertullian or in any other writer before the middle or end of the 3rd century.

3. The expression, "Catholic church" appears first in Ignatius.

4. The term "Invisible church" is found for the first time in Hegesippus, but this is not the early predicate used by the earliest writers.

5. The independence of the local churches had, he says, wide scope in the end of the second and far into the third century.

6. The invisible church idea would have produced a greater lapse from pure Christianity in those early ages, than the idea of the Holy Catholic church.

7. Cyprian was the father of the Roman Catholic church idea of an aristocratic government of the church.

8. Clement of Rome was the first to compare the pastors of the early churches to "priests," the last quarter of the 2nd century.

9. Infant baptism is of human origin of obscure date and grew out of the idea of baptism being indispensable to salvation.

10. Child communion originated at the same time as child baptism.

These are the testimonies of one of the greatest living church historians and in the main agree with most if not all historians of the early church.—AMERICAN BAPTIST FLAG, March 13, 1902, issue.

ITEM V

A POPE AND A KING

Here is one of the innumerable instances where popes have shown their disdain for civil authority.

William Jones says—

"To avoid the odium of this impending trial (King) Henry took the strange resolution of suddenly passing the Alps, accompanied only by a few domestics, and of throwing himself at the feet of Gregory, in order to implore his absolution. The pontiff was at that time on a visit to the countess or duchess Matilda, at Canosa, a fortress on the Appenines.

"At the gate of this mansion, the emperor presented himself as an humble penitent. He alone was admitted within the outer court, where, being stripped of his robes, and wrapped in sackcloth, he was compelled to remain three days, in the month of January (A.D. 1077) barefoot and fasting, before he was permitted to kiss the feet of his holiness!!

"The indulgence was, however, at length granted him —he was permitted to throw himself at the feet of the haughty pontiff, who condescended to grant him absolution, after he had sworn obedience to the pope in all things, and promised to submit to his solemn decision at Augsburgh; so that Henry reaped nothing but disgrace and mortification from his journey, while the pontiff, elate with triumph, and now considering himself as the lord and master of all the crowned heads in Christendom, said in several of his letters, that it was his duty to pull down the pride of kings."

—History of the Christian Church, Jones, page 264.

ITEM VI

ROGER WILLIAMS NEVER A BAPTIST

Roger Williams and his wife left the port of Bristol, England, in 1630 on the ship Lyon. They arrived in Boston February 5, 1631. He was about 30 years of age. He was an avowed separatist and spoke freely his views.

He refused to join the Boston Congregation because they had not completely separated from the Anglicans. The Liberal Church at Salem called him, but the Court of the Colony interfered. This caused Roger to go to Plymouth. He pastored the Pilgrim's Church for two years and became a member of it. According to Governor Bradford, "He was freely entertained, according to our poor ability, and exercised his gifts among us; and after sometime was admitted a member of the Church among us and his teachings well approved."

"To term Roger Williams the founder of the Baptist Church in America, and the church he founded "the venerable mother of American Baptist Churches" as often done, is historically incorrect, for after all the part played by Williams in American Baptist history is extremely small, and the church he founded bore no living children."—William Warren Sweet, **The Story of Religions in America,** 1930 P. 98-99.

Mr. Roger Williams was brought up in the church of England. Coming to America he became an assistant, and later pastor, of a church in Salem; the said church being comparable to the present day Congregationalists.

1. He was not a Baptist because, in the view of Baptists, he never had scriptural baptism. He had been bap-

tized by Ezekiel Holiman, an unbaptized man himself. In the convictions of Baptists this is unscriptural. No orthodox Baptist today would approve it. That it was considered irregular and unscriptural by Baptists we cite the following.

The Philadelphia Baptist Association is very renown. One hundred years history of this group of Baptists is recorded in the minutes of said body bound in one volume comprising the years 1707 to 1807. In these minutes we find the following:

"In the year 1732 a question was moved whether a person, not being baptized himself, and presuming in private (i.e. without the knowledge or consent of a church) to baptize another, whether such pretended baptism be valid or not, or whether it might not be adjusted a nullity?

"Resolved, we judge such baptism as invalid and no better than if it had never been one."—Minutes Philadelphia Baptist Association, page 33.

In 1744 we find this query and answer:

"Suppose a person, baptized by a man, who takes upon himself to preach the gospel, and proceeds to administer the ordinances without a regular call or ordination from any church, whether the person so baptized may be admitted into any orderly church—yea or nay?

"Resolved, we can not encourage such irregular proceedings, because it hath ill-consequences every way attending it; it is also opposite to our discipline (i.e. revolutionary). We, therefore, give our sentiments that such administrations are irregular, invalid and of no effect." This is the kind of baptism that Roger Williams had, and no other. It was not Baptist Baptism. He was immersed by a man who had not only not been ordained but one who had himself never been baptized, and was not a member of a Baptist church. Nothing could be more invalid from a Baptist viewpoint.

On page 104 of the same minutes of the Philadelphia Baptist Association we find that in 1768 another such query came from New York. We quote: "In answer to a query from New York, it was agreed that baptism administered by a person not ordained, was invalid and disorderly."

Again in 1792—"A query respecting the validity of baptism administered by an unordained and unbaptized administrator was taken up and determined in the negative." Ezekiel Holiman was not a baptized man and was not ordained when he baptized Roger Williams.

In the minutes of the Elkhorn Association, for the year 1822 we find the following:

"The committee, to whom the following querys from the First Baptist Church, Lexington, we referred, viz. 1. Can a person baptized on a profession of faith, by an administrator not regularly ordained, be received into our churches under any circumstances whatsoever, without being again baptized?"

"Report in answer to the first query, that it is not regular to receive such members. In the minutes of 1802, this Association defined valid baptism to consist in the administration of the ordinances by an administrator legally called to preach the gospel and ordained as the Scriptures direct, and that the candidate for baptism make a profession of faith in Jesus Christ, and that he be baptized into the name of the Father, and of the Son, and of the Holy Ghost, by dipping the whole body in water.

> Signed: J. Vardaman,
> E. Waller,
> James Fishback,
> John Edwards,
> Jacob Creath."

It can be readily seen that the Baptism of Roger Williams was not Baptist baptism in any manner. Not being a Baptist he could not very well organize a Baptist church at Providence, or any other place.

It also follows that when Williams baptized Holiman and several others after being baptized himself by Holiman that he did so without authority. Therefore the Providence church was unscriptural because baptism is admitted by all a prerequisite for church membership.

2. Roger Williams never belonged to a Baptist church in his life. There is no question but that the "church" he formed at Providence died in four months after its "organization." Williams renounced his own baptism, said the world was without the true church and true ministry. He lived for many decades after the failure of the Providence effort but never was identified with any Baptist church. If he had been a Baptist at heart undoubtedly he would have joined the church at Newport or some other place.

3. Williams was not a Baptist in that he contended that the true church no longer existed and that it was necessary for some special authority from heaven to re-establish it. He became a seeker and familist waiting for some such demonstration which, of course, never came. Baptists believe that Jesus meant what he said when he said the gates of hell should never prevail against His church. **"Upon this Rock I will build my church and the gates of hell shall not prevail against it,"** Matthew 16:18. Baptists have ever believed this. Roger Williams believed that the gates of hell did prevail.

Mr. S. Adlam, one time pastor of the First Church, Newport, made an investigation of the claims of both the Newport and the Providence churches and then published his findings. We quote: "There is one writer whose testimony is of the highest value on the subject. I allude to Thomas Lechford, who was in New England from 1637 till August, 1641; and, among other places, he visited Providence, somewhere, I judge, about the close of 1640, or the beginning of 1641. He inquired, with great diligence, into the ecclesiastical affairs of the country, and gave a faithful account. Against the Baptists he had no special prejudices more than against the Congregationalists, for he was an Episcopalian. But whatever were his own convictions, I have gained, in many respects, a more exact view of New England during these four years from him than any other person. When speaking of Providence he says, "At Providence, which is twenty miles from the said island (Rhode Island) which he visited, lives Master Williams and his company, of divers opinions; most are Anabaptists.

They hold there is no true, visible church in the Bay, nor in the world, nor any true ministry."

These are not the doctrines of Baptists.

4. He was critical of Baptist baptism as performed by Dr. John Clarke and others. While he said it was the nearest to the Scriptural way, he could not wholly approve of the manner of it. This shows he was not a Baptist. No Baptist would criticise regular Baptist baptism.

5. Williams was not the first to preach liberty of conscience in religious matters, despite a plaque on the wall of the church in Providence to that effect. In fact, the pact he fathered for the colony did not guarantee such freedom. It actually adopted the laws of England, which permitted the abuse of liberty.

Christ and all the apostles and believers from that day until now have believed in and fought for liberty of conscience. Many confessions of faith had been adopted by people of Baptist sentiments previous to Roger Williams' coming to America. We readily grant that Williams held these views but it takes more than this to make a Baptist.

THE ORGANIZATION OF WILLIAMS AT PROVIDENCE WAS NOT A BAPTIST CHURCH

To be a scriptural church it must be formed of scriptural members. In the view of Baptists this means persons who have been saved from their sins by the grace of God, born-again ones. Second, they must be baptized upon a profession of their faith by one who himself is qualified as an administrator. A qualified administrator is one who has been ordained by a Scriptural church and authorized by that church to administer the ordinance of baptism.

When Williams and his friends came to Providence they came as excluded members of the church at Salem. Neither of them having baptism. Ezekiel Holiman baptized Williams and then Williams baptized the remainder. No ordination, no church authority . . . and Jesus gave the Commission to baptize to His CHURCH, Matthew 28:19-20. These not being regularly baptized, even granting they were saved, were not qualified to form a Baptist church. Had they had regular Baptist sentiments they could have joined the church at Newport, some 20 miles away, been Scripturally baptized and then obtained letters, as Baptists do today, and scripturally organized a Baptist church at Providence.

THE CHURCH AT PROVIDENCE DIED IN FOUR MONTHS

We know from many and reliable historical sources that the "church" Williams and some others formed at Providence died in about four months. Williams at that time renounced his own baptism and the baptism of the others and became a self confessed "seeker" or familist, contending that the church (true church) had become extinct and that it would take a revelation of authority from the Holy Spirit for it to be reconstituted. He waited for such a demonstration which, of course, never came.

Cotton Mather, a contemporary historian, a Methodist, a scholar, one that was on the ground and who knew the facts as they existed in that day testified: "One Roger Williams, a preacher, arrived in New England about the year 1630; was first an assistant in the church at Salem and afterwards its pastor. This man—a difference happening between the Government and him—caused a great deal of trouble and vexation. At length the Magistrates passed the sentence of banishment upon him; upon which he removed with a few of his own sect and settled at a place called Providence. There they proceeded not only unto the gathering of a thing like a church, but unto the renouncing their infant baptism. After this he turned seeker and familist, and the church came to nothing."—Mathers' Eccl. History of New England, Page 7 and Crosly, Vol. 1, Page 117. Notice that the "thing like a church" came to nothing. And notice that he renounced the whole thing and became a seeker and familist. So, the "church" he established has no succession.

A writer in the CHRISTIAN REVIEW condenses some facts as follows:

1. Roger Williams was baptized by Ezekiel Holiman,

March 1639; and immediately after, he baptized Mr. Holiman and ten others.

2. These formed a church, or society, of which Roger Williams was the pastor.

3. Four months after his baptism—that is, in July following—Williams left the church, and never afterwards returned to it. As his doubts respecting baptism and the perpetuity of the church, which led to this step, must have commenced soon after his baptism, it is not likely that he baptized any others.

4. The church which Williams formed, came to nothing, or was dissolved soon after he left it.—Ray's Baptist Succession, Page 61.

SECOND ORGANIZATION AT PROVIDENCE

Sometime after the dissolution of the "thing like a church" originated by Williams, a second effort was made to establish a church in Providence. Thomas Olney became its pastor and continued, it is said, until 1682. Olney was one of Williams' original group. This church also finally ceased to exist.

About 1652 there was a division in the church and three brethren by the name of Brown, Dexter and Wickenden (also known as a Wiggington, probably by the way the name was pronounced) took the lead in organizing another church.

"Not long after the dissolution of the Roger Williams society, which only existed a few months, Thomas Olney, one of the persons baptized by Williams, gathered a church at Providence. Some historians have made Olney the successor of Williams in the pastorship over the Williams church. He was the successor of Mr. Williams as pastor in Providence, not over the Williams' church, but over one gathered some time after the Williams' church came to nothing. So, Olney's church was the **Second** formed in Providence, over which he officiated as pastor until his death in 1652. A division occurred in the Olney church; a number of members broke off and formed another church under the leadership of Elders Dexter, Wickenden and

Brown, who were Elders together in its formation, and succeeded each other in the pastorship of this church. That there were two Baptist churches in Providence as early as 1652 or 1653, is an undisputed fact. Mr. Adlam introduces the testimony of Mr. Staples, as follows: "Staples, in his annals of Providence, says: "There were two Baptist churches in Providence as early as 1652; one of the six-principle, and the other of the five- principle Baptists. This appears from a manuscript diary kept by John Comer, a Baptist preacher at Newport."

A Mr. Callender says the same thing except he places the date of the organization of the second church in either 1653 or 1654.

The church formed by Elders Dexter, Wickenden and Brown is the existing church, the second becoming extinct. Quoting Ray's Baptist Succession, page 54: "Thus it is shown that the present Providence church, which was organized in 1652, by Wickenden, Dexter and Browne, has taken, instead of her own date, the date of the Roger Williams Society. But what became of the old Olney five-principle church? Mr. Adlam says: 'A melancholy interest invests the last notice we have of this ancient church. It continued until early the last century, when it became extinct, leaving NO RECORDS, and but few events in its history behind. The fullest information of it I have found, is in a note by Callender, on page 115 of his discourse.' Speaking of this church, he adds below: 'This last continued till about twenty years ago, when, becoming destitute of an elder, the members were united with other churches.'" This was written in 1738.

WILLIAMS AND CONTINUITY

The following is taken from J. M. Cramp's History:

"He denied that any ministry now exists, which is authorized to preach the Gospel to the impenitent, or to administer the ordinances. He believed that these functions belonged to the Apostolic race of ministers, which was interrupted and discontinued when the reign of Antichrist commenced, and which will not, as he thought, be restored, till the witnesses shall have been slain and raised again (Rev. xi. 11) . . . He says in his **Hireling Ministry None of Christ's,** published in 1652:—'In the poor small span of my life, I desired to have been a diligent and constant observer, and have been myself many ways engaged, in city, in country, in courts, in schools, in universities, in church, in Old and New England, and yet cannot, in the holy presence of God, bring in the result of a satisfactory discovery, that either the begetting ministry of the Apostles or messengers to the nations, or the feeding or nourishing ministry of teachers, according to the first institution of the Lord Jesus, are yet restored and extant. The only ministry which, in my opinion, now exists, is that of prophets, i.e. ministers, who explain religious truths, and bear witness against error.' "—J. M. Cramp's History of The Church.

Mr. Benedict himself, later in life, admitted that the more he studied the matter the more he was confused about the priority of the organizations of the two churches, Newport and Providence. Not that it makes any real difference, of course, since we know the Providence church was not organized until 1639 and died four months later. Abundant evidence shows that it never was and could not have been a Baptist church, because it did not have Baptist material with which to build.

THE PROVIDENCE CHURCH HAD NO CREED

"The church at Providence never had any creed or any covenant; till the year 1700 it had no meeting house, but, in fine weather, worshipped in a grove, and, when inclement, in private houses. Not till the year 1775, had it any regular records. Can we be surprised that, in tracing the history of such a body, a hundred years after its origin, unless ancient writers are carefully studied, that material errors will be made."—First Baptist Church in America, Adlam. Quoted by Ray, page 45.

We quote John Marsh on this point:

"Roger Williams, who left his Congregational church in Salem and contended with the Government and churches in Massachusetts, on points of discipline, established himself at Providence, **with no particular church order.**"—Epitome Eccl. History, page 410.

CELEBRATE AN UNKNOWN DAY

One of the orators on the occasion of an anniversary said: "We celebrate, after all, an **Un-known** Day. There is no record of the exact date of our beginning." This was said by a Dr. Caldwell April, 1889.

Dr. Caldwell further says: "No records before the coming of Manning, in fact, prior to 1775, have been preserved of the Providence church. They may have departed with Winsor and his church, and disappeared, we know not where. One hundred and fifty years of the story now told has had to be taken where ever it could be found, and not from any records preserved and authenticated by the church itself." He said this in his two hundred and fiftieth anniversary address.

A Dr. Manning was president of Brown College for years and was pastor of the Providence church as well. He says of John Stanford's visit there in search of historical material:

"During the brief period of his stay here Reverend John Stanford gathered such facts as he could find, and his account was inserted in the Book of Records. It has been quoted by Benedict and other writers, as if it had the authority of original records. BUT IT CONTAINS MANY ERRORS. It was published by Dr. Rippon in his Baptist Annual Register, in 1801-2, with a picture of the meeting house. The publication, for some reason, was delayed for several years."—Manning and Brown University, 440.

DR. JOHN CLARKE AND THE NEWPORT CHURCH

Dr. John Clarke was one of the most eminent Baptist ministers of all time. HE ORGANIZED THE FIRST BAPTIST CHURCH IN AMERICA.

Some years ago Dr. J. R. Graves, a noted author of Baptist papers and books, and one of the greatest of scholars, and one always interested in pure facts, resolved to investigate the matter of which was the first Baptist church to be organized in America.

Dr. Graves was a man who had had many religious discussions, especially with Pedobaptists. He had met constantly with the assertion that the Baptists began in America with Roger Williams. He knew better than this and determined to learn the truth about the first Baptist church in America.

A book of S. Adlam, a pastor of the First Baptist Church, Newport, Rhode Island, had come into the hands of Dr. Graves. Dr. Adlam had made intensive investigation of the claims of the Providence church and had come to the conclusion, after deliberate weighing of all evidence, that the "church" organized by Williams had come to naught in a few weeks. He further learned that the present Providence church was indeed the THIRD church of the place. It was this third church that appropriated to itself the Roger Williams' date.

Dr. Graves traveled to Providence and Newport in quest of more information. He visited Dr. Adlam who took him to the neglected grave of Dr. John Clarke. Let him tell his story:

"Under the guidance of Dr. Adlam I sought the neglected grave of Dr. John Clarke, and digging away a mould, which had accumulated at the foot of the tombstone, I read as follows: To the Memory of DOCTOR JOHN CLARKE, one of the founders of the FIRST BAPTIST CHURCH of Newport, its first pastor, and munificent benefactor; He was a native of Bedfordshire, England, and a practitioner of physic in London. He, his associates, came to this island from Mass., in March 1638, O. S. and on the 24 of the same month obtained a deed thereof from the Indians. He shortly after gathered the church aforesaid and became its pastor; in 1651, he, with Roger Williams, was sent to England, by the people of Rhode Island colony, to negotiate the business of the Colony with the British Ministry. Mr. Clarke was instrumental in obtaining the charter of 1663 from Charles II, which secured to the people of the State free and full enjoyment of judgment and conscience in matters of religion. He remained in England to watch over the interests of the Colony until 1664. Mr. Clarke and Mr. Williams, two fathers of the colony, strenuously and fearlessly maintained that none but Jesus Christ had authority over the affairs of conscience. He died April 20, 1676, in the 66th year of his age, and is here interred.'

"Granting that the Roger Williams' group was a New Testament Church, which it wasn't; and granting that it continued to live, which it didn't, and granting that the date was 1639, still it could not have been the First Baptist Church in America. There is no doubt but that honor belongs to the Newport church and the founder Dr. John Clarke. The Newport church was by all measure at least one year the older.

"Mr. Adlam quotes John Comer as follows: 'Comer, the first, and, for the early history of our denomination, the most reliable of writers, ascribes, distinctly and repeatedly, this priority to the Newport church. He had formed the design, more than a hundred and twenty years ago, of writing the history of the American Baptists; and in that work, which he only lived to commence—but which embraces an account of this church—he says in one place 'that it is the first of the Baptist denomination.' (i.e. in America)." Closing his history he says: "Thus I have briefly given some account of the settlement and progress of the First Baptist Church in Rhode Island, in New England, and the first in America."—Ray's Succession, pages 55, 56.

MORE EVIDENCE

From the Minutes of the Philadelphia Baptist Association we have the following: "When the First church in Newport, Rhode Island, was one hundred years old in 1738 (Note, it was 100 years old in 1738) Mr. John Callender, their minister, delivered and published a sermon on the occasion." This shows conclusively that the Newport church was organized in 1638, one year BEFORE the Providence "thing like a church" was organized by Roger Williams.

THE ENEMIES HAVE WRITTEN

One of the reasons for so many errors in the history of the Baptists is because most of the history that we have was written by their enemies. The student should remember that while Baptists were burning at the stake their records were also being destroyed. Fox's "Book of the Martyrs" contains much proof that Baptist people have been martyrs in the ages past. When hate is strong enough to murder it is certainly strong enough to destroy books and papers. It is obvious that the enemies of Baptists would not go to a lot of trouble to correct some historical document if doing so would discredit them or give credit to Baptists.

WARREN ASSOCIATION ACTION

"The matter of the formation of the First Baptist Church was brought before the Warren Association at its meeting in 1847, and at the annual meeting of the Association in 1848 the following votes were passed by that body:

"**First**—That the date of 1638, inserted under the name of the First Baptist Church in Newport, contained in the tabular **estimate** in the minutes of last year, be stricken out and the date (1644) be inserted, as in the minutes of the years preceding.

"Second—That a committee, consisting of T. C. Jameson, J. P. Tustin, and Levy Hale, be appointed to inquire into the evidence as to the date of the First Baptist Church in Newport, with instructions to report at the next session of the Association.

"This committee reported in 1849, that they are of the opinion that this church was formed certainly before the 1st. of May, 1639, and probably on the 7th. of March, 1638.

"This called out a review of the forenamed report by a committee of the First Baptist Church in Providence, whose report is dated August 22, 1850, which led Rev. S. Adlam, who had just settled over the First Baptist Church in Newport, to make a thorough investigation of the matter, which resulted in his book upon the First Baptist Church in Providence.

"It was expected that this book would call out a reply from some one of the First Baptist Church in Providence, as there were several very able members of that church professors in Brown University, but as no reply came, Mr. Adlam asked one of their ablest men (I am reliably informed) when his little book was to be answered. He replied, 'It is unanswerable.' "—Asa Hildreth, Clerk of First Baptist Church, Newport, R. I.

The above was taken from First Baptist Church in America Not founded by Roger Williams, by Graves and Adlam, footnote, page 161.

Mr. William Cathcart, in Baptist Encyclopaedia, page 228, 840, says of Dr. Clarke and the Newport church, "A Church was gathered in 1638, probably early in the year, of which Mr. Clarke became pastor or teaching elder. He is mentioned (in 1638) as "preacher to those of the island," as "their minister," as "elder of the church there," by Mr. Lechford writing in 1640, after having made a tour through New England, that "at the island . . . there is a church where one Master Clarke is pastor."

Mr. Cathcart says further of Mr. Clarke, "His views of christian doctrine have been pronounced so clear and scriptural that they might stand as the confession of faith of Baptists today, after more than two centuries of experience and investigation." He has, and perhaps not inaptly, been called the "Father of American Baptists."

For a further study of this subject get The First Baptist Church In America by Graves and Adlam.

BIBLIOGRAPHY

History of the Christian Church, William Jones, 1831
Distinctive Principles of Baptists, J. M. Pendleton, 1882
Ecclesiastical History, Ancient and Modern, John Lawrence Mosheim, 1824
A Concise History of the Christian Church, Martin Ruter, 1840
The Church of Christ, in Its Idea, Attributes, and Ministry, Edward Arthur Litton, 1856
Close Communion, John T. Christian, 1892
Scenes From Christian History, William Crosby, 1852
A History of American Baptist Missions, E. F. Merriam, 1890
Epitome of General Ecclesiastical History, John Marsh, 1835
History of Virginia Baptists, Robert B. Semple, 1810
A Concise History of Foreign Baptists, G. H. Orchard, 1855
Cook's Story of the Baptists, Richard B. Cook, 1889
Baptist Succession, D. B. Ray, 1887
Fox's Book of Martyrs, John Fox, written about the middle of the 16th Century
The Church That Jesus Built, Roy Mason, 1923
Sketches of Church History, James Wharey, 1840
History of Christianity, Charles W. Rishell, 1891
The Baptist Way-Book, Ben M. Bogard, 1945
Baptist Pamphlets, George B. Ide, 1851
Did Jesus Command Immersion? J. Gilchrist Lawson, 1915
Church History, H. T. Besse, 1908
A Pictorial History of Ancient Rome, S. G. Goodrich, 1862
Dr. Brewer's History of France, Dr. E. Cobham Brewer, 1893
The Form of Baptism in Sculpture and Art, John T. Christian, 1907
A General History of the Baptist Denomination in America, David Benedict, 1848
The Gospel in Water, W. A. Jarrell
History of the Baptists, Thomas Armitage, 1889
First Baptist Church in America, Graves and Adlam, 1887
A View of the Organization of the Primitive Church, A. B. Chapin, 1867
Neander's Memorials of a Christian Life, Augustus Neander, 1822
History of the Christian Church, Edward Burton, 1845
Eusebius' Ecclesiastical History, Pamphali Eusebius, 324 A.D.
Davis' History of the Welsh Baptists
New Church Manual, J. E. Cobb
Ancient British and Irish Churches, Life, and Labors of St. Patrick, William Cathcart, 1894
Church Manual, J. M. Pendleton
The Christian Church During First Three Centuries, J. J. Blount, 1869
Baptist Short Method, Edward T. Hiscox, 1868
Baptist Encyclopedia, William Cathcart, 1881
The Origin of the Baptists, S. H. Ford

A Short History of the Baptists, Henry C. Vedder, 1897
Immersion the Act of Christian Baptism, John T. Christian, 1891
The Decline and Fall of the Roman Empire, Edward Gibbon
Discourses on the Apostolical Succession, W. D. Snodgrass, 1844
History of the Great Reformation, J. H. Merle D'Aubigne, about 1850
Baptist Doctrines, edited by C. A. Jenkins, about 1880
Duruy's General History of the World, Victor Duruy, 1889
Christian Repository, Dr. S. H. Ford, Editor, about 1875
Antiquities of the Jews, Flavius Josephus, first century
The Sumter Discussion, Dr. J. J. Porter
History of the Church, J. M. Cramp
The Lord's Supper, J. R. Graves, 1881
What Is It to Eat and Drink Unworthily, J. R. Graves, 1881
Trilemma, J. R. Graves, 1881
The Memorial Supper, J. M. Frost
Church Communion, W. W. Gardner
A History of the Baptists, Robert G. Torbet, Fifth Edition, 1963
The Churches of the Valley of Piedmont, Samuel Moreland, 1658, Reprint by Dale Kesner and Ellis G. Yoes, 1955
The Voice of Truth, J. M. D. Cates, 1876
History of the Christian Church, Philip Schaff, 1888
Institutes of the Christian Religion, John Calvin
History of the Baptists, John T. Christian, 1922
Baptists and the American Republic, Joseph Martin Dawson, 1956
Miller's Church History, Andrew Miller
General History of the Christian Religion, Augustus Neander
The American Church History Series, 1895
Baptism, Translated from the German by G. H. Lang, Johannes Warns
Martyrs Mirror, Thieleman J. Van Braght translated by Joseph F. Sohm of edition 1660
History Of The Church In the Eighteenth And Nineteenth Centuries, by K. R. Hagenbach, 1869
The History of Christianity, by John S. C. Abbott, 1877

 1DollarScan

1dollarscan.com (zLibro, Inc.)
1590 Oakland Rd. B105,
San Jose, CA 95131

I agree with the following things:

1) I am using 1dollarscan.com services based on my own request.

2) I agree to Terms and Conditions at 1dollarscan.com, http://1dollarscan.com/terms.php and my use of 1dollarscan's services will be within the scope of the Fair Use Policy (http://www.copyright.gov/fls/fl102.html). Otherwise, meet at least one of the following;

   a) I am the copyright holder of this content.
   b) I have the permission from copyright owner.

3) I understand that 1dollarscan shall have no liability to me or any third party with respect to their services.

NAME: Scott Atteberry

Signature: _____

Date: 5/3/10

This sheet should be inserted at the last page of each file generated by 1dollarscan.com scanning services.

www.ingramcontent.com/pod-product-compliance
Lightning Source LLC
Chambersburg PA
CBHW081413160426
42811CB00096B/825